Camus, Philosophe

Social and Critical Theory

A CRITICAL HORIZONS BOOK SERIES

Editorial Board

John Rundell (*University of Melbourne*)
Danielle Petherbridge (*University College Dublin*)
Jeremy Smith (*Federation University*)
Jean-Philippe Deranty (*Macquarie University*)
Robert Sinnerbrink (*Macquarie University*)

International Advisory Board

William Connolly
Manfred Frank
Leela Gandhi
Agnes Heller
Dick Howard
Martin Jay
Richard Kearney
Paul Patton
Michel Wieviorka

VOLUME 18

The titles published in this series are listed at *brill.com/sct*

Ancient Rhamnous, Attica, looking down from the Temple of Nemesis, taken by the author, August 2013

Camus, Philosophe

To Return to Our Beginnings

By

Matthew Sharpe

BRILL

LEIDEN | BOSTON

This paperback was originally published in hardback as Volume 18 in the series SCT.

Library of Congress Cataloging-in-Publication Data

Sharpe, Matthew, 1975-
  Camus, philosophe : to return to our beginnings / Matthew Sharpe.
    pages cm.—(Social and critical theory, ISSN 1572-459X ; VOLUME 18)
  Includes bibliographical references.
 ISBN 978-90-04-30233-4 (hardback : alk. paper)—ISBN 978-90-04-30234-1 (e-book) 1. Camus, Albert, 1913-1960. 2. Philosophy, French. I. Title.

B2430.C354S53 2015
194—dc23

2015023763

Typeface for the Latin, Greek, and Cyrillic scripts: "Brill". See and download: brill.com/brill-typeface.

ISSN 1572-459X
ISBN 978-90-04-32841-9 (paperback, 2016)
ISBN 978-90-04-30233-4 (hardback, 2015)
ISBN 978-90-04-30234-1 (e-book, 2015)

Copyright 2015 by Koninklijke Brill NV, Leiden, The Netherlands.
Koninklijke Brill NV incorporates the imprints Brill, Brill Hes & De Graaf, Brill Nijhoff, Brill Rodopi and Hotei Publishing.
All rights reserved. No part of this publication may be reproduced, translated, stored in a retrieval system, or transmitted in any form or by any means, electronic, mechanical, photocopying, recording or otherwise, without prior written permission from the publisher.
Authorization to photocopy items for internal or personal use is granted by Koninklijke Brill NV provided that the appropriate fees are paid directly to The Copyright Clearance Center, 222 Rosewood Drive, Suite 910, Danvers, MA 01923, USA. Fees are subject to change.

This book is printed on acid-free paper and produced in a sustainable manner.

To Marion, our 'Austral-Silesian' Grenier
And to Marcus Albert ('al-bear'), my son
καὶ τὸ ποτήριόν σου μεθύσκον ὡς κράτιστον.

∴

What we are, what we have to be, are enough to fill our lives and occupy our strength. Paris is a glittering cave, and its inhabitants, seeing their own shadows reflected on the far wall, take them to be the only reality there is. The same is true of the strange, fleeting fame this town dispenses. But we have learnt, far from Paris, that there is a light behind us, that we must turn around and cast off our chains in order to face it directly, and that our task before we die is to seek through words to identify it.
  ALBERT CAMUS, *"The Enigma"* (1950)

Contents

Acknowledgements XIII
Abbreviations XVI

Introduction: Camus, *Philosophe*? 1
1 Enigma 1
2 Four Causes of the Camus Renaissance, after Post-Structuralism 7
3 But Camus, a Philosopher? 18
4 Camus, Neohellenic Philosopher, Neoclassical Humanist 28
5 Ancient *and* Modern: Camus as Post-Enlightenment 'Philosophe' 37
6 Why a *Philosophe* Writes Novels (and Plays, Lyrical Essays …) 41
7 The Desire for Unity and Communion: Camus' Eudemonism 47
8 Prospectus and Limits 54

PART 1
Cave & Critique

1 **Plague Power: Camus with and against the Critiques of Instrumental Reason** 61
   1 "Plague Power", from *La Peste* to *L'État de Siège* 61
   2 The Plague and the Panopticon: Camus with Foucault 68
   3 *Nouvelle Philosophie Avant La Lettre*? Another 'Dialectic of Enlightenment'? 76
   4 Totality on Trial 83
   5 Concluding Remarks 95

2 **Theodicy Now? Camus with and against the Secularisation Thesis** 98
   1 Introduction: Camus, Nihilisms, and the Returns to Theology 98
   2 The Problem of Evil and Modern Metaphysical Rebellion 105
   3 The Existence of Evil Rationalised: Evangelical, Gnostic, Augustinian Theodicies 114
   4 'Too Big a Word for Me': Jacques Othon, Father Paneloux, and Doctor Rieux 118
   5 From Rebellion to Revolution, Unity to Totality: All or Nothing 125
      5.1 *Absolute Negation* 131
      5.2 *Absolute Affirmation* 132

6 Against Secularised Messianism: Camus' Critique of Marx's Prophetism 135
7 Concluding Remarks: *Nuancer?* 143

PART 2
Turning Around, the Rough Ascent

3 Between All or Nothing: Camus with and against the 'Deconstruction of Western Metaphysics' 149
  1 Contradictions: Situating the First Camus 149
  2 Deconstructing Logocentrism, Philosophical Suicide 153
  3 The Middle Path between Irrationalism and Rationalism 164
  4 Excursus: Absurd Heroes? Meursault and Caligula with Sade 171
  5 *Je suis revenu à mon commencement*: The Irreducibility of the Subject and the Primacy of Ethics 180
  6 Concluding Remarks: Camus' Socratism, between Philosophy, Autobiography, and Literature 191

4 From Revolution to Rebellion: Camus with and against the Theorists of Dialogic Ethics 198
  1 Beyond Nihilism, Sympathetic Imagination: Camus with Levinas 198
  2 'I Rebel, Therefore We Are': A Primary Post-Metaphysical Value 211
  3 Between Formal Virtue and Historicism—not 'against History' 220
  4 Political Suicide? On Camus' Concrete Political Philosophy 228
  5 Concluding Remarks: Camus and the Legacy of Modern Sceptical Humanism 241

PART 3
Going Back Down

5 Excluding Nothing: Camus' NeoHellenic Philosophy of *Mesure* 253
  1 From Political Messianisms to Philosophical Naturalim 253
    1.1 *Camus, beyond 'the Political'?* 253
    1.2 *A Greece of the Flesh* (la chair) 266
    1.3 *The Two Sides of Camus' "New Mediterranean Culture", and of His Greeks* 273
    1.4 Contra *Philosophies of History,* Pace *Secular Messianisms* 284

    2   *Mesure* and Nature   294
          2.1   *Camusian* Mesure, *a Thought that Excludes Nothing*   294
          2.2   *Prometheus Reclaimed: From the Philosophers to the Poets*   301
          2.3   *All is Well? The Consent within Revolt and the Black Side of the Sun*   307

6 After the Fall, the First Man   318

    1   Judgment, *The Fall*, and the Post-Prophetic Philosopher   318
          1.1   *Exile and Algeria: The Post-colonial Case against Albert Camus*   318
          1.2   *Camus' Fall, the Judge-Penitents, and the Mandarins*   326
          1.3   *For a Civil Truce: The Post-Prophetic Philosopher as Stand-in and Mediator*   346
    2   Philosophy, the Virtues, Love and Wonder   355
          2.1   *Literature and Philosophy as a Way of Life, the Camusian Virtues*   355
          2.2   *The First Man as Algerian Text: Camus' Fictional True Algeria*   375
          2.3   *Childhood, Poverty, and Wonder*: The First Man *as Literary-Philosophical Exercise*   382

Appendix One: *L'Homme Révolté* **in 40 Premises**   393
Appendix Two: Camusian *Mesure***: Philosophic, Aesthetic, and Political**   403
Appendix Three: Philosophy United to Rhetoric: The 'Master Argument' in "Letters to a German Friend"   406

Bibliography   412
Index   437

Acknowledgements

In the balance of things, this is the book the author has long wanted to write. The story has grown in the telling. In many ways, it is not the book he had imagined (or even that he had promised Brill in 2013). It is the book that Doctor Marion Tapper has urged him to write for well over a decade, in which nearly everything has changed in both our lives. She has gone into the heartlands, I into the academy. The gods alone know which is best, Socrates might say.

The author scarcely remembers when he first read Camus. I must have been 16. A boy raised in the sunshine, on the beaches of a settler society in the antipodes, in the thick pall of an unbalanced youth's metaphysical angst, I savoured little more than the mood in the copy of *The Stranger* I pilfered from my English teacher, or borrowed from a first intellectual friend. Some time later, the Penguin *Selected Essays and Notebooks* introduced me to the lyrical essays and to the *Carnets*. From that time on, Camus' voice has been so much a part of my inner life, like many millions of others', that I don't know where my own sensibilities begin that were not taken from what I took to be his. There were ten years there when, as an undergraduate then Honors student, I studied modern German and twentieth century French thinking: nothing of Camus. Then, in this new light, I returned to write my honors thesis on Camus' philosophical thought, alongside Derrida and Foucault. (Some of the materials from Chapters One and Three draw from that thesis, in a hopefully far better written and informed shape).

Another decade passed, near enough, darkened by the fear-driven excesses of the 'war on terror,' in which I became steadily more disillusioned with the ethical, political, and epistemic credentials of the theorists in whose works my generation of students had been encouraged to seek an unspeakable salvation in conditions of growing anxiety and progressive despair. Wayward paths during that time led me back to the study of classical thought my schoolboy and undergraduate glimpses of Plato and Aristotle's ethics had suggested. Around 2008, by way of a very fine course by Doctor Ashley Woodward at the Melbourne School of Continental Philosophy, I discovered the great gift of Pierre Hadot's *Philosophy as a Way of Life* and through it, the quiet wisdom and admirable, unachievable serenity of the Roman Stoics.

It was the 50th anniversary of Camus' death, and the conference to mark the same organised by my colleague Associate Professor Russell Grigg at Deakin University in 2010 that brought me back to Camus a second time. Rereading *The Rebel, Nuptials, Summer* and the *Carnets* after having read and taught many of the classical sources Camus himself had read as a young man completely transformed the experience, and enhanced my appreciation of (as it seems still to me) his singular voice in 20th century thought. It seemed to me from that time onwards, amidst all the heated political talk of preserving the West's 'JudaeoChristian heritage' and theoretical 'returns to Saint Paul' and to theology of different stripes that a return to the measured wisdom of the classical Greeks, rooted in a deep sense of the fragile balance of nature and an undeniable human sociability this side of irresolvable metaphysical claims was every bit as vital as when Camus conceived something like it in the 1940s and 1950s. It might also make a worthwhile contribution to contemporary scholarship.

I do not know what Camus would think of the resulting study, which follows now. *Camus, Philosophe* is after all a work of criticism not creation; and when he died too soon in January 1960, Camus wanted to have made an end to polemic and criticism. The author has tried within it to do all the justice and honour he is able to someone who seems to him a rare and genuinely admirable human being, and also (so the argument runs) a much more interesting and profound, observant thinker than has widely been credited, at least within academe. Not all great men or women are philosophers, by a long stretch, but there is a perilous amount of truth to Camus' June 1937 observation that "philosophies are worth the philosophers who make them. The greater the man, the truer his philosophy": at least when it comes to ethical and political matters. Readers will each judge how successful the book is, if successful at all.

To name all the people who have made possible whatever virtues *Camus, Philosophe* can claim has would take far too long. (The shortcomings I claim as my own). Like Marcus Aurelius' opening in the *Meditations*, it would amount to little less than a list of all the author's benefactors. I single out my old South African English teacher, John Mason at Mentone Boys' Grammar school. The author will always a debtor to the remarkable man who (alongside probably my copy of *The Stranger*) started issuing me the great books 'contraband' in Year 11, and taught me George Orwell, Kenneth Slessor, Athol Fugard, and that "a man is always a Lion away from home" (at home, he is just a man). Alongside the impishly irreverent Reverend Christopher Winter, my first classical history teacher, 'Mr. Mason' gave me my first, indelible impression of the life of the mind, and the grand adventure of teaching young people. To Doctor Marion Tapper, the first dedicatee of this book: you were the first, outside of the tiny world of a suburban grammar-school, to have faith in me and make me start to believe I was someone who could not only work hard. To Associate Professor John Rundell, who came closely next, I owe every bit as much. Thanks for all your learning, your legendarily enthusiastic teaching, that incredible honours class on 20th century French anthropology and social theory, your continuing professional counsel, and your unflagging critical support for this book.

There are many people to thank for more particular points of assistance. Thanks to my MSCP (Melbourne School of Continental Philosophy) Camus class of 2013, where many of the ideas in Chapters Five and Six were generated. Your enthusiasm (and sheer number) made it clear to me how much interest remains 'out there' in Camus, beyond the academy. A thank you to Deakin University and the School of Humanities and Social Sciences for two periods of teaching relief in 2011 and 2014. These enabled me to first think up, and then to write up this book. A thank you is due also to the (mostly-critical) reviews of drafts of Chapters and spin-off ideas: the sting removed, the critical ones are the most helpful, even when this is not the intention. For their research assistance, gratitude to Mr. Scott Thomas and the now-Dr Andrew Sims: the former, for work on post-colonialism, the latter for work on the history of the *vita contemplativa*, and for sharing in so many ironies on the new clouds or birds. For reading chapters and commenting on them, thank yous to Peter Cryle, Patrick Stokes, Marion Tapper, John Rundell, Geoffrey Boucher, Mr. Nick Scott and Daniel Brennan. For their moral and professional support, finally, my measureless gratitude is owed to Dr. Will Altman and Professor Ian Hunter. Being urged to persevere with open eyes is not the least valuable advice you can get. Nor is it the least Camusian.

On a personal note, I want to thank my wife for being so gracious in affording me the time to write *Camus, Philosophe*: a labour of love but still a labour, and sometimes a preoccupation (especially when it came down to the footnotes). For your love and support, and patient acceptance of the absent-mindedness and occasional ill-temper which comes from brooding over something so far away for so long: *eucharisto!*, as they say in the sun-white streets of the *Hora* on Naxos. To my parents, thank you again, on the record, for everything. You can read this book to know a little more of who your son became after that summer between years 11 and 12 all those years ago in Bodley Street. Finally, to my little boy, Marcus Albert Sharpe, just crawling as I write this and pulling at my trouser hems, gratitude for more than everything—and the book itself. Thank you for reminding everyone who meets you how not simply philosophy begins in wonder.

Abbreviations

The following are the abbreviations used in the footnotes for Albert Camus' books, after their first full citation in the notes. I give paginations for both the French and English editions of the *Carnets* and Camus' philosophical essays, since these are the central texts for this book, where it has been particularly vital to have worked from the originals. Camus' literary, lyrical, and journalistic writings I cite in their English translations, including the pieces in *Resistance, Rebellion, and Death*. I indicate in these cases when I have altered the translation by recourse to the French-language originals. Lyrical essays and interviews cited more than once are cited according to their specific titles within *Lyrical and Critical Essays* and the *Oeuvres Complètes*. Otherwise, quotes from these collections are assigned only their page number within the larger volume. Finally, readers should note that, after giving both titles in fist mentions of a given text, I use either the French or English titles of Camus' books.

AC *Algerian Chronicles* translated Arthur Goldhammer with an Introduction by Alice Kaplan (Cambridge, Massachusetts: Belknap Press, 2013).

AT "The Almond Trees" (from *Summer*), *Albert Camus: Lyrical and Critical Essays*, edited by Phillip Thody, translated by Ellen Conroy Kennedy (Vintage: New York, 1987), 134–137.

BYN "Between Yes and No" (from *The Wrong Side and the Right Side*), in *Lyrical and Critical Essays*, 30–39.

CAC *Camus at Combat: Writing 1944–1947* ed. Jacqueline Lévi-Valensi, trans. Arthur Goldhammer, with a Foreword by David Carroll (Princeton: Princeton University Press, 2006).

C I *Carnets I, mai 1935–février 1942* (Paris: Gallimard, 1962).

C II *Carnets II, janvier 1942–mars 1951* (Paris: Les Éditions Gallimard, 1964).

C III *Carnets III. mars 1951–décembre 1959* (Paris: Les Éditions Gallimard, 1989).

C I Eng. *Carnets 1935–1942*, translated with Introduction & notes by Philip Thody (London: Hamish Hamilton, 1963).

C II Eng. *Carnets 1942–1951*, translated with Introduction & notes by Philip Thody (London: Hamish Hamilton, 1966).

C III Eng. *Notebooks 1951–1959*, translated with Introduction & notes by Ryan Bloom (Chicago: Ivan R. Dee, 2008).

ABBREVIATIONS

CD	"Create Dangerously", in *Resistance, Rebellion, Death* trans. Justin O'Brien. Vintage, New York: 1960, pp. 249–272.
CH	"La Crise de L'Homme (28 mars 1946)", in *Albert Camus Oeuvres Complètes II 1944–1948* (Gallimard Bibliothèque de la Pléiade, Paris: 2006), 737–749.
CMN	*Christian Metaphysics and Neoplatonism*, translated with Introduction by Ronald Srigley (Columbia & London: University of Missouri Press, 2007).
D	"The Desert" (from *Nuptials*), in *Albert Camus: Lyrical and Critical Essays*, 93–105.
E	"The Enigma" (from *Summer*), *Lyrical and Critical Essays*, 154–161.
Ess	*Essais*, Édition de Louis Faucon et Roger Quilliot; Introduction de Roger Quilliot. (Collection Bibliothèque de la Pléiade (no. 183), Gallimard, 1965).
EE Pref.	"Preface, 1958" (to *The Wrong Side and the Right Side*), in *Albert Camus: Lyrical and Critical Essays*, 5–18.
EK	*Exile and the Kingdom* translated by Justin O'Brien (Penguin, London: 1962).
F	Albert Camus, *The Fall* translated Justin O'Brien (New York: Vintage, 1956).
FC	*The First Camus: Youthful Writings* with an Introduction by Paul Viallaneix, translated by E.C. Kennedy. (New York: Vintage, 1977).
FM	*The First Man* translated David Hapgood (London: Penguin, 1996).
HE	"Helen's Exile" (from *Summer*) in *Lyrical and Critical Essays*, 148–153.
HR	*L'Homme Révolté* (Éditions Gallimard, Paris, 1951).
IS	"Intelligence and the Scaffold", in *Lyrical and Critical Essays*, 210–218.
LCE	*Albert Camus: Lyrical and Critical Essays*, edited by Phillip Thody, translated by Ellen Conroy Kennedy (Vintage: New York, 1987).
LFT	"Lecture in Athens on the Future of Tragedy," in *Lyrical and Critical Essays*, 295–310.
LGF	"Letters to a German Friend", in *Resistance, Rebellion, Death*, trans. with an Introduction by Justin O'Brien (New York: the Modern Library, 1974), 2–32.
LL	"Love of Life" (from *The Wrong Side and the Right Side*), in *Lyrical and Critical Essays*, 52–57.
LTM	"A Letter to the Editor of *Les Temps Modernes*," in *Sartre and Camus: A Historic Confrontation*, edited and translated by David A. Spritzen (Humanity Books: New York, 2004), 107–130.

MSO	"The Minotaur, or Stopping in Oran" (in *Summer*) *Albert Camus: Lyrical and Critical Essays*, 109–133.
MS	*Le Mythe de Sisyphe* (Paris: Gallimard, 1942 [2008]).
MSe	*Myth of Sisyphus*, translated by Justin O'Brien (London: Penguin, 1978).
OC I	*Albert Camus Oeuvres Complètes I 1944–1948* (Gallimard Bibliothèque de la Pléiade, Paris: 2006).
OC II	*Albert Camus Oeuvres Complètes II 1944–1948* (Gallimard Bibliothèque de la Pléiade, Paris: 2006).
OC III	*Albert Camus Oeuvres Complètes III 1949–1956* (Gallimard Bibliothèque de la Pléiade, Paris: 2008).
OC IV	*Albert Camus Oeuvres Complètes IV 1957–1959* (Gallimard Bibliothèque de la Pléiade, Paris: 2008).
NMC	"The New Mediterranean Culture" in *Lyrical and Critical Essays*, 189–198.
NT	"Nuptials at Tipasa" (from *Nuptials*), in *Lyrical and Critical Essays*, 65–72.
NVE	"Neither Victims nor Executioners", in *Camus at Combat*, 255–276.
P	*The Plague*, translated Stuart Gilbert (London: Penguin, 1971).
PU	"Prometheus in the Underworld" (from *Summer*), in *Lyrical and Critical Essays*, 138–142.
R	Albert Camus, *The Rebel*, revised and complete translation by Anthony Bower, with a Foreword by Sir Herbert Read (New York: Vintage, 1956).
RG	"Reflections on the Guillotine" in Albert Camus, *Resistance, Rebellion, Death*, trans. with an Introduction by Justin O'Brien (New York: the Modern Library, 1974), 173–234.
RRD	*Resistance, Rebellion, Death*, trans. with an Introduction by Justin O'Brien (New York: the Modern Library, 1974.
RT	"Return to Tipasa" (from *Summer*) in *Lyrical and Critical Essays*, 162–171.
S	*The Stranger* translated by Stuart Gilbert (New York: Vintage, 1946).
SA	"Summer at Algiers" (from *Nuptials*) in *Albert Camus: Lyrical and Critical Essays*, pp. 80–92.
TL	"Le Témoin de la Liberté", *Oeuvres Complètes II*, 488–495.
TM	"Le Temps des Meurtrieurs", in *Oeuvres Complètes III*, 351–364.
WD	"Wind at Djemila" (from *Nuptials*) in *Lyrical and Critical Essays*, 73–79.
WG	"Wager of our Generation" in A. Camus, *Resistance, Rebellion, Death*, 237–348.

INTRODUCTION

Camus, *Philosophe*?

1   Enigma

"My profession is double, like the human being",[1] Jean-Baptiste Clamence tells us in *The Fall* (*La Chute*), at the end of our first day with him at the *Mexico City*. Like nearly everything in this archest of Albert Camus' books, these words can be read as an ironic confession of the author himself. As Clamence taunts us: "I know what you're thinking: it's very hard to disentangle the true from the false in what I'm saying."[2]

Certainly, the reader who returns to Camus' *oeuvre* today, especially if she looks to do this by availing herself of the voluminous critical responses it has provoked, soon enters a forest of contradictions. From the very beginning, the two most famous, lay understandings of Camus (each in fact reflecting a different stage in his short life's work) completely negate each other. On one side, Camus is still today a "prophet of the absurd," especially for many culturally conservative critics. He is to be aligned with Beckett, the surrealists, and before them Nietzsche, as one more way-station on the West's long path towards the nihilistic abyss. Yet for Breton, Jeanson, and Sartre in the early 1950s, as differently since for figures like Bronner, Camus represents less a "nihilist" than an incorrigible moralist:[3] in the title of Jeanson's famous polemic, a *belle âme* too beautiful for political life, if not the eloquent high priest of bourgeois reaction against Marxism, the inescapable political horizon of our times.[4]

---

1   Albert Camus, *The Fall* translated Justin O'Brien (New York: Vintage, 1956), 9.
2   F, 119. For a more detailed assessment of *The Fall*, see Chapter Six.
3   Stephen Eric Bronner, *Camus: Portrait of a Moralist* (Chicago: University of Chicago Press, 2009). See Robert Zaretsky, *Albert Camus: Elements of a Life* (USA: Cornell University Press, 2010), 144; Norman Podhoretz, "Camus and his critics", in *New Criterion* 1982, at www-site http://www.newcriterion.com/articles.cfm/Camus-and-his-critics-6546, last accessed January 2015.
4   Francis Jeanson, "Albert Camus, or the Soul in Revolt", in *Sartre and Camus: An Historic Confrontation*. Edited and translated by David A. Spritzen (Humanity books, New York, 2004), pp. 79–106. For a recent authoritative account of the pre- and post-history of the Jeanson/Sartre-Camus confrontation, and the confrontation itself, see Ronald Aronson, *Camus and Sartre: The story of a Friendship and the Quarrel that Ended It* (Chicago: Chicago University Press, 2004); also David A. Sprintzen, Salam Hawa, Bernard Murchland, and Adrian van den Hoven, "Historical and Critical Introduction: From Friendship to Rivals" in *Sartre and Camus: An Historic Confrontation*, 31–78. For an earlier account, see Nicola Chiaramonte, "Sartre

The paradoxes in Camus reception only begin there. On the religious question, for instance, Camus stands condemned or celebrated by many critics for being a doctrinaire atheist, alongside Sartre and many others of his time. Yet other commentators, including deeply religious authors like Thomas Merton,[5] continue to find in Camus an interlocutor almost uniquely open to the sacral dimensions of human experience in a century whose most renowned intellectuals were often pre-emptively anti-theological.[6]

In the literary field, Maurice Blanchot, considering only Camus' earliest cycle of works, already expressed consternation that Camus could so well depict the absurd "divorce" between human beings and their world in *L'Étranger* and *Le Mythe de Sisyphe*, only to end the latter meditation by imagining his absurd icon, Sisyphus, *heureux*.[7] For André Breton and his surrealist followers at *Arts* and *Libertoire*[8] (and with some variation, also George Bataille)[9]

---

versus Camus: A Political Struggle", in *Camus: A Collection of Critical Essays* ed. Germaine Brée (Englewood Cliffs, N.J.: Prentice-Hall, 1962), 51–57.

5 Thomas Merton, "Seven Essays on Albert Camus" in *The Literary Essays of Thomas Merton*, edited by Brother Patrick Hart (USA: New Direction, 1995), 181–304.

6 As Moya Longstaffe has put it: "Nor can Camus's attitude to Christianity be reduced, as here, simply to an acceptance of Nietzsche's contemptuous epithet: slave religion (i.e. fit only for women!) Camus's contacts with the Dominicans and Bruckberger, or with the Jesuit Didier, his rebuke to an interviewer in 1948 ('Je réfléchirais avant de dire comme vous que la foi chrétienne est une démission. Peut-on écrire ce mot pour un saint Augustin ou un Pascal?', Essais, Édition de Louis Faucon et Roger Quilliot; Introduction de Roger Quilliot. (Collection Bibliothèque de la Pléiade (no. 183), Gallimard, 1965), p. 380) amply show that while he refused Christianity, he never failed to respect it...", in Moya Longstaffe, *"'Ces forces obscures de l'âme': Women, Race and Origins in the Writings of Albert Camus* (review)", *French Studies: A Quarterly Review* Volume 63, Number 2, April 2009 pp. 233–234. See Chapters Two, Five and Six below for adumbrations of Camus' attitude towards Christianity: respect for its altruism, proximity to its account of solidary non-erotic love, its commitment to cultivating a difficult way of life, and finally respect and affection for Jesus as a man: as against its theodicy and eschatology, as well as recurrent tendencies within it towards a denial of the natural beauty of the body and sexuality. See the still-authoritative Thomas L. Hanna, "Albert Camus and the Christian Faith", in Germaine Brée ed. *Camus: Critical Essays* (Englewood Cliffs, N.J.: Prentice-Hall, 1962), 48–58.

7 See Jonathan Degenève, "'Quelle absence!': Blanchot lecteur de Camus," at www-site http://www.blanchot.fr/fr/index.php?option=com_content&task=view&id=134&Itemid=41, last accessed January 2015; & Albert Camus, *Le mythe de Sisyphe* (Paris: Gallimard, 1942 [2008]), 168.

8 Cf. Camus, "Révolte et conformisme (*Arts* 19 octobre 1951)", *Oeuvre Complètes III 1949–1956* (Gallimard Bibliothèque de la Pléiade, Paris: 2008), 392–394; "Révolte et conformisme (suite), (*Arts*, 18 novembre 1951)", 394–397.

9 George Bataille, "Le Temps de Révolte", reproduced at www-site http://www.pileface.com/sollers/article.php3?id_article=938, last accessed January 2015.

similarly, Camus' later works on rebellion betray his earlier explorations of the absurd. Camus scandalously tries to align revolt against the indignities of the human condition and the banalities of bourgeois society with a philosophical appeal to *mesure* which for these intellectuals almost *defined* such banality. If Camus' interpretation is so divided, such critics have suggested, we should look to the causes of this division in alleged inconsistencies in Camus' texts, or the incompetence of their author.[10]

Camus, for his part, repeatedly denied the *idée fixé* that he was an existentialist, just as he refused the label of atheist so often pinned to his breast. He even laughingly planned at one point immediately following the war to co-author a piece with Sartre explaining the differences between them:[11] differences which would become all-too-serious after Camus' publication of *L'Homme Révolté* in 1951, seeing Camus' virtual exile from the kingdom of the Parisian *rive gauche*. All that notwithstanding, Camus continues to be anthologised as an existentialist: "since it is more convenient to exploit a cliché than a nuance, I am a prophet of the absurd as before".[12] And he is taught as such in those *classes terminales* and sophomoric "introductions to philosophy" that one Sartrean critic (echoing the words of his master, and the assessment of most of the Anglophone philosophical profession since) suggested represent the highest pedagogical level to which Camus' thought can aspire.[13] The almost-complete critical silence (outside of dedicated 'Camus studies' circles) concerning Camus' philosophical thought from around the time of his death until the fall of the Berlin wall (certainly in the English-speaking world, but mostly also in France) reflects this widespread grouping of Camus with Sartre et al. as an existentialist, if not as a "philosopher of the subject."[14] Camus' reflections

---

10 Cf. Jorn Boisen, "Hédonisme et éthique: un paradoxe camusien?" in Christine Margerrison, Mark Orme, Lissa Lincoln eds., *Albert Camus in the 21st Century: A Reassessment of His Thinking at the Dawn of the New Millennium* (Amsterdam, New York: Editions Rodopi B. V., 2008), 123, 125, 127, 129.

11 Albert Camus, "Three Interviews" ("No, I am not an existentialist"), *Albert Camus: Lyrical and Critical Essays*, edited by Phillip Thody, translated by Ellen Conroy Kennedy (Vintage: New York, 1987), 345. "... the only book of ideas that I have ever published, *Le Mythe de Sisyphe*, was directed against the so-called existentialist philosophers..."

12 Albert Camus, "The Enigma", LCE, 159. For a recent example, see Avi Sagi, "Is the absurd the problem or the solution? *The Myth of Sisyphus* reconsidered", in Stephen G. Kellman ed. *Critical Insights: Albert Camus* (USA: Salem Press, 2012), 195–198, where Camus is read through the prism of Heidegger and others.

13 Jean-Jacques Brochier, *Camus, Philosophe pour Classes Terminales* (Paris, La découverte, 1970/1979).

14 Cf. Jeanyves Guerin, "Camus, Philosophe pour Classes Terminales?", 98–99 assigns Camus' oversight in both the period of existentialist Marxism and structuralism to his resistance

on the absurd, evil, revolt, and other humanistic themes became completely *dépassé* in the heroic eras of structuralism and post-structuralism after 1960 in France, and the generations of the "theoretical turn" influenced by these movements in the UK, US, Australasia and globally.

For many commentators, indeed, Camus cannot be considered a philosopher at all, whether existentialist or no.[15] Camus' fictional works continue to be accepted and categorised as 'philosophical' novels, plays, and stories. A just criticism of his plays in particular (one which, ironically, he levelled as a young man against Sartre's *Nausea*)[16] is that their *mises en scenes* are too transparently set-pieces for Camus to explore the celebrated themes of his philosophical reflections: *viz*. the absurd, revolt, limits, the legitimacy of political violence, or the need for dialogue.[17] Nevertheless, critics vie with each other to dismiss Camus' pretensions to the august title of '*philosophe*', as against a gifted *littérateur*. To cite for the moment just one eminent recent case of Camus' sidelining as a *philosophe*, Jacques Derrida, in one of his last seminars on the death penalty, maintained that no philosopher had written, *qua* philosopher, against *la peine de mort*. What then to make of the seemingly striking counter-example of Camus' 1956 "Reflections on the Guillotine," a key piece behind Camus' award of the Nobel Prize one year later?[18] In a way which sits very uneasily with Derrida's earlier 'deconstruction' of the philosophy-literature divide, Derrida

---

of the impulse to systematisation. Cf. also the brusque assessment of Marc Blanchard, "Editor's Introduction", *MLN* Vol. 112, No. 4, French Issue (Sep., 1997), pp. 497–498, on Camus' thought as paradoxically "unjustly neglected and canonized" (p. 497), at p. 498: "Almost two generations past Camus's much derided 1957 Nobel, the balance sheet remains on the whole negative. One major biography, by an American historian. But no major works of criticism on Camus, except for one famous 1960 article by Rene Girard in PMLA and one broad brush intellectual survey by Germaine Brée in the early sixties; no displays of curiosity among French or American glitterati-only dull admiration for the canonical bravura of the universally translated *L'Étranger*. One exception: the combined *ressentiment* of Conor Cruise O'Brien's and Edward Said's postcolonial discourses." This assessment of Camus' neglect, albeit itself arguably excessive, no longer holds true, even in part, even in the anglosphere.

15 Representatively, *The Cambridge Companion to Camus* edited by Edward J. Hughes (Cambridge: Cambridge University Press, 2007) contains no article on *L'Homme Révolté*, or on Camus as a philosopher, with Chapter 4 by David Carroll on *Le Mythe* (David Carroll, "Rethinking the Absurd: *Le Mythe de Sisyphe*", 53–66....). The volume is part of the Cambridge University Press series on European literature.

16 Albert Camus, "On Jean-Paul Sartre's *La Nausée*" LCE, 199–202.

17 See Henry Popkin, "Camus the Dramatist" in *Camus, A collection of critical essays*, 172.

18 Camus, "Reflections on the Guillotine", in *Resistance, Rebellion and Death*, trans. with an Introduction by Justin O'Brien (New York: the Modern Library, 1963), 133–179.

simply numbers his great Algerian predecessor (with whom he is elsewhere deeply sympathetic) as a *litterateur*, not a *philosophe*.[19]

The list of contradictions or (adapting one of Camus' own terms) of 'enigmas' surrounding how to read Albert Camus' *oeuvre* and how to understand its reception could go on. The opening wager of this book is that these manifold contradictions in the way people have read Camus' works are not indices of the author's incompetence, deep inconsistencies, inability to make up his mind, or to stick to any program. They are so many indices of Camus' work's abiding originality and complexity, as well as his ongoing philosophical evolution from the early 1930s to his death in early 1960. Camus' divided reception bespeaks the singularity of Camus' thought and writing as an author both Algerian *pied noir* and proudly republican; both Mediterranean and European; philosophically trained yet famed as a *litterateur*; deeply 'of his times' yet drawn to ancient paradigms; a man of sentiment yet legatee to "a certain kind of dry, plain, contemplative rationalism, which is typically French";[20] a *résistant* moved by solidarity with the political struggles of his contemporaries, while longing for the solitary leisure characteristic of what less interesting times called the *vita contemplativa*; hedonist and humanist;[21] a thinker inveterately sceptical of all totalising philosophical systems, yet an unfailing defender of the life of the mind; one of the first, most powerful critics of French barbarities in Algeria, yet unable to endorse complete French withdrawal from its colonial possession; a man of the Left, yet increasingly anti-Stalinist; a figure acutely moved by what one early essay names "the love of life,"[22] but a love whose *envers* in all his writings is a nearly-tactile sense of the transience of things, the reality of senseless suffering, and the proximity of death.[23]

Faced with almost all of the ways people have tried to categorise Camus drawing on their own pre-existing understandings, there is something about Camus' *oeuvre* that does not fit the mould. Moments, indeed, whole strata of his work can be cited to support reading Camus as an atheist, or an existentialist,

---

Not to mention "La crise de l'homme" of 1946 and "Le temps des meurtrieurs" of 1949: see Chapter Four below, section "Political Suicide? On Camus' concrete political philosophy".

19   Jacques Derrida, *The Death Penalty* translated by Peggy Kamuf (Chicago: University of Chicago Press, 2013), 30.
20   Jean-Paul Sartre, "Camus' 'The Outsider' ", *Literary and Philosophical Essays* translated by Annette Michelson (London: Hutchinson & Co., 1968), 25.
21   Cf. Jorn Boisen, "Hédonisme et éthique: un paradoxe camusien?", 121–132.
22   Albert Camus, "Love of Life", in LCE 52–57. "There is no love of life without despair of life," writes the young Camus at LCE 58.
23   See in particular the essays in *Nuptials* (*Noces*), notably "Wind at Djemila", and "The Desert", LCE 73–79, 93–105.

or a modernist, an anti-Christian, an "absurdist" or a nihilist. At the same time textual support can be, and has been, adduced to position Camus as an opponent to existentialism and modern thought more widely: as either a pagan adept or pseudo-Christian on the verge of final conversion; as a vehement opponent of political reaction as he saw it embodied amongst the Algerian *colons* and Vichy France, and as the kind of "reactionary" that Sartre, Hervé and Jeanson denounced him for in 1952, or which Nora, O'Brien, Said, Haddour and others later charged against his Algerian stance.[24]

As we shall be underlining, the heart of Camus' philosophy is encapsulated in the Jansenist thinker Pascal's enigmatic claim that "nothing is true which compels us to exclude": "what else can I desire than to exclude nothing and to learn how to braid with white and black thread a single cord stretched to the breaking-point?"[25] Although the passion and the logic of polemical debate unfailingly push interlocutors towards "all-or-nothing" stances (the opponent, as enemy, must be wholly mistaken or culpably blind) according to Camus' deeply classical perspective, people err through not weighing all relevant considerations or hybristically overvaluing their own perspective. Rarely are they wholly misdirected, fallen or malignant. In just this way, we will argue, existing accounts of Camus have each partly grasped the unfolding import of his thought, in ways which reflect their own preoccupations and presuppositions. They are not wholly wrong. From a Christian perspective, Camus' agnosticism or naturalistic sense of the sacred can only appear as "atheistic", despite his disavowals that such "... words say nothing to me: for me they have no meaning. I do not believe in God and I am not an atheist."[26] For the *Marxissant*, Camus' enduring fascination with "imagining [sic.] the sacred without a belief in immortality"[27] can only appear as a kind of theism *manqué* and failure of critical nerve. In other cases like Blanchot's, Bataille's, or recently Ronald Srigley's, we will argue, critics have been drawn too quickly to assert Camus' deep

---

24   Cf. Conor Cruise O'Brien, *Albert Camus* (Great Britain: Collins/Fontana, 1970); Edward Said, *Culture and Imperialism* (London: Vintage, Random House Group Limited, 1994); Pierre Nora, *Le Française d'Algérie* (Paris: René Julliard, 1961); Azzedine Haddour, *Colonial Myths: History and Narrative* (UK: Manchester University Press, 2000) & Chapter Six below.

25   Albert Camus, "Return to Tipasa", LCE, 169. See Chapters Five & Six below.

26   Albert Camus, *Carnets III, mars 1951–décembre 1959* (Paris: Les Éditions Gallimard, 1989), 128; *Notebooks 1951–1959*, translated with Introduction & notes by Ryan Bloom (Chicago: Ivan R. Dee, 2008), 112.

27   Albert Camus, *Carnets II, janvier 1942–mars 1951* (Paris: Les Éditions Gallimard, 1964), 21; *Carnets 1942–1951*, translated with Introduction & notes by Philip Thody (London: Hamish Hamilton, 1966), 7.

inconsistency: or to infer from the free rhetorical form of Camus' writings that they can contain no coherent, if always developing, theoretical perspective.[28] What is attested by their claims, we will maintain, is the way that Camus was striving towards a philosophical position which challenges the presuppositions shaping regnant later modern interpretive frameworks by drawing on different cultural, philosophical, and biographical inheritances.

In order to try to philosophically reconstruct Camus' position, and to show why he has been so 'partially' received, this book argues for a single hypothesis. We argue that Camus should be understood as a *philosophe*, in a neoclassical, humanistic and also an 'enlightened' French sense that it will be our task in the Introduction to preliminarily explain.

2   Four Causes of the Camus Renaissance, after Post-Structuralism

Camus, Philosophe is situated in a 'Camus renaissance', in honour of one of Camus' own key terms. Of course, Camus' classical works of fiction, led by *L'Étranger, La Peste* and *La Chute* have continued in print since first appearing in 1941, 1947, and 1956 respectively. It is worth remarking that, despite all the changed political circumstances since Camus' untimely death—thus, to take France alone: the fall of Algeria, May '68, the *gauchisme* of the early 1970s and the new social movements, the '74 revelations of Solzenitzyn and the anti-communism of the later 1970s, the 1980s' "liberal turn" and the collapse of the PCF (*Partie Communiste Francaise*) as a viable electoral force, etc.—despite all these things, Camus' *romans* and *récits* continue to speak to new generations of readers.[29] Yet, in 1994, *Le Premier Homme*, the semi-autobiographical novel on which Camus was working at the time of his death was published in its incomplete form. This literary event provoked renewed critical attention to Camus' work and its importance in the 1990s.[30]

---

28 Cf. George Bataille, "Le Temps de Révolte", reproduced at www-site http://www.pileface.com/sollers/article.php3?id_article=938, last accessed January 2015; Ronald Srigley, *Albert Camus' Critique of Modernity* (Missouri: Missouri University Press, 2011), esp. 32–33, 76.

29 Cf. Maurice Weyembergh, "Réflections sur l'(in)actualité de Camus", in Christine Margerrison, Mark Orme, Lissa Lincoln eds., *Albert Camus in the 21st Century: A Reassessment of His Thinking at the Dawn of the New Millennium* (Amsterdam, New York: Editions Rodopi B. V., 2008), 24–32.

30 See for example the dedicated issue of *MLN* 112: 4, September 1997: French Issue, *Special Issue: Camus* 2000. Special Editor: Marc Blanchard.

More than this, with the fall of the Eastern bloc after 1989, and with it the fall of the last vestiges of communism's credibility as a global political force, Camus' stances against Leninism and Stalinism in the immediate post-war era came to seem uncannily ahead of their time. Perhaps, figures like Jeffrey C. Isaac in the English-speaking world now begun to argue[31] (as had the *nouveaux philosophes* and others in France over a decade before)[32] the time had come to reconsider the verdict about Camus' defeat as a political philosopher by Sartre on the Stalinist issue in 1952. Perhaps, with *Le Premier Homme* now in print, we would need also to query the verdict passed by Said, O'Brien, Haddour and others about Camus' irredeemability in an age of post-colonial criticism, as a *pied noir* who could never accept either the violent means or political ends of the FLN (*Front de Libération Nationale*), and who would hold on to the dream of an Algerian French-Arab federation until his passing, despite the tide of events.[33]

Meanwhile, the "new world order" of untethered, globalising free markets heralded by US President George H. Bush has only gathered momentum following 1989 and the fall of the capitalist West's inveterate foe. Yet, despite its celebrants' frenetic or solemn pledges, this new dispensation has not delivered global peace or lasting economic security. Instead, the world economy has experienced a series of increasingly steep boom-bust cycles, culminating in the near-catastrophic "great recession" following 2008. Camus' call for new political forms in which substantive social justice might be balanced with the civic and political freedoms falteringly enjoyed in the liberal-capitalist nations remains very much the Left's task today, in a world whose glittering postmodern-consumerist metropoles, high tech gadgetry and ubiquitous financialization have been purchased at the cost of deunionisation and declining civic participation, the cheapening of public cultures in thrall to "market forces" and the logics of media concentration, the corporate colonisation of the universities, the atrophy of democratically-elected national governments' ability to control the economic forces upon which their peoples' material well-being depends,

---

31 Jeffrey C. Isaac, *Arendt, Camus, and Modern Rebellion* (Yale: Yale University Press, 1994).
32 Cf. Jeanyves Guérin and Diane S. Wood, "Albert Camus: The First of the New Philosophers", *World Literature Today* Vol. 54, No. 3 (Summer 1980), pp. 363–367. For Camus' distance from the *nouveaux philosophes*, much more heavily influenced by the total critiques of modern reason issuing from Foucault et al., and before them Heidegger, see Chapter One below, section "*Nouvelle philosophe avant la lettre?*"
33 See David Carroll, *Albert Camus the Algerian: Colonialism, Terrorism, Justice* (USA: Columbia University Press, 2008).

growing inequalities between rich and poor within developed nations, and the continuing superexploitation of the populations of the global South.[34]

People systematically robbed of all economic security and political dignities, Camus knew, can be expected (in Camus' eyes, indeed, they have an inalienable *right*) to rebel.[35] And if they perceive that all peaceable avenues of redress, defence, and for having their grievances heard are closed to them, they can be expected to be 'radicalised': that is, attracted to ideological visions which promise a definitive end to their sufferings, and license for this event the messianic use of force. And so it is that the darker underside of the globalised neoliberal order which emerged after 1989 has again and again involved the emergence of militant political and religious movements—headlined by the fundamentalist Sunni networks Al Qaida or Al Shebaab or more recently ISIL (Islamic State in the Levant). These movements have shown themselves willing to deploy spectacular violence against civilian targets, animated by eschatological visions of the total overthrow of the present global order. Such terroristic movements are indeed, in many ways, contemporary spiritual legatees of the nineteenth century Russian nihilists to whom Camus devotes several sections of *L'Homme Révolté*, moved to use terroristic violence in order to overthrow the regime of the Tsar.[36] Islamist terrorists' willingness to suspend the civilian-military distinction to prosecute their cause (and, as Camus would have us add, the US' and her allies' willingness to use waterboarding and other manners of torture against them, as well as targeted assassinations, air strikes with inevitable 'collateral damage', etc.) meanwhile hearken back darkly to the atrocities committed by both sides in the Algerian war following 1954: a conflict which Camus confided affected him "as others feel pain in their lungs".[37] Concerned commentators following legal developments in the United States, United Kingdom, Australasia and elsewhere—not to

---

34   See Thomas Picketty, *Capital in the Twenty-First Century* (USA: Harvard University Press, 2014).

35   This is important to underline, alongside Camus' distance from absolute pacifism, given widespread images from the Left of Camus as conservative, in one form or another (as we will underline in Chapter Four). See for an excellent account, to which we are indebted, John Foley, "Albert Camus and Political Violence" in Christine Margerrison, Mark Orme, Lissa Lincoln eds., *Albert Camus in the 21st Century: A Reassessment of His Thinking at the Dawn of the New Millennium* (Amsterdam, New York: Editions Rodopi B. V., 2008), 209–221.

36   Cf. Albert Camus, *L'Homme Révolté* (Paris: Gallimard, 1952), "Le Terrorisme Individuel", 193–226; Albert Camus, *The Rebel* translated by Anthony Bower, with a Foreword by Sir Herbert Read (New York: Vintage Books, 1971), 149–176.

37   AC 113. See Ronald Aronson, "Camus and Sartre on Violence—the unresolved Conflict", *Journal of Romance Studies* Vol. 6, no. 1 & 2 (2006), esp. 66–70, & 75–76. Cf. Albert Camu,

mention recent disclosures about the extent of government electronic surveillance of their own (and other nations') populations—have drawn attention to the anguishing paradox Camus already noted in the wartime censorship of *Alger républicain*, the newspaper for which he worked in Algeria in 1939–1940.[38] This is that it is almost always in the name of 'national security' against enemies, domestic and foreign (or some cognate version of an hypostasised, imperilled 'general will') that democratic polities come to accept dictatorial, unchecked powers of control, ironically embodying the illiberal features they claim to be defending their subjects from.

In the world after '9/11', the very questions that divided Camus from Merleau-Ponty and Sartre after the war, and which underlay the split over Stalinism, have again become questions of public debate: questions concerning 'means and ends', the possible legitimacy of political violence and the suspension of civil and political liberties to promote visions of a better world. The new millennium's reflections by theologians, philosophers, media commentators and politicians about the nature of evil, again prompted in large measure by the recurrent violent actions of governments and radicalised sects, meanwhile revisit themes long sidelined by academic theory and philosophy, but at the heart of Albert Camus' thought after 1942.

In the recent works by Orme, Carroll, Margerisson, Srigley, Sherman, Zaretsky, Sagi and others,[39] together with the critical collections edited by Lyotard, Margerisson, Orme and Lincoln, Walker and others, however, too little

---

Algerian Chronicles translated Arthur Goldhammer with an Introduction by Alice Kaplan (Cambridge, Massachusetts: Belknap Press, 2013) 113.

38 On this episode, see Emmett Parker, *Albert Camus, the Artist in the Arena* (USA: Wisconsin Press, 1966), 46–47.

39 See Mark Orme, *The Development of Albert Camus's Concern for Social and Political Justice: "Justice pour un Juste"* (Madison, NJ: Fairleigh Dickinson University Press, 2007); David Carroll, *Albert Camus the Algerian: Colonialism, Terrorism, Justice* (New York: Columbia University Press, 2007); Aicha Kassoul and Mohamed Lakhdar Maougal, *The Algerian Destiny of Albert Camus* (Ann Arbor, MI: Academica Press, 2006); John Foley, *Albert Camus: From the Absurd to Revolt* (Stocksfield: Acumen, 2008); Christine Margerrison, Mark Orme & Lissa Lincoln (eds), *Albert Camus in the 21st Century: A Reassessment of his Thinking at the Dawn of the New Millennium.* (Amsterdam: Rodopi, 2008); Adrian Van der Hoven & Sprintzen, David A. (ed. and trans.) *Sartre and Camus: A Historic Confrontation.* (Amherst, NY: Humanity Books, 2004); David Sherman, *Albert Camus* (London: Wiley-Blackwell, 2008); Ronald Srigley, *Camus' Critique of Modernity.* (Columbia, MO: University of Missouri Press, 2011); Dolorès Lyotard, *Albert Camus Contemporain* (Lille: Septentrion Presses Universitaires, 2009); Stephen G. Kellman ed., *Critical Insights: Albert Camus* (Pasadena, California: Salem Press, 2012).

attention has arguably so far been given to a 'fourth cause' for Camus' renewed relevance (alongside *Le Premier Homme*, the fall of Stalinism, and the war on terror). *Camus, Philosophe* aims to redress this shortcoming most of all. It hails from how, in the anglosphere, the widespread intellectual hegemony is passing that was won across numerous academic disciplines by the works of subsequent generations of French thinkers under the loosely-defined titles of 'Theory,' 'post-modernism', or 'post-structuralism'. This hegemony, taught to generations of undergraduate students in the humanities, had worked to sideline voices like Camus' or Sartre's: many of whose ideas, concerns and literary preoccupations were foreign to its own. Indeed, as Gary Gutting or Niilo Kauppi have each suggested,[40] it can be argued that the French university philosophers who came to maturity after 1960 metaphorically 'killed their masters,' and the post-war generation's signature existentialism and humanism. This Oedipal act was necessary if the new theorists were to establish their professional identities, in a context where the academy's insulation from popular "mediocratic" culture was imploding[41] and the urge for constant theoretical novelty, radicality, and subversion was being enshrined.

The history remains largely still to be written of what one disenchanted volume calls "Theory's Empire",[42] referring to the enormous influence wielded in the United States, the United Kingdom, Australasia, and elsewhere of French thinkers led by Claude Lévi-Strauss, Louis Althusser, Jacques Lacan, Luce Irigaray, Michel Foucault, Jacques Derrida, Julia Kristeva, Luce Irigaray, Gilles Deleuze, Jean-Francois Lyotard, and Jean Baudrillard, and more recently figures like the Italian Giorgio Agamben and, to a lesser extent, Jacques Rancière and Alain Badiou. Within France, it is well known that these thinkers were never entirely 'of a piece,' or at peace. Foucault and Derrida, for just one instance—but also Irigaray and Lacan, Baudrillard and Foucault, Rancière and Badiou . . .—had acrimonious disagreements, sometimes touching fundamental points of philosophical or hermeneutic principle. By 1976, in any event, the moment of the post-'68 *désiderants* led by Deleuze and Guattari was passing. Derrida's never-wholly-intergalactic hexagonal star was already on the wane.

---

40   Gary Gutting, *Thinking the Impossible: French Philosophy since 1960* (Oxford University Press, Oxford and New York, 2011); Niilo Kauppi, *French Intellectual Nobility: Institutional and Symbolic Transformations in the Post-Sartrian Era* (USA: State University of New York Press, 1996).

41   Dominique Lecourt, *The Mediocracy: French Philosophy since the Mid-1970s*, translated Gregory Elliot (London: Verso, 2002).

42   Daphne Patal and Wilfrido Corrall, *Theory's Empire: An Anthology of Dissent* (USA: Columbia University Press, 2005).

Lacan's seminars had become an impenetrable shadow of their former gallic glories. Foucault was writing in support of the *nouveaux philosophes* and moving, via a return to the ancients and Immanuel Kant, towards a qualified defence of *les droits de l'homme*.[43] Lyotard, Derrida and others (increasingly influenced by Emmanuel Levinas) had abandoned post-68 *gauchisme* to begin experimenting with an 'ethical' then a 'theological turn'.[44]

As Minerva's owl would have it, it was at just this historical moment of the late 1970s that 'deconstruction' was beginning its remarkable conquest of anglophone literary theory. By the mid-1980s, alongside the genealogical works Foucault produced in the wake of May '68 and the French prison revolts, the works of Deleuze and Guattari, then Lyotard's diagnoses of "the postmodern condition" were having a huge say in shaping literary criticism and what came soon to be called 'cultural studies.' From this bridgehead, 'French theory' (as it is sometimes polemically labelled) has since determined a much wider climate of academic thought pushing into philosophy, sociology, political science, criminology and anthropology.

Great distances often stand between what the Anglophone reception of the French master thinkers' works has made of them, shaped by divergent cultural and political settings, and the authors' original *oeuvres*.[45] The hegemonic climate of thought their authority has been widely drawn upon to establish, however, has served to marginalise philosophical and wider interest in Camus. This hegemony has several agreed features we need to identify to set up our reading of Camus as a voice worth re-hearing today. The first is a scepticism concerning the idea of the modern, autonomous or transcendental subject, commanding a genderless, ahistorical rationality wholly transparent to itself and to the world. According to an 'anti-humanism' paradigmatically announced by Foucault's *Les Mots et les Choses*' closing remarks on the "erasure" of "man",[46] the 'modern subject' is held to have been shown to be an

---

43 Cf. Julian Bourg, *From Revolution to Ethics: May 1968 and Contemporary French Thought* (USA: McGill, Queen's University Press, 2007); Richard Wolin, *The Wind from the East: French Intellectuals, the Cultural Revolution, and the Legacy of the 1960s* (USA: Princeton University Press, 2012).

44 See Dominique Janicaud, *Phenomenology and the 'Theological Turn': The French Debate* (USA: Fordham University Press, 2000).

45 See Robert C. Holub, *Crossing Borders: Reception Theory, Poststructuralism, Deconstruction* (USA: University of Wisconsin Press, 1992).

46 Michel Foucault *The Order of Things: An Archaeology of the Human Sciences* (Oxford and New York: Routledge, 1989), 386–7: "One thing in any case is certain: man is neither the oldest nor the most constant problem that has been posed for human knowledge. Taking a relatively short chronological sample within a restricted geographical area—European

ideological illusion by developments in anthropology, psychoanalysis, linguistics, Nietzscheanism, Hegelianism and Marxism. Instead, secondly, varieties of social or political constructivism are endorsed: whereby the subject "we are invited to free"[47] is shown to be the contingent product of transindividual economic, political, linguistic structures, *dispotifs* or forms of power. Thirdly and equally, the West's age- or ages-long faith in reason as a means to render the self, society and world harmonious or amenable to human control is denounced as one more "great hoax."[48] Indeed, Western rationalism has come to be widely depicted as hybristic, secretly gendered, closed to genuine difference or 'Otherness,' destructive of the natural world, and at base a ready instrument for objectifying human beings and instituting forms of highly intrusive, even totalitarian, forms of political control. Fourthly, then, what might be called the 'Theoretical *endoxa*' is predicated on a deep scepticism about Western societies' long sequence of claims to have established, through philosophy or the sciences, any context-transcendent Truth about the world, or viable ethicopolitical norms. Progress in science, as in politics or ethics, is another ideological or 'metanarratival' illusion, alongside that of the transcendental Cartesian subject. Instead, varieties of radical epistemic perspectivism, relativism and historicism are pronounced, often looking directly back to Friedrich Nietzsche. Students educated in the humanities over the last 20 years will be familiar with the claim that there is no knowable Truth. Granting this hyper-sceptical premise, it must follow that all claims by people to *have*

culture since the sixteenth century—one can be certain that man is a recent invention within it. It is not around him and his secrets that knowledge prowled for so long in the darkness. In fact, among all the mutations that have affected the knowledge of things and their order, the knowledge of identities, differences, characters, equivalences, words—in short, in the midst of all the episodes of that profound history of the Same—only one, that which began a century and a half ago and is now perhaps drawing to a close, has made it possible for the figure of man to appear.... As the archaeology of our thought easily shows, man is an invention of recent date. And one perhaps nearing its end./ If those arrangements were to disappear as they appeared, if some event of which we can at the moment do no more than sense the possibility—without knowing either what its form will be or what it promises—were to cause them to crumble, as the ground of Classical thought did, at the end of the eighteenth century, then one can certainly wager that man would be erased, like a face drawn in sand at the edge of the sea..."

47 Michel Foucault, *Discipline and Punish*, translated by Alan Sheridan (New York: Vintage, 1977), 30.
48 Maurice Blanchot, "The Great Hoax", in *The Blanchot Reader* edited with an Introduction by Michael Holland, with translations by Susan Hanson, Leslie Hill, Michael Holland, Roland-François Lack, Ian Maclachlan, Ann Smock, Chris Stevens, and Michael Syrotinski (Oxford: Blackwell, 1995), 157–166.

established some 'truth' or other can only exemplify so many instances of self-misunderstanding. These validity-claims can then *themselves* be productively studied, at the second order, as so many claims to cultural or political power.[49] Often enough, again following Nietzsche, martial metaphors—of discourse or politics as war, involving the 'deployment' of ideas in 'interventions'... —are endorsed to describe the resulting kaleidoscope of competing, incommensurable power claims.

Progressive critics led by Nancy Fraser, Jürgen Habermas, Alex Callinacos, Thomas McCarthy, Terry Eagleton,[50] and soon enough culture warriors and more reputable critics on the neoconservative Right like Leo Strauss' students[51] have powerfully decried the potentially stifling philosophical, ethical and political implications of these views.[52] A central problem the critics of 'post-modernism' have again and again identified is that any such

---

49 Although on what epistemic basis these second-order claims can themselves claim authority becomes problematic. See for example Christopher Norris, *Against Relativism: Philosophy of Science, Deconstruction and Critical Theory* (Oxford: Blackwell Publishers, 1997).

50 See Nancy Fraser, "Foucault on Modern Power: Empirical Insights and Normative Confusions," Praxis International 1 (October, 1981): 272–287; Jürgen Habermas, *The Philosophical Discourse of Modernity: Twelve Lectures* translated T. McCarthy (Massachusetts: MIT Press, 1990); Alex Callinacos, *Against Postmodernism: A Marxist Critique* (London: Polity Press, 1990); Terry Eagleton. *The Illusions of Postmodernism* (London: Wiley-Blackwell, 1996); Thomas McCarthy, "The Critique of Impure Reason: Foucault and the Frankfurt School", *Political Theory* Vol. 18, No. 3, (Aug. 1990), 437–469; Thomas McCarthy, "The Politics of the Ineffable: Derrida's Deconstructionism in Hermeneutics in Ethics and Social Theory," *Philosophical Forum* 21 (1–2): 146–168 (1989).

51 Strauss' key criticism of "historicism" comes, notably, in the opening chapter of *Natural Right and History* (Chicago: Chicago University Press, 1953).

52 It is worth underscoring, nevertheless, one thing that conservative critics, moved by the moral panic of the culture wars, have rightly stressed. This is that 'Theory' was in part born from, and draws its powerful normative appeal, from the 'cultural turn' towards forms of identity politics (which politicise race, gender, and sexuality, as well as class) in the developed countries in the wake of the turbulent 1960s. (This is a key point of Eagleton's qualified defence in Terry Eagleton, *After Theory* (London: Basic Books, 2003). Social constructivism, even in the seemingly pessimistic form it takes in Foucault's genealogical works, has been interpreted in the light of the emergence of these new social movements as unqualifiedly liberating. For this kind of perspectivism promises to show (indeed it just *is* the view) that hitherto-dominant social, cultural, and political practices, ideas and institutions are in no way the inevitable embodiments of an unchallengable rationality, Truth, or human nature. They are constructs, embodying contestable normative and epistemic claims. Accordingly, they can be critically or genealogically challenged. Historical institutions and practices which seemed unchangable can be politically challenged or

thorough-going scepticism about normative claims to justice, rightness, fairness, the virtues...—as well as brooking well-known forms of performative contradiction[53]—threatens to pull the normative rug from under the feet of the disadvantaged groups it intends to defend. If "power is everywhere", as Foucault famously opined, likewise "everything is dangerous."[54] Any alternative practice, perspective or institution can only be every bit as groundless, or closed to Otherness, as that which it replaces. Unlike Robin Hood, relativism do not rob only from the rich. After three decades of Theory, it can seem that what we are in any case left with is as far as imaginable from a revitalised global and local set of resistances to neoliberal capitalism's unprecedented economic and cultural hegemony. Instead, students are introduced to a series of more or less incommensurable variations upon what Terry Eagleton once called "pessimistic libertarianism": capable of sustaining at least the semblance of radical, critical distance, but unable to concretely prescribe, or normatively justify, alternative visions of political justice or the good life.[55]

---

replaced by alternatives which promise to be more open to the perspectives of groups hitherto disadvantaged, excluded or marginalised.

53 The key claim in Habermas, *The Philosophical Discourse of Modernity* of post-structuralist theories that engage in a total critique of reason, drawing on forms of critical rationality. See eg 276–286 on Foucault.

54 Michel Foucault, *History of Sexuality: Volume 1, The Will to Knowledge* trans. R. Hurley (London: Penguin, 1998), 93; Michel Foucault, "On the Genealogy of Ethics: An Overview of Work in Progress," in Hubert L. Dreyfus and Paul Rabinow, Michel Foucault: Beyond Structuralism and Hermeneutics, Second Edition With an Afterword by and an Interview with Michel Foucault (Chicago: The University of Chicago Press, 1983), 231; cf. Peter Dews, "The Nouvelle Philosophie and Foucault", *Economy and Society*, Volume 8, Issue 2 (1979), 127–171.

55 See Terry Eagleton, "Where do postmodernists come from?" *Monthly Review* 47(3), July 1995: 59–70. As per Eagleton's diagnosis, already twenty years old, on one side, theorists compete in offering pessimistic diagnoses of the entire social or historical world (nature, usually, is off limits, alongside the natural sciences) as comprising institutions, practices, and beliefs founded on the more or less violent exclusion of everything they cannot control. On the other side, since appeal to the normative languages of rights, virtues, justice, freedom, progress, democracy, socialism, liberalism... have all been sceptically 'deconstructed' as implicated in forms of violent exclusion, all that *can* be valorised to oppose the "carceral archipelego" (Foucault), "society of control" (Deleuze), "technological age" (Schmitt, Heidegger), "state" (Badiou), "police" (Ranciere), or "biopower" (Agamben) are increasingly amorphous, liminal phenomena: difference (with or without an 'a') *per se*, alterity or Otherness itself, schizophrenia or nomadism, Events *defined* by their being wholly beyond the purview of existing institutions and categories, decisionistic Acts which will allegedly, fideistically bring into being the principles with reference to

As new generations of critical thinkers today call into question the philosophical, ethical and political limits of this 'poststructuralist' constellation of opinions, our point is, the space is opened up to reconsider the work of authors like Albert Camus with new eyes. On the one hand, as the first four chapters of this book will be devoted to showing, Camus anticipates many of the epistemic, ontological and political claims of later "post-structuralist" theorising. Like the 'post-structuralists', his works contain a strong critique of rationalistic modern philosophies (Chapters One and Two), one which implicates them in the Promethean or Caesarian program realised most completely under Stalinism: of "gradually enlarging the stronghold where, according to his own rules, man without God brutally wields power."[56] Likewise, Camus' thought is founded on a profound scepticism towards claims people make to have discovered absolute Truth or salvific Meaning. (Chapter Three) The philosophy of the absurd, no less than Derrida's account of *différance* or Lyotard's "incredulity towards metanarratives",[57] is founded on the claim that such Truth is unavailable to us. People who have hitherto claimed access to such Truth, Camus agrees, have submitted to "cheat" (*tricher*) or made a "leap" (*un saut*) which intellectual probity should caution us against.[58] In place of philosophies which claim to explain everything, Camus is instead attracted to forms of philosophising and writing open to the complexity, plurality, and differences of human experience and political life. Indeed and of course, Camus' work famously contests the philosophy-literature divide given which theoretical philosophising has often been held (by philosophers, incidentally) to lead to truth. Last but not least, behind both Camus' thought and most of the post-structuralist thinkers', there stands the ambiguous influence of Friedrich Nietzsche: a figure whom Camus would never leave behind (he literally died with *The Gay Science* in his bag), despite articulating one of the bluntest political criticisms of the prophetic dimensions of Nietzsche's *oeuvre* of the last century.[59]

---

which they can be justified, or forms of apophatic theology and utopian messianism of a more radical kind, as we shall see, than Camus already set himself against from the later 1940s. (Chapters Five & Six)

56   HR 134; R 102.
57   Jean-François Lyotard, *The Postmodern Condition: A Report on Knowledge* (US: University of Minnesota Press, 1984).
58   Albert Camus, *Le Mythe de Sisyphe* (Paris: Gallimard, 1942), 21, 54–63; *The Myth of Sisyphus*, translated by Justin O'Brien (New York: Vintage, 1991), 6, 33–41; see Chapter Three below.
59   HR 91–108; R 65–80. On Camus' critique of Nietzsche, see Isaac, *Arendt, Camus, and Modern Rebellion*, 98–102. We should not neglect, as we will not in Chapter Six, Camus' embroiling in the Algerian issue: on whose importance in shaping poststructuralism, see Pal Ahluwalia, *Out of Africa: Post-Structuralism's Colonial Roots* (USA: Routledge, 2010).

And yet... while Camus in these ways can look remarkably like a 'post-modernist', as several critics have realised,[60] the foundations of his thinking and its normative directions differ markedly from the later Parisian *maîtres penseurs*: as well as the thought of the *nouveaux philosophes*, their "mediocratic" children.[61] As we will draw out in Chapter One, Camus' criticism of the role of philosophical and theological systems in shaping the ideologies wielded by Hitler's Nazis and Stalin never gives way to a total criticism of reason *per se*.[62] Again, although Camus argues that the totalitarianisms of Left and Right which he targets in *L'Homme Révolté* are decisively modern phenomena with philosophical antecedents reaching back to Turgot, Condorcet and Rousseau in the 18th century, Camus never gives way to the kind of totalising pessimistic critique of the "modern age" *en toto* which today licenses the kinds of return to theology prominent within and outside the academy. (Chapter Two) While deeply critical of modern political ideologies, and of the economic injustices and cultural cheapening of advanced liberal-capitalist societies,[63] Camus always defended the political values of liberty and social justice, the importance of multi-party political regimes with a free and plural press, churches separated from the repressive arms of the state, and the rule of law, not men, backed by judiciaries independent of the executive powers. (Chapter Four) Camus would thus never waver in his insistence upon the decisive political differences of all forms of liberalism, democratic republicanism, and social democracy from the total, single-party states of Right or Left. The "nomos" of the modern world, for Camus, is not that of the concentration camp (indeed, he would likely reject such a pseudo-metaphysical category);[64] just as for him "to know" is not the same thing as "to dominate", as André Glucksmann breathlessly rejoined

---

60 See for examples: David Sherman, *Albert Camus*, 6–7 (cf. also his "Epilogue", 207–210); Raquel Scherr Salgado, "Memoir at Saint-Brieuc" *MLN*, Vol. 112, No. 4, French Issue (Sep., 1997), pp. 576–594, esp. 577–78. 588; cf. Azzedine Haddour, *Colonial Myths—History and Narrative* (Manchester: Manchester University Press, 2000), 84.

61 Cf. again Lecourt, *Mediocracy*, cited above. Cf. "However, in its honesty and seriousness, his work has never participated in the intellectual conundrums that devalue everything, including the idea of postmodernism itself...", Salgado, "Memoir at Saint-Brieuc," 578.

62 Cf. Georges Pascal, "Albert Camus ou le philosophe malgré lui" in Anne-Mari Arriot & Jean-Françpos Mattéi dir. *Albert Camus et la philosophie* (Paris: Presses Universitaires de France, 1997), 173–185.

63 See Chapter Two below.

64 Cf. Giorgio Agamben, *Homo Sacer: Sovereign Power and Bare Life*, translated by Daniel Heller-Roazen (USA: Stanford University Press, 1998).

in the 1970s.⁶⁵ Finally, although Camus would be deeply sympathetic with the causes and motives underlying the forms of new Left that emerged after his death in France and elsewhere (indeed, in the US, he was a hero of the 1960s student rebels); and although Camus grounds his political philosophy in a defence of the importance of *revolt* against unjust powers, Camus always underlined that rebellion involves the affirmation ("Yes!") of normative limits circumscribing goods the rebel wants to defend. (Chapters Three & Four) Revolt is not exhausted in the impassioned rejection ("No!") of all forces which threaten this "primary value". If a political philosophy of revolt is to be fruitful and not collapse into chaos ("also a form of servitude")⁶⁶ or the kinds of inefficacious dandyism Camus decried in the romantics (attracting Breton's chagrin),⁶⁷ it must be able to do more than say "No!" to illegitimate claimants to political authority.⁶⁸ It must also be able to furnish a coherent, affirmative language in which the reasons behind this revolt can be articulated, and the values or institutions it aims to enshrine be preserved and promoted. (Chapter Four) But for Camus, unlike the great theorists of succeeding French generations, such affirmative values should be sought in the West's classical and early modern heritages, properly reunderstood, not in 'returning' to theological categories he saw as deleteriously continuous with the ideological excesses of the last century: whether Leninist, Stalinist, or paraNietzshean.

3   But Camus, a Philosopher?

We have seen four opening reasons for Camus' recent renaissance, to which this book hopes to contribute. Each of these four causes speaks to the value of reconsidering Camus' thought and *oeuvre* seriously, despite over 50 years having passed since his death, and the continuing academic sidelining of his thought. In order to re-read Camus in the light of contemporary debates in a way which can recapture the complexity of his thought

---

65   André Glucksmann, cited in Fatos Tarifa, "The Poverty of the 'New Philosophy'", *First principles ISI Web Journal*, at www-site http://www.firstprinciplesjournal.com/articles.aspx?article=1661&theme=home&page=4.
66   HR 97–98; R 71.
67   HR 109–130; R 80–89; cf. Camus, "Révolte et conformisme (*Arts* 19 octobre 1951)", *Oeuvre Complètes III 1949–1956* (Gallimard Bibliothèque de la Pléiade, Paris: 2008), 392–394; "Révolte et conformisme (suite), *Arts*, 18 novembre 1951)", 394–397.
68   See Aronson, *Camus and Sartre*, 132–134 for a recent account of the Camus-Breton argument and *rapprochement*.

from more simplistic accounts, we have said that this book argues for a specific claim: that Albert Camus is best understood as a *philosophe* of a very specific kind. The claim that Camus was a philosopher worthy of the name seems scarcely less controversial than the claim that we can still learn anything from Camus' *oeuvre*. Due to reasons of health, although he completed the *Diplôme de Hautes Études* in Algiers, Camus was prevented from attempting the *khagne*, let alone winning the kudos associated with being a *normalièn*.[69] Most importantly, indeed decisively, Camus never aimed even his most theoretical works solely or primarily at a scholarly, academic audience. His most conventionally philosophical works do not develop a recondite technical vocabulary. The sense that Camus gives to his key terms in his philosophical essays ("absurd", "revolt", "freedom", "guilt"...) grow out of, rather than overturn, commonplace usages. *Le Mythe de Sisyphe* and *L'Homme Révolté* are not presented in the jargon of an academic specialist. Indeed, their language is more often a model of classical clarity. No more than Descartes, Montaigne, Plato, Aristotle, Bacon, Kant or Hegel does Albert Camus scrupulously cite his sources, in ways reflecting later modern academic convention.[70] As Jeanson and others were duly to criticise, Camus' philosophical books often soar to heights of hortatory rhetoric, most notably of the closing stanzas of *L'Homme Révolté* on *la pensée du midi*.[71] Then there are his lyrical essays: a genre which Camus very much made his own, somewhere between autobiography, meditation, theoretical reflection, critical analysis, travelogue and musical poetry.

Camus for his part almost everywhere denied that he was a philosopher.[72] "Why I am an artist and not a philosopher?", Camus asks himself in October 1945: "Because I think by words and not by ideas."[73] In an interview with *Servir* of the same year, he explains that "I do not believe sufficiently in reason... to

---

69 Cf. Gutting, *Thinking the Impossible* (UK: Oxford University Press, 2011); Edward Baring, *The Young Derrida and French Philosophy, 1945–1968* (Cambridge: Cambridge University Press, 2011).
70 Cf. Amiot & Mattei, "Avant-Propos," *Albert Camus et la Philosophie*, 2–3.
71 Francis Jeanson, "Albert Camus, or the Soul in Revolt", 81–83.
72 At other times, by the same token, he denies any strong distinction between these two "disciplines": "to anyone who is convinced of the mind's singleness of purpose, nothing is more futile than these distinctions based on methods and objects. There are no frontiers between the disciplines that man sets himself for understanding and loving. They interlock, and the same anxiety merges them." MS 133; MSe, 96–97; see below, esp. Chapter Six.
73 Albert Camus, *Carnets II, janvier 1942–mars 1951* (Paris: Les Éditions Gallimard, 1964), 146; *Carnets 1942–1951*, translated with Introduction & notes by Philip Thody (London: Hamish Hamilton, 1966), 73.

believe in a system."[74] In his *Discourse de Suede* ("Create Dangerously") delivered on receiving the Nobel Prize, it was as an "artist" that Camus spoke and reflected.[75] "The evil geniuses of contemporary Europe bear the label of philosopher. They are Hegel, Marx, Nietzsche...", Camus commented in an interview, reflecting one of his key claims in *L'Homme Révolté*.[76] From even before his falling out with Sartre, who came for Camus to epitomise the kind of intellectual he did not want to be (Chapter Six), Camus entertained grave doubts about the *persona* of the twentieth century university *philosophe*. As early as 1948, under the *nom du plume* "Antoine Bailly", Camus produced a never-published *Impromptu des Philosophes*, a biting satire in the tradition of Lucian and Aristophanes of the existentialist *philosophie de la mode*.[77] "Yes, he is a philosopher, I bought him in Paris...," reads one note in the *Carnets* from 1952.[78] It is likewise from Paris that the suspiciously-named *Monsieur Néant* comes to deliver his weighty tome on human freedom and nothingness to the provinces in the *Impromptu*.

Academic philosophers, for their part, have largely returned Camus' scepticism, when it comes to assessing his intellectual credentials.[79] Sartre, here as elsewhere, heads the list. But A.J. Ayer's early review of Camus' "absurds", which position the "philosopher-novelist" lightly as a poetic "metaphysician" in thrall to unanswerable, because badly formulated, mysteries expresses well how Camus is weighed by most academicians today.[80] Already in his generally

---

74 Albert Camus, "Interview à *Servir*", *Oeuvres Complètes II* (Gallimard Bibliothèque de la Pléiade, Paris: 2006), 659; see Pascal, "Albert Camus ou le philosophe malgré", 173.
75 Albert Camus, "Create Dangerously", in *Resistance, Rebellion, Death* trans. Justin O'Brien. Vintage, New York: 1960, pp. 249–272.
76 Albert Camus, "Three Interviews", LCE 354.
77 Albert Camus / Antoine Bailly, "*Impromptu des philosophes*", OC II, 769–795.
78 C III, 186; C III Eng, 171.
79 As Jacob Golomb has noted: "Of the few scholars still interested in Camus, most esteem his literary genius but denigrate his importance as a philosopher", in his *In Search of Authenticity: Existentialism from Kierkegaard to Camus* (London: Routledge, 1995), 168. As Guérin notes, Camus is not anthologised in most leading French-language encyclopedias, dictionaries, and works on twentieth century philosophy such as Vincent Descombes *Le même et l'autre*: at Jeanyves Guérin, "Camus: Philospohe pour classes terminals?", in *Albert Camus et la philosophie*, 85. The same holds true, only 'more so,' in English-language histories of philosophy.
80 See Roger Mclure, "Autour de la vérité avec Camus, Ayer et le barman", in David H. Walker ed., *Albert Camus: Les Extremes et l'Equilibre*, 75–88. Assessments like Ayer's are commomplaces amongst critics. Even for his biographer Patrick McCarthy, "Although he wrote a great deal, only a small part of his work remains alive. He was a bad philosopher and he has little to tell us about politics. His plays are wooden even if his novels

favourable review of Camus' first cycle of works, Sartre comments disdainfully of his younger contemporary that: "[a]s to the doubts raised by Camus about the scope of our reasoning powers, these are in the most recent tradition of French epistemology...": so there is first of all nothing new here. Moreover, "Camus shows off a bit by quoting passages from Jaspers, Heidegger and Kierkegaard, whom, by the way, he does not always seem to have quite understood."[81] So not only is there nothing new, but much of what is presented is scarcely accurate, even as exegesis. Sartre's disdain would grow in the "Response to Albert Camus" regarding *L'Homme Révolté* that definitively ended their friendship. "You detest difficult thought and hastily declare there is nothing to understand in it", Sartre charges there, "in order to avoid the criticism that you did not understand it."[82] Decades later, in 1970 and again in 1979, following the first French Camus revival in the period of the *nouveaux philosophes*, Jean-Jacques Brochier would expand his master Sartre's diagnosis, underscoring that despite Camus' continuing repute, Camus was at most a philosopher *pour classes terminals*, forgetting seemingly that Bergson and Plato amongst others have also commanded this role in France.[83]

There can be no question that Camus was not a philosopher in the contemporary, professional academic sense of this term. It truly would be absurd to deny this. After all, Camus' *oeuvre*, far from being restricted to the journal articles and monographs assigned to university philosophers today,[84] is from its beginning divided across a remarkable range of intersecting literary genres:

(i) literary fiction (*L'Étranger* [*The Stranger*], *La Peste* [*The Plague*], *La Chute* [*The Fall*], *Exil et Royaume* [*Exile and the Kingdom*], *Le Premier Homme* [*The First Man*]),

---

are superb." At Podhoretz, "Camus and his Critics", at www-site http://www.newcriterion.com/articles.cfm/Camus-and-his-critics-6546. Cf. Raymond Gay-Crosier, "De l'*Homo faber* à l'*Homo ludens*: défence et illustration de la pensée de midi", in *Albert Camus, Contemporain*, 30–31.

81 Jean-Paul Sartre, "Camus' Outsider", in *Literary and Philosophical Essays* translated by Annette Michelson (Great Britain: Hutchinson & Co., 1968), 26.

82 Jean-Paul Sartre, "Response to Albert Camus," in *Sartre and Camus, A Historic Confrontation*, 145.

83 Jean-Jacques Brochier, *Camus, philosophe pour classes terminales*, éd. A. Balland. (Paris: Différence; Discordance edition, 1970, 1979).

84 Maurice Weyembergh, *Camus: ou la mémoire des origins* (Paris: de Boeck & Larcier s.a. 1998), 17: "if it is necessary to write treaties to be a philosopher, then Camus is not a philosopher, assuredly." Again, neither is Plato or Plotinus, Petrarch or Cicero.

(ii) plays (*Caligula, The Misunderstanding, The Just*) and adaptations of novels for the stage (Dostoevsky's *Possessed*, Faulkner's *Requiem for a Nun*);
(iii) philosophical reflections on art and creation ("Essay on Music", "Art in Communion", "The Absurd and Art", "Rebellion and Art", "Create Dangerously"),
(iv) extended philosophical "essays" (*Myth of Sisyphus, Rebel*),
(v) political journalism,
(vi) critical essays on contemporary and historical fiction,
(vii) lyrical essays (*Noces* [*Nuptials*], *L'Été* [*Summer*]),
(viii) autobiography or *anamnesis* (*L'Envers et L'Endroit* ["The Wrong Side and the Right Side"], *Le Premier Homme*,
(ix) notebooks or *Carnets*.

Nevertheless, there are three pillars to our claim that Camus is a *philosophe*, one who (like the great 18th century *philosophes* in France his work often recalls, per Chapter Four) did not shirk from exploring multiple genres of writing in order to develop, explore, and convey his evolving perspectives, and try to reach different audiences. The first of these pillars we will address in this section: the second and third in what follows.

The first side to our contention is that, in and behind Camus' different modes of writing, there is a coherent, original, arguably profound body of philosophical thought (Camus' "philosophical discourse", as we will call it)[85] about the natural and political world and the place of human beings within it. This thought addresses a host of fundamental questions which we would be hard-pressed to deny have philosophical dimensions, unless we subscribe to the

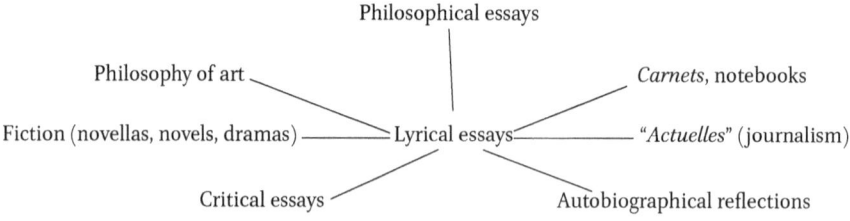

FIGURE 1   Camus' œuvre *pictured, with lyrical essays at intersection of all Camus' genres (as they incorporate elements of each).*

---

85   The distinction between philosophy and "philosophical discourse" is drawn from Pierre Hadot, *What is Ancient Philosophy*, trans. M. Chase (USA: Belknap Press, 2002), 172–236. See below.

most aridly narrow view of what philosophy is.[86] These questions remain pertinent culturally and politically, for individuals and more widely,[87] although some of them have disappeared from more formal academic reflection:

1. Can suicide ever be rationally justified, especially after the "death of God" (the loss in the West of shared faith in a transcendent, providential, salvific creator deity) diagnosed by Nietzsche in the late 19th century?
2. Can murder, for political or religious reasons (capital punishment, terrorism, targeted assassinations, drone strikes, etc.), ever be justified or should it always be opposed on principle?
3. Can ethical and political values be founded without recourse to a transcendent God, whose attributes and intentions seem beyond the scope of uncoerced, universal human agreement?
4. Is despair or "nihilism," the view that there are no lasting epistemic or ethical limits or norms, inevitable for thoughtful non-believers in such a *theos*?
5. Is a criticism of capitalism's excesses and systematic injustices possible, which does not rely either on a return to theology (although it may), or the embrace of Marxist-Leninist principles which arguably secularise many *motifs* from Christian theodicy and eschatology, replacing the last judgment with utopian visions of an 'end of history'?
6. Why (as of circa 1950) has two centuries of modern revolt against the perceived implausibilities and injustices of theologically-sanctioned churches and states not ended civil and international conflict, while furnishing political and military organisations with vastly expanded destructive technologies?
7. What is the relationship between the West's monotheistic (Jewish, then Christian) heritage, and its classical (Hellenic, then Roman) legacies, and what are the defining values and virtues of each which we might call upon in a modern world?

---

86   Cf. Jacqueline Lévi-Valensi, "'Si tu veux être philosophe…'", *Albert Camus et la philosophie*, 27.
87   Cf. Maurice Weyembergh, "Sur l'(in)actualité de Camus," *Albert Camus in the 21st CenturAlbert Camus in the 21st Century*, 33–35. Also see Thomas Landon Thorson, "Albert Camus and the Rights of Man" *Ethics*, Vol. 74, No. 4 (Jul., 1964), 281–291: 282 ("Political philosophy will never die for the simple reason that it is far too important for men in society.") One needn't accept all of Thorson's position to accept for instance that questions 2, 3, 6, and 8, and other of Camus' questions, like that concerning the relationship between freedom and justice, are perennial, albeit articulated in different theoretical and natural languages.

8. How can peoples of different cultural and religious backgrounds peaceably cohabit, in the absence of a single, universally agreed set of metaphysical or theological assumptions?
9. What is the relationship between human action, political life (or "history") and the natural world, and have Western theological and philosophical positions systematically under-weighed the extent to which human beings are natural (albeit speaking, rational) creatures?

In response to these questions, this book will argue, Camus' thought turns around a single, 'master argument' which he develops between the late 1930s through to the 1950s. This argument can be presented in a way which should satisfy even the most convinced sceptic about Camus' philosophical credentials, if by such credentials we mean the ability to coherently unfold a rationally constructed, evidentially based argument, and apply it across a range of different topics.[88] Camus' master argument:

> (i) begins semantically (and in order of publication) with the famous post-metaphysical agnosticism of *Le Mythe de Sisyphe*. Camus argues that we cannot, without making "leaps" of faith, claim to know either that there *is* a single, theological or rationalistic Meaning explaining human life, *or* that there is *no* such absolute Meaning. This philosophical starting-point is described by Camus, including in *L'Homme Révolté*, in Cartesian terms. However greatly Camus' thought, as it develops, takes on the distinctly classical *mien* which has led several critics (recently Ronald Srigley in the Anglophone world) to dub Camus *un ancien*,[89] the absurd *skepsis* is supposed by Camus to guarantee a philosophical foundation as indubitable as Descartes intended his *cogito sum* to be.[90] Yet;
>
> (ii) Camus does not infer from such a post-metaphysical starting point the kind of nihilistic despair often associated with his name. Camus argues, on the contrary, that suicidal despair would only be rationally justifiable if it *could* be definitively established that human life did have no Meaning. But this is not so (i). Instead, Camus argues that philosophical "honesty" or "decency" demands a kind of chastened epistemic ethics:

---

[88] See Appendix One, which presents *The Rebel*'s argument in 41 sequential, numbered premises; and also Appendix Three, wherein an illustration of how the argument operates in "Letters to a German Friend", one of the texts it is easy to read as "not philosophical".

[89] Srigley, *Camus' Critique of Modernity*; Francois Bousquet, *Camus L'Ancien, Camus Le Mediterraneen* (Sherbrooke, Quebec, Canada: Éditions Naaman, 1977).

[90] HR 38; R 22; & Chapter Three below.

one of "living only with what we can know,"[91] continually awake to, and animated to honestly confront, honor and preserve, the "absurd" divorce between the human longing for absolution and its unavailability, unless we philosophically "cheat".

(iii) On the basis of this epistemic ethic, Camus argues in *L'Homme Révolté* that the murder of others can no more be justified than killing oneself, absent the sanction of an absolute theological or philosophical perspective. Thus, metaphysical scepticism does not necessitate moral nihilism. It points towards an unrelativisable primary value: that of solidarity with other human beings whom we *know* to exist, this side of all metaphysical disputes and confabulations:[92] "In the light, the earth remains our first and our last love. Our brothers are breathing under the same sky as we; justice is a living thing."[93] Accepting this living, presentist, non-messianic value thus proscribes forms of premeditated, rationalised deceit, slavery, and murder, each of which destroys "that small part of reality (*l'être*) that can be conquered by living men...";[94]

(iv) Instead of continuing to aim for "all-or-nothing," absolute perspectives, Camus contends that a consistently post-theological position must cultivate a perspective which would "exclude nothing" of what does inescapably present itself to human experience. No single truth or exigency (above all, the human longing for unity and order, *or* the final opacity of reality to total rational comprehension) can fully explain or comprehend all elements of the human condition. Rather (and to clarify):

(v) a consistently post-metaphysical philosophy will:

(a) vindicate a neoclassical philosophy of *mesure*, 'balance' or 'moderation.' This position recognises the importance of, and tries to comprehensively balance *both* sides of the oppositions that Western thought has lurched uneasily between, excluding no evidently salient dimension of our shared condition: nature–history; reason–affect; justice–love; political duty–happiness; individual–collective; exile–kingdom;

---

91 MS 77–78; MSe 53.
92 This is what David Sprintzen calls a "minimal evaluative standpoint", although his description of this as a "metaphysical base" is ambiguous, at David Sprintzen, *Camus: A Critical Examination* (Philadelphia: Temple University Press, 1998), 133.
93 HR 381; R 306.
94 HR 354; R 283.

sacred–profane; contemplation–action; withdrawal–engagement; innocence–guilt; assent–negation or revolt; unity–difference;[95]

(b) thus point towards a philosophy of wider ethical and political limits, rooted in the epistemic limits identified in *The Myth of Sisyphus* which deny us total comprehension of our condition. As Camus argues in *The Rebel* and "Reflections on the Guillotine," reprising almost to the letter sceptical claims for religious toleration made in the earlier modern period by Bayle, Montaigne, and Voltaire, epistemic humility makes imperative in the political realm a principled opposition to rationalised murder or the death penalty: not in the name of God or an essentialist doctrine of human nature, but in the name of the primary, inalienable ethical solidarity with our contemporaries "in error and aberration"[96] against all ideologies which claim the right to silence, enslave, systematically deceive or kill.

(c) be a philosophy of dialogue: which recognises that, no person or perspective having a monopoly on Truth, it is incumbent upon political institutions to organise our shared life in such a way as to enshrine the communication between different perspectives, and peaceful cohabitation between their adherents;

(vi) Given (i) through (v), Camus defends a neoclassical comprehension and criticism of human evil, including the totalitarian experiments of the 20th century. In contrast to secularised versions of the claim that human nature is fallen or 'radically evil', Camus sees evil in post-Socratic terms. This makes it the product of passion-bound ignorance, partiality, finitude and error. In particular, political evil for Camus results from perpetrators' 'excessive' attempts to 'monologically' absolutise some single perspective or value, and impose it on the 'totality' of reality: the history of class struggle over the manifold differences between human beings; justice at the expense of liberty; solidarity at the expense of the individual, economic over political liberties, etc. For Camus' philosophical perspective, each such totalising perspective is partially legitimate. Despite all polemics, there is next to no philosophy or theology under the sun that does not answer to real human exigencies (the need for community; the shaping role of history in human experience, the importance of social justice, attachment to place …) It is just that, by pursuing this perspective and its aims to the exclusion of all competing or opposing considerations

---

95 See Appendix Two below, and Chapter Five.
96 Albert Camus, "Reflections on the Guillotine" in RRD, 173–234., at 217.

(the need for individual liberties to pursue the good life, to respect the shaping role of nature in human experience, cross-cultural commonalities between peoples…), it will illegitimately obviate other important constituents of the human condition, when it does not license forms of messianic violence in order to totalise its vision and impose it on recalcitrant reality.

It would be excessive to suggest that Camus' many critical and admiring readers have not to different degrees circled this core philosophical argument in Camus. But we do want to claim here that the logical, para-Cartesian rigor of this position has, certainly in English-language criticism, been widely overlooked: above all, due to Camus' mode of presenting his philosophical ideas (see below). Frederic Worms in France for one has recently situated "Camus' moment" as a decisive turning point in the evolution of twentieth century French philosophy.[97] For Worms, whose brief reading of Camus seems to us admirably insightful, Camus is no less "philosophical" than Sartre and Merleau-Ponty. Indeed, Worms underlines that, "as much as and even more than these others… the position of Camus… has a force and a specifically *philosophical* coherence…."[98] As Worms reads Camus' philosophical position, his thought responds to three tasks:

1. "to return to the existential facts of the absurd and then of revolt, considered in themselves… not as simple facts, but as complex, divided exigencies [and] tendencies of the human condition."
2. "to critique the abusive forms of reasoning which pretend to lean on these 'simple facts' in ways which lead to human beings' murderous follies…" Then:
3. "to comprehend the sense that these facts take on when we unshackle them from these [false modes of] reasoning; to understand why they then appear for what they really are: testimony to a condition which is not simply difficult, absurd, 'scandalous', but also an experience which is simple, world-affirming, *heureux*. [For Camus] human existence is not only defiance but also joy, not only unhappiness but also sunlight and the sea, not only indignation but dignity or justice."[99]

---

97   Frederic Worms, *La philosophie en France au XXe siècle. Moments* (Paris: Broché, 2009).
98   Worms, *La philosophie*, 321.
99   Worms, *La philosophie*, 324. The numbering of the *partitio* here is ours.

To underline what Worms discerns here, that is, Camus' philosophical thought not only involves a set of descriptive and explanatory claims concerning the human condition. This comprehensive perspective also provides a framework to explain why it is that other philosophers have failed to achieve its classically measured understanding. The result thus answers to what Aristotle, long ago, argued was one mark of a convincing philosophical perspective, able readily to dialectically defend its claims, since:

> … we must not only state the true view, but give the reason why of the false one [why anyone would think it true], since that furthers confidence. For when we have a clear and good account of why a false view appears true, that makes us more confident of the true view.[100]

4 Camus, Neohellenic Philosopher, Neoclassical Humanist

If Camus' *oeuvre* does harbour such an elegantly coherent philosophical perspective at its core, it will be asked why this perspective has not been more widely recognised and criticised. Why has Camus instead been much more often dismissed as not a philosopher at all, but an admirable author, or a pious moralist whose public stances rested on nothing more weighty than his own generously democratic or socialistic dispositions? The principal reason for this has already been mentioned several times. It lies in Camus' literary style, or rather styles, of writing, even in the philosophical essays *The Myth of Sisyphus* and *The Rebel*. Here as elsewhere, Jeanson's barbs against *L'Homme Révolté* (that its writing was too beautiful to be taken seriously as philosophy or as politics)[101] have bitten. Or rather, Jeanson's criticisms of Camus' style reflect deep-set later modern preconceptions about who a philosopher is, and how she must write, engage, and argue which Camus did not conform to. Even Camus' biographer Olivier Todd has argued that Camus' writing, for instance in *The Myth of Sisyphus*, was not "philosophical" so much as "rapid, punchy, and fluid. He sought a certain lucidity without attaining it."[102]

---

100 Aristotle, *Nicomachean Ethics*, VII 14, 1154a22–25.
101 Jeanson, "Albert Camus, or the Soul in Revolt," 79–83.
102 Olivier Todd, *Albert Camus: A Life* trans. B. Ivry (New York: Carroll & Graf, 2000), 144. Or again, compare Zaretsky (amidst a reading of Camus with which we are generally sympathetic): "*The Myth* is an essay, similar to those written by one of Camus' models, Michel de Montaigne. In its pages, Camus pursues the perennial prey of philosophy—the questions of who we are, where and whether we can find meaning, and what we can truly know

To introduce the second pillar to our contention that Camus is rightly understood as a specific kind of philosopher, we can cite Camus' responses when asked to clarify his distance from the regnant existentialism of the post-war period. One way he did this was to highlight that his own philosophical background and predilections differed markedly from the standard *paideia* of his Parisian contemporaries. "I am not an existentialist, although of course critics are obliged to make categories," Camus commented: "I got my first philosophical impressions from the Greeks, not from nineteenth century Germany."[103] Understanding the kind of Hellenic or Hellenistic impressions Camus received as a young man, as he grew up in the fierce sunlight of colonial Algeria, is vital to understanding the shape of his mature *oeuvre*, his identity as a *philosophe* and his distance from almost all other 20th century French thinkers.[104]

Camus always recalled his origins as a working class *pied noir* Algerian in tones of great tenderness,[105] as we will return to in Chapter Six. The son of an illiterate, nearly deaf mother and a father who perished when Albert was

---

about ourselves and the world—less with the intention of capturing them than continuing the chase. Camus no more worried that there remained "something provisional" to his work than Montaigne did that his self-portrait kept changing. In fact, Camus achieves with the *Myth* what the philosopher Maurice Merleau-Ponty claimed for Montaigne's *Essays*: it places "a consciousness astonished at itself at the core of human existence." Robert Zaretsky, *A Life Worth Living* (Harvard University Press. Kindle Edition, 2013), 13.

103 At Todd, *Albert Camus*, 379. Cf. "Non, je ne suis pas existentialiste........." (15 Novembre 1945) in *Oeuvres Complètes 1944–1948*, 655–656; with Albert Camus, "Pessimism and Courage": "I do not much relish the all too celebrated existentialism and to be honest, I find its conclusions false," in *Resistance, Rebellion, Death*, translated with Introduction by Justin O'Brien (New York: Vintage, 1960), 58. As Aronson comments, Camus became concerned after 1945 to not be perceived only as Sartre's shadow, at Aronson, *Camus and Sartre*, 51: which is not to deny that there were substantive reasons behind Camus' taking his distance (on the contrary, in this case).

104 In making this case, we will be again be joining but reframing a rush of recent works and events. There were five conferences on Camus' classical and Mediterranean heritage held between 1997 and 2006 alone, as per http://webcamus.free.fr/conferences.html: '*Albert Camus: parcours méditerranéens*' (Jerusalem, 1997); '*Camus et le rêve méditerranéen: de l'Algérie à la Grèce*' (Marseille, 2003); '*Les valeurs méditerranéennes dans l'œuvre d'Albert Camus*' (Algiers, 2003); "); '*Albert Camus: Oran, l'Algérie, la Méditerranée*' (Oran, 2005) and '*Albert Camus, précurseur: Méditerranée d'hier et d'aujourd'hui*' (University of Madison-Wisconsin, 2006). In the English language, there is the important study of Ronald Srigley, *Camus' Critique of Modernity* published in 2011 which will be an ongoing interlocutor in this book.

105 See *The First Man* translated David Hapgood (London: Penguin, 1996), with *Between the Wrong Side and the Right Side* in LCE, 3–62 and Chapter Six below.

barely one on the Marne in 1914, Camus' precocious abilities were first discovered by Louis Germain, his school teacher. Under Germain's guidance, Camus completed his *baccalaureate*. Camus was then introduced to philosophy by his university instructor, the philosopher and author Jean Grenier. Under Grenier's influence, the young Camus (enamoured of Bergson and Nietzsche, and already experimenting with a variety of literary media)[106] was introduced to many of the philosophical and literary classics of the ancient world. In their settings and sensibilities, Camus sensed a deep kinship to his own Mediterranean provenance. As Grenier would reflect: "it is necessary, when one speaks of him [Camus], to never forget his native country."[107] In 1935–'36, Camus wrote his thesis for the *Diplôme d'Hautes Études* on no less a topic than the monumental cultural transition between paganism and Christendom at the end of the antique world.[108] Camus was thus familiar with the works of Plotinus, the evangels and Saint Augustine before he encountered Hegel, Husserl, and Heidegger, the presiding Germanic forefathers of French existentialism. Meanwhile, although the young Camus briefly joined the Algerian Communist Party, a note on "Grenier on communism" from this time—"should one, for an ideal of justice, accept stupid ideas?"[109]—suggests that already Camus felt Marxism's philosophical trajectory alien, despite his working class allegiances. "I will never place a copy of Marx's *Capital* between life and my fellow men," Camus would write during this period to a friend.[110]

In the French language, Bousquet in 1977 devoted an extended study to Camus as a thinker whose career hearkens back to "ancient," "Mediterranean" paradigms. Different strains of his *oeuvre* echo Stoic, Epicurean, tragic and

---

106 Cf. Albert Camus, *The First Camus: Youthful Writings* with an Introduction by Paul Viallaneix, translated by E.C. Kennedy. (New York: Vintage, 1977).
107 Jean Grenier, cited at Monique Crochet, *Les Mythes dans L'Oeuvre d'Albert Camus* (Paris: Éditions universitaires, 1973), 26.
108 Albert Camus, *Christian Metaphysics and Neoplatonism*, translated with an Introduction by Ronald Srigley (Columbia & London: University of Missouri Press, 2007). On Camus' education, see Herbert Lottman, *Albert Camus: A Biography* (London: Picador, 1979); Toby Garfitt, "Situating Camus: the formative influences", in *The Cambridge Companion to Camus* (Cambridge: Cambridge University Press, 2007), 26–38.
109 C I 16; C I Eng 8. Cf. Parker, *Albert Camus: the Artist in the Arena*, 6–8.
110 At Zaretsky, *Albert Camus: Elements of a Life*, 26–29. See on Camus' fall out with the Algerian communists, Ronald Aronson, *Camus and Sartre: The story of a friendship and the quarrel that ended it*, 24–25; Herbert Lottman, *Albert Camus: A Biography*, 147–160; and on his early activism, Stephen Bronner, *Camus: Portrait of a Moralist*, 19–30.

pre-Socratic motifs, as we will confirm.[111] Archambault's *Camus' Hellenic Sources* has critically documented the extent of Camus' borrowings from ancient Hellenic, Hellenistic, and Roman sources, and contemporary studies of the ancients.[112] More recently, Ronald Srigley's *Camus' Critique of Modernity* likewise situates Camus as decisively a 'Greek' or philhellenic thinker. Srigley highlights how Camus' formative influences lay in Greek poetry, drama, the historians and the philosophers, in contrast to the West's Christian legacies, although he continually engaged with the latter. Camus would even ironically joke in interview: "The truth is that it is a hard fate to be born in a pagan land in Christian times. This is my case. I feel closer to the values of classical world than to those of Christianity. Unfortunately, I cannot go to Delphi to be initiated!"[113]

The present study stands in the lineage of these works on Camus *"l'ancien"* by Bousquet and Srigley, as well as essay-length studies by Ward and Richardson and those collected in the invaluable collections, *Albert Camus et la Grèce* and *Albert Camus: Les Extremes et L'Equilibre*.[114] As Camus was well aware, his defence of classical *mesure* in 1940s and 1950s France paradoxically placed him in an exceptional position, relative to the prevailing cultural directions of *les temps modernes*. Yet we will see, in spades, that Camus did attempt such a defence, placing the ancient value of *sophrosyne* (the Delphic "nothing too much") on new, 'modern', metaphysically agnostic premises.[115]

This study, in addition, brings to the interpretation of Camus' neoclassicism or neoHellenism[116] a specific conception of ancient philosophical culture, new

---

111 François Bousquet, *Camus le méditerranéen, Camus l'ancien* (Sherbrooke, Québec: Éditions Naaman, 1977).

112 Paul Archambault, *Camus' Hellenic Sources* (Chapel Hill: University of North Carolina Press, 1972).

113 Albert Camus, "Interview with Gabriel d'Aubarède *in Les Nouveles Littéraire*, May 10, 1951", in "Three Interviews", LCE 357.

114 A. Fosty (ed.), *Albert Camus et la Grèce* (Paris: Broché, 2008); David H. Walker ed., *Albert Camus: Les Extremes et l'Equilibre* (Actes du colloque de Keele, 25–27 mars 1993. Amsterdam: Rodopi, 1994); Bruce Ward, "The Recovery of Helen: Albert Camus's Attempt to Restore the Greek Idea of Nature", *Dionysius* 14 (1990): 169–194; Luke Richardson, "Sisyphus and Caesar: the opposition of Greece and Rome in Albert Camus' absurd cycle", *Classical Receptions Journal* Vol. 4: 1 (2012) 66–89.

115 "What distinguishes modern sensibility from classical sensibility is that the latter thrives on moral problems and the former on metaphysical problems…" Camus comments intriguingly at MS 142; MSe, 104. Since the 19th century at least, this is generally how Hellenistic and Roman philosophy alone, as against the entire classical world has been conceived. Camus' early focus on late antiquity may be in play here.

116 'Neo-*hellenism*', for as we will specify in Chapter Five, Camus lastingly distanced himself from the Rome of Caligula, the Caesars, and the European Right's imaginings. On which,

to work on Camus. This metaphilosophical idea is indebted to the work of the French classicist Pierre Hadot published since 1970 (and after 1995 in English translation).[117] In a series of works written between 1970 and his death in 2011, Hadot argued powerfully that to be a philosopher in classical antiquity, from the pre-Socratics to the later Imperial period, was a very different thing than to be an academic philosopher in the recognised senses of this term today, or in Camus' time. Hadot was a key influence on the 'last Foucault''s interest in ancient Greek and Roman practices of self-formation.[118] His famous claim is that philosophy was conceived, and practiced, by the ancients as a way of life. In this conception of philosophy, the production of theoretical discourses about the world, knowledge, and political matters was not the self-standing, sufficient goal of philosophical activity. This is not (implausibly) to deny that the construction, dialectical examination and defence of theoretical understandings was not, then as now, a defining, necessary feature of *philosophia*. But the rational theoretical systems developed in the different classical pagan schools were each adduced as a means to justify, comprehend, reflect and direct "spiritual exercises" in which the philosopher would try to discipline his or her own (and students') beliefs, actions and passions. The goal was to shape their psyches as kinds of living reflections of the world as each school's theoretical perspective conceived it to be. In one of Hadot's favourite formulations, classical philosophy aimed at the formation of human beings, as well as the conveyance of information. It was thus not unusual for ancient philosophers, dedicated to this care of the self, to like Socrates write nothing at all, let alone to restrict themselves to the recognised academic forms of exegesis and argumentation accepted today. "No, I am not a philosopher," Camus explained in another of his key statements on this issue, but went on immediately to stipulate that this was because of his *Socratic* preoccupations, "What

---

see Richardson, "Sisyphus and Caesar: the opposition of Greece and Rome in Albert Camus' absurd cycle" *Classical Receptions Journal* Vol. 4: 1 (2012) 66–89.

117 I note that Arriot and Mattei, in the conclusion to their "Avant Propos" to *Albert Camus et la philosophie* also link Camus with Hadot's metaphilosophical reflections, at 17–18. But they do not develop the thought, which several of the collected articles nevertheless circumscribe. See Matthew Lamb, "Philosophy as a Way of Life: Albert Camus and Pierre Hadot.", *Sophia* 50 4 (2011): 561–576, the only dedicated comparative piece on the two figures (which arguably overplays Hadot's metaphysical commitments and Platonism, contra Camus).

118 On Foucault's later concern with Greek and Roman thought, see the excellent secondary study by Edward F. McGushin, *Foucault's Askesis: An Introduction to the Philosophical Life* (USA: Northwestern University Press, 2007).

interests me is to know how one must conduct oneself."[119] In a passage remarkably anticipating Hadot in the *Carnets* (Camus is reflecting on the great medieval scholar Étienne Gilson), we can see in fact that Camus was cognisant of the kinds of differences between ancient and modern philosophers that also struck Hadot:

> Philosophers in the ancient world ... thought much more than they read. That is why they stuck so close to concrete cases. Printing has changed that. People read more than they think. We don't have philosophers any more but merely commentaries. This is what Gilson says in arguing that the age of philosophers concerned with philosophy has been followed by the age of professors of philosophy concerned with philosophers. This attitude contains both modesty and impotence. And a thinker who began his book with the words: 'And let us take things from the beginning' would raise some smiles. We have reached the point where a book of philosophy published nowadays that did not rely on authority, quotation, commentary, etc., would not be taken seriously. *And yet ...*[120]

Ancient Greek and Roman philosophy, when it was written at all, was characterised by a remarkable divergence of literary forms, Hadot has stressed.[121] To take only the leading examples, Plato and Aristotle, Cicero and Plutarch wrote dialogues; while Seneca wrote letters, dialogues and tragedies. Even Socrates was said in ancient times to have assisted Euripides in producing his iconoclastic tragic dramas.[122] The reason for this proliferation of genres and the openness of the *philosophoi* to writing in different ways, Hadot persuasively argues, reflects how these thinkers did not yet take their role to be restricted to the production of theoretical understandings. They understood their goal, in line

---

119   Camus, "Interview à *Servir*", OC II 659. See Robert Sasso, "Camus et la refus du système", *Camus et la philosophie*, 207–8.
120   C II 88; C II Eng, 44. See Robert Sossa, "Camus et la rfus du systèeme", 215–216.
121   Cf. especially Pierre Hadot, "Forms of Life and Forms of Discourse in Ancient Philosophy" in *Philosophy as a Way of Life* translated M. Chase (London: Wiley-Blackwell, 1996), 49–70 and the *compte rendu* of Hadot's course of 1979–1980 on philosophical genres, at Pierre Hadot, *Études de Patristique et D'Histoire des Concepts* (Paris: Le Belles Lettres), "Année 1979–1980", 162–167. For a general account, see Matthew Sharpe, "Hadot, Pierre", *Internet Encyclopedia of Philosophy* (2011) at www-site http://www.iep.utm.edu/hadot/, last accessed February 2015.
122   Diogenes Laertius, *Lives of the Eminent Philosophers*, translated by C.D. Yonge, paragraph 11, at www-site http://classicpersuasion.org/pw/diogenes/dlsocrates.htm, last accessed January 2015.

with inherited Greek ideals of *paideia*, to lie in the cultivation in aspirants of a *bios theoretikos*, or at least an examined *life*. The philosophical student in the ancient schools aspired not, or not only, to write good speeches or books (the profession of the sophists). They aspired to be a good and wise man: ideally a sage like Socrates, Epicurus, the younger Cato or Pyrrho. Philosophical discourse for the ancients, in Hadot's words, was "a privileged means by which the philosopher can act upon himself and others: for if it is the expression of the existential option of the person who utters it, discourse always has, directly or indirectly, a function which is formative, educative, psychagogic, and therapeutic."[123] In modern language, we might say that these ancient philosophical authors, when they chose to write at all, aimed to produce a host of different perlocutionary effects in different audiences in different contexts, relative to the anticipated aptitudes and preoccupations of audiences, and the different subjects and aims of their texts. Such differentia, notably, were the very matters philosophically examined in the treatises on rhetoric written by ancient thinkers led by Aristotle, Cicero and Quintillian.[124]

The reader can thus see the sympathies between this ancient understanding of philosophy with a modern figure like Camus. Classical philosophy, from before Plato, embraced both philosophical and literary modes of writing.[125] It did so in the light of an expanded, humanistic conception of philosophical practice, as touching the lives and experiences of philosophers. If Camus has so often been understood as an existentialist, and if his writings still attract new generations of readers, one reason is because of the way his philosophical reflection and literary writings so clearly reflect his own personal and political concerns. The questions we listed above around which Camus' philosophical discourse develops are not the product of what we today call a 'research program' unaffected by the existential and political struggles of their author. He is rather what Sagi, following Germaine Brée, has termed a "personal thinker." This is "a philosopher who takes his personal experience as his point

---

123 Pierre Hadot, *What is Ancient Philosophy?*, 176.

124 HR 377–382; R 302–306. These latter in turn lay at the heart of the European renaissance and early modern humanistic education and culture which Camus evokes in his call for a second renaissance, "beyond nihilism."

125 As Camus recognised, as per "Helen's Exile"'s *bon mot*: "whereas Plato contained everything—nonsense, reason, and myths—our philosophers admit nothing but nonsense or reason, because they have closed their eyes to the rest. The mole is meditating…", at 151.

of departure. This experience becomes the focus of his thinking, and Camus explicates it through philosophy."[126]

We have seen Camus thus distancing himself from a mode of intellectual life which he came after 1952 to see embodied in Sartre (Chapter Six). It is nevertheless notable that, from early on in his *Carnets*, Camus was open to accepting a more Socratic description of his intellectual *persona*: if by this epithet we mean "someone whose mind watches itself. I like this, because I am happy to be both watcher and watched. 'Can they be brought together?' [someone will ask] That is a practical question. We must get down to it."[127] The *Carnets* themselves, as the author has argued elsewhere,[128] can be seen in one of their registers as a modern instantiation of the kind of "self-writing' of *hypomnémata* (memory notes, reminders) that Hadot has shown Marcus Aurelius' *Meditations* to have been: a form of "spiritual exercise" in which the author, addressing himself, tries to call to mind and apply to his life the philosophical precepts he has theoretically accepted as true: to, as it were, give these ideas their pound of flesh.[129]

Certainly, when Camus writes concerning existential despair in *Le Mythe de Sisyphe*, it is because he finds the "absurd" "an idea in the streets of my time," rather than in the corridors or seminar halls of the Sorbonne or ENS.[130] A chronological reading of his developing thoughts in the 1940s, moreover, shows that Camus' philosophical defence of revolt as a 'source of values' was rooted first of all in his own, and his French contemporaries', passionate experiences of rebellion against the Nazi occupation. In the 1950s, it is fair to say, following Audi, that an animating affect for Camus was *guilt* following the falling out

---

126   Abraham Sagi, *Albert Camus and the Philosophy of the Absurd* (Rodopi, 2002), ch. 2, p. 16. See Orme, *Development of Camus' Concern*, 170–171, 162 on *The Rebel*, where this is made a point of criticism in a "therapeutic" reading.

127   C I 41; C I Eng. 15.

128   Matthew Sharpe, "Camus' *Askēsis*: reading Camus in light of the *Carnets* (and his *L'Impromptu des philosophes*), *Philosophical practice*, vol. 8, no. 1 (2013), pp. 1149–1164.

129   See Hadot, "Spiritual Exercises" and "Marcus Aurelius" in *Philosophy as a Way of Life*, 81–125 & 179–205; and Pierre Hadot, *The Inner Citadel: The Meditations of Marcus Aurelius*, translated by M. Chase (USA: Harvard University Press, 1998). On Camus' proximity to this conception of philosophy, with specific reference to the stoics and also Cicero, see Robert Sasso, "Camus et la refus du système", 210. On writing in particular as a technique in self-formation, see Michel Foucault "Self Writing" in *Dits et écrits*, pp. 415–430, at www-site http://foucault.info/documents/foucault.hypomnemata.en.html, last accessed February 2015.

130   E 159; see MSe ("Preface" (1955)), 5.

with Sartre, his wrestling with the Algerian *événements* after 1954, as well as his own personal failings towards his second wife. (Chapter Six)[131]

One further dimension of Camus' understanding and practice of philosophy as a way of life, we thus see (and a further reason why many critics dismiss him as a philosopher *per se*) is Camus' refusal of the hard-and-fast separation between heart and mind, reason and the passions. Like all the ancient philosophers, we hasten to specify, Camus deeply suspected the untethered passions. He associated the unmastered passions with forms of epistemic imbalance and behavioural 'excess' that need to be moderated through individual and collective reflection and struggle, not visited upon the world.[132] Nevertheless, alongside Martha Nussbaum amongst more recent thinkers (and indeed like Aristotle or the Stoics) Camus held that the heart nevertheless has its reasons that philosophical reason is foolish to ignore.[133] Emotions like indignation against cruelty, compassion at the suffering of others, or wonder before natural beauty embody for Camus potentially revelatory forms of intelligence and sources of reflection.[134] They are not blind forces somehow disconnected from agents' wider cognitive assessments of the world. If it is a question of understanding and speaking to what actually *does* motivate the vast majority of human beings, meanwhile, Camus agreed with the ancient teachers of rhetoric that the politically engaged philosopher, especially when he is a political journalist or advocate, cannot reasonably eschew forms of poetic and rhetorical language.[135] For it is such language that appeals to readers' passions and imagination, the wellsprings of their motivations. This is not to deny that it is vitally important that she should be able to proffer clearly stated arguments

---

131 Paul Audi, *Qui témoignera pour nous? Albert Camus face à lui-même* (Paris: Éditions Verdier, 2013).

132 HR 376; R 301.

133 Cf. Martha Nussbaum, *Upheavals of Thought: The Intelligence of Emotions* (Cambridge: Cambridge University Press, 2003).

134 Cf. Amiot & Mattei, "Avant Propos", 8 ("... and what made Camus think, like the Socrates of the *Thaeatetus*, is admiring wonder, the *thamazein*, before the beauty of the world and its naked presence..."; also Maurice Weyemberg, "Camus et la Genie du consentement," in *Albert Camus et La Philosophie*, 117–132 and Chapter Six below.

135 Cf. Cicero, *De oratore*, 1.51.22; cf. 1.5.17; 1.14.60; 1.46.202; or amongst the renaissance thinkers, Francis Bacon, *Advancement of Learning* II.XVII.1–5: "in regard of the continual mutinies and seditious of the affections, *Video meliora, proboque, Deteriora sequor*. [I see and approve of the better, but I follow the worse]: reason would become captive and servile, if eloquence of persuasions did not practise and win the imagination from the affections' part, and contract a confederacy between the reason and imagination against the affections; for the affections themselves carry ever an appetite to good, as reason doth."

for the critical assessment of her audience, if she is not to be a mere demagogue or sophist. It is just that, to again cite an early reflection from the *Carnets* which clearly links Camus' philosophical persona with a humanistic recognition of the need to tailor how philosophical ideas are presented to different audiences, most people "think in images." They are moved more by narratives than by syllogisms. Thus "if you want to be a philosopher, write novels."[136] We need only to add: if you want to be a philosopher whose primary audience is not solely scholars, but the wider reading and philosophising public, then you need to write in ways that can engage this wider audience.

5 Ancient *and* Modern: Camus as Post-Enlightenment *'Philosophe'*

Already we thus see how Camus' *oeuvre*, itself an argument for Pascal's claim that "a man does not show his greatness by being at one extremity, but rather by touching both at once"[137] is as good as its word. Camus does not accept the accepted polarity of philosophy versus literature. His life and work contests the separation of wholly theoretical philosophy versus a lived philosophising rooted in the Socratic *gnôthi seauton*. He equally challenges the opposition between reason and emotion. Our claim is that Camus' bridging of these accepted polarities goes some way to explaining how often he has been partially read hitherto. If we do not accept that Camus' thought and activity challenges these inherited oppositions, we are bound to read him as *either* a philosopher *or* a poet, a sentimentalist *or* a rationalist... an atheist *or* a theological thinker, a rebel *or* a reactionary, an ancient *or* a modern...—even when such readings can only be vouchsafed by overlooking countervailing evidences found elsewhere in Camus' diverse production. Srigley, for instance, argues that the evidence speaking to Camus' deep allegiance to Greek thought (evidence we have started to give here) speaks in favour of reading Camus' work as involving a total critique of the modern age.[138] Camus at one point in his *Carnets* does declare that "no, I am not a modern"[139] and *The Rebel* proffers

---

136   C I 23; C I Eng. See Lévi-Valensi's invaluable, "Si tu veux être philosophe...," which turns around understanding this fecund note.
137   Pascal cited as epigraph for "Letters to a German Friend", at RRD, 1.
138   See esp. Srigley, *Albert Camus' Critique of Modernity*; and Hanna, "Albert Camus and the Christian Faith", in Germaine Brée ed. *Camus: Critical Essays*, 48–58.
139   This quote is also stressed by Samantha Novello, "La liberté de ne pas être moderne: le paradigm tragique de l'action politique dans l'oeuvre d'Albert Camus", in *Albert Camus et la Grèce*, 125–142. Like Srigley, Novello must place great weight on Camus' comment, made

a powerful critique of fascism, Marxism-Leninism and elements of modern liberal societies. Yet in "Helen's Exile" and elsewhere, Camus is critical of figures like Saint-Exupéry to the extent that they despaired of the times.[140] Again, the closing arguments of *The Rebel* criticise nothing so much as people who turn away from "the fixed and radiant point of the present" in the name of idealisations of what the present is decried to lack, in more or less elegiac or apocalyptic strains.[141]

The opposition ancient-modern, we would rather suggest (one which must always trade in unsustainable historicising generalisations) is one more opposition that Camus' thought straddles. In fact, the word *'philosophe'* that features in our title, in Camus' native French, is not only the generic term for philosophers of all times and places. It resonates specifically with the generations of French *lumières* spanning from Montesquieu through to d'Holbach, led by Diderot and Voltaire, but looking back via Pierre Bayle to Michel de Montaigne, and sideways (across the channel) to the 'moral sentiment' thinkers of the British enlightenment, and the empiricists in train of Bacon, Locke and Newton. As Peter Gay in particular has argued, the thought and activity of these definitive "moderns," the enlighteners, involved their attempt to revitalise the modern West's pagan, classical heritage in the context of the advent of the modern natural sciences.[142] It is just such a project that Camus, his own still small voice, advocates for in the twentieth century.

---

in light of a contrast between Greek thought as beginning in a sense of beauty while for "Europeans," beauty is at most a goal, "Je ne suis pas moderne," at Albert Camus, *Carnets II, janvier 1942–mars 1951* (Paris: Les Éditions Gallimard, 1964), 240. See ensuing note.

140   "I will answer Yes to the challenges of my century", Camus writes in *Summer* and rejects the "I hate my time" of Saint Exupéry, respectively in "Prometheus in the Underworld," *Lyrical and Critical Essays*, 141; and "Helen's Exile," *Lyrical and Critical Essays*, 151–152: "But, however upsetting that exclamation, coming from him who loved men for their admirable qualities, we shall not accept responsibility for it. Yet what a temptation, at certain moments, to turn one's back on this bleak, fleshless world! But this time is ours, and we cannot live hating ourselves."

141   Camus' avowal of the need to ground an ethics in the "fixed and radiant point of the present" (*L'Homme Révolté*, 381) needs also to be read with Camus' sympathetic reading of the early modern revolts against theologically-sanctioned monarchies in *L'Homme Révolté*, 41–45, betrayed by the excesses of Sade, the dandies, and the later modern thinkers. I have argued elsewhere (Matthew Sharpe, "A Just Judgement? Considerations on Ronald Srigley's *Camus' Critique of Modernity*," *Thesis Eleven*, vol. 120, no. 1 (2014), pp. 43–58) that Srigley does not rightly weigh Camus' commitment to the early moderns: see Chapters Three and Four below.

142   Peter Gay, *The Enlightenment: An Interpretation, Volume 1: The Rise of Modern Paganism* (London: W.W. Norton and co., 1966).

Like Camus, also, these men would challenge the hard-and-fast oppositions between *theoria* and *praxis*, the intellectual and political life.[143] Their hero was above all Cicero: politician and orator, but also philosopher; the author or timeless works of *theoria* who repeatedly returned to the forum to fight Cataline, Clodius, Caesar, then Antony.[144] The *lumières* tried through their writings (and through their sponsorship of the emerging bourgeois "public sphere")[145] to bring the fruits of philosophical and scientific inquiry to the wider population, just as Camus did through writing philosophically-informed literature. Voltaire was pamphleteer as well as novelist, playwright, historian, critic, advocate, and philosopher.[146] Diderot had a similarly eclectic or Protean literary profile, ranging from the sublime and recondite to the erotic and profane.[147] Finally, as recent work by Gordon, Lloyd, Rasmussen and others has highlighted,[148] one entire strand of the enlightenment tradition (despite postmodern or reactionary images) shares with Camus his epistemic scepticism, his grounding of ethics in sensibility, his critique of all forms of totalising rational philosophy and theodicy, and his defence of democratic political institutions as bespeaking this far-ranging *modestie*.[149] In Peter Gay's words,

---

143   Gay, *Enlightenment*, 103–109, 155–156, 163–4, 192–5. See Kevin Newmark, "Tongue-Tied: What Camus' Fiction couldn't teach us about Politics", in *Camus in the 21st century*, 109: who notes that the first half of the 20th century, in figures like Malraux, Sartre and Camus, represented the greatest highpoint since the enlightenment in French letters of authors engaged in "a mutually productive concatenation between figural and discursive modes of writing...".

144   Gay, *Enlightenment*, 47–56, 62–68, 105–109.

145   Cf. notably Jürgen Habermas, *The Structural Transformation of the Public Sphere* (USA: MIT Press, 1991); Antoine Lilti, "Private lives, public space: a new social history of the Enlightenment" in Daniel Brewer ed., *Cambridge Companion to the French Enlightenment* (Cambridge: Cambridge University Press, 2014); Craig Calhoun, ed. *Habermas and the Public Sphere* (USA: MIT Press, 1993).

146   Cf. Gay, *Enlightenment*, 197: "...the philosophes did not disdain pure art, as we know; and treatises like Kant's *Critiques* and Condillac's essays on linguistics are among [the enlightenment's] lasting monuments. Yet the most characteristic mode of its expression was witty, informal, and didactic at once; it was Lichtenberg's aphorisms, Diderot's *Rêve de d'Alembert*, Lessing's *Nathan the Wise*, and Voltaire's *Candide*..."

147   Cf. Will & Ariel Durant, "Diderot Proteus", in *The Age of Voltaire* (New York: Simon & Schuster 1965), 650–679.

148   Dennis Rasmussen, *Pragmatic Enlightenment* (Cambridge: Cambridge University Press, 2013); Genevieve Lloyd, *Enlightenment Shadows* (Oxford: Oxford University Press, 2013); Daniel Gordon ed. *Postmodernism and the Enlightenment: New Perspectives in Eighteenth-Century French Intellectual History* (London: Routledge, 2000).

149   See "Démocratie et modestie", *Oeuvres Complètes II*, 427–429, and Chapter Four below.

in the *philosophes*' "glorification of criticism and their qualified repudiation of metaphysics, the Enlightenment was not an Age of Reason but a Revolt against Rationalism."[150] Camus in *L'Homme Révolté* elevates this revolt to the central point of his philosophical ethics and politics, as well as his understanding of the legitimacy of the modern, post-theological age.

And so we have arrived at our third pillar undergirding the ways Camus should be read as a *philosophe*, despite his ambivalence about the term. Camus' thought, this book argues, contains (first, as above) a deeply coherent, identifiable and urbane set of philosophical claims (his philosophical discourse) spanning epistemology, ethics, and political philosophy. This philosophical discourse is nevertheless rooted in a wider sense of philosophy as answering to the questions posed by his own and his contemporaries' lives and experiences in a way which reflects the ancient, Socratic conception of philosophy as a way of living (the second pillar to *Camus, philosophe*). Thirdly, Camus' profuse philosophical and literary *oeuvre* aligns with an august 18th century heritage in French letters either ignored or unjustly represented by the post-structuralists and their legatees, including the *nouveaux philosophes*: that of the more sceptical, humanistic or 'moderate' branch of 18th century *lumières*.[151] Like Cicero or the philosopher depicted in *Republic* VII who has seen the True Ideas (in Camus' case, the joys of art, contemplation, friendship, and nature), Camus nevertheless "went back down" into the city, moved by his sense of the import of justice and belonging with ordinary people, in ways many philosophers do and are not. The concluding remarks of one of his important 1939 articles on the misery of the Kabyle people of the Algerian highlands encapsulates this double-identity as philosopher-*politique*, or simply '*philosophe*', perfectly. "For now, I must end this survey of the suffering and hunger of an entire people...", Camus reflects:

> What have we done about it, and do we have the right to avert our eyes? I am not sure anyone will understand. But I do know that after returning from a visit to the 'tribe' of Tizi-Ourou, I climbed with a Kabyle friend to the heights overlooking the town. From there we watched the night fall. And at that hour, when the shadows descending from the mountains across this splendid land can soften the hardest of hearts, I knew there was no peace for those who, on the other side of the valley, were gathered

---

150 Gay, *Enlightenment*, 141.
151 Aurelian Craiutu, *A Virtue for Courageous Minds: Moderation in French Political Thought, 1748–1830* (USA: Princeton University Press, 2012); and Dennis Rasmussen, *Pragmatic Enlightenment* (Cambridge: Cambridge University Press, 2013).

around eating a spoiled barley cake. I also knew that it would have been comforting to surrender to the startling grandeur of that night, except that the misery gathered around the glowing fires across the valley placed the beauty of this world under a kind of ban. 'Let's go down, shall we?', my friend said.[152]

6   Why a *Philosophe* Writes Novels (and Plays, Lyrical Essays ...)

Camus, Philosophe wants to come to terms with Camus' *oeuvre* as a body of philosophical thinking and philosophically informed writing, and with Camus himself as a philosopher of a certain kind. Camus' *oeuvre*, we have noted, spans at least eight different literary genres: philosophy, aesthetics, fiction, dramas, lyrical essays, critical essays, political journalism and reflective self-writing. Readers of Camus will in addition know that, from the early 1940s, Camus conceived of his diverse productions as belonging to prospective stages or cycles. The *Carnets* of February 21, 1941, tell us that "the three absurds [*Caligula, Myth of Sisyphus, Outsider*] are now complete. Beginnings of liberty."[153] The *Carnets* in May or June 1950 project three stages: "I *The Myth of Sisyphus* (absurd) II the myth of Prometheus (revolt) III The Myth of Nemesis."[154] Camus elsewhere gives a more expansive, five-stage plan, which his own premature death was to prevent him from completing:

> First series. Absurd: *The Stranger-Myth of Sisyphus-Caligula* and *The Misunderstanding*
> Second series. Revolt: *The Plague* (and annexes)—*The Rebel*—*Kaliayev* [*Les Justes*]
> Third series: judgment—*The First Man?*
> Fourth series. Love sundered [?]: the stake (*le bûcher*) [?]—on love—the seducer/charmer (*le séduisant*) [?]
> Fifth series. Creation corrected or The System: Big novel + great meditation + unplayable play [?]"[155]

---

152   *Algerian Chronicles* translated Arthur Goldhammer with an Introduction by Alice Kaplan (Cambridge, Massachusetts: Belknap Press, 2013), 46.
153   C I 224; C I Eng 107.
154   C II 328; C II Eng 168.
155   C II 201; C II Eng 103–4.

What we do know, given what Camus was able to complete, is that each cycle in this almost Platonic or Wagnerian conception of his life-work embraced several different genres of writing. Each cycle considers a predominant theme or subject (absurd, revolt, judgment, love, 'creation corrected'). It turns around a framing pagan myth (Sisyphus, Prometheus, Nemesis). It examines a thematic with biblical resonances (exile, rebellion, the fall, the first man). The biblical resonances become more explicit in the 1950s. Each cycle involves, finally and above all, a novel or short stories, a play or plays, a philosophical discourse, and lyrical essays.[156] All the while, Camus continuously wrote critical essays on contemporary and classical literature; kept the notebooks or *Carnets*; and wrote political journalism for a variety of outlets. The resulting scheme, pictured in **table 1**, shows both the extraordinary ambition of Camus' work, and its vast distance from representations of him as a second-rank nihilistic prophet or moralising preacher.

As things stand, even in the works Camus was able to publish, his work is less one more expression of post-war French existentialism, than a bold and singular attempt to trawl through the entire cultural memory and unconscious of the modern West, seeking the causes of its *malaises*, and those resources it could draw upon to move "beyond nihilism" towards a second renaissance.

We have proffered above the beginnings of an interpretation of why Camus, *because* he was a philosophical thinker in the classical humanist tradition (which, contra Heidegger et al., of course has much less to do with a "Cartesian subjectivity" assigned improbable cultural significance than Ciceronian, Plutarchian or Senecan *humanitas*),[157] should have chosen to undertake such a diverse literary production. In Camus' philosophical reflections on art, and his own artistic practice, however, we find Camus drawn to a further kind of justification for his abiding identification, as primarily an artist. To approach our understanding of the unity of Camus' *oeuvre*, which lies in Camus' philosophical postulate of an inalienable human desire for unity, we need now to clarify this justification.

Camus' philosophical evaluation of literary writing anticipates Martha Nussbaum's more recent defences of the value of reading novels in courses of philosophical ethics.[158] It looks back to the classical sense announced in

---

156 I am unabashedly indebted here to Srigley, *Albert Camus' Critique of Modernity*, 4–7.
157 Cf. esp. Gay, *Enlightenment*, 107–108.
158 Martha Nussbaum, *Love's Knowledge* (Oxford: Oxford University Press, 1992). Nussbaum is here reprising a classical humanist tradition, drawing on her preeminent example, Aristotle. See for a contrasting renaissance example Francis Bacon, *Advancement of Learning* II.XXII.6 on the "poets" as superior sources to the philosophers concerning the

Aristotle's *Nicomachean Ethics* and explored in the ancient poets and historians, that ethical and political life is "most immersed in matter,"[159] and thus so diverse as to be recalcitrant to comprehension by one or other rational scheme or all-purpose "decision-procedure".[160] In *The Myth of Sisyphus*, in the important culminating Part on "Absurd Creation," Camus develops an epistemic inference that he has skirted in his earlier examination of the philosophical idea of the absurd. This is the idea that if reason is powerless to comprehensively explain the *totality of* human experience, this limit in no way speaks against our rational capacity to lucidly *describe* the different elements *within* our experience: in art or the sciences.[161] In "Absurd Creation", in the same vein, Camus posits a very minimal, austere account of the kind of art accepting the absurd will license. This ties creation to what Camus had in early essays called *témoinage*: lucid testimony to all aspects of human experience.[162] Nothing, from the sublimities of nature and experiences of joy and wonder, to the humblest realities of a hospital in a poor quarter, the lonely desperation of an aging woman in a home, the idle boasts of a forgotten man, or the dreams of a young child growing up poor in the sunlight are beneath the interest of the absurd creator.[163]

---

emotions; and narrative histories and the letters of engaged men as superior sources concerning civil affairs, *Advancement* II.XXIII.8: "... the form of writing which of all others is fittest for this variable argument of negotiation and occasions is that which Machiavel chose wisely and aptly for government; namely, discourse upon histories or examples. For knowledge drawn freshly and in our view out of particulars, knoweth the way best to particulars again. And it hath much greater life for practice when the discourse attendeth upon the example, than when the example attendeth upon the discourse..."

159   Cf. Bacon, *Advancement of Learning*, II.XXIII, 1: civil knowledge is "most immersed in matter and hardliest reduced to axiom"; to be compared with Aristotle, *Nicomachean Ethics*, I.3; II.2.

160   This is the key argument for contemporary virtue ethics, given paradigmatic expression in Bernard Williams, *Ethics and the Limits of Philosophy* (London: Routledge Classics [reedition], 2011).

161   Camus for this reason had expressed enthusiasm earlier in *Le Mythe* for the purely descriptive phenomenology of Husserl of the *Logical Investigations*: "[t]hat apparent modesty of thought that limits itself to describing what it declines to explain, that intentional discipline whence results paradoxically a profound enrichment of experience and the rebirth of the world in its prolixity..." MS 66; MSe 43–44. See Chapter Three below.

162   See Paul Viallaneix, "The First Camus", in *Youthful Writings: The First Camus*, translated by Ellen Conroy Kennedy (New York: Alfred A. Knopf, 1970), esp. 28–40; esp. Camus, "Art in Communion", 215–224.

163   Readers of Camus will know that I am reprising here the subjects of the stories of "The Wrong Side and the Right Side", LCE 19–62, as well as "The Hospital in a Poor Neighbourhood", FC, 211–214.

TABLE 1   *Camus' works by genre and cycle*

	Pagan myth	Biblical motif	<u>Novel(a)</u>	<u>Plays</u>
1932–37			Happy Death (unpublished)	Revolt in the Asturies; adaptation of Malraux's Tem du Mépris…
1937–'42	Sisyphus	Alienation, exile	L'Étranger (Outsider)	Caligula Misunderstanding
1943–52	Prometheus	rebellion	La Peste (The Plague)	– State of Siege (1948) – Les Justes (The Just, 1949)
1952–1958		Guilt, the fall; exile & the kingdom; John the Baptist, Christ	La Chute (The Fall)	Adaptations of *The Possessed* (Dostoevsky); & Faulkner's *Requiem for a Nun*
1958–	Nemesis	The Kingdom	Le Premier Homme	Don Faust? Christ-Pan?

If we can, without nostalgia or regret, give up on ever fulfilling the aspiration to totally understand the world, this sceptical renunciation is liberating. "On this score," accepting the absurd "is stirring. On this score, everything resumes its place and the absurd world is reborn in all its splendour and diversity."[164] Sceptical suspension of judgment about things in the heavens and beneath the earth, as Camus echoes Montaigne's example, frees the thinker to deal more sensitively with this world as it presents itself to us in the full range of human experiences.[165] Where concepts, being universal, stumble and buckle before

---

[164] MS, 92; MSe, 65.
[165] Probably the paradigmatic statement is the last essay: Michel de Montaigne, "Of Experience" in *The Complete Essays of Montaigne* translated Donald Frame (Stanford:

osophical essays	Lyrical essays	Theme(s)	Journalism, notebooks, criticism
istian Metaphysics & olatonism (1935-6 ôme de'études Supérieures sis)	L'envers et endroit	irony 'the bright side and the dark side' Pagan versus Christian (thesis)	1937–Sep. 1939: Alger-Républicain
h of Sisyphus	Noces (Nuptials)	Absurd suicide	1939–1940 Le Soir Republicain 1943–45: Combat
Rebel (L'Homme Révolté)	Summer (L'Été)	Rebellion murder (pagan v Christian)	Articles for Combat, until 1948; Actuelles I, II
lections on the Guillotine"; lections on the Future of ʒedy in Athens"	?	Guilt judgment pagan versus Christian	articles for Express, Le Monde, Actuelles III (writings on Algeria)
h of Nemesis (?); ilosophico-poetic essay on ." (?)	?	love(?) moderation (?) "creation corrected" [?]	

the particularities of existential and ethical life, there literature can continue philosophy's reflective calling as a "school of patience and lucidity,"[166] aiming to give testimony to the whole truth. This is why Camus claims in his Preface to Chamfort's works something very like what Nussbaum skirts claiming in *Love's Knowledge* and *Poetic Justice*, that "[o]ur greatest moralists are not makers of

---

Stanford University Press, 1971). For Camus 'with' Montaigne, see Daniel Stern, "The Fellowship of Men that Die: The Legacy of Albert Camus", *Cordozo Studies in Law and Literature*, Vol. 10, No.2 (Winter, 1998), 183–198; and Matthew Sharpe "On a Forgotten Argument in French Philosophy: Sceptical Humanism in Montaigne, Voltaire and Camus", *Criticial Horizons* January 2015.

166 MS 156; MSe 115.

maxims—they are novelists."[167] As we might say, art can give testimony to the variety and often-tragic complexity of the human condition which philosophical systems too often trample roughshod over. Such literature is a continuation of philosophy *qua* love of wisdom or of the world by other means.

In technical language, as it seems to us, Camus is an epistemic pluralist. He feels acutely what Aristotle professes, that "precision is not to be sought for alike in all discussions, any more than in all the products of the crafts."[168] Despite continuing dreams of some *mathēsis universalis*, whether psychoanalytic, physical, or set-theoretical, different subject-matters demand different modes of experience, comportment and description, if their specific features are to be honoured. Thus "it is evidently equally foolish to accept probable reasoning from a mathematician as to demand from a rhetorician scientific proofs."[169] Camus carries this kind of pluralistic, fundamentally *realist*, insight very far.[170] He in effect accepts, for example (and gives creative trial to the thought) that the best way to examine the vicissitudes of guilt and murderous desire is through monologues like those he gives us in *The Fall* and "The Renegade".[171] He explores the idea that a particularly revealing way to examine the varieties of human response to senseless suffering will be through the testimony of an imagined, dispassionate observer like the physician Rieux in a town struck by the plague. At the time of his death, Camus was undertaking to explore, and capture, the reality of love through the autobiographic anamnesis of *Le Premier Homme* ("to speak of those I loved. And of that only: Intense joy").[172] He had also envisaged a never-to-be-completed essay on love "in the philosophico-poetic manner of Nietzsche, and in a Nietzschean spirit,"[173]

---

167   Albert Camus, "Introduction aux *Maxims et anecdotes* de Chamfort", *Albert Camus Oeuvres Complètes I 1944–1948* (Gallimard Bibliothèque de la Pléiade, Paris: 2006), 923–932: 924. Cf. Nussbaum, *Love's Knowledge*, esp. "Form and Content, Philosophy and Literature", and Ch. 1 "The Discernment of Perception: An Aristotelian Conception of Public and Private Rationality". See also, Martha C. Nussbaum, "Exactly and Responsibly: A Defence of Ethical Criticism", *Philosophy and Literature* 22: 2 (1998): 343–365.
168   Aristotle, *Nicomachean Ethics* 1.3.
169   Aristotle, *Nicomachean Ethics* 1.3.
170   We mean "empirical realism," not the Platonic sense of realism (about universals), about which Camus remains sceptically agnostic, as per his response to Husserl in *Le Mythe de Sisyphe*, 67; MSe 45.
171   Albert Camus, "The Renegade", in *Exile and the Kingdom* translated by Justin O'Brien (New York: Vintage 1958), 33–61;); Albert Camus, *The Fall* translated Justin O'Brien (New York: Vintage, 1956).
172   FM 250.
173   Camus, cited at Crochet, *Les Mythes*, 31.

seemingly moved by the same sense of love's affective and poetic dimensions that would go some way to explaining why Plato's two dialogues on love are also supreme works of literature.[174]

Differently, Camus accepts that literary and theoretical treatments of a single theme like the absurd can reveal different dimensions of this phenomenon. The feeling of absurd is thus made especially vivid in the fate, and "writing degree zero" that Camus places in the laconic mouth of Meursault.[175] Its moral ambiguity, and the different ways people can respond to the absurd, is better shown in situation-plays like *Caligula* and *Malentendu*; while, again, the existential parameters and logic that underlie the "absurd feeling" can only be revealed by the kind of philosophical reflection Camus undertakes in *The Myth of Sisyphus*. In this way, the conception of Camus' lifework in great cycles around a theme, a myth, and works in different genres, *itself* finds an expanded philosophical (or 'metaphilosophical') rationale.

7   The Desire for Unity and Communion: Camus' Eudemonism

It is vital, though, to emphasise from the start that Camus' openness to the irreducible plurality of the world as it is revealed to us in the different varieties of human experience, in no way pushes him towards the kind of abstract celebrations of difference *per se* that the "thinkers of '68" would later champion. As we will examine in Chapter Three, in *The Myth of Sisyphus*, Camus chastises Chestov and Kierkegaard for falsely inferring from a true disclosure of the limits of reason to the alleged, fundamental irrationality of the world.[176] What is at stake here is the key difference which (as we will see in Chapter Two) runs through *L'Homme Révolté*, but which hearkens back to Camus' earliest work, between the inalienable human desire for unity, and excessive claims to comprehend the "totality" of human experience, history and ethical life. For Camus, in perhaps the over-riding principle of his philosophy of *mesure*: "[t]he real is not entirely rational, nor is the rational entirely real.... the desire for unity not only demands that everything should be rational..."[177] (Chapter Five) As in the attentive descriptive work of the novelist or scientific observer, this desire for unity "... also wishes that the irrational should not be sacrificed..."

---

174   I.e. Plato, *Symposium*; Plato, *Phaedrus*.
175   Roland Barthes, "Réflections sur le style de *L'Étranger*," *Oeuvres Complètes* Vol. 1 (Paris: Seuil, 1994), 60–63.
176   MS 53–63; MSe 32–41.
177   HR 369; R 296.

but patiently attested.[178] Although it is important to stress just how *minimal* Camus wants his sceptical, philosophical foundations to be—"[t]here will be found here merely the description, in the pure state, of an intellectual malady. No metaphysic, no belief is involved in it for the moment," the Preface to *Le Mythe* protests[179]—it is fair to say that Camus' most fundamental claim concerning the human being is that we are creatures who demand that our experience has some unifying sense. This "mania for unity," as it is described in one of his first published essays,[180] is as irreducible and inalienable as the Stoics thought their *hegemonikon* to be.[181] Alongside the arationality of the world which refuses wholly to yield to it, it forms of one of the two irreducible sides of the absurd: fidelity to which will base Camus' entire ethical reflection. "I continue to believe the world has no ultimate meaning," Camus writes to his *ami allemand* in the culminating of the four, open wartime letters he penned: "But I know that something in the world has a meaning and that is man, because he is the only creature to insist on having one. The world has at least the truth of man, and our task is to provide its justification against fate itself."[182] The epistemic and ethical spade has turned, and as in Descartes, it has turned performatively, on the basis of a kind of lucid or philosophical self-reflection, as we will stress in our central chapters. (Chapter Three and Four)

This desire for unity for Camus underlies not only our cognitive, theoretical pursuits. It is no less apparent in our bodily needs and desires than in the idols of the mind. As Hegel then Marx rightly saw, it finds expression also in all forms of bodily labour, as indeed in the most elementary efforts of human beings to eke out spaces to conduct their shared lives (tents, houses, towns, cities, nations…) shielded as far as possible from the inundations, plagues or earthquakes that nature from time to time visits upon us. (Chapter Five)

---

178 HR 368; R 296.
179 MS, 16; MSe 2: Camus protests, of course, in vain: at least in how he has been read by many respondents who are inclined to claim that all thought is metaphysical or theological, either openly or without self-knowledge. (Cf. Camus' comment at C I 72; C I Eng 31: "If you say 'I don't understand Christianity, I want to live without consolation', then you are narrow minded and prejudiced. But if, living without consolation, you say: 'I understand and admire the Christian position', you are a shallow dilettante. I am beginning to grow tired of being concerned by what people think.")
180 FC 221.
181 The *hegemonikon* or ruling faculty of the psyche for the Stoics holds within it the power to give or withhold assent to ontological and normative claims. It cannot be involuntarily moved, even by the Gods or under torture, since it is the very agency of volition. Camus' proximities to Stoicism will become clear in Chapter Six below.
182 LGF 2, 28.

According to Camus, as the important section on "Rebellion and Art" in *The Rebel* attests, perhaps the highest expression of this human desire for unity is to be found in the creative labours of artists. For Camus, artists' business it is to selectively take up and transform elements of experience into artificially unified "creative" canvases, gestures, or stories. Great works of art are in this way so many instances of "creation corrected," between formalistic excesses and the hopeless dreams of a perfected, prolix realism.[183] *L'Homme Révolté* as a whole argues that, despite the way that "rebellion" is usually associated with forms of negation alone (or lamented as a specifically modern, Western aberration in reactionary criticism) revolt in the name of ideals which contest *le monde comme il va* is a fundamental expression of the universal, transcultural human desire for unity. By the end of *L'Homme Révolté*, Camus has come close to identifying rebellion with value-creation *per se*: "In every rebellion is to be found the metaphysical demand for unity, the impossibility of capturing it, and the construction of a substitute universe. Rebellion, from this point of view, is a fabricator of worlds."[184]

In a way which reflects Camus' early engagement with the neoPlatonician Plotinus (the subject of a surprisingly sympathetic depiction in his 1936 *Diplôme* thesis),[185] Camus throughout his life will even describe this animating desire for unity as directed at a fugitive kind of "communion" with, or "participation" in, the world:

> It is always wrongly thought that the notion of reason is a one-way notion. To tell the truth, however rigorous it may be in its ambition, this concept is nonetheless just as unstable as others. Reason bears a quite human aspect, but it also is able to turn toward the divine. Since Plotinus, who was the first to reconcile it with the eternal climate, it has learned to turn away from the most cherished of its principles, which is contradiction, in order to integrate into it the strangest, the quite magical one of participation.[186]

---

183 HR 317–345; R 253–277; CD 249–263. The *Carnets* attest how early these arguments concerning art as "creation corrected" (between 'transcended' and 'wholly accepted') came in the process of Camus' thinking concerning *The Rebel*, hailing from his ongoing reflection on his practice. (C II 117 "Mon œuvre. Terminer suite d'œuvres sur livre sur le monde créé: 'La création corrigée [creation corrected].'), cf. C II 131, 132, 146, 157, 163, 190, 198, 201.
184 HR 320; R 255.
185 CMN 88–114.
186 MS 71; MSe 48.

We hasten to reassure the reader, as we so often will have to do explaining Camus' consistently two-sided philosophical discourse, that this is not an endorsement by Camus of 'magical' obfuscation.[187] His entire philosophy, as we will see, is drawn simultaneously towards such unity and to clear-sightedly critique forms of unjustifiable 'leaping' to embrace it. Moreover and of course, contra Plotinus and most of the Platonic tradition, Camus remained a resolutely immanent thinker, albeit with his own almost mystical side. So, even in those moments when he most sympathetically speaks of Plotinus' sense that the philosophical quest for understanding points beyond abstract ratiocination towards a participatory communion with the world—even a sense of the sacred—Camus locates this fugitive *royaume* very much within the bounds of our mortal, natural condition:

> ... there are moments when everything [in us] aspires to this homeland (*patrie*) of the soul: 'Yes, this is the place to which we must return'. [But] this union, which for Plotinus so ardently wished—what is so strange about finding it on this earth, where unity expresses itself in terms of sun and sea?'[188]

In one more, final feature reflecting Camus' deep proximities to the Greek thinkers he admired from his youth, we see, Camus remained convinced that the unifying goal and justification of literature, philosophy, and living lay in the possibility of the kinds of happiness glimpsed in such "moments" as Camus describes in these neoPlatonic terms in "Summer in Algiers". Such moments dot his *oeuvre*. In one more mark of his singularity amidst much 20th century philosophy, Camus' works are replete, in fact, with language he shares with the "eudemonistic" classical philosophers (Chapter Six). He strove as a thinker and a writer to engender and speak a language which would allow for the evocation and exploration of phenomena like love, joy, the virtues, the sacred, communion, testimony, and beauty: phenomena which psychoanalytic, Marxist, and Foucaultian frameworks have taught generations of students to be highly

---

187 For one thing, the immediate context of this passage is *The Myth of Sisyphus*' argument that reason, as descriptive and reflective, can and should always monitor and temper this *eros* for "participation", which if allowed to override "the most cherished of principles" leads to the kinds of all-or-nothing positions Camus' *oeuvre* is dedicated to opposing. (Camus is here meditating on "the apparent paradox that leads thought to its own negation by the opposite paths of humiliated reason [Kierkegaard] and triumphal reason [Husserl]").

188 Camus, "Summer in Algiers", LCE, 90.

sceptical, and sometimes pre-emptively cynical about.[189] "Cynicism," Camus noted pithily in the *Carnets*, represents "the temptation shared by all forms of intelligence."[190] After the long round of his critical debates over *The Rebel* was finished, Camus documented his desire that the time of criticism, in his own intellectual life at least, should be over:

> I am tired of criticism, of disparagement, of the spitefulness of nihilism, in short. It is essential to condemn what must be condemned, but swiftly and firmly. On the other hand, one should praise at length what still deserves to be praised. After all, that is why I am an artist, because even the work that negates still affirms something and does homage to the wretched and magnificent life that is ours...[191]

Camus' dream in this period was "to create literature like Mozart creates music."[192] In Bruce Ward's words, despite being compelled to 'go back down' into the strife of his time,[193] "Camus is exceptional amongst major twentieth-century writers in the loving attention he bestowed on the beauty of the natural world."[194] The beaches, coasts, and waves of the Mediterranean remained for him the living images of a happiness with which he aligns the realities of love, friendship, liberty, rebellion, creation and beauty, in order to counter-pose these against the divisions and murderous violence of 20th century European politics. Although he felt as if he needed almost to apologise for this in contemporary Paris, and without for one moment ceding a concern for social justice, he writes in his May 1959 reflection on his love of the theatre: "I am tempted to believe that it is necessary to be strong and happy in order to aid those who

---

189 See Abbou, "L'actualité de Camus, demain," *Camus in the 21st century*, 183–187, who attributes Camus' continuing 'actuality' for new generations of readers to this ahistorical or non-historical dimension to Camus' concerns.
190 C I 116; C I Eng 54.
191 Albert Camus, "The Wager of Our Generation," in RRD, 239.
192 Albert Camus, "Albert Camus parle Nicola Chiaramonte (octobre 1948)", OC II 718–719. Cf. Albert Camus, "Remerciement à Mozart" (2 fevrier 1956)", OC III, 1078–1080.
193 Cf. William Altman, *Plato the Teacher: The Crisis of the Republic* (USA: Lexington, 2013) which makes the argument that this is the key Platonic idea of justice (a philosopher who nevertheless, like Socrates, 'goes back down' into the city), signalled by the book's and Socrates' first word: "I went down [*katebēn*]..."
194 Bruce K. Ward, "Christianity and the Modern Eclipse of Nature: Two Perspectives", *Journal of the American Academy of Religion* Vol. 63, No. 4, Winter, 1995: 823–843. 825.

are unhappy."[195] For Camus, as we again hasten to stress, it is not a matter of wilfully suspending critical acumen or blinding ourselves to the forms of natural calamity and sociopolitical malignities that beset individuals, groups, and societies. "[I]t is essential to condemn what must be condemned...," and to defend the pen against the sword, the life of the mind against philistinism, and the lives and aspirations of ordinary men and women against the soulless machinations of oppressive economic and political systems, and the hybristic excesses of ruling cliques.[196] But Camus rebels against the idea that, in doing this, we should somehow ascetically suspend all talk of liberty, justice, love, artistic creation or happiness as so many scams.[197] The most needful criticism presupposes, and itself finds its orientation, in prior positive values which Camus believes it is the task of the philosopher and creator to seek out and give a form—alongside genealogically unmasking the ways these and other ideals have been betrayed or abused.

Camus knows well the passion for justice that leads many of the best of each generation to reject any compromise with *le monde comme il va* and long for a complete messianic redemption of the present world:

> Those who have not insisted, at least once, on the absolute virginity of human beings and of the world, who have not trembled with longing and impotence at the fact that it is impossible, and have then not been destroyed by trying to love half-heartedly, perpetually forced back upon their longing for the absolute, cannot understand the realities of rebellion...[198]

Nevertheless, Camus' philosophy of *mesure* applies to these considerations too. "Shakespeare without the shoemaker serves as an excuse for tyranny," Camus

---

195 Albert Camus, "Pourquoi je fais du theatre", in *Oeuvres Complètes IV, 1956–1959* (Gallimard Bibliothèque de la Pléiade, Paris: 2008), 604. Camus repeats that his aim is to serve life and *bonheur*, as at "Entretiens sur la révolte," 401.

196 Cf. Albert Camus, "Almond Trees", LCE, 134–137.

197 "To know how to say 'no', to require each in his place to create the living values without which any renaissance cannot pass, to preserve what wants to live, to prepare what deserves to live, to attempt to be happy in order to soften the terrible taste for justice: these are the motifs of renewal and of hope." Albert Camus, "Interview non publiée", OC II, 481–2. "When I do happen to look for what is most fundamental in me, what I find is a taste for happiness." Camus, "Three Interviews", LCE 351.

198 HR 327; R 261–2.

agrees with vulgar-Marxist aesthetic criticism in "Rebellion and Art".[199] Art and its *promesse de bonheur* always stands accused of being a heartless deception or distraction in societies characterised by avoidable, basic injustices. By the same token, *l'envers et l'endroit*: "the shoemaker without Shakespeare is absorbed by tyranny when he does not contribute to its propagation."[200] In other words, political or philosophical programs which, in the name of an ideal of justice, deny the legitimacy of the human longing for happiness and love and beauty, or would deprive us of the vocabulary to articulate these desires are equally to be resisted as tragically one-sided. Camus' lyrical essay "Return to Tipasa" (which itself dramatizes Camus' return as a mature man to the site of his youthful, neopagan *"noces"* with nature and North Africa's classical past), perhaps puts Camus' difficult *eudemonism* best:

> In everything I have done or said up to now, I seem to recognize these two forces, even when they work at cross-purposes. I have not been able to disown the light into which I was born and yet I have not wanted to reject the servitudes of this time. It would be too easy to contrast here with the sweet name of Tipasa other more sonorous and crueller names. For men of today there is an inner way, which I know well from having taken it in both directions, leading from the spiritual hilltops to the capitals of crime. And doubtless one can always rest, fall asleep on the hilltop or board with crime. But if one forgoes a part of what is, one must forgo being oneself; one must forgo living or loving otherwise than by proxy. There is thus a will to live without rejecting anything of life, which is the virtue I honor most in this world. From time to time, at least, it is true that I should like to have practiced it. Inasmuch as few epochs require as much as ours that one should be equal to the best as to the worst, I should like, indeed, to shirk nothing and to keep faithfully a double memory. Yes, there is beauty and there are the humiliated. Whatever may be the difficulties of the undertaking, I should like never to be unfaithful either to one or to the others.[201]

Perhaps the most elevated task of *Camus, philosophe*, to which we will duly return in the final pages, will be to tease out the lineaments of Camus'

---

199 HR 341–2; R 274.
200 HR 341–2; R 274; cf. CD 249–262.
201 RT 169–170.

conceptions of happiness, communion, and the constituents of the good life, honouring his neoHellenistic *philosophia*.

8   Prospectus and Limits

Before commencing, let me briefly specify the structure and anticipated readerships of this book. This task is vital, not simply because it accords with Camus' humanistic sense of the importance of tailoring one's discourse to audiences, contexts, and ends. It also provides the author with the chance to signal his very real sense of the book's limits, located as it is between disciplines (literature, French studies, philosophy, history of ideas) and their respective readerships, and reclaiming (at least for the philosophers in the mix) the singular, academically neglected author of a tragically unfinished *oeuvre*, in the face of powerful prejudgments concerning his place in 20th century culture.

First of all, it is necessary to underscore that the primary focus of this book is on Camus' lyrical essays, *Carnets*, political writings, and extended theoretical or philosophical essays, *The Myth of Sisyphus* and *The Rebel*. This is that part of his *oeuvre* which I am arguing remains least well appreciated, as well as that which the author (a trained philosopher and social theorist) happens to be best qualified to comment on. For this reason, while sections of the book focus on Camus' "State of Siege", *The Stranger, The Plague, The Fall* and *The First Man*, readers will not find in this book an exhaustive examination of all of Camus' fiction. (I should have liked to give more time to *Les Justes, Exile and the Kingdom* and *The Plague*, as well as his aesthetics, but that would require a different book, and there are besides many fine studies of these by now). Throughout *Camus, Philosophe*, in the text and extensive notes, I signal my debts to, agreements with and divergences from the less voluminous, but significant critical literature on Camus' political and philosophical writings.

To establish the positive exegetical claims of the book, these claims will be presented in dialogue with recent, important works on Camus' political and philosophical writings, notably those by Srigley, Orme, Sessler, Carroll, Aronson and Zaretsky. Special dialogic and critical attention will however be given, unapologetically, throughout the book firstly to the widespread *endoxa* that Camus was 'not a philosopher', so that his texts (notably *The Rebel*) are scarcely coherent, except as rhetorical performances; secondly, to the crucially influential *Marxissant* criticisms of Camus' work articulated by de la Vigerie, Sartre and Jeanson, and thirdly, to the almost-equally-influential post-colonial criticisms of O'Brien, Said, Dunwoodie, Haddour and others. These positions are constant interlocutors in all that follows quite simply because, by themselves or combined, they have done most to motivate Camus' continuing marginalisation in academic studies of 20th century European philosophical culture.

The next point responds to a recognition that there have been many, valuable examinations of Camus' life and work which treat these matters chronologically. Such studies examine his texts and deeds starting from his youthful efforts and finishing with the final notebooks, *Exile and the Kingdom* or *The First Man*.[202] To avoid reinventing the wheel, and out of respect for these works, this book is not structured in that way, although Chapter Six does end with Algeria, *La Chute* and *Le Premier Homme*. Nor are its audiences and aims the same as these works'. *Camus, Philosophe* instead is planned around a philosophical structure recalling the famous cave allegory of Plato's *Republic* VII, which Camus himself recalls in the key 1950 essay "The Enigma" and its reflections on the reception of his work on the eve of *L'Homme Révolté*.[203]

The philosopher begins within his city or cave (what we would call his context, times or culture). If s/he is to turn people's souls around towards the truth, as s/he vocationally wishes to, Plato's allegory suggests that this *philosophe* must begin by engaging in and with her own times' political and philosophical concerns. Socrates thus famously discoursed as much or more on training horses, raising children or captaining ships as he did on anything so august as the Platonic Ideas, or even the Athenians' more mundane ideas of justice, moderation, or the other virtues.[204] In just this way, with an eye towards a student, lay and professional readership educated within the tertiary humanities in the epoch of post-structuralist hegemony, the first four chapters of this book place Camus in dialogue with more recent, more celebrated French thinkers—at the same time as they begin with Camus' darkest, historical concerns with the total modern States of the far Left and Right in his times. It is by putting Camus into dialogue with Foucault, the 'new philosophers' and the Frankfurt School concerning disciplinary and instrumental rationality and totalitarianism (in Chapter One); the 'returns to theology', Hans Blumenberg's work, and debates concerning the 'legitimacy' of modernity (in Chapter Two); Derrida's post-Heideggerian deconstruction of Western metaphysics (Chapter Three); then Levinas' and Habermas' dialogic forms of ethics (in Chapter Four)

---

202 As Christine Margerrison has remarked, "the narrative of Camus's life has been told so often that some of its predictable milestones have become banal from overuse…." Christine Margerrison, "*Albert Camus: Elements of a Life* (review)," *French Studies: A Quarterly Review*, Volume 65, Number 2 (April 2011), 268.

203 E 161.

204 See Alcibiades' famous lament in the Platonic *Symposium* 215a–217e.

that we will reconstruct Camus' 'master argument' and 'philosophical discourse' introduced above (see "But Camus, a philosopher?").

Some of the claims we make in this dialectical "rough ascent" towards Camus' neoHellenistic philosophy of *mesure* will by themselves seem unsurprising to different readerships. I aim to present Foucault, Derrida, Badiou, Levinas, Habermas and other later critical thinkers faithfully, not maverically: while necessarily focussing only on those aspects of their work most conversant with Camus' in ways which will invite criticisms from relevant specialists. The full extent of the book's 'post-Camusian critique' of post-structuralism's dispositional messianism will emerge clearly enough as we proceed. It will have become very clear to readers by the ends of Chapters Five and Six. *Mutatis mutandis*, readers from within Camus scholarship may find many of the claims concerning *Le Mythe de Sisyphe* and *The Rebel* uncontroversial (although disputes still surround how to interpret these, like the literary texts). To these readers, I hold to the framing claim that few critical authors hitherto have done adequate philosophical justice to the paraCartesian form of Camus' 'master argument' and the way that it structures *The Rebel*, as well as the extent of Camus' debt to the classical Greek and Roman philosophical legacy. Once the distinction between form and content is made, the flowing rhetoric and resonant symmetries of Camus' writing do not preclude his texts' containing 'serious argumentation'. For both of these academic readerships, and so for all, it is the project of putting Camus into critical dialogue with subsequent French thought, as a philosophical thinker who had anticipated many of its signal concerns, that I proffer firstly as unique; secondly as a source of renewed appreciation for Camus as a thinker; and thirdly as a contribution to emerging currents of thought that will be genuinely post-post-structuralist, re-awake to entire strata in our classical and early modern cultural heritage that much recent academic work has misrepresented, screened out, or consigned to increasingly-closed-off Classics and History of Ideas departments.

With the cave *eikon* in mind, the first four Chapters of *Camus, Philosophe* do represent its "rough ascent." Only in Chapter Five do we leave the "glittering cave" of Parisian thought,[205] and present Camus' own neoHellenistic perspective which undergirds his critical, genealogical and political positions unfolded in Chapters One to Four. It is accordingly only in Chapters Five and Six of *Camus, Philosophe* that we return back to what was 'first for Camus' both biographically and 'by nature' (as well as in most accounts of his work), but so unique to him amongst later modern French thinkers: his orienting expe-

---

205 E 161.

riences in North Africa and his decisive, abiding love for classical Greek literature, history and philosophy dating from these formative years. Chapter Five brings to an end our reconstruction of Camus' philosophical discourse. It does so by examining Camus' untimely defence of classical *mesure*, rooted in his acute aesthetic or contemplative sensitivity to the beauty of the natural world in pointed contrast to what could be termed the recent 'messianic turn' in post-Heideggerian critical thinkers.

Chapter Six then, passing beyond 'discourse alone', takes up the second, framing pillar of *Camus, Philosophe*'s titular argument: the Hadotian idea that Camus saw philosophy, in the Greek sense, as a way of life; as well as in a post-enlightenment sense, as bound to try to progressively engage in the troubles of its times. Here we look at Camus' 'going back down', as Plato enjoins of his philosopher in the *Politeia*: his attempts to reimagine or recreate a language capable of speaking to and about the classical virtues, rooted in his own biographical attempt to philosophically cultivate himself as a writer, a thinker, and a human being. It is in Chapter Six, above all, that our concern with Camus' literary writing will recur, notably concerning his writings of the later 1950s. We will also (continuing from Chapter Five) examine Camus' difficult personal and political stances on Algeria, and the widespread criticism he has received on this issue. Camus' *The First Man* was of course going to be Camus' lengthiest literary statement concerning the Algerian situation, his political writings on which were published in *Actuelles III*. Nevertheless, it has been claimed that Camus' *The Fall* and his *Exile and the Kingdom* in different ways reflected a deep change in orientation by Camus, moved by his sense of guilt about his identity as a *pied noir*, and the increasingly inevitable end of the French Algerian world in which he grew up. In Chapter Six, we will claim that Camus' political stances (a) remained consistent with the philosophy that came out of his resistance to European fascism; and (b) that they exemplify his 'post-prophetic' conception of the philosopher, in stark contrast to the kind of "judge-penitent" he derisively portrayed in *La Chute*, with Sartre's and Jeanson's 1952 prosecution of him as "Chief Prosecutor" in "the Republic of Beautiful Souls" in mind.[206] However much Camus' vision of a federated Algeria may have been rooted in nostalgia and a sense of mourning, we will argue, it is simply too simple for us from an untroubled distance to see this Algerian tragedy as invalidating

---

206 Jean-Paul Sartre, "Response to Albert Camus," in *Sartre and Camus, A Historic Confrontation*, 137. Compare for this conception of the role of the intellectual in Camus' Algerian texts Norman Jacobsen, *Pride and Solace: The Functions and Limits of Political Theory* (Berkeley: University of California Press, 1978), 146 ff. and Chapter Six below.

his key philosophical positions: any more than, for instance, Cicero or Cato's failure to save the Roman republic shows the republican tradition bereft, or the historical success of many post-colonial movements alone bespeaks their wider justice.

Finally, let me say that the attempt here to reclaim Camus as a serious *philosophe* does not aim to suggest that 'he had all the answers.' Seemingly one of those beloved of the gods, Camus died young. It is impossible for us to ever know what a man as dynamic, observant, thoughtful and passionate as Camus would have achieved given a natural span of life: how he would have responded to the Evian accords, the social and cultural unrest of the 1960s or the intellectual positions that hailed from it...Camus' own testimony, and what he was able to complete, attest both to the man's integrity and to the continuing concentrated unfolding of his thought around the key concerns and ideas this book aims to reconstruct with a just critical charity. Doubtless, Camus' contemplative philosophical naturalism and philosophy of *mesure* is incomplete or only a beginning: in itself; relative to the differing levels of theoretical complexity demanded for different tasks and by different audiences; and relative to the kinds of new theoretical thinking and political advocacy needed in the face of the problems facing us today: ecological collapse, resource shortages, species extinctions, the superexploitation of the South, the liberal-plutocratic eclipse of democratic will-formation, the rise and rise of forms of state-based and extremist terrorism, and the growing of states' security and surveillance apparati. Camus was always profoundly uncomfortable with people looking to him as a saviour, prophet or master. Indeed, we will see in Chapters Five and Six how his thought challenges all forms of messianism, prophetism and hero-worship. Honouring this humility, and paraphrasing *The Rebel*, let us finally then say of our 'defence' of Camus in *Camus, Philosophe* (since that is how it will unavoidably be read) that 'naturally, it is not a question of deifying Camus as a master-thinker, but only of arguing that his is a kind of measured, neoclassical naturalism and humane thinking that the world today cannot very much longer do without...'

PART 1

Cave & Critique

∴

CHAPTER 1

Plague Power: Camus with and against the Critiques of Instrumental Reason

1 "Plague Power", from *La Peste* to *L'État de Siège*

It is ironic that Albert Camus always remained so fond of *L'État de Siège*, amongst all his dramatic productions. The play, first staged in Paris in October 1948, was almost a complete failure, critically and at the ticket office. Written by the author of *La Peste*, which had been a grand success the previous year, many theatre-goers apparently expected Camus' new play, co-authored with director and lead actor Jean-Louis Barrault, to be a direct adaptation of the novel. Critics found its action ponderous, its characters unconvincing and one-dimensional, and the elaborate stage design and effects over the top.[207] Moreover, the form and action of the play is very distant from that of Greek tragedy, the dramatic form which Camus would always valorise in his critical essays as the highest form of literary art.[208] As a young man in Algiers, Camus had staged and acted in an adaptation of Aeschylus' *Prometheus Unbound* and written an hortatory essay on Nietzsche's *Birth of Tragedy from the Spirit of Music*. Two decades later, in 1956, Camus would deliver a "Lecture on the Future of Tragedy" in Athens in which the ancient dramatic form is favourably counter-posed to the morality plays of the medieval period, as being more morally complex, and thus closer to reality. Yet *L'État de Siège* is knowingly created on the model of medieval French morality plays, and the Spanish *autos sacramentales*, in which Catholic dogmata on sacral and secular matters was propagated to the masses. Far from denying the play's intention "to create a myth which could be intelligible to all spectators of 1948", Camus would "plead guilty to all charges of creating symbolic characters in this play" in the Preface to the American edition.[209] No one

---

[207] See Edward Freeman, *The Theatre of Albert Camus* (London: Methuen & Co., 1971), 76–77. "A shorter, revised version of parts of this chapter is to appear in *Thesis Eleven* as "The Plague and the Panopticon".

[208] As a young man in Algiers, Camus staged an adaptation of Aeschylus' *Prometheus Unbound* and written an hortatory essay on Nietzsche's *Birth of Tragedy from the Spirit of Music*. In 1956, Camus delivered his "Lecture in Athens on the Future of Tragedy" (LCE 295–310) which valorises the ethical and metaphysical complexity of this dramatic form.

[209] At Freeman, *Theatre of Camus*, 78.

in 1948 or since can mistake its ethical and political message. *State of Siege* is a kind of garish neo-baroque allegory about the need for individuals and groups to revolt against the excesses of totalitarian modes of government.

Camus' *The Plague* had also been an experiment in literary genre which aimed at coming to terms with the new forms of tyrannical government facing twentieth century Europe, and the question of how they might be resisted. On one side, the text was clearly intended by its author as an allegory on a very specific set of historical events and experiences: those of the French people under occupation by the Nazis between 1941 and 1944, and the struggles of the resistance movement in which Camus, as editor at *Combat*, had played a role.[210] On the other hand, the 'novel', if it bears the term, is composed of a chronicle of dispassionate observations of a single character, the Doctor Rieux, who only reveals his identity as narrator towards the end of the tale. Camus' story, which follows what transpires in the Algerian town of Oran, struck by the plague unaccountably "in 194–" for almost exactly a full year, draws on the precedent of Defoe's *Chronicle of a Year of Plague*. Yet some critics, led by Archambault, have noted (drawing on his *Carnets* after 1941) that Camus is also clearly, here as elsewhere, emulating classical models: notably, the dispassionate accounts of the Athenian plague of 431–427 BCE given first by Thucydides, an eye-witness and survivor, in his *History of the Peloponnesian War* and then by Lucretius at the end of *De Rerum Natura*.[211]

For critics of the novel like Roland Barthes or the Marxist commentator Emmanuel d'Astier de la Vigerie, the two dimensions of Camus' extraordinary literary experiment in *The Plague* do not balance each other.[212] The use of this medical or metaphysical subject matter, a plague striking the coastal North African town, to allegorise the National Socialist occupation of continental Europe, does not really succeed. The French resistance was after all not a struggle against a natural or metaphysical force which disappeared as unaccountably as it arrived, heralded only by the sudden appearance of rats dying in stairwells, beneath doorways, and on the streets of *la ville*. Almost no one will deny the uprightness of the responses of Camus' heroes or anti-heroes,

---

210 See Aronson, *Camus and Sartre*, 34–38.

211 Cf. P. Archambault, 'Camus' Hellenic Sources', *University of North Carolina Studies in Languages and Literatures*, 119 (1972). See Albert Camus, "Les Archives de La Peste", OC II, 271–284.

212 See Albert Camus, "Letter to Roland Barthes on *The Plague*," LCE 338–341; and "Deux réponses à Emmanuel d'Astier de La Vigerie", OC II, 457–474; also, on Sartre's belated criticisms in 1952, Aronson, *Camus and Sartre*, 54–56..... This case has been reprised by Orme, *Development of Camus' Concern* chapter 1, see also 252–3, n. 30.

Grand, Rieux, Rambert, and Tarrou, who form the *équipes sanitaires* to fight the plague in Oran, since this resistance involves a struggle against a faceless physical "abstraction" (as Rieux calls it), rather than a political regime. Yet the situation of French men and women contemplating resistance to the occupiers was, tragically, more morally ambiguous, given the Nazis' proven, brutal willingness to target civilian populations in reprisal for the *resistants'* activities. The National Socialist regime was not a force of nature, however much Hitler and his celebrants came to believe in the Fuhrer's star. It was the product of a complex of historical, economic and political factors; of ruthless and desperate men able to galvanise entire populations behind them by boldness, fortune, propaganda and terror. Was not Camus' assimilation of this totalitarian form of government with a kind of natural or metaphysical evil an exercise in obfuscating the specifically historical and political nature of the resistance and progressive politics more widely?[213]

In response to Barthes and de Vigerie, Camus in no way denied that, by choosing the motif of the plague to allegorise the Nazi occupation, he aimed at the same time to propose a reflection on the human response to "existence in general" as on this specific historical event

> I want to express through the medium of the plague the suffocation from which we have all suffered and the atmosphere of menace and exile with which we have all lived. I want at the same time to extend this interpretation to the notion of existence in general. The plague will give the image of those in this war who have had the part of reflection, of silence—and that of moral suffering.[214]

Yet the political meaning of Camus' depiction of the plague in *La Peste* is arguably a good deal more complex than Barthe et al.'s criticism captures. To be sure, the plague's arbitrariness and inhumanity, its being "no respecter of persons,"[215] allegorise for Camus the pitiless brutality of the Nazi regime. But very soon into the novel, Camus makes it clear that it is not only—and in some ways, even less—the horrors of the plague *itself* that Camus is targeting as the force people need to rebel against. What causes the characters' anguish in *La Peste*, almost as much as the plague itself, are the measures the political authorities in Oran make to combat this grave threat to public health or

---

213 See Freeman, *Theatre of Camus*, 82–84.
214 At Freeman, *Theatre of Camus*, 84.
215 Albert Camus, *The Plague* trans. S. Gilbert (London: Penguin, 1948), 140.

'national security'.[216] It is a case of what Jacques Derrida has more recently dubbed "auto-immunity".[217] After a good deal of bureaucratic debating concerning how the plague should be named or categorised, Part I of the novel ends with the words of the urgent telegram Rieux receives from the town prefect: "Proclaim a state of plague stop close the town."[218] Dotted throughout Parts II and IV of Rieux's chronicle, and then in the single key chapter of the central Part III, Camus makes us see the kind of political world the advent of the plague in Oran has called forth, in the name of public health and security. Oran becomes a city walled off, with gated, guarded entrance points; subject to quarantine, rationing, and curfews; with a population deprived of all luxuries, possibilities of travel, or even of communicating with people on the outside. After several incidents involving the crazed relatives of plague victims, sufferers themselves, or people attempting to escape, a state of exception is declared, and martial Law is put in place.[219] Police action is militarised, including the normalisation of executions for dissent. Police officers are made eligible for military decorations ("plague medals") for their service.[220] Increasingly, all aspects of the Oranais' lives are subject to red tape, bureaucratese, and official intrusion, a situation Camus uses the exiled journalist Rambert's attempts to win release from the town in order to stage. Affected areas of the town are periodically segregated, and the houses of victims closed off.[221] Individuals taken by the illness are isolated even from their own family members, for their own safety. Soon, even public burials are prevented: "Thus the disease, which apparently had forced on us the solidarity of a beleaguered town, disrupted at the same time long-established communities and sent men out to live, as individuals, in relative isolation."[222] In Part IV, we learn of the existence of an "Isolation camp" at the Municipal Sports Ground: for French readers a chilling reminder of June 1942's Operation Spring Breeze (*Opération Vent printanier*) in which some 28,000 Jews were interred by the Nazis in Paris' *Velodrome d'Hiver* before being deported, including 13,152 to Auschwitz.[223] Finally, as the

---

216 Cf. Jacques Derrida, "Autoimmunity: Real and Symbolic Suicides," trans. Pascale-Anne Brault and Michael B. Naas, *Philosophy in the Time of Terror: Dialogues with Jürgen Habermas and Jacques Derrida*, ed. Giovanna Borradori (Chicago: Chicago University Press, 2003), 85–136.
217 Jacques Derrida, "Autoimmunity: Real and Symbolic Suicides", 85–136.
218 P 56.
219 P 57–65 (Part II, ch. 1).
220 P 140.
221 P 138–152 (Part III).
222 P 141.
223 P 195–199.

numbers of dead grow towards the epidemic's height, the regime finds it necessary "to find new space and strike out in a new direction" to maintain public health. The authorities reopen the old crematoria to the East of Oran. Bodies of the dead are moved there *en masse* by train in closed streetcars, shielded as far as possible from the sight and mind of the surviving citizenry:

> Thereafter only when a strong wind was blowing did a faint, sickly odour coming from the east remind them that they were living under a new order and that the plague fires were taking their nightly toll...What with the gunshots echoing at the gates, the punctual thuds of rubber stamps marking the rhythm of lives and deaths, the files and fires, the panics and formalities, all alike were pledged to an ugly but recorded death,...amidst noxious fumes and the muted clang of ambulances...[224]

If the identification of the "plague" to be resisted with forms of totalising political control were not direct enough in *La Peste*, however, *The State of Siege* of the following year fairly shouts Camus' political message at audiences. After some troubling astrological portents, the play begins with a single man on stage, then two others placed in the audience, dropping dead with disease, accompanied by the droning of air sirens. A man appears with a Secretary, wearing "a military uniform with a medal" (in the first performance, this was an SS uniform).[225] The man, who is bald and in no way distinguished to look at, asks politely of the governor of Cadiz, the play's Spanish setting, whether he might take over the government of the city. When the governor protests and asks who the newcomer is, the man replies calmly: "the plague, if you really must know..."[226] His Secretary, whom we find out to be none other than 'Death' herself, then eliminates one of the city guards with the stroke of a pen in her administrative notebook. What follows in Part I of the play is what might today be called a "regime change," in which the personified Plague and Death close the city gates, declare a "state of siege" for "the control and charitable succour of all citizens infected with disease..."[227] They then go about governing the town through their puppet, the town's First Alceste, with the notable complicity of many of Cadiz' leading citizens.

While the device of personifying the Plague and Death, together with many elements of the ensuing "total spectacle" borrow heavily from medieval

---

224 P 152.
225 Albert Camus, "State of Siege" in *Caligula & Three Other Plays* (USA: Knopf, 1958): 135.
226 Camus, "State of Siege", 136.
227 Camus, "State of Siege", 171, 165.

conceits,[228] as *State of Siege* proceeds it becomes very clear that Camus has a very specific, modern kind of political power in his sights in the play. No less than *La Peste*, set "in 194–",[229] the play is contemporary political comment. The Plague himself laughingly observes that people would like their villains or oppressors spectacular, like the romantics' Satan, or pre-modern monarchs adorned in the pomp and purple of ceremonial rule:

> Well, they won't be satisfied this time. I don't wield a sceptre or anything like that. In fact I prefer to look like a quite ordinary person, let's say a sergeant of a corporal. That's one of my ways of vexing you ... so now your king has black nails and a drab uniform. He doesn't sit on a thrown, but in an office chair. His palace is a barracks and his hunting lodge a court house.[230]

"In any case, when I say I rule ... I rule in a rather special way," this new dictator explains, "it would be more correct to say that I function."[231] Of course, the Plague is as good as his Secretary's name, and wields absolute power of life and death over all his subjects. Yet in the new Cadiz even death has become banal: "administered". When someone is to be eliminated, this is achieved by Death's striking their name off the directory of every inhabitant she carries around with her. Besides, the Plague explains, too much open violence is neither salutary nor efficient: "the great thing is to ensure a majority of slaves by a minority of well-selected deaths. And thanks to our new technique, we can bring that off..."[232] The Plague indeed prides himself on leaving nothing to custom or chance, criticising the old powers and the old God, for "playing fast and loose [sic.] with logic."[233] By contrast with such quaint inefficiencies, the "plague power" of *State of Siege* works by generating new kinds of intimate knowledge of every aspect of peoples' lives. One of the first measures of the new government sees a sinister observation tower erected in the centre of Cadiz, to ensure the entire population can be constantly, efficiently, surveyed.[234]

---

228   Jennifer Stafford Brown, "Prison, Plague, and Piety: Medieval Dystopia in Albert Camus's *The Plague*", in The *Originality and Complexity of Albert Camus's Writings*, edited by Emmanuelle Anne Vanborre (Palgrave Macmillan, division of St. Martin's Press LCC, New York, NY, 2012), 94–110.

229   P 5.

230   Camus, "State of Siege", 191.

231   Camus, "State", 170.

232   Camus, "State", 227.

233   Camus, "State", 227.

234   Camus, "State," 175.

PLAGUE POWER   67

Death meanwhile carries out an exacting administrative census, animated by her happy scientistic conviction that "everything can be expressed in terms of figures, formulas."[235] "[W]e're not against slaughterhouses—quite the contrary," she explains: "Only we apply to them the latest methods of accounting."[236] Every aspect of life in Cadiz is soon subject to these "latest methods". All citizens are listed, numbered and badged by the authorities, moved by their hatred of "untidiness and irrationality."[237] Anyone who resists the idea must wear a second kind of badge to indicate this resistance: "that way we see at once with whom we have to deal"[238] One citizen makes the error of thinking that he can withhold a 'private' matter from the authorities. "Your private concern, do you say?," he is reprimanded: "These words don't mean anything to us. What interests us is your public life, and that as a matter of fact is the only life you are allowed by us to have."[239] All people infected with the disease are assigned black stars with long rays, bearing the Orwellian inscription 'we are all brothers.' All food is centrally requisitioned, to be distributed "to all those who can prove their adhesion to the new social order."[240] No one is to help others stricken by plague, except by reporting the case to the authorities. Reporting on family members is especially encouraged by a double "good citizenship" ration. A 9 p.m. curfew is applied to prevent nocturnal assemblies, and no one is allowed in public without a permit, "to be admitted only in very special cases and at our good pleasure."[241] "The whole point of our regime is that you need a permit to do anything whatsoever," Death again explains:[242] and indeed, as the action proceeds, we are introduced to citizens' needs to always have at hand their "certificates of existence", which are "temporary and of short duration," again subject to the authorities' executive discretion.[243]

It is not that there are no pay-offs for this kind of rule. Indeed, the Plague specifies that one advantage of his new mode of governance is a kind of maximisation of the working efficiencies of the population: "the dead man is refreshing enough, but he's not remunerative; not nearly so rewarding as a slave..."[244] Nada, the aptly-named nihilist who makes her peace with the new

---

235   Camus, "State," 206.
236   Camus, "State," 175.
237   Camus, "State", 172.
238   Camus, "State," 172, 178–9.
239   Camus, "State," 176.
240   Camus, "State," 166.
241   Camus, "State," 179–180.
242   Camus, "State," 175, 178.
243   Camus, "State," 175, 178.
244   Camus, "State," 226.

regime, is reprimanded at one point for supposing that the role of this kind of power is solely negative, to "suppress everything."[245] If he were asked to give one word to describe his highest goal for the people of Cadiz, the Plague candidly avows that it would be "discipline, my friend, discipline."[246]

2 The Plague and the Panopticon: Camus with Foucault

Anyone even distantly familiar with the great motifs of Foucault's 1976 masterpiece *Surveillir et Punir* [*Discipline and Punish*] will hear in the Plague and Death's declamations in *State of Siege* an uncanny echo of many of the means of "disciplinary power' that this work would later patiently document. *Discipline and Punish* is of course a very different work from Camus' 1940s' novel and play allegorizing the take-over and administration of fascistic forms of government in France or Spain in the period surrounding the second world war. Its proximate goal is to analyse the emergence of modern forms of punishment and penitentiary institutions, pre-eminently in liberal or republican regimes like the author's native France. Foucault had been animated and informed in this research by his participation in the Maoist *Group d'Information des Prisons* formed in the years following May 1968. This group, a support group for imprisoned Maoists, aimed also to provide the prisoners with a means of describing their own experiences, according to Maoist principle that "one must descend from the horse in order to smell the flowers."[247] The book followed on the heals of revolts in the French prisons in the period following the *événements* of 1968: revolts which Foucault describes as not simply protests against poor conditions, or the cruelty of the guards, "but ... also revolts against model prisons, tranquilisers, isolation, the medical and educational services."[248] Nevertheless, Foucault's book, the first fruits of his adaptation of the Nietzschean methodology of "genealogy"—"if one wanted to be pretentious, you would say that what I am doing is writing the genealogy of morals"[249]—has much wider implications. The book opens out on to, and has most often been read as proffering a new theory of specifically modern forms of power, of which the Fifth Republic's

---

245 Camus, "State," 212, cf. 163.
246 Camus, "State," 185.
247 Wolin, *The Wind from the East*, 32.
248 Michel Foucault, *Discipline and Punish* trans. A. Sheridan (New York: Vintage Books, 1979), 30.
249 Michel Foucault, *Power/Knowledge: Selected Interviews and Other Writings, 1972–1977*, ed. Colin Gordon (New York: Pantheon, 1980), 53.

penitentiary system is but a local example. "Discipline may be identified neither with an institution nor with an apparatus," Foucault clarifies concerning one of his key terms in the book: "it is a type of power, a modality for its exercise, comprising a whole series of instruments, techniques, procedures, levels of application, targets: it is a physics or anatomy of power, a technology."[250]

Foucault's work has had such a huge impact across the humanities in the last three decades that we need here only to briefly recount the key theses of his genealogical period of the middle 1970s, with an eye back to Camus' Oran and Cadiz. *Discipline and Punish* opens with the vivid documentation of what the reader is tempted to think of as an incomparable pre-modern barbarism: the spectacular public dismemberment and execution of the prisoner Damiens as his *amende honourable* before God and Louis XIV, the sun King. Damiens' "tortured, dismembered, amputated body, symbolically branded on face and shoulder, exposed alive and dead to public view"[251] outside the doors of the Church of Paris is presented by Foucault as representative of a kind of political power the modern era has supplanted. In *History of Sexuality, Volume 1*, this will be called sovereign power:[252] the power of the monarch to publically kill all those who, like Damiens, he deems to have committed *lèse-majesté*, amidst an almost carnivalesque display of the might and fearful glory of throne and altar. In the France preceding the revolution (the *amende honorable* was first abolished in 1791), there was no dedicated police force. The power of the state to surveil its citizens was characterised by a comparatively "irregular and inadequate extension;"[253] a fact that itself can be taken as one more expression of the sovereign indifference of the monarch to his subjects. When a person was apprehended and incarcerated, after whatever trial or torture the King's men felt it fit to subject them to, they were in effect left to rot or stew in the darkness of dungeons—"the old simple schema of confinement and control—thick walls, a heavy gate that prevents entering and leaving"[254]—until the hour of their humiliation or release according to His Majesty's Good Grace. No knowledge concerning the prisoner's biography, his upbringing, his deeper motives, his relationship with family members, or his socio-political circumstances was sought after or produced. No statistics listing and tabulating such information

---

250 Foucault, *Discipline*, 215.
251 Foucault, *Discipline*, 8. See James Miller, "Carnivals of Cruelty: Foucault, Nietzsche, Cruelty", *Political Theory* Vol. 18, no. 3 (1990), 470–492.
252 Michel Foucault, "Right of Death and Power over Life," in *The Foucault Reader* ed. P. Rabinow (London: Penguin, 1984), 259.
253 Foucault, *Discipline and Punish*, 219.
254 Foucault, *Discipline*, 190.

across multiple cases was solicited or maintained. It was sufficient that the threat to the sovereign had been neutralised, removed from public life, and placed at the disposal of the King's *voluntas*. "Knowledge of the offence, knowledge of the offender, knowledge of the law: these three conditions made it possible to ground a judgment in truth", at least to the satisfaction of the sovereign: and no more was required.[255]

All this changes in the kinds of modern regimes that have come into being in the West since the end of the 18th century, Foucault famously argues. Damiens' spectacular execution is followed immediately in *Discipline and Punish* by Leon Faucher's meticulous and exacting rules "for the House of young prisoners in Paris" from only 80 years later. These rules do not stipulate the means of physical torture to which prisoners are to be subjected. Instead, they plan in advance the prisoners' every action (including nine hours of productive labour), from six in the morning until half-past seven or half-past eight at night, down to five minute allotments ("at five minutes to one, at the drumroll, they form into work teams. Art 24: At one o'clock they must be back in the workshops...", etc.)[256]

"We have, then, a public execution and a timetable," Foucault crisply summarises a contrast that he presents as emblematic of what his book goes onto document by meticulous recourse to the archives of documents concerning the conception, planning, and day-to-day workings of modern prisons, schools, military camps, barracks, factories and hospitals.[257] For this kind of exacting timetable that Faucher envisages for the young Parisian prisoners in language akin to the detached reportage of a scientific lab, Foucault presents as typifying a new modality of the exercise of political control over subjects which emerges in the modern era. What is at stake in this new kind of power is a veritable "political anatomy," "anatomopolitics" or "microphysics" of power:[258] the proliferation of regimes of exercises, examinations, requirements to work, solicitations to talk and objectify oneself as a 'case' and a 'history,' or to observe oneself and monitor one's own every movement. This new kind of power, as Foucault documents its different exemplifications, completely supplants the *éclat* characterising pre- and early modern sovereigns' exercise of their august prerogatives. Indeed, at every level, it represents a different kind of power over

---

255 Foucault, *Discipline*, 19.
256 Foucault, *Discipline*, 6–7.
257 See the rightly celebrated statement of Foucault's neoNietzchean method in this period, Michel Foucault, "Nietzsche, Genealogy, History." *The Foucault Reader*, edited by Paul Rabinow (New York: Pantheon, 1984), 76–100.
258 Foucault, *Discipline*, 215.

subjects. Its object has changed: from the subject's body alone, as the markable flesh capable of bearing witness in its torments and dismemberment to the glory of the King, to his more hidden 'soul'—not the immortal soul imagined by Christian and other religions, mind you, but that 'psyche' that becomes the object studied by the new would-be 'human sciences' of psychology, criminology, and in time psychoanalysis. The methods of its exercise have changed: from the splendid, violent imposition of the will of the monarch, with his power over life and death, to the near-constant surveillance, monitoring, checking, testing, and documenting (usually behind closed institutional doors) of subjects' movements, habits, behaviours, and where possible their impulses and thoughts. Its means have moreover altered: from the actions of the personalised font of power and His representatives to bureaucrats, drills, examinations, timetables, and the very architecture of buildings—"the geometry of the paths, the number and distribution of the tents [or offices, workstations, desks], the disposition of files and ranks."[259] Foucault cites the minute, almost machine-like regimentation of individual behaviour in military drills, or documents extolling the most precise arrangement of seating and desks in school classrooms as exemplifying the far more intimate control exerted by this "disciplinary power" over individuals in modern prisons, barracks, or factories: "exercising upon the body a subtle coercion, of obtaining holds upon it at the level of the mechanism itself—movements, gestures, attitudes, rapidity; an infinitesimal power over the active body."[260] "The peculiarity of these disciplines [sic.]," Foucault summarises, is threefold. Firstly, they "obtain an exercise of power" over individuals' behaviour:

> ...at the lowest possible cost: politically by its discretion... its relative invisibility, the little resistance it arouses; second, [they] bring the effects of this social power to their maximum intensity and... extend them as far as possible, without either failure or interval; thirdly, [the disciplines] link this economic growth of power with the output of the apparatuses (educational, military, industrial or medical) within which it is exercised; in short, to increase both the docility and the utility of all the elements of the system.[261]

Famously, however, the kind of epitome or paradigm of modern disciplinary power Foucault asks us to see resembles very much the watch tower the Plague

---

259   Foucault, *Discipline*, 171.
260   Foucault, *Discipline*, 137.
261   Foucault, *Discipline*, 218.

has assembled at the centre of Camus' Cadiz, in one of his inaugural decrees as the town's new governor.[262] It is the panopticon imagined by Jeremy Bentham: namely, the vision of an ideal, circular prison with inmates' enclosures on the outside, all overseen constantly by a single central watchtower, from whence a light would shine which makes the prisoners constantly visible, while rendering any overseers in the central towers invisible to their charges. The French Minister for the Interior in 1841 describes with some enthusiasm this "intelligence of discipline in stone" (as Foucault cites Lucas),[263] at once terrifying and perfectly anaesthetic:

> The central inspection hall is the pivot of the system. Without a central point of inspection, surveillance ceases to be guaranteed, continuous, and general: for it is impossible to have complete trust in the activity, zeal, and intelligence of the warder who immediately supervises the cells... the architect must therefore bring all his attention to bear on the object: it is a question of both discipline and autonomy.[264]

In the vision of a panoptical, ideal prison, what Foucault calls the economy of visibility has been completely reversed from pre-modern to modern, disciplinary power. Traditionally, Foucault reflects, "power was what was seen, what was shown", while "those on whom it was exercised could remain in the shade; they received light only from that portion of power that was conceded to them..."[265] In the panoptical factory, barracks, workhouse or town, it is the subject who is visible, while power has become completely impersonal, and ideally invisible. "For a long time, ordinary individuality remained below the threshold of description," Foucault observes:

> To be looked at, observed, described in detail, was a privilege. The chronicle of a man, the account of his life... formed part of the rituals of his power. The disciplinary method reverses this relation, lowered the threshold of describable individuality, and made of this description a means of control and a method of domination. It is no longer a monument for future memory, but a document for future use, and this describability is all the more marked in that the disciplinary framework is a strict one; the child, the patient, the madman, the prisoner were to become

---

262 Camus, "State," 175.
263 At Foucault, *Discipline*, 249.
264 Foucault, *Discipline*, 250.
265 Foucault, *Discipline and Punish*, 187.

with increasing ease from the eighteenth century... the object of individual descriptions and biographical accounts...[266]

In *The Will to Knowledge*, the first volume of Foucault's never-completed *History of Sexuality*, this new visibility of subjects to the authorities epitomised by the panopticon—and this new *interest* of authorities in the minutae of subjects' lives, actions, dispositions, and capacities—underlies Foucault's influential conception of "biopower". This book highlights what is already one key feature of the account of modern power in *Discipline and Punish*: namely, the overturning of the idea that power is wholly negative, as Nada in *State of Siege* still supposed, evidently reckoning on something like the older sovereign conception of power as what says "no".[267] At least in the modern period of the disciplines, Foucault stresses that power is productive. Its regimes of exercise, observation, timetabling and examinations produce new kinds of subjects, "docile bodies" as he bleakly describes them; thoroughly domesticated and rendered calculable by constant surveillance and regimentation. This functioning of power also produces new kinds of knowledge: psychological, criminological, sociological. In the eighteenth century, *Volonté de Savoir* contends, a "threshold" is crossed, from the sovereign's power to kill to a new form of power interested in monitoring, preserving, and channelling subjects' capacities as living bodies.[268] Through the new population or "demographic" sciences based in the compilation of statistics concerning birth rates and death rates, differential life expectancies, patterns of migration and the like, modern forms of governmentality for the first time, Foucault explains: "brought life and its mechanisms into the realm of explicit calculations and made power-knowledge an agent of transformation of human life."[269] Individuals' sexuality, in this constellation, far from being "repressed"—as sexual libertarians of different stripes continue to claim—takes on unprecedented new importance. Camus' Jean-Baptiste Clamence jokes acidly in *The Fall* that modern men and women will be remembered for doing nothing more than fornicating and reading the newspapers.[270] Foucault's *History of Sexuality* would have us add that we are also the age which became obsessed with observing and talking about our sex, as the key to our selves and our pathologies: whether to doctors or to analysts, in magazines, on

---

266   Foucault, *Discipline*, 191.
267   Camus, "State," 212.
268   Foucault, "Right of Death and Power over Life," 265.
269   Michel Foucault, *The History of Sexuality, vol. 1. An Introduction* (London: Allen Lane, 1979), 179.
270   Albert Camus, *The Fall*; trans: J. O'Brien (London: Vintage, 1956), 6–7.

television and now the internet. In earlier political regimes, the reproductive potency of the sovereign in generating male heirs was perhaps the only sexual matter of public concern in the entire realm. In Foucault's modern period, by contrast, "it was essential that the state know what was happening with its citizens' sex, and the use they made of it ... between the state and the individual, sex became an issue, and a public issue no less..."[271]

The reader will by now have been seeing the wide-ranging parallels between Camus' depiction of the new forms of totalitarian power in *State of Siege* and *The Plague* in the late 1940s, and Foucault's genealogical analyses of modern disciplinary power in the middle-1970s.[272] Of course Camus, even in his most extended treatment of Hitlerism and Stalinism in *The Rebel* which we will examine momentarily, never undertook such an extensive documentary work as Foucault's extraordinarily ambitious, minute studies of the modern disciplines and modes of 'governmentality.' Yet Camus' descriptions of the exactions of what we might call 'plague power' exemplify that attention to the particular we saw in the Introduction that *The Myth of Sisyphus* extols as recommending literature as a post-metaphysical form of intelligence.[273] They also bespeak Camus' own almost lurid fascination with all the forms of human cruelty, from the "little ease" of *La Chute* to the death penalty: the traumatic effects of whose witnessing by Camus' father was recalled to Albert in one of the few memories his *maman* could relay of the man.[274]

Certainly, in Camus' post-war fiction we already find the evocation of forms of power which, far from being merely prohibitive, work by actively surveying individuals, disciplining their ways of thinking, acting, working and loving, all the while compiling and applying new forms of knowledge in conjunction with these means of control. If the parallels we have so far documented were not direct enough, however, it is remarkable—albeit very little remarked[275]—that Foucault's famous central chapter in *Discipline and Punish* on the

---

271   Foucault, *History of Sexuality*, 25–6.
272   Parallels, remarkably, which have not been made, as far as the author has been able to find, excepting in Lissa Lincoln, "Discours du juste, ou juste un discours?" in *Camus in the 21st century*, 168–175: which places the focus on epistemology, not their accounts of modernity and the darker potentials of modern rationalisation.
273   Albert Camus, *Myth of Sisyphus*, trans. J. O'Brien (London: Penguin, 1978), 87–88, 26–27.
274   Cf. F 98, 109–11; P 201–210; FM 62–65.
275   Camus' invisibility in Foucault and the post-structuralists would itself be an interesting study in the history and formation of French ideas, but not something which is our specific concern in this book. The centrality of the example of the plague has been recognised by Peter Dews, *Logics of Disintegration: Post-structuralist thought and the claims of critical theory* (London: Verso, 1987), 186–187.

panopticon, which begins by seeking out the "ignoble" *enstehung* of modern forms of disciplinary power,[276] strikes upon the shutting down of the plague-stricken town of Vincennes at the end of the 17th century. As in Camus' Oran (whose imagining certainly drew on similar historical sources as Foucault later cites[277]) Vincennes was segregated off from the outside world by gated walls, and its internal space was divided into quarters administered by attendants. In this "segmented, immobile frozen space", inspection became more or less continuous, with guards posted at the city gates to prevent escape, and syndics responsible for each street who would at the end of each day call upon houses individually, armed with exhaustive lists.[278] The regime thus put in place "a system of permanent registration: reports from the syndics to the intendants, from the intendants to the magistrates or mayor."[279] In this system, even "the relation of each individual to his [own] disease passed through the representatives of power...," as Foucault puts it: regardless of, and supplanting all familial, erotic or philial ties.[280] Faced with the matter of understanding modern power's specific physiognomy, Foucault thus at this decisive point in his most famous genealogy echoes Camus' choice of the plague as a means to allegorise and analyse modern, total forms of government. As Foucault intones in a characteristic, near-Ciceronian sequence of antinomies which, their flowing prose notwithstanding, might almost have come from the pen of Dr. Rieux in *The Plague*:

> But there was also a political dream of the plague...: not the collective festival, but strict divisions; not laws transgressed, but the penetration of regulation into even the smallest details of everyday life through the mediation of the complete hierarchy that assured the capillary functioning of power; not masks that were put on and taken off, but the assignment to each individual of his 'true' name, his 'true' place, his 'true' body, his 'true' disease. The plague as a form, at once real and imaginary, of disorder had as its medical and political correlative discipline. Behind the disciplinary mechanisms [of modern prisons, schools, barracks, hospitals, asylums] can be read the haunting memory of 'contagions', of the plague, of rebel-

---

276 See Michel Foucault, "Nietzsche, Genealogy, History," in *Foucault Reader*, 83, with 77–81.
277 On Camus' historical researches for *La Peste*, see esp. "Commentaire de Stephan sur Thucydide et Lucrèce. Fragment du chapitre v, IIIeme partie", & "Les Archives de *La Peste*", OC II, 258–261, 271–284.
278 Foucault, *Discipline*, 196.
279 Foucault, *Discipline*, 196.
280 Foucault, *Discipline*, 196–7.

lions, crimes, vagabondage, desertions, people who appear and disappear, live and die in disorder.[281]

3   *Nouvelle Philosophie Avant La Lettre*? Another 'Dialectic of Enlightenment'?

Michel Foucault always remained tellingly qualified about his assessment of what Camus and others in the post-war period dubbed the 'totalitarian' states of National Socialism, Stalinism, or later Mao's China in the period of the cultural revolution. There remains interpretive room to move and dispute concerning how his analysis of the disciplinary 'carceral archipelago' related to these most openly and completely oppressive of modern regimes. Certainly, the competing theorisations of totalitarianism that emerged in the 1940s and 1950s (amongst which Camus' political novels, drama and theory should be numbered) tended to focus on the question of state power.[282] Camus cites Mussolini's "nothing outside the State, nothing above the State" as illustrating the kind of "State Terror" he means to document in *The Rebel*.[283] To the extent that this is the case, these theories of totalitarianism seem to represent the kinds of theorisations of power which, in Foucault's happy phrase, have yet "to lop off the head of the King":[284] still conceiving power as a hierarchical, more or less substantial thing concentrated, possessed, and deployed by individuals or parties.[285] Yet Foucault's genealogical work in the 1970s is both predicated upon, and duly discovers, the existence of kinds of "micro" or "capillary" forms of power we have seen. These are neither necessarily (although they are sometimes) personalised. Nor are they hierarchized or substantial. They concern instead the implementation of bodily exercises, schedules and examinations, and the planning of the very architecture of public institutions. Such insights enshrine Foucault's break with more traditional political theories. They seem also to speak against any association of Foucault's works, principally on modern liberal regimes, and Camus' work targeting Hitlerism and Stalinism.

---

281   Foucault, *Discipline*, 197–198.
282   See Isaac, *Arendt, Camus and Modern Rebellion*, 37–75; cf. Foucault, *Discipline*, 308; also Mitchell Dean, *Governmentality: Power and Rule in Modern Society* (London: Sage, 2010 [2nd ed.]), "Authoritarian governmentality", 155–174.
283   HR 233; R 182.
284   Foucault, *History of Sexuality*, 88–89.
285   See 140–1 of Peter Dews, "The '*Nouvelle Philosophie*' and Foucault", *Economy and Society*, 8:2 (May 1979), 127–171.

Nevertheless, we are not the first here to associate Foucault's genealogical critique of modern forms of power with a criticism of totalitarian modes of political rule. Notoriously, the *nouveaux philosophes* led by André Glucksmann and Bernard Henri-Lévy built the criticisms of Stalinism they developed in the wake of the 1974 translation of Solzenitzyn's *Gulag Archipelago* in France by way of key recourse to Foucault's genealogical work and his earlier book on *The History of Madness*. All the while, as Lecourt and others have noted, they claimed Camus' anti-Stalinism and critique of totalitarian forms of government as an inspiration for their own theories of rebellion, and sometimes-defences of human rights.[286]

Critics of the 'new philosophers' have been at pains to distance Foucault from any affiliation with these "mediocratic" young Turks. They point to Foucault's genealogical turn away from any focus on the State (the object of the *nouveaux philosophes*' ire) which we have just mentioned. There is also the materialism of his genealogical accounts which situate the production of ideas—effects as much as causes—in wider *assemblages* of institutions, practices, and rituals. The new philosophers' accounts of Marxism by contrast focus on it as a set of political doctrines ("the most formidable doctrine of Order the West has ever invented").[287] These ideological doctrines are held to have more or less by themselves "caused" the gulags. Accordingly the new philosophers' positions seem prize exemplars of a kind of idealistic political theory Foucault rejects:[288] one which holds that "thought makes reality," instead of observing the way that forms of power, rooted in institutional settings and practices, themselves produce kinds of knowledge-claim. When Lévy or Glucksmann meanwhile assert that, even if Marx's (or Fichte's, or Plato's) teachings are not directly responsible for the camps, these atrocities embody the necessary political unfolding of their ideas, they seem to exemplify the exact kind of 'essentialist', idealising understanding of history (which sees it as the necessary unfolding of one or other essential power, like Hegel's *Geist* or Heidegger's *Sein*) which Foucault's

---

286   Lecourt, *Mediocracy*, 176–178. See Gayatri Chakravorty Spivak & Michael Ryan, "Anarchism Revisited: A New Philospohy. Contra le Nouvelle Philosophie", *Diacritics* Vol. 8, No. 2 (Summer 1978), 66–79.

287   Peter Dews, "The New Philosophy and the End of leftism", in *Radical Philosophy Reader*, ed. R. Edgley et al. (London: Verso, 1985): 381.

288   See in particular André Glucksmann, *The Master Thinkers*, translated by Brian Pearce (New York: Harper & Row: 1980) and Bernard Henri-Lévy, *Barbarism with a Human Face* translated by George Holoch (New York: Harper & Row, 1979). See Julian Bourg, *From the Revoltution to Ethics*, 289–295.

Nietzschean methodology, open to the contingency and complexity of historical events, powerfully contests.[289]

Yet it remains that Foucault himself was far from dismissing the *nouveaux philosophes* (alongside his friend Gilles Deleuze and many on the Marxist Left). He spoke out in Glucksmann's and his friends' defence, praising *Les Maîtres Penseurs'* "*éclat*, its fits of rage, its thick clouds and its laughter."[290] Underscoring his own career-long ambivalence concerning Marxism,[291] Foucault also lauded the young philosophers' refusal to "buy" Marxists' exonerations of Marxism *per se*, by presenting Stalinism as an historically specific, politically and philosophically reprehensible "deviation."[292] Just so, as Peter Dews in particular has argued, if we look for arguments in Foucault's work that do seem to licence the kinds of anti-Marxist positions Lévy and Glucksmann were to take, several plausibly present themselves. Foucault's very claim that the disciplinary mechanisms he documents in *Discipline and Punish* are kinds of "technologies of power," which do not need to be manned and implemented by any particular kind of sovereign implies what Foucault in fact openly avows: that they can operate "in the most diverse political regimes, apparatuses or institutions," including outside of the liberal regimes in which they emerged.[293] Indeed, in "Subject and Power" Foucault claims that the two "diseases of power" of fascism and Stalinism both "used and extended ... the ideas and devices of our political rationality", i.e. that of the modern liberal West.[294] Then there is the uneasy proximity between Foucault's critique of "power-knowledge" and the *nouveaux philosophes'* further signature hyperboles, that "to conceive is to dominate" and "to theorise is to terrorise," underlining their attacks on the *maîtres penseurs* Marx, Hegel, Fichte, or even (in Lévy's case) Plato and "the Greeks."[295]

As Dews has argued in an essay which in part tries to rescue Foucault from guilt by association with Glucksmann, Lardreau and Jambet, Clavel or Lévy, there are distinct proximities to Foucault in such 'hyper-pessimism' about

---

289   Foucault, "Nietzsche, Genealogy, History", 76–85.
290   Foucault, quoted at Lecourt, *Mediocracy*, 53.
291   See Michel Foucault, "Two Lectures" (1976) in *Power/Knowledge: Selected Interviews and Other Writings, 1972–1977* ed. Colin Gordon (Brighton: Harvester 1980), 76–108.
292   Peter Dews, "The 'Nouvelle Philosophie' and Foucault", *Economy and Society*, 8: 2 (1979): 140.
293   Foucault, *Discipline* 221, 204.
294   Michel Foucault, "The Subject and Power", in *Critical Inquiry*, Vol. 8, No. 4 (1982), 777–795: at 779.
295   See Dews, "The 'Nouvelle Philosophie' and Foucault", 141–145–153; Bourg, *From the Revolution to Ethics*, 297–298.

'Western rationality' and the modern State. Foucault, famously, remained as coy about his own final epistemological commitments as he was politically guarded or ambiguous. Nevertheless, Foucault again and again after 1970 tries to show how the modern "human sciences" (or at least certain of them, as McCarthy specifies)[296] are not the progressive products of a neutral or benign will to know, so much as the products of "the mechanisms of examination,... the formation of the mechanisms of discipline.... the modern play of coercion of bodies, gestures, and behaviours."[297] In their defence, Glucksmann, Lévy et al. are far from the only readers who take Foucault's work to have licensed an openly sceptical, politicising epistemological position wherein all claims to "scientificity" are in truth (forgive the wording) so many manifestations of, and bids for, forms of power. Dews notes, in a related point, how Foucault oscillates uneasily between (a) his minute, genealogical accounts of specific forms of disciplinary or biopower and (b) larger claims about "Power" per se.[298] This latter hypostasisation comes in his work (and in the work of many of his students) to take on an inescapable, almost metaphysical status. By the time "power is everywhere", for Foucault—"coextensive with the entire social body"[299]—we can see how such a gloomy assessment can be readily applied to the analysis of totalitarian forms of government. Indeed, this assessment threatens at every moment to collapse all differences between ostensibly liberal states founded on the civil, political, and economic liberties, and the total states of the 20th century. Foucault does not shrink from describing the liberal subject whom "humanism invites us to free" as "already the effect of a subjection much more profound than himself."[300] On the face of it, this looks a wholly determinist position which leads Foucault into the notorious difficulties encapsulated in the paradoxical claim (which Lévy echoes) that even *resistance* is a product of the power it ostensibly rebels against.[301] The disciplines which can operate

---

296 Thomas McCarthy, "The Critique of Impure Reason," *Political Theory*, Vol. 18, No. 3 (Aug., 1990): 437–469 (on this issue of the scope of Foucault's claims, see 449–450).
297 Foucault, *Discipline*, 191.
298 Dews, "Nouvelle Philosophie", 141: "It is Jacques Rancière who has suggested the solution to this puzzle—that Foucault's and Glucksmann's conceptions of power are in fact mirror-images of each other. Foucault's elusive power, which is 'everywhere' (Foucault...) and yet 'does not exist' (Foucault...) is ultimately no different from Glucksmann's power, which radiates from the Panopticon state into every interstice of a civil society which is simultaneously a network of resistances..."
299 Foucault, *Discipline*, 213.
300 Foucault, *Discipline*, 30.
301 Dews, "The nouvelle philosophie", 162; cf. Nancy Fraser, "Foucault on Modern Power: Empirical Insights and Normative Confusions", *Praxis International* issue 3, 1981: 272–281;

with equal effect in liberal and total states, Foucault in this vein argues are "the foundation of the formal, juridical liberties" the liberal West has long valorised as its point of difference from these other regimes. They are "the other, dark side" of the ostensible protections of law whose promise of liberty they render illusory in advance.[302]

Why though do we draw attention here to Foucault's uneasy *rapport* with the hyperventilating excesses of the *nouveaux philosophes* against Western rationality, Marxism and the modern State?

We do so firstly because Marxist critics of the new philosophers like Dominique Lecourt were quick to espy commonalities between Camus' anti-Stalinism and that of this later generation of thinkers of nearly three decades later.[303] Secondly, we do so since we want to now set up a vital set of questions concerning Camus' account of totalitarian power as it is developed in *The Rebel*. These questions will be the subject both of the final section of this Chapter and of Chapter Two.

The importance of the trauma for European civilization represented by the atrocities committed by Germany under Adolf Hitler and Stalin in Eastern Europe can scarcely be overstated. The Solzhenitsyn affair in France in the mid-1970s, which launched the new philosophers' "*reductio ad absurdem* of a decade of French thought in which the concepts of reason, theory and history have been subject to incessant critique",[304] is but one chapter in the continuing history of intellectual and political attempts to come to terms with this trauma in later modern Western history. Camus was of course one of the first public voices in the post-war period to try to theorise both the enormity and specificity of Hitlerism and Stalinism, in "Neither Victims nor Executioners",[305] the speeches he gave in the United States in 1946, then in *The Rebel*—as well as in the post-war fictions we have introduced. There is a lasting temptation faced by any such attempt to analyse total forms of power: one, to which we would argue the *nouveaux philosophes* accede but Camus does *not*. It lies in

---

      Thomas McCarthy, "The Critique of Impure Reason," *Political Theory*, Vol. 18, No. 3 (Aug., 1990): 437–469 (on this issue, 449–450).

302   Foucault, *Discipline*, 222.

303   Cf. Lecourt, *Mediocracy*, 176–178.

304   At 381 in Peter Dews, "The New Philosophy and the End of leftism", in *Radical Philosophy Reader*, ed. R. Edgley et al. (London: Verso, 1985): 361–384.

305   Albert Camus, "Neither Victims nor Executioners", in *Camus at Combat*, 255–276. This 'piece' was in fact eight serialised articles appearing in *Combat* between November 19 and 30, 1946, the only of Camus' contributions to the paper of that year.

kinds of despair as ironically bleak and totalising as what we have set out to comprehend.

The workings and atrocities of the total states exert an unmistakable, horrifying fascination. It becomes possible under the sway of this fascination to see these regimes' rule as all-but-inescapable or inevitable. Differently, since these regimes have arisen in the modern period which had hoped to supplant forms of mythical and Christian forms of authority with 'the light of reason'—and since these regimes did deploy new political and other technologies unique to the modern age—it can seem truth-preserving and urgent to assign causal responsibility for these regimes to 'modernity', 'liberalism,' 'reason' or 'the enlightenment' themselves. Whatever their specific weaknesses and the specific political effect of their media-fuelled emergence at a specific moment in French political history, Lardeau, Jambet, Clavel, Glucksmann, and Lévy are not alone in propounding this kind of *kulturpessimismus*. (The often frantic and sensationalised tones or "*éclat*" with which they publicised their anti-Stalinist message are a different, more specifically post-'68 Parisian matter.)[306] If as one recent commentator has claimed, almost all contemporary political theory, from postmodern Left to neoconservative Right, belongs to an "anti-enlightenment project,"[307] it is above all because the modern age and its celebrated Reason has been so widely suspected of being 'in essence' totalitarian. At the least, the West's vaunted modernity was unable to prevent the great State-led crimes of the last century. More strongly, the philosophical and technical advances of the post-enlightenment period are arraigned by critics from Right and Left for furnishing the ideological justifications and technological means for the genocidal atrocities of the first half of the twentieth century. We need only recall, to illustrate this wider climate of critical thinking, the great theses of Adorno and Horkheimer's *Dialectic of Enlightenment*, written from Californian exile in the darkest hours of the second world war. Modern rationality, this extraordinary text claims, does not escape mythical violence, as its progenitors had dared to dream. It engenders new forms of abstraction and instrumental control that come, perversely, to take on all the impersonality

---

306 On the peculiar sociology of French academe, see Niilo Kauppi, *Radicalism in French Culture: A Sociology of French Theory in the 1960s* (Ashgate: Surrey, 2012); and earlier, on the 1960s "moment", with the implosion of distance between "high" theoretical and philosophical study and the media culture, Niilo Kauppi, *French Intellectual Nobility* (Albany: State University of NY Press, 1996).

307 Dennis Rasmussen, "Contemporary Political Science as an Anti-Enlightenment Project" at www-site http://www.brown.edu/Research/ppw/files/Rasmussen_PPW.pdf, accessed November 2014.

and inhumanity of the ancient fates.³⁰⁸ In fact, as reading Homer's *Odyssey* is supposed to show us, the West's founding myths had already anticipated (witness wily Odysseus' polytropic guiles) the genesis of forms of rationality whose vocation to domesticate the chthonic forces of external nature is bought at the price of increasing inner repression and alienation from others, deafly manning the oars of the administered Western state.³⁰⁹

Adorno and Horkheimer may not so baldly state, in the over-heated phrases of the *nouveaux philosophes*, that "to conceive is to dominate," that "the Prince is the other name of the World," or that "the idea of the good society is an absurd dream."³¹⁰ But the kinship is clear between this kind of sensationalised Spenglerism and Adorno and Horkheimer's tracing back of the totalitarian *désatre* to Homer's epics. Each leaves us a thoroughly pessimistic prospect of any escape from such a tri-millenial 'dialectic of enlightenment.' As Horkheimer would later reflect in a passage which echoes, even to the exclamation mark, *Barbarie et le visage humain*: "we have reached the conclusion that society will evolve towards a totally administered world: that everything will be regulated, everything!... [Hitler and Stalin just] tried to carry out a too-brutal unification, and exterminated all those who did not submit."³¹¹

It will be decisive for us here, by contrast, to show how (Camus' reclamation as "moral exemplar" by Lévy and Glucksmann notwithstanding) Camus' position in *The Rebel* and more widely does not represent another version of the 'dialectic of enlightenment.' As we saw above in Camus' phenomenological descriptions of totalitarian power, Camus accepts the imbrication of modern, technical forms of rationality in the great totalitarian crimes of the last century.³¹² Asked in 1956 in a seminar on "The Future of European Civilization" to discuss the threats facing the West, Camus expostulated on whether "the

---

308 Theodor Adorno and Max Horkheimer, *The Dialectic of Enlightenment*, translated by John Cumming (NY: Continuum, 1989), 3–80.
309 Adorno and Horkheimer, *The Dialectic of Enlightenment*, 81–119.
310 Citations from Dews, "The New Philosophy and the End of leftism", 380.
311 Horkheimer, cited at Luc Ferry, *Political Philosophy 1: Rights, the New Quarrel Between Ancients and Moderns* (Chicago: University of Chicago Press: 1990), 2.
312 In several addresses Camus gave leading up to *L'Homme Révolté*, beginning with "La Crise de l'homme" in March 1946, Camus argues that this contemporary crisis is manifest in the proven ability of men of different regimes to kill other human beings without any sense of horror: but "coldly and scientifically (sic.)," "in the name of logic," as "an affair of statistics and administration." (Albert Camus, "Les Temps des Meurtriurs," *OC III*, 351–2: see Chapter Four below)

singular success of occidental civilization in its scientific aspect was not in part responsible for the singular moral flaw [*echec*] of this civilization":[313]

> The universe of technology, by itself, is not a bad thing, but considered as the most important mechanical agency of a civilization, [it] finishes by provoking a sort of perversion, at the same time in the mind and in morality...[314]

But Camus, we will argue, does not infer from these theses a wholesale rejection of the modern age, or of the West's Greek (and Christian) inheritances. Nor, as Isaac has pointed out,[315] does Camus accede to a total criticism of reason as "instrumental", "technological," or "disciplinary" all the way down: implicated from the beginning, and the beginnings of Western history, in the objectification and oppression of human beings and destruction of everything the exceeds "the reign of quantity."[316] In order to show this, we turn first to his account of Stalinism and Hitler's tyrannical regime in *L'Homme Révolté*, before examining his account of the ideological causes of these regimes in Chapter Two.

4 Totality on Trial

Camus was one of a host of authors who, in the period of the second world war and the decade afterwards, contended that the crimes and workings of the National Socialist and Stalinist regimes were so unprecedented as to demand a new political category: 'totalitarianism'.[317] The term was meant to capture the novelty of these single-party regimes which commanded total economic and political control, a monopoly of the use of force and internal communications, sophisticated secret police apparati and purportedly "scientific" ideological justifications. From its beginning, 'totalitarianism' was a controversial category. Critics of the term's scientific value have long argued, with Barber, that "the mood of political crisis and ideological urgency that surrounded such studies [of 'totalitarianism' as Camus', Arendt's, Neumann's, etc.] naturally

---

[313] Camus, "L'Avenir de la civilization européenne", OC III, 996–997.
[314] Camus, "L'Avenir de la civilization européenne", OC III, 997.
[315] Isaac, *Arendt, Camus and Modern Rebellion*, 70–73.
[316] HR, 293; R 234.
[317] Isaac, *Arendt, Camus,* and *Modern Rebellion*: 38. See in general for Camus on the total states, Isaac, *Arendt, Camus, and Modern rebellion*, 37–67.

gave totalitarianism a controversial, sometimes polemical aura from which the term has never been satisfactorily emancipated."[318] From the time of Hannah Arendt and Albert Camus in the late 1940s and early 1950s to Slavoz Žižek's more recent polemics, 'totalitarianism' has stood accused by *Marxissant* critics of being an ideological sledgehammer with which the liberal West has tried to bludgeon political alternatives into silence.[319]

Camus' depiction of the Stalinist and Hitlerian regimes in *L'Homme Révolté*, as in *La Peste* and *L'État de Siège* bespeak a definite philosophical and political urgency. The question is whether Camus' description of these regimes accurately captures their decisive features, and then whether those features do not demand urgent rejection. How such rejection is used by interested parties is an in principle independent question.

For Camus, these regimes' uniqueness resides first of all in their ideological and political ambition to conquer what he terms "totality", a term which is in fact used a good deal more often in Camus' works than "totalitarian" or "totalitarianism".[320] "Totality is, in effect, nothing other than the ancient dream of unity common to both believers and rebels [against the deity], but projected horizontally onto an earth deprived of God," Camus writes.[321] "The originality of the 20th century revolution" for its part "lies in the fact that, for the first time, it openly laid claim to realise [this] ancient dream of the unity of the human race, and at the same time, the definitive consummation of human history."[322] Stalinism at least (see below) was for Camus the political instantiation or 'immanentisation' of a deeply theological or philosophical ambition, "to control the world and introduce a universal rule", if not "to annex all creation" in the name of a unifying, definitive vision of human history.[323] It is impossible to deny, then, that many of Camus' declarations in the late 1940s and early 1950s

---

318 Benjamin Barber, at Isaac, *Arendt, Camus and Modern Rebellion*, 38. Cf. for a more recent polemical statement of this position, Slavoj Žižek, *Did Anybody Say Totalitarianism?* (London: Verso, 2011).

319 Isaac, *Arendt, Camus and Modern Rebellion*, 38–39.

320 As Maurice Weyenbergh has helpfully counted, "totality" is used 40 times in *The Rebel*, "totalitarian" only 7. (Weyenbergh, "La tentation du 'tout est permis': Camus entre 'détour' et 'rétour' ", in D. Lyotard ed. *Camus, Contemporain*, 73).

321 HR, 292; R 233.

322 HR 142; R, 107.

323 HR 135; R 103. The term 'immanentisation' is Eric Voegelin's, and I use it here as its semantics are not as loaded as 'secularisation' which carries the polemical, historical reference to the early modern monarchs' expropriation of Church properties. See Eric Voegelin, *The New Science of Politics* (Chicago: University of Chicago Press, 1987); also Robert M. Wallace "Translator's Foreword" to Hans Blumenberg, *The Legitimacy of*

concerning totalitarian government do skirt becoming both metaphysical and every bit as pessimistic as the declamations of Adorno and Horkheimer from this period. From the 18th century to 1951, Camus for instance writes in the section "Nihilism and History" in *L'Homme Révolté*, the West's purported progress:

> ... has consisted of gradually enlarging the enclosure where, according to his own rules, man without God brutally wields power. In defiance of the divinity, the frontiers of this stronghold have been extended, to the point of making the entire universe a fortress erected against the fallen deity. Man, at the culmination of his rebellion, incarcerated himself: from Sade's lurid castle to the concentration camps, man's greatest liberty consisted only of building the prison of his crimes.[324]

Nevertheless, the deciding features of Camus' writings on totalitarianism emerge from his close analyses of the workings of these regimes' control over subject populations. In "Totality and Trial," devoted to analysing Stalinism, as well as in "State Terrorism and Irrational Terror" on Nazism, Camus descends from grandiose philosophical generalisations.[325] Instead, we are given analyses of the mechanisms of 'totalitarian' rule which more closely approach the kinds of descriptive, 'proto-Foucaultian' claims about specific forms of modern power we saw him staging in *State of Siege* and *The Plague*. These regimes, Camus repeats in *L'Homme Révolté*, set about turning the entire political life of their people into "the factory and barracks of the world."[326] Under Stalinism in particular, this was achieved by setting out to control the "three dimensions" of human political life; space, time, and people: by the militarisation of everyday life, the use of propaganda, torture and terrorism.[327]

Hitler and Nazism, alongside Mussolini's Italian fascism, Camus observes, "lacked the ambition of [spatial or human] universality." "At the very most," he explains, "Hitler, astonished by his own victories, was diverted from the purely provincial origin of his movement towards the indefinite dream of an empire of the Germans that had nothing to do with the universal City."[328] Lenin's and Stalin's regimes, by contrast, had recourse to the Marxist philosophy of

---

      the Modern Age translated by R.M. Wallace (USA: MIT Press 1997) and Blumenberg, *The Legitimacy of the Modern Age*, 22–25.

324   HR 134; R 102–103.
325   HR, 292–306; R 233–245.
326   HR 231; R 180.
327   HR 293; R 235.
328   HR 228; R 177, 186.

history to justify their exactions. This philosophy of course does claim that communism both should and will follow capitalism—in principle, globally. Nevertheless, it soon became clear to Lenin and the Bolsheviks after 1917 that their success in Russia would not, automatically, trigger global communist revolution, including in the more advanced capitalist economies. Indeed, socialism "in one country" attracted the concerted opposition of the Western liberal-capitalist states.[329] Meanwhile, the revolutions ardently hoped for in Italy, France and Germany in the days following the end of World War I failed to materialise. The only means to attain universal communist rule, or even a federation of communist states, thus became through prosecuting defensive war, and then imperialist expansion of the kind Stalin undertook *de facto* in Eastern Europe as the Red Army drove back the *Wehrmacht* after Stalingrad. Camus cites Bakunin's *Appeal to the Slavs*, in a passage which Engels approved, stipulating that "the next world war will cause the disappearance from the surface of the globe ... of whole races of reactionaries. This also is a part of progress" as illustrating the kind of World-Historical, quasi-prophetic thinking in play here.[330] Indeed, if progress can only mean the achievement of a global superstate or federation of communist states, then "war, cold and lukewarm, is the slavery imposed by world empire": so long as at least one state or people resists this dispensation.[331]

We saw how in *L'État de Siège*, the Plague wore a military uniform, and how in *La Peste* policing in plague-stricken Oran becomes morphed into a species of military action. The militarisation of everyday life, putting everything on a war footing, for Camus, is a characteristic mark of both the Stalinist and the National Socialist regimes. Externally, all nations that oppose communist rule, or in Hitler's case, the ambitions of the Germanic master race to win *lebensraum* throughout Europe and to the East, are in principle enemies, when they have not accepted alliances or ceded their independence. Internally, all

---

329 HR 294; R 234: due to the contingent fact of what Camus calls "the cynical intervention of the armies of the Western powers against the Soviet revolution." This acknowledgment is significant, as it recognises the non-inevitability of Stalinism, as against seeing it as the product of some larger metaphysical process operating wholly behind the backs of the political and international agents. This is worth saying, although readers of Camus' political journalism in the *Algerian Chronicles* will be awake to his measured, empirical approach to assessing contemporary events, and reluctance to assign them metaphysical or fate-like significances. See Isaac, *Arendt, Camus, and Modern Rebellion*, 87 who notes that Camus' account of the Russian revolution is more judicious than his critics have painted it to be.

330 Bakunin, cited by Camus at HR 294–295; R 235.

331 HR 295; R 235.

individuals or groups who oppose the rule of the Party or the Leader in effect become 'enemies of the state'. They are to be combatted like external enemies threatening national security, using all the repressive means at the disposal of the ruling clique and its apparatus, whose suspension of all ordinary forms of legality these real or manufactured 'enemies' in turn justifies. This is why terrorism, exercised first of all by the State on its own peoples (and justified always by charges of the terrorism of others) is a further defining characteristic of totalitarian regimes. In Camus' assessment:

> As long as enemies exist, terror will exist; and there will be enemies as long as the dynamic exists to ensure that 'all the influences liable to undermine the sovereignty of the people, as exercised by the *Führer* with the assistance of the party ... must be eliminated'. Enemies are heretics who must be converted by preaching or propaganda, exterminated by the inquisition or by the Gestapo. The result is that man, if he is a member of the party, is no more than a tool in the hands of the Fuhrer, cog in the apparatus, or, if he is the enemy of the Fuhrer, a waste product of the machine.[332]

So we arrive at the definitive dimension of totalitarian power: that of control over subject populations, which makes these regimes resemble nothing so much as "armed camps (*camps retrenchés*)".[333] While global revolution or the bucolic realm of the Nordic farmer-warriors awaits the conquest or extermination of recalcitrant elements, "the dream of empire, put in check by the realities of time and space, gratifies its desires on humanity."[334] For Camus, like both George Orwell and Hannah Arendt, totalitarianism represents an unprecedented attack on the nature and liberties of human beings: using the best available means of technological and political manipulation. The workings of these police states in effect suppose the negation of any constant human nature not subject to historical forces. Foucault, as we have commented, claims that the subjects imagined by modern humanisms are the products of forms of power that exceed their control; so that at most we can hope that the latter somehow generate their *own* forms of resistance. At a general philosophical level, Camus disputes this claim, forcibly, as we will be seeing. He nevertheless accepts that it can stand as an accurate description of the ambition of the

---

332 HR 234; R 183.
333 HR 284; R 226.
334 HR 297; R 237.

totalitarian regimes which set out to ideologically deny, and politically crush, any dimensions of human experience not subject to their control.

Propaganda in these regimes ("the first step towards hell," as Frank avowed)[335] is the principal, least directly coercive means for this total political domination. At its limits, the proselytising of this propaganda, using the most advanced aesthetic and psychological techniques and mass media, approximates for Camus to a kind of ongoing political "experiment" testing the hypothesis that "if there is no human nature, the malleability of man is, in fact, infinite."[336] The ruling regimes commandeer a complete monopoly of the press, and as far as possible survey, monitor and censor all forms of communication between people: a situation we note has again become disturbingly contemporary in the post-9/11 world. This means that the regimes' freedom of violent and coercive action is in effect doubled, and protected, by a similarly total control over the means whereby their subjects can understand and monitor historical reality. Government communications are carried out in increasingly lifeless, scholastic jargon closed to understanding by subjects outside of the ruling elites: so the regime no longer kills or murders, but undertakes "forcible relocations", "resettlements in the East", a "final solution to the Jewish problem", etc. This ensures that these elites have the maximum freedom to coordinate actions without provoking dissent, since the population is increasingly in the dark as to what is being done in their name.[337] Nada, the Plague's collaborator in *L'État de Siège* explains that the regime's extraordinary measure of placing vinegar pads on subjects' tongues serves the goal of "fixing things up in such a way that nobody understands a word of what his neighbour says. And let me tell you, we are steadily nearing the moment when nothing anybody says will rouse the least echo in another's mind..."[338] Inconvenient truths that cannot be concealed or obfuscated away behind walls of 'scholastic' jargon are simply denied. Thus, Goebbels would continue announcing imminent German triumph as Soviet tanks and ammunitions were bombarding Berlin in 1945;

---

335   At HR 232; R 182.
336   HR 297; 297–299; R 237; 237–239.
337   On monologue as language of domination, and Camus' defence of dialogue or a "théorie de la communication" *avant la lettre* ("Conférence au convent de Latour-Marbourg", OC II, 509), cf. HR 300, 354; R 283, 291; "Le Dialogue et le Vocabulaire", OC III, 1105–8; "Démocratie et modèstie" and "Dialogue pour le Dialogue", OC II, 427f; 479f; "Le Témoin de la liberté", OC II, esp. 490–491 ("Il n'y a pas la vie sans dialogue"). This will be the subject of Chapter Four below, and resurface in Chapter Six as we look at *The Fall*.
338   At Isaac, *Arendt, Camus and Modern Rebellion*, 53. The proximities to George Orwell, writing at nearly the exact same time, are clear, although it appears the men never met, and Camus does not comment on Orwell, as far as the author is aware.

just as the inveterate ideological opposition between National Socialism and Stalinism was promptly denied by both regimes' propaganda machines in 1938, when Hitler and Stalin signed their non-aggression pact, only to be reaffirmed in June 1941, when the *entente cordiale* ended and Operation Barbarossa began.

For anyone who dares to challenge official versions of events or to question the justice of the regimes' actions, these regimes of course had no scruples about the use of terror and torture to change people's minds. Indeed, Camus sees the barbarous willingness of totalitarian regimes to use torture as one more illustration of their ambition to treat human beings as "only an interplay of forces that can be rationally influenced"[339] and, when faced with dissent, to forcibly 'prove' this reductively determinist hypothesis by either destroying or converting all would-be 'counter-examples.' Under Stalinism at its height, dissenters led by Bakunin were made to publically repent their 'errors' in the spectacular show trials, or else (under National Socialism) they were simply deported or 'disappeared'. The reason is that their continued existence and visibility, as unrepentant prisoners, "would be a silent protest and might cause a fissure in the totality". But this is an unacceptable prospect, and a bad example for future "terrorists" or "enemies of the *volk*."[340] Torture, Camus notes, targets human beings insofar as they are embodied animals, with the intention of using physical harm or its threat to "allow the object to subdue the person in the soul of man."[341] In a passage which closely again evokes Foucault's formulations, Camus comments:

> From this point of view, the only psychological revolution brought about in our time since Freud's has been brought about by the NKVD and the political police in general. Guided by a determinist hypothesis which calculates the weak points and the degree of elasticity of the soul, these new techniques ... thrust aside one of man's limits and have attempted to demonstrate that no individual psychology is original and that the common measure of all human beings is matter. They have literally created the physics of the soul.[342]

---

339 HR 297; R 237.
340 HR 298; R 239.
341 HR 299; R 239.
342 HR 299–300; R 239–240. Compare Hannah Arendt, *Origins of Totalitarianism* (USA: Harvest, 1976), 443, 457. See also David Sprintzen, *Camus: A Critical Examination* (Philadelphia: Temple University Press, 1998), 182–184.

At this ultimate point of Camus' account of Stalinism, however, the extent to which his account of totalitarian power remains distant from another totalising 'dialectic of enlightenment'-style account needs to be preserved. Camus is in fact very clear, contra the *nouveaux philosophes* or Adorno and Horkheimer, that reason itself is not on the dock, when it comes to understanding totalitarian rule, in order to condemn what must be condemned. "What does Galileo say, in fact, at this moment?", Camus can instead ask rhetorically concerning the fate of Marxism-Leninism's proposed historical science: evoking this archetypal martyr for scientific independence censored by the Roman Catholic Church.[343]

Camus' defence of modern rationality becomes clearest when we consider the third dimension of the "totality" the National Socialist and Stalinist experiments in absolute historical power aimed to master: that of time. In claiming that these regimes aimed at dominating time, as well as space and people, Camus refers to the remarkable enterprise epitomised by Stalin's attempt to not simply assassinate Trotsky, but retrospectively 'write him out' of the history of the Russian revolution. "Year by year, sometimes month by month, *Pravda* corrects itself, and rewritten editions of the official history books follow one another off the presses",[344] Camus observes of a process whose apparent insanity also intrigued George Orwell. If pushed, we can say that this kind of wholesale deception has a certain strategic 'rationality' to it. The Nazis, when they simply wiped all traces of the town of Ludice from the map,[345] like *Pravda* expunging Trotsky from the pages of history, aimed by these actions to establish in the public mind that the present order never faced resistance or challenge. But if there is this kind of rationality at stake here, it violates the function almost universally assigned to this faculty of reflecting, monitoring, and coordinating our responses to a mind- or (let us say) 'regime-independent' factual reality. Instead, as in the cynical Orwellian hypothesis that 'he who controls the future controls the past', we witness the almost complete triumph of 'truth' as coherence, at the price of disavowing or eliminating all discordant data, over truth as correspondence.[346] "At this point, comparison [of the totalitarian regimes] with religious obscurantism is no longer even fair," Camus comments:

---

343 HR 268; R 212.
344 HR 296; R 236.
345 HR 235–6; R 184–185.
346 The comparisons with Arendt, *Origins*, 384, 436, 445, 465 (wherein Arendt cites Camus, whom she considered the 'best man' in France (per a letter, cited in Isaac, *Arendt, Camus and Modern Rebellion*, 17)) are again striking.

so far are we for him from the necessary or ultimate culmination of the dreams of a Bacon, Bayle, Spinoza, Montaigne, Locke, Montesquieu or Voltaire:

> ... the fabrication of truth, ... accomplished at this pace, becomes pure fantasy. As in a fairy story in which all the looms of an entire town wove the empty air to provide clothes for the King, thousands of men whose strange destiny it is, rewrite a presumptuous version of history which is destroyed the same evening while waiting for the calm voice of a child to proclaim suddenly that the King is naked.[347]

Here as elsewhere far closer to Arendt's *Origins of Totalitarianism* than to *The Dialectic of Enlightenment*, for Camus the salient image to describe totalitarian power is not that of the gradual freezing and solidification of an increasingly lifeless, iceberg-like technocratic crystal palace.[348] Totalitarianism is more like the destructive force of a hurricane, landslide or tsunami, uprooting and overturning streets, villages, towns and cities, leaving a wake of devastation behind it. It is like what Rieux at the conclusion of *La Peste* describes as "the slow, deliberate progress of some monstrous thing crushing all in its path,"[349] including subjects' very ability to establish, and publically verify, what is real and what is fiction. Contra Adorno and Horkheimer, it was not the philosophy of the enlightenment that pre-scripted totalitarianism or "wrote it on the wall."[350] The total regimes were rather the embodiments of what Camus calls an "irrational furor" betraying the genuine normative legacy and promise of the modern legacy of rebellion.[351]

The irrational dynamism of this kind of rule is clearest, indeed Camus notes that it is explicit, in many of the statements of the Nazi ideologues concerning the National Socialist "movement". Rauschnig's *Revolution of Nihilism* identified the Hitlerian revolution with an "unadulterated dynamism". Frank at the Nuremberg trials emphasised the "hatred of form" that animated Hitler. Junger declaimed on how "becoming is far more important than living," in an almost direct rendition of one of the celebrated theses of libertarian Nietzscheanism.[352] To be sure, the first and most obvious difference between the fascists and communists lay in how the former, at the level of ideological discourses, "chose to

---

347 H R296; R 236–7.
348 Arendt, *Origins of Totalitarianism*, 398, 411, 429, 445, 465.
349 P 148.
350 Adorno and Horkheimer, *Dialectic*, 86.
351 HR 299; R 239. See Chapter Two below.
352 HR 229–233; R 178–181.

deify the irrational, and the irrational alone" in the biologistic philosophy of the historical struggle between races.[353] Stalinism, by contrast, found its justification in a Marxist narrative for which national and racial differences are epiphenomenal, and the forces and relations of economic production primary. Nevertheless, beneath the level of ideology, the concentration of political powers in the hands of Stalin's inner clique—including the supplanting of public language by propaganda and officialese, the destruction of a judiciary independent of direct executive control, the power to detain, torture, deport or "disappear" individuals without trial, the capacity to retrospectively criminalise hitherto permitted actions...—for Camus all attest to the irrational madness of this species of political rule as well.

Camus does grant the Marxist point that fascist regimes were able to collaborate with existing forms of big capital, whereas under the communist regimes, these interests were expropriated and the relations of production changed. The willing collaboration of many of Cadiz' leading citizens with the new powers is one feature of the Plague regime in *The State of Siège* which marks it off as more fascist than Stalinist. Nevertheless, the experience of living in Stalinism for ordinary men and women much more closely approximated that of subjects living under Nazism than that of subjects in the liberal West, Camus emphasises.[354] In both, as in Rieux's Oran, isolation and disorientation became in effect the new *esprit des lois*: "the august silence that prevails in all perfect social orders," predicated on subjects' living in constant anxiety about their own, and their loved ones', futures.[355] With the absence of any checks on the actions of the State, there were equally no stable standards in these regimes establishing what or who was at any given time going to be declared "objectively guilty" in the eyes of the Party. As we have seen, edicts defining these matters, and even naming the regimes' external enemies, could always be retrospectively changed. When the hero Diego in *L'État de Siège* asks refuge from the Plague from Judge Cassado, citing the criminality of the new regime as justification of his rebellion, the Judge's response epitomises the mad legal positivism at stake here, *pereat mundus*: "I do not serve the law because of what it says but because it is the law...If crime becomes the law, it ceases

---

353   HR 228; R 177–178.
354   See P 246: the narrator of our story, like Camus more widely, "...has deliberately taken the victims' side..."
355   Nada in *The State of Siege* cited at Isaac, *Arendt, Camus and Modern Rebellion*, 53. On the spirit of fear and anxiety in these regimes, see also NVE 257–8 "The Century of Fear"; cf. also Franz Neumann, "Anxiety and Politics" in *The Democratic and Authoritarian State* (Glencoe: Free Press, 1957), 270–300.

being crime."³⁵⁶ The condition of the subject under totalitarian rule is thus the condition of what Giorgio Agamben has called the *homo sacer*, subject to a "ban" which delivers them, shivering and defenceless, up to the executive discretion of the sovereign.³⁵⁷ In *La Peste*, when Rieux ends up reflecting on the best way to describe what the plague's ravages had made of the people of Oran, he hits upon the idea that they had become as exiles, emigrants, or refugees in their own city.³⁵⁸ It is significant that in *The Rebel* Camus underscores that the title of his 1948 drama, "state of siege", accurately describes these political regimes. Fascist and Stalinist regimes, for Camus, implement a permanent state of exception or emergency, rather than embodying legal and political rationalisation in any meaningful sense:

> ...the regimes which have issued from these ideologies are precisely those which, systematically, proceed to uproot [entire] populations, [and] parade them over the surface of Europe as bloodless symbols which have only a derisory existence in the figures of statistics. Since these beautiful philosophies have entered into history, enormous masses of human beings... are definitively buried under the two initials of 'displaced persons', which this world, so logical, has invented for them.³⁵⁹

Totalitarian power, at its base, in Camus' more specific terminology, works by "the affirmation of general culpability" or "universal guilt" in all subjects, excluding only the Leader and his present ruling clique or "gang":³⁶⁰ "we start by the premise that you are guilty. But that's not enough, you must learn to feel yourself that you are guilty."³⁶¹ We will see in Chapter Six, when we look at *La Chute* in particular, how important this psychological category of guilt becomes for Camus, and his attempts to understand the causes why people

---

356 Camus, *State of Siege*, 189–190.
357 Giorgio Agamben, *Homo Sacer*; and *State of Exception* translated Keven Ateill (Chicago: University of Chicago Press, 2005).
358 P 243–244. The anticipations in Camus of Agamben's thought would make for an interesting scholarly study, although Agamben's debts to Heidegger push his thoughts in different, messianic directions. See my "Only Agamben Can Save Us? Against a recent messianic turn in post-Heideggerian critical theory", *Bible and Critical Theory* 5: 3 (2011) and for a devastating critique Jef Huysmans, "The Jargon of the Exception—on Schmitt, Agamben and the Absence of Political Society", *International Political Socology* (2008), 2: 165–183.
359 TL 491.
360 HR 229; R 179.
361 Camus, "State of Siege", at Isaac, *Arendt, Camus, and Modern Rebellion*, 57.

actively embrace forms of political oppression and servitude.³⁶² Our point here is only that, by asserting that all subjects are in principle guilty, independent of their intentions, but for instance on grounds of their race alone (in Nazism) or because of the allegedly "objective" effects of their action, measured against the Party's present interpretation of History,³⁶³ we are in the presence of a cynical 'pseudo-rationality.' This is anything but an inevitable reflection of modern scientific modes or reasoning and inquiry:

> Therefore the history of contemporary nihilism is nothing but a prolonged endeavor to give order, by human forces alone and simply by force, to a history no longer endowed with order. The pseudo-reasoning ends by identifying itself with cunning and strategy, while waiting to culminate in the ideological Empire. What part could science play in this concept? Nothing is less determined on conquest than reason. History is not made with scientific scruples; we are even condemned to not making history from the moment when we claim to act with scientific objectivity. Reason does not preach, or if it does, it is no longer reason. That is why historical reason [as proclaimed by the total regimes] is an irrational and romantic form of reason, which sometimes recalls the false logic of the insane and at other times the mystic affirmation of the Word.³⁶⁴

Indeed, far from Foucault and the new philosophers,³⁶⁵ Camus in *The Rebel* decisively adduces the kinds of rationality the sciences strive towards, answerable to factual reality and subject to the uncoerced agreement of independent observers, as a key basis for his criticism of these terrifying forms of counter-enlightenment:

> The objective criminal is, precisely, he who believed himself innocent. His actions he considered subjectively inoffensive, or even advantageous for the future of justice. But it is demonstrated to him that 'objectively'

---

362 See Chapter 6 below.
363 For a definitive, terrifying account of National Socialist "legality", cf. Otto Kirchheimer, 'Criminal Law in National Socialist Germany' in W. Scheuermann (ed.) *The Rule of Law Under Siege* (Berkeley: University of California Press, 1996).
364 HR 278; R 221.
365 As in fact *The Myth of Sisyphus* of 1942 had philosophically defended descriptive rationality, despite (or because of) his metaphysical scepticism MS 48–74; MSe 28–50. Again see Chapter Three below, and the Introduction above, section "Why a *philosophe* writes novels".

his actions have been harmful to that future. Are we dealing with scientific objectivity? No, but with 'historical objectivity'. How is it possible to know, for example, if the future of justice is compromised by the unconsidered denunciation of present injustice? Real objectivity would consist in judging by those results which can be scientifically observed and by facts and their general tendencies. But the concept of 'objective culpability' proves that this curious kind of objectivity is only based on results and facts which will only become accessible to science in the year 2000, at the very earliest. Meanwhile, it is embodied in an interminable subjectivity which is imposed on others as objectivity: and that is the philosophic definition of terror.[366]

5 Concluding Remarks

The philosophical and ethicopolitical importance can hardly be overstated of stressing Camus' distance from those pessimistic accounts of the total states of the twentieth century which assert one or both that:

(a) the totalitarian regimes of the last century successfully enshrined for the first time the complete, incontestable dominance of scientific and technological rationality over entire societies;
(b) such power represented the more or less inevitable unfolding of the true meaning and destructive potentials of Western rationalism, or at least the modern age.

For Camus, as we have seen, these regimes deploy a host of political technologies that aimed at cynically reducing human beings to calculable "planetary bacilli"[367] in unprecedented ways. "The concentration-camp system of the Russians has, in fact, accomplished the dialectical transition from the government of people to the government of objects, but by identifying people with objects," Camus ironises.[368] But such political programs would only be 'rational' in any larger sense if we were to agree with the totalitarian premise that human beings could, or should, ever be completely reduced to calculable marionettes. And it is far from clear that Camus does, or thinks we should, accede to such reductionist analyses. Moreover, despite several momentarily despairing

---

366   HR 303–304; R 243. Again, compare Arendt, *Origins*, 383, 409, 415, 424, 427–9, 431, 436.
367   Hitler, cited at HR, 235; R 183.
368   HR 298; R 238.

formulations, neither does he think that these regimes can in fact ever succeed in their distorted Promethean or finally Caesarian ambitions.[369] The reason is that Camus rejects the historicist or determinist claim about infinite human malleability on which the totalitarian regimes have wagered: "in so far as human nature to date has never been able to live by history alone and has always escaped from it by some means."[370] The human beings we are invited to free, in Camus' works, are not wholly the products of the political forces and technologies that are brought to bear by and upon them. Thus, even the totalitarians' deployment of terror, torture, and propaganda themselves in Camus' eyes attest obliquely to the existence and political pertinence of dimensions of the world and human experience that "do not come under the reign of quantity" and which as such can only be violently subdued:[371]

> Totality is not unity. The state of siege, even when it is extended to the very boundaries of the earth, is not reconciliation. the claim to a universal city is supported in this revolution only by rejecting two thirds of the world and by denying, to the advantages of history, both nature and beauty and by depriving man of the power of passion, doubt, happiness, and imaginative invention...[372]

Camus' critical work, we will repeatedly see, is founded upon the affirmation of a series of realities—here, nature, beauty, and the human powers to feel, doubt, and create—which always "escape the Empire" of political power. In *The State of Siege*, thus, the Plague and Death, representing totalitarian governance, and Nada and Judge Cassado, representing forms of nihilistic collaboration are met by Diego, who represents rebellion against these powers and Victoria, who (however clumsily) is meant to give figure to the joys and promises of erotic love and private happiness.[373] *The Plague* for its part assembles a famous panoply of characters each representing a basis for that "stubborness against evil" the book valorises:[374] Rieux, embodying scientific

---

369   HR 305–6; R 244–245.
370   HR 297; R 237.
371   HR 293; R 234.
372   HR 300–301; R 240.
373   See Jerry L. Curtis, "Camus' Portrayal Of Women in 'The State Of Siege': Exegesis and Explication", *Orbis Litterarum* 1998: 53, 42–64.
374   Jean Grenier to Albert Camus December 6, 1947, in *Albert Camus & Jean Grenier, Correspondence 1932–1960* translated with an Introduction by Jan E. Rigaud (USA: University of Nebraska Press, 2003), 108.

impartiality and measured classical sobriety; Tarrou, the lapsed revolutionary now pursuing "Sainthood without God," whose friendship with Rieux—baptised in their final swim together in the ocean—provides some of the more moving moments in the chronicle; Rambert, the journalist in exile who longs for private happiness, but chooses the collective struggle; Paneloux, who represents the ambiguities of the Christian faith, wrestling with the mysteries of providence (see Chapter Two); and the ironically named "Grand," who joins the sanitary teams out of an unassuming sense that it is the only decent thing to be done when plague appears. The exploration and attempt to recoup these realities from forms of historicism which deny them forms the affirmative basis of what Camus' mature work strives to achieve in the European maelstrom of the 1940s and 1950s.

Nevertheless, before we can turn our attention to this positive Camusian philosophy and its foundation in his earlier philosophical reflections on the absurd, we need to examine in more detail Camus' wider understanding of modernity. In particular, we need to turn from Camus' account of the nature of totalitarian power to the historical or genealogical question concerning the ideological origins of these forms of total political power. Camus' denial that the totalitarian regimes represented the culmination or epitomisation of modern or Western rationality implies a rejection of (b) above, and the claim of the *nouveaux philosophes*, Adorno and Horkheimer and many others that these regimes represent the predestined culmination of this rationality—whether conceived as instrumental reason, disciplinary or biopolitical rationality, a technological forgetting of *Sein*, etc. Nevertheless, we have glimpsed how there are entire strata in Camus' work which justify Ronald Srigley's recent claim in *Albert Camus' Critique of Modernity* that Camus' work is at its base a concerted, more or less totalising criticism of modernity. In Chapter Two, our work will be to unpack these tensions and to draw out Camus' characteristically two-sided defence of the legitimacy of the modern age. This is a defence which, we will see, involves his locating in the early modern rebellions against 'throne and altar' a permanent dimension of the human condition ("that part of man which refuses to submit (*ne veut pas s'incliner*)")[375] that can also be drawn upon to decry the excesses of the total states, at the same time as it looks backwards to ancient antecedents and forwards to our present concerns.

---

375   HR 140; R 105.

CHAPTER 2

Theodicy Now? Camus with and against the Secularisation Thesis

1   Introduction: Camus, Nihilisms, and the Returns to Theology

The title of Robert Solomon's book on Albert Camus and Jean-Paul Sartre, *Dark Thoughts, Grim Times*, captures well one popular image of Camus' oeuvre.[376] As we have seen in Chapter One, from 1938 onwards Camus' thought and writings increasingly wrestle with the grim realities of fascism, then Stalinism. Invited to speak in the United States in March 1946, Camus spoke to the title "La crise de l'homme" ("The Crisis of Man"). "The men of my age in France and in Europe," Camus could reflect in the cognate address "Le temps des meurtrieurs" ("The Time of Murderers") of 1949:

> … were born just before or during the first great war, arrived at adolescence at the moment of the global economic crisis and were twenty years old when Hitler seized power. To complete our education, we were offered the war in Spain, Munich, the war of 1939, the [French] defeat and four years of occupation and clandestine struggle. To top things off, we are [now] promised the conflagration of atomic war. I thus suppose that we are what is called 'an interesting generation'.[377]

We contended in Chapter One that Camus' accounts of fascism and Stalinism cannot be assimilated with total criticisms of modern rationalism or modernity *per se*, akin to those issuing from near-contemporary German thinkers like Schmitt, Spengler, or Heidegger. Put simply, Camus disputes whether the excesses of totalitarian power are wholly continuous with the deepest logics of Western civilization rather than the excessive, unbalanced manifestations of particular ideological and technological currencies within it. Many of Camus' statements from the 1940s and in the "Introduction" to *L'Homme Révolté* come closer to what is a competing 20th century tradition explaining the aetiology of totalitarianism. This tradition, represented for instance by Hannah Arendt in

---

376 Robert C. Solomon, *Dark Feelings, Grim Thoughts: Experience and Reflection in Camus and Sartre* (Oxford: Oxford University Press, 2006).
377 Albert Camus, "Le Temps des Meurtrieurs", OC III, 353.

The Origins of Totalitarianism, presents Hitlerism and Stalinism as the products of an unprecedented *rupture* with established traditions, not the culmination of an unbroken occidental decline.378 This rupture was caused by a number of increasingly destabilising geopolitical realities: the accelerated imperialism and colonialism of the 19th century, the catastrophes of the first world war and years immediately following, and the creation therefrom of a 'front generation' of shell-shocked returned soldiers, fatherless children and grieving widows, to many of whom all old ideologies and religious credos (if not the banality of peacetime life itself) seemed a valueless sham.379 Camus in *The Rebel* notes "the epidemic of suicides" which afflicted Germany after defeat and Versailles. These indicate "a great deal about the state of mental confusion" which made the population more susceptible to Hitler's radical, reactionary movement. Otherwise, Nazism's "reactionary modernism" and celebrations of redemptive war might never have gained traction.380 For "to those who despair of everything reason cannot provide a faith, but only passion, and in this case it must be the same passion that lay at the root of the despair, namely humiliation and hatred."381 In "Le temps des meurtrieurs", Camus stresses that for the people of his generation (even those born on the side of the victors) all of the old cultural, normative and political standards indeed seemed bereft:

> The literature of this time involved a revolt against clarity, narrative, and even the phrase itself. Painting was a revolt against representation [*le sujet*], reality, and simple harmony. As for the philosophy of the times, it taught that there was no truth, only phenomena...The moral attitude of this generation was again more categorical: nationalism appeared to them as a truth *dépassé*, religion an exile, twenty years of international politics taught them to doubt all purities...And the traditional morality of society? It appeared to them as what it has not ceased to be, that is to say a resignation [*démission*] or a monstrous hypocrisy.382

---

378   Arendt, *Origins of Totalitarianism* Parts I and II, 3–304; see also Hannah Arendt, "Tradition and the Modern Age", *Between Past and Future* (London: Penguin, 2006), 17–40.
379   Arendt, *Origins of Totalitarianism*, 267–340, esp. "Chapter Ten: A Classless Society", 305–340.
380   See Jennifer Herf, *Reactionary Modernism: Technology, Culture, and Politics in Weimar and the Third Reich* (Cambridge: Cambridge University Press, 1986).
381   HR 229; R 178–179.
382   TM 354.

Camus' predominant term in the 1940s and 1950s to describe this state of affairs is one he shares with Friedrich Nietzsche and theological critics of modernity like, in our time, John Milbank and the radical othodoxasts: *viz.* "nihilism".[383] Nietzsche described this "uncanniest of guests" in *The Will to Power* as the cultural situation in which the question "why?" to do or not do anything can find no compelling answer.[384] Camus' starkest formulations of this 'nihilism,' a contested and often polemical term (which should be noted, as often it is not) echo Nietzsche's formulations. "For if one does not believe in anything...," "Le temps des meurtriers" for instance again reflects:

> ... if nothing has any sense and if we cannot affirm any value, then everything is permitted and nothing has any importance. So, there is neither good nor bad, and Hitler for example was neither wrong nor reasonable. Malice and virtue are chance and caprice. One can send millions of innocent people to crematoria as we can dedicate ourselves to the care of lepers. One can equally well honour the dead as throw them into the rubbish. All this is equivalent.[385]

For Milbank and other, anti-liberal theological critics of modernity,[386] this inability to answer to the "why?" question is the inevitable result of modern man's heretical experiment of trying to live without God: the transcendent ground of meaning and being. It is the bitter harvest of modernity's aspirations to shape wholly secular political and cultural institutions, without orienting reference to the *theos*.[387] Milbank's work and his school does not stand alone in this and like opinions. Charles Taylor's more recent *opus The Secular Age* for instance has argued that the modern self, pre-emptively closely to all transcendent sources of value, has become increasingly empty and "buffered."[388] This is a situation which, with and differently to Milbank et al., Taylor traces back to changes in later medieval Europe which have made our modern *malaises* inevitable. For Milbank and the radical orthodoxasts' highly idealist

---

383   Cf. John Milbank, *Theology and Social Theory* (Oxford: Blackwell, 2006 [2nd edition]).
384   Friedrich Nietzsche, *The Will to Power*: In *Science, Nature, Society and Art*. (USA: Random House, 1968), sec. 1.
385   TM, 354–55.
386   On the different strands of political theology within the Christian tradition, see Elizabeth Phillips, *Political Theology: A Guide for the Perplexed* (London: Bloomsbury, 2012).
387   See John Milbank, Catherine Pickstock &Graham Ward eds. *Radical Orthodoxy: A New Theology* (London: Routledge, 1998).
388   Charles Taylor, *A Secular Age* (Cambridge, Massachusetts: Harvard, 2007), 378–9.

account,[389] the 'fall' occurs due to the disastrous advent of nominalist theology in the Fransciscans Duns Scotus and William of Ockham;[390] while in Taylor's more Catholic rendition, it is the Protestant reform movements that have set Western men and women on their long path to becoming today's "industrious, disciplined...mutually predictable" subjects, living in a wholly disenchanted, immanentised world.[391] Post-Marxist literary critic Terry Eagleton is yet to offer a comparable narrative of cultural decline. But he has argued that Marxism should look for regeneration to the example of Christ's sacrificial martyrdom and ministry to the *anawin* or outcasts of ancient society.[392] Giorgio Agamben, differently, has coupled his highly-pessimistic account of the evolution of modern societies into a permanent "state of exception"[393] with an anomic messianism drawing inspiration from the ancient gnostics, Sabbatai Zevi, or Saint Paul:[394] the same founder of institutional Christianity to whose example and *Romans* Alain Badiou has drawn students' attention as a model for a militant, post-Maoist "politics of truth."[395] In a more recent book, Agamben has repackaged the "secularisation thesis" announced by Carl Schmitt in 1923's *Political Theology*, central also to Milbank et al.'s thought: the claim that all decisive concepts of modern economics, society and government have a 'theological genealogy': 'secularising' ideas developed within the West's Christian-theological past, rather than expressing anything culturally novel or legitimate on their own terms.[396]

This brief list of recent thinkers who have coupled their critical accounts of modern culture, politics, or society with 'returns to theology' could be

---

389 "Idealist" used here in the sense of describing a view which assigns great causal significance in human behaviour to people's ideas, in abstraction from their historical, economic, social, political and other contextual factors.
390 Milbank, *Theology and Social Theory*, 14–23.
391 Taylor, *Secular Age*, 106, 373.
392 See on Eagleton's Christological turn, and its roots in his youthful Catholicism, Roland Boer, "The Apostasy of Terry Eagleton", in *Criticism of Heaven: On Marxism and Theology* (Leiden, Boston: Brill, 2007), 275–334.
393 Agamben, *Homo Sacer: Sovereign Power and Bare Life*; "Part Three: the Camp as Biopolitical Paradigm of the Modern", 69–106.
394 Giorgio Agamben, *Time that remains: A commentary on the Letter to the Romans*, translated by Patricia Dailey (Stanford: Stanford University Press, 2005).
395 Alain Badiou, *Saint Paul: The Foundation of Universalism*, trans. R. Brassier (Stanford, Stanford University Press, 2003).
396 Giorgio Agamben, *The Kingdom and the Glory: For a Theological Genealogy of Economy and Government* trans. Lorenzo Chiesa (Stanford: Stanford University Press, 2011); cf. again the paradigmatic work by Milbank, *Theology and Social Theory*.

multiplied. This new public visibility of religious ideas, long considered to have been sidelined in the modern West, represents one of the more remarkable marks of the contemporary situation. In this Chapter, we want to examine Camus' diagnosis of the ideological genealogies of the total states in *L'Homme Révolté* and his wider account of modern thinking against the background of this new religious visibility: one which has led some commentators to speculate that we are witnessing the advent of a 'post-secular age'.[397] For Camus' sense of the breakdown of the West's vital religious and cultural traditions did not lead him to the conclusion that the West could return to its theological heritage in search of renewal. "After all," he notes to his "German Friend," seemingly with the Naz's concordat with the Catholic Church in mind, "the Christian tradition is only one of the traditions that made this Europe..."[398] Besides, "[i]t is perfectly vain to say to us: you must believe in God or in Plato or in Marx, when justly we do not have this kind of faith."[399] 80% of Europeans live "beyond grace," outside of any Church, Camus claims in November of that year, and the number of authentic Christians amongst those who declare their faith is much smaller: figures which recent statistics broadly bear out.[400] None of this is to deny that Camus' thought developed in continual, decisive dialogue with Catholic writers like François Mauriac, nor the Christian tradition, as we will continually see.[401] Yet Camus remained deeply sceptical of calls to 'return to religion' like to those which had played a very large role under Petain's regime in Vichy France. Camus even at one point in his *Carnets* jests darkly that, if we are to be asked to "make history go backward", we may as well be asked to

---

397   See for example Jürgen Habermas, "Secularism's Crisis of Faith: Notes on Post-Secular Society", *New perspectives quarterly*, vol. 25 (2008), 17–29; Manav Ratti, *The Postsecular Imagination: Postcolonialism, Religion, and Literature* (London and New York: Routledge, 2013); Alessandro Ferrara, "The separation of religion and politics in a post-secular society", *Philosophy & Social Criticism* vol. 35. (2009), 77–92.

398   LGF 22.

399   CH 743. With that said, many have continued to say each of these three things.

400   Camus, "Intervention à la table ronde de 'Civilization'", OC II 681; TM 359.

401   See Albert Camus, *Camus at Combat*, and the articles from 1944 to January 1945 responding to Mauriac (CAC 80–81, 88–90, 106, n. 231, 163–165), wherein Camus goes from his acceptance of the death penalty for leading collaborators, in the name of a justice without mercy, to his famous, stringent opposition to it: "I have come to admit to myself, and now to admit publicly here, that for the fundamentals and on the precise point of our controversy, François Mauriac was right." Camus, "The Unbeliever and Christians", in RRD, 70. See also Camus' sympathetic "Portrait of a Chosen Man" (on *Le Portrait de M. Pouget*), LCE 219–227.

return to "Pharaoh,"[402] suggesting his deep scepticism about the reactionary potential of such calls:

> The modern mind is in complete disarray. Knowledge has stretched itself to the point where neither the world nor our intelligence can find a foothold. It is a fact that we are suffering from nihilism. But what is most amazing are the 'back to' sermons. Back to the Middle Ages, back to primitive mentality, back to the land, back to religion, to the arsenal of old solutions. To give these soothing potions the slightest efficacy we would have to behave as if we had forgotten all our knowledge... pretend, in fact, to wipe out what is indelible. With one stroke of the pen we should have to cross out the contribution of several centuries, together with the undeniable gains of a mind which... recreates progress for its own sake...[403]
>
> In short, we were worth nothing during the Renaissance, the 18th century and the Revolution. We counted for something only from the 10th to 13th century... thus whole centuries of history, the hundred or so great names that have handed down to us a tradition, a national life, love...: all this has been in vain, it is all nothing. And it is we who are nihilists![404]

As we shall see, Camus' attitude to Christianity is complex. It seems to us too much to follow Srigley (who ironically echoes many of Camus' harshest theological critics) when he decries Camus as an unregenerately anti-Christian thinker.[405] What is decisive for us at this point is only this. Beginning from *Le Mythe de Sisyphe* in 1941, Camus' diagnosis of modern nihilism does not lead him to infer that 'the only way out,' critically speaking, is to deconstruct the entire modern secularising heritage, obviating its classical nonChristian antecedents. On one side, Camus' observation that such cultural disorientation had produced both Nazism *and* the many men and women he had struggled alongside in the resistance opened him to the ways that new sources of virtues and values can be found 'this side' of metaphysical theologies. The vital human capacities for shared joy, wonder, love, friendship, solidarity and beauty do not depend on peoples' possessing a shared, totalising metaphysics. On the other hand, Camus repeats that to long to escape the times in which we live, rather than to engage in their struggles represents its own form of

---

402   C II 210; C II Eng 108.
403   C II 26; C II Eng. 9.
404   C II 101–102; C I Eng 52.
405   Srigley, *Camus' Critique*, esp. 83–85.

cowardice, rather than the portal to higher, redemptive virtues. "This is why we have sought these reasons" for new forms of life, Camus specifies, "within the same revolt" whose 20th century devolutions had issued into the forms of political and cultural modernism Camus critiques.[406] As we will see in Chapters Three and Four, indeed, Camus became increasingly convinced that "it is possible, within the bounds of nihilism, to go beyond nihilism."[407] Specifically, Camus argues that there is a normative legitimacy and promise at the basis of the founding modern philosophical and historical rebellions against theological modes of legitimating political regimes that is imperative the later modern world does not forget. This normative promise within modern revolt was not fulfilled by the fascist and Stalinist disasters. It must be reclaimed despite them, and the kinds of intellectual and political excess they embody:

> My response is different... Revolt does not conduce to domination and it is by a perversion of intellectual pride that we have drawn such frightful consequences [in the total regimes of the 20th century]. Nothing justifies this rage of destruction if not the blindness of an indignation which can no longer see even its own reasons.[408]

In order to understand Camus' history of modern rebellion and his aetiology of later modern, revolutionary nihilism, accordingly, we want to clearly situate Camus' mature position in light of his wider engagement with Western theology, hailing back to his 1936 *Diplôme* thesis on *Christian Metaphysics and Neoplatonism*. In particular, we need to comprehend how Camus' critical thinking concerning totalitarianism reflects his life-long wrestling with questions posed in the West under the heading of 'theodicy': *viz*, the problem of evil, what it is, and whether and how we should understand and respond to it. It is remarkable that in nearly all of the recent meta-theological literature of the last decades, attempts to wrestle with this existentially vital issue—of how a posited omnibenevolent God could create a universe in which senseless suffering perdures—is singularly absent. Yet this issue, touching people's lives and experiences in the most intimately tragic ways, is vital in understanding why people take up, or give up, their faiths: as against, for instance, competing attempts to renarrate modern ideological or institutional histories. Responding to the perdurance of evil and useless suffering was also vital, Camus reminds us, in understanding the genesis of the modern age in ways we would do well

---

406   CH 743.
407   MSe v; cf. PC 59.
408   TL 359.

today not to forget, particularly since the different versions of the 'secularisation thesis' to a man pass over this vital issue.

2 The Problem of Evil and Modern Metaphysical Rebellion

'Camus hates God more than he hates the bourgeois': thus, in effect, protested Jean-Paul Sartre in his very public falling out with his friend over Camus' 1951 work *L'Homme Révolté*.[409] We met this kind of criticism of Camus in Chapter One concerning *La Peste*. The idea that struggling against fascism could be allegorised by the struggle against an outbreak of plague in a walled Algerian city was attacked by de la Vigerie, Barthes, Jeanson and others. For the plague is a form of what was called 'natural evil' in medieval Christendom: as against the political reality of National Socialism and kindred regimes.[410] But just as *La Peste* was intended by Camus to dramatise both political and philosophical questions, so *The Rebel* as a work of philosophical criticism openly spans "metaphysical revolt" (to which it devotes its second of five Parts); and the "historical revolt" of political movements from the Jacobins to Stalin (in the longest, central Part).[411] Asked by Émile Simon concerning the foundations of his thinking in 1948 as he built towards the final text of *The Rebel*, Camus gave what can appear as a surprisingly 'ahistorical' answer, given our sense of Camus as wholly *dépassé* or 'of his time'. Camus replied to Simon that, beneath the questions concerning totalitarianism, "the insurmountable obstacle appears to me to be the problem of evil. There is the death of innocents which signifies

---

409 Jean-Paul Sartre, "A Reply to Camus," in David A. Spritzen & Adrian van den Hoven eds. and trans. *Camus and Sartre: A Historic Confrontation* (Humanity Books: New York 2004), esp. 148–153. And compare Francis Jeanson, "Albert Camus, or The Soul in revolt", *Camus and Sartre: A Historic Confrontation*, 95–96.

410 See Albert Camus, "Letter to Roland Barthes on *The Plague*," LCE 338–341; and in "Deux réponses à Emmanuel d'Astier de La Vigerie", in *Albert Camus Oeuvres Complètes II 1944–1948* (Paris: Gallimard Bibliothèque de la Pléiade, 2006): 457–474; also Edward Freeman, *The Theatre of Albert Camus* (London: Methuen & Co., 1971, 82–84. Jeanson reprised this critique in Francis Jeanson, "Albert Camus, the Soul in Revolt", in David A. Spritzen & Adrian van den Hoven eds. and trans. *Camus and Sartre: A Historic Confrontation* (Humanity Books: New York 2004), 82–84: "the plague was already a transcendental chronicle..." and for a recent restatement of the critique, Susan Neiman, *Evil in Modern Thought: An Alternative History of Philosophy* (Princeton: Princeton University Press, 2004), 291–298.

411 HR 39–136; 137–314; R 23–100; 105–252.

the arbitrariness of the divine, but there is also the murder of infants which embodies [*traduit*] human arbitrariness."[412]

In the period following 11 September 2001, we might be a good deal less unsettled by Camus' response than many of his contemporaries were. For the kinds of Marxism to which Jeanson, Sartre, and Merleau-Ponty were attracted in the post-war period had long held any concern with 'the moral question' under suspicion of obscuring the decisive economic and political determinants shaping human life. For the last decade of his life and beyond, Camus would be pursued by the accusation brought by de la Vigerie, Jeanson and Sartre: that he was defending an inefficacious, eloquent retreat from 'history' and politics.[413]

Accompanying today's returns to theology, although (remarkably) not generally in the same texts, another feature of today's conjucture involves a renewed interest in the problem of evil.[414] In order to better situate Camus' thought closer to present-day debates, for this reason, we can helpfully position *The Rebel's* argument alongside Susan Neiman's remarkable 2003 contribution to this literature, *Evil in Modern Thought*. In this book, Neiman defends a bold synoptic thesis which brings her unmistakably close to Camus' account of modernity in *The Rebel*, ironically despite her own arguable misreading of him later in the text.[415] Neiman argues that modern philosophy is not best understood as it is most often understood within academic studies. The standard view sees modern thought as shaped primarily by the epistemological questions that seem front and centre in Bacon, Descartes, Locke, or Kant. "On literary grounds alone," Neiman comments, "that narrative is flawed, for it lacks what is central to dramatic movement anywhere: a compelling motive."[416]

---

412 Camus, "Trois Interviews", OC II 476.
413 Jeanson, "The Soul in Revolt" 82–84, 87–88, 92–94, 98–100; Sartre, "Reply to Albert Camus", 144–147 (147: "he has gone into a corner by himself to sulk"), 149–150; 155–158.
414 See for examples of the recent flood of continental-philosophical studies and collections: Maria Pia Lara (ed.), *Rethinking Evil: Contemporary Perspectives* (Berkeley: University of California Press, 2001); Richard Bernstein, *Radical Evil: a philosophical interrogation* (Malden, MA: Polity Press 2002); Maria Pia Lara, *Narrating Evil: A Postmetaphysical Theory of Reflective Judgment* (Columbia: Columbia University Press, 2007); Peter Dews, *The Idea of Evil* (Oxford: Blackwell, 2008); Martin Beck Matuštík. *Radical Evil and the Scarcity of Hope* (Bloomington/Indianapolis: Indiana University Press, 2008); Sharon Anderson-Gold and Pablo Muchnik (eds). *Kant's Autonomy of Evil: Interpretive Essays and Contemporary Applications.* (New York: Cambridge University Press, 2010); C. Card, *Confronting Evils: Terrorism, Torture, Genocide* (Cambridge: Cambridge University Press, 2010).
415 Susan Neiman, *Evil in Modern Thought: An Alternative History of Philosophy* (Princeton: Princeton University Press, 2004), 291–298.
416 Neiman, *Evil in Modern Thought*, 6.

Academic philosophers may be moved by epistemological concerns 'in themselves', and these have their own intrinsic importance. But if such concerns are to become culturally ascendant, Neiman (like Popkin and others) has suggested,[417] other ethical, political and religious issues must underlie the 'epistemological turn'.

According to Neiman, then, to best understand the trajectory of modern philosophy, we need to place at its traumatic head not abstract concerns about knowledge, but a very concrete event or set of realities: namely, the Lisbon earthquake of November 1755, followed by the attempt of the Churches to explain this horrific catastrophe on the basis of the still-regnant Augustinian theodicy. The Lisbon earthquake, Neiman argues, had as profound a shaping, disorienting effect on early modern thought as the confrontation with Auschwitz would have on the 20th century:

> Eighteenth and nineteenth-century philosophy was guided by the problem of evil. Like most short statements, this one is too simple. Nevertheless... as an organising principle for understanding the history of philosophy, the problem of evil is better than alternatives. It is more inclusive, comprehending a far greater number of texts, more faithful to authors' stated intentions, and more interesting. Here 'interest' is not merely an aesthetic category, important as that is, but also an explanatory one, which answers Kant's question: what drives pure reason to efforts that seem to have neither end nor result?[418]

The story of Lisbon 1755 and its cultural aftermath will be known to the reader. "The quake had come on All Saints' day, the churches had been crowded with worshippers, and death, finding its enemies in close formation, had reaped a rich harvest."[419] Between 30,000 and 80,000 people, including women and children of all denominations were indiscriminately killed, while many (including some Moslem unbelievers) were spared.[420] The different denominations'

---

417 Cf. Richard Popkin, *The History of Scepticism from Savonarola to Bayle*. Third enlarged edition (Oxford: Oxford University Press, 2003). Neiman's (very plausible) observation is that questions about the nature and limits of what we know simply do not engage the passions of the many, except insofar as modern attempts to sceptically limit epistemic claims, from very early on, profoundly impacted on the hegemonic theological and metaphysical legitimations of political and cultural authority.

418 Neiman, *Evil in Modern Thought*, 7.

419 Will Durant, *The Story of Philosophy* (USA: Simon & Schuster, 1937), 225.

420 See Peter Gay, *Voltaire's Politics: The Poet as Realist* (USA: Yale University Press, 1988).

attempts to blame the wickedness of their rivals for calling down God's evident rage at the Lisbonites thus seemed particularly implausible and mutually cancelling.[421] Reflecting after Lisbon on the arguments of Leibniz' 1709 text *Theodicy*, that "all is well" and that "we live in the best of all possible worlds,"[422] Voltaire meanwhile headed a chorus of voices, breaking forth in a long poetic *cri de coeur* whose eloquent indignation would soon blossom into *Candide's* satirical outrage:

> I am a puny part of the great whole. / Yes; but all animals condemned to live, /All sentient things, born by the same stern law, / Suffer like me, and like me also die. / The vulture fastens on his timid prey, / And stabs with bloody beak the quivering limbs: / All's well, it seems, for it. But in a while / An eagle tears the vulture into shreds; / The eagle is transfixed by shaft of man; / The man, prone in the dust of battlefield, / Mingling his blood with dying fellow-men, / Becomes in turn the food of ravenous birds. / Thus the whole world in every member groans: / All born for torment and for mutual death. / And o'er this ghastly chaos you would say / The ills of each make up the good of all! / What blessedness! And as, with quaking voice, / Mortal and pitiful, ye cry, "All's well," / The universe belies you, and your heart / Refutes a hundred times your mind's conceit...[423]

Significantly, Voltaire's scepticism looks back to "the learned Bayle",[424] author of the *Historical and Critical Dictionary*. Bayle is little known today outside of circles of historians of ideas. Yet this *Dictionaire* was perhaps the most widely read book of the 18th century amongst the lumières, and the model of Voltaire's own *Philosophical Dictionary* of 1764. Bayle has been widely touted as the "father of the enlightenment" and of modern philosophical vindications

---

421 See Jonathan Israel, *The Democratic Enlightenment: Philosophy, Revolution and Human Rights 1750–1790* (Oxford: Oxford University Press, 2011), 39–55.

422 G.W. Leibniz, *Theodicy: Essays on the Goodness of God, the Freedom of Man and the Origin of Evil*, edited with an Introduction by Austin Farrer, Fellow of Trinity College, Oxford, Translated by E.M. Huggard from C.J. Gerhardt's Edition of the Collected Philosophical Works, reproduced as Project Gutenberg EBook at www-site www.gutenberg.org/files/17147/17147-h/17147-h.htm, last accessed October 2014; cf. Neiman, *Evil in Modern Thought*, 21–31.

423 Voltaire, "Poem on the Disaster at Lisbon," translated by Joseph McCabe, *Voltaire: Selected Texts* (London: Watts & Co., 1948), 4.

424 Voltaire, "Poem", 6.

of religious toleration.[425] Certainly, Bayle's *Dictionary* was the specific target of Leibniz's 'capital R' Rationalistic arguments in his *Theodicy*.[426] In the famous entries on "Manicheanism" and the "Paulicians," Bayle had argued that the Manichean solution to the problem of evil, by simply positing an Evil God alongside the Good Deity, was more rationally convincing than anything the different variants of Augustinian Christianity can provide. The best thing the Christian can do, faced with events like Lisbon, is to point to the text of the Bible as the unquestionable Word of God, and acknowledge the severely limited scope of fallen human understanding.[427] "What is the verdict of the vastest mind?," Voltaire asks likewise in the Lisbon "Poem": "Silence: the book of fate is closed to us. / Man is a stranger to his own research…."[428] One thing only is sure: faced with the undeniable evil of the suffering of masses of innocents, the traditional Christian postulate of an all-Good, all-powerful, and all-knowing God begins to waver:

> But how conceive a God supremely good, / Who heaps his favours on the sons he loves, / Yet scatters evil with as large a hand? / What eye can pierce the depth of his designs? / From that all-perfect Being came not ill: / And came it from no other, for he's lord: / Yet it exists. O stern and numbing truth![429]

Neiman traces two strands of modern thought in response to the problem of evil so violently posed by Lisbon. The first is represented by Leibniz, Rousseau, Kant and Hegel. All of these thinkers in different ways tried to reconcile themselves to the realities of natural and human evil while preserving a sense of a larger rational or providential order. Bayle, Voltaire, Hume and de Sade by contrast took the reality of natural catastrophes like Lisbon to call into question either God's omnipotence or His omnibenevolence. It is this kind of thinker who "condemns the architect"[430] that Camus in Part II of *L'Homme Révolté* calls the early modern "metaphysical rebels".[431] Europe's medieval and early

---

425 Cf. Peter Gay, *The Enlightenment: The Rise of Modern Paganism* (UK: W.W. Norton, 1995), 291–2; Jonathan Israel, *The Radical Enlightenment: Philosophy and the Making of Modernity, 1650–1750* (Oxford: Oxford University Press, 2001), 331–341.
426 Leibniz, *Theodicy*, 62–63, 92–94, 98–99, 127–128.
427 Pierre Bayle, *Historical and Critical Dictionary*: Selections trans. R. Popkin (London: Hacket, 1991), entries "Manicheism", "Paulicians".
428 Voltaire, "Poem", 6.
429 Voltaire, "Poem", 5.
430 Neiman, *Evil in Modern Thought*, 113–202.
431 HR 39 ff.; R 23 ff.

modern regimes were political regimes whose ideological legitimations (as against their economic and political realities) remained theological. Beginning with the King, understood as God's embodied representative on earth at the head of the realm, the latter was conceived in its turn as a microcosm of the larger world of Creation. Writing of the early modern, absolute monarchies headed by Louis XIV (the 'Sun King') in France or Henry VIII or Elizabeth in Britain, Camus writes that the monarch in such regimes "... dispenses his protection and his assistance if and when he wants to. One of the attributes of grace is that it is discretionary. Monarchy in its theocratic form is a type of government which wants to put grace before justice."[432] Modern times, as Camus puts it, thinking like a good Frenchman of 14 July 1789, "begins to the accompaniment of the crash of falling ramparts."[433] The ramparts here were metaphysical and metaphorical, as well as political and physical. Kings had many times been deposed in the annals of European history. To overhaul monarchy itself, a crime which Kant for one thought too horrible to even conceive,[434] presupposed a metaphysical challenge to that institution's theological foundations.[435] Such a challenge, as it unfolds itself in the 18th and 19th centuries, Camus calls "metaphysical rebellion". This kind of revolt "disputes the ends of man and of creation" as these had been laid down by Christian theology in the Latinate West since Nicaea and Saint Augustine.[436]

And why this metaphysical dispute? Is it only a matter of human pride writ large, the inevitable consequence of an anomic impiety which refuses any authority greater than the I? Modern metaphysical rebellion, for Camus, responds to that problem of theodicy which had so struck Bayle, and then Voltaire after Lisbon. It is an issue of justice pitted against grace:

> ...[m]etaphysical rebellion is the *justified claim* of a desire for unity against the suffering of life and of death—in that it protests against the incompleteness of life, expressed by death, and its dispersion, expressed by evil.[437]

---

432   HR 148; R 113. For what seems to us a very misplaced interpretation of Camus as sympathetic to Louis XVI and absolute monarchy, see Susan Dunn, "Camus and Louis XVI: An Elegy for the Martyred King", *French Review* 62 (1989).
433   HR 45; R 26; cf. HR 153–157; R 120–121 on the killing of the "King-priest" Louis XVI.
434   Immanuel Kant, *The Metaphysics of Morals* translated and edited by Mary Gregor (Cambridge: Cambridge University Press, 2003), note at 97–98.
435   HR 147–148; R 112–113.
436   HR 41; R 23.
437   HR 42; R 24, compare HR 147–8; R 105–6.

In *L'Homme Révolté*'s examination of modern metaphysical rebellion, this is why Camus gives a paradigmatic status to the troubled character Ivan Karamazov's protest in Dostoevsky's masterpiece *The Brothers Karamazov*.[438] Ivan's rebellion begins not with an earthquake, nor even a plague visiting his town. It commences with the senseless murder of a single innocent child. As a Christian, Ivan wrestles with how to reconcile this paradigm example of senseless suffering with the all-benevolent, all-powerful God posited by his faith. In the beginning at least, Ivan does not conclude from this innocent suffering that God cannot exist. Ivan concludes first of all only that "even if God existed, Ivan would never surrender to Him in the face of the injustice done to man." This agnostic "even if" is stressed by Camus: "[h]e says that if revealed truth [or God] does exist, it can only be unacceptable." And why is this? It is for Ivan not about 'I versus Thou', as it were: but: "[b]ecause it [the suffering of innocents] is unjust. The struggle between truth and justice is begun here ... ; and it will never end."[439]

The Marquis de Sade as Camus reads him had reckoned likewise. His bizarre exaltations of evil began reasonably enough, Camus argues (see Chapter Three). They commenced with Sade's own assessment of the same kinds of evidence that disturbed Ivan Karamazov. Sade argues that if God exists, given the world as it is, then He can evidently only be "a criminal divinity who oppresses and denies mankind".[440] A similar sense of indignation at the stubborn realities of natural and political evil, Camus contends, underlies the romantics' fascination with Milton's Satan and "the outlaw, the criminal with the heart of gold, and the kind brigand."[441] These iconic counter-cultural modernist figures all refuse to consent to the injustices of the human condition (Hamlet's "oppressor's wrong, the proud man's contumely, / The pangs of despised love, the law's delay, / The insolence of office and the spurns / That patient merit of the unworthy takes...")[442] Instead, they make of themselves or their art[443] so many standing protests against this condition and the powers-that-be sanctified within it.

The key point is that, far from seeing the early modern metaphysical rebels like Bayle or Voltaire as nihilistic egoists interested in rivalling the Creator, Camus sees these figures as moved primarily by a legitimate sense of justice

---

438 In the dedicated section "The Rejection of Salvation," at HR 79–86, 55–62.
439 HR 81; R 56.
440 HR 58; R 37.
441 HR 73; R 50.
442 William Shake-speare, *Hamlet* Act III, scene 1.
443 On this theatrical dimension of dandyism, see esp. HR 75–76; R 51–52.

and compassion towards other human beings.[444] These ideals were previously identified, in eminent form, with the Deity Himself. In early modernity, they are levelled against the Latinate Christian tradition's conceptions of Him. In Camus' understanding, the metaphysical rebel, initially at least, is no atheist. His rebellion is agnostic and ethical, before it is totalising or metaphysical. The rebel "defies more than he denies... he does not suppress God, he merely talks to Him as an equal," Camus underlines:[445]

> ...he draws this superior power into the same humiliating adventure as himself... he subjects it to the power of our refusal, bends it to the unbending part of human nature,... and finally drags it from its refuge outside of time and involves it in history...[446]

The key thing is that it is a *justified* "demand for unity (*revendication d'unité*)" that operates in these early modern "rejection[s] of salvation" in Camus' eyes:[447] whatever perverse, hybristic consequences these rebels or their successors subsequently drew from their initial rebellions. For Camus, human beings have an inalienable right to resist all forms of evil or the imposition of innocent, useless suffering. They have a legitimate right to contest all forms of theological or philosophical theodicies whose proponents propose to rationalise away the immovable scandal represented by such suffering. This is why Camus will not, in his later Part of *The Rebel* on "Historical Rebellion", totally dismiss the Jacobin criticism of theocracy and what he terms Rousseau's "submitting God to justice" in his Savoyard Curate's declaration.[448] Camus likewise sees the lineage of this legitimate modern metaphysical rebellion in Hegel's criticism of the Thermidorean terrorism practiced by the Jacobins in the name of wholly formal values.[449] Indeed and importantly, as we will stress below, Camus never denies the force of Marx's criticisms of the way these same bourgeois

---

444   Compare Isaac, *Arendt, Camus and Modern Rebellion*, 72–73. Isaac seemingly goes wrong on 74 when he assigns a 'grand narrative' to Camus: to the extent that he means Camus' narration of the modern revolutionaries' betrayal of early modern revolt, this is true: but to evoke Lyotard's 'grand narratives' is to assign an Historical inevitability which Camus always remained agnostic about epistemically, and ethicopolitically opposed to.
445   HR 43; R 25.
446   HR 43; R 24.
447   HR 132; R 101.
448   HR 150–153; R 114–117.
449   HR 173–178; R 133–137.

values have been appealed to in order to "mystify" concrete social injustices.[450] On the contrary, in a way which again shows his distance *avant la lettre* from the "new philosophical" anti-Marxists of the 1970s,[451] Camus consistently defends the critical side of Marxism as a legatee of legitimate modern metaphysical rebellion:

> The very core of [Marx's] theory was that work is profoundly dignified and unjustly despised. [Marx] rebelled against the degradation of work to the level of a commodity and of the worker to the level of an object. He reminded the privileged that their privileges were not divine and that property was not an eternal right. He gave a bad conscience to those who had no right to a clear conscience, and denounced with unparalleled profundity a class whose crime is not so much having had power as having used it to advance the ends of a mediocre society deprived of any real nobility...[452]

If Camus opposes Marxism, as we will see later in this Chapter, the reason lies not in this critical dimension of Marx's *oeuvre*. Nor does it reside in Marx's rebellion against the avoidable, systematically reproduced forms of injustice imposed by capitalism. The reason for Camus' opposition to Marxism-Leninism and its Stalinist legatee instead hails from what he calls its "prophetic" dimension: or what can be called, in the language of wider contemporary debates, 'the secularisation of theodicy' or 'political messianism'. It is to the genealogy of such a 'secularisation', as Camus sees it, that we turn now.

---

450 In passages which again distance him from the later, cruder anti-Marxism of the *nouveaux philosophes* who claimed his legacy, Camus thus can write that: "[Marx's] theory of mystification is still valid, because it is in fact universally true, and is equally applicable to revolutionary mystifications. The freedom of which Monsieur Thiers dreamed was the freedom of privilege consolidated by the police; the family, extolled by the conservative newspapers, was supported by social conditions in which men and women were sent down into the mines, half-naked, attached to a communal rope; morality prospered on the prostitution of the working classes. That the demands of honesty and intelligence were put to egoistic ends by the hypocrisy of a mediocre and grasping society was a misfortune that Marx, the incomparable eye opener, denounced with a vehemence quite unknown before him..." HR 254, 263–264; R 200–201; 208–209.
451 See Chapter One, "*Nouvelle Philosophe avant la lettre*? Another 'Dialectic of Enlightenment'?"
452 HR 263–4; R 209.

3 The Existence of Evil Rationalised: Evangelical, Gnostic, Augustinian Theodicies

Camus' career-long, agonised wrestlings with the realities of evil and the suffering of ordinary people puts him at greatest distance from the many contemporary callers for a 'return to theology'. In fact, from his earliest philosophical work, the *Diplôme de Hautes Etudes* thesis on "Christian Metaphysics and Neoplatonism" (1936), Camus' thought was shaped by an ongoing critique of the Augustinian Christianity central to the Catholic and Protestant Churches in the Latinate West, turning on the theodical issue.[453] As Ronald Srigley has stressed,[454] Camus always held that the subject of this thesis, the transition between classical pagan antiquity and Christianity, marked the decisive turning point in Western history: a turning point like to whose magnitude he felt the later modern West was in his times reentering.[455] Throughout his fictional and philosophical *oeuvre*, different strands of Camus' critique of Christianity emerge: epistemological (concerning the limits of human knowledge (Chapter Three)), ontological (concerning the value of the natural world, sexuality and the body, and the nature of history (Chapter Five)), and ethical or political. But as we have begun to appreciate, it is above all at the ethico-political level, "as a religion of injustice" that Camus takes his distance from Christianity, "even if" its Theistic claims could be somehow agreed upon.[456] To put thing simply, Camus lastingly sympathises with the early moderns' revolt against the "sacred world" of medieval Christendom: a world in which "metaphysic is replaced by myth. There are no more questions, only eternal answers and commentaries…"[457]

What though, more exactly, does Camus mean by claiming that Christianity is 'a religion of injustice,' and what historical evidence does he adduce to support this striking claim? The later antique period in which evangelical Christianity

---

453 See James W. Woefel, *Camus: A Theological Perspective* (New York: Abington, 1975); Hanna, "Albert Camus and the Christian Faith", in Germaine Brée ed. *Camus: Critical Essays*, 48–58.

454 Srigley, *Camus' Critique of Modernity*, 138.

455 C II 342; C II Eng 176; "Intervention à la table ronde de 'Civilisation' ", OC II 684.

456 "What I reproach Christianity with is being a doctrine of injustice." C II 112; C II Eng, 56; cf. 63, 92. Cf. Albert Camus, "September 8, 1944 Justice and Freedom" in *Camus at Combat*, 32: "Christianity is in essence a religion of injustice (and that is, paradoxically, the source of its greatness). It is founded on the sacrifice of the innocent and the acceptance of that sacrifice." Cf. HR 51–55; R 31–34; & on the sacrifice of the innocents reported in the gospels as, for Camus' Clamence, a source of Jesus' own alleged guilt: F 112–113.

457 HR 36; R 21.

(today's 'Jesus movement') arose, the young Camus agrees with most commentators, was characterised by a growing sense of cultural disorientation. This phenomenon accompanied the expansion of the Roman empire, the increasingly heinous corruption of the Roman elites, and the unprecedented confrontation of "an extraordinary incoherence of races and peoples" the later Empire brought about. "Few periods were as distressed as that one."[458] It was a world in which the question of the good was receding before the quest for God, Camus turns an aphorism.[459] The acceptance of 'this world' common to all Greek schools (barring the metaphysical forms of Platonism which became ascendant in syncretic forms after 200 CE) receded before a growing sense of the world's irredeemable misery and evil. The flipside of this devaluation of the material and political worlds lay in the forms of longing for other-worldly salvation attested by the rising popularity of the pagan mystery religions, then Christianity itself.[460]

The evangelical early church is the subject of Camus' opening chapter in *Christian Metaphysics and Neoplatonism*. It was characterised by strong world-rejection and the vivid eschatological sense that this world was imminently to end. The profound pessimism was reflected in the sentiment expressed in Paul's *Romans* 3:23 that "All have sinned."[461] "This idea of an imminent death, closely bound moreover to the second coming of Christ, obsessed the entire first Christian generation."[462] Faced with the evils of this "vale of tears," the early Christians posited the need for grace made possible through the bodily, expiatory sacrifice of the saviour: in contrast to works, the cultivation of the virtues, or initiatory gnosis.[463] Indeed, the early Church writers including Paul are deeply anti-speculative and anti-intellectual.[464]

From very early on in its history, however, the evangelical movement was faced with gnostic splinter groups, the subject of Camus' second chapter in *Christian Metaphysics and Neoplatonism*. The gnostics, like the early Christians, "were obsessed with the problem of evil."[465] However, influenced by forms of Platonism, the gnostics claimed that the solution to this problem lay in

---

458 CMN 42.
459 CMN 42.
460 CMN 42–43.
461 CMN 49.
462 CMN 47.
463 CMN 48–49.
464 CMN 50–51, 56, 60.
465 CMN 67.

elevated forms of initiatic knowledge.[466] Theoretically, as Bayle stressed in his entries on the ancient Manicheans, the problem of explaining evil was 'solved' by figures like Marcion and Basilides by positing that this material world was evidently the creation of a malign lesser God or Deities. The God of salvation from this world, whose gnosis they believed Jesus came to teach, was simply not the same creator God described for us in the *Torah*.[467]

Like Hans Blumenberg, whose reading of the later antique world in *Legitimacy of the Modern Age* Camus strikingly anticipates—and like Pierre Bayle in the late 17th century whom he consistently echoes—Camus is struck by the cogency of the gnostic two-God solution to the problem of evil, for which Marcion was able to adduce apostolic support.[468] Camus notes that, however much the Church tried to suppress gnosticism's radical Dualism, it forms a recurring heretical tendency in the history of the Latin Churches: most spectacularly with the Catharism of the 13th century brutally suppressed by a first Holy Inquisition, but continually in lasting popular conceptions of the devil.[469] The gnostic solution to the problem of evil would only be officially supplanted, and the Christian West's orthodoxy on the problem of evil be stabilised, with Saint Augustine in the fourth century. Augustine's systematic theology represents for this reason what Camus calls a "second revelation,"[470] of absolutely monumental significance in shaping Western culture. He dedicates the last chapter of *Christian Metaphysics and Neoplatonism* to its examination.

Augustine's theology arose after two centuries in which, faced with the task of proselytising, the early Christians had increasingly reframed their faith in response to the wider, Hellenised Mediterranean culture in which they had come to proselytise.[471] Drawing on categories taken from neoPlatonic philosophy, notably the ideas of emanation and the hypostases, Augustine undertook to give systematic, metaphysical foundations to evangelical beliefs concerning the Father, Son, and Holy Spirit.[472] At the same time, Camus stresses, "the problem of evil was for Augustine, as for the gnostics, a kind of obsession": a fact reflected in the Saint's own biographical trajectory through Manicheanism.[473]

---

466   CMN 68.
467   CMN 71–75.
468   CMN 73–74.
469   CMN 44; for Camus on the Albigensian heresy, see HR 242; R 190.
470   CMN 115.
471   CMN 44. See James Shiel, *Greek Thought and the Rise of Christianity* (New York: Barnes & Noble, 1968); Werner Jaegar, *Early Christianity and Greek Paideia* (Harvard: Harvard University Press, 1961).
472   CMN 117–8, 124–7.
473   CMN 119.

Having broken with the Manichees after the famous conversion documented in his *Confessions*, Augustine attempted to explain the existence of evil while preserving a notion of an omnibenevolent, salvific, creator God. Natural evil in events like Lisbon 1755 or the death of innocent children, Augustine invited believers to see as both inevitably tied to all matter (a neoPlatonic inheritance) and necessary in order for the Greater Providential Good to manifest Itself (a Christianised Stoic notion).[474] More than this, and in a way which arouses Camus' own metaphysical rebellion, Augustine expostulated that such suffering is the inherited punishment of human beings for the sin of the first man, Adam and his consort, Eve. For Augustine as for the evangelicals, contra Pelagius and the pagan philosophers, man can never attain perfection or salvation, or live truly well, through cultivating good works, virtue, or knowledge. Indeed, the virtues pursued outside of the one thing needful, a love of God, even or especially amongst the philosophers, give body only to the sin of pride.[475] God has moreover in His Goodness given us free will. It is this power which allows Augustine to explain human, political and moral evil and justify God's punishment of human beings. Augustine nevertheless disagrees with Pelagius on the scope of this freed will. Indeed, in a way which Bayle had seen threatens at every moment to make God's punishment of the wicked seem irredeemably unjust, Augustine maintains that, after the fall, human beings cannot but choose the evil for which they shall also be judged and punished.[476]

As Blumenberg argues in *The Legitimacy of the Modern Age*, so Camus contends that Augustinian theodicy only ever 'resolved' the problem of evil unstably: leaving a worm of doubt or fundamental contention at the heart of the medieval theological edifice. It did so, first of all, by gravely burdening human beings with the cosmic weight of bringing evil into Creation. At stake here is the teaching that *nemo bonus* (no one is good) because of original sin and the fall. According to this doctrine, Adam's sin is responsible even for the natural evils that befall later generations, which take on the aspect of punishments for our inherited guilt.[477] The Augustinian idea of inherited guilt would also come, in time, to vindicate the Catholic Church's long-held teaching that unbaptised

---

474   CMN 119. On the Stoic account of providence, see Marcus Tullius Cicero, *De Natura Deorum*, II.XXX-LII.

475   CMN 120, 121–2. See Christopher Brooke, *Philosophic Pride: Stoicism and Political Thought from Lipsius to Rousseau* (Princeton: Princeton University Press, 2012), 1–11 ("Augustine of Hippo").

476   CMN 122–123. Bayle, *Dictionary*, "Manicheans", "Paulicians".

477   I have developed this comparison between Camus and Blumenberg in Matthew Sharpe, "The Black Side of the Sun: Camus, Theology, and the Problem of Evil," in *Political Theology*, 2014.

infants will be eternally damned.[478] It is fair to say that Camus, throughout his life, found this latter idea as ethically and metaphysically unconscionable as Ivan Karamazov found the notion that the suffering of innocents might be a necessary price of Providential Truth. In a talk Camus gave to Dominicans at Latour-Marbourg in 1946, Camus thus protested against his depiction by theological and Marxist critics as a pessimistic thinker in these precise terms:

> … what right has a Christian or a Marxist to accuse me of pessimism? It is not I who invented the 'misery of the creature', nor the terrifying formulas of divine malediction. It is not I who exclaimed '*nemo bonus*' (Mark 10:18), nor I who preached the damnation of unbaptised children. It is not I who said that man was incapable of saving himself and that from the depths of his misery his only hope was in the grace of God.[479]

Camus' protest against the idea of inherited original sin represents the fundamental 'dikaiostic' basis of Camus' critique of Augustinian Christianity as a religion of injustice. Camus' most vivid staging of his criticism of Augustinian Christianity however comes in his great 1947 novel, *La Peste*, to which we accordingly now briefly turn.

4   'Too Big a Word for Me': Jacques Othon, Father Paneloux, and Doctor Rieux

As Jennifer Stafford Brown has argued, the Jesuit Father Paneloux is particularly important in terms of the political and wider meanings of *The Plague*.[480] Before the plague had come to Oran, Paneloux had a reputation even amongst non-believers on the basis of some pieces of trenchant social critique he had

---

478   CMN 123.

479   Camus, "Unbeliever and Christians", RRD 72–73. In a note in his *Carnets* in the weeks preceding this 1946 speech, Camus had reflected similarly: "The only great Christian mind to look at the problem of evil in the face was Saint Augustine. His conclusion was the terrifying '*nemo bonus*'. Since then, Christianity has spent its time giving the problem temporary solutions. The result is there for everyone to see. It took time, but men are today poisoned by an intoxication that dates back two thousand years. They have had enough of evil, or they are resigned to it, which amounts to pretty much the same thing. But at least they can no longer put up with deception (*le mensonge*) on that subject." C II 179; C II Eng 92.

480   See Jennifer Stafford Brown, "Prison, Plague, and Piety: Medieval Dystopia in Albert Camus's *The Plague*" in *The Originality and Complexity of Albert Camus's Writings*, 95–110.

written for "a wider, non-specialist public" on "present-day individualism."[481] Although we are not made privy to the texts in question, the contents of Paneloux's sermons make it clear that they would almost certainly have echoed motifs today recounted in Taylor, Milbank, and others. Yet Paneloux's passion, Camus' chronicler tells us, was his "research work on St. Augustine and the African Church that had won for him a high place in his Order."[482] This is a fact which, given Camus' *Diplôme* thesis, can hardly be a matter of chance.

So it is that when the plague strikes, Paneloux is ready in his first sermon to deliver a classically Augustinian reading of the Oranais's sufferings. As the Catholic Church had interpreted the Lisbon quake, so Paneloux tells his flock that the plague they were facing was assuredly a sign of God's wrath at Oran's impiety.[483] "Calamity has come on you, my brethren, and, my brethren, you deserved it...," the Father begins in thundering form, echoed by the rain storm beating down outside the Church:

> The first time this scourge appears in history, it was wielded to strike down the enemies of God. Pharaoh set himself up against the divine will, and the plague beat him to his knees. Thus from the dawn of recorded history the scourge of God has humbled the proud of heart and laid low those who hardened themselves against Him. Ponder this well, my friends, and fall on your knees...[484]
>
> No earthly power, nay, not even, mark me well, the vaunted might of human science can avail you to avert that hand once it is stretched toward you. And winnowed like corn on the blood-stained threshing-floor of suffering, you will be cast away with the chaff.[485]

While the town's governing magistrate, Monsieur Othon, assures Rieux that he finds the sermon "absolutely irrefutable",[486] in Part IV of *La Peste*, Othon's and Paneloux's faith is put to the severest test. Camus uses his imaginative license as a novelist to stage the most extreme challenge possible to the

---

481 P 78.
482 P 78.
483 *La Peste* perhaps suggests the lineage of the plague, *qua* senseless disaster, in the Lisbon quake when Camus has Cottard, the collaborator figure who celebrates the disease's arrival express his desire early in the piece for "An earthquake! A big one—to smash everything up..." at P 53.
484 P 78.
485 P 81–82.
486 P 85.

Augustinian attempt to make peace with natural evil as an instrument of God's justice: the agonising death of Monsieur Othon's own son in a school-come-makeshift-hospital with Paneloux, Tarrou and Rieux watching helplessly at the bedside. This episode is perhaps the most famous, striking exemplification of Camus' use of literature to bear witness, very directly, to the concrete, sometimes deeply uncomfortable consequences of abstract thinking. As such, it stands very much in the lineage of Voltaire's *Candide* and its staging *ad absurdem* the kinds of horrors a Leibnizian theodicy is committed to accepting as "necessary evils":[487]

> They had already seen children die, for many months now death had shown no favouritism, but they had never yet watched a child's agony minute by minute, as they had now been doing since daybreak. Needless to say, the pain inflicted on these innocent victims had always seemed to them to be what in fact it was: an abominable thing. But hitherto they had felt its abomination in, so to speak, an abstract way; they had never had to witness over so long a period the death-throes of an innocent child. / Paneloux gazed down at the small mouth, fouled with the sores of the plague and pouring out the angry death-cry that has sounded through the ages of mankind. He sank on his knees, and all present found it natural to hear him say in a voice hoarse but clearly audible across that nameless, never ending wail: 'My God, spare this child!' But the wail continued without cease and the other sufferers began to grow restless. The patient at the far end of the ward, whose little broken cries had gone on without a break, now quickened their tempo so that they flowed together in one unbroken cry, while the others' groans grew louder. A gust of sobs swept through the room, drowning Paneloux's prayer, and Rieux, who was still tightly gripping the rail of the bed, shut his eyes, dazed with exhaustion

---

[487] This is a feature of Camus' work we will highlight at the start of Chapter Four below. Cf. Roger Pearson, *Fables of Reason: A Study Of Voltaire's Contes Philosophiques* (Oxford: Oxford Scholarship online, 1993). Camus' use of fiction here is very close to that used by Voltaire, as Pearson captures it at *Fables of Reason*, 35: "Paradoxically Voltaire uses fiction (in the sense of invented stories) to provide the empirical evidence, the facts of life, upon which the initial, illusory system founders, with the result that both protagonist and reader are brought to believe not in a theory or an abstraction but in the evidence of their own eyes (even if, like the *'crocheteur borgne'*, Memnon, or Pangloss, they have only one). They are subjected to what Jean Starobinski calls *'la riposte du monde à l'euphorie du système.'*"

and disgust. / When he opened them again, Tarrou was at his side. 'I must go,' Rieux said. 'I can't bear to hear them any longer.'[488]

What follows, when Paneloux follows Rieux out the door, is a direct confrontation between the doctor, representing modern metaphysical revolt, and Paneloux's medieval Augustinian position:

> Rieux was already going out of the ward, walking so quickly and with such a look on his face that when he overtook Paneloux, the priest held out his arm to restrain him. 'Come now, doctor,' he said. Without stopping as he swept along, Rieux turned round and spat out: 'Ah, now that one, at least, was innocent, and you know it as well as I do!'[489]

Paneloux persists. He follows Rieux outside to the schoolyard, catching up with him in the poignant setting of the children's deserted play equipment:

> 'Why did you speak to me with such anger just now?' said a voice behind him. 'I, too, found that unbearable to watch.' Rieux turned round to Paneloux. 'That's true,' he said. 'Forgive me. But tiredness is a form of madness. And there are times in this town when I can only feel outrage and revolt.' 'I understand,' said Paneloux. 'It is outrageous because it is beyond us. But perhaps we should love what we cannot understand.' Rieux sat up abruptly. He looked at Paneloux with all the strength and passion he could muster and shook his head. 'No, Father,' he said. 'I have a different notion of love; and to the day I die I shall refuse to love this creation in which children are tortured.'[490]

Camus makes clear that Paneleux is as profoundly traumatised by the death of the child Jacques as is Rieux, a fact which sympathetic Christian critics led by Merton have duly noted.[491] For the first time, he tells the doctor, he has fully

---

488 P 176–177.
489 P 177.
490 P 177–8.
491 See Thomas Merton's important reading of Paneloux in his "*The Plague* of Albert Camus: A Commentary and Introduction", in *The Literary Essays of Thomas Merton*, 209–211. Camus always respected Christianity as a way of life: but he associated it with the acceptance of grace, which means also accepting what for him was unacceptable. See C II 116: "Les Grecs n'auraient rien compris à l'existentialisme—alors que, malgré le scandale, ils ont pu entrer dans le Christianisme. C'est que l'existentialisme ne suppose pas de conduite."

understood what is meant by talk of grace, and begins to reflect on whether it could ever be justified for a Priest to consult a secular physician.[492] Soon after, the Jesuit Father delivers his second, more halting sermon, addressing the congregation with a 'we', not 'you'.[493] In it, Paneloux withdraws from his initial, strident Augustinian claims that the plague was justified punishment for Oran's sins. Now, shifting theological ground, he falls back upon Augustine's conception of Predestination, as explained by Camus in these terms in *Christian Metaphysics and Neoplatonism*:

> ...Saint Augustine constantly returns to the gratuity of this doctrine. The number of the chosen, just as that of the outcasts, is set once and for all and invariably. Only then does God consider our merits and demerits in order to determine the degree of our punishment. What we cannot know is the reason why this is so...Augustine's final word on this subject, vital to a Christian, is an admission of ignorance. Divine arbitrariness remains intact.[494]

Just so, Paneloux now tells his congregation that there can be no Divine justification within the scope of human understanding for the death of a child like Jacques:

> 'My brethren,' Father Paneloux said at last, announcing that he was coming to an end, 'the love of God is a difficult love. It assumes a total abandonment of oneself and contempt for one's person. But it alone can wipe away the suffering and death of children, it alone makes them necessary because it is impossible to understand such things, so we have no alternative except to desire them. This is the hard lesson that I wanted to share with you. This is the faith—cruel in the eyes of man, decisive in the eyes of God—which we must try to reach. We must try to make ourselves equal to this awful image. On this peak, everything will be confounded and made equal, and the truth will break forth from apparent injustice...'[495]

---

492 P 180.

493 P 182.

494 CMN 123, 121. This 'justification of the ways of God to men' by way of God's unfathomable separation of the chosen elect from all others, Blumenberg argues, represents a relocation of the Gnostic dualism 'in the bosom of mankind.' Blumenberg, *Legitimacy of the Modern Age*, 132–136.

495 P 186.

We can accordingly say that Paneloux moves after the death of the Othon boy from what Hans Blumenberg in *The Legitimacy of the Modern Age* calls the "first" to the "second" medieval attempt at "warding off Gnosticism" as the evidently best theistic solution to the problem of evil.[496] As if recharting the history of the medieval Church and the shift from Thomism towards forms of scholastic voluntarism in the 14th century, Paneloux now embraces the very kind of (still Augustinian) solution the later medieval nominalists would defend, and against which the early modern metaphysical rebels in the 17th and 18th centuries would set their demands for justice. Faced with the senseless ravages of the plague, Paneloux hypostasises God's omnipotence at the cost of rendering his providential omnibenevolence wholly beyond human understanding. From a doctrine of consolation, Christian faith at this stretching point becomes the difficult basis for a heart-rending, unquestioning acceptance of the fundamental, divinely willed injustice of Creation.

Camus' position on Christianity, like Blumenberg's, thus powerfully challenges the elegiac supposition deposited in Milbank's or Taylor's anti-modern metanarratives. The supposition in question improbably suggests that medieval Christendom, at some point between the 11th and 14th centuries, was an unproblematically unified, coherent and consummately humane and just social order—if only at the level of its legitimising theologemes. According to Camus and Blumenberg, by contrast, the perdurance of evil posed a lingering, never satisfactorily resolved, absolutely fundamental problem for Christian thought. Thus, if the later scholastics, against whose theological doctrines the early moderns revolted, were drawn to hypostasize God's *voluntas* to such fearsome proportions, this was not the unaccountable 'fall' into nihilism that Milbank's story for one suggests.[497] It was because, pious Christians as these Fransiscans and Protestants were, they had inherited from the Augustinian 'secularisation' of eschatological, evangelical Christianity the worm of division and doubt represented by the problem of evil.[498] In the face of the undeniable malignities of the world, they saw that the fundaments of Christian faith could only be preserved, within the Augustinian world-frame, by conceptually elevating God's Will far above what was called His intellect: shaping the world as a beautifully ordered, humane and rationally comprehensible cosmos. In Camus' *L'Homme Révolté*, the early moderns' metaphysical rebellion

---

496   Blumenberg, *Legitimacy*, 132–141.
497   Milbank, *Theology and Social Theory*, 14–23, in which nominalism seems a second fall, rather than an attempt to reclaim Jerusalem from Athens, and a coherent explanation of evil in the context of omniscience.
498   Blumenberg, *Legitimacy*, 137–143, 170–2, 178–9, 181–5, 191, 194–196.

thus represents what Blumenberg calls a new, limited "self-assertion" against a world whose providential, humane ordering had become impossible to maintain, and whose Deity had come to take on the proportions of an inscrutable Cosmic Tyrant.[499]

It is indeed notable, in a further remarkable testimony to Camus' anticipations of the key theses of *The Legitimacy of the Modern Age*, that Blumenberg's narration of the emergence of the early modern "sufficient rationality" of the empirical modern sciences draws central attention to Descartes' *cogito sum*.[500] For Blumenberg, contra Heidegger and those influenced by him, the Cartesian *cogito* does not represent the unbounded hypostasisation of man in the 'onto-theological' place of the fallen Deity.[501] Historically, it emerges as a kind of minimal bulwark of rationality set against the post-nominalistic collapse of any sense of humanly-comprehensible order in Creation, personified in the conceptual drama of Descartes' *Meditations* by the vertiginous trickery of the *malin genie*.[502] Camus also, as we shall stress in our central Chapters, lays claim to a kind of neoCartesian minimal foundationalism in his mature philosophical reflections. (Chapters Three and Four) As *The Rebel* puts it, "I rebel" against all legitimations or rationalisations of evil, "therefore we exist."[503] The community of living human beings, this side of all metaphysical speculation, is the basis for a political ethics which resists all rationalisations of senseless suffering. Camus like the early modern rebel rejects salvation; but not, contra the Augustinian critiques (and the fond dreams of fascism and messianic Marxism), in the name of his own, the race's or the species' aspirant divinity. His rebellion is at first a scrupulously limited defiance of any divinity which would demand unjustifiable human suffering as the price of His or Its adherence. As Camus reflects in an important note from the time of writing *La Peste*:

> Grace? We should serve justice because our condition is unjust, increase happiness and joy because this world is unhappy. Similarly, we should

---

499 Blumenberg, *Legitimacy*, 138, 158, 178–185.
500 Blumenberg, *Legitimacy*, 74–75, 183–187.
501 See Martin Heidegger, "Modern Science, Metaphysics and Mathematics", in David Farell Krell ed., *Martin Heidegger Basic Writings* (San Fransisco: Harper, 1998), 296–305. It is notable how close this reading of Heidegger's is to Augustinian ideas, arguably reflecting Heidegger's profound debts in the decisive years of the early 1920s to protestant theology, on which see Theodore Kisiel, *The Genesis of Heidegger's Being and Time* (London: University of California Press, 1995), 149–219 ("The Religion Courses, 1920–1921").
502 Blumenberg *Legitimacy*, 137–143, 170-2, 178–9, 181–5, 191, 194–196.
503 HR 38; R 22.

sentence no one to death, since we have been sentenced to death. The doctor [Rieux is] God's enemy: he fights against death.[504]

The last word in this section, however, should go to Doctor Rieux himself, this paradigmatic Camusian figure who brings together a neoStoic fortitude with the philanthropic practice of modern medicine. After Rieux's *cri de coeur* that "that one at least was innocent," Paneloux's questioning draws out the Doctor's scrupulously limited form of human self-assertion in precise post-metaphysical terms:

> A shadow of profound distress passed across Paneloux's face. 'Ah, doctor,' he said sadly. 'I have just understood what is meant by God's grace.' But Rieux had slipped back onto his bench. From the depths of his returning exhaustion, he replied more gently: 'Which I don't have, I know. But I don't want to discuss this with you. We are working together for something that unites us at a higher level than prayer or blasphemy, and that's all that counts.' Paneloux sat down beside Rieux. He seemed moved. 'Yes,' he said. 'Yes, you too are working for the salvation of mankind.' Rieux tried to smile. 'Salvation is too big a word for me. I don't go that far. What interests me is man's health, his health first of all.'[505]

5   From Rebellion to Revolution, Unity to Totality: All or Nothing

For Camus, then, the limited self-assertion of the early modern rebels against Christian theodicy is justified: a noble defence of human dignity in the face of the inhumanity of nature, and the injustices visited by human beings on each other. If the price of the 'returns to theology' being advertised today is that we will soon enough be asked to embrace forms of resigned, fideistic acceptances of the suffering of innocents, then Camus like Ivan Karamazov, Rieux or Voltaire does not think we should pay this price. The pagan deity Prometheus, rebel against Olympian Zeus and bringer of fire to human beings, hero of Aeschylus' *Prometheus Unbound*,[506] remains the presiding divinity to whom Camus' *L'Homme Révolté* looks back, even as the book details the baleful

---

504   C II 129; C II Eng 65.
505   P 178.
506   Lottman, *Albert Camus*, Chapter 13 ("Theatre d'Équipe"); Todd, *Albert Camus* 51–53; Zaretsky, *A Life Worth Living*, 65–67.

evolution of the modern Prometheans into tyrannical *ersatz* Caesars.[507] As Camus concludes Part III of *L'Homme Révolté*, using the ancient myth to pictorially dramatise his assessment of the troubling careers of the modern revolutionary movements of far Left and Right:

> Here ends Prometheus' surprising itinerary. Proclaiming his hatred of the gods and his love of mankind, he turns away from Zeus with scorn and approaches mortal men in order to lead them in an assault against the heavens. But men are weak and cowardly; they must be organized. They love pleasure and immediate happiness; they must be taught to refuse, in order to grow up, immediate rewards. Thus Prometheus, in his turn, becomes a master who first teaches and then commands. Men doubt that they can safely attack the city of light and are even uncertain whether the city exists. They must be saved from themselves. The hero then tells them that he, and he alone, knows the city. Those who doubt his word will be thrown into the desert, chained to a rock, offered to the vultures. The others will march henceforth in darkness, behind the pensive and solitary master. Prometheus alone has become god and reigns over the solitude of men. But from Zeus he has gained only solitude and cruelty; he is no longer Prometheus, he is Caesar. The real, the eternal Prometheus has now assumed the aspect of one of his victims. The same cry, springing from the depths of the past, rings forever through the Scythian desert.[508]

How though does Camus understand, philosophically, this surprising revolutionary itinerary which takes us from the Promethean *cri de coeur* of a Voltaire, a Rieux or an Ivan Karamazov, moved by compassionate indignation against Priestly rationalisations of epidemics and natural catastrophes, to the later modern, Caesarian universe of show trials and camps, in which ideologically rationalised murder has 'secularised' divine inscrutability?

The argument turns around Camus' related distinctions between rebellion and revolution, and unity and totality. Legitimate rebellion, Camus argues, is

---

507 See Chapter Five for Camus' view of Prometheus, as opposed to Satan in the Christian world-frame.

508 HR 305–6; R 244–245. We underscore again that it is such a mythical *denouement*, not the alleged unfolding of Odysseus' strategic cunning into the instrumental rationality involved in organising the camps that defines Camus' task in *L'Homme Révolté*. (For Camus, indeed, Odysseus' refusal of immortality on Calypso' island, and longing to return home to his mortal wife, Penelope, and homeland, Ithaca, is a profoundly edifying tale.) At HE 152; cf. Zaretsky, *Life Worth Living*, 93–96.

the expression of the desire for unity and belonging in the world innate in each human being we met in the "Introduction". This desire, "common to both believers and rebels",[509] although capable of different symbolizations,[510] is also for Camus the ground of our inalienable dignity, as we will highlight in Chapter Three. This desire for unity confronts its own limits in realities like useless suffering or, differently, the inhuman majesty of the natural world. The longing for totality, a concept we met in Chapter One underlying Stalinism's ambition for global revolution, is a contingent excessive manifestation of this desire for unity. It sets out to deny, reduce or destroy everything that exceeds its present control. In a key phrase, Camus aligns this longing for totality with forms of 'all or nothing' thinking.[511] He opposes all such totalising 'all or nothing' claims to more moderate ways of thinking which allow for the suspension or moderation of assent and denial.[512] "I rebel" against forms of senseless suffering, the rebel proclaims, "therefore we are." The 'all or nothing' revolutionary, in different forms, adds to this the metaphysical claim: "and we are alone."[513] He or they thereby pass from blasphemy and defiance, challenging human or divine powers by recourse to an independent standard of justice; to outright atheism or denial of any such higher principles. From this denial, the willingness to suspend the commitment to justice and 'do whatever it takes' to overthrow the enemies' powers follows. It is above all this revolutionary willingness 'to do whatever it takes', given which the taking of human life becomes a matter of indifference that Camus will finally call 'nihilism'.[514]

It has to be said, as critics have said, that Camus' explanation of this 'nihilism' and thus of the universe of the concentration camp remains pitched at the level of ideas, and flirts substantively with overvaluing their role in human motivation.[515] Camus is moved by the (fundamentally Socratic)[516] supposition that people act on the basis of reasons. So when they act extremely, violating the 6th Mosaic commandment, we must assume that they do so on the basis of justifications they have taken to be compelling: whether passionate or ideo-

---

509   HR 292; R, 233.
510   HR 132–133; R 101;cf. Srigley *Camus' Critique*, 71.
511   HR 36, 80–81, 128, 142, 203, 313; R 21, 56–57, 97, 107, 157, 251.
512   See for different aspects of this opposition, epistemic and ethical, Chapters Three and Five.
513   HR 135 (literally, the last words of "La Révolte Métaphysique"), 312; R 104, 250.
514   See HR 350; R 280: "This is the extreme of nihilism; blind and savage murder becomes an oasis, and the imbecile criminal seems positively refreshing in comparison with our highly intelligent executioners."
515   See for examples TM 353, 361.
516   TM 353, 361; cf. Camus, "Conférence au couvent de Latour-Marburg", OC II 509.

logical, or both. Camus explicitly avows this limit to his analyses: the way that *L'Homme Révolté* largely by-passes economic and social factors in explaining the origins of totalitarianism,[517] leaving the question of other causal factors to other studies.[518] In his "Letters to a German Friend" written during 1943–1944 and published in the clandestine press, Camus thus presents the Nazis as having responded primarily to a sense of the meaninglessness of human life—as against specific historical, economic and political realities—when they exalted power as the only *de facto* rule. "You never believed in the meaning of the world," Camus writes his *ami allemand*:

> ...you therefore deduced the idea that everything was equivalent and that good and evil could be defined according to your [or the Führer's] wishes... You supposed that in the absence of any human or divine code, the only values were those of the animal world—in other words, violence and cunning.[519]

The communist position, as Camus develops it in his post-war addresses, follows a different 'ideologic', although it leads to the same kind of theoretical vindication of lethal political violence. Given the posited absence of any values outside of the history of class struggle (and in the light of the Marxian critique of bourgeois appeals to theological and formal ideals to obfuscate material injustices), the Leninist affirms as the one supreme value this historical struggle itself. But in this struggle, any means may be necessary (and, absent any external checks, legitimate) to succeed on behalf of the working classes: ergo, violence and cunning again. "It is not legitimate to identify the ends of Fascism with the ends of Russian Communism," *The Rebel* thus reflects:

> The first represents the exaltation of the executioner by the executioner; the second, more dramatic in concept, the exaltation of the exe-

---

517   Although we saw above the role he, like Arendt, sees being played by the first world war, and the resulting chronic instabilities in Europe.

518   This methodological stipulation comes on the opening page of Camus' examination of fascism, and then the ideological origins of the Stalinist State, at HR 227; R 177; "To the editor of *Temps Modernes*", 113. With Jeanson, Sartre and others, we can agree that the exclusive heuristic focus on political and philosophical ideas does often flirt with a substantively idealistic account of history and human motivation, overvaluing the role of ideas in shaping political life. With that said, Camus' Algerian writings of 1945 and 1954 give more than due weight to economic factors, a fact which has attracted post-colonial criticism. See AC 59–80; 90–99.

519   LGF 27. See Appendix Three.

cutioner by the victims. The former never dreamed of liberating all men, but only of liberating a few by subjugating the rest. The latter, in its most profound principle, aims at liberating all men by provisionally enslaving them all. It must be granted the grandeur of its intentions. But, on the other hand, it is legitimate to identify the means employed by both with the political cynicism that they have drawn from the same source, moral nihilism.[520]

The central part ("Historical Rebellion") of *L'Homme Révolté* provides Camus' most detailed examination of the causes and ideological constellations of fascism and Stalinism. It is in these key Camusian analyses of de Sade and the romantics, Jacobinism and Rousseau, Stirner and Nietzscheanism, the German idealists, Hegelianism, Marxism and Leninism, in fact, that Camus' thought can best be shown to be far from the vague, incoherent, or illogical *mélange* critics after Sartre have invariably contended.[521] If there is a fault in Camus' reconstructions of these positions, we would contend, this fault is that Camus skirts an excessively schematic logicisation of complex positions, moved by his ardent interest in the problem of evil and the propensity of modern ideologies to vindicate forms of lethal violence. Although Camus would urge caution about the thought, the academic reader can be oddly reminded as s/he reads Camus' exegetical reconstructions in *L'Homme Révolté* of Hegel's similarly idiosyncratic 'reconstructions' of the 'figures of spirit' in *The Phenomenology of Geist*.[522] In both cases, the later author reconstructs earlier thinkers' positions with an eye to a problematic that is their own, and which is not necessarily

---

520   HR 308; R 246–247.
521   As we commented in the "Introduction", Sartre in his "Reply to Camus" at p. 145 claims of Camus: "You detest difficult thought and hastily declare that there is nothing in it to understand, in order to avoid in advance that you did not understand it." For two representative cases of such an assessment, consider Susan Tarrow in her (excellent) *Exile from the Kingdom* (USA: University of Alabama Press, 1985), 144–145; and more recently Mark Orme, *The Development of Albert Camus' Concern for Social and Political Justice*, 152–157, 170–172, 178–180; with Orme's summary of critical responses at 152–153. See Appendix One below, as well as what follows here and in Chapters Four and Five.
522   To recognise one, formal similarity between Camus and Hegel is not to say that Camus is "the same" as Hegel, or an Hegelian in the decisive senses. A red car has little more than its colour in common with a red kangaroo or a red book. Camus finds Hegel's dialectical philosophy of history, and the underlying principle that "man is made for history, not history for man", "detestable" (CH 741) as we shall be seeing: indeed he assigns Hegel, as read by him (like most of his contemporary compatriots) through Kojève, in many ways the decisive position in his account of the devolution of modern rebellion into 20th century

in the foreground of the original authors' intentions. In each case, citation of original texts takes back stage to the commentators' own philosophical reconstructions of what they take to be the essential logics of the earlier positions: reconstructions whose adequacy as complete readings of the thinkers in question specialists have accordingly questioned.[523] It is just that, where Hegel sees these figures succeeding one another towards a utopian terminus of Absolute Knowledge and the End of History, *Camus reads each with an eye to whether and how their positions come to sanction the forms of deceit, servitude or violence modern metaphysical rebellion initially opposed.*

Camus is quite explicit about this methodology: and in his defence we can note that, in the works of both Sartre and Merleau-Ponty of this period (including *Humanism and Terror*, one of Camus' targets) a similarly urgent preoccupation with the legitimacy of political violence is manifest.[524] It is fair to say that the question of rationalised murder, like the question of suicide in *Le Mythe de Sisyphe*, became for Camus in the period of Auschwitz and the revelations concerning the gulags the *sine qua non* of serious reflection.

---

revolutionary ideologies. HR 173–192; R 133–148; cf. Orme, *Development of Camus' Concern*, 162–168.

523   See Évelyne Pisier & Pierre Bouretz "Camus et le marxisme" in *Revue française de science politique*, 35e année, no. 6, 1985. pp. 1047–1063; on Rousseau, Suzanne Hélein-Koss, "Albert Camus et le 'Contrat Social' ", *Studies on Voltaire and the Eighteenth Century* 161 [1976]; Jorn Schosler, "Rousseau, Camus et le nihilism: sur l'actualité de Rousseau", *Orbis Litterarum* 40 (1985): 97–110. For a recent article vindicating Camus' reading of Rousseau as bringing a messianic component into republicanism, see Keith Michael Baker "Transformations of Classical Republicanism in Eighteenth-Century France", *The Journal of Modern History*, Vol. 73, No. 1 (March 2001), 32–53. Camus does not attempt an exhaustive reading of these authors' *oeuvres*, but one directed towards his ethical concerns, and with the total regimes in view. The question is not whether reading *The Rebel* could be a stand in for reading the originals, or whether it could be recommended to students for an authoritative account of an *oeuvre* as diverse, for instance, as Marx's. The issue is whether, in making a division between prophetic and critical components in Marx or Nietzsche, and arguing that the prophetic component of these positions can and has led, along the historical and inferential chains Camus traces to the justifications of redemptive political violence, Camus has made a wholly illegitimate move. As he might point out, and as indeed he does suggest, it would be inaccurate to suggest that the agents of Lenin or Stalin's regimes were close, scholarly readers of the Marxian *oeuvre*.

524   See Phillipe Sabot, "Les Mésaventures de la dialectique: Camus critique de Kojève dans *L'Homme Rèvoltè*" in Dolorès Lyotard ed. (Paris: Les Presses Universitaires des Septentrion, 2009), 45–60. On Camus' break with Merleau-Ponty, as early as 1946 on this question, see Aronson, *Camus and Sartre*, 66–67.

According to Camus, if modern rebellion's "achievements are sometimes ignoble," we must seek the causes for this betrayal of the normative promise of early modern revolt in what he calls, in a characteristically classical turn of phrase, "an intemperate recourse to absolutes."[525] Such is the clarity of Camus' reasoning, beneath the flowing prose, that we can present his analyses of the key modern metaphysical, cultural and political revolutionaries' 'intemperances' as each responses to one conditional thought or 'protasis' (to use an old Stoic term). This is the thought prompted by moderns' confronting the reality of undeniable evil against the background of the inherited Christian categories: *viz*. 'what if natural and human evil are necessary to God or in nature, His creation? What *then?*...' As in the postwar addresses, in what is a recurring pattern in Camus' thinking, there are two broad species of revolutionary nihilism he opposes in *The Rebel*. The first is associated with species of "absolute negation" ('all *or nothing*'); the second, symmetrically, with species of "absolute affirmation" ('*all* or nothing'):

> Each time that [rebellion] deifies the total rejection [of the world as the rebel finds it], rebellion destroys. Each time that it blindly accepts what exists and gives voice to an absolute assent, it destroys again. Hatred of the creator can turn to hatred of creation or to exclusive and defiant love of what exists. But in both cases it ends in murder and loses the right to be called rebellion. One can be a nihilist in two ways, in both cases by having an intemperate recourse to absolutes.[526]

5.1 *Absolute Negation*

All forms of 'absolute negation' ('all *or nothing*') deny any values above those of force and efficacy. They deny any larger normative order to the world out of a founding indignation at the perceived injustices of the human condition or present political regimes. In each case, Camus argues, the resulting position is neither valid nor sound, except at the level of the passions involved. They each involve what *Le Mythe de Sisyphe* calls a "leap" of logic, smuggling in an unjustified or unjustifiable premise.[527] Correlatively, in all cases, absolute negation ends by justifying the kinds of injustice and violence rebellion initially protested against.

---

525 HR 133; R 101–102.
526 HR 133; R 102.
527 MS, 21, 54–63; MSe, 6, 33–41.

TABLE 2.1   *Species of absolute negation, as reconstructed in* L'Homme Révolté

Protasis: "If natural and human evil seem necessary to God or in nature, His creation…"

De Sade: "… *then* God must wish for destruction";
- we must, 'surely' [*i.e.* this is what Camus will call a 'leap'], follow this wicked God or do His will;
- And *thus* we must become his willing, pitiless executioners/*jouisseurs*."[528]

Romantics, surrealists: "*then* we, like Milton's Satan, are the victim of injustice;
- and we should make our lives (in dandyism) and our art a standing protest against His Order [the 'leap'], even down to the formal negation of all representational norms…;
- *Thus* crime is justifiable as a form of indignation, the criminal a martyr, and excess the portal of higher revelations…"[529]

Ivan Karamazov: "*then* He [God] does not deserve to exist;
- so He cannot exist [Ivan's 'leap'];
- Thus everything is permitted, including murder, parricide [a second 'leap']".[530]

From Rousseau to the Jacobins: "*then* morality must not come from, or depend upon, either a transcendent Deity or Nature;
- It must come from the single, virtuous General Will of citizens; the true basis of normative authority hitherto invested in God (Rousseá's political-theological 'leap');
- All factions, criminals against the General Will, may thus be "compelled to be free";
- Thus 'either virtue or the terror' ".[531]

5.2   *Absolute Affirmation*

All forms of what Camus terms 'absolute affirmation' ('*all* or nothing') involve the affirmation of the world *comme il va*, in defiance of a fallen or absent deity. After Hegel's historicising turn, in Marx and differently in Nietzsche, such positions defy not simply the transcendent deity. They also reject the abstract-'bourgeois' or 'life-denying' post-Christian values which have historically

---

528   HR 58–70; R 37–47. See Chapter Three below.
529   HR 70–78, 109–130; R 47–54; 81–100.
530   HR 79–86; R 55–62.
531   HR 70–78, 109–130; R 114–117; 121–132.

abetted structural injustices (Marx) or calumniated this, the only true world (Nietzsche).[532] The protasis to which such positions respond is the same as in the forms of absolute negation. The reasoning deployed in response to this problem in Hegel, Nietzsche, Marx and the fascists however differs profoundly both from the absolute negations, and between themselves. Fascism, in its National Socialist variety, propounds a pseudobiologistic philosophy of history; Hegel (certainly in the Kojevian form familiar to Camus) deems history as essentially the struggle for Universal Recognition and *Geist*'s achievement of Absolute Knowledge; and Marxism sees history as staging the ongoing dialectic of the class struggle, based in social relations rooted in labour as our definitive species-being. Decisive again for Camus is however that, "[i]f Nietzsche and Hegel serve as alibis to the masters of Dachau and Karaganda, that does not condemn their entire philosophy. But it does lead to the suspicion that one aspect of their thought, or of their logic, can lead to these appalling conclusions..."[533] This "aspect" of their thought or logic, Camus proposes, is in each case the absolute affirmation of political or natural history without balance or reserve:

TABLE 2.2 *Species of absolution affirmation, as reconstructed in* L'Homme Révolté

Protasis: "If natural and human evil seem necessary to God or in nature, His creation..."

Nietzsche: "*then* God's only excuse is that he does not exist...;
- any values that do exist cannot come from Him, or from any other Transcendent Other-worldly source;
- this sad and suffering, but also magnificent, world alone—the world of will to power—is true;
- thus the highest value, to be embodied by the Overman, must be to totally affirm this world;
- and this means the pitiless, anti-Christian fortitude to affirm, as forms of destiny, hierarchy, exploitation, and murder..."[534]

---

532   HR 91–96; R 65–70 (on Nietzsche as critic, as against prophet of the overman); & HR 173–178, 238–9, 254–5; R 133–137, 197–201 on the critical components in Hegel and Marx respectively.
533   HR 178; R 137.
534   HR 91–108; R 65–80.

TABLE 2.2   *Species of absolution affirmation, as reconstructed in* L'Homme Révolté *(cont.)*

Fascism ("irrational revolution"): "*then* there is no higher Meaning to this world;
- the suffering of the weak, and the triumph of the strong, must be an ineradicable part of the world order;
- Thus, the strong (those capable of seeing and seizing this without illusions) should do whatever they must (murder, exploitation, deceit) to achieve rule for themselves or their kind.'[535]

Marxism (via Hegel, "rational revolution"): "*then* … any values that do exist cannot come from Him, or from any other Transcendent Other-worldly source;
- indeed, theological and formal, transcendent principles have been used to rationalise and mystify real injustices, the Jacobin terror (Hegel) or bourgeois exploitation (Marx);
- so human History alone, the long story of the struggle for recognition (Hegel) or of the class struggle and the evolution of means and relations of production (Marx) alone is true;
- Thus, the one thing needful is to do whatever it takes (including murder, hierarchy, vanguardism, deceit) to overthrow existing forms of injustice, and expedite the end of historical struggle in the classless society (not 'we are' but 'we shall be').[536]

Hence we arrive at Camus' glib synopsis in the section "Rebellion and Revolution" at the culmination of *The Rebel's* central Part:

> Those who rush blindly to history in the name of the irrational, proclaiming that it is meaningless, encounter servitude and terror, and finally emerge into the universe of concentration camps. Those who launch themselves into it, preaching its absolute rationality, [likewise] encounter servitude and terror and emerge into the universe of the concentration camps.[537]

---

535   HR, 227–238; R 177–187; the other key engagement of Camus with fascist nihilism is Albert Camus, "Letters to a German Friend", RRD 5–32, esp. 13–14, 27–28. See Appendix Three.
536   HR 173–192, 25–265, 284–291; R, 133–148, 197–210, 226–232.
537   HR 307; R 246.

6 Against Secularised Messianism: Camus' Critique of Marx's Prophetism

Formalising Camus' readings of the figures that he critiques over the space of several hundred pages in *L'Homme Révolté*, as we have just done, has the advantage of clarity. It highlights the logical, 'propositional' spine that underlies Camus' freely moving style, with its balanced cadences and resonant clauses. Camus protested against Jeanson's remarks on this book's style (in *The Rebel*, Camus' young critic had written, "art may have won out over protest";[538] the book is "too beautiful, too sovereign, too sure of itself, too much in harmony with itself... formulas tirelessly follow formulas...")[539] Only a puritanical viewpoint could assume that writing well must speak against the content conveyed. An attractive style, we know Camus appreciated, can serve to render accessible otherwise prohibitively dense and dry materials to wider audiences. But our presentation in Tables 1 and 2 of the key claims of Camus' reconstructions has the inevitable disadvantage of over-schematising Camus' engagements with key modern texts and political traditions. Avoiding the Scylla of viewing Camus as an overheated *litterateur*, we have sailed close now to the Charybdis of presenting him, as per one of Jeanson's other charges, as an unregenerate idealist: "he...limits himself to considering revolutions from the point of view of a metaphysician",[540] so what we get is "pseudo-philosophical pseudohistory".[541] To close this Chapter, given that it was above all the issue of Camus' reading of Marxism-Leninism that caused the *scandale* surrounding *The Rebel*, we want to examine in detail this key critical engagement in *L'Homme Révolté*. In doing so, we will also bring Camus' critique of Marxism-Leninism, so indebted in his case to Jean Grenier and Arthur Koestler,[542] back into relation with Camus' critique of Christian theodicy, and Camus' remarkable anticipation of Blumenberg's criticism of all versions of the theological 'secularisation thesis'.

We saw above in fact how Hans Blumenberg in *The Legitimacy of the Modern Age*, like Camus, protests that early modern "self-assertion" represents a break with a theological heritage doubled over under the weight of its own attempts to resolve the theodical question: not 'more of the same'. For Blumenberg, the formal resemblance between the Marxist-Leninist notion of History (as a lin-

---

538 Jeanson, "The Soul in Revolt", 81.
539 Jeanson, "The Soul in Revolt", 82.
540 Jeanson, "The Soul in Revolt", 87.
541 Jeanson, "The Soul in Revolt", 101.
542 See Aronson, *Camus and Sartre*, 85–89.

ear process culminating in an immanent End) and earlier Christian theologies of history (as a linear process leading to a transcendent End) does not bespeak the 'secularization' of a continuous theological content.[543] Marxism for him instead 'reoccupies' the fallen cultural place of medieval theology. The argument is that, contra the theological critiques, modern thought inherits from its medieval predecessors a set of 'debts' or framing problems; not solutions.[544] Blumenberg's idea (so close to Camus' defence of the metaphysical rebellion of Voltaire et al.) is that the early moderns' self-assertion, and their fledgling efforts to establish empirically-based forms of natural and social science, challenged and broke with the theological tradition whose crippling theodical difficulties we have seen. Accordingly, modern thought, an essentially agnostic affair, did not intrinsically *need* to answer the questions Christian theology had proposed itself as the millennial solution for: including that of yielding up a single Meaning of a similiarly single, linear, salvific History.[545] Yet the lingering cultural weight of the theological frameworks modernity succeeded remained. So again and again—as with Marxism's claims to have discerned the meaning of "The history of all hitherto existing society"[546]—European men were tempted to try to make modern thought solve Christian problems and resolve eschatological dilemmas.

Camus' critique of the prophetic dimensions of Nietzschean and Marxian philosophies in *L'Homme Révolté* anticipates Blumenberg's "reoccupation" claim exactly. Of course, here as elsewhere, we need to proceed very precisely to get this claim right. Ronald Srigley has astutely observed in *Camus' Critique of Modernity* how several formulations in *L'Homme Révolté* suggest, contra Blumenberg's kind of account, that Camus accepts something very like the secularisation thesis: and beneath it, the Augustinian claim that, if human beings call God into question, this must necessarily be because they aspire themselves to take the Creator's place. The aspirations and hopes invested for so long in Christian theology, Srigley echoes Blumenberg, exerted their weight even on Camus. They "had established themselves as the sole locus of meaning in the West for more than fifteen hundred years. So powerful was their influence that even critics [like Camus] tend to accept them as the paradigm of meaning."[547] Although Hegel or Nietzsche both call into question the existence of a transcendent creator God, Camus thus comments in Augustine

---

543   Blumenberg, *Legitimacy*, 37–38, 49–50.
544   Blumenberg, *Legitimacy*, 48–49, 59–61, 64–65.
545   Wallace, "Translator's Introduction", xx–xxi.
546   *Viz.* the opening words of Chapter 1 of *The Communist Manifesto*.
547   Srigley, *Camus' Critique*, 76.

mode, "nothing can discourage the appetite for divinity in the heart of man."[548] This suggests a metaphysical zero-sum game, between submission to God and hybristic *apotheosis*, with no *terium datur*.[549]

Nevertheless, we have seen how Camus' account of early modern rebellion (with which Srigley has some difficulties),[550] alongside his defence of the desire for unity (against totality), aims exactly to open up such a *tertium datur* between God and the overman or a deified 'species being': "Saint Augustine or Hegel," as Camus put it in interview.[551] Camus in no way denies the force of claims that modern modes of totalitarian thinking effectively 'reoccupied' the cultural 'positions' (and, more's the point, claims to legitimate lethal violence) vacated by Christian thought.[552] It is just that, in a remarkable inversion of how the secularization thesis is often presented by reactionary critics beginning with Schmitt (namely, as a premise to conclude the illegitimacy of secular institutions), Camus' criticisms of Nietzscheanism, fascism and revolutionary Marxism *begin at the exact moment when these modern forms of thought come (unnecessarily and illegitimately, as he sees things) to 'reoccupy' theological positions*.[553] As Stafford Brown has argued, one resonance of the use of 'the plague' in La Peste and L'État de Siège by Camus (alongside those we saw in Chapter One) lies in his "rebelling against something preached over and over by the Vichy government: the idea of a return to the Middle Ages..."[554] Rebellion

---

548 HR 190; R 147. In Camus' defence, he is talking here of Hegel, which makes it ambiguous as to whether he is describing Hegel's position, or his own. Given his wider reflections, I opt against Srigley for the former reading.

549 Or consider Camus, responding in his analysis of Ivan Karamazov on "the only question that interests us: can one live and stand one's ground in a state of rebellion?" Here, Camus similarly rehearses a seemingly Augustinian (or, *les extremes touchent*, Nietzschean) reply: "Ivan allows us to guess his answer: one can live in a state of rebellion *only by* pursuing it to the bitter end. What is the bitter end of metaphysical rebellion? Metaphysical revolution. The master of the world, after his legitimacy has been contested, must be overthrown. Man *must* occupy his place." HR 83; R 58 (italics mine).

550 See Srigley, *Camus' Critique*: Srigley has to argue that Camus repented of his praise for the early moderns, whom he equates with Christian metaphysics, at least in longing for 'all or nothing' style positions (8–9, 51). See for the terms of our agreements and disagreements Sharpe, "A Just Judgment?" *Thesis Eleven* (2014).

551 Camus, "Interview à *Servir*" OC II, 659.

552 See RG 228; and Chapter Four below.

553 For an important, profoundly convergent reading of National Socialism, see Uriel Tal, *Religion, Ideology and Politics in the Third Reich: Selected Essays* (London: Taylor & Francis, 2004), esp. ch. 4 "Structures of German 'Political Theology' in the Nazi Era", 87–121.

554 Brown, "Prison, Plague, and Piety: Medieval Dystopia in Albert Camus's The Plague", 96–97.

must in 1950 "return again (*se retremper*) to its sources" in early modern revolt. It must do so insofar as 20th century revolutionary dogmata in effect immanently reembodied the excessive, eschatological ambitions of the West's medieval worldview.[555]

This is the fundamental basis of Camus' criticism of Marxism and of Bolshevism as secularised forms of Christian messianism: "Believe me, they all are, even when they set fire to heaven. Whether they are atheists or churchgoers, Muscovites or Bostonians, all Christians from father to son."[556] As Camus protested after Jeanson's response to *L'Homme Révolté*, any adequate response to his text must indeed address Camus' key claim that there is, deleteriously, a precritical, immanentised prophetic dimension to Marxist thought.[557] For, as we commented above, Camus repeatedly emphasises that there is also in Marx as he reads him, alongside this unreconstructed prophetism, "the most valid method" which reflects his legitimate philosophical modernism:[558]

> To him we owe the idea which is the despair of our times... that when work is a degradation, it is not life, even though it occupies every moment of a life. Who, despite the pretensions of this society, can sleep in it in peace when they know that it derives its mediocre pleasures from the work of millions of dead souls? By demanding for the worker real riches, which are not the riches of money but of leisure and creation, [Marx] has reclaimed, despite all appearance to the contrary, the dignity of man.[559]

Camus even ironically enlists his own immanent critique of Marx in *The Rebel* under the Marxian heading of the critique of "ideological mystification": although Marx's celebrated dictum that the critique of religion is the beginning of all critique is also not far away here. The ideological dimension to which Lenin and Stalin were able to appeal to justify their political crimes, Camus contends, comes from how Marx:

---

555 HR 367; R 294.
556 F 134. Cf. C II 165; C II Eng 84.
557 Camus, "A Letter to the Editor of *Les Temps Modernes*", 120–123. See Aronson, *Camus and Sartre*, 142–143.
558 Glibly, Camus even observes in *L'Homme Révolté* that "[w]e now know that the Marx-Engels Institute in Moscow ceased, in 1935, the publication of the complete works of Marx while more than thirty volumes still remained unpublished; doubtless the content of these volumes was not 'Marxist' enough." Marx was not a Marxist, someone said. Cf. HR 240; R 188.
559 HR 263–4, cf. 254; R. 209, cf. 201.

> ... could blend in his doctrine the most valid critical method with a utopian messianism of highly dubious value. The unfortunate thing is that his critical method, which, by definition, should have been adjusted to reality, has found itself farther and farther separated from facts to the exact extent that it wanted to remain faithful to the prophecy.[560]

Despite Marx's unparalleled critical insight and sympathetic concern with the dignity of human labour, Camus observes, he remained a man of the 19th century, responding to the most brutal forms of capitalism in Britain prior to the legalisation of trade unionism. Marx did not (and indeed, as a finite man, he scarcely could have) foreseen Capital's ability to adapt from the relatively primitive industrial state which Engels and he observed; through the great 20th century compromises between business, unions and states; the continual generation of intermediary and smaller capitals; the creation of joint stock companies and other, more sophisticated 'financial instruments' to sustain productivity and disseminate ownership; and more.[561] The great mobilisations of 1914 and then again under the fascist states (and under Stalin) showed that Marx underestimated sadly the resilience of the ideological appeal of nationalism to the masses, disseminated by compliant news media and educational bases.[562] As we saw in Chapter One, Camus also echoes many Western Marxists (as well as Schmitt, Heidegger and others on the Right) in suggesting that Marx underestimated the cultural and political effects of the increasing dependency of modern economies on technological development: generating new managerial and technocratic classes in the advanced nations, rather than a democratisation of peoples' abilities to manage the means of material production and social reproduction.[563] Most devastatingly of all, Marx's prediction of global revolution (whether uttered as provocation to the ruling classes, spur to the workers, supposedly scientific prediction, or all of these things at once) failed after World War 1 to prove true.

If Leninism succeeded in predominantly agricultural Russia, and her alone, Camus reasons, it was to spite Marxism's credentials as a predictive, fallible science of history. What remained in the social science's place, as a source of ideological legitimation, was Marxism as an unfalsifiable prophecy of the end of alienation, class struggle, and of all human history (or 'prehistory'). The failure of Marxism's predictive claims "brought into the open the difference

---

560 HR 239; R 188.
561 Cf. HR 265–284, esp. 268–269; R 210–226, esp. 212–213.
562 HR 269; R 213.
563 HR 270–272; R 214–216.

between scientific reason, that fruitful instrument of research, of thought, and even of rebellion, and historic reason which German ideology invented by its negation of all principles."564 The sciences since the advent of relativity, Camus notes, had after all challenged many of the fundamental physical principles accepted by the Second International's 'dialectical materialism'. Under Stalin, while the new science was hence officially *verboten*, Soviet scientists were forced to steal atomic physics from the US to build the 'proletarian bomb' and Lamarkian biology was mandated by the Central Committee. As Camus comments drily, it furthermore became necessary "to entrust Lyssenko with the task of disciplining chromosomes…" in order to produce a biology consistent with Stalinism's positing of a wholly historical human nature.565

As we recall from Chapter One, Stalinism for Camus involved not science, but an indefensible species of ideological "historic reason."566 The determinist faith that economic development, by itself, would meaningfully liberate all human beings Camus sees as a "bourgeois" inheritance which Marx shares with Turgot, Renan and Comte.567 If we ask from whence the guarantee could come that the impoverished, alienated modern proletarian will be the agent of revolutionary liberation, Camus ironises: "the guarantee lies in Hegel".568 As Christ had to lose everything in order to fulfil his salvific mission (and as Hegel presents his succession of the different figures of *Geist* as the "Golgotha of Absolute Spirit")569 so Marxism in its utopian aspect maintains that the proletarian's universal messianic mandate comes from the completion of its misery:

> … capitalism, by driving the proletariat to the final point of degradation, gradually delivers it from every decision that might separate it from other men. It has nothing, neither property nor morality nor country. Therefore it clings to nothing but the species of which it is henceforth the naked and implacable representative. In affirming itself it affirms everything

---

564 HR 277; R 220.
565 HR 279; R 221–222.
566 HR 277–279; R 220–222. As Camus specified, it was not logic he questioned, but "ideology which substitutes for living reality a logical succession of reasonings", at Pascal, "Albert Camus ou le philosophe malgré lui", 174.
567 HR 241, 245–250; R 189, 193–197.
568 HR 259; R 205.
569 G.W.F. Hegel, *Phenomenology of Spirit*, translated by J.B. Baillie, at www-site https://ebooks.adelaide.edu.au/h/hegel/phenomenology_of_mind/complete.html: closing words: "Both together, or History (intellectually) comprehended (*begriffen*), form at once the recollection and the Golgotha of Absolute Spirit, the reality, the truth, the certainty of its throne, without which it were lifeless, solitary, and alone. 'Only the chalice of this realm of spirit/ Foams forth to God His own Infinitude' (Schiller)."

and everyone. Not because members of the proletariat are gods, but precisely because they have been reduced to the most abjectly inhuman condition. 'Only the proletariat, totally excluded from this affirmation of their personality, are capable of realizing the complete affirmation of self.' That is the mission of the proletariat: to bring forth supreme dignity from supreme humiliation. Through its suffering and its struggles, it is Christ in human form redeeming the collective sin of alienation. It is, first of all, the multiform bearer of total negation and then the herald of definitive affirmation.[570]

In this definitively prophetic appeal to hopeless hope, Camus notes, lies the genesis of communists' ambivalence or bitter hostility towards all forms of social democratic reformism.[571] As for what the End of History will look like, Camus notes that Marx is troublingly short on details. He equivocates concerning the likely duration of the posited "dictatorship of the proletariat" before the State will supposedly "wither away": truly in spite of all human history hitherto or since. But this historical or political uncertainty is the corollary of a higher Certainty that the proletarian revolution will resolve and transcend all class struggle. Although Marx challenges all 'vertical' transcendence, that is, he 'horizontally' relocates the predicates of Divinity or *Beatitudo*, traditionally consigned to Heaven or the Kingdom after the destruction of this physical world, to a point in the future. These eschatological predicates now attach to a proletarian utopia. As Camus quotes the Marx of the *1844 Economic and Philosophical Manuscripts*:

> Communism in so far as it is the real appropriation of the human essence by man and for man, in so far as it is the return of man to himself as a social being—in other words, as a human being—a complete conscious return which preserves all the values of the inner movement. This communism, being absolute naturalism, coincides with humanism: it is the real end of the quarrel between man and nature, between man and man, between essence and existence, between externalization and the affirmation of self, between liberty and necessity, between the individual and the species. It solves the mystery of history and is aware of having solved it...[572]

---

570 HR 259–269; R 205.
571 I.e. insofar as these (by alleviating present sufferings of workers and encouraging forms of organisation within the framework of capitalist economies) are held "objectively" to harm the cause of revolution.
572 At HR 263; R 208.

Camus replies that it is only the terminology that differs between such a declaration and Second Isaiah's eschatological vision of the sheep lying down with lions, and men beating their swords into plough-shares. "It is only the language here that attempts to be scientific.... The eternal springtime of mankind is foretold to us in the language of an encyclical."[573] And what does Camus, to draw in the threads, think that such a 'political eschatology' has to do with political violence, and the universe of terror and trial into which Stalinism descended after 1930? The argument is that, by removing all standards for judging actions good or bad 'this side' of the End of History; and by elevating this End of History as the one thing needful, Marxism's political eschatology licenses political cynicism and Machiavellianism on a grand scale:

> Marx destroys all transcendence, then carries out, by himself, the transition from fact to duty. But his concept of duty has no other origin but fact. The demand for justice ends in injustice if it is not primarily based on an ethical justification of justice; without this, crime itself one day becomes a duty. When good and evil are reintegrated in time and confused with events, nothing is any longer good or bad, but only either premature or out of date. Who will decide on the opportunity, if not the opportunist? Later, say the disciples, you shall judge. But the victims will not be there to judge...[574]

The "prodigious", "generous" ambitions of Marxism are so disproportionate to, and distant from, history as we find it, Camus comments, that it can readily be seen how "hope on such a scale leads to the inevitable neglect of problems that therefore appear to be secondary..."[575] Faced with working classes who, still, have not risen to their salvific Historical vocation, such hopes mandate forms of vanguardism: "absolute secrecy, meticulous care in the choice of members, [the] creation of professional revolutionaries": Lenin's "Young Turks of the revolution... with something of the Jesuit added," charged to make the revolution the proletariat is unwilling or unable to make themselves, and in the meanwhile to jealously guard and proselytise dogma.[576] As for the means this vanguard might use to accelerate this End, Camus cites Lenin's *What is to be done?*:

---

573   HR 263; R 208.
574   HR 265; R 218–219.
575   HR 262; R 207–208.
576   HR 286; R 228. On the comparison of Marxist theory, as the revolutionary Event began to seem a distant prospect, with the establishment of the Church, led by Saint Paul, see HR 266; R 211.

> One must be prepared for every sacrifice, to use if necessary every stratagem, ruse, illegal method, to be determined to conceal the truth, for the sole purpose of penetrating the Labour unions... and of accomplishing, despite everything, the Communist task.[577]

At this point, Camus' argument is, the prophetic dimension of Marx's thought has trumped not only its critical and scientific credentials. Marxism has become a kind of secular theodicy justifying 'redemptive' violence, oppression and deceit. The revolutionary circle full-turned, we are now tasked with prosecuting ourselves exactly the kinds of crimes and injustices that had animated the modern challenges to medieval Christian dogmata, thrones and altars at the inception of modernity:

> In any event, when the bourgeois class has disappeared, the proletariat will establish the rule of the universal man at the summit of production, by the very logic of productive development. What does it matter that this should be accomplished by dictatorship and violence? In this New Jerusalem, echoing with the roar of miraculous machinery, who will still remember the cry of the victim? The golden age, postponed until the end of history and coincident, to add to its attractions, with an apocalypse, ... justifies everything.[578]

7 Concluding Remarks: *Nuancer?*

It isn't difficult to see why Camus' criticism of Leninism and Stalinism in *L'Homme Révolté* should have outraged Sartre, Merleau-Ponty, and the intellectuals at *Les Temps Modernes*.[579] The book positions Leninism's ruthless political vanguardism as the logical, pragmatic consequence of the former's eschatological, prophetic ideological claims. Then it situates Stalin's excesses, up to and including the gulags, as just a more ruthless attempt to 'push for the end' of salvific History, to adapt an old messianic phrase.[580] Sartre and

---

577 Lenin, *What is to be done?*, at HR 284–285; R 226.
578 HR 262; R 207–208.
579 Aside from the aside against the "existentialists" as "subjected for the moment to the cult of history and its contradictions" in HR 310; R 249 ("Rebellion and revolution"); cf. Aronson, *Camus and Sartre*, 126.
580 Gershom Scholem, *The Messianic Idea in Judaism, and Other Essays on Jewish Spirituality* (London: Allen and Unwin, 1971), 14–15. Cf. "In opposition to [all such ideas] stands

Merleau-Ponty at this time, although not members of the PCF, had come to something very like the principle that, ironically, Camus had broadcast from the sheets of *Combat* in October 1944: namely, that all forms of anti-communism are the beginnings of reaction.[581] Sartre was more forthright, as his "Reply to Albert Camus" reflects: "an anti-communist is a dog."[582] Merleau-Ponty in *Humanism and Terror* of 1947, drawing on the same para-Hegelian reading of Marx by Alexandre Kojeve Camus is indebted to,[583] advocated for exactly the kind of distinction between legitimate, redemptive violence leading to the proletarian revolution, and other forms of political violence that Camus denies in *L'Homme Révolté*: "we don't have the choice between purity and violence, but between different sorts of violence... what counts and what it is necessary to discuss is not violence, it is its sense, and its future."[584]

However contemporary Parisian opinion assessed Camus' 1952 falling out with Sartre (see Chapter Six), Merleau-Ponty by 1956 and *The Adventures of the Dialectic* had already moderated his earlier position. After Hungary, Sartre too broke from the more or less uncritical proximity to Stalinism that had seen him publically condemn Camus only four years earlier.[585] Even Sartre in his last years was to undertake an "ethical turn." In interviews late in his life, Sartre revised his long-standing belief (still very much in place at the time of the Algerian war) that revolutionary violence could usher in a future fraternity of human beings[586] in terms which must have called his *pied noir* friend of the 1940s to mind. As we said in our Introduction, the fall of the Berlin wall and Soviet bloc after 1989 have made Camus' anti-Stalinism retrospectively seem unquestionably far-sighted, for all but a minority of extreme voices.

Paradoxically more pressing than Camus' anti-Stalinism in our present intellectual conjuncture, wherein the ethical turn of the 1970s has given way to theological recuperations, are the theoretical bases of Camus' critique of

---

the... powerful sentiment that the Messianic age cannot be calculated. This was most pointedly expressed in the words of a Talmudic teacher of the third century: 'three things come unawares: the Messiah, a found article, and a scorpion'." Scholem, *The Messianic Idea*, 11.

581 Camus, *Combat* October 7, 1944, at CAC 62.
582 Sartre in 1952 (following the arrest of two protesting PCF leaders, cited at Ian H. Birchall, *Sartre against Stalinism* (USA: Berghahn Press, 2004), 134. For Sartre's drift in 1948–1950 from existentialism as a counter to Marxism, to an existentialist Marxism willing to 'take sides' and espouse emancipatory violence, see Aronson, *Camus and Sartre*, 106–109.
583 Sabot, "Les Mésaventures de la dialectique: Camus critique de Kojève dans *L'Homme Rèvolté*", 45–60.
584 Merleau-Ponty cited at Sabot, "Les Mésaventures de la dialectique", 47.
585 Aronson, *Camus and Sartre*, 201–203.
586 See Bourg, *From Revolution to Ethics: May 1968 and Contemporary French Thought*, 320.

modern totalitarian regimes: not, to say it once more, as the deracinating, rationalising destroyers of religious transcendence but as the immanentised political bearers of the West's legacy of monotheistic messianism. For this is the very lineage of Western thought presently being widely revalorised amongst many post-Marxian theorists as the only basis to contest global neoliberalism.

Camus' fundamental ethical concern is that forms of political messianism can too readily allow proponents to rationalise very concrete, very real forms of political violence. They do this by appealing to transcendent claims, hopes and standards not subject to public, rational, dialogic agreement, given which really-existing human beings' claims to dignity can be 'strategically', violently pushed aside. Relative to today's theological turn, Camus' project announced in "Neither Victims and Executioners" to "define the conditions for a political position that is modest—i.e. free of messianism and disencumbered of nostalgia for an earthly paradise"[587] remains as untimely as Camus found it to be in Paris, 1951. An idea Camus flirts with in the *Carnets* at the time of his ongoing critical engagements over *L'Homme Révolté* for a "*comedie sur la presse*" jokes: "Be moderate (*nuancer*)? If I find a word like that again in your vocabulary, I will kick you out the door!"[588] Today, we can well imagine this speech coming from the mouths of a Žižek, a Badiou or one of their more militant intellectual admirers: whose forms of secularised political theology (as we will examine in Chapter Five) in fact offer us far less concerning what dispensation will follow the salvific Event than Marx, while inheriting earlier revolutionaries' scorn for any or all conceptions of 'moderation' as hopelessly irredeemable. In his never-published "Defence of *The Rebel*," Camus jokingly proposes that his position would doubtlessly have found a more favourable audience had he framed his appeal to classical *mesure* in the language of "hand to hand combat (*corps à corps*)" to "satisfy the thirst for strategy and heroism one finds in our literary society."[589]

To understand what Camus did and did not positively advocate, how and why, as his thought developed in the final two decades of his life is the task that now awaits us.

---

587 NVE 261 (end of second instalment, "November 20, 1946: Saving our Skins").
588 C III 43; C III Eng 31.
589 Albert Camus, "Défence de *L'Homme Révolté*", OC III 374.

PART 2

Turning Around, the Rough Ascent

∴

CHAPTER 3

Between All or Nothing: Camus with and against the 'Deconstruction of Western Metaphysics'

1   Contradictions: Situating the First Camus

At some time in 1933, the 19-year old Albert Camus, having published his first tentative essay on music the year before,[590] penned the following extraordinary meditative fragment. Suitably, it is entitled "Contradictions." Readers can glimpse within it many of the opposing considerations and exigencies Camus would spend the remainder of his short life wrestling with, and whose presence in Camus' works have continually invited partial understandings:

> Accept life, take it as it is? Stupid. The means of doing otherwise? Far from our having to take it, it is life that possesses us and on occasion shuts our mouths.
> Accept the human condition? I believe that, on the contrary, revolt is part of human nature.
> To pretend to accept what is imposed on us is a sinister comedy. First of all we must live. So many things are capable of being loved that it is ridiculous to seem to desire pain.
> Comedy. Pretence. One must be sincere. Sincere at any price, even to our own detriment.
> Neither revolt nor despair, moreover. Life with what it has. To accept it or revolt against it is to place oneself in opposition to life. Pure illusion. We are in life. It strikes us, mutilates us, spits in our face. It also illuminates us with crazy and sudden happiness that makes us participants. It is short. This is enough. Still make no mistake: there is pain. Impossible to evade. Perhaps, deep within ourselves, life's essential lot.
> Our contradictions. The mystics and Jesus Christ. Love. Communion. Certainly, but why waste words? More later.[591]

Ten years later, Camus' life had almost completely changed. No longer in his beloved native Algeria, Camus found himself living as an exile from his wife

---

590   See Albert Camus, "Essay on Music", FC 130–155.
591   Albert Camus, "Contradictions", FC 210.

and homeland, amidst the cold and stony facades of Paris. 1943 was the year Camus would join *Combat* and, despite his continuing literary ambitions, actively throw himself into the French resistance against the Nazi occupation. No longer an unknown from the colonies, the son of an impoverished and illiterate mother, the young author, journalist and *philosophe* had by 1943 gone a long way to becoming 'Camus'. His first novel *L'Étranger* appeared in 1941, and had been a *success de scandale*. Its accompanying philosophical essay, *Le Mythe de Sisyphe*, published in near-complete form soon afterwards (excepting the section on the Jewish author Kafka, censored under Vichy) was also enjoying notoriety. By the end of the year, Camus had begun his famous friendship with Sartre and Simone de Beauvoir, and been invited into the Parisian *rive gauche*'s most exclusive 'scene'.[592] Camus' first and most successful play, *Caligula*, was completed: awaiting the end of the occupation for its first successful Parisian season.[593]

These three works, especially *The Myth of Sisyphus*, remain famous to this day for expounding the notion of the 'absurd' which was to follow Camus in the popular mind until his death and beyond it. In the 1950 piece "Enigma" in *L'Été*, Camus would indeed complain of the way his name had become indissolubly tied to this term, many of whose implications he now rejected:

> ...the modern mania for identifying an author with his subject matter does not allow him to enjoy [any] relative liberty. Thus one becomes a prophet of the absurd. Yet what did I do except reason about an idea which I found in the streets of my time?...[594]

When the name Albert Camus is mentioned in most circles, this idea of him as a 'prophet of the absurd' is still the understanding. Camus is supposed to have held that the world was a godless, meaningless place: something like the sterile promontory Prince Hamlet lamented in Shakespeare, and which the younger Sartre sometimes evoked under the headers of 'being-in-itself' and the 'nausea' its naked confrontation can engender. In such a world, Sartre had argued, human beings enjoy the paradoxically inescapable responsibility to

---

592   Aronson, *Camus and Sartre*, 9–10, 19–21.
593   There are many authoritative accounts of Camus' life. For the war years in particular see Parker, "The Plague Years", in *Artist in the Arena*, 46–68, Lottman, *Albert Camus: A Biography*, Chapters 19–27; Olivier Todd, *Albert Camus: A Life* (USA: Alfred A. Knopf, 1997), Chapters 19–30.
594   E 159.

make up their own lives, and assign what passing meanings to them they can.[595] Condemned to be free, they can as well kiss or kill, both of which Meursault does in Camus' *The Stranger*, soon after impassively attending his own mother's funeral, as blank and murderous as the North African sun. At most a heroic ethics is possible in this metaphysical arrangement, shadowed everywhere by the incompletely-mourned absence of the fallen, providential, salvific Deity. Existentialism on this view (and Camus, on this view, is alongside Sartre one of the two definitive voices of post-war atheistic existentialism) may not be a humanism, although Sartre claimed this, and Camus ambivalently skirted the term.[596] It is a kind of dark romanticism.[597] The reader can think of reactionary critic Leo Strauss' depiction of later modern thinkers, after Nietzsche, as rebelling against the inherited Christian and monotheistic religions: not in the name of a joyous life-affirmation, but out of a grim "probity" that almost suspects the old faiths to the very extent they had provided consolations against the awful truth.[598]

It cannot be stressed enough that Camus always denied his existentialist credentials, and that this is 'a difference that makes a difference'.[599] His 1939 review of Sartre's *Nausea* already affirmed a basic difference of sensibility and worldview to his own: "it is the failing of a certain literature to believe that life is tragic because it is wretched. [But] life can be magnificent and overwhelming—*that* is its whole tragedy."[600] The "Contradictions"

---

595   Jean-Paul Sartre, *Being and Nothingness: An Essay on Phenomenological Ontology*, translated by Hazel E. Barnes (New York: Washington Square Press, 1984).

596   Jean-Paul Sartre, "Existentialism is a Humanism", *Existentialism from Dostoyevsky to Sartre*, ed. Walter Kaufman (Meridian Publishing Company, 1989); Aronson, *Camus and Sartre*, 47–48; cf. for Camus' ambivalence about the label, for example C II 172; C II Eng: 88 "I have nothing against humanism, of course. I find it inadequate, that is all" (alongside the claim, to which we will return in Chapter Five that "Greek thought for example was something other than a humanism. It was a thought that gave everything its place.") Compare C III 71–2; C III Eng 58, where Camus differentiates his admiration for some men, as against an abstract love of men in general—Camus seems inclined to associate "humanism" with an ideological abstraction, if not the disastrous ideological abstractions of the 20th century, although unsurprisingly he can and does differentiate "classical humanism" more favourably at C III 274; C III Eng 253.

597   See for instance the reading of Protestant theologian Harvey Cox in his *The Secular City: Secularisation and Urbanisation in Theological Perspective* (New York: Macmillan CO, 1965), 72–74 ("man doesn't simply discover meaning [for Camus] ... he originates it ...")

598   Leo Strauss, *Philosophy and Law* translated with Introduction by Eve Adler (USA: Suny 1995), 18–19.

599   See E 159–160; and Introduction above.

600   Camus, "Review of Jean-Paul Sartre's *Nausea*," LCE 201).

above already named love, communion, the mystical or Christ as "so many things... capable of being loved that it is ridiculous to seem to desire pain."[601] In an editorial in *Combat* in 1945 defending Sartre, Malraux and others against Christian critics' charges of promoting despair (and thereby Nazism), Camus affirmed that "I do not have much liking for the too famous existential philosophy, and, to tell the truth, I think its conclusions false."[602] We saw in Chapter Two how, faced with similar charges of being a pessimistic thinker, Camus turned the charge around against the pessimistic Augustinian anthropology.[603] Indeed, as we shall see in Chapter Six, Camus came more and more after 1945 to turn the categories of both existentialists and Christian critics on their heads: arguing that, if he is not an existentialist, it is because existentialism secularises or 'reoccupies' the Augustinian pessimism as to man, and as to the natural world. In a 1950 interview, Camus specified that it was a mistake to treat existentialism with levity, as if it might be a passing fad. It was in his eyes a very serious form of philosophical research whose origins reach back to Saint Augustine.[604]

This Chapter, which begins to mark out the spine of Camus' positive philosophical position, will continue challenging the popular images of Camus as existentialist, 'absurdist' or nihilist. In line with our work in the first two Chapters, reading Camus in light of more recent, more celebrated philosophical positions, here we want to use Jacques Derrida's "deconstruction of Western metaphysics" as our hermeneutic foil. Our aims will be several-fold. First, we will see how Camus' reflections on the absurd in *Le Mythe de Sisyphe* anticipate the key impulses underlying the later Algerian thinker's post-Heideggerian critiques of both Western philosophical rationalisms, and of attempts (in thinkers like Nietzsche, Bataille, or Levinas) to leave this tradition behind altogether. If we can do this work, given Derrida's influence in the Anglophone world since the mid-1970s, we shall once more have won significant ground in recovering Camus' credentials as a 'serious thinker'. Second, tracing Camus' reflections 'with and against deconstruction' will allow us to see very precisely the different critical and ethical trajectory Camus' work takes, in contrast to the later post-structuralist criticisms of Western philosophy: politically towards forms of democratic socialism, philosophically towards a renovated classicism.

---

601 Camus, "Contradictions", FC 210.
602 Camus, "Pessimism and Courage", 58.
603 Camus, "Unbeliever and Chrsitians", RRD 72.
604 Camus, "Interview au *Diario* de São Paulo (6 août 1949)" OC III 867.

2 Deconstructing Logocentrism, Philosophical Suicide

1933 was a very different year for the great philosopher Martin Heidegger than it was for the young Albert Camus, bumping up against his internal contradictions on the way to finding a literary and philosophical voice. Heidegger had long since made his name as the leading proponent of existentialist philosophy: a title which, in this way perhaps alone like Camus, he would deny.[605] 1927's *Sein und Zeit* remains a definitive work in 20th century European thought.[606] But on January 30, 1933, Adolf Hitler had come to power in Germany. Heidegger, soon after, in the first flushes of the National Socialist *Gleichschaltung*, very publically took on the position of *Führer-Rector* at Freiburg University.[607] His infamous rector's speech of May 1933, far from denouncing the barbarism of the Nazi regime, celebrated its advent in *Deutschland* as a moment of the highest spiritual import for the German people, and thereby for Europe.[608] Alongside Carl Schmitt, the leading jurisprudential and political thinker who joined the Nazi cause (following prompting from Heidegger), Heidegger's *imprimatur* would go some way to establishing the larger intellectual legitimacy of the National Socialist regime. The following year, shortly after the "Night of Long Knives," Heidegger would resign his rectorship: not without making significant efforts to reform Freiburg University. The 1935 "Introduction to Metaphysics" lectures (republished with the great thinker's approval in 1953) speak still of the "inner truth and greatness" of the Nazi regime.[609] The continuing publication of his Nazi-era lectures of the 1930s into the 1940s show the full, troubling dimensions of Heidegger's proximities to this radically anti-modern, radically bellicose regime.[610] Heidegger would never resign his Party card. He retained

---

605 Martin Heidegger, "Letter on Humanism", in David Krell ed. *Basic Writings* (New York: Harper and Row, 1977), 189–242.
606 Martin Heidegger, *Being and Time* translated by J. Macquarie and E. Robinson (London: Blackwell, 1978).
607 Cf. esp. Hugo Ott, *Martin Heidegger: A Political Life* trans. Allan Blunden (New York: Basic, 1993).
608 See Martin Heidegger, "Self-Assertion of the German University" in Richard Wolin *The Heidegger Controversy* (USA: MIT Press, 1993), 29–39.
609 Martin Heidegger, *Introduction to Metaphysics* trans. Gregory Fried and Richard Polt (Yale: Yale University Press, 2000), this sentence, excised from this edition, is cited in the Preface at p. xv; cf. William H.F. Altman, *Leo Strauss: The German Stranger* (USA: Lexington, 2010), 172–180; and by the same author, *Martin Heidegger and the First World War: Being and Time as Funeral Oration* (USA: Lexington, 2012).
610 See Emmanuel Faye, *Heidegger: The Introduction of Nazism into Philosophy in Light of the Unpublished Seminars of 1933–1935*, Michael B. Smith (tr.), Yale University Press, 2009;

a near-complete silence concerning the atrocities of the Shoah, despite the ardent requests of several of his former students and admirers.[611]

Whereas Heidegger's thought was for a long time untouchable in Germany after the war, the decades following the Second World War saw Heidegger's work increasingly welcomed across the Rhine. Alongside Nietzsche, another thinker whose appropriation by the Nazis made him more controversial in Germany, Heidegger is one of the key thinkers underlying the 'post-structuralist' generation of authors in Paris following 1960 led by Derrida, Foucault, Lyotard, and Gilles Deleuze. 1987's publication of Victor Farias' *Heidegger and Nazism*, revealing to the French reading public the extent of Heidegger's political commitments, hence caused a shock of comparable magnitude to that of Solzenitzyn's *Gulag Archipelago* of a decade before.[612] Although Farias' book contained little that was factually new relative to what had appeared in Germany, and although the author's own questionable philosophical credentials formed an easy diversion for Heidegger's defenders, Farias' work made French neoHeideggerians confront a burning issue. How could one of the most important philosophers of the century, and someone whose legacy had been appealed to in the wake of the fall of Marxism to ground a good deal of critical reflection in France have been an outspoken advocate of fascism? If, as Foucault had written in his 1977 "Preface" to Deleuze and Guattari's *Anti-Oedipus*, it was above all a matter of "getting rid of the fascism in our heads",[613] how could we have been attempting this by appropriating motifs from thinkers who were vociferous philosophical advocates for Adolf Hitler's Third Reich?

For all of the thinkers who tried (and continue to try in different ways) to 'save Heidegger's name', the dating of Heidegger's National Socialist activities was decisive. For some time in the decisive Nazi years of 1933–1936, Heidegger

---

Dominic Losurdo, *Heidegger and the Ideology of War: Community, Death and the West* (USA: Humanity Books, 2001).

611   The exception, until 2015 and the already-notorious *Black Books*, is another controversial remark equating mechanised agriculture with the *shoah*, as both reflections of modern *gestell*: "Agriculture is now a mechanised food industry, in essence the same as the manufacturing of corpses in gas chambers and extermination camps, the same as the blockade and starvation of nations, the same as the production of hydrogen bombs..." This extraordinarily blithe and ambiguous passage was first published by Wolfgang Schirmacher, *Technik und Gelassenheit: Zeitkritik nach Heidegger* (Freiburg and Munich, 1983), at p. 25. It is cited in Tom Rockmore, *On Heidegger's Nazism and Philosophy* (Berkeley – Los Angeles, Oxford: University of Califiornia Press, 1991), 241, note 128.

612   See Chapter One above, setion *"Nouvelle philosophe avant la lettre?"*.

613   Michel Foucault, "Preface" to *Anti-Oedipus: Capitalism and Schizophrenia* Translated from the French by Robert Hurley, Mark Seem, and Helen R. Lane (Minneapolis: University of Minnesota Press, 1983), xii.

scholars mostly agree, the great thinker's thought underwent a 'turn' or *kehre*. His earlier work, to which many French Heideggerians now pointed in accusation, had been 'existentialist'. It led up to the valorisation of a formal, decisionistic choice that an individual or collective *dasein* needed to make, in order to wrest its authenticity from the mediocrity of modern urban culture. This kind of position, it was argued by recourse to "Heidegger II" (the Heidegger of after his *kehre*, as "historian of Being") remained in sway to the kind of "philosophy of subjectivity" that in France, under Heidegger's influence, Sartre would celebrate in *L'Être et Néant*.[614] Yet, it was argued, it was just such a 'metaphysical' position, whose *'destruktion'* had been announced in the "Introduction" of *Being and Time* but not completed by 1933, that the later Heidegger's work on the "history of Being" was supposed to decisively deliver us from.

Jacques Derrida, the most famous French post-Heideggerian thinker outside of the Hexagon, argued a particular variation of this apologetic position in *De l'Esprit* of 1987.[615] For Derrida, if we look at the rhetoric of Heidegger's Nazi speeches, we find a series of unreconstructed commitments to notions like "spirit" ("the hymn to the freedom of the spirit.... across the European network")[616] which Heidegger had allegedly insufficiently 'deconstructed' in *Sein und Zeit*, in a way which allowed for his disastrous dalliance with National Socialism. For Derrida, in a variety of the total critiques of modernity and reason we met in Chapter One, it was "the transcendental teleology of European humanism" that underlay the Nazi adventure. According to this position, as paradoxical as this can sound, Nazism was a 'humanism'.[617] "Even if all forms

---

614   Luc Ferry and Alain Renaut, *Heidegger and Modernity* (Chicago: Chicago University Press, 1990), 31–54.

615   Jacques Derrida, *Of Spirit: Heidegger and the Question* trans. A. Bloomington and R. Bowlby (Chicago: Chicago University Press, 1989).

616   Jacques Derrida, "Heidegger: The Philosopher's Hell," in *Points. Interviews 1974–1994*, edited by Elizabeth Weber, translated by Peggy Kamuf et al., 181–90, (Stanford, Calif: Stanford University Press, 1995), 186.

617   Ferry and Renaut, *Heidegger and Modernity*, 31–54. One needs to understand how, following Heidegger, humanism in the post-structuralist context comes improbably to be identified (a) with "modernity" as the age of *technik* and (b) with Cartesianism (whose scientific and cultural stocks had run low by the late 17th century, following the Newtonian revolution. This for instance can be clearly seen in Voltaire's hugely influential *Philosophical Dictionary* of 1764, in which Descartes is presented as a speculative romançier, whose physics is a fantasy, and the only part of whose philosophy remains viable is the methodological scepticism (cf. Voltaire, *Philosophical Dictionary*, "Atoms," "Ovid," "Philosophy", "Poets," "Sensations," "Soul", trans. William F. Fleming: at www-site https://ebooks.adelaide.edu.au/v/voltaire/dictionary/complete.html, last accessed December 2014). While we cannot pursue this here, the post-structuralists' blindness or partiality

of complicity" with this teleology of European humanism "are not equivalent," Derrida concedes, "they are irreducible: a complex and unstable skein I try to unravel by recognising the threads shared by Nazism and non-Nazism."[618]

Derrida's defence of Heidegger in the "Heidegger Wars" drew directly on his own, post-Heideggerian project for the 'deconstruction of Western metaphysics' or 'logocentrism'—to arrive now at the point where our comparison with Camus will, more directly, commence. According to this position (one which as Thomas McCarthy notes, Derrida always claimed was of political import),[619] the agonies of the twentieth century European experience were related to "something ancient and hidden in [the West's] history."[620] Adopting Heidegger's post-war reflections on modernity as the age of *technik*, Derrida at times spoke of the West's "principle of integral calculability," operative in its "purportedly 'modern' reason and technoscience."[621] However, like his teacher (and like the secularization theorists we met in Chapter Two), Derrida relativised modern thought's claim to originality, as the inverted commas around 'modern' here attest. Modern technoscience, he followed his teacher Heidegger, was but "the verbal formulation of a requirement present since the dawn of Western science." This was the requirement which Derrida calls "logocentrism," aspiring ultimately to "technical mastery over the totality of what is."[622] Its origins, just as Heidegger had claimed, lay in Plato if not the pre-Socratics,[623] long before this logocentrism issued more or less inevitably in the modern technological and political dispensations. If we are to understand the peculiar violence of the twentieth century (which we have seen Camus very much wanted to do) Derrida assigns this to a "rapport of violence with the Other" allegedly embedded in Western philosophical conceptuality. This philosophical "violence," he argued, lies in "structural solidarity" with the concrete

---

towards the French 18th century is remarkable in a predominantly French generation of thinkers.

618   Derrida, "Philosopher's Hell," 186.
619   See Thomas McCarthy, "The Politics of the Ineffable", *Philosophical Forum*, Volume XXI, Nos 1 and 2, Fall-Winter, 1989–90; pp. 146–7, 163–4; cf. Peter Dews, *Logics of Disintegration: Poststructuralist Thought and the Claims of Critical Theory* (London: Verso, 2006), 35.
620   Jacques Derrida, in interview with Richard Kearney: "Deconstruction and the Other", in Richard Kearney ed., *Dialogues with Contemporary Continental Thinkers* (Manchester: University Press, 1984), 112.
621   Jacques Derrida, "Principle of Reason: The University in the Eyes of its Pupils", *Diacritics* XIX (1983): 3–20, at 14.
622   Derrida, "Principle of Reason", 8; cf. 9–10; "Deconstruction and the Other", 114.
623   Jacques Derrida, *Dissemination* translated with an Introduction and additional notes by Barbara Johnson (London: The Athlone Press, 1981).

violences of the Western "defensive and offensive security establishment."[624] Deconstruction's calling into question of "that which ... continues to be based on the principle of reason"[625] for this reason is not politically neutral. It intervenes at the point of a "trembling" of Western identity, or so Derrida claims in "The Ends of Man", a talk delivered in the fateful year of 1968, as Derrida makes a point of underlining.[626]

What deconstruction *does* during this intervention, famously, is a variety of the Heideggerian critique of 'ontotheology.' Deconstruction shows how the claims to conceptual clarity, transparency, and mastery Western philosophers have made cannot be rightly accepted. Decisive for Derrida's thought, very much of its moment in the French milieu after Levi-Strauss' *Pensée Sauvage*, is a claim for the irreducible primacy of language to both thought and meaning. This claim emerges in his decisive 'deconstruction' of the founding phenomenologist Edmund Husserl's work in his ground-breaking "Introduction" to Husserl's *Origins of Geometry*. Like Heidegger's before him, Derrida's account of the temporal dimension of meaning-formation is anticipated in Husserl's account of internal time-consciousness: in which the phenomenologist had observed how our ability to understand present things rests upon a series or retentions and protentions which also already *divide* the living present.[627] Husserl famously claimed that meaning emerges for human beings through the meaning-bestowal of transcendental consciousness, which intuits the atemporal essences of what it perceives. Yet, Derrida argues, when Husserl comes to reflect on the transmission of such alleged 'essential,' consciously-constituted and present meanings, and on the preservation of stable "geometrical ideality" across time, he is forced to admit the role of language: "no longer simply [as] the expression of that which would, without it, already be an object," but as something that plays a role in "constituting the object and [being] a juridical condition of its truth."[628]

---

624   Derrida, "Principle of Reason", 13–14.
625   Derrida, "Principle of Reason," 16.
626   Jacques Derrida, "Ends of Man", *Margins of Philosophy* trans Alan Bass (Chicago: Chicago University Press, 1986), 134–5; Jacques Derrida, *Of Grammatology* trans Gayatry Chakravorty Spivak (Baltimore and London: John Hopkins University Press, 1976), 3–5; Jacques Derrida (and Rohard Kearney) "Deconstruction and the Other," 116–7; Jacques Derrida, *Positions* translated and annotated by Alan Bass (London: Athlone Press, 1981), 91.
627   Jacques Derrida, *Speech and Phenomena* (Evanston: The John Hopkins University Press, 1973), 50–54; *Of Grammatology*, 62.
628   Jacques Derrida, *Edmund Husserl's 'Origin of Geometry': An Introduction* by trans. John P. Leavey (USA: University of Nebraska Press, 1989), 76 [sic.]).

The force of this concession, for Derrida, is monumental. For language, here admitted into the transcendental processes underlying meaning-bestowal, is trans-individual. Beyond the intentionality of any transcendental, individual subject, it is a changing historical and material medium. As such, it always enshrines the possibility of a radical loss of meaning in its "primordial purity," as imagined or intuited by an isolated subject.[629] Indeed, in written language, a person's words can continue circulating and generating untold responses long after the author is dead.

Derrida's positive account of language, meanwhile, hails not from phenomenology, but from structuralism. As he had done with Husserl, Derrida reads Saussure's structuralist linguistics 'against himself' or Saussure's own intentions. These held to a priority of "living speech" (and behind it, a meaning-constituting subject) over writing as the basis for understanding language.[630] Yet Derrida, with and against the master, takes very seriously Saussure's demonstration that meaning in language can only be generated from material signifiers (vocables, written marks, hand gestures, whatever). Signification emerges on this model only on the basis of these signifiers' structured differences from other such signifiers in a given linguistic system. If we take this discovery seriously, Derrida maintains, it stands to upset the founding "logocentric" suppositions of Western philosophy: since philosophical thinkers have again and again argued that meaning rested upon stable, unchanging "transcendental signifieds": grand ideas like God, the subject, essences, or the Platonic Ideas. If Saussure is right, Derrida claims, "no element can function as a sign without referring to other elements."[631] Each sign, whatever its ostensible referent, is constituted differentially, all the way down, without substantive remainder. Philosophers who have tried to stabilise rational systems by assigning unchangeable meanings to key 'transcendental signifieds' stand accused of a grand *méconnaissance*. They try, impossibly, to "uproot the presence of meaning from difference"[632] or "regulate the circulation of signs, drawing along with it all the reassuring signifieds, reducing all the ... out-of-bounds shelters..."[633] For Derrida, whose founding debt to Husserl here recurs, behind these attempts we are to see a "transcendental illusion": that of a sovereign

---

629 Derrida, *Edmund Husserl's 'Origin of Geometry'*, 88; *Of Grammatology*, 37–40; "Signature, Event, Context", *Margins of Philosophy* tr. Alan Bass (Chicago: Chicago University Press, 1982) 316 ff.
630 Derrida, *Of Grammatology*, 3–73.
631 Derrida, *Positions*, 26; cf. Derrida, "Differance", *Margins of Philosophy*, 5, 10–12, 15–16; *Of Grammatology*, esp. 48–52.
632 Derrida, *Positions*, 32.
633 Derrida, *Of Grammatology*, 7.

subject who "hears itself speaking", and in an exercise of metaphysical 'auto-affection', fancies itself in complete Godlike control of its own meanings.[634] Importantly for Derrida and for us, deconstruction is premised on the way that such attempts must fail. Their failures leave textual traces or marks, points of undecidability or simple logical inconsistency, which the astute 'deconstructive' reader can seek out and decry.

What though have Derrida's 'deconstructive' premises to do with Albert Camus' thought, from a full generation earlier? Camus' *Myth of Sisyphus*, it will be protested, opens by posing the distinctly 'existential,' individual or subjectivistic question of whether suicide is ever rationally justifiable.[635] It declares that all other questions (amongst which we must presumably include Derrida's concerning language or 'logocentrism') are by comparison not "truly serious".[636] Camus' famous delineation of the absurd, moreover, begins phenomenologically, examining what Camus calls several "unconscious feelings in the face of the universe" which can strike us,[637] before he turns to the philosophical notion of the absurd. If 'feeling' is a category at all in Derrida's texts, it is a marginal one. It seems to carry with it the kind of focus on subjective experience disqualified by his post-structuralist sense of the subject's secondary status, behind that of language. Yet here is Camus:

> It happens that the stage sets collapse. Rising, streetcar, four hours in the office or the factory, meal, streetcar, four hours of work, meal, sleep, and Monday, Tuesday, Wednesday, Thursday, Friday and Saturday according to the same rhythm—this path is easily followed most of the time. But one day the "why" arises and everything begins in that weariness tinged with amazement.[638]

We then get a delineation of three kinds of experience in which the absurd feeling is encountered. The first, approaching the younger Heidegger (whom Camus, for nearly the only time in his *oeuvre*, evokes) is the anticipation of death:

> ... a day comes when a man notices or says that he is thirty. Thus he asserts his youth. But simultaneously he situates himself in relation to time.

---

634 Derrida, *Of Grammatology*, 7–9; *Positions*, 22; "Deconstruction and the Other", 115–116.
635 MS 7; MSe 3.
636 MS 7; MSe 3.
637 MS 34; MSe 17.
638 MS 29; MSe 12–13.

> He takes his place in it. He admits that he stands at a certain point on a curve that he acknowledges having to travel to its end. He belongs to time, and by the horror that seizes him, he recognizes his worst enemy. Tomorrow, he was longing for tomorrow, whereas everything in him ought to reject it.[639]

A look at Camus' earlier *Carnets* and the essay "Wind at Djemila" in *Noces* of 1938 confirms a biographical basis of Camus' analysis here. Told at 17 that he suffered from tuberculosis, Camus' experience from this time was coloured by an unusually intimate sense of the proximity of death, periodically heightened by his relapses of the disease. He was personally acquainted with what he terms "the physical terror of the animal who loves the sun"[640] or what *Le Mythe* calls "the revolt of the flesh." This remains one wellspring of his ethical sensibility.[641]

Next in *The Myth of Sisyphus*, there is the following remarkable passage concerning an element of "absurdity" Camus thinks confronts us when we are moved by the beauty of nature (a passage to which we will return in Chapter Five):

> At the heart of all beauty lies something inhuman, and these hills, the softness of the sky, the outline of these trees at this very minute lose the illusory meaning with which we had clothed them, henceforth more remote than a lost paradise. The primitive hostility of the world rises up to face us across millennia, and for a second we cease to understand it because for centuries we have understood in it solely the images and designs that we had attributed to it beforehand, because henceforth we lack the power to make use of that artifice.[642]

Finally, Camus tells us that the absurd feeling (one whose proximity to the comic he duly notes)[643] can strike us when we perceive this same uncanny "inhumanity" in human beings, or even ourselves:

> Men, too, secrete the inhuman. At certain moments of lucidity, the mechanical aspect of their gestures, their meaningless pantomime makes

---

639   MS 30; MSe 13–14. It is fair to say that the force of this reflection on death, although Heidegger is mentioned, is not derivatively or specifically 'Heideggerian'. See Chapter Six below on the *memento mori* as spiritual exercise.
640   Camus, "Wind at Djemila," LCE 77.
641   MS 30; MSe 14.
642   MS 30; MSe 14.
643   MS 49–50; MSe 29–30.

silly everything that surrounds them. A man is talking on the telephone behind a glass partition; you cannot hear him, but you see his incomprehensible dumb show... Likewise the stranger who at certain seconds comes to meet us in a mirror, the familiar and yet alarming brother we encounter in our own photographs is also the absurd.[644]

At this point, however, I want to contend that the seemingly vast distance between Camus' phenomenological analyses of the absurd and Derrida's structuralist-informed ruminations on the uncanny *"differance"* which underlies ordinary sense-making begins to diminish. To be sure, Camus later in *Le Mythe de Sisyphe* goes to some trouble to situate his reflections with critical reference to the existentialist heritage of the first decades of the 20th century, one hearkening back to Kierkegaard and Zarathrustra.[645] Yet, however so much Camus' descriptive method owes to phenomenology (and indeed, we will see that he like Derrida finds much to praise in the descriptive, rather than systematic, dimensions of Husserl's work),[646] what this phenomenology uncovers is not the sovereignty of an individual subject, in full command of its meanings and surrounds. Camus depicts for us a subject struck from time to time by the *collapse* of its sense of established order in the world, and periodically affronted by the mechanical, uncannily foreign aspect to its own body and movements, and those of its fellows. As the young Camus had said, "life strikes us, mutilates us, spits in our face." It can present the visage of a "sinister comedy".[647] It is as if in such moments, indeed, that life is at once too close (consider the "mathematical" aspect of the aging of our own bodies Camus describes above), yet utterly remote and inhuman: "it eludes us since it has returned to itself again."[648]

"The criticism of rationalism has been made so often that it seems unnecessary to begin again," Camus acknowledges.[649] Yet, two decades before his great Algerian successor (and sometime admirer)[650] who would begin it again, Camus admits the sympathy of his approach with "those paradoxical systems

---

644 MS 31; MSe 14–15.
645 MS 41–47; MSe 22–28.
646 MS 64–66; MSe 43–44; see below.
647 Camus, "Contradictions", FC 210.
648 MS 30–31; MSe 14.
649 MS 41; MSe 22–23.
650 Edward Baring, "Liberalism and the Algerian War: The Case of Jacques Derrida", *Critical Inquiry* Vol. 36, No. 2 (Winter 2010), pp. 239–261.

that strive to trip up the reason as if truly it had always forged ahead."[651] He is unconvinced of the capacity of science, or any philosophical system, to answer to all human beings' epistemic needs:

> ... all the knowledge on earth will give me nothing to assure me that this world is mine. You describe it to me and you teach me to classify it. You enumerate its laws and in my thirst for knowledge I admit that they are true. You take apart its mechanism and my hope increases. At the final stage you teach me that this wondrous and multi-coloured universe can be reduced to the atom and that the atom itself can be reduced to the electron. All this is good and I wait for you to continue. But you tell me of an invisible planetary system in which electrons gravitate around a nucleus. You explain this world to me with an image. I realize then that you have been reduced to poetry: I shall never know.[652]

However, in a way that provides the most direct point of comparison with Derrida, it is Edmund Husserl who stands as representative in *The Myth of Sisyphus* of the kind of philosophical rationalism Camus opposes. Even the two sides of Camus' reading of Husserl reflect, albeit in a much more condensed form, the kinds of 'two-handed' readings of philosophers Derrida would later become famous for.[653] Evidently thinking of the kind of purely descriptive phenomenology Husserl undertook in *The Logical Investigations*,

---

651 MS 40; MSe 22.

652 MS 37–38; MSe 19–20. As we have seen, that science does not deliver metaphysical essences does not mean for Camus that it does not have relative, progressive, descriptive credentials that should not be dismissed.

653 I refer to the famous statement in Derrida, "Signature, Event, Context", 329–330: "Deconstruction cannot limit itself or proceed immediately to a neutralization: it must, by means of a double gesture, a double science, a double writing, practice an overturning of the classical opposition and a general displacement of the system.... Each concept, moreover, belongs to a systematic chain, and itself constitutes a system of predicates. There is no metaphysical concept in and of itself.... Deconstruction does not consist in passing from one concept to another, but in overturning and displacing a conceptual order, as well as the nonconceptual order with which the conceptual order is articulated. For example, writing, as a classical concept, carries with it predicates which have been subordinated, excluded, or held in reserve by forces and according to necessities to be analyzed. It is these predicates... whose force of generality, generalization, and generativity find themselves liberated, grafted onto a 'new' concept of writing which also corresponds to whatever always has resisted the former organization of forces, which always has constituted the remainder irreducible to the dominant force which organized the— to say it quickly—logocentric hierarchy...".

Camus is impressed with Husserl's description of phenomenological method. He is attracted to the idea of practicing an "intentional discipline" that "limits itself to describing what it declines to explain"; but "aims to elucidate what it cannot transcend"; "awakening... a sleeping world and... making it vivid to the mind."[654] In a transport of enthusiasm, Camus compares Husserl almost to a philosophical Proust who:

> ... reinstate[s] the world in its diversity... The rose petal, the milestone, or the human hand are as important as love, desire, or the laws of gravity. Thinking ceases to be unifying or making a semblance familiar in the guise of a major principle. Thinking is learning all over again to see, to be attentive, to focus consciousness; it is turning every idea and every image... into a privileged moment.[655]

Nevertheless, the way Husserl then reflectively, metaphysically categorises what this phenomenological description brings to light attracts Camus' critical ire, no less than it later provoked Derrida. Camus specifically targets Husserl's key claim that conscious intuition can unearth the unchanging essences of the things it perceives. When Husserl begins to talk of "eidetic intuition" after 1900, Camus claims, we meet with a kind of modern metaphysical Platonism. It is just that, as against Plato (or Plotinus) to the extent that they elevated the Good above all other ideas, in Husserl there are as many "essences" as there are different natural kinds. Husserl's is "a formal army composed exclusively of generals," in Camus' lovely phrase.[656] "Platonic realism becomes intuitive, but it is still realism," Camus observes.[657] When Husserl posits an idea of eternal natural and psychological laws, above and beyond possible human experience, for Camus this is nothing else than a highly abstract "metaphysic of consolation... after having denied the integrating power of human reason, [Husserl] leaps by this expedient to eternal Reason."[658] But for a mind imbued with the experience of the absurd, Camus argues, this is beyond what can justly be assented to: "That geometrical place (*lieu*) where divine reason ratifies mine will always be incomprehensible to me."[659] What will be required is a modern form of *eucatalepsia*: the reflective, sceptical suspension of judgment before

---

654 MS 65; MSe 43–44.
655 MS 65; MSe 43.
656 MS 67–68; MSe 45.
657 MS 67; MSe 45.
658 MS 68; MSe 46.
659 MS 68; MSe 46.

what exceeds understanding, which we will see lies at the heart or basis of Camus' positive philosophy.

3 The Middle Path between Irrationalism and Rationalism

Camus' criticism of a figure like Husserl in *Le Mythe de Sisyphe*, like his later critique in *L'Homme Révolté* of Hegel's notion of Absolute Knowledge and an End of History, underlie his popular image as a kind of philosophical irrationalist or 'nihilist'. Is not his avowal of the absurd a definitive philosophical hymn to the nihilistic view that "nothing is clear, all is chaos…",[660] leaving man abandoned, a metaphysical exile in an alien cosmos? Following Ronald Srigley's incisive recent analysis, I want to show now both that this is *not* Camus' position and that, nevertheless, there *are* statements in *The Myth of Sisyphus* and elsewhere which can encourage commentators to form this idea. There is a way of setting up the problems with which Camus is concerned, inherited from Christian theology (as Hans Blumenberg would alert us).[661] This way suggests that the world, in order to have any 'meaning', must have a providential purpose, willed by a transcendent deity. To be 'meaningful' here means not simply to be ordered and rationally comprehensible (something science has not ceased affirming of the world, in principle and fact). It means to have been created for some larger, and anthropocentric, purpose by a volitional, soter Deity. We will return to this vital stipulation in Chapter Five, whose importance is staggering.

Camus, certainly, denies that we could ever *know* whether there is such a providential order and such a Transcendent Deity. In Chapter Two we saw that Camus thinks the reality of senseless suffering calls into question the justice, love, or wisdom of any such Transcendent Deity. With that said, throughout *The Myth of Sisyphus* Camus as it were 'falls back' at different points to a theological way of framing his position, asserting ontological-sounding claims that, without a knowable salvific deity, the world 'has no meaning'. He can evoke "this chaos, … sovereign chance and … divine equivalence which springs from anarchy", "this mad world", "this ridiculous reason that sets me in opposition to all creation."[662] He can ask rhetorically: "A stranger to myself and to the world, armed solely with a thought that negates itself as soon as it asserts, what is this condition in which I can have peace only by refusing to know and to live, in

---

660   MS 46; MSe 27.
661   See Chapter Two above.
662   MS 75; MSe 51.

which the appetite for conquest bumps into walls that defy its assaults?"⁶⁶³ Yet, this being the other side of Camus' seeming 'contradiction' here, in the same passages it becomes clear that Camus does not take himself to be licensed to make any such metaphysical claims. His intention is a more measured epistemological claim: *viz.* that, whether or not such a higher theological 'meaning' exists, *it is unavailable to us*. "I don't know whether this world has a meaning that transcends it," Camus at one point specifies: "But I do know that I do not know that meaning and it is impossible for me just now to know it."⁶⁶⁴ Elsewhere, he checks his manner of speaking ontologically: "I said that the world is absurd, but I was too hasty. This world in itself is not reasonable, that is all that can be said."⁶⁶⁵

So what then is Camus' absurd, if not a defiant claim for something like Sartre's "senseless passion" of human existence or of the senselessness of the world? Actually, as Camus would protest, *The Myth of Sisyphus* is clear enough. When we call something "absurd," we are not dismissing it by itself, as 'without meaning'. The idea is comparative. A peasant girl who wants to marry a prince has an 'absurd' dream. For what she wants is hopelessly out of proportion with her real prospects. Likewise Don Quixote tilting at the windmill is absurd; in the sense that his self-conception is so wildly out of touch with reality: "[i]n each of these cases, the magnitude of the absurdity will be in direct ratio to the distance between the two terms of my comparison," not in either term itself, Camus observes.⁶⁶⁶ Just so, when it comes to the absurd in the philosophical sense relevant to assessing whether life is worth living, we are dealing not with an absolute claim about reality, but a comparative claim about some agent's or agents' relationship with reality. "The absurd ... lies in neither of the elements compared; it is born of their confrontation."⁶⁶⁷

And what are the elements compared in this philosophical case? Camus specifies: "the absurd is not in man (if such a metaphor could have a meaning) nor in the world [we note this especially], but in their presence together."⁶⁶⁸

---

663   MS 38; MSe 20.
664   MS 75; MSe 51.
665   MS 39 ("Ce monde en lui-même n'est pas raissonable, c'est tout ce qu'on en peut dire ..."); MSe 21. It is a similar kind of deflationary logic in play when Camus reflects of the notion of original sin in the *Carnets*: "The revolutionary mind rejects original sin. By so doing, it sinks into it. The Greek mind does not think of it. By so doing, it escapes from it." C II 339; C II Eng 174. We will see in "Prometheus Reclaimed: from the philosophers to the poets" in Chapter Five below the larger basis for this claim on behalf of the Greeks.
666   MS 50; MSe 29.
667   MS 50; MSe 29.
668   MS 50; MSe 30.

We touch here upon the immovable basis of Camus' philosophical position. Human beings, for Camus, are beings who need, cognitively and viscerally, to unify their experience:

> The mind's deepest desire, even in its most elaborate operations, parallels man's unconscious feeling in the face of his universe: it is an insistence upon familiarity, an appetite for clarity. Understanding the world for a man is reducing it to the human, stamping it with his seal..... The truism "All thought is anthropomorphic" has no other meaning. Likewise, the mind that aims to understand reality can consider itself satisfied only by reducing it to terms of thought. If man realized that the universe like him can love and suffer, he would be reconciled. If thought discovered in the shimmering mirrors of phenomena eternal relations capable of summing them up and summing themselves up in a single principle, then would be seen an intellectual joy of which the myth of the blessed would be but a ridiculous imitation.[669]

Camus never cedes on the idea that "that nostalgia for unity... illustrates the essential impulse of the human drama."[670] This position, which we saw in the "Introduction" he associates from his early work with Plotinus' philosophical psychology,[671] sees him sympathetically disposed towards religious claims of a certain kind, in ways which differentiate him from Sartre and many others. Nevertheless, what experiences of the *unheimlich* elements of our lives and others' attests (alongside what we confront philosophically when we acknowledge the limits of reason) is that "the fact of that nostalgia's existence does not imply that it is to be... satisfied."[672] No more than the fancy of every peasant girl to marry the prince guarantees her royal nuptials can we take the evidence of the "appetite for the absolute"[673] in the human mind and heart to attest to the satiability of this appetite. The absurd is what results from the "confrontation" between the human desire for unity and a world in which "the key words,

---

669   MS 34; MSe 17.
670   MS 34; MSe 17.
671   See Camus, "Summer in Algiers", 90; with *Christian Metaphysics and Neoplatonism*, 90; & I.H. Walker, 'Camus, Plotinus, and *'Patrie'*: the Remaking of a Myth', *Modern Language Review*, 77: 4 (October 1982), 829–39.
672   MS 34; MSe 17.
673   MS 34; MSe 17.

the final secrets, are not in man's possession."[674] It is "essentially a divorce" between our metaphysical hopes and reflective awareness of our own limits. Initially at least, "it binds [the person and the world] as only hatred can weld two creatures together," Camus dramatically proclaims.[675]

As a direct inferential consequence of this measured critique of Rationalisms, we see Camus anticipating a further theme of Derrida's post-Heideggerian deconstruction: one which it is easy to read as more culturally conservative than radical,[676] but which echoes themes in Foucault and Lacan from the same period. We mean Derrida's second critical claim, which is to assert that while the "logocentric" or "phonocentric" ambition of a fully consistent, world-disclosing philosophical system is ill-conceived, the attempts of figures from Nietzsche through Bataille and Levinas to wholly escape from "Western metaphysics" and its founding commitments are equally impossible to achieve. "I do not believe in decisive ruptures, in an unequivocal 'epistemological break'", Derrida explains, using a phrase made fashionable by Althusser's structuralist rereading of Marx: "...the risk of metaphysical reappropriation is ineluctable..."[677] Derrida is for instance deeply sympathetic with Emmanuel Levinas' attempts to challenge "Greek" philosophical conceptuality, founding an account of the subject on our responsibility to the Other, rather than the alleged sovereignty of consciousness or the subject (see Chapter Four).[678] Likewise, he finds Bataille's search for a "general economy" opening out onto un-recuperated excess congenial, as an anticipation of that "dissemination" of sense his own deconstructive readings of philosophical and literary texts aim at.[679] Nevertheless, Derrida's readings of these figures (for example, in the magnificent essay "Violence and Metaphysics" on Levinas) are largely devoted to showing that it is not so easy to avoid, or to overcome, the West's founding metaphysical oppositions of self-Other, high-low, light-dark, peace-violence, male-female, ideal-real...[680] To merely reverse the priorities

---

674   Camus, "Roger Martin du Gard" LCE 286: "...but man retains the power to judge and to absolve".
675   MS 39; MSe 21.
676   E.g. Dews, "Nouvelle Philosophie and Foucault", 163–165.
677   Derrida, *Positions*, 58; 24; Derrida, "Principle of Reason", 17; 19; Derrida, "Ends of Man", 134 ff.
678   Jacques Derrida, "Violence and Metaphysics" in *Writing and Difference* trans. Alan Bass (Chicago: Chicago University Press, 1978), 79–153.
679   Jacques Derrida, "From Restricted to General Economy: An Hegelianism without Reserve", *Writing and Difference* trans. Alan Bass (Chicago: Chicago University Press, 1978), 317–350.
680   Derrida, "Violence and Metaphysics" in *Writing and Difference* trans. Alan Bass (London: Routledge Classics, 2001), 97–192.

in these, usually hierarchically-coded binaries (by following Nietzsche for instance, and prioritising becoming over being), is for Derrida to reproduce the dominant system one is resisting:[681] just as if Camus, in our case, were the facile atheist he is accused by theological critics of being who maintained that the world must be bereft of any sense, since he denies the knowability of the God the West long extolled. While Derrida thus in "Signature, Event, Context" admits a provisional value in moves like Nietzsche's prioritising becoming over being, what deconstruction aims at is a moving beyond such oppositions.[682] The logic here is closer to Nietzsche's declamations in *Twilight of the Idols* on "how the true world became a fable": "The true world—we have abolished. What world has remained? The apparent one perhaps? But no! With the true world we have also abolished the apparent one."[683] Thus, Derrida's founding move in *Of Grammatology*, for instance, is not simply to valorize writing as somehow 'prior to' speech, although he has been taken to be asserting this. It is to argue that both speech and writing are forms of a transcendental *archéécriture* whose generative '*differance*' without positive terms conditions their possibility.[684]

Camus' position on the 'existentialists' he examines in *Myth of Sisyphus* anticipates exactly this kind of deconstructive position. Confronting the absurd through experiences of the extra-rationality of the world and its non-transparency to our rational control, for Camus, involves a kind of spiritual test (see Chapter Six). The test invokes a basic normative and epistemic standard which in a certain sense can be said to underlie all of Camus' thinking: "If I judge that a thing is true, I must preserve it," Camus explains: "If I attempt to solve a problem, at least I must not by that very solution conjure away one of the terms of the problem."[685] Faced with the competing demands of a political dispute, for instance, to simply ignore one or more sides of the quarrel will be unjust; just as to count only evidences supporting one's preconceived (meta)physical notions, when more relevant evidence becomes available, is epistemically unconscionable. Just so, Camus argues, the test involved

---

681 Derrida, "Signature, Event, Context" (A communication to the Congrès international des Sociétés de philosophie de langue francaise", Montreal, August 1971) from *Margins of Philosophy*, tr. Alan Bass (Chicago: Chicago University Press, 1982), 307–330.
682 Derrida, "Signature, Event, Context", 329 cited above, at note 653.
683 Nietzsche, "How the true world finally became a fable. The History of an error", in *Twilight of the Idols (Die Götzen-Dämmerung)* Text prepared from the original German and the translations by Walter Kaufmann and R.J. Hollingdale, at www-site http://www.handprint.com/SC/NIE/GotDamer.html#sect4, last accessed January 2015.
684 Derrida, *Of Grammatology*, 6–73.
685 MS 51; MSe 31.

in any adequate response to the absurd is "to be faithful to the evidence" the absurd confrontation involves.[686] "Any other position implies for the absurd man deceit and the mind's retreat before what [it] had brought to light."[687] This evidence suggests that I can well doubt or "negate" every metaphysical claim to be able to reveal the total Meaning of the world or experience. However, this fact *in no way* negates "this desire for unity, this longing to solve, this need for clarity and cohesion" that animated the inquiry in the first place.[688] To recognise the limits of the human desire for understanding (the fact that it cannot comprehend all experience) is just *not* the same thing as contending that reason cannot explain anything of worth. Camus here stands close to the legacy of Kant's *Critique of Pure Reason* amongst academically recognised philosophers: although he never mentions this text that similarly defends the limited, but still sizable, province of the understanding and modes of fallibilistic inquiry.[689]

By contrast, Camus argues, if we look at the religious existentialists Shestov or Kierkegaard, "I see all of them without exception suggest evasion" of the two-sided reality of the absurd.[690] Kierkegaard, Jaspers or Shestov, like Camus' Husserl in his descriptive aspect, encounter the limits of human rationality, faced with the world. But then, having argued that reason is unable to find a totalising significance in life, Jaspers for one asks, rhetorically: "does not the failure reveal beyond any possible explanation or interpretation, not the absence but the existence of transcendence?"[691] Likewise Shestov begins with what, for Camus, is the veridical acknowledgement of the limits of the human mind. But he then turns this acknowledgment of the irrational itself into a form of fideism: "[t]he only true solution ... [lies] precisely where human judgment sees no solution. Otherwise, what need would we have of God? We turn towards God to obtain the impossible."[692] According to Camus, decisively, any such embrace of the impossible involves a kind of "leap": a leap both of logic ("nothing logically prepares this reasoning") and of the spirit more widely: "thus the absurd becomes god ... and the inability to understand becomes the existence that illuminates everything."[693] By such a "juggler's emotional trick

---

686 MS 73; MSe 50–51.
687 MS 73; MSe 50.
688 MS 75; MSe 51.
689 See my "Invincible Summer: Camus' Philosophical Neoclassicism", *Sophia*, Volume 50, Issue 4 (December 2011), 577–592.
690 MS 32; MSe 52.
691 Jaspers, at MS 53; MSe 32–33.
692 MS 54; MSe 34.
693 MS 53–54; MSe 33.

(*un tour pathétique de jongleur*)",⁶⁹⁴ the absurd in these thinkers (initially only a truthful confrontation with the finitude of our hopes) "has been turned into eternity's springboard."⁶⁹⁵

Such positions, as against Camus', are forms of Irrationalism. They do not just soberly acknowledge the extra-rational, so much as revelling in "the intoxication of the irrational and the vocation of rapture…"⁶⁹⁶ Yet in Camus' eyes, recognising the limits of reason does not mean accepting its complete, fallen powerlessness: any more than Derrida's deconstructive thought amounts to an apophatic, negative theology.⁶⁹⁷ "Here…intervene the notion of limit and the notion of level," Camus comments: pointing up what become two of his central notions in *The Rebel* and all his later work.⁶⁹⁸ By contrast, with Kierkegaard's or Shestov's extolling of an absolute that exceeds all limits and human comprehension, we witness a symmetrical double of Husserl's celebration of Reason's allegedly absolute power to discern the timeless essences underlying phenomena. What such cases attest is that "[r]eason and the irrational lead to the same preaching. In truth the way matters but little, the will to arrive suffices…" In these instances, this will has run ahead of the critical intellect, echoing Thomas' famous definition of faith.⁶⁹⁹ On one side, we have Husserl's ceding the arationality of elements of experience and the world to his desire to unify and comprehend. On the other side, for the religious "existentialists" Camus examines, the human desire for unity is ceded before an equally exclusive, comparably one-sided celebration of the irrational. In both cases, "[n]ostalgia is stronger…than knowledge."⁷⁰⁰ The absolute rationalistic and apophatic termini thus achieved are, for Camus, all-too-human. They attest that, short of the most demanding "lucidity", reason will always tend to remain "…an instrument of thought and not thought itself. Above all, a man's thought is his nostalgia."⁷⁰¹

---

694 MS 56; MSe 35.
695 MS 56; MSe 35.
696 MS 56–57; MSe 35.
697 On Derrida and negative theology, cf. *Derrida and Negative Theology*, edited by Harold Coward, Toby Foshay (New York: SUNY 1992), especially Jacques Derrida, "How to Avoid Speaking", 73–142.
698 MS 57; MSe 36. See Chapters Four through Six below.
699 MS 70–71; MSe 47–48. For Thomas, "the act of believing is an act of the intellect assenting to the Divine truth at the command of the will moved by the grace of God", *Summa Theologica* second part of the second part, art. 2, question 9, answer to obj. 1. At www-site http://www.newadvent.org/summa/3002.htm#article9, last accessed February 2015.
700 MS 70–71; MSe 47–48.
701 MS 71; MSe 48.

4 Excursus: Absurd Heroes? Meursault and Caligula with Sade

So what then is the relationship between Camus' analysis of the absurd and his critique of forms of philosophical suicide in *The Myth of Sisyphus* with the fictional "absurds": notably, the hugely successful drama *Caligula* (1938, then 1944) and Camus' most perennially popular text, *The Stranger* (1941). Sartre's remarkable "Explication of the Stranger", although considerably more astute than sometimes thought by some 'Camusians', does at one point approach a simplistic idea that other less subtle readers have not failed to elaborate: "Camus distinguishes, as we have mentioned, between the notion and the feeling of the absurd," Sartre writes: "*The Myth of Sisyphus* might be said to aim at giving us this idea, and *The Stranger* as giving us this feeling."[702] On this kind of reading, Meursault at least (and Caligula in Camus' play) are considered as "illustrations" of the absurd feeling, if not ethical or existential paradigms to emulate. Hence, Robert Solomon tells us about *The Outsider* that:

> Meursault is a philosophically fantastic character who, for the first part of the novel, is an ideal Sartrean pre-reflective consciousness, pure experience without reflection... but then, in the second part of the novel [after he is imprisoned and condemned at his trial to be executed]...[the] threat of imminent death forces him into a Heideggerian celebration of the 'privilege of death' and the 'happy death' which is a constant theme to Camus' novels.[703]

Christian critic Paul Archambault in *Camus' Hellenic Sources* makes the argument that it is not Meursault but Caligula who shows us the truth of Camus' rebellion against metaphysical thought. He sees in Camus' Caligula's crazed longing to bring the moon down to earth, make the sun set in the East, and achieve a dark benediction by embracing Evil an illustration of Camus' deep Gnosticism.[704] "The gnostic themes of cosmic evil, of liberation through knowledge, and of the need for an initiating teacher" are all present in *Caligula*,

---

702 Jean-Paul Sartre, "Camus' Outsider", in *Literary and Philosophical Essays* translated by Annette Michelson (Great Britain: Hutchinson & Co., 1968), 32.
703 Robert C. Solomon, *Dark Feelings, Grim Thoughts: Experience and Reflection in Camus and Sartre* (New York: Oxford University Press, 2006), 16.
704 Albert Camus, "Caligula", in *Caligula and Other* Plays (London: Penguin, 2007), 39–40, 45, 48.

Archambault observes. And these are all so many "forerunners of modern nihilism," like to that which he sees as characteristic of Camus.[705]

It is to be hoped that, should such readings identifying Camus with Meursault or Caligula be found true, that this would go some way to discrediting his work as a political and ethical thinker. For as improbable as this sounds given Camus' biography, such readings ask us to see Camus' anomic 'stranger', condemned to die after senselessly shooting an innocent man or a crazed Roman Emperor who dedicates himself to theatrically terrorising his own population as the kinds of amoral termini to which Camus' post-theological thought would lead readers. Certainly, there are reasons to think that Camus is expressing *something* of his own self in these protagonists, despite attempts to completely distance Camus from this thought.[706] *L'Étranger*, Camus could reflect in his *Carnets*, "describes the nudity of man in face of the absurd."[707] There is a good deal of Camus, and of those Algerians marooned in a limbo at the edge of European history he affectionately describes in "Summer in Algiers"[708] in this enigmatic, laconic 'Meursault'. Meursault's cathartic *anagnorēsis* and refusal of the metaphysical "escape" proffered him by the Priest in the novel's famous culminating action is, just as Sartre suggests, unmistakably close to that "divine availability of the condemned man before whom the prison doors open in a certain early dawn" in whom Camus affirms, in his own name, "the only reasonable freedom" in *Le Mythe*.[709] Equally, the reader of the philosophical essay cannot but be struck by Caligula's embodiment of several of the celebrated themes Camus analyses in *Le Mythe*: notably this "divine freedom" of the man who has revolted against all consoling myths and the "divine equivalence" of all things seen outside of societies' traditional evaluative categories (see below).[710] As we know from the "Introduction", Camus numbered *Le Mythe de*

---

705   Paul Archambault, *Camus' Hellenic Sources* (University of North Carolina Press: Chapel Hill, 1972), 120, 134.
706   Cf. Matthew Lamb, "Reexamining Sartre's Reading of The Myth of Sisyphus", *Philosophy Today* 56, 1 (Feb. 2012) who goes a long way in this direction.
707   C II 36; C II Eng 15, See Crochet, *Les Mythes*, 133.
708   SA, 80–92. For a strong post-colonial criticism of this and related essays on colonial Algeria, as expressing Camus' evasion of colonial, violent and expropriative historical relations, see Haddour, *Colonial Myths*, 33–34, with 86–87.
709   MS 85; MSe 59–60.
710   MS 75, 87–88, 96–97; MSe 56–60, 64–65. Caligula's edifying theatrics are in part dedicated, he tells us, to making others understand truly what a "freedom without frontier" could involve, as the one free man in Rome. Camus, "Caligula," *Caligula and Other Plays*, translated Stuart Gilbert (London: Penguin, 2006), 48, 49.

Sisyphe alongside *L'Étranger* and *Caligula* in his first cycle of the absurd: again suggesting the thematic kinship of these different works.[711]

Yet these readings of Camus' fiction as 'illustrations' of his philosophical thought skirt, or tread roughshod over, the difficult larger issues concerning the relationship between Camus' conceptual and literary productions. We do well to keep in mind Camus' explicit resistance in *Le Mythe* to the idea that great literature could ever be like a "thesis-novel", playing out conceptual thought better expressible in the dispassionate, denotational language of a treatise.[712] Significantly, such criticism of the idea of the 'thesis-novel' underlay the young Camus' criticism of Sartre's *Nausea* in *Alger républicain*. In Sartre's first novel, "the balance" between philosophical ideas and literary autonomy had been "broken", so "the theories do damage to the life," Camus complained.[713] Then there are more general concerns about identifying an author with any one of his characters, even within a given work, which Camus duly raises in the 1950 essay "Enigma".[714] Camus is the creator not simply of Meursault, but Raymond, Masson, Marie, Celeste, and *maman* in *L'Étranger*; of Caligula but also Cherea, Caesonia, Scipio in *Caligula*: just as Shakespeare is behind Othello and Iago, Posthumus, Polonius, and the entire cast of characters in the plays and poems...[715]

How then are we to read the two "absurd" fictions, if not as either completely unrelated to the 'theses' of *The Myth of Sisyphus*,[716] or else (the other extreme here) derivative literary illustrations of Camus' crystallising 'absurdist philoso-

---

711   C I 224; C I Eng 107.
712   MS 137–8; MSe 115–116.
713   Sartre, "Review of *La Nausée*", LCE 199.
714   E 155–159.
715   To balance the ledger, "Philosophy and the Novel," the subsection which opens Part III of *Le Mythe de Sisyphe*, goes a considerable way to denying a hard-and-fast distinction between philosophy and literature, as Cruickshank has stressed. MS 129–141; MSe 93–104; cf. John Cruickshank, *Albert Camus and the Literature of Revolt* (New York: Oxford University Press, 1959), 143.
716   At the opposite end of the spectrum to Sartre or Archambault on this issue, we find positions like that of Thomas Hanna who argues that: "Those who have tried to make a direct correspondence between the novel and the subsequent philosophical essays succeed only in confusing the proper structure of this novel, which deals with the absurd, but in a manner completely independent of the essay..." Thomas Hanna, *The Thought and Art of Albert Camus* (Chicago: Regnery, 1958), 55: compare Matthew Lamb, "Reexamining Sartre's Reading of The Myth of Sisyphus", *Philosophy Today* 56, 1 (Feb. 2012), 102, who likewise rebels against any sense that the philosophical material in *Le Mythe* could inform the literary texts.

phy'? On this point, as I have argued at greater length elsewhere,[717] I think a reflection in Camus' essay on one of his literary heroes, Roger Martin du Gard, gives a revealing insight into Camus' own artistic practice which can help:

> A novelist certainly expresses and betrays himself through all of his characters at the same time: each of them represents one of his tendencies or his temptations. Martin du Gard is or has been Jacques, just as he is or has been Antoine: the words he gives them are sometimes his own, sometimes not...[718]

That is to say, there is a clear middle ground between equally partial affirmations that Camus' absurd anti-heroes in *The Stranger* and *Caligula* 'illustrate' his philosophy, or else that their stories have *no* relation to this theoretical discourse. The middle path here is to see these characters as representing particular "temptations" or "tendencies" Camus felt within himself, as he underlines in "The Enigma", rather than 'the man himself'.[719] On this kind of reading, Meursault and Caligula would dramatically embody different responses to "the absurd sensitivity which can be found widespread in the age" (here we agree with Solomon et al.).[720] And these responses are meant, like characters in those classical myths in which Camus attested that he felt "most at ease",[721] to have more than particular significance. But, contra the simple idea that Camus' heroes must represent his own ethical ideals, it seems clear that they are meant to embody the kinds of *tentations* Camus sees as timelessly presenting themselves to us in the absurd divorce or "desert" between our deepest hopes and reality.[722] As we saw in the previous section concerning Camus' symmetrical critiques of Husserl and Shestov (with Jaspers and Kierkegaard), these temptations pre-eminently include forms of "evasion",

---

717 Matthew Sharpe, "Meursault (and Caligula) avec de Sade: On the relations between the Literary Absurds and Camus' Philosophical Discourse", *Journal of Camus Studies* (2014) makes the present case at greater length, accompanied by wider reflections on Camus' artistic practices and intentions.
718 Camus, "On Roger Martin du Gard", LCE 271–272.
719 E 159.
720 MS 16; MSe 2; See E 159.
721 C II 224; C II Eng 317.
722 Camus comments in the *Carnets* that he was "without doubt and until now...not a novelist in the widely accepted sense. But above all [I am] an artist who creates myths to the measure of his passion and of his anguish..." Camus at Arthur Scherr, "Marie Cardona: An Ambivalent Nature-Symbol in Albert Camus's *L'étranger*," *Orbis Litterarum*, vol. 66, no. 1 (Feb. 2011), 12.

"leap" or "suicide". Camus' identifying of such forms of 'evasion' in his philosophical essay has suggested to no one his 'identification' with them (far from it). Just so, it seems to us that Camus' narrations of the "undoing" of Meursault[723] and Caligula's murderous excesses are Camus' pointed narrations of existential forms of evading 'the truth, the whole truth, and nothing but the truth' of the absurd *denouement* analysed in *Le Mythe*: not celebrations or models to be emulated.

In fact, as Heffernon has shown, Camus can be seen to have placed many cues to alert us to this meaning in *The Stranger*, to begin with the more famous novel. As we will highlight shortly, Camus' ethical ideal is a kind of wakeful attentiveness to life. Yet Meursault from beginning to near the end of *L'Étranger* is wracked by drowsiness and periodic lapses into somnolence.[724] Camus valorises an attentive weighing of experience, including ongoing practices of self-reflection, to maintain a fidelity to what we have acceded to as true.[725] When he is asked at trial concerning his motives, Meursault by contrast "replied that I had pretty much lost the habit of analyzing myself": he is an anti-Socrates.[726] Most of all, Meursault until the very end of *L'Étranger* is presented as less someone who soberly weighs the inhuman indifference of the natural world than someone who is in effect *more and more violently overcome by it* to the point where he finds himself pulling a trigger and killing a man—because of "the sea and the sun", as he improbably explains at his trial.[727]

It is in the register of light, above all, that Meursault has particular difficulties. In the novel's opening pages, it is "the glare of light" off the road and from the sky that makes Meursault want to sleep on the bus to maman's home.[728] The glare in the "bright, spotlessly keen" mortuary and off its white walls leads Meursault to ask his hosts if they cannot turn the lights down a little—in response to which he is told that they are "all or nothing" (a phrase whose significance for Camus we know).[729] When maman's friends arrive and Meursault is awoken:

---

723 S 39.
724 I am indebted to George Heffernan, "'Mais personne ne parraissait comprendre': Atheism, Nihilism, and Hermeneutics in Albert Camus' *L'Étranger/The Stranger*" *Analecta Husserliana* CIX (2011), 133–152.
725 MS 29; MSe 13; MS 65; MSe 44–45; MS 131; MSe 94–95. See Chapter Six below.
726 Camus, *The Stranger*, 40.
727 S, 64: "I tried to explain that it was because of the sun, but I spoke too quickly and ran my words into each other. I was only too conscious that it sounded nonsensical, and, in fact, I heard people tittering..."
728 S 4.
729 S 6, 7.

> I had a feeling that the light had grown even stronger than before.... Never in my life had I seen anyone as clearly as I say these people: not a detail of their clothes or features escaped me.[730]

At maman's funeral, again, the sky is described by Meursault as "a blaze of light": a furnace with "the air stoking up rapidly...."[731] It becomes so intrusive as to threaten to obliterate all possibility of human inhabitancy: "now, in the full glare of the morning sun, with everything shimmering in the heat haze, there was something inhuman, discouraging, about this landscape."[732] Things famously culminate, however, in the dreadful moment of the murder of the arab man on the beach. Camus' narration makes it clear that, at this fateful moment, Meursault is veritably assaulted by "the same sort of heat as at my mother's funeral";[733] blinded to the human significance of who he is and what he is doing by the violent epiphany of the sun:

> A shaft of light shot upward from the steel, and I felt as if a long, thin blade transfixed my forehead. At the same moment all the sweat that had accumulated in my eyebrows splashed down on my eyelids, covering them with a warm film of moisture. Beneath a veil of brine and tears my eyes were blinded; I was conscious only of the cymbals of the sun clashing on my skull, and, less distinctly, of the keen blade of light flashing up from the knife, scarring my eyelashes, and gouging into my eyeballs. Then everything began to reel before my eyes, a fiery gust came from the sea, while the sky cracked in two, from end to end, and a great sheet of flame poured down through the rift. Every nerve in my body was a steel spring, and my grip closed on the revolver. The trigger gave, and the smooth underbelly of the butt jogged my palm. And so, with that crisp, whipcrack sound, it all began...[734]

---

730 S 8.
731 S 11. We note that the sand under their feet "stokes up" on the day of the murder (S 33); it was hot like a furnace on the beach (S 36), and that the sky is starting to "stoke up" again at exactly the time of day when Meursault's trial properly begins, at S 54. The sun in this way has something like the role of the classical choruses in the tragedies, framing the action: except that it is also an active agent in shaping the protagonist, in this sense more like an actual character in the story.
732 S 11.
733 S 38.
734 S 38–39.

Meursault in *The Stranger* thus represents anything but a Camusian ideal, however immovable this idea will remain in the popular mind. Rather than lucidly weighing the human desire for sense against the inhuman dimensions of our condition, he is instead someone increasingly overwhelmed by this inhumanity, until he becomes its murderous, unthinking avatar.[735] To be sure, *Le Mythe*'s 'suicide' is not the right word for this unlikely murderer. For one thing, it implies a sense of volition that Meursault attests to having lost, particularly after he is imprisoned and placed on trial to watch helplessly as he is categorised by his colonial contemporaries as a veritable anti-Christ and condemned to die.[736] Thinking back to Chapter Two and Camus' typology of responses to the existence of senseless suffering in *The Rebel*, we would indeed suggest, Meursault's fatal blindness comes closest to anticipating the kind of "absolute negation" Camus ascribes to the romantics and the Marquis de Sade, and which we will see presently perfectly describes the figure of Camus' Caligula.[737]

So what, then, in more detail than we have hitherto given, does Camus in *The Rebel* say concerning the romantic dandies, the surrealists, and the Marquis de Sade, that unlikely "man of letters"? According to *L'Homme Révolté*, what marks off these figures' metaphysical rebellion is their 'leap' from the supposition that the reality of evil represents proof positive that God's order is inhumane, to their own literary celebrations of transgression against this order as an end in itself. "In order to combat evil, the rebel renounces good, because he considers himself innocent, and once again gives birth to evil."[738] This form of metaphysical revolution, Camus argues, can be seen equally in Milton, Vigny and Lermontov's sympathy for the devil, as in Lermontov's Maldador, whose copulations with a shark and attack on the Creator in the form of an octopus are "are clear expressions of an escape beyond the frontiers of existence and of a convulsive attack on the laws of nature."[739]

---

735 See Raquel Scherr Salgado, "Memoir at Saint-Brieuc" *MLN*, Vol. 112, No. 4, French Issue (Sep., 1997), pp. 576–594: p. 592.

736 E.g. S 62: "It is always interesting, even in the prisoner's dock, to hear oneself being talked about. And certainly in the speeches of my lawyer and the prosecuting counsel a great deal was said about me; more, in fact, about me personally than about my crime..."

737 The author has since writing this become acquainted with the confirming argumentation of J. Larson, "Albert Camus' *Caligula* and the Philosophy of the Marquis de Sade", *Philosophy and Literature*, Volume 37, Number 2, October 2013. See Chapter Two above, section "From rebellion to revolution, unity to totality: all or nothing".

738 HR 71; R 47.

739 HR 114; R 85.

The Prince amongst these 'men of letters', however, is Sade. Sade as Camus sees him does not propose attacking the unjust Deity: far from it. As Jacques Lacan discerned a little after Camus (with common reference to Klossowski's *Sade, mon prochain*),[740] having surmised that God evidently must *desire* the senseless suffering with which this world is replete, Sade instead 'sides with' this evil "big Other", as the only effectively pious thing to do.[741] The fortresses of crime his characters thus dream up have more of the convent about them than their segregation from the profane world wherein men senselessly give way to untethered desires. Sade for instance can have one of his spokespersons stipulate that all the *jouisseurs* should periodically confess concerning their exactions and infamies. As definitively perverse as all this is, these "strongholds of debauchery where a kind of bureaucracy of vice rules over life and death"[742] are engaged in doing Sade's God's work. Rather than impotently denying the Will of the malign deity and dreaming hopelessly of good, Sade's criminals see themselves as engaged in the Holy work of carrying out the violent edicts of this "... lawless universe where the only master is the inordinate energy of desire."[743] To be true to this libidinal order, it is true, we are called upon to give up on all our merely whimsical pleasures, no less so than in a Catholic convent or Kant's deontological morals:[744]

> It is a curious kind of pleasure, no doubt, which obeys the commandment: 'We shall rise every morning at ten o'clock'! But enjoyment must be prevented from degenerating into attachment, it must be put in parentheses and toughened. Objects of enjoyment must also never be allowed to appear as persons. If man is 'an absolutely material species of plant,' he

---

740   Cited at HR 61; R 39.
741   Compare Jacques Lacan, "Kant With Sade": "Sade...stopped at the point where desire and the law became bound up with each other [se noue]. / If something in him lets itself remain tied to the law in order to take the opportunity, mentioned by Saint Paul, to become inordinately sinful, who would cast the first stone? But Sade went no further./ It is not simply that the flesh is weak, as it is for each of us; it is that the spirit is not willing not to be deluded. [Sade's] apology for crime merely impels him to an oblique acceptance of the Law. The Supreme Being is restored in Evil Action [le Maléfice]," at Jacques Lacan, *Ecrits: The First Full Edition in English* translated by Bruce Fink et al. (New York, London: W.W. Norton and co., 2006), 667.
742   HR 65; R 42.
743   HR 64; R 41.
744   Adorno and Horkheimer, "Juliette, or the Enlightenment and Morals," *Dialectic of Enlightenment*.

can only be treated as an object and as an object for experiment. In Sade's fortress republic, there are only machines and mechanics.[745]

So what, on these terms, do Sade's fortress republics have to do with Camus' *Caligula* and that unhappy Emperor's Rome? The proximity between Camus' absurd anti-hero and this Sadean position is actually much more direct than in the more listless case of Monsieur Meursault of Algiers. Like Sade, with whose clear-sighted apprehension that "murder is an attribute of... divinity" Camus lastingly agrees,[746] Caligula's eyes are opened by Drusilla's death to the reality "that nothing lasts",[747] despite the ways that social conventions seem designed to conceal this larger reality of our condition. It is his visceral recognition of this truth that explains the emperor's "devastating scorn" for all social conventions:[748] and his equally Olympian disdain for others' all-too-human cravings for wealth, status, power, love, recognition, or happiness. Camus' Caligula declaims nihilistically that "everything's on an equal footing", "the world has no importance..."; "it all comes to the same in the end"; darkly echoing moments in *Le Mythe de Sisyphe* and the form of magnaminity we will see always remained Camus' classical, almost neoStoic ideal.[749] Yet, as Camus was to reflect in his Preface to the American edition of the play: "*Caligula* is the history of a higher suicide. It is the history of the most human and the most tragic of errors."[750] In Caligula's own words, "killing is not the solution."[751] The issue is that, like Sade's, Caligula's rebellion against mortality in Camus' play 'leaps' over almost immediately into a definitively perverse, homicidal conclusion.[752] Evidently the only thing left to do, in this order wherein death is the eventual Law, is to consciously take on the violences of which we are otherwise merely the passive victims. In this way, far from rejecting the inhumanity of the world that provokes his rebellion, Caligula 'sides with' this Irrationality, no less than

---

745   HR 65; R 42.
746   HR 59; R 37.
747   Camus, "Caligula", 102; see also 101.
748   Camus, "Caligula," 69, 102.
749   Camus, "Caligula," 43–44, 46; Camus, *Stranger*, 74; Camus, "Caligula," 64. See Chapter Six, section "Literature and philosophy as a way of life, the Camusian virtues".
750   Camus, "Caligula," 43–44, 46; Camus, *Stranger*, 74; Camus, "Caligula," 64 Camus, "Author's Preface" to *Caligula and Three other plays* trans. Justin O'Brien (New York: Alfred A. Knopf, 1958), vi.
751   Camus, "Caligula," 72.
752   Cf. Camus, "Caligula", Act III, Caligula's recognition that he is not always 'logical': "that's true. But for once I want to contradict myself. It will harm no one, and it's good to contradict oneself occasionally. It relaxes a person."

Camus sees Shestov or Kierkegaard doing in the realm of ideas. He accordingly sets about using his absolute imperial power as a kind of pedagogical theatre[753] to open the eyes of his dullard contemporaries to the full dimensions of their fate. Caligula will "prove to the imaginary gods that any man, without prior training, can play their absurd role to perfection... all that's needed is to be as cruel as they."[754] He will indeed "play the part of Fate," visiting natural or divine violence on unwitting human beings, just as Sade had dreamed for his libertines.[755] In a phrase inescapably significant in the *oeuvre* of the author of a 1947 work entitled *La Peste*, Camus' crazed Emperor clarifies: "it's I who replace the epidemics..."[756]

5 *Je suis revenu à mon commencement*: The Irreducibility of the Subject and the Primacy of Ethics

What then do Camus' 'absurds' positively point us towards, in contrast to the forms of philosophical and existential suicides *Myth of Sisyphus*, *Outsider* and *Caligula* each document? We cited above an important passage from *Le Mythe de Sisyphe* expressing Camus' sense that purely objective scientific inquiry can deliver descriptive truths about the natural world. Yet they can never satisfy that eros that "this world is mine" which, for him, unites our cognitive with our wider pursuits.[757] In the context of describing this metaphysical disappointment, Camus uses a telling phrase. The inquiry, having striven outwards or upwards to encompass the whole world in its categories, is 'returned to its beginnings'. *"Je suis revenu à mon commencement,"* Camus writes: "I am returned to my beginnings"[758] This self-reflective movement of thought in Camus, we propose, is pivotal in understanding all of Camus' *philosophie*: both as a reasoned discourse and the basis for a reflective, examined *modus vivendi*.

However understandably lovers of Camus are tempted to denounce him, Sartre once more was right about his old friend in his 'Eulogy' of 1960, when he suggested that Camus stands in a long tradition of sceptical French *moralistes* dating back in the modern period to Michel de Montaigne and Pierre

---

753 Camus, "Caligula," 49.
754 Camus, "Caligula," 74–75.
755 Camus, "Caligula," 92.
756 Camus, "Caligula," 92, cf. 75.
757 MS 34; MSe 17.
758 MS 38; MS 20.

Bayle.[759] But for Camus, sceptical doubt remains a methodological and ethical starting-point (and by itself, a temptation). It is not epistemically or ethically a terminus: "it is useful to note at the same time that the absurd, hitherto taken as a conclusion, is considered in this essay as a starting-point," we are warned at the very start of *Le Mythe*.[760] There are limits to scepticism. They lie on this side of 'nihilism', conceived as the happy but finally chimerical attempt to claim that 'nothing has any meaning.' "All thought, and primarily that of non-signification, signifies something," Camus observes.[761] As he comments in "The Enigma":

> ...there is likewise no total nihilism. As soon as you say everything is nonsense, you express something that is meaningful. Refusing to see the world as meaningful would amount to abolishing all value-judgments. But living and eating, for example, is a value judgment. You choose to stay alive the moment you do not allow yourself to die of hunger, and consequently recognise at least a relative value.[762]

The immediate consequence of recognising the absurd divorce between (1) the human desire for meaning and (2) the ultimate resistances of the world to this desire, is not (per Kierkegaard or Caligula) the real or willed negation of (1). We have not arrived at the world-alienation that Sartre declaimed, when he called human subjectivity a "useless (*inutile*) passion".[763] For Camus, the consequence of this recognition of our finitude is at once epistemic and ethical. It lies in what he calls "a rule of method," here as elsewhere echoing Cartesian language.[764] In short, Camus' founding interest in *The Myth of Sisyphus* is a deeply Socratic one: "to live solely with what [one] knows":[765]

---

759   In his moving tribute to Camus on the latter's death, Sartre reflected that Camus was "in our time the latest example of that long line of moralists whose works constitute perhaps the most original element in French letters". Jean-Paul Sartre, "Tribute to Albert Camus," in *Camus: A Collection of Critical Essays*, ed. Germaine Brée (Englewood Cliffs, NJ: Prentice-Hall, Inc., 1962), 173. We will return to this idea, principally in the closing section of Chapter Four.
760   MS 16; MSe 2.
761   HR 323; R 254.
762   E 159–160. Cf. HR 21–22; R 8–9 "To breathe is to judge..."
763   Sartre, *Being and Nothingness*, 615.
764   MS 50–51; MSe 30.
765   MS 77–78; MSe 53.

If I judge that a thing is true, I must preserve it. If I attempt to solve a problem, at least I must not by that very solution conjure away one of the terms of the problem.[766]

Mutatis mutandis, "[e]verything that destroys, conjures away, or exorcises these requirements... ruins the absurd and devaluates the attitude that may then be proposed..."[767] The absurd *skepsis* can as it were never get back behind the desire for meaning and unity (1) which motivated it, and opened the inquirer up to the acknowledgement of her own limits (2). A "Descartes of the absurd" just as Sartre saw,[768] Camus in *Le Mythe* uses scepticism as a means, not an end: "it is not this discovery which interests us, but the consequences and the rules of action that we can draw from it."[769] He wants like the great Cartesian to find an immovable, indubitable foundation for a new mode or living and inquiring—without ever hoping on this basis, like Descartes, that he could 'know the whole world', as it were. For this Camusian Neocartesian foundation is not metaphysical or timeless: some 'thinking thing' equipped with a God-given *lumen natural* and helpfully acquitted with inherited scholastic categories.[770] It is living, performative, and as transitory as the embodied and passionate desire for sense and unity which had, in the first place, motivated the search for certainties.[771] To borrow a term from Lacanian psychoanalysis and linguistics, Camus' foundation involves the subject of enunciation, as against any content the subject enunciates, whether affirmatively or in an attitude of doubt. For Camus, echoing Descartes' *Meditations on First Philosophy*, everything else can be doubted except the subject that (at that moment) doubts. Camus adds to Descartes that this doubting subject remains faced with the immovable reality of a world whose recalcitrant realities finally elude its longing for "this homeland (*patrie*) of the soul... for which Plotinus so ardently wished."[772]

In the decisive final "Letter to a German Friend" Camus published in *Combat*,[773] Camus recurs to exactly this neoCartesian logic from *Le Mythe*

---

766   MS 51; MSe 31.
767   MS 51; MSe 31.
768   Sartre, "Tribute to Albert Camus", *Camus: A Collection of Critical Essays*, ed. Germaine Brée (Englewood Cliffs, N.J.: Prentice Hall, Inc., 1962), 174.
769   Camus, "Review of Sartre's *Nausea*", 201–202.
770   See Heidegger, *Being and Time* sec. 18–21.
771   See Isaac, *Arendt, Camus, and Modern Rebellion*, 120.
772   SA 90.
773   See for a good recent account Orme, *The Development of Albert Camus' Concern for Social and Political Justice*, 119–124; for a criticism of the articles for not rating the evil of the Nazis sufficiently gravely, Neiman, *Evil in Modern Thought*, 296–297. At stake here, in

to differentiate his response to the arationality of the world from that of his fascist (former) friend. The fascist, following Rauschnig and others,[774] Camus positions as an active nihilist: as we saw in Chapter Two, someone who infers from the absence of a providential deity the rule of force and will alone, as if there could be no balancing middle ground. Camus by contrast responds that *even if* "I continue to believe that the world has no ultimate meaning... I know that something in it has meaning, and that is man, *because he is the only creature to insist on having* this meaning."[775]

In effect, even after the most radical doubt, we are for Camus always returned to our beginnings. This means, as inquirers and as human beings, we are faced again with the task of thinking and living well, despite the unavailability of a total metaphysical theory of everything. And this reflexivity, precisely (one which does not relativise or eschew a finite subject, but recognises at once *both* its epistemic limits *and* its performative irreducibility) is the decisive feature differentiating Camus' 'deconstruction of metaphysics' (if that title can heuristically stand) from those we find in Derrida and other post-Heideggerian thinkers. Camus' affirmation of the inalienable dignity of each inquirer arguably has decisive political implications down the inferential line, glancing now back to *our* beginnings in this Chapter with the decisive year of 1933, as lived so differently by Camus and Heidegger. According to Camus, recognising the limits of reason and the subject's aspirations to total comprehension is not a premise from which we must infer that this subject should be seen as the 'constructed' epiphenomenon of wholly transpersonal structures, relations of power, the abyssal *glissement* of the signifier or the incalculable destinies of the History of Sein.[776] What ultimately eludes the "all or nothing" claims of totalising reason, Camus makes clear, is not any wholly extra-subjective reality which is claimed to overdetermine and undermine the human claim to meaning and limited control over its environs. First of all, what transcends or *remains* 'this side' of competing, vaulting metaphysical claims is the enunciating

---

Camus' recognition of the Nazis' responding to a similar European cultural situation as the resistance fighters (that of nihilism) is another instantiation of Camus' view of evil as error: in this case, what he terms the inability, fuelled by passions, to make a few "fine distinctions." See Appendix Three below for an analysis of the philosophical content of these letters, and their relation to Camus' wider thinking.

774   On Rauschnig and Nazism, see HR 228–229; R 177–179; cf. Altman, *Leo Strauss and National Socialism* (on Strauss' article on "German nihilism", 301–348).
775   See Introduction; Appendix Two. RRD 21 (italics ours).
776   I have made this argument in Sharpe, "Invincible Summer" *Sophia* December 2011, Volume 50, Issue, 50: 577–592.

subject itself, and its insatiable demand for a total unity which, on a first level, eludes it.

To deny 'meaning', a meaningful claim itself, is for Camus to submit oneself to a *performative* contradiction which is also a form of philosophical self-forgetting. We are 'counting our own claim out' of what our judgment claims to describe. Camus rehearses this type of claim, central also to Jürgen Habermas' critiques of post-structuralist and related critiques of reason, at several decisive points of his criticisms of other Western philosophies.[777] Each of these philosophies, at the exact moment they claim an 'all or nothing' total validity, fall into a comparable performative contradiction, Camus observes. In rejecting the idea of vulgar, metaphysical materialism in the context of his reading of Marxism in *L'Homme Révolté*, Camus thus notes that the proposition "everything is material" *itself* is the first place we should look for evidence of realities which elude what the universal quantifier claims about the totality of things.[778] In *The Myth of Sisyphus*, Camus' premier examples of the "absurd walls" enclosing the capacities of reason to comprehend the world likewise both involve performative contradictions, whose famous logic (or illogic) characterises the liar's paradox. The first is Aristotle's reflections on the claim that "all is true" in the *Metaphysics*: "The often ridiculed consequence of these opinions is *that they destroy themselves*," Camus writes.[779] We again stress the self-reflexivity in play:

> For *by asserting that all is true* we assert the truth of the contrary assertion and consequently the falsity *of our own thesis* (for the contrary assertion does not admit that it can be true). And if one says that all is false, *that assertion is itself* false.[780]

Camus' second example is drawn from Plato's *Sophist*, and Plato's stranger's refutation of Parmenides' "all is one" position, although Camus characteristically does not cite the source. The thing to note is that it is again the *claim itself* that performatively refutes what the claim wants to assert about the world:

---

777 Cf. Habermas, *Philosophical Discourse of Modernity*, 119, 127, 185–6, 193.
778 "We can immediately remark, with Berdyaev, on the impossibility of reconciling the dialectic with materialism. There can be a dialectic only of the mind. But even materialism itself is an ambiguous idea. Only to form this word, it must be admitted that there is something more in the world than matter alone." HR 251; R 198.
779 MS 33; MSe 16.
780 MS 33; MSe 16 (italics ours).

> ... if, bridging the gulf that separates desire from conquest, we assert with Parmenides the reality of the One (whatever it may be), we fall into the ridiculous contradiction of a mind that asserts total unity *and proves by its very assertion its own difference and the diversity it claimed to resolve* ...[781]

Camus then does not proffer any kind of affirmative, metaphysical theory of the self: whether it is substantial or insubstantial, immortal or mortal, tied to or freed from the body.... His 'subject' (if we can import this technical term into his work for exegetical purposes) is the bearer of an inalienable demand for meaning which emerges most clearly at the precise instant when we claim the ability to negate or deny it. Yet Camus' positing of this inalienable demand for meaning is decisive in differentiating Camus' post-metaphysical position from Derrida's and other post-structuralist critiques of the world-mastering modern Cartesian subject: tied, however erroneously by them, to the West's very different, rhetorical, sceptical and literary humanist tradition. Within the context of *The Myth of Sisyphus*, Camus' defence of this irreducible subjectivity marks what we might term the 'switch over' from Camus' more epistemic reflections on the limits of knowledge to the concerns of the second half of the book. Part II of *Le Mythe* does not develop a theory of language or a philosophy of history within which we could re-place the finite, founded and self-misunderstanding efforts of modern subjects to claim total sense or mastery.[782] Instead, Part II of *Le Mythe* is a deliberation on the ethical question of how to live.[783] As Camus announces at the end of Part I, "An Absurd Reasoning": "The preceding merely defines a way of thinking. Now, the point is to live (*Maintenant, il s'agit de vivre*)."[784]

Indeed, what Camus' absurd reasoning has highlighted is that philosophical or theological meditation, however august, can never exhonerate individuals of the responsibility to live in the world about which they declaim. Nor, theoretically, can it justify our inveterate propensities to 'count our own position of enunciation out' of what we assent to intellectually. Systems of thought, to the extent they claim totalising knowledge, should be resisted first of all since,

---

[781] MS 35; MSe 17–18 (italics ours).
[782] Inviting the powerful kind of criticism Habermas has made in *Philosophical Discourse of Modernity* that in these thinkers power, language, or the other determinative structures take on the predicates assigned in 'the philosophy of the subject' to the individual subject: rather than challenging the paradigm more fundamentally.
[783] This primacy of ethics is stressed in Matthew Lamb, "Reexamining Sartre's Reading of The Myth of Sisyphus", *Philosophy Today* 56, 1 (Feb. 2012).
[784] MS 92; MSe 65. Cf. D 97.

by claiming to explain everything, they "debilitate me at the same time. They relieve me of the weight of my own life, and yet I must carry it..."[785] This is why Camus calls *both* the move of a Husserl (announcing that conscious intuition accesses the timeless essences of natural kinds and laws) and symmetrically that of a Kierkegaard (in whom "the inability to understand becomes the insight that illuminates everything")[786] forms of "philosophical suicide." As the real suicide, often enough, leaps and ends his own attempts to give his life form, so in both these metaphysical positions, the theorising subject 'counts itself out'. He does so either by affirming a world whose seamless rational order renders his own want for unity an unaccountable or illusory exception; or in the despairing affirmation of our condition as so totally opaque to humane sense as to render this desire futile, in order to then make of this humiliation its own sublime solution.

As readers will know, Camus' answer in *Le Mythe de Sisyphe* to its famous opening question about whether suicide can ever be rational is a resounding 'no'. Suicide is not rendered reasonable by the absence of a knowable transcendent Meaning of life. On the contrary, "I cannot conceive that a metaphysical scepticism can be joined to an ethic of renunciation."[787] Suicide, either by physical act or through acceptance of an absolute rationalism or irrationalism involves for Camus a kind of ethically compromising "repudiation."[788] What remains this side of any such repudiation, for Camus, is a difficult spiritual denouement:

> ...a total absence of hope (which has nothing to do with despair), a continual rejection (which must not be confused with renunciation), and a conscious dissatisfaction (which must not be compared to immature unrest).[789]

"The absurd does not deliver, it binds," Camus reflects: "It does not authorise all actions."[790] If we ask of Camus what ethical attitude(s) the "absurd man" should actively cultivate, *Le Mythe de Sisyphe* gives us three answers: the first, an attitude of revolt, the second, a species of freedom, and the third, a kind of

---

785 MS 80; MSe 55.
786 MS 53; 33.
787 MS 80; MSe 55.
788 MS 80; MSe 55.
789 MS 75; MSe 51.
790 Camus MS 96; MSe 67; cf. Montgomery, "Plus loin que la morale", 125.

quantitative ethic (to live as much of life as one can)[791] which Camus will reject after 1942 as, indeed, too close to the amoralisms of Meursault and Caligula.[792]

Concerning the freedom that interests him, the decisive contrast with Sartre's contemporary, phenomenological ascription of the freedom of the 'for itself' as a basic ontological feature of consciousness is again illustrative of Camus' distance from his great contemporary, and the depth of his philosophical scepticism. "In order to remain faithful to my method, I have nothing to do with the problem of metaphysical liberty," Camus states forthrightly: "Knowing whether or not man is free [in this sense] doesn't interest me. I can experience only my own freedom."[793] The 'freedom' that interests Camus is not ontological or necessarily given: it is a spiritual attribute to be contingently, ethically won by specific human beings. As Thomas Merton has noted, its model in *Le Mythe* is religious and mystical[794] like to the mode of life consciously assumed by the Franciscan monks at Fiescole whose sombre meditations upon mortality Camus' 1937 essay "The Desert" extol as the unlikely kindred of the young bathers on Mediterranean beaches, in love with the ephemeral life of the body and the Mediterranean sun.[795] To understand absurd freedom, Camus tells us, we must think of mystics who "find freedom in giving themselves" to their God without reserve.[796] The absurd man however gives himself over to this life he sees, touches, and experiences: now newly awake at all times to the transience of things and of his own life: "[C]ompletely turned towards death … the absurd man feels released from everything outside that passionate attention crystallising in him. He enjoys a freedom with regard to the common rules."[797] His freedom is a new mode of awareness, as much as a species of action: and we cannot but note here what we will duly stress in Chapter Six: the lineage of Camus' thinking in Stoic and Epicurean meditations on mortality (alongside

---

791 MS 86–92; MSe 60–65.
792 It arguably continues to inform his reflections on art. We mean, as described above, the role of art as testifying to the whole truth, avoiding nothing: what for Camus is also an ethical imperative for living well.
793 MS 81; MSe 56. Herein lies the sorce of Cruickshank's inability to see anything worthwhile in Camus' concept of freedom in *Le Mythe*: he expects a positive ontological account of freedom, which Camus is not concerned with. Cruickshank, *Albert Camus*, 71–72. As per Chapter Four, Camus has a robust account of political freedom, whose relations with this ethical freedom are not simple.
794 MS 84 MSe 58–59. See Thomas Merton, "Camus: Journals of the Plague Years", in *Literary Essays of Thomas Merton*, 230–231.
795 D 99–100.
796 MS 84 MSe 58–59.
797 MS 84; MSe 59.

Montaigne)[798] as a means to weigh and enhance life for what it is.[799] Absurd liberty is a return to wakefulness, "escape from everyday sleep"[800] in complete contrast with Mersault's somnolence, or Caligula's megalomaniacal dreams of changing the order of things. Indeed, in a way that evokes the old philosophical ideal of seeing things *sub spaecie eternitatis* (what Hadot calls the 'view from on high (*en haut*)'),[801] Camus talks evocatively of becoming "sufficiently remote from one's life to increase it and take a broad view of it..."[802]

As for the "revolt" in play here, it is of course the key term linking *Le Mythe de Sisyphe* to Camus' subsequent political texts, led by *L'Homme Révolté*.[803] So we again need to be careful not to misunderstand its specific lineaments. This term "rebellion," evoking as it does in Christian culture the narrative of the Fall, evokes images of the Adamic or Satanic revolt against God and, through him, His creation. Such a reading positions Camus' "absurd man" as a kind of Miltonian figure, grimly setting out to forge meaning by Will alone (and so in effect, a *petit* voluntarist God *manqué*). The universe, meanwhile, can *ex hypothesi* only be a blank slate awaiting the Satanic rebel to paint it what colours his defiant Will lists. As we commented above, Camus often does speak in a manner that suggests just this atheistic kind of existentialism: "I said just now that this world has no meaning..."[804] Nevertheless, we have by now also seen that Camus denies we can know whether God *does not* exist, any more than we can be sure that He does. Camus attentively acknowledges the arationality of elements of human experience, measured relative to pre-reflective human hopes and purposes. The absurd, like Lucretius' teachings, is at first a bitter pill. It needs the wormwood of reflection, and a certain discipline, to soften its impact upon our prephilosophical, culturally sanctioned aspirations for metaphysical absolutes or certainties.[805]

---

798   Cf. C II 197: "Montaigne. Changement de ton au chap. XX du liv. 1ᵉʳ. Sur la mort. Étonnantes choses qu'il dit de sa peur devant la mort."; C II Eng 101.
799   Cf. Hadot, *Philosophy as a Way of Life* 58; 68–69; 93–101 and Chapter Six below.
800   MS 84–5; MSe 59.
801   Hadot, *Philosophy as a Way of* Life, 138–149.
802   MS 84; MSe 59. We will return to these thoughts in Chapter Six below.
803   See Weyembergh, "Réflexions sur l'(in)actualité de Camus," in *Camus in the 21st century*, 30.
804   MS 71; MSe 51 and above.
805   "...the verses I compose about dark matters are so luminous, investing all things with poetic grace. And that, too, does not seem unreasonable. For just as healers, when they try to give young children foul-tasting wormwood, first spread sweet golden liquid honey round the cup, so at this age the unsuspecting child, [940] with honey on his lips, may be deceived and in the meantime swallow down the drink of bitter gall... if, with such a

But we know by now how for Camus, accepting the arationality of the world does not license the totalising nihilistic claim that 'therefore everything is chaotic/meaningless/without worth...' Interceding between the mirroring, totalising "all or nothing" positions, we have seen, is the human desire for unity. *Pereat mundus*, Camus suggests (and despite all temptations to accept such "all or nothing" doctrines as we encountered in Chapter Two in *The Rebel*) the absurd man must not cede on this desire, and the need to honestly or lucidly face up to the extra-human order of the world. For Camus, our postmetaphysical situation is akin to those fragments in which the Stoic Marcus Aurelius ponders whether the Epicurean doctrine of atoms, void, and hazard may not be true. Faced with this prospect, Marcus regathers himself: "But if it [the world] is ruled by chance, don't you too be ruled by chance." Even if the world is not providentially ordered, Marcus reflects, "it would be possible for there to be order in you, and for disorder to reign over the All."[806] This Stoic or neoStoic 'here I stand', not despite, but *even if* the world has no providential order, is what Camus calls "revolt" in *The Myth of Sisyphus*.[807] It is interesting that, shortly after the war, Camus aligns his emerging political philosophy

---

method, I could perhaps get your attention on my verse ... until you perceive the entire nature of things—how it is shaped and what its structure is." (Lucretius, *De Rerum Natura* I. 933–950).

[806] Marcus Aurelius, *Meditations*, IV.27; cf. XII.14. See Camus' letter to himself, or to a despairing friend, in the *Carnets*, after the outbreak of the war. It brings together many of the arrows in Camus' philosophical quiver. First, the defence of reason, while recognising the force of affects: "you cannot stay on in despair. And feelings must give way to a clear view of things. We must 'see the truth as reason presents it to you' ... [not as] we see it in the flesh." Then, secondly and as ever, there is the return to the self, and neoStoically, what one can actually do, as against pining about what we cannot change: "Every man has at his disposal a certain zone of influence [the classic Stoic principle, focusing on what is within one's control only] ... you can convince ten, twenty, or thirty men that this way is not inevitable..."—and already despair is giving way to a lucid, limited self-assertion. C I 178–182; I Eng 83–85. Marcus Aurelius, *Meditations*, IV.27; cf. XII.14.

[807] MS 78–85; MSe 53–60: "To abolish conscious revolt is to elude the problem. The theme of permanent revolution is thus carried into individual experience. Living is keeping the absurd alive. Keeping it alive is, above all, contemplating it. Unlike Eurydice, the absurd dies only when we turn away from it. One of the only coherent philosophical positions is thus revolt. It is a constant confrontation between man and his own obscurity. It is an insistence upon an impossible transparency. It challenges the world anew every second. Just as danger provided man the unique opportunity of seizing awareness, so metaphysical revolt extends awareness to the whole of experience. It is that constant presence of man in his own eyes. It is not aspiration, for it is devoid of hope. That revolt is the certainly of a crushing fate, without the resignation that ought to accompany it."

of revolt with a renewed Stoicism, comparing the 20th century breakdown of civilizational consensus with that affecting the later Roman empire which Camus had researched in his *Diplôme* thesis.[808]

Characteristically, such Camusian revolt involves both a no and a yes: "at the heart of my revolt, a consent lay dormant."[809] What is rebelled against or refused here is not this life or this mortal condition, despite Camus' oscillations.[810] The absurd man rebels first of all against all doctrines which claim to explain everything, and thus hide from us the whole truth of this life as we find it. The absurd man aims to "live without appeal" to such doctrines.[811] These Camus compares to the veils placed between the condemned man and the scaffold, shielding the full force of the truth until the last moment.[812] Far from robbing life of meaning, Camus' strongest statements suggest that it is only through confronting the truth of our limited condition without such veils that "the body, creation, action, [and] human nobility will resume their places…"[813] What theological discourses see as the sufficient condition for the loss of all value ("the world eluding us because it becomes itself again")[814] Camus' perspective reframes as the precondition for the virtues. "[T]here is no finer sight than that of the intelligence at grips with a reality that transcends it," Camus writes.[815] Aristotle in book X of the *Nicomachean Ethics* ventures that all of the political virtues (courage, practical wisdom, justice, and moderation) presuppose need, uncertainty, and the possibility that the agents who will be praised for them also may act badly. (These virtues, unlike contemplation, are thus beneath the gods.)[816] Camus' position agrees, on its own more modern

---

808 Camus, "Intervention à la table ronde de 'Civilisation'", OC II 684.

809 D, 105. Again, this idea of revolt involving always an affirmation, beneath the negation, is central to *L'Homme Révolté, Part I*: "L'Homme Révolté". See also the essays of Walker, *Albert Camus: Les Extremes et l'Equilibre* (1993), collected around this Camusian theme: notably Maurice Weyembergh, "L'unité, la totalité, et l'énigme ontologique", 33–50; Ines de Cassagne, "Tension et equailibre des extremes dans l'idéal classique de Camus", 171–188; & Jacqueline Lévi-Valensi, "Roman, mesure et démesure", 245–259.

810 See Chapter Two above, and Srigley's explanation of these oscillations as reflecting the heavy weight of theological conceptualisation even on Camus.

811 MS 78; MSe 53. Here, see Cruickshank, *Albert Camus and the Literature of Revolt*, 70–71.

812 MS 78; MSe 53.

813 MS, 78; MSe 52.

814 MS 31; MSe 14.

815 MS 80; MSe 55.

816 Aristotle, *NE* X, 8; cf. Martha Nussbaum, *Therapy of Desire* (Princeton: Princeton University Press, 1993), and the argument of her chapter "Mortal-Immortals: Lucretius on Death and the Voice of Nature", 192–238.

terms, that the highest human virtues, far from being negated, *presuppose* a non-providential world beyond our measure. We cannot know in advance that we are destined to win. This is why "there is an absurd side to all the great virtues."[817] According to Camus, in another paradox, the very "inhumanity" of the world, and its transcendence of our comprehension and control is the precondition of the highest human excellences. To venture to explain everything is "to impoverish that reality whose inhumanity constitutes man's majesty."[818] Claiming total insight into a providential order, far from securing what is finest in man, is "tantamount to impoverishing man himself."[819] This is why Camus can go as far as proclaiming:

> It was previously a question of finding out whether or not life had to have a [total metaphysical] meaning to be lived. It now becomes clear, on the contrary, that it will be lived all the better if it has no [such] meaning."[820]

We will return to these decisive considerations in Chapter Five, in the context of comprehending Camus' ontological debts to Greek philosophical and poetic thought.

6 Concluding Remarks: Camus' Socratism, between Philosophy, Autobiography, and Literature

The importance of *The Myth of Sisyphus* for understanding all of Camus' other and subsequent work can scarcely be over-stated. In this Chapter, we have seen how Camus' criticism of the rationalism of a Husserl anticipates the celebrated *motifs* of Derrida's deconstruction of metaphysics. We have now also seen how, far from making this critique of rationalism the launching pad for the kind of apophatic turn he critiques in Shestov or Kierkegaard, Camus like Derrida urges caution about 'leaping' from recognising the limits of human intelligence into a glorification of the irrational. Camus' philosophical discourse points towards a difficult position 'between' absolute rationalisms or systematic theological explanations of the 'All' (*Tout*), and nihilistic attempts to claim that '*Nothing*' (*Rien*) has any significance. This situating of his position in a middle ground 'between' absolute rationalism and irrationalisms is in fact the earlier basis of

---

817 C II 39; C II Eng 17.
818 MS 80; MSe 55.
819 MS 80; MSe 55.
820 MS 78; MSe 53.

what will become Camus' mature appeals to classical moderation (*sophrosyne* or *mesure*).[821] For Camus as for Aristotle and the Greeks more widely, there are typically at least two ways to go wrong. There is in every human being, on the basis of our innate "insistence upon familiarity ... [or] appetite for clarity"[822] the seeds of those forms of excess (*démesure*) he associates with 'all or nothing' philosophical positions: and after 1942, the ethical and political stances which license murder.[823] Camus' fictional 'absurds', we argued above, aim to explore different possible *tentations*, responding to the "starting point" of the recognition of the natural limits of human knowledge and desire. Like the absolute rationalists and fideistic existentialists Camus critiques in *Le Mythe*, neither the hero of Camus' Roman melodrama *Caligula*, nor he of his first Algerian *roman* represent Camusian ethical paragons. Each instead accedes to what Camus will later in his career call the human "desire for death":[824] an all-too-human desire to escape from the complexities associated with the human condition: an *"entre-deux"*, in Weyembergh's term,[825] supended ontologically and ethically as we are between angels and beasts, absolute innocence and terminal guilt, and all of the "other antinomies of rebellious thought".[826]

What then remains for Camus, on the other side of his critiques of earlier metaphysical and mystical philosophies and theologies? Three things at least, each of which is of the greatest weight in understanding the different aspects of Camus' developing philosophical position and persona which will concern us in the second half of our journey here.

First, at the level of Camus' philosophical writings, there is what we have stressed in this Chapter: Camus' insistence that what resists the most corrosive metaphysical doubt is *the subject herself who doubts*, as the bearer of an inalienable desire for meaning. As we have seen, this form of post-metaphysical subject operates in Camus' work as the point of a near-constant 'switch over' between ontological and epistemological concerns, on one side, and ethical and political concerns, on the other: at the same time as it marks his trajectory off from Derrida's post-Heideggerian post-structuralism. If the subject must

---

821 See chapter Five. The *locus classicus* is the section "Mesure et Démesure" in *L'Homme Révolté* 367–376; *Rebel* 204–301.
822 MS 34; MSe 17.
823 HR 36, 80–81, 128, 142, 203, 313; R 21, 56–57, 97, 107, 157, 251.
824 RG 191.
825 Maurice Weyembergh, "La tentation du 'tout est permis': Camus entre 'détour' et 'rétour'", in D. Lyotard ed. *Camus, Contemporain*, 76.
826 Camus, "Minotaur, or stopping at Oran" [1939–40, published 1953], LCE 130–3. HR 369; R 295.

'count itself in' to the 'all' it would declaim about, the philosophical attempt to know the world for Camus ought always to be tied to the Socratic 'know thyself.' Socrates duly emerges around 1946 as an iconic figure for Camus.[827] In *The Myth of Sisyphus*, we have seen how this 'counting oneself in' is already the basis for his rejection of suicide: since without the doubting subject, one irreducible side of the absurd and its "wager" could not continue.[828] In *The Rebel*, this principled sceptical repudiation of suicide is extended to become a basis for Camus' philosophical and political opposition to all forms of rationalised, premeditated murder, as we will see in Chapter Four.

If, returning once more to *our* beginnings in this Chapter, we were to pinpoint the decisive differentiating feature between Camus and anything like Martin Heidegger's ontological 'thought of Being,' it lies in the primacy of ethics in his thought. This primacy of ethics is based on Camus' defence of the inalienable legitimacy of the individual's demand for meaning. *'Even if it could somehow be shown that there was a singular, fatefully unfolding history of Sein,'* Camus might retort to Heidegger, *'human beings always have the capacity and the right to resist its Evental 'destinings'. And if such 'destinings' (however discerned, by whichever prophetic authority)*[829] *sanction salvific violences to achieve their World-Historical ends, we must imperatively rebel against them. History is not God, and certainly not an omnibenevolent God, even when it is decked out in the purple of a 'History of Sein' Itself.'*[830]

In *Le Mythe de Sisyphe*, Camus' switch over from epistemological to ethical concerns is reflected in the structuring of the book itself. Part II, entitled "The

---

827 CH 746; cf. TM 364; "Unbeliever and Christians," RRD 74. See also the profoundly important note at C II 79: "l'occasion force au choix. C'est ainsi qu'il parait nécessaire à Nietzsche d'attaquer avec des arguments de force Socrate et le Christianisme. Mais c'est ainsi au contraire qu'il est nécessaire que nous défendions aujourd'hui Socrate, ou du moins ce qu'il représente, parce que l'époque menace de les remplacer par des valeurs qui sont la négation de toute culture et que Nietzsche risquerait d'obtenir ici une victoire dont il ne voudrait pas..."
828 MS 77; MSe 52.
829 See Max Horkheimer, "Theism and Atheism", *The Critique of Instrumental Reason* (London: Continuum, 1974), at www-site https://www.marxists.org/reference/archive/horkheimer/1963/theism-atheism.htm, last accessed February 2015: "but...Being...does not say anything, which has been tried recently and which is supposed to deliver its oracles through the mouths of professors. The place of God is taken...by an impersonal concept..."
830 This thought shapes Camus' unlikely admiration for the Russian terrorist Kaliayev and the other 'just assassins' of 1905, in their willingness to accept their own death as the price of their willingness to kill others in the name of political reform.

Absurd Man", is concerned to present us with images or possibilities concerning how to *live* in the "desert" of the absurd.[831] And as we shall see in Chapter Six, Camus' *Carnets* from their earliest entries can be read, in one of their strata, as a document in what Michel Foucault has called an author's 'self writing': a reflective practice of writing "daily or as often as possible"[832] points of observation or principle you want to recall and reactivate, in order to try to actually *live* an examined life.[833] The continuing autobiographical dimension to Camus' literature, culminating in the extraordinary anamnesis of *Le Premier Homme*, intersects with the philosophical motivations underlying his keeping of the *Carnets*. It reflects Camus' Socratic concern from *Le Mythe* that knowledge should also involve, return to, or expand its votary's self-knowledge. In this light, Camus' denial that he was an academic philosopher in the *Servir* interview of 1945, on grounds that he remained interested in the Socratic question of "knowing how we must conduct ourselves," is completely *apropos*.[834]

The second direction that emerges from Camus' Socratic position in *Le Mythe de Sisyphe* concerns the place of reason. We have been emphasising this feature in Camus, since it also is decisive if we are to differentiate Camus' from the anti-humanist philosophical paths taken by so much post-Heideggerian French and European thought. The 'reason' Camus insists on defending is of course no longer the vehicle for the construction of absolute, 'all or nothing' metaphysical perspectives: any more than Derrida thinks that such logocentric systems can be allowed to uncritically stand. But for Camus (again as for Derrida), we have now seen how the inability of reason to explain the 'All' does not license the inference that it can describe 'nothing' well: any more than the imbrication of rational techniques, and Rationalistic ideological claims in 20th century totalitarianism discredits all forms of reason *per se*.[835] Accepting reason's limits does not rob reason, coupled with sympathetic imagination, of its contemplative and descriptive capabilities:

---

831   MSe 16; MS 39–40; MSe 22.
832   C I 107; C I Eng 48.
833   See Michel Foucault, "Self Writing" in *Dits et écrits*, pp. 415–430 at www-site http://foucault.info/documents/foucault.hypomnemata.en.html, last accessed February 2015. Vol. IV., 1983. And cf. Pierre Hadot, *The Inner Citadel: The Meditations of Marcus Aurelius*, translated by M. Chase (USA: Harvard University Press, 1998). Pierre Hadot, "La Physique Comme Manière de Vivre" in *Exercises Spirituels et Philosophie Antique* (Paris: Broché, 2002), 149:
834   Cf. Pascal, "Albert Camus ou la philosophe malgré lui", 188.
835   See Chapter One. Also, Pascal, "Albert Camus ou la philosophe malgré lui" 173–174, on the philosophical nature of Camus' critique of systems, and his defence of a reason aware of both its powers and its limits.

> If I recognise the limit of the reason I do not thereby negate it, recognising its relative powers. I merely want to remain in the middle path where the intelligence can remain clear... in the subtle instant that precedes the leap.[836]

In particular, as in the early Husserl (and pre-eminently in the modern world, in the poets and novelists)[837] rationality for Camus remains as a faculty of description. Like Montaigne, one of Camus' august early modern inspirations, it is just that rationality is now freed to expend the energy it had hitherto exhausted trying to scale the metaphysical Jacob's ladder in observantly, humanely, exploring what transpires on the lower rungs we presently inhabit:

> Describing—that is the last ambition of an absurd thought. Science likewise, having reached the end of its paradoxes, ceases to propound and stops to contemplate and sketch the ever virgin landscape of phenomena. The heart learns thus that the emotion delighting us when we see the world's aspects comes to us not from its depth but from their diversity. Explanation is useless, but the sensation remains and, with it, the constant attractions of a universe inexhaustible in quantity...[838]

This is why, for instance, Camus tells us that: "[t]he absurd mind cannot so much expect ethical rules at the end of its reasoning as, rather, illustrations and the breath of human lives."[839] We see also why Camus will later be willing to accept the charge of being a moralist or director of conscience only if we acknowledge that today the true moralists are novelists, devoted to describing rather than judging the world.[840]

Thirdly and finally, we can see now how Camus' position avoids those notorious performative difficulties that attend all forms of total criticism of reason—since, for instance, *The Dialectic of Enlightenment* draws on reasoned arguments, appeals to evidence, to establish the plausibility of its case against 'the enlightenment'... In *Le Mythe de Sisyphe* as later in the critical parts of

---

836 MS 73–74; MSe 50 (cf. MSe 38–9, 34, 42).
837 See Milan Kundera, *The Art of the Novel* (USA: Harper Perennial Classics, 2003).
838 MS 131; MSe 94–95.
839 MS 98; MSe 68. He then gives us, in the figures of Don Juan, the actor and the conqueror just such imaginative mythopoetic sketches of different ways of living consistent with the absurd. Cf. MS 99–126; MSe 69–92.
840 Camus, "Introduction aux *Maxims et anecdotes* de Chamfort"; OC I 923–5. Again, as per the "Introduction" above.

The Rebel on "Metaphysical Rebellion" and "Historical Rebellion", Camus is instead himself *practicing* exactly the kind of post-metaphysical rationality he preaches: 'counting himself in'. His critical analyses embody a critically Socratic use of reason, alongside the descriptive attentiveness that Camus will develop and exercise in his journalism and fictive writings. As again in Derrida's work, analytical reason in Camus keeps its credentials for examining and showing up the ways that philosophers and theologians, in order to license their metaphysical commitments, have to illegitimately help themselves to unexamined or un-establishable premises (like Husserl's *eidai* or Kierkegaard's non-Camusian fideistic 'absurdity'). Or else, as Camus agrees with Derrida, they must have recourse to false forms of inference which a critically lucid reason can disclose.

Probably the key example of this kind of 'proto-deconstructive' analysis in Camus' *oeuvre* comes in his section in *The Rebel* on Dostoevsky's Ivan Karamazov, and the section "Nihilism and History" ending Part II of the text.[841] Driven by indignation at the suffering of innocents, Ivan (Camus shows; and see our schematisation in Chapter Two above) falsely "leaps" away from the ('rebellious') view that a creator-God who allows children to suffer senselessly "does not deserve our faith."[842] "A longer contemplation of this injustice, a more bitter approach," Camus observes, leads Ivan to falsely take this evidence attesting to the injustice of our condition to license the unestablishable, atheistic and 'revolutionary' conviction that "there is no God."[843] The problem is that a reasoned, *sine ira* analysis shows that the existence of evil simply does not prove the non-existence of God: only His injustice, measured by human standards. In Ivan's case, nevertheless, this 'leap' is taken, and through it (and then by presupposing another suppressed, culturally specific premise: *viz*. that a salvific *theos* is the precondition for any morality) Ivan arrives at his infamous claim, echoed since a thousand times by theists and atheists alike, that "without God, everything is permitted."[844] For Camus, everything is not permitted. Philosophically, for one thing, we must be on our critical, self-reflective guard against the kinds of impermissible, despairing 'leaps' that Ivan so poignantly exemplifies.

Having examined these different directions of Camus' work, all spanning out from its nodal self-reflexivity staged in *Le Mythe de Sisyphe*, we are ready to turn to Camus' more explicitly political works on revolt written after 1942 and Camus' involvement, as editor of *Combat*, in the French resistance. As we shall

---

841   HR; 79–86; R 55–62.
842   HR 134; R 102.
843   HR 134; R 102.
844   HR 134; R 102.

see, in strongest contrast with the Heideggerians and closer here to Emmanuel Levinas' and Jürgen Habermas' perspectives, the primacy of ethics in *Le Mythe* develops by the late 1940s into a political philosophy that reframes classical and Christian perspectives, and points towards a vindication of a form of modern democratic socialism.

CHAPTER 4

From Revolution to Rebellion: Camus with and against the Theorists of Dialogic Ethics

1   Beyond Nihilism, Sympathetic Imagination: Camus with Levinas

"Yes, there is a crisis of man when the death or torture of a [human] being can in our world be examined with a sentiment of indifference or of amiable curiosity ..., or with simple passivity ...," Albert Camus proclaimed to his American audience at the McMillan Theatre on 28 March 1946.[845] Characteristically, rather than launch into declamations concerning first principles or exegesis of august authorities, Camus illustrated his meaning by narrating four concrete examples. All of these had been related to him by victims or witnesses. They dated from the six years of the European war, then finished for less than one year.

In the first, an SS guard, after torturing his two charges in what today would be called an 'enhanced interrogation' session, calmly took his *petit déjeuner* in front of the battered men. Reproached by one of them for the derisive inhumanity of this action, the guard replied calmly that "he never pays any mind to his lodgers"—for the make-shift prison was a requisitioned tenement building. Camus' second example came from one of his resistance comrades. This man had his ear torn off, in another 'enhanced interrogation session' with the Nazis. His tormenter then approached him, leaned close to his bandaged head and asked with affected concern: "how are your ears?" Camus' third story involved a classic Sophie's choice: the kind of bizarre, catastrophic situation that still exercises moral philosophy classes. An aging Greek woman was forced by a German officer to choose which of three of her countrymen should be saved from execution: an impossible choice which served to make her inescapably complicit in the assassination of two others. The fourth story reads as uncannily contemporary in our world of unwanted asylum seekers. It involved a group of French women deported by the Germans. After the war ended, the women were to be repatriated to their homeland via Switzerland. Nevertheless, having arrived in this neutral nation, they found themselves shunted immediately,

---

845   Camus, "La Crise de l'Homme" OC II, 739.

there also, into civil detention. It was just as if they were already corpses, one of the women commented.[846]

What these examples illustrate for Camus is nothing short of a spiritual *maladie* affecting Europe. Its gravity Camus tries to impress upon his young American audience, in their relative peace and plenty, in precise terms:

> Europe is sick when to put to death a human being is conceived otherwise than with the horror and scandal which it should arouse, when the torture of men there is admitted as a service which is a little irksome (*ennuyeux*), comparable to resupplying an inventory or the obligation to form a queue in order to obtain a ration of butter.[847]

If we are tempted, faced by the sheer enormity of the problem in a period "which, in a space of fifty years, uproots, enslaves, or kills seventy million human beings"[848] to treat such atrocities "philosophically" Camus reminds us that any such stance of resigned acceptance is unthinkable for the victims: "... I believe it is impossible for those who have known torture to be able to say calmly... that after all it has always been thus..."[849] For Camus, here again closely approaching ideas Hannah Arendt would soon explore, it is the sheer *banality* that organised, state-sanctioned crime assumed in the middle decades of the 20th century ("when death has become an affair of statistics and administration")[850] that makes the period at once so unique and profoundly horrifying. "It is not today as when Cain killed Abel!", Camus reflected in 1949's "Time of Murderers": "today... Cain kills Abel in the name of logic and then claims the Legion of Honour..."[851]

L'Homme Révolté, Camus' most extended philosophical essay of 1951, brings together the fruits of his political and philosophical reflections of the previous decade, including the decisive speeches: "The Crisis of Man", "The Witness of Liberty", and "The Time of Murderers". Yet, thinking of the kinds of examples he brought to audiences' attention in these pieces, this 'book of ideas' begins with an ethical urgency which marks it off from most *livres* of its genre. *The Rebel*'s opening gambits indeed recall the tone in which Camus' younger

---

846 CH 738–9.
847 CH 739.
848 HR 16; R 4.
849 Camus, "Sommes-Nous des Pessimistes?", OC III 750.
850 TM 353–4.
851 TM 352. See Hannah Arendt, *Eichmann in Jerusalem: The Banality of Evil* (London: Penguin Classics, 2006).

self had proposed that suicide was the only really serious philosophical problem in *Le Mythe de Sisyphe*:

> There are crimes of passion and crimes of logic. The boundary between them is not clearly defined. But the Penal Code makes the convenient distinction of premeditation. We are living in the era of premeditation and the perfect crime. Our criminals are no longer helpless children who could plead love as their excuse. On the contrary, they are adults and they have a perfect alibi: philosophy, which can be used for any purpose—even for transforming murderers into judges... In the age of negation, it was of some avail to examine one's position concerning suicide. In the age of ideologies, we must examine our position in relation to murder. If murder has rational foundations, then our period and we ourselves are rationally defensible. If it has no rational foundations, then we are insane and there is no alternative but to find some justification or to avert our faces. It is incumbent upon us, at all events, to give a definite answer to the question implicit in the blood and strife of this century. For we are being interrogated.[852]

The language here is at once analytically precise and powerfully emotive. What it underlines is that engaging with the question of the legitimacy of murder in 1951 was for Albert Camus not the aleatory choice of an unconstrained inquirer who happens to have a taste for morbid subjects. "The important thing, therefore, is not, as yet, to go to the root of things, but, the world being what it is, to know how to live in it," Camus writes. 'Going to the root of things', or attempting to write any kind of "System" (as one of Camus' notes enigmatically promises for "1500 pages" in a fifth stage of production)[853] must await better times, if these times ever arrive. For the moment, this world and the burning ethical questions posed by a scenario in which "every dawn masked assassins slip into some cell...", "bind us, and so firmly that we can no longer choose our own problems. They choose us, one after another, and we have no alternative but to accept their choice."[854]

The pinning force of these questions is indeed such as to exert a shaping influence upon all of Camus' thinking from 1942 onwards. From this time, centrally, when Camus talks of "nihilism" and the need for European civilization to pass beyond it, he no longer means only the collapse of all universally

---

852   HR 15; R 3.
853   C II 201; C II Eng 103–104.
854   HR 17; R 5.

agreed metaphysical or theological bases of moral and political order.[855] "Nihilism" for Camus, *pace* both the Nietzschean and theological usages, has an irreducibly ethical meaning, directed towards how we relate to really-existing Others: not to ideas of any species or another. It means the condition in which killing other human beings has lost all horror, as if they were so many marionettes, *homini sacrii* or administrative abstractions to be shunted between queues, columns and rail-yards and exterminated in the name of competing ideological doctrines:

> In more naive times, when the tyrant razed cities for his own greater glory, when the slave chained to the conqueror's chariot was dragged through the rejoicing streets, when enemies were thrown to the wild beasts in front of the assembled people, the mind did not reel before such unabashed crimes and judgment remained unclouded. But slave camps under the flag of freedom, massacres justified by philanthropy or by a taste for the superhuman, in one sense cripple judgment.[856]

There could scarcely be a clearer statement than the opening pages of *L'Homme Révolté* of the kind of primordial ethical responsibility about which Camus' near-contemporary, the Lithuanian-French Jewish thinker Emmanuel Levinas, was to elevate to the centre of his concerns. In a series of writings beginning, like Camus' political texts, from the end of the second world war (during which Levinas was held in an internment camp and lost family in the *Shoah*), Levinas undertook what Jacques Derrida has called "a discreet but irreversible mutation, one of those powerful, singular, and rare provocations in history."[857] Levinas' argument was that all of Western philosophy has been marked by a certain closure to, or disavowal of, the demands placed upon us as subjects shaped by, and called to respond to, an Other or Others. Always assigning his teacher Martin Heidegger's 'thought of Being' paradigmatic significance as representative of the Western philosophical heritage, Levinas argues that in this 'Athenian' legacy, ontology or 'the question of being' (delineating what is, and how it can be known) has been paramount.[858] Ethics or morality, concerning our dealings with other human beings, has meanwhile appeared

---

855   CH 737–8.
856   HR 16; R 3–4.
857   Jacques Derrida "Adieu to Emmanuel Levinas" in *Adieu to Emmanuel Levinas* translated by Pascale-Anne Brault & Michael Naas (Stanford: Stanford University Press, 1999), 9.
858   Emmanuel Levinas, "Is Ontology Fundamental?" in *Basic Philosophical Writings* edited by Simon Critchley et al. (Bloomington: Indiana University Press, 1996).

as only one sub-branch of philosophical inquiry. This is when it has not (as in Heidegger's work and life) almost completely disappeared behind philosophers' ontological preoccupations.

By contrast, in the works that followed his first *chef d'oeuvre*, *Totality and Infinity*, Levinas' thought centres upon a phenomenological analysis of what transpires when we are confronted with another person. The Other, as an Other, for Levinas, eludes the kind of objectification characteristic of theoretical or scientific modes of inquiry. In this much, of course, he agrees with Jean-Paul Sartre's analysis of the Other in *Being and Nothingness*. But for Levinas, taking his leave from the younger Sartre, the Other's alterity (which he terms infinite or excessive, relative to our standard concerns and self-understanding) is experienced primordially in a kind of axiological demand. *Totality and Infinity* identifies this demand with the absolute prohibition of murder codified in the 6th Mosaic commandment: "Thou Shalt Not Kill".[859] To the extent that we so much as speak, for Levinas (or are exactly *moved* to speak) it is always by way of responding to this animating demand hailing from the alterity or in-finity of the Other. Long before we have thought to pen philosophical systems or construct ontologies, we have been sons, brothers, sisters, friends, nieces, or fathers: the subject and object of the care of Others. Ethics is thus for Levinas "first philosophy," if we insist on such a 'Greek' designation at all. Increasingly, indeed, Levinas argued that this primacy of ethics over ontology, and of our responsibility to Others over the ontological pursuit of truth, represents the deepest meaning of the Bible.[860] According to him, such an ethical challenge to the 'Athenian' or 'Greek' tradition of secular rational inquiry in the name of the infinity of the Other is the call posed by West's second founding city, the 'Jerusalem' of monotheistic revelation.

Given the urgent primacy that Camus affords to the subject of the 6th Mosaic commandment in *The Rebel* and nearly every philosophical essay he penned after 1942, it is not surprising that there are by now several works recognising Camus' *rapport* with Levinas.[861] Tal Sessler's *Levinas and Camus: Humanism*

---

859 Emmauel Levinas, *Totality and Infinity: An Essay on Exteriority*, translated by Alphonso Lingis (Duquesne: Duquesne University Press, 2011), 89.

860 See especially Emmanuel Levinas "God and Philosophy", in *Of God Whom Comes to Mind* (Stanford: Stanford University Press, 1998), 55–78 and Levinas' work of biblical scholarship, Emmanuel Levinas *Difficult Freedom: Essays on Judaism* (USA: John Hopkins University Press, 1997).

861 Tal Sessler, *Levinas and Camus: Humanism for the Twenty-First Century* (UK: Bloomsbury, 2008); cf. my own Matthew Sharpe, "Reading Camus with, or after, Levinas: rebellion and the primacy of ethics", *Philosophy Today*, vol. 55, no. 1, (Spring 2011), 82–95. Cf. also Raylene Ramsay, "Colonial/Postcolonial hybridity", in Christine Margerrison, Mark Orme, Lissa

for the Twenty-First Century follows the parallels between Camus' and Levinas' different criticisms of "totality", or totalising philosophical thought.⁸⁶² One limitation of Sessler's account, however, which focuses heavily on *L'Homme Révolté, La Peste* and *La Chute*, is his unwillingness to closely consider the development of Camus' ethical and political positions in his journalism and activism. For what considering this development throws into relief, more strongly than Sessler's account, is the full extent to which Camus' journey towards his mature opposition to all rationalisations of murder passed by way of his own coming to feel increasingly subject to a kind of impassioned, Levinasian sense of responsibility to defend Others against injustice, at whatever personal cost.

Camus is indeed clear, at several points, about the *passionate* nature of his decision to become involved in the French resistance to the Nazis, as we commented in our Introduction. Camus' resistance was born out of a kind of pre-reflective response to National Socialist barbarisms, rather than a carefully planned out, systematically grounded commitment. As he would reflect in *Combat* in September 1944:

> What carried the resistance for four years was a sense of revolt. That is, the obstinate refusal—almost blind in the beginning—to accept an order that sought to bring men to their knees. Revolt is first of all courage.⁸⁶³

In several kindred statements from the heated period following the liberation of France, Camus recurs to a *"passion* for justice" to justify his historical stance in joining *Combat* and aiding the resistance.⁸⁶⁴ Camus is equally clear that, biographically, his passionate rebellion preceded, anticipated, and shaped his later, increasingly philosophically worked-through reflections on the illegitimacy of political murder: "through a rebellion of the heart, [the resistance] brought together certain truths of the intellect," and not the other way around.⁸⁶⁵ The same sentiment forms a first basis for Camus' resistance to the active nihil-

---

Lincoln eds., *Albert Camus in the 21st Century: A Reassessment of His Thinking at the Dawn of the New Millennium* (Amsterdam, New York: Editions Rodopi B.V., 2008), 75. Levinas was deeply influenced by one of Camus' interlocutors and admirers, the philosopher Martin Buber, philosopher of the 'I-Thou' relation. On Camus' proximities to Buber, see Fred H. Willhoite, *Beyond Nihilism: Albert Camus' Contribution to Political Thought* (Baton Rouge: Louisiana State University Press, 1968), 67–71.

862   Tal Sessler, *Levinas and Camus: Humanism for the Twenty-First Century* (UK: Bloomsbury, 2008). See Chapter Two above.
863   Camus cited at Parker, *Artist in the Arena*, 76.
864   *Combat* 22/11/44, in CAC 118–9.
865   *Combat* 8/10/44, in CAC 65.

ism he attributes to his *"ami allemand"* ' in the famous "Letters to a German Friend" published clandestinely in *Revue Libre, Cahiers de la Liberation, Liberté*, then *Combat* between 1943 and 1944. "To tell the truth," Camus reflects in the first instalment: "I, believing I thought as you did, saw no valid argument to answer you except a fierce love of justice..."[866]

Since this has been questioned, it is worth again underscoring the 'modernism' underlying Camus' affective revolt here, recalling our claims in Chapter Two. If Camus' appeal to this kind of *thymos* (or indignation) bears the weight it does for him in the mid-1940s, it is because Camus feels at this time that neither he nor others of his generation could appeal to any unbroken philosophical, normative or theological traditions in order to justify resistance to fascism. The breakdown of European consensus concerning moral, political, and even aesthetic norms after two centuries of metaphysical and historical revolt he examines in *L'Homme Révolté* was too complete. Faced with "the triumphs of the beasts who were exalted at the four corners of Europe," the men and women who resisted Nazism "knew instinctively that they could not cede." Yet, Camus continues, "they did not know how to justify this obligation that they felt under. This was the malady of Europe, that whereas for a long time, bad actions needed justification, ... today, it is the good..."[867] "It is a problem of civilisation," "Pessimism and Tyranny" pronounces at around the same time: "it is essential for us to know whether human beings, *without the help of either the eternal or rationalistic thought*, can unaided create their own values."[868] In all the subsequent development of Camus' thought, we would argue, his insistence that "this is why we tried to find these reasons in our revolt itself" holds true.[869]

---

866   LGF 4, 27. In his own case, like that of Cherea in *Caligula* or the exiled journalist Rambert in *La Peste*—both of whom long for an impossible private happiness—Camus attests that yielding to this "fierce love" was not a personally comfortable experience. He needed to overturn the longing (that he would always acutely feel) of pursuing private happiness and artistic creation. An important fragment from the *Carnets* dating from the opening days of the war shows both the extent of Camus' attraction to such withdrawal, and his burgeoning indignation (as the drums of war began to beat) at any such possibility: "... more and more, when faced with the world of ours, the only reaction is one of individualism. Man alone is an end unto himself. Everything one tries to do for the common good ends in failure. Even if one likes to try it from time to time, decency requires that one do it with the required amount of scorn. Withdraw into oneself, and play one's own game. *Idiotic*." (C I 203; C I Eng 96).

867   TM 354.

868   Camus, "Pessimism and Courage", RRD 58.

869   CH 743. See for example HR 24; R 10.

There is however a further key component to what we might call the affective (or, evoking the 18th century sense, 'sentimental') bases of Camus' philosophy of revolt in the decisive texts of the resistance and immediate post-war period. This is the decisive role of sympathetic imagination in shaping and motivating political resistance. We started this Chapter by citing one instance of Camus' frequent recourse in his political writings to concrete examples, with this important component of his position in mind. If we ask: what is it exactly that those people who became complicit in the Nazi atrocities in France and elsewhere lacked, which allowed them to make peace with this regime and become its willing executioners?, Camus severally answers that these people suffered above all from a "lack of imagination."[870] This seems an oddly disproportionate response, except when we see that what Camus had in mind was the specific ability to concretely envisage the consequences of the Nazis' exactions upon their victims: "imagination when it comes to other people's deaths."[871] Speaking of Pierre Pucheu, a leading Vichy functionary, Camus thus explains his meaning:

> He believed, for example, that the government after the defeat was a government like any other and that the words 'minister', 'power', 'laws', 'condemnation' did not change their sense when France changed her visage.... He believed that everything could continue as before, that he was still in the [same] administrative and abstract system where he had always lived ... where one signed these laws behind which there was nothing to imagine. And these laws that he signed amidst everyday décor, in a comfortable and anonymous office; he did not have enough imagination to see *really* that they would be transformed into early mornings of agony for innocent French men and women whom they delivered over to their deaths...[872]

Again, the Levinasian resonances of this position are clear, although Levinas remained hesitant about such psychological categories as the imagination. Here as elsewhere, we also note Camus' proximity with species of criticism of instrumental reason proffered by Theodor Adorno and others. (see Chapter One) The political ideologies Camus opposed drew from the philosophical

---

870   NVE 260, see 266. Cf. Camus, "The Age of Contempt, *Combat* (August 30, 1944)", CAC 20; Albert Camus, "Tout ne s'arrange pas," in OC I 922.
871   NVE 260.
872   "Tout ne s'arrange pas", OC I 922. Cf. Robert Zaretsky, *Albert Camus: Elements of a Life*, 66–68; Parker, *Artist in the Arena*, 80–81.

categories of Rousseau, Nietzsche, Hegel and Marx to construct grand pictures of the course of European History and its underlying necessities. Acting in the name of these necessities, fascists and Stalin's functionaries felt licensed to deport, enslave and kill entire groups of human beings, deemed 'guilty' not of any specific crimes, but in the light of ideologies which more or less completely effaced their individuality by reference to their race, creed, political or lifestyle choice or class. By contrast, Camus protests, those moved to join the anti-Nazi resistance "had the necessary imagination when confronted with the thousands of reports of our arrested, deported, massacred or tortured brethren."[873] Unlike the collaborators, they could understand concretely what these reports signified for these men and women and their loved ones, and were not wholly cowed by Nazi terror.

From the time of the important series of articles Camus wrote in June 1939 for *Alger-Républicain* on the impoverished state of the Arab and Berber population of the Kabylia region in Algeria, Camus was attracted to the potential of journalism, like literature, to speak from and to individuals' sympathetic imagination.[874] Unlike systematic philosophy, such writing concerning *actuelles* has the capacity to present the reality of particular examples, beneath the shifting abstractions of political and philosophical polemic. Good journalism can ask us, like good fiction, to put ourselves inside the situations reported or in the shoes of the protagonists. It can prompt us to re-ask then, as if we were participants or victims, what we would sanction or proscribe: unto others as to ourselves. We saw above Camus' depiction of the death of Monsieur Othon's son in *La Peste* (a concrete example of the kinds of real suffering that accepting the notion of particular providence commits us to accepting). The young Camus' 1939 Kabyle articles likewise, alongside statistical, economic, and institutional analyses to satisfy the most hardened materialist,[875] are replete with clear but quietly urgent descriptions of the abjection of the Kabylie people concealed behind complacent imperialist, claims about the "inferiority of the indigenous workforce":[876]

---

[873] Camus, at Parker, *Artist in the Arena*, 81.

[874] See Zaretsky, *Elements of a Life*, 35–41; Parker, *Artist in the Arena*, 25–45; Jeanyves Guerin, "Camus the Journalist", in *Cambridge Companion to Camus*, 79–92; Martin Crowley, "Camus and Social Justice", *Cambridge Companion to Camus*, 94–96.

[875] Haddour, *Colonial Myths*, 120–121 which critiques Camus for over-valuing the economic as a means of obfuscating the political: ironically, given his Marxist critics.

[876] See Camus, *Algerian Chronicles*, 51: "these arguments are beneath contempt…" Cf. Chapter Six below.

> In the early hours, I have seen in Tizi-Ouzou children fighting with dogs in Kabylie over the contents of a garbage can. To my questions a Kabyle resident responded: 'It's like that every morning'... I knew that the stem of the thistle constituted one of the basic Kabyle food sources. I later verified that this was true pretty much everywhere. But what I did not know is that last year, five small Kabyle children of the region of Abbo died following the consumption of poisonous roots...[877]

Another illustrative example of Camus' appeal to sympathetic imagination is his recounting of the death of his friend and resistant comrade René Leynaud. Camus' tribute to his friend was published in a series of *Combat* articles, entitled significantly "The Flesh" (*La chair*). On 13th June 1944, Reynaud was one of 19 resistants executed by the Nazis near Villeneuve. By itself, and as one amongst many such atrocities, Reynaud's execution is a footnote in the pages of universal History. Camus' *Combat* description, by contrast, gives the event its 'human face', as we might say with Levinas in the frame:

> We know the names of only eleven of them. Between five and six a.m., Leynaud and 18 of his fellow prisoners were gathered together in the courtyard. They were served coffee and then handcuffed. One by one, they climbed into a truck which took them to the Gestapo Headquarters in Place Bellecour. They waited three quarters of an hour in the cellar of that building. When they were finally called, their handcuffs were removed and they were made to climb into a truck again with some German soldiers armed with machine guns. The truck drove out of Lyons in the direction of Villeneuve. At 11 a.m. it crept through Villeneuve and encountered a group of children returning from a walk. The prisoners and the children looked at each other for a time but didn't exchange a word. Just beyond Villeneuve, opposite a grove of poplars, the truck stopped, the soldiers lead to the ground and commanded the men to get out and go towards the words. A first group of six left the truck and started towards the trees. The machine guns immediately crackled behind them and mowed them down. A second group followed, then a third. Those who were still breathing were put out of their misery by a final shot. One of them, however, although frightfully wounded, managed to drag himself to a peasant's house. From him we learned the details.

---

877 AC 44, 47.

Leynaud's friends simply wonder whether he was in the first group or one of the later groups.⁸⁷⁸

This capacity of literature and journalism to give "flesh" to the particular, and to human beings as embodied, affective beings remains at the heart of Camus' identity as an artist, and his philosophical defence of the ethical value of literary art. In his important 1944 Preface to Chamfort's *Maxims and Anecdotes*, as we have commented, Camus contends that "the novel alone is faithful to the particular".⁸⁷⁹ This is why, he argues, our "true moralists", if we define the latter as people "who feel the passion of the human heart... [which] is the least general thing in the world," are writers who "do not make phrases, they see and they see themselves. They do not justify, they paint."⁸⁸⁰ Camus criticises Rochefaucauld's well-turned maxims for their almost mathematical symmetries and striking generalisations: "one can always perhaps, as in algebra, draw from one of these combinations some presentiment concerning experience. But nothing is real here, because all is general."⁸⁸¹ For Camus, the reality of individual human lives cannot be captured in abstract generalisations, and sometimes these abstractions become lethal. Camus thus concludes his 1939 series on the misery of the Kabyle people by arguing that their situation, confronted 'face to face', cannot be captured by "glib phrases. It is. It cries for our attention, and it despairs of getting it."⁸⁸² It is the kind of economic and social emergency that, seen aright, demands that we put aside 'business as usual'. "Some progress is made any time that a political problem is replaced by a human problem," Camus argues.⁸⁸³ "We do not want a politics without morality," Camus rejoins in a short but characteristic piece "*Au service de l'Homme*" published in *Résistance Ouvrière* in December 1944,⁸⁸⁴ "because we know that this morality is alone what justifies politics... The day will come when politics will be moral, when politics will have served men, rather than degraded them."⁸⁸⁵

---

878 Camus, "The Flesh", RRD 46–47.
879 Camus, "Introduction aux *Maximes et anecdotes* de Chamfort" OC I 923–932: 924.
880 Camus, "Introduction aux *Maximes*" OC I 924.
881 Camus, "Introduction aux *Maximes*" OC I 925.
882 AC 46; cf. AC 49: "What could I possibly add to facts such as these? Mark them well. Imagine the lives of hopelessness and desperation that lie behind them. If you find this normal, then say so. But if you find it repellent, take action. And if you find it unbelievable, then please, go and see for yourself."
883 AC 82.
884 OC I 1417.
885 OC I 934.

As Barthes, de la Vigerie, Jeanson and Sartre protested against Camus, nevertheless, real questions face any attempts to ground a political philosophy in such a 'moralising' appeal to ethics. This is never more true than when ethics, in its turn, is grounded in more or less pre-reflective, more or less immediate, affective responses to the sufferings of others. Far from wanting to deny the force of these critical queries, the remainder of this chapter will expound Camus' mature political thought in their light. First of all, there is the simple observation that not all of Camus' contemporaries were moved to action by Camus' sense (or that of his character Grand in *La Peste*)[886] that there was simply 'no choice' to join the struggle against the plague of the National Socialist occupation. However admirable was Camus' sense that "in all clear-sightedness...it was my duty",[887] many others lacked Camus' sympathetic imagination and what he sometimes called this "simple reaction of an honour which has been humiliated."[888] Or else, they were silenced by the overwhelming forces of terror Camus describes ably in *La Peste*, *L'État de Siège* and *L'Homme Révolté*. Camus notes that the kinds of "compassion which is the sister of [a sage] ignorance" animating the *resistants*'[889] emerged alongside an equally visceral "temptation to hatred" in the occupied nation: one which lasted well into the cold war.[890] Camus himself wrestled with the justice of a post-war purge to execute the worst Vichy collaborators. Indeed, like Tarrou in *La Peste*, Camus initially, vociferously demanded the heads of leading collaborators in the name of a justice "without charity", until he came to see that this purge was licensing acts as barbarous as those of the occupying power.[891] "The most difficult battle to be won against the enemy in the future", Camus would thus reflect, "must be fought within ourselves, with an exceptional effort that will transform our appetite for hatred into a desire for justice."[892] Camus seems

---

886 See P 112: "When Rieux thanked him with some warmth, [Grand] seemed surprised. 'Why, that's not difficult! Plague is here and we've got to make a stand, that's obvious. Ah, I only wish everything were as simple!' And he went back to his phrase..."
887 At Orme *Development of Albert Camus' Concern*, 118.
888 Camus at *Combat* (CAC 142), cited at Orme *Development of Albert Camus' Concern*, 125.
889 Albert Camus, "Exhortation aux Medicins" OC II 285 (last words of the exhortation).
890 Orme, *Development of Albert Camus' Concern*, 122.
891 See Zaretsky, *Albert Camus: Elements of a Life*, 47–78 for a good recent account of Camus' 1944–'45 course. Here is its end, in a concession to Mauriac and the public that he had been wrong:"There can no longer be any doubt that the postwar purge has not only failed in France but is now completely discredited. The word 'purge' itself was already rather distressing. The actual thing became odious...The failure is complete" Albert Camus, *Combat* August 30, 1945, at CAC 252.
892 Camus, "Unbeliever and Christians", RRD 62–3.

to us typically astute in asserting the powerful motivating role of moral sentiments in ethicopolitical life: the problem of moral motivation facing Kant's or any other deontological appeals to formal imperatives in ethical life is real. Yet the conclusion remains that, unless Camus' ethical *sympatheia* is grounded in appeal to rationally defencible moral principles, this sympathetic imagination seems an insufficient philosophical basis for what Camus optimistically calls "the only effective force in this world ... that of justice."[893]

Secondly, as Barthes and Jeanson were to criticise Camus, any defence of an ethics rooted solely in the 'first response' to particular human sufferings runs the risk of leading to an apolitical, or wholly politically impractical, set of stances. Warming to his polemical charge, Jeanson accused Camus of propounding a "red cross morality": one which celebrates the "mystery of inefficacity," retreating into beautiful, moralising condemnations, rather than informing efficacious political responses.[894] Putting aside Jeanson's colourful denunciations, a para-Levinasian focus on the pressing suffering of particular individuals and groups, if and when it becomes exclusive, can serve to occlude the larger political, economic and cultural causes leading to this suffering. *Marxissant* criticisms of the "returns to ethics", from Sartre et al. in 1952 to Žižek, Jameson et al. today[895] have continually highlighted how fetishising the vulnerable Other, outside of all the mediations of historical context, can be unwittingly problematic in this way. If the sufferings of the Kabyle Arabs and Berbers are to be prevented, such criticisms aver, we will need to strike at

---

893 At Orme, *Development of Albert Camus' Concern*, 124. Cf. AC 112.

894 Jeanson, "Soul in Revolt", 93; for another of his responses to similar charges, see Camus, "Response to Roland Barthes", LCE 339–341.

895 See for example Fredric Jameson: "In our time, ethics, wherever it makes its reappearance, may be taken as a sign of an intent to mystify, and in particular to replace the more complex and ambivalent judgments of a more properly political and dialectical perspective with the more comfortable simplifications of a binary myth." Fredric Jameson, *Fables of Aggression* (London and New York: Verso, 2008 [1979]), 56. Cf. Slavoj Žižek, in Slavoj Žižek, Judith Butler and Ernesto Laclau, *Contingency, Hegemony, Universality* (London: Verso, 2000), 127: "the moment one shows a minimal sign of engaging in political projects that aim seriously to change the existing order, the answer is immediately: 'benevolent as it is, this will necessarily end in a new gulag.' The 'return of ethics' in today's political philosophy shamefully exploits the horrors of the gulag or holocaust as the ultimate bogey for blackmailing us into renouncing all serious radical engagement'." Compare his "Against Human Rights" in *New Left Review* 34, July–August 2005, at www-slte http://newleftreview.org/II/34/slavoj-Žižek-against-human-rights, wherein Žižek attacks human rights as "Alibi for militarist interventions, sacralization for the tyranny of the market, ideological foundation for the fundamentalism of the politically correct", last accessed January 2015.

the causes of such suffering. But these lie in colonial injustices and an unjust international order. Camus' kind of humanitarian journalism merely shows this suffering as a cause for lament (perhaps, these days, alongside appeals from charitable NGOs for first world moneys). It is at most one precondition for redressing the effects of this unjust order. At worse, it can function as an ideological distraction.[896] When Camus talks of turning a political problem into an humanitarian one, or of a true revolution reinstating ethics in the political realm, doesn't this apparently noble position deprive us of the specifically political and historical categories which will be needed to overcome structural injustices and violences?[897]

We turn now to Camus' developing political philosophy from 1946 onwards, very much awake to these criticisms. Our intent will be to show that, in Camus' case, they purchase their cogency by simplifying his complex and evolving position. For very soon after 1944, this position moves from heart to mind, and from an ethics of rebellious indignation to the articulation of a principled political universalism.

2   'I Rebel, Therefore We Are': A Primary Post-Metaphysical Value

We have several times referred to Ronald Srigley's important study *Camus' Critique of Modernity*. Srigley's work, drawing on the author's background in the thought of Eric Voegelin, has the merit of taking Camus seriously as a philosophical thinker. Srigley asks us to read Camus' *oeuvre* as a whole, awake to the breadth of Camus' background in classical and Christian thought as a self-conscious attempt to draw on the Greek tradition in particular to challenge the totalitarian excesses of his times.[898] Yet Srigley argues that Camus'

---

896 Slavoj Žižek, *On Violence* (London: Picador, 2008), 2–4, 21–23.
897 The problem can be seen, precisely, in Levinas' ethical philosophy, when he comes in *Otherwise than Being or Beyond Essence* to consider the tension between an ethics of responsibility to the immediate Other, and wider justice towards many others ("the third") in complex historical and institutional conjunctures. Here Levinas appeals to a notion of justice, and 'comparing the incomparables', but he does not then engage with the long philosophical and political heritages considering the nature of justice and its institutional forms: and how, if at all, reframing the comparative dimensions of justice with reference to an infinite Other implies changes in the ways we think about the institutional and other political preconditions of justice. Emmanuel Levinas, *Otherwise than Being or Beyond Essence* translated by Alphonso Lingis (Pittsbrgh: Duqesne University Press, 1998), 16–17, 81–82, 127, 150, and esp. 157–162.
898 Srigley *Camus' Critique of Modernity* 1–16.

recourse in *Le Mythe de Sisyphe* and *L'Homme Révolté* to Cartesian language to describe his emerging philosophy is problematic. It is also a commitment which Camus renounced in the 1950s: alongside his 'modern' attraction to rebellion as the founder of political values and virtues.[899] According to Srigley, it was in the period after *The Rebel*, as a response to his own growing sense of the limitations of this study, that Camus' criticism of the modern age of rebellion was radicalised: a radicalisation which culminated in the biting satire of *La Chute* of 1956. Admiration for his book aside, we disagree with Srigley on this point and on his assessment of the modern age, as Chapters One and Two have fleshed out. What we want to argue now is that Camus' paraCartesianism, his desire to construct a new philosophical and political position on the basis of the far-reaching doubt precipitated by the modern crisis is what gives his thought its philosophical cogency, and makes it of continuing relevance in the present post-secular or post-postmodern period. Despite legion critical claims alleging philosophical laxity or contradictions in Part V of *The Rebel*, or its reversion back to wholly "personal" solutions,[900] we will also show that

---

899   Srigley, *Camus' Critique of Modernity*, 80–83, 99–100.
900   See the paradigmatic expression of this position by John Cruickshank: "near the end, the book begins to fall apart. Despite Camus' eloquence and ingenuity it is difficult to find a genuine link between the criticisms he has made and the conclusions he draws. The final pages strike one as an unsuccessful attempt to turn a fundamentally negative argument into a positive one... after 350 pages of admirably clear and direct prose, Camus allows himself a series of lyrical flights." John Cruickshank, *Albert Camus and the Literature of Revolt*, 116. Camus' doctor at the time opined that the last pages' hymns to life had a biographical basis, in Camus' wrestling with the relapse of his tuberculosis between 1949 and 1950 (see Lottman *Albert Camus*, 485). Compare more recently Orme, *The Development of Albert Camus' Concern*, 152–157, 170–172, 178–180. Orme takes Camus' grounding of *The Rebel* in his own experiences in the resistance, and his "misguided idealism" (170) to speak against the book's conclusions' philosophical generalizability. For Orme, who becomes increasingly critical towards Camus as the book proceeds, the final part of the book is "nebulous philosophy which offers a response incommensurate with the actual crises portrayed in the rest of the book..." Orme, *The Development of Albert Camus' Concern*, 172–3. I am clearly arguing against this kind of view which I think takes the stylistic change, into an exhortatory mode, to exclude ordered cognition; but this is not necessarily the case, nor is it the contingent case here. Exhortation in the finale of an engaged piece of philosophical writing can even seem to be in order, if the book (as here) is not aimed primarily at professional scholars. Tarrow concurs that "the final chapter "Thought at the Meridian" is an unsatisfactory piece of writing in which logic is transformed into lyricism and proofs into metaphor." Tarrow, *Exile from the Kingdomi*, 147, cf. 144–145. For a formalisation of Camus' argument, up to and including Camus' political prescriptions in Part V, which challenges these readings see Appendix One below.

Camus' political philosophy (founded on the very concrete, three-fold prohibition of rationalised murder, deceit, and exploitation) follows clearly from this paraCartesian position, articulated in the Introduction and Part I of *L'Homme Révolté*, and defended *per via negativa* in the central Parts on metaphysical and historical rebellion. To be clear: if Camus' position did not have such a philosophical foundation but was grounded only in his *bonhomie*, or even what Isaac calls an optative "hypothesis about how we might best organise our common condition",[901] it would not deserve the reconsideration we are advocating for here.

At issue is the way that Camus, in the "Introduction" to *L'Homme Révolté* as in the earlier piece "Le Meurtre et L'Absurd" published in April 1949,[902] is at pains to establish a direct methodological and substantial link between the arguments of *The Myth of Sisyphus* and *The Rebel*. Camus is clear enough, in fact, that *The Rebel's* extended meditation on the history of modern rebellion, animated by his ethical concern with the problems of murder and human evil (Chapter Two), begins with his meditations on the absurd.[903] The "Introduction" to *The Rebel* begins where *Le Mythe* ended, by asking what a philosophical recognition of the absurd can bring to the ethicopolitical question of political violence, with which this new book is concerned. By itself, Camus now argues, "the absurd, considered as a rule of life, is contradictory."[904] To recognise the limits of human aspirations and understanding before a world whose scale and grandeur surpasses us "does not provide us with values which will enable us to decide whether murder is legitimate or not."[905] Yet Camus feels that it is "necessary" to begin with the absurd. For he in no way thinks that the horrific decade of the 1940s has done anything to upset *Le Mythe*'s cogency as a description of the post-traditional intellectual denouement of contemporary European life (as we opened this Chapter by stressing). This shared cultural starting point of scepticism and unbelief, Camus states, is "the equivalent on the plane of existence of methodical doubt". It "wipes the slate clean" of any transcendent, inherited legitimations to ground his ethicopolitical reflections.[906]

---

901   Isaac, *Arendt, Camus, and Modern Rebellion*, 122.
902   Camus, "Le Meurtre et l'Absurd", OC III 344–350.
903   As Woelfel noted in 1975, this point tends to have been elided by critics, then and since, at Woelfel, *Camus, A Theological Perspective*, 92–98.
904   HR17, 22; R 5, 9.
905   HR 22; R 9.
906   HR 23; R 10.

However, as in Descartes, this 'wiping clean' of all inherited positions is only of provisional value for Camus. It is a means, not an end. The *Meditations* does not end after the first day, or the second. Like Descartes' methodical doubt, Camus' project also is *to reason only on the basis of what we cannot doubt on the basis of experience* (the thought "returning upon itself" which we saw in Chapter Three, and which Camus duly invokes in the *Rebel*'s Introduction).[907] He wants to give shape to a new, rigorous post-metaphysical reflection that takes as little as possible for granted as it looks to construct new ethical and political values.[908] The radicality of Camus' neoCartesian ambition here, in the opening pages of his philosophical *chef d'oeuvre*, can then hardly be overstated. Yet it has been almost universally passed over in talk of Camus as *littérateur* alone, in readings of Camus from within literary criticism, and (as we said) in Srigley's recent philosophical book. *L'Homme Révolté* aims at the same kind of self-reflexive transparency, assuming nothing, that sees Heidegger's *Being and Time* taking the questioner ('dasein') him/itself as the first object of investigation, or Hegel in the *Phenomenology* beginning with the bare act of someone pointing and saying "This!"[909]

Now: while considering the absurd itself can provide no bases for addressing normative questions, *Le Mythe de Sisyphe* had nominated the ethical stance of revolt as "one of the only coherent philosophical positions" on the basis of the absurd, as we saw in Chapter Three.[910] Indeed, Camus argued that a self-critical revolt against all wishful consolations was the ethically necessary basis for remaining faithful to the absurd and not committing real or philosophical suicide. And so it is that Camus now insists, in the philosophical as well as the wider cultural context of 1951, that "it is absolutely necessary that rebellion finds its reasons within itself, since it cannot find them elsewhere":[911]

> Deprived of all knowledge, incited [in the period of the two wars and total states] to murder or to consent to murder, all I have at my disposal is this single piece of evidence, which is only reaffirmed by the anguish

---

907 HR 23; R 10: "But like methodical doubt it can, *by returning to itself*, open up a new field..."
908 HR 23; R 10.
909 Heidegger, *Being and Time*, section 4, "Theontic priority of the question of Being"; Hegel, *Phenomenology of Spirit*, A. 1 "Certainty at the Level of Sense-Experience—The 'This', And 'Meaning'", "This", And 'Meaning'"Meaning". See Gay-Crosier, "De l'*Homo faber* à l'*Homo ludens*: defence et illustration de la pensée de midi", in *Albert Camus, Contemporain*, 32–34.
910 MS 78; MSe 53.
911 HR 24; R 10.

I suffer. Rebellion is born of the spectacle of irrationality, confronted with an unjust and incomprehensible condition. But its blind impulse is to demand order in the midst of chaos, and unity in the very heart of the ephemeral. It protests, it demands, it insists that the outrage be brought to an end, and that what has up to now been built upon shifting sands should henceforth be founded on rock...[912]

We recall from Chapter Three that it was Camus' refusal to cede this desire for unity, when confronted with a world which finally resists it, that led *Le Mythe de Sisyphe* to its life-affirming argument against suicide. The transition to the normative heart of *The Rebel*'s life-affirming argument against murder follows from the same premises. The "most important deduction" of the most far-reaching, lucid metaphysical scepticism conceivable is that suicide cannot be philosophically defended on the basis of a post-metaphysical thinking. The reason is that "suicide would mean the end of the encounter [between desire for unity and world], and absurdist reasoning considers that it could not consent to this without [self-reflectively] negating its own premises."[913] However, as *The Rebel*'s "Introduction" now continues, faced with the moral question of the legitimacy of killing someone else, the same argument proscribes taking the life of any other. To kill another, as oneself, is to end their awareness of our shared condition. It is to definitively snuff out their desire for meaning, and end their adventure of reckoning this desire against a world which finally resists its satiety. Thus, murder betrays the only living truth which can be indubitably affirmed this side of all metaphysical expostulations. And, as Camus asks rhetorically:

> How is it possible, without making remarkable concessions to one's desire for comfort, to preserve exclusively for oneself the benefits of such a process of reasoning? From the moment that life is recognized as good, it becomes good for all men. Murder cannot be made coherent when suicide is not considered coherent...[914]

So, whereas the absurd man's "revolt" against the symmetrical consolations of absolute, "all or nothing" despair (Irrationalism) and hope (Rationalism) was in *Le Mythe de Sisyphe* mustered to oppose suicide, *L'Homme Révolté*'s rebellion is posited as an indubitable human datum which *ought* to set itself

---

912   HR 23; R 10.
913   HR 18; R 6.
914   HR 18; R 6.

against all ideological, theological or philosophical legitimations of murder. As Camus reflected in the *Carnets* concerning the novels of his first two "stages": "*L'Étranger* described the nudity of man facing the absurd. *La Peste* [described] the profound equivalence of individuals' points of view in face of the same absurd."[915] Part I of *L'Homme Révolté* thus ends, famously, by highlighting the foundational, paraCartesian status of Camus' argument against murder in the context of a cultural setting wherein all appeals to grounding absolutes have become uncertain: "In our daily trials, rebellion plays the same role as does the *cogito* in the category of thought: it is the first clue ... rebellion is the common ground on which man bases his first values. *I rebel—therefore we exist.*"[916]

The subject matter *L'Homme Révolté* concerns itself with then equally follows more or less immediately from this paraCartesian beginning. For if rebellion is the subject, then historically speaking, "two centuries of rebellion, either metaphysical [Part II] or historical-political [Part III], present themselves for our consideration..."[917] All this, to stress again, Camus proposes as following from his paraCartesian meditations without importing any external, unexamined matter or presupposition. *The Rebel* sets about examining the two centuries of modern metaphysical and political revolt, framed by his initial paraCartesian deduction of the illegitimacy of all personal, political or philosophical rationalisations of murder, and Camus' phenomenological account of rebellion in Part I, to which we will come presently.

A sceptical reader can certainly wonder about how compelling Camus' inference is from the rational proscription against nihilistic suicide to the impermissibility of murder in the opening pages of *The Rebel*.[918] As a matter of sheer statistics, there have been a good deal more human beings killed by others in history than have chosen to take their own lives. Many people, it thus seems, are instinctively less inclined to take their own lives than they are willing, in certain circumstances, to kill others.[919] Most political systems have enshrined deep-set normative distinctions between classes of people

---

915   C II 36; C II Eng 15.
916   HR 34; R 22.
917   H 24; R 10. See Appendix One below for our systematic presentation of the argument.
918   See Cruickshank, *Albert Camus and the literature of revolt*, 94–95 ("a poor argument"); or Colin Davis, "Violence and Ethics in Camus", in *Cambridge Companion to Camus*, 111–113. We note in passing that Davis' claim that Camus' rhetoric in *The Rebel* is "altericidal" is a very strong claim. Compare Raymond Gay-Crosier, "De l'*homo faber* à l'*homo ludens*: défence et illustration de la pensée de midi", in *Albert Camus, Contemporain*, 35–36.
919   Cf. Pascal, "Albert Camus ou le philosophe malgré lui", 184–5.

positioning some as morally more important than others, and legitimating the continuing willingness of rulers to send others to kill and die, while exempting themselves from fighting on grounds of hereditary, providential or other claims to higher worth.

Camus' argument in the opening pages of *L'Homme Révolté* is however neither naïve nor closed to these critical considerations. We can see this by tracking the phenomenological analysis of rebellion which he undertakes in the foundational Part I of the essay. "What is a rebel?," Camus begins by asking, in Socratic clip. He answers that any rebel, no matter what the cause, is "a man who says no, but whose refusal does not imply a renunciation."[920] The rebel says "no" to some particular action or infraction: the imposition of a pay cut, the assassination of a leader, the removal of health or other forms of social insurance, the corruption of a government, the invasion of a territory, the murdering of innocents, etc. But this "no" is never the whole story. In contrast to many of his post-1960 French successors, Camus was never really tempted to celebrate either dissidence, difference, dispersion, alterity, *as such*: or the pure, irruptive Event of Negation by itself. These form but one half of the whole truth of what is engaged in genuine rebellion, as Camus sees it. Indeed, Camus notes that phenomenologically, for the rebel's "no!" to even be coherent, it must always presuppose an affirmation or 'Yes'. *When* the rebel says "no" to a perceived injustice, this is because s/he has, if only tacitly, recognised now a normative limit: some point or boundary or principle which is "so far, but no farther…"[921] As Camus notes, perhaps s/he has hitherto let violations of this principle pass. But the moment of her rebellion just *is* the affirmation of a normative limit. Far from being a nihilistic action in anything like a literal sense, Camus thus sees rebellion as either the creator or discoverer of values, principles, rights, or an implicit sense of justice. "Not every value leads to rebellion," he writes in a characteristic symmetry, "but every rebellion tacitly involves a value."[922]

And here is the decisive thing, relative to the critical concerns we raised above. Camus' next claim is that this "Yes" of the rebel always involves "something inside him that does not belong to him alone."[923] In this way, Camus asks us to reject any kind of Augustinian idea that human beings must either love a God that transcends them, or idolise their own self, now aspiring to usurp His place.[924] If we look at the history of human rebellion, Camus notes, we see that

---

920   HR 26; R 13.
921   HR 26; R 13.
922   HR 27; R 14.
923   HR 32–33, 37–38; R 15–16; 22.
924   See Chapter Five below.

human beings have very often (throughout both ancient and modern history) shown themselves willing to die for a whole range of causes larger or wider than their own self-love.[925] People can and have rebelled for the sake of a violated principle: like a sense of justice, or of the importance of its specific institutional embodiment, a city or a nation. They have often done so at the highest cost to themselves and their personal felicity, as when Diego at the culminating moment of *State of Siege* willingly sacrifices himself in place of his lover;[926] or when Kaliayev, historically and in Camus' 1949 play *Les Justes*, accepts his own death as the price for his revolutionary terrorism.[927] Differently, people can and often have rebelled, at similarly ultimate personal cost, because of others' suffering. Camus cites Russian militants who suicided in protest against comrades' treatments.[928] Today many more sad examples can be cited of hunger strikes amongst refugees in offshore detention camps dotted around the globe.

For Camus, this overwhelming historical evidence suggests that it is simply wrong to think of rebellion *per se* as either a solely negative, or a wholly egoistic, order-destroying action. Very often if not always, the affirmative moment in revolt (for instance, against the kinds of dehumanising penitentiary logics denounced in Foucault's *Discipline and Punish*, or against the kinds of states of exception declared by Western governments after 9/11) involves a transcendence of agents' egoistic self-concern. Indeed, such rebellions involve acts of often passionate, sympathetic identification with others' interests, struggles, and concerns: forms of imaginative identification of the very kind we have seen Camus trying to engender through his literature and political journalism. Rebellion, Camus writes (countering a claim made by Scheler) involves a "passionate affirmation" of what we are, not resentful envy of what we are not.[929]

So to tie in the threads, Camus wants us to recognise in the self-transcending "Yes" he uncovers in the phenomenological analysis of rebellion *per se* in *L'Homme Révolté* Part I an avatar of that "demand for clarity and for unity... an aspiration for order..."[930] we have seen at the basis of the affirmative argument

---

925   HR 32–33; R 15–16. Cf. Francis Bacon, "On Death" (*Essays, Civil and Moral*. The Harvard Classics. 1909–14), at www-site http://www.bartleby.com/3/1/2.html, last accessed January 2015: cited by Camus in support of this point in RG 190.
926   Camus, "State of Siege", 228–9.
927   Camus, "The Just", trans. H. Jones & J. O'Brien (London: Penguin 1970); cf. HR 211–221; R 164–173.
928   HR 31; R 17.
929   HR 33–34; R 19. In fact, as we will examine in Chapter Five, rebellion's analysis is going for Camus "to lead... to the suspicion that, contrary to the postulates of contemporary thought, a human nature does exist, as the Greeks believed" HR 30; R 16.
930   HR 41; R 23.

of *Le Mythe de Sisyphe*, this side of any metaphysical consolations. "Essentially, then, we are dealing with a perpetual demand for unity", he claims,[931] or "desire for the true life":[932] what a later collection calls a human *royaume* or kingdom, communion or a homeland. "What [the rebel] is seeking, without knowing it, is a moral philosophy or a religion … If the rebel blasphemes, it is in the hope of finding a new god …," Camus can even write, here again upsetting easy images of his supposed dogmatic atheism.[933]

At the same time, importantly, we observe at this point the proximity of Camus' account of rebellion to the kind of moral psychology expounded by the early modern moral sentiment theorists[934] led by Hutcheson, Shaftesbury, Ferguson, Smith, and Hume. There are always as many reasons to admire as to despair of people, Doctor Rieux will argue at the end of his chronicle in *La Peste*, as Camus was urging his working class comrades in December 1944.[935] For Hume, Hutcheson et al. likewise, alongside our self-interested egoism, we are the bearers of the kind of sympathetic imagination we saw Camus extolling above as of paramount ethical importance, as for the Stoic tradition upon which Hutcheson and Shaftesbury drew, our innate sociability is rooted in the kind of powerful self-effacing love parents inescapably feel for their progeny, insulated from implication.[936]

---

931 HR 132; R 101.

932 HR 103; R 102.

933 HR 132; R 101. Far from being atheistic, Camus is willing here to call rebellion a kind of "disillusioned religious experience…": just as we saw him comfortable in seeking precedents in *The Myth of Sisyphus* for absurd freedom in the religious ascesis of Christian mystics given over wholly to their God. Compare SA 90 and MS 84; MSe 58–59.

934 See Jennifer Riskin, *Science in the Age of Sensibility: The Sentimental Empiricists of the French Enlightenment* (Chicago: Chicago University Press, 2002); cf. James Schimdt, "The Legacy of the Enlightenment", *Philosophy and Literature* Vol. 26: 2 (October 2002), 432–442; "… it would be mistaken to think of reason as the rallying cry of Enlightenment thinkers except in so far as it was opposed to faith, and the Age of Reason opposed to the Age of Superstition. If one's gaze shifts away from the battles with *l'Infâme*, then the 'Age of Sentiments,' 'Sentimentality,' 'Feelings,' 'Passions,' 'Pleasure,' 'Love' or 'Imagination' are apter titles for the movement of ideas in the eighteenth century …" Sylvana Tomaselli, "Reason", in *The Blackwell Companion to the Enlightenment*, ed. John W. Yolton (Oxford: Blackwell, 1991), 446.

935 Camus, "Au service de l'homme", OC I 935; Cf. P 251.

936 Cicero, *De Fin. III*, 20–21, 63, 67–9; Diogenes Laertius, *Lives of the Eminent Philosophers* VII 107; Stobaeus *Anthologion Ioannis Stobæi Florilegium* 2 II 79. See Troel Engberg-Pederson, "Discovering the Good: Oikeiosis and Kathekonta in Stoic Ethics", *The Norms of Nature: Studies in Hellenistic Ethics*, edited by Malcolm Schofield and Gisela Striker (Cambridge: Cambridge Uni. Press 1986), 145–184.

Thus Camus, by the end of Part I of *The Rebel*, brings together the two seemingly disparate argumentative strands at play (respectively) in the "Introduction" and this opening phenomenological account of revolt. Camus argues that the prohibition on murder he has drawn from his paraCartesian meditations on the absurd (Introduction) speaks directly to the 'moral-sentimental' side of his thought (Part I) which we saw in the previous section predated and preshaped his mature philosophical formalisations. For "the first progressive step for a mind overwhelmed by the strangeness of things", Camus argues: "... is to realize that this feeling of strangeness is shared with all men and that human reality, in its entirety, suffers from the distance which separates it from the rest of the universe. The malady experienced by a single man becomes a mass plague (sic.)...":[937] or at least, it can become such a *peste*, if humans do not respond with principled solidarity.

3 Between Formal Virtue and Historicism—not 'against History'

Citing Klaus Heinrich (and thinking of Jean-Baptiste Clamence's derisive claim in *The Fall* that he no longer has friends, but legion accomplices),[938] the primary value towards which Camus' mature philosophical discourse points could accordingly be termed a "universal confederation against betrayal, without which the idea of enlightenment is meaningless."[939] As David Carroll has put it:

> Camus' anti-ideological stance is rooted not in the belief that there exists an alternate form of politics that would be in itself completely pure or nonideological [...] It is rather based on the conviction that because life has precedence over politics, politics cannot be allowed to determine life ... [Camus'] refusal to legitimize murder [...] [is] the founding principle of Camus' critical perspective on politics, both his increasingly militant anticommunism and his refusal to defend the use of terrorism in the cause of national liberation in Algeria or torture and murder in France's counterterrorist strategy.[940]

Two things, straight away, need to be stressed about this primary value of pre-metaphysical, predogmatic human fraternity or solidarity, if we are to correctly

---

937   HR 38; R 22.
938   F 73.
939   At Habermas, *Philosophical Discourse of Modernity*, 325.
940   Carroll, *Camus the Algerian*, 100, 101.

appreciate its philosophical force and status. The first is the simple inaccuracy of Jeanson's and Sartre's attempt to position Camus as a defender of a purely formal morality in the tradition of Rousseau, Kant, or the Jacobins.[941] As both men must have known, Camus sets out in his section "The Regicides" in Part III of *The Rebel* to critique this 'bourgeois' tradition. As he sees things, with the doctrine of the General Will, Rousseau asks us to replace the demands of a transcendent God with those of a transcendent rational morality.[942] It is this tradition's valorisation of transcendent norms and virtue above living human beings, Camus argues, that allowed figures like Saint-Just and Robespierre to vindicate the material actions of Madame Guillotine.[943] The bourgeois theorists' formal morality is in fact the first example Camus cites in "Historical rebellion" of the kind of crime that has "assumed all the aspects of the syllogism" which the entire book opposes:

> Saint-Just sets the example; even his tone is definitive. That cascade of peremptory affirmatives, that axiomatic and sententious style, portrays him better than the most faithful painting. His sentences drone on; his definitions follow one another with the coldness and precision of commandments. 'Principles should be moderate, laws implacable, principles without redress.' It is the style of the guillotine…. Saint-Just dreams of an ideal city where manners and customs, in final agreement with the law, will proclaim the innocence of man and the identity of his nature with reason. And if factions arise to interrupt this dream, passion will exaggerate its logic. No one will dare to imagine that, since factions exist, the principles are perhaps wrong. Factions will be condemned as criminal… Whoever criticizes [the republic] is a traitor, whoever fails to give open support is a suspect. When neither reason nor the free expression of individual opinion succeeds in systematically establishing [national] unity, it must be decided to suppress all alien elements. Thus the guillotine becomes a logician whose function is refutation…[944]

Camus is clear that, while rebellion may discover values which challenge the historical reign of power and expediency celebrated by fascist ideologues (and

---

941   Jeanson, "Soul in Revolt" 91 ("as soon as eternal principles, nonincarnated values, and formal virtue are put in doubt… nihilism is established, and Caesar triumphs…"); Sartre, "Reply to Albert Camus" 140: "why must you surround yourself with a universe of intangible values…" etc.
942   HR 151–2; 158–159; R 116; 121–122.
943   "La morale, quand elle est formelle, dévore." HR 161; R 124.
944   HR 162–163; R 125.

sanctified still under the august name of 'political realism'), these values are not formal. Nor, contra Jeanson's implications, do they wholly transcend their origin in human struggles:

> Man's solidarity is founded upon rebellion, and rebellion, in its turn, can only find its justification in this solidarity. We have, then, the right to say that any rebellion which claims the right to deny or destroy this solidarity loses simultaneously its right to be called rebellion... [T]his solidarity, except in so far as religion is concerned, comes to life only on the level of rebellion. And so the real drama of revolutionary thought is announced. In order to exist, man must rebel, but rebellion must respect the limit it discovers in itself—a limit where minds meet and, in meeting, begin to exist.[945]

At the end of *L'Homme Révolté*, Camus reaffirms this point. His thought is neither an absolute materialism, nor an absolute historicism. But this does not condemn his thought to the cloudless or clouded dreams of a beautiful soul. The primary value of solidarity Camus postulates is located, always, in the present *hic et nunc*: "the fixed and radiant point of the present," in contrast to utopian hypotheses and nostalgic reveries.[946] The political ideologies or theodicies we have seen him opposing in Chapters One and Two, by contrast, always promise a "we shall be" to justify their exactions, or an elegiac "we once were," in the name of which present, really-existing people can be branded enemies, traitors, nihilists, etc. and dealt with accordingly.[947] Camus ties his ethicopolitical universalism to *la chair* or "the flesh" we saw him invoking in his tribute to Leynaud above, and which remains a constant term of reference in his work, from his earliest lyrical exercises and *The Happy Death*. Camus' is a universalism of the body, based in the affects: human beings' capacities both to suffer and experience joy, love, solidarity and fecundity. By the same token, then, despite Sartre's charge that "Camus evades history" (which Margerisson comments "is so familiar that we are likely to accept it as self-evident"),[948] Camus always affirmed that "[i]t is true that we cannot 'escape History', since we are in

---

945 HR 37; R 21–22.
946 HR 380–381; R 305. See Pascal, "Camus, philosophe malgré lui", 186–7.
947 HR 352; R 282.
948 Christine Margerisson, "Algeria's Others" in Stephen G. Kellman ed. *Critical Insights: Albert Camus* (USA: Salem Press, 2012), 31.

it up to our necks."⁹⁴⁹ What *The Rebel* seeks out is a middle ground between all cynical positions, whether of Left or Right, which end by equating Right with might or historical fact; and on the other side, the elevation of formal, fleshless values standing judgment over human affairs in place of the absent God:

> In the same way [rebellion] defined, in contradiction to nihilism, a rule of conduct that has no need to await the end of history to explain its actions and which is, nevertheless, not formal. Contrary to Jacobin morality, it made allowances for everything that escapes from rules and laws. It opened the way to a morality which, far from obeying abstract principles, discovers them only in the heat of battle and in the incessant movement of contradiction. Nothing justifies the assertion that these principles have existed eternally; it is of no use to declare that they will one day exist. But they do exist, in the very period in which we exist...⁹⁵⁰

In delineating the status of Camus' primary political value of solidarity, between cynical realism and formal world-denials, in fact, we are rejoining Camus' major, paraCartesian argument and its attempt to found a political ethic which can withstand the most scathing sceptical critique. This is the second thing that needs to be stressed if we are to understand the philosophical stakes of Camus' mature political philosophy. In elevating a primary human solidarity leagued against natural and human injustices, Camus' political philosophy aims at a rigorous post-metaphysical, self-reflexive position. Its philosophical credentials, he thinks, can accordingly be shown *per via negativa* by the same kind of argument we saw him making in Chapter Three concerning the "leap" involved in assenting to Rationalist or Irrationalist positions. According to Camus, we recall, one accedes to such 'all or nothing' positions only by wishfully accepting more than what experience can attest or *denying* salient 'negative instances' facing one's position (and not least, often disavowing one's own position of enunciation). The price of such "intemperate recourse to absolutes",⁹⁵¹ in other words, is inconsistencies and obfuscations of the kind that Derrida has since honed in upon in his deconstructive writings on systematic philosophers. In the same way as we have seen Camus critiquing Ivan Karmazov's passionate 'leap' to an atheist nihilism permitting everything, Camus argues that all forms of modern ideological justification for murderous

---

949 NVE 275; compare Sartre's "up to our noses" in "Reply to Albert Camus," 157. See Chapter Five.
950 HR 353–354; R 283.
951 HR 133; R 101–102 (and Chapter Two above).

political action, by violating the "we are" of presently-existing human beings their revolt initially affirmed, decisively betray *themselves* at the same time as they visit violence on others.

Just how far Camus is willing to go in this suggestive line of thinking calling upon rebels to continually return to their beginnings is indicated in the decisive section of *The Rebel*, "Rebellion and Revolution." Coming at the end of *L'Homme Révolté*'s longest part on "Historical Rebellion", here Camus approaches a position which sounds unmistakably like Jürgen Habermas' later claims on behalf of the "ideal speech situation." As readers will know, Habermas argues that, even when the worst scoundrel misrepresents himself, lies or withholds relevant information, the efficacy of these speech acts *themselves* turns on the auditors' presuppositions that they aimed to speak truly, respectfully and honestly.[952] Of course, the kind of ideal situation in which all parties actually *do* speak and act in such complete good faith, with complete relevant information, only rarely or perhaps never transpires. But this does not, by itself, speak against the normative force of the ideal *qua* ideal. Nor, before that, does it speak against Habermas' quasi-transcendental claim that, *in speaking*, we presuppose such a counterfactual ideal, all the time, and trade upon it even in our most mendacious monologues.[953]

Just so, Camus argues in *The Rebel*, in one of the book's most beautiful formulations, that *"parler, répare"*: "to speak heals".[954] Even our greatest criminal excesses presuppose and bespeak the longing for the fugitive kingdom of a solidary humanity, as an ideal normative horizon. "In every word and in every act,

---

[952] Jürgen Habermas, *Philosophical Discourse of Modernity*, 199–204, 206–209; 247–248, and esp. 311–326; *The Theory of Communicative Action*. Vol. I: *Reason and the Rationalization of Society*, T. McCarthy trans. (Boston: Beacon, 1984), 3–23; *Justification and Application*, trans. C.P. Cronin (Cambridge, MA: MIT Press, 1993), ch. 1; "Reflections on the linguistic foundations of sociology: The Christian Gauss Lectures (Princeton University, February-March 1971)", in Habermas, *On the Pragmatics of Social Interaction*, trans. B. Fultner (Cambridge, MA: MIT Press, 2001), 1–103.

[953] Compare the early Jacques Lacan on good faith as the basis of social exchange in *Ecrits* "As a rule everyone knows that others will remain, like himself, inaccessible to the constraints of reason, outside an acceptance in principle of a rule of debate that does not come into force without an explicit or implicit agreement as to what is called its basis, which is almost always tantamount to an anticipated agreement to what is at stake... I shall expect nothing therefore of these rules except the good faith of the Other, and, as a last resort, will make use of them, if I think fit or if I am forced to, only to amuse bad faith..."..." Jacques Lacan, *Ecrits: The First Full Edition in English*, 430–431.

[954] HR 21; R 8. See Gay-Crosier, De l'*Homo faber* à l'*Homo ludens*: défence et illustration de la pensée de midi", in *Albert Camus, Contemporain*, 35–36.

even though it be criminal," Camus writes, "lies the promise of a value that we must seek out and bring to light..."⁹⁵⁵ This value of human fraternity (*le royaume*) is surely something very close to that "obscure...joy" Camus allows us to glimpse in the final scene of *Exile and the Kingdom* in his character d'Arrast in "The Growing Stone". It is "a fresh beginning in life" represented in the story by d'Arrast's taking on of the symbolic burden of the cook, carrying his huge weight for him back to the latter's hearth. Here d'Arrast is welcomed almost wordlessly by the cook's humble people "whose credence in a supernatural deity he cannot share": " 'sit down with us' ".⁹⁵⁶ Reflecting on the secular theodicies to which Camus assigns ideological responsibility for the state terrorisms of the last century, he explains:

> Man wants to reign supreme through the revolution. But why reign supreme if nothing has any meaning? Why wish for immortality if the aspect of life is so hideous?... The destruction of man once more affirms man. Terror and concentration camps are the drastic means used by man to escape solitude. The thirst for unity must be assuaged, even in the common grave. If men kill one another, it is because they reject mortality and desire immortality for all men. Therefore, in one sense, they commit suicide. But they prove, at the same time, that they cannot dispense with mankind; they satisfy a terrible hunger for fraternity. 'The human being needs happiness, and when he is unhappy, he needs another human being.' Those who reject the agony of living and dying wish to dominate. 'Solitude is power,' says Sade. Power, today, because for thousands of solitary people it signifies the suffering of others, bears witness to the need for others. Terror is the homage the malignant recluse finally pays to the brotherhood of man...⁹⁵⁷

We see why Srigley seems in error when he comments that, for Camus, there is nothing recognisably human about the actions of the people who built and operated the concentration and death camps.⁹⁵⁸ For Camus, the desire for

---

955 HR 310; R 248. Compare: " 'Obey', said Frederick the Great to his subjects, but when he died his words were: 'I am tired of ruling slaves.' ", at HR 313; R 251.
956 "The Growing Stone", EK 211–212; Wilhoite, *Beyond Nihilism*, 70.
957 HR 308–309; R 248.
958 Srigley argues, contra Camus, that "... neither the presence of good in all lives nor the permanent possibility of recognising that good and cultivating it—makes *these* lives good. There is no necessity, logical or otherwise, that the totalitarian dictator will turn the inescapable good of his soul to account or that the metaphysical rebel will desist

unity and fraternity is universal to all humans, as we have seen. This desire is also the ground of their inalienable dignity: "there is not one human being who, above a certain elementary level of consciousness, does not exhaust himself in trying to find formulas or attitudes that will give his existence the unity it lacks."[959] For Camus' profoundly classical position,[960] this will include even the men who organised the *Shoah* and the gulags, many of whom were (this being what is most disturbingly uncanny) family men and lovers of fine music, and fancied themselves men of culture.[961] The desire for totality evinced in the modern totalitarian regimes and their crimes, to be sure, is historically contingent and avoidable, ethically condemnable and politically to be opposed. It is prompted by claims to absolute metaphysical or Historical knowledge which Camus thinks epistemically illegitimate, and gravely ethically problematic. Totalitarian thinking is thinking which 'leaps' over the bounds of what the desire for unity should honour, including everything about natural and human reality which "exceeds the reign of quantity".[962] But it is in this sense alone that Camus talks of "... an evil, undoubtedly, which men accumulate in their desire for unity."[963] The evil remains an excessive misshaping of the inalienable, universal human need to give unity to the world.

---

from his revolt against 'the whole of creation' and there is no hidden goodness or moderation in either of these excessive revolts against the good." Srigley *Camus' Critique*, 52. I have argued that this is not Camus' position at greater length than we can here in Sharpe "A Just Judgment?", *Thesis Eleven*, vol. 120, no. 1 (2014), 43–58.

959   HR 327–328; R 262; see introduction.
960   See for example the profoundly Socratic passage in Epictetus, *Discourses* I. 28: "it is the very nature of the understanding to agree to truth, to be dissatisfied with falsehood, and to suspend its belief, in doubtful cases." "What is the proof of this?," Epictetus asks rhetorically. "Persuade yourself, if you can, that it is now night": [respondent] "It is impossible." "Dissuade yourself from the belief that it is day." [respondent] "Impossible." "Persuade yourself that the number of the stars is even or odd. [respondent] "It is impossible." "Well, then; have we, in actions, anything correspondent to this distinction between true and false?" [respondent] "Right and wrong; advantageous and disadvantageous; desirable and undesirable; and the like." "A person then, cannot think a thing truly advantageous to him, and not choose it?" [respondent] "He cannot." Of course, people can be wrong about what is truly desirable, however. Camus, we know from Carl A. Viggiani, read Epictetus in hospital ("*Il m'aide à tenir...*"), cited at Bousquet, *Camus le Méditerranéen*, 35.
961   See Thomas Harding, *Hans and Rudolf* (London: Random House, 2013) and Harding's quiet narration of the disturbing, because so incredibly mundane life of Rudolf Höss, commandant of Auschwitz.
962   HR 293; R 234.
963   HR 378; R 303.

As such, it is less monstrously inhuman than destructively inhumane, and all-too-human.[964]

In Chapter Five, we will see how this position is one component of the deeply Greek bases of Camus' ethical philosophy: for it aligns evil with weakness, ignorance, or error, as against an irredeemable or incurable fallenness or sin. For now we need only stress the deeply Socratic form of Camus' argument. The striving for totality, by which men accord to themselves the right to judge, condemn and kill other human beings, for Camus involves also a kind of self-betrayal or self-forgetting: if not a negligence in the work implied by Socrates' injunction to *gnôthi seauton*. In killing others, we violate and betray what is best in ourselves, and compromise whatever causes we serve, however otherwise just: as we will see, a key consideration in Camus' *Algerian Chronicles*.[965] Political rebellion, and modern metaphysical rebellion, for Camus affirms the human need for unity and order, at the same time as it says 'no' to incursions against the primary, promissory value of living human solidarity—at least in its beginnings. For this reason, Camus entire critique in *L'Homme Révolté* is not directed at the "revolutionary spirit" of modern Europe from the outside, as if he were in possession of some external, transhistorical standpoint of the kind Jeanson et al. polemically attributed to him. The book is a form of immanent critique. It calls upon "the revolutionary spirit in Europe..., for the first and last time, [to] *reflect upon its own principles*, ask itself what the deviation is which leads it into terror and into war, and rediscover with the reasons for its rebellion, its faith in itself."[966] As in *Le Mythe de Sipyphe*, Camus thus deploys a language of ethical fidelity and of memory to articulate his position: "... the real drama of revolutionary thought is announced. In order to exist, man must rebel, but rebellion *must respect the limit it discovers in itself...*":[967]

> At this exact point the limit is exceeded, rebellion is first betrayed and then logically assassinated, for it has never affirmed, in its purest form, anything but the existence of a limit and the divided existence that we

---

964 While Srigley at one point does mark Camus' distinction between unity and totality in *The Rebel* (Srigley *Camus' Critique*, 74), the weight of his argument is to occlude the way that for Camus, totality perverts—but still in this way bespeaks—the desire for unity. "A human being who has such excessive desires and acts on them" as the ill-begotten desire for a final political solution, Srigley claims, "is simply not the same type of human being as one who does not." (Srigley, *Camus' Critique*, 52).

965 See Chapter Six below.

966 HR 366; R 293 (our italics).

967 HR 38; R 22.

represent… When rebellion, in rage or intoxication, adopts the attitude of 'all or nothing' and the negation of all existence and all human nature,… *it denies itself.* Only total negation justifies the concept of a totality that must be conquered. But the affirmation of a limit, a dignity, and a beauty common to all men only entails the necessity of extending this value to embrace everything and everyone and of advancing toward unity *without denying the origins of rebellion*…[968]

4   Political Suicide? On Camus' Concrete Political Philosophy

Most readers today are likely to be much more sympathetic with the Camus of 1951–'52, *contra* Jeanson and Sartre, in the wake of the end of the Cold War. It remains that the latters' polemical critique of Camus has largely shaped reception (or non-reception) of Camus' mature political philosophy, outside of the circles of Camus scholarship. As we have said, where Camus' philosophical essays are read at all, criticisms of *L'Homme Révolté* as rhetorically cogent but philosophically insubstantial roll from the pens or word processors of critics, alongside complaints that the final affirmative part of the work on "*Le Pensée de Midi*" is hopelessly opaque: a triumph of style or sentiment over substance and applicability in the 'real world'.[969] On one level, such criticisms raise the broader question of the role of philosophical reflection in politics. How much practical detail can we rightly ask of a philosopher *qua* philosopher, to complain that a book like *The Rebel* does not offer us more? To what extent do the types of abstract cognition we demand of philosophers pull against the production of point-by-point prescriptive schemes, as they pull away from particularity towards universalities? Leaving such meta-questions aside, it can be reasonably asked: just how *just* are the continuing criticisms of Camus' alleged political naivety, alongside concomitant attacks on the supposedly complete impracticality and rhetorical emptiness of his political philosophy?

Let us say straight away that, on the basis of his affirmation of the primary value of "the mutual recognition of a common destiny between human beings",[970] Camus says a good deal concerning politics at a general or 'philosophical' level. He also says a very great deal, as a journalist and a political agent, concerning the specific situations in which he intervened: much more,

---

968   HR 313; R 251.
969   For one further example (but see below), Aronson, *Camus and Sartre*, 123 says the book has "a frequently arbitrary, eccentric quality", amidst an otherwise balanced and sympathetic reading.
970   HR 353; R 283.

in fact, than many another, more recognised philosopher. As soon as we have arrive at human solidarity as a primary political value, and we ask accordingly how the "shared dignity, a communion of men" can be promoted in political life,[971] Camus' philosophical discourse allows him and us to change gear from abstract speculation towards political engagement. What is needed politically, both in itself and in order to do honour to the rebels who have died glimpsing this promissory universal value is a society founded on the principle of dialogue. What is demanded philosophically, in its turn (and here as above, Camus anticipates Habermas' dialogic turn after *Knowledge and Human Interests*) is what he calls a "theory of communication."[972] Such a theory could formalise the features of such a society of dialogue, stipulate its institutional preconditions, and dialectically defend its justice and principles against all adversaries.

Camus had begun to make his way towards philosophically articulating his political position by the time of March 1946's "La Crise de L'Homme" in the United States. He advocates for a radicalised democratic socialism in France and more widely.[973] This position is developed in "Neither Victims nor Executioners" in 1947, "Le Temps des Meurtrieurs" of 1949 and a host of occasional pieces throughout these years, before finding its definitive statement in the subsection "Nihilistic Murder" in Part V of *L'Homme Révolté*.[974] Importantly, although Camus' defence of a "new social contract" for a *"civilisation de dialogue"*[975] or a "community of reflection and dialogue"[976] anticipates Habermas' later, more systematic statements on this subject, Camus' primary justification for it is political, not transcendental—once, that is, we have accepted Camus' paraCartesian defence of the primary value of human solidarity. Dialogue for Camus is the only realistic alternative to forms of political thought which sanction Machiavellian means in order to attain their ideologically-nominated ends: "The mutual understanding and

---

971 TM (OC III) 360.
972 Camus, "Conférence au couvent de Latour-Marbourg", OC II 509.
973 Cf. CAC 55 (*Combat* October 1 1944), where the Scandinavian social democracies are cited; CAC 63 (October 7 1944) where Camus endorses communism's "collectivist ideal and social program, their ideal of justice, and their disgust with a society in which money and privilege occupy the front rank..."; and CAC 121 (November 20, 1944) where Camus appeals to a French, nonMarxist tradition of socialism which "has always made room for individuals and that owes nothing to philosophical materialism." As per Chapter Two, at both CAC 63 and 121 it is Marxism's secularised philosophy of history that Camus criticises, as the basis for political cynicism.
974 HR 353–367; R 282–286.
975 NVE 270, 273.
976 TM 363.

communication discovered by rebellion can survive only in the free exchange of conversation."[977] The twentieth century has learnt this the hard way, witnessing the systematic attempt of the total states to close down all uncoerced dialogue, and censor independent thought and artistic creation. We saw in Chapter One how, for Camus, "the language peculiar to totalitarian doctrines is always a scholastic or administrative language..."[978] The *esprit* of these regimes is one of atomisation and terror. They set out in a more or less openly cynical way to suppress the "the implicit and untrammeled dialogue through which we come to recognize our similarity and consecrate our destiny."[979] Far-Right ideology, for instance, touts such dialogue as indecisive and unworldly; and far Left propaganda presents it as "bourgeois" and hopelessly complicit in the structural injustices of the capitalist order.[980] Challenging both extremes, Camus proclaims in *L'Homme Révolté* that "Plato is right and not Moses and Nietzsche":

> Dialogue on the level of mankind is less costly than the gospel preached by totalitarian regimes in the form of a monologue dictated from the top of a lonely mountain. On the stage as in reality, the monologue precedes death...[981]

Camus puts it more simply elsewhere: politically speaking, in the age where states can muster unprecedented lethal force against their subjects, "there is no life without dialogue."[982] So what does Camus have to say concerning the content of this political dialogue and its political preconditions? Is its defence, indeed, anything more than a pleasant-sounding, substantively empty chimera?

First, a progressive political philosophy should oppose the proliferation of specialised, managerial jargon: "every ambiguity, every misunderstanding, leads to death; clear language and simple words are the only salvation" from it.[983] Clearly, Camus *qua* artist cannot mean to proscribe metaphoric, lyrical, and mythical modes of expression. Yet Camus is attuned to what Habermas, once more, has since called the role of systematically distorted communication in

---

977 HR 354; R 283.
978 HR 354 note; R 283 note.
979 HR 354; R 283.
980 See for instance Carl Schmitt, *Political Theology: Four Chapters on the Concept of Sovereignty*. Translated by Guy Oakes (Cambridge, Mass.: MIT Press), 62, 85.
981 HR 354; R 283–4.
982 TL 490.
983 HR 354; R 283.

political life.⁹⁸⁴ Commentators today talk of 'spin', 'weasel words' and the like: meaning language distorted by its proponents' economic and political interests, compelling them to misrepresent or distort what they say. And despite Camus, Orwell, Chomsky and others like them, the role of 'spin doctors' in contemporary liberal plutocracies has become, alongside marketing 'madmen', an utterly respectable, lucrative profession. When it comes to political matters involving harming, killing, and expropriating (or, in better times, distributing the peaceable risks, costs, burdens and benefits of social life) Camus maintains that unclear, allusive or misleading vocabularies made up of administrative shibboleths ('we defend freedom', 'there was collateral damage', 'national security is paramount,' etc.) function most often as or alongside forms of the Machiavellian 'noble lie'. They conceal or misrepresent relevant information from those affected by the proposed actions, in order to manufacture a political pseudo-consensus. *Pace* the venerable tradition recently defended by Leo Strauss and his students which would sanction such deceit as a necessary instrument of policy for 'the wise',⁹⁸⁵ in his important, brief "Reflections on a Democracy without Catechism", Camus contends that:

> All thought, all definition which risks adding to the deceptions or entertaining them is unpardonable. It is enough to say that in defining a certain number of key-words [the article takes 'democracy' as its subject], in rendering them sufficiently clear today so that they will tomorrow be effective, we are working towards liberation...⁹⁸⁶

---

984 Jürgen Habermas, "On systematically distorted communication", *Inquiry* Volume 13, Issue 1–4, 1970: 205–218. Cf. Donald Lazere, "Camus on Doublespeak" *The English Journal*, Vol. 66, No. 7 (Oct., 1977), 24–26.

985 "Strauss' view certainly alerts one to the possibility that political life might be closely linked to deception. Indeed, it suggests that deception is the norm of political life, and the hope—to say nothing of the expectation, of establishing a politics that dispense with it is the exception." G. Schmitt and A. Shulsky, 'The World of Intelligence (By Which We Do Not Mean *Nous*)', *Leo Strauss, the Straussians, and the American Regime* (USA, Rowman and Littlefield, 1999), pp. 410–11. Although it is not our concern here, the remarkable, idiosyncratic and positive role Strauss assigns to the bellicose sophist Thrasymachus in the *Republic* is important here, at Strauss, *City and Man* (Chicago: Chicago University Press, 1963), 78–80, 86–7, 115–16, 123–4. Interested readers in this controversial, influential figure can look to Leo Strauss, *Natural Right and History* (Chicago: Chicago University Press, 1953), 158 for his 'teaching' there on the need for rulers to misrepresent merely general rules as universally binding, an exigency for which religious doctrine is serviceable.

986 Camus, "Réflexions sur une démocratie sans catéchisme," OC II 718.

Secondly, Camus argues that to maintain a culture of political dialogue requires the willingness to treat those with whom we disagree on political and other matters with a minimum of respect. That is to say, we must reject all paraSchmittian definitions of 'the political' as inescapably a world of friends and enemies as a far Right definition of "the political" masquerading as social science.[987] The other may be an adversary. We may not always agree with his reasons. Sometimes, we will question his motives, especially when his reasons are weak, evidently partial, and mustered in defence of unstated interests. But to treat the other as an enemy is to reserve the right to not credit whatever reasons he is able to give; and to license oneself to ignore, simplify or misrepresent her position and motivations. In short, it is to license oneself and one's 'friends' to do whatever it takes to defeat the other: through deceit and calumny where possible, and where necessary through exile, excommunication or "physical killing".[988] At times, Camus will reflect upon his own distaste for politics conceived in this extremist way, since he professes himself unable after 1945 to any longer wish for and celebrate the physical killing of adversaries.[989]

If the twentieth century is the age of monologic ideologies, for Camus it is also "the age of polemic and insult": far from the apolitical reign of a toothless liberal consensus sometimes lamented by critics.[990] Polemic is what remains of dialogic respect, when one or more parties believe themselves alone exclusively in possession of the definitive Truth. In the absence of any shared vocabulary, Camus laments:

> From millions of voices, day and night, each pursuing on his side a tumultuous monologue, pours a torrent of mystifying discourses, attacks, defences, and exaltations ... [But] he whom I insult, I no longer know the colour of his regard ... Having become three quarters blind due to our polemics, we no longer live amongst human beings but amongst silhouettes.[991]

---

[987] Franz Neumann, "The Concept of Political Freedom", *The Democratic and Authoritarian State* (Glencoe: the Free Press, 1957), 160–200.

[988] TM 357; cf. Carl Schmitt, *Concept of the Political* translated with a Introduction by George Schwab, Preface by Tracey Strong (Chicago: Chicago University Press, 1996), 33, 48–49.

[989] Camus, "Projet de Preface" (to *Actuelles II*) OC II 499.

[990] TM 357; "La Témoin de la liberté" OC II 490–491; NVE 258: "Today, no one is talking (except for those who repeat themselves) ..."

[991] TL 490–491.

To defend a culture of *"dialogue pour dialogue"* is thus in Camus, two decades before post-structuralism, to defend plurality. "I am for the plurality of positions ... In any case I do not insult those who are not with me. It is my sole point of originality," he claimed ironically.⁹⁹² Yet for Camus, as we have remarked, to defend Plurality or Difference with the capital letters, as pseudo-metaphysical finalities, is never a temptation. Neither, as we contended in Chapter One, is Camus tempted (as post-structuralist thinkers and their legatees continue to be) to deny or collapse the distinction between liberal-democratic or liberal-plutocratic states and the fascist or Stalinist regimes. Politically more engaged, Camus thinks that to defend plurality in practical terms means accepting the reality, first of multi-party political states, in which no single group can claim an unchecked, permanent possession of executive power; and second, of a free press, not under the control of any single party or perspective.

"The first thing to define totalitarian society whether of the Right or Left is the single party, and the Single party has no reason to destroy itself," Camus observes in his response to the Hungarian events in 1956, "Kadar had his Day of Fear":

> This is why the only society capable of evolution and liberalisation, the only one that deserves both our critical and our active support is the society that involves a plurality of parties as part of its structure. It alone allows one to denounce, hence to correct, injustice and crime.⁹⁹³

Equally, the executive branch of government needs to be subject to what social democratic theorist Franz Neumann, writing around the same time, argued was the changed modern function of the law: not as an instrument to exercise rulers' *voluntas* and privileges over subjects, but as a means of protecting the liberty of those subjects from this *voluntas* in the forms or arbitrary arrest, imprisonment, expropriation, or execution.⁹⁹⁴ "The limit where freedom begins and ends is where its rights and duties come together, and is called the Law, and the state must bow to the Law," Camus affirms.⁹⁹⁵ The rule of laws and not of men is the precondition for any democratic polity—which of

---

992   Camus, "Dialogue pour la dialogue (Défence de l'Homme, juillet 1949)", OC II 479.
993   Camus, "Kadar had his day of fear", RRD 161.
994   Franz Neumann, "The Changing Function of Modern Law", in *Democratic and Authoritarian State*, 23–68. It is fair to say that this changed function of modern law, in principle although not always in practice, from instrument of executive will towards a means to check executive force, is overlooked in many critical studies.
995   Camus, "Homage to an Exile," RRD 101.

course does not mean that any such rule of law, even one which does check the powers of states, is sufficient for the kind of autonomy Camus valorised.[996]

As for a free press (and journalism, Camus' lifelong democratic vocation, first in Algeria, then in France) Camus' argument here again is close to long-standing liberal and democratic arguments, albeit founded on the different philosophical grounds we have seen:

> Not that the press is in itself an absolute good... a free press can of course be good or bad, but most certainly without freedom it will be bad... with freedom of the press, nations are not sure to go towards justice and peace. But without it, they are sure of not going there. For justice is done to peoples only when their rights are recognised, and there is no right without expression of that right...[997]

We are in the presence, contra Srigley's reading of Camus (and contra all total critiques of an abstract 'modernity') of a passionate defence of the always imperfect, threatened modern democratic political legacy. The author of a celebrated, if controversial, study of this modern tradition after all, Camus urges us to recall:

> ...in particular, [that] the few democratic liberties we still enjoy are not unimportant illusions that we can allow to be taken from us without a protest. They represent exactly what remains to us of the great revolutionary conquests of the last two centuries.[998]

To be sure, Marxism (and since Marxism, Foucaultian and other branches of critical theorising) have continued to show us the ways in which "bourgeois liberty is a hoax".[999] Continuing appeals to freedom in the liberal-capitalist states serve to promote policies which necessarily engender structural economic inequalities, and conceal the proliferation of insidious micro-forms of dehumanising surveillance and control. But while this is all true, Camus urges, it is false to infer from the premise that "bourgeois liberty is a hoax" to the idea that political liberty *per se* "is a bourgeois hoax."[1000] Indeed, as Orme has

---

996 See Camus "Dialogue pour le Dialogue", OC II 480, and Camus' opposition to retroactive law-making. See also Issac, *Arendt, Camus, and modern rebellion*, 148–149, on Camus' opposition of Roman legalism with Greek autonomy.
997 Camus, "Homage to an Exile", RRD 102.
998 Camus, "Bread and Freedom", RRD 93.
999 Camus, "Bread and Freedom," RRD 90.
1000 Camus, "Bread and Freedom", RRD 90 (See "Introduction" above).

noted, increasingly after 1945, as Camus continues to talk of balancing freedom against justice, he becomes particularly concerned with the forms of personal freedom involved in the liberal civil rights, and democratic freedoms for political participation.[1001] This is because, although such freedoms are in no way ends in themselves (like justice and all the virtues, they are a subordinate value, below the primary post-metaphysical end of human solidarity we have seen) civil and political freedoms are necessary if other virtues are to be cultivated and other political values to be defended. "One might even have to fight a lie in the name of a quarter truth," Camus argues: "That is our situation today. However, the quarter truth contained in Western society is called liberty... without liberty, heavy industry can be perfected, but not justice or truth."[1002] The primacy of freedom comes from how, "even when justice is not realised, freedom preserves the power to protest and guarantees human communication."[1003]

This, however (*l'envers et l'endroit*), is not to say that Camus is a political libertarian of any stripe. Freedom, Camus argues, must always be balanced against justice. This tension of freedom and justice is the key political instance of what he will call the kind of balance or *mesure* between competing demands that his neoHellenic philosophy extols.[1004] From 1946 onwards, Camus famously insisted that a prohibition on the *peine de mort* ought to be the first statute of any post-metaphysical and post-totalitarian political dispensation: limiting the freedom even of States in fidelity to the normative promise implicit in the modern tradition of political rebellion.[1005] If Europe is serious about being post-theological, Camus argues, it must forthwith remove the sovereign powers of nation-states, so amply enjoyed in the first half of the 20th century, to torture and execute enemies and their own citizens.[1006] As *L'Homme Révolté* explains, in a passage that underlines Camus' distance from Georges Bataille whose celebration of sovereign excess drew him to target Camus on this point:[1007]

1001 Orme, *Development of Albert Camus' Concerns* 30–131; cf. Aronson, *Camus and Sartre*, 82–3.
1002 Camus, "The Wager of our Generation," RRD, 248. See on the balance of freedom and justice in *The Rebel*, Isaac, *Arendt, Camus and modern rebellion*, 128–9.
1003 HR 363; R 291.
1004 HR 362–363, 367–371; R 290–291, 295–296. See Chapter Five below.
1005 CH 744; "Interventions à la table ronde de 'Civilisation'", OC II 681; TM 361.
1006 See RG 226–228.
1007 Bataille, "Le Temps de la Révolte", section 7. "La révolte, la souveraineté et le caractère criminel et rebelle de la royauté", at www-site http://www.larevuedesressources.org/le-temps-de-la-revolte,1491.html, last accessed February 2015.

> Every rebel, solely by the movement that sets him in opposition to the oppressor, therefore pleads for life, undertakes to struggle against servitude, falsehood, and terror, and affirms, in a flash, that these three afflictions are the cause of silence between men, that they obscure them from one another and prevent them from rediscovering themselves in the only value that can save them from nihilism—the long complicity of men at grips with their destiny. In a flash—but that is time enough to say, provisionally, that the most extreme form of freedom, the freedom to kill, is not compatible with the sense of rebellion. Rebellion is in no way the demand for total freedom. On the contrary, rebellion puts total freedom up for trial. It specifically attacks the unlimited power that authorizes a superior to violate the forbidden frontier. Far from demanding general independence, the rebel wants it to be recognized that freedom has its limits everywhere that a human being is to be found—the limit being precisely that human being's power to rebel...[1008]

The reader can see that there is nothing utopian about these Camusian political proscriptions, however often Camus is accused of mealy-mouthed idealism. If anything, they point towards the other side to the criticism of *L'Homme Révolté* hailing from the communists and surrealists in the early 1950s. This is that Camus' book on modern revolt ends by making rebellious politics concrete enough; but concretely conformist, sanctioning a political order very much like to that which the mainland France of 1950 had already achieved. Yet for Camus, rebellion's primary value opposes all forms of servitude. So justice, limited by the need to institute forms of freedom, remains in the front rank of its political aspirations: "[The rebel] is not only the slave against the master, but also the man against the world of master and slave."[1009] His reasoning, as ever, turns on appeal to the primary Camusian political value:

> There is, in fact, nothing in common between a master and a slave; it is impossible to speak and communicate with a person who has been reduced to servitude. Instead of the implicit and untrammelled dialogue through which we come to recognize our similarity and consecrate our destiny, servitude gives sway to the most terrible of silences...[1010]

1008 HR 355; R 284.
1009 HR 355; R 284.
1010 HR 354; R 283.

This is why, despite all attempts to claim Camus *qua* anti-Stalinist (and as a defender of the modern democratic political legacy) for the neoconservative Right, Camus always remained a dissident of the Left.[1011] He remained faithful to what he understood socialism *per se* to stand for: the principled opposition to egregious and unnecessary forms of social injustice.[1012] In the days immediately following the liberation, *Combat* would proclaim its staunch opposition to all forms of anti-communism as "the beginning of dictatorship."[1013] Camus never wavers in his fidelity to the critical component to Marxism, as we saw in Chapter Two. Like Marxist critics, he tirelessly condemns the cheapening of political values in marketised-capitalist societies and the exploitation of labor, alongside criticising the kinds of colonial institutions that condemned Meursault, and that were immiserating the Arabs of Algeria.[1014] "There is no possible freedom for a man tied to his lathe all day long who when the evening comes crowds into a single room with his family," Camus can write: "... this fact condemns a class, a society and the slavery it assumes..."[1015] We know that what he consistently opposes in Marxism is what, in many contemporary forms of post-Marxism and post-structuralism is most celebrated: namely, its more or less openly prophetic component as a secularised political theodicy promising a liberating redemptive Event.

Beyond his critique of modern political theologies, Camus' positive political thought continually wrestles after 1944 with the need to balance the demand for justice (what he sometimes, after Dostoevsky, calls the bread of earth) with political liberty, the bread of heaven.[1016] Economic liberty for each is also liberty for the banker and the avaricious, Camus notes in *Combat* 8 September 1944: *"voila injustice restaurée."*[1017] Camus' great hope in the post-war period is that France might "realise without delay a true popular democracy. We think in effect that all politics which is separated from the working class is vain and that France tomorrow will be what its working class will be."[1018] Such appeals to an "aristocracy of labour"[1019] or, per *The First Man*, of the common people

---

1011 Cf. Camus, "The Artist and His Time", MSe 209. See Chapter Six on Camus' "heroes" up to the *pied noir* "first men" and his mother.
1012 See especially Camus, "Socialism of the Gallows", RRD 165–171; "The Wager of Our Generation", 239–241, 244–245.
1013 CAC 63 (October 7 1944).
1014 Cf. Carroll, *Camus the Algerian* 26–35 and Chapter Six below.
1015 Camus, "Bread and Freedom", RRD 90.
1016 Camus, "Bread and Freedom", RRD 87–91.
1017 Camus *"Combat* 8 September 1944", at OC II 390 (CAC 32).
1018 Camus, *Combat* 1 octobre 1944, OC II 540 (CAC 55).
1019 Camus, "Bread and Freedom", RRD 94–95.

and dispossessed of the earth is not a neoconservatism, or a conservative politics in any sense.[1020]

Nevertheless, the model of social change here, drawing on the model of the passing solidarity between Christians, communists, socialists and patriots forged in the resistance, is discursive and bottom-up: not violent and vanguard-down. Even "if revolutions can only be made by violence, they can only be maintained in dialogue," Camus maintains.[1021] Camusian revolt eschews prophetic-philosophical or theological guarantees, and embraces risk.[1022] It is the Leninist model for social change, led by an inner clique of intellectuals animated by a sense of the transcendent Justice of violent actions to overthrow the existing order in a single Event that Camus increasingly opposes. This is not a political messianism, as we have seen: indeed, Camus meets Agamben, Benjamin and others' fascinations with messianism with the consistent claim that *"Il y a les actions messianiques et les actions réfléchie* (there are messianic actions and considered actions)".[1023] Camus instead points to the different syndicalist legacies Leninism's eventual triumph served to suppress in the European Left after 1917:

> The history of the First International, when German Socialism ceaselessly fought against the libertarian thought of the French, the Spanish, and the Italians... The commune against the State, concrete society against absolutist society, deliberate freedom against rational tyranny, [and] finally altruistic individualism against the colonization of the masses...[1024]

1020 See Chapter Six below. Cf. Camus, "The End of a World, *Combat* (September 6, 1944)", CAC 28: "we now have a new definition of the word 'aristocracy': that part of the nation that refuses to be enslaved or to enslave others."

1021 TM 365.

1022 See Gay-Crosier, "De l'*Homo faber* à l'*Homo ludens*: défence et illustration de la pensée de midi", in *Albert Camus, Contemporain*, 36–44.

1023 C II 220; C II Eng 113.

1024 HR 371–372, n. 2 at 372; R 297–298, note 2 at 298. See Peter Dunwoodie, "Albert Camus and the Anarchist Alternative", *Australian Journal of French Studies* 30 (1993), 84–103; Neil Foxlee, *Albert Camus's "The New Mediterranean Culture": A Text and Its Contexts* (Bern: Peter Lang, 2010), 255–260; "Camus, Albert and the anarchists", *Organise!* Magazine, at www-site https://libcom.org/library/albert-camus-anarchists, last accessed February 2015; and for more critical assessments, Ian H. Birchall, "The Labourism of Sisyphus: Albert Camus and Revolutionary Syndicalism", *Journal of European Studies* 20 (1990), esp. 151; also his "Neither Washington nor Moscow? The rise and fall of the Rassemblement Démocratique Révolutionaire", *Journal of European Studies* 29 (1999): 365–404; Orme, *the Development of Camus' Concern for Justice*, 178–180.

Neither, as John Foley has authoritatively shown,[1025] is Camus wholly against violence, although he has been widely claimed by pacifists, and reviled in these terms by Emmanuel d'Astier de la Vigerie and Jeanson.[1026] In a world where injustice continues to be violently visited upon peoples, Camus repeats that only a faith in another life could justify absolute non-violence. Koestler's yogi, who completely renounces the right to deploy defensive violence, is in such a world the passive accomplice in the crimes of the Commissars he does not deign to oppose.[1027] Camus specifies again and again that it is only the *legitimation* of political violence (violence made "comfortable"[1028] or administrative at the hands of totalising, theodical ideologies) that any post-metaphysical, rebellious thought must unconditionally oppose.[1029] Camus is not, superbly, against the political or historical world *per se*. He is, viscerally, opposed to "a world where murder is legitimate, and where human life is considered trifling."[1030] What this leaves, as Foley shows, is a wide enough range of situations when violence is legitimate: firstly, in self-defence; secondly, when it pits its proponents against tyrants like Caligula or tyrannical regimes wherein; thirdly, peaceable avenues of redress against injustices, deceit, or violences have been prohibited; fourthly, that such violence be discriminate, not targeting non-combatants; and finally, that the violence be perpetrated by the rebel "in close proximity to his victim," not called down upon victims from distant offices by appeal to ideological abstractions.[1031]

Here, indeed, we recall Camus' controversial celebration of the Russian terrorist Kaliayev and his friends in 1905: those *"meurtrieurs délicats"* who consented to sacrifice their own life, having assumed the right to kill others in the name of overthrowing the Tsarist State.[1032] There are many issues with this

---

1025 John Foley, "Albert Camus and Political Violence" in Christine Margerrison, Mark Orme, Lissa Lincoln eds., *Albert Camus in the 21st Century: A Reassessment of His Thinking at the Dawn of the New Millennium* (Amsterdam, New York: Editions Rodopi B.V., 2008), 209–221.
1026 See particularly Albert Camus, "Deux réponses à Emmanuel d'Astier de la Vigerie," OC II 457–469.
1027 HR 360; R 288. The Yogi represents the inefficacity of abstention, in a world in which violence continues, and he does nothing to stop it. "La nostalgie du repos et de la paix doit elle-même être repousse", HR 310; R 248.
1028 TM 361.
1029 See for example, Camus "Deux réponses à Emmanuel d'Astier de la Vigerie," OC II 457–458.
1030 NVE 259.
1031 Foley, "Albert Camus and Political Violence," 212–214. We will recur to this vital delineation of forms of legitimate violence in Chapter Six. Vitally, it is not capacious enough to include the FLN's actions against ordinary *pied noirs* in 1945 and following August 1955.
1032 See Albert Camus "Le meurtrieurs délicats", OC III 338–345; and HR 211–221; R 164–173.

position, especially in an age of murderous suicide bombers.[1033] A vital note in the *Carnets* in fact makes it clear that Camus found Kaliayev's "life for a life" arguments strictly "*faux*". Intriguingly, though, he is content to defend the position as salutary. He does so precisely to the extent that it demands that any would-be militant or state operative take seriously the exceptional gravity of visiting violence or death upon others: whereas "today murder [is only] done by proxy [*procuration*]. No one pays."[1034] What Camus' celebration of the Russian terrorists of 1905 certainly underscores, that is, is the extent to which any defensible ethics, for him, must be grounded in the injunction to 'count oneself in' the actions and consequences one's thought would sanction or visit upon others. (see above, Chapter Three) "Neither Victims nor Executioners" of 1947, for this reason, pointedly poses the question of political violence to its readers in the second person, as Kaliayev and his fellows had asked it to themselves:

> Before anything can be done, two questions must be put: 'Do you, or do you not, directly or indirectly, want to be killed or assaulted? Do you or do you not, directly or indirectly, want to kill or assault?'[1035]

1033 See for criticisms Crowley, "Camus and Social Justice," *Cambridge Companion to Camus*, 102–103. Herbert Hochberg, "Albert Camus and the Ethics of Absurdity", *Ethics* 75 (1965), 87–102. Hochberg sees a contradiction in Camus' opposition to principled murder and capital punishment, and the "just assassins'" acceptance of their own state-assisted suicide: "[O]n the basis of the absolute value of life Camus has rejected suicide, capital punishment and murder. He ends by acquiescing in certain cases to all three, for the suicide of the just assassin is self-imposed capital punishment": at p. 100. Philip Thody offers a practical criticism, against the seeming idealism of this "life for a life" stance: "to recommend that all conscientious rebels commit suicide after they have been obliged to kill in the service of the revolution is rather an impractical solution. No political organisation fighting against a tyranny could possibly succeed if its leaders follow Kaliayev's example." Phillip Thody, *Albert Camus, 1913–1960* (New York: Macmillan, 1980), 127; cf. George Kateb, *Utopia and Its Enemies* (New York: Free Press, 1963), 39 for a comparable criticism. Critics from Blanchot onwards have noted an assymmetry between the life of the targeted, involuntary oppressors, and the consciously-chosen death of the "meurtrieur délicat", if Camus is serious about a "life for a life". See Foley, "Albert Camus and Political Violence", 217; Geraldine F. Montgomery, "Plus loin que le morale", in *Camus and the Twenty First Century*, 139–140.
1034 Camus, *Carnets II* [Fr.], 199.
1035 NVE 259.

5 Concluding Remarks: Camus and the Legacy of Modern Sceptical Humanism

We have in this Chapter tried to unfold Camus' mature political theory, responding to charges that it is incoherent, or that it is based on nothing more substantial than Camus' upstanding moral sentiments. Camus' political philosophy rests instead on his paraCartesian defence of a minimal, post-metaphysical value. On this philosophically demanding basis, assuming no pre-existing traditions and invoking no unexamined premises, Camus' philosophy sanctifies as a primary post-theological value the community of living human beings. This community is circumscribed by what Camus calls a 'limit': a prohibition against murder, systematic deceit, and exploitation. Politically, this philosophy prescribes, as the legitimate and real gains of the modern legacy of metaphysical and historical rebellion, the separation of executive from the judiciary and legislature; the importance of a plural, open public sphere and independent, critical 'fourth estate' (the media); and the cultivation in citizens of a series of modest democratic virtues: the honesty to recognise one's limits, the equanimity to accept others may disagree, the liberality to see that they will have their reasons, however weak, alongside the right to pursue their own conceptions of the good, consistent with not harming others. At the very basis of Camus' political philosophy, that is—the deepest inference from his critique of modern secularised political messianisms—is a defence of the separation of Churches (whether secular-immanent or sacral-transcendent in metaphysics) from the repressive arms of the State. In response to what one critic has enigmatically called the "theologico-political problem", apparently meaning the relations between revealed religions and political authorities, Camus chooses a version of the centuries-old liberal solution Leo Strauss never countenanced except to one-sidedly reject.[1036] Each particular Church should have the right to proselytise and practice so that individuals remain free to choose their own faith. No creed should have the legal right to impose its perspective on all, including the capacity to suppress alternative creeds and practices. Doubtlessly this is one reason, alongside Camus' *modestie*, underlying Camus' repetitions in the late 1940s that his own political prescriptions should be taken as preliminary, subject to revision and contestation,[1037] and in this sense, "relative" as opposed to absolute:

1036 Leo Strauss, "Preface to the English Translation," *Spinoza's Critique of Religion* (Chicago: University of Chicago Press, 1997), 31.
1037 Egs Camus, "*Combat* 19 septembre 1944" OC II 532; "Remarques sur le politique internationale" II 651; "Interventions à la table ronde", OC II 682–684; TM 360, 363.

> Rebellion itself only aspires to the relative and can only promise an assured dignity coupled with relative justice. It supposes a limit at which the community of man is established. Its universe is the universe of relative values. Instead of saying, with Hegel and Marx, that all is necessary, it only repeats that all is possible and that, at a certain point on the farthest frontier, it is worth making the supreme sacrifice for the sake of the possible...[1038]

Looked at in the wider perspective of debates in political philosophy, Camus' clear and distinct advocacy of political toleration in the context of a political philosophy of dialogue, we would argue, is worth recalling. This is perhaps true now as much as ever, in our period of declining public faith in liberal institutions, occasioned by the increasing sidelining of nation-based democratic institutions and forms of will formation in the neoliberal, globalising era.

Alan Levine, in an important essay on "The Prehistory of Toleration and the Varieties of Scepticism" has noted the difficulties attending contemporary liberal-philosophical attempts to justify toleration metaphysically, politically, or prudentially.[1039] Metaphysical appeals to an absolute or "self-evident" basis for the liberal civil rights, or democratic political rights fall prey to continuing sceptical criticisms concerning the plausibility of such metapolitical foundations. Virtually any account of human nature which lays claim to universality can be (and has been) shown to tacitly select for some particular features, races, gender, or virtues, and thus to license excluding some others as not fully 'human'.[1040] If, accepting this, we try to justify tolerance merely politically, on the basis of an appeal to Hobbesian self-interest ('it is in everyone's best interest to cooperate, thus...'), we run the risk of sanctioning the types of free-riding mendacity of those who deem their self-interest 'above the law' or by 'natural right' above the social contract they generously agree should apply to everyone else.[1041] When, however, Richard Rorty or more recently John Rawls have tried to justify liberal rights simply because they happen, historically, to be ours, their position is sub-philosophical. Indeed, it is formally comparable

---

1038   HR 362; R 290. Before any reader cries 'relativism', they should note the logic of the claim here: Camus is not saying beliefs are relative to individuals or cultures (from the bottom-up, as it were), but 'relative' in contrast to 'absolute' (from the top-down), in terms of their ability to plumb the single, existent, culture-transcendent truth.
1039   Alan Levine, "The Prehistory of Toleration and the Varieties of Scepticism" (USA: Lexington, 1999), 1–19.
1040   Levine, "The Prehistory of Toleration and the Varieties of Scepticism", 3.
1041   Levine, "The Prehistory of Toleration and the Varieties of Scepticism", 3–4, 5.

to the most illiberal or repressive forms of particularism that can likewise argue, concerning their own practices and prejudices: "it is good, because it is ours," not "it is ours, because it is good."[1042]

Camus' philosophical discourse aims at what he repeatedly designates as a new "universalism"—even if it turns out to be a "folly of men" no less preposterous, in the eyes of 'realists', than the old "folly of God."[1043] Nevertheless Camus' universalism, we have seen, presupposes no more robust account of human nature than one which acknowledges that all human beings, from very early in their lives, seek out unifying forms of meaning to their experiences.[1044] Nothing more metaphysically contentious is called upon, although by the end of *Ther Rebel* Camus argues that more is implied. Camus' 1957 "Reflections on the Guillotine," the last decisive statement of his broader political theory, accordingly makes clear that Camus does not share Rousseau's faith in the alleged goodness of human nature, any more than he accepts 'realistic' paeans to man as a "dangerous" animal *à la* Schmitt et al.:[1045] "of course [man] is not [completely good] (he is worse or better). After twenty years of our magnificent history, we are well aware of this."[1046] If we insist on talk of foundations, we must say that the 'foundation' for Camus' political universalism lies in that epistemic scepticism we traced back in Chapter Three to *Le Mythe de Sisyphe*. In *The Rebel*, as we saw, Camus ties his phenomenological account of rebellion (as involving an affirmative 'Yes' at the basis of the rebel's 'No' to perceived injustices) to his account of the post-metaphysical rebellion of the absurd man in *Le Mythe*. The absurd man already 'rebels' there against all forms of metaphysical or habitual consolation in face of a world whose extra-human density resists his efforts at final comprehension and control. Camus' later political philosophy, likewise, is based on what "Reflections on the Guillotine" calls a "solidarity of all men in error and aberration."[1047] He does not venture any more directly positive, essentialist account of what human beings have in common. If the death penalty is to be opposed, it is not because many guilty men still elude punishment, given the fallibility of human justice.[1048] It is because this same fallibility means that innocent men, from time to time, have been

---

1042 Levine, "The Prehistory of Toleration and the Varieties of Scepticism", 4–5.
1043 Camus, "Sommes-nous des pessimistes?", OC II 753.
1044 HR 327–328; R 262.
1045 Schmitt, *Concept of the Political* 58, 95–97, 100.
1046 RG 222, 224.
1047 RG 217.
1048 See Thorson, "Albert Camus and the Rights of Man", *Ethics*, Vol. 74, No. 4 (July 1964) 289–290.

and will be falsely executed. "The unpunished crime, according to the Greeks, infected the whole city," Camus writes: "But innocence condemned or crime too severely punished, in the long run, soils the city just as much."[1049] We know in the age of the 'war on terror', in which centuries-old Western civil liberties have been rapidly rolled back (and many falsely imprisoned or tortured) 'to defend freedom', just how radically progressive this position continues to be.

Camus' 'dogmatically minimal' political foundation eludes the important criticisms of essentialism that have been proffered over the last decades from post-colonial, feminist, and post-structuralist perspectives. All of these draw us to see hidden, particular biases and violences behind appeals to forms of political universalism: whether in the form of the modern disciplines multiplying in the interstices of liberal polities, Europeans' imperialist exactions upon subject populations, or instrumental reason's rendering pyrrhic of the enlightenment's claim to have banished mythical fatality... We have seen how Camus agrees with such critical perspectives that, "from the humanitarian idylls of the 18th century to the bloodstained gallows the way leads directly."[1050] Camus maintains that the predominant forms of modern political ideology have each, as of 1951, failed to secure ethical progress comparable to the technological progress achieved in the same centuries.[1051] At the same time, Camus was never tempted by the kinds of ethical and cultural relativisms that have become, very often, the aporetic termini for these kinds of criticisms of political universalism. For the physical killing of a human being, Camus insists, is a metaphysically grave, unrelativisable affair. Murder is the one form of absolute action (absolute, since it destroys any and all future possibilities for the person killed) uncontroversially available to human beings, independent of their cultural or historical settings. It involves what Camus terms a "fundamental scission" in reality.[1052] If capital punishment is to be opposed, Camus argues, it is above all because "capital punishment upsets the only indisputable human solidarity—our solidarity against death";[1053] "[i]t kills the small part of existence that can be realized on this earth through the mutual understanding of men..."[1054] As such, only the appeal to now-unavailable religious absolutes, and in particular the Churches' beliefs in the posthumous judgment of an immortal body or soul, could excuse violating this "extreme limit" to human

---

1049 RG 216.
1050 RG 230.
1051 See Albert Camus, "L'Avenir de la civilisation européene", OC III 996–998.
1052 Camus, "Conference au convent...", OC II 509.
1053 RG 222.
1054 RG 222; HR.

solidarity, and the irrevocably final judgment on the other that it implies. Yet, Camus notes quietly, since the 18th century, European nations ostensibly have "lost all contact with the sacred."[1055] The issue is that, as we saw in Chapter Two, "society begun in the 19th century to find a substitute for religion by proposing itself as an object of adoration."[1056]

> One kills for a nation or a class that has been granted divine status. One kills for a future society that has likewise been given divine status. Whoever thinks he has omniscience imagines he has omnipotence. Temporal idols demanding an absolute faith tirelessly decree absolute punishments. And religions devoid of transcendence kill great numbers of condemned men devoid of hope.[1057]

It follows from this, in Camus as in the legacy of early modern thinkers beginning with Pierre Bayle and Michel de Montaigne, that metaphysical scepticism does not require or imply moral or ethical scepticism. On the contrary, it forms the basis of a new, tolerant moral universalism. We may legitimately doubt the reasons of others, when they lay claim to absolute truths or warrants. Yet we cannot doubt their existence; nor the legitimacy of their desire for the same kinds of unifying explanations of our shared condition we also seek. As Pierre Bayle had asked at the end of the 17th century: "Which of us is so sure to know the Truth that they can justifiably injure another who differs in opinion?"[1058] The Socratic acknowledgment of metaphysical ignorance that

---

1055 RG 225.
1056 RG 225. We rejoin here Camus' critique of secularised political theodicy as rationalising murder. In the later modern period, men have consented to take on the power of life and death traditionally reserved to the fallen deity.
1057 RG 228. Although, as we will see, one component of Camus' work after 1940 is his continuing attempt to rehabilitate in French thought the language of the classical virtues, his position shares decisive features with his great predecessor Montaigne, in denouncing the "*folie de vertu*" in the modern age as the source of by far the greatest and most reprehensible crimes: *viz.* not the folly of unrestrained passions targeted by Socrates and his successors, but the fanaticism of people convinced of the exclusive nobility or historical mandate of their position. Camus, "Projet de preface", OC II 500.
1058 On Bayle and toleration, see Pierre Bayle, "A Philosophical commentary on these words of the Gospel, *Luke 14.23*: 'Compel them to come in, that my house may be full'" edited by John Kilcullen and Chandran Kukathas (Indianapolis: Liberty Fund, 2005); Gianluca Mori, "Pierre Bayle, The rights of the conscience, the 'remedy' of toleration." *Ratio Juris* 10, no. 1 (1997): 45–60; John Christian Laursen, "Baylean Liberalism: tolerance requires non-tolerance" in *Beyond the persecuting society: Religious toleration before the Enlightenment*,

Camus increasingly comes after 1945 to cite as ethically exemplary[1059] thus has profound political implications. It involves an opening to the possibility that others, as fellow human beings (not "existentially something different or alien")[1060] may have reasons we could profit from considering:

> The decadence of the Greek world commenced with the assassination of Socrates. And we have killed many more Socrates' in Europe for many years now. It is a sign. It is a sign that only the Socratic spirit of indulgence towards others and rigor towards oneself [from the *Sophist*] is dangerous for civilizations given over to murder. It is thus the sole spirit that can regenerate the world.[1061]

With Camus, it is just as with Montaigne's *Essais*, whose legendary scepticism concerning the things in the heavens opened out the space for Montaigne's observant *jugment* to curiously attend the particularities of human experience, in the very period after Saint Bartholemew, amidst France's continuing religious wars.[1062] Increasingly in his own post-war period, we see Camus stressing the importance of "*modestie*" as both a political, as well as an epistemic virtue.[1063] Democracy, Camus agrees with Churchill, may only be the 'least bad' form of political regime. But if it is less bad than other regimes, it is to the extent that it asks citizens to internalise and practice a sociable modesty: "it is the social and political exercise of such modesty":[1064]

> The men who do not have the absolute Truth do not wish to kill anyone and they ask that others do not kill them. They ask only to search for the truth and as a consequence they have need of a certain number of historical preconditions which permit them this search. It is what I call the conditions of a modest thinking.[1065]

---

   edited by John Christian Laursen and Cary J. Nederman (Philadelphia: University of Pennsylvania Press, 1998), 197–215.

1059 Camus, "Démocratie et modestie", OC II 428; TL 494; CH 746; cf. TM 357, 364.
1060 Schmitt, *Concept of the Political*, 27.
1061 CH 746; cf. TM 364.
1062 See the author's "On a Forgotten Argument in French Philosophy: Sceptical Humanism in Montaigne, Voltaire and Camus," *Critical Horizons* Vol. 16, No. 1 (Feb. 2015).
1063 Camus, "Réflexions sur une démocratie sans catéhisme", OC II 717.
1064 Camus, "Réflexions sur une démocratie sans catéhisme", OC II 716.
1065 Camus, "Interventions à la table ronde", OC II 681.

It is no surprise then, that in the same period that we find Camus adducing the authorities of both Socrates and Montaigne, he also adduces the "*grand mot*" of that other tireless, sceptical advocate of religious and political toleration, Voltaire: "I do not think as you do, but I will fight for your right to express your thought."[1066] It is true that no ancient political philosopher advocated toleration. As the lumières were wont to stress, the civic and "ortho-praxical" bases of the pagan cults provided a practical basis for Greek and Roman eclecticism and syncretism which found its limits only with the advent of the new Christian religion's exclusive claim to salvific Truth.[1067] Yet appeals for religious toleration on the sceptical bases found in thinkers like Bayle, Montaigne, Charron, Montesquieu, and others emerged during the early modern period of conflict between Protestants and Catholics across Europe.[1068] What is remarkable is that these highly influential appeals have received a good deal less academic attention than the natural law and social contract traditions. Camus' decisive, lifelong recourse to classical Greek precedents, which we have now to examine, ought not then to blind us to the extent that he is also the legatee of a powerful tradition of modern sceptical humanism in French letters.[1069] We recall one last time that, in *L'Homme Révolté*, Camus is profoundly sympathetic with the first premise of the early modern metaphysical rebels who, like de Sade and Voltaire, call into question the justice of a providential Deity who could create an order in which innocents senselessly suffer and die.[1070] It is only when, armed with indignation and the exhilarating sense of having broken with divine constraints, the moderns set about imagining political-theological foundations of their own that Camus argues the normative promise of modern rebellion betrays itself, and comes to mimic the divinely-sanctioned injustices it began by opposing.

* * *

1066 Camus, "L'Avenir de la civilisation européene", OC III 997.
1067 See Rebecca Kingston, "Religion" in *Montesquieu dictionary* at www-site http://dictionnaire-montesquieu.ens-lyon.fr/en/article/1377637039/en/, last accessed December 2014; also Roger B. Oake, "Montesquieu's Religious Ideas", *Journal of the History of Ideas*, Vol. 14, No. 4 (Oct., 1953), pp. 548–560; Gay, *Enlightenment*, 167–170.
1068 Cf. Richard Popkin, *A History of Scepticism: From Savoranola to Bayle* (Oxford: Oxford University Press, 2003); Alan Levine ed., *Early Modern Scepticism and the Origins of Toleration*.
1069 Cf. Matthew Sharpe, "On a Forgotten Argument in French Philosophy: Sceptical Humanism in Montaigne, Voltaire and Camus", *Critical Horizons*, Vol. 16, no. 1 (Feb. 2015).
1070 See Chapter Two above.

It is customary for book-length studies on Camus the man or the author to end with the subject of Camus' political career and his failures in Algeria (see Chapter Six below). Camus' accidental death in 1960 means that Camus' unresolved wrestling with his own *pied noir* identity and Algerian independence from France came chronologically last for him. There is also however a wider tendency to assess a thinker in terms of their political commitments, as if these were the truest tests of a philosophy and politics the arbiter of theoretical reflection per se. This book takes as its object Camus as a *philosophe*, however. And as per our Introduction, in claiming Camus as a *philosophe*, we are situating him in a very specifically classical heritage that conceived philosophy as a way of life, as well as the early modern legacy we just recalled. Yet within this classical tradition, it was widely recognised that the activity of philosophising, or of living contemplatively or reflectively, stands at some distance from political activity, and has its own relatively autonomous goods.[1071] *La politique* is concerned with deciding the more or less urgent, more or less practical matters *du jour*, subject by their nature to an unformalisable diversity of competing interests and opinions. "But it is not the same thing, I think, the life of a contemplative philosopher as that of a statesman...," Plutarch can comment off-handedly, reflecting *en passant* on the relationship between Pericles and his philosophical mentor, Anaxagoras.[1072] Perhaps the *locus classicus* sanctifying this distinction between the *vita activa* and *vita contemplativa* comes in Aristotle and his *Nicomachean Ethics*. Here, after nine books on the civic virtues, Aristotle changes gear to announce that the best way of life is one characterised by theoretical pursuits requiring the minimum of the external goods at stake in political conflict, including the recognition and endorsement of others.[1073]

[1071] There is, contra well-known historicising polemics, no one 'ancient' view on these matters, and the political life-theoretical life distinction is parsed differently by the different philosophical schools, not to mention wider poetic and civic culture, and the roman republic tradition that in part shapes someone like Cicero. To state things briefly: the sense of the division or choice between the two modes of life is strongest in the Epicurean and peripatetic schools, and also the neoplatonicians, although Plato famously thinks the philosopher must 'go back down' into the city; but any strong division or necessary choice of life is contested amongst the Stoics, on the basis of their strong emphasis on human community and appropriate action, and is differently 'deconstructed' in the sceptical schools.

[1072] Plutarch, "Life of Pericles," *The Parallel Lives* trans. Bernadette Perrin (published in Vol. III of the Loeb Classical Library edition, 1916), at www-site http://penelope.uchicago.edu/Thayer/E/Roman/Texts/Plutarch/Lives/Pericles*.html, last accessed February 2015.

[1073] Aristotle, *NE* X.10*.

Although Camus' philosophical claims differ very greatly from 'the philosopher''s, we do want to claim that like Aristotle and other ancients, Camus calls into question the ultimacy or sufficiency of politics and the political life in his vision of the human condition. Sartre is characteristically astute when he suggests in 1952 that Camus' involvement in political life was always experienced by his longtime friend as minimally involuntary: a duty as much as an inclination.[1074] Camus tells us as much, challenging the enthusiastic existentialist celebration of "commitment" in his Nobel Prize speech and several other pieces.[1075] Camus would never deny his longing for at least periodic withdrawal from the political arena, both as a minimal precondition for the creation of works of art and as a means to recover a sense of the beauty of the natural world *au-delà l'histoire*.[1076] Even in the decisive series of addresses Camus gave in his most politically active period after 1944, Camus at several points stipulates that one feature of modern thought that he opposes is exactly its sense that "everything is political." "More and more, we are politicised," Camus observes in his 1946 "Interventions à la table ronde de 'Civilisation' ".[1077] Yet this is one of five features of the contemporary world Camus thinks needs *challenging* in light of the disasters of fascism, the two world wars, the gulags and the atomic bomb. As we skirted in Chapter Two, what the oft-celebrated 'primacy of the political' means in normative terms is the acceptance that the highest goods (for instance, perfect social justice, an end to history, the triumph of the master race...) are at stake, and can be achieved or forfeited in the political arena. Camus by contrast contends, repeatedly, that whatever the absolute highest Good for human beings may consist in (if, indeed, there is such a Thing, and it could be known), it cannot be realised or exhausted in political action: for instance, in the form of a once-and-for-all utopian dispensation. To the extent that political parties take on such Ends, Camus instead warns us (whether they are religious, nationalist, communist, or prophetic-philosophical), they take on a license to deceive, oppress and murder which rebellion legitimately sets its face against.[1078] For Camus, our lives rightly belong, in large measure, to others: we are political animals. But just as we each must individually die,

---

1074 Sartre, "Reply to Albert Camus", esp. 150–152.
1075 CD 249: the artist in the later modern world is "impressed" into history, whether he likes it or not.
1076 Camus professes his natural inclination being away from politics in Albert Camus, "Lettre à Marcel Ayme," OC II 734. See also RT 169–170.
1077 Albert Camus, "Interventions à la table ronde de 'Civilisation' " OC II 679.
1078 CH 744.

Camus disputes the idea that we are *wholly* political animals, without reserve or remainder.[1079]

If anything like a renaissance beyond the kinds of nihilistic disregard for human life that led to the Nazi and Socialist camps is to be possible, Camus repeats in *"La Crise de L'Homme"* and his speech at Latour-Marbourg in 1946, "politics must be put in its true place." That place, however, is "secondary".[1080] In other words, his teaching of the limit does not only operate within politics, but to limit politics' total claims over human lives and cultures:

> The absolute is not attained nor, above all, created through history. Politics is not religion, or if it is, then it is nothing but the Inquisition. How would society define an absolute? Perhaps everyone is looking for this absolute on behalf of all. But society and politics only have the responsibility of arranging everyone's affairs so that each will have the leisure and the freedom to pursue this common search...[1081]

With this much said concerning Camus' critique of the omnipresence of 'the political' in human affairs, we are ready to turn now to Camus' philosophical neoHellenism. For this position, as we will see, involves his singular attempt in the 20th century to rehabilitate a philosophical naturalism, calling into question this ultimacy of 'the political'. Significantly, it rests on a teaching of classical *mesure* very like to that which, still in the 18th century, 'moderns' like Mounier, Necker, Mme de Staël, and Benjamin Constant could appeal to as an ethicopolitical ballast for large commercial regimes, and Montesquieu in their front rank would appeal to as a principle governing the separation of powers in his great work, *L'Esprit des Lois*.[1082]

1079 CH 744; HE 150–151; cf. OC 469, 481; OC III 463.
1080 Camus, "Conférence au convent de Latour-Marbourg", OC II 510. See Stern, "Fellowship of Men that Die", 185–186.
1081 HR 377; R 302.
1082 Cf. Aurelian Craiutu, *A Virtue for Courageous Minds: Moderation in French Political Thought, 1748–1830* (USA: Princeton University Press, 2012). See p. 14, Cariutu's description of the moderate enlighteners (and not Camus, whom he does not mention): "The question remains: what do moderates stand for? It would seem to me that they affirm three basic attitudes. First, they defend pluralism [...] Second, moderates prefer gradual reforms to revolutionary breakthroughs, and they are temperamentally inclined to making compromises and concessions on both prudential and normative grounds. [...] Third, moderation presupposes a tolerant approach which refuses to see the world in Manichean terms that divide it into forces of good (or light) and agents of evil (or darkness)..."

PART 3

Going Back Down

CHAPTER 5

Excluding Nothing: Camus' NeoHellenic Philosophy of *Mesure*

> *If, in order to go beyond nihilism, we have to go back to Christianity, then we may very well follow the movement, and go beyond Christianity into Hellenism.*[1083]

1 From Political Messianisms to Philosophical Naturalim

1.1 *Camus, beyond 'the Political'?*

"But this still resembles a moral code, and we live for something that goes farther than morality...",[1084] Camus' 1954 essay "Return to Tipasa" reflects. Camus has been describing what the essay sets up as two polarities of his intellectual career and persona. The first is a passionate love of natural beauty with which his life, and artistic and philosophical work, had begun. "Forsaking beauty and the sensual happiness attached to it, exclusively serving misfortune, calls for a nobility I lack," Camus confesses, as he reflects on the terrible years which had passed between his youthful visit (in 1936) and present return (1954) to the classical ruins at Tipasa, on the Mediterranean coast of Algeria.[1085] The second side of this persona is what Camus avowed as his "fierce love of justice" beginning in that "... obstinate refusal ... to accept any order that seeks to bring men to their knees" whose terms we have been examining.[1086]

Most of the work we have done throughout the first four chapters bringing Camus into critical dialogue with Foucault, the *nouveaux philosophes* and the Frankfurt School (Chapter One), Hans Blumenberg and the 'secularisation thesis' (Chapter Two), then Emmanuel Levinas and Jürgen Habermas (Chapter Four) has explored only the latter, more political side to Camus' thought and work. The subject of natural beauty has emerged only briefly at a crucial point

---

1083 C II 233; C II Eng 120. See C II 342; C II Eng 176. "Revise the transition from Hellenism to Christianity, the genuine and sole turning point (*véritable et seul tournant*) in history. Essay on destiny (Nemesis?)."
1084 RT 170.
1085 RT 165.
1086 CAC 42.

in Chapter Three, as we tried to clarify Camus' notion of the absurd. This notion, we saw, is far from excluding a deep aesthetic appreciation of the wonder of the natural world: contemplating a landscape furnishes Camus one of his examples of the feeling of the absurd.[1087] Yet Camus' readers know what a large part this aesthetic sensibility, and love of natural beauty, plays in shaping his *oeuvre*, from the earliest essays and notes in the *Carnets*, via *Noces* into *L'Été* and a host of later works, up to the incomplete *Le Premier Homme*. Again, in Camus' criticism of the longing for "totality" he accuses Stalinism of enshrining, we briefly glimpsed what can be called this other, neoclassical side to Camus' philosophy. (Chapter One) Camus counterposes an idea of unity (as against one of difference, becoming, the messianic, or the Event) against the spirit of totality. Then Camus names a series of dimensions to the human condition which the political bid to "annex all creation" must violently suppress, since they resist such political control:

> Totality is not unity. The state of siege, even when it is extended to the very boundaries of the earth, is not reconciliation. The claim to a universal city is supported in this revolution only by rejecting two thirds of the world and by denying, to the advantages of history, both nature and beauty and by depriving man of the power of passion, doubt, happiness, and imaginative invention...[1088]

This anatomisation of 'two thirds of the world' that totalitarian governments must suppress: featuring nature and beauty, on the one hand, and the human powers of passion, doubt, happiness, and imaginative invention, on the other, is highly characteristic of Camus' thought after 1942. At several key points in his political and philosophical speeches and writings, we find Camus counterposing what he terms 'history' (following Hegel, meaning human social and political life) to the beauty of non-human nature.[1089] He then aligns this beauty of non-human nature with the human longing for happiness, the need for leisure and recreation,[1090] our capacities for a series of classical virtues (notably courage, intelligence, honesty, justice and friendship), forms of love or generosity, and the capacities to doubt, dialogue, and produce enduring works of art. In his important interview with *Servir* in 1948, Camus reflected that he

---

1087 See below.
1088 HR 300–301; R 240.
1089 Camus, "Deux réponses", OC II 469; "Dialogue pour le dialogue", OC II 481; "Conférence au couvent" OC II 510; TM 363; HE 150–152.
1090 "[F]ecund work and reflective leisure..." TM 363.

had increasingly come to search for an alternative to the seemingly "zero-sum" choice between forms of Augustinian faith and modern historicisms which declaim human beings and their creations solely the products of their cultural, historical, or political circumstances:

> We do not believe any longer in God, but we believe in history. For my part, I understand well the interest of the religious solution, and I perceive very clearly the importance of history. But I do not believe in either the one or the other, in an absolute sense. I query myself and it bothers me very much that we are asked to choose absolutely between Saint Augustine and Hegel. I have the impression that there must be a defencible truth between the two.[1091]

In a vital series of reflections in the second volume of his *Carnets* between 1944 and 1947, we can see Camus beginning to eke out the shape of this supportable *tertium datur*, between theology and historicism, despite manifold doubts and all the difficulties associated with striking out on an independent philosophical course. "There is no objection to the totalitarian attitude other than the religious or moral one. If this world has no meaning, they [Christian authors] are right... It is our task to create God",[1092] Camus reflected at the end of 1944. However, with this familiar post-theological dilemma stated (either a salvific God or totalitarianism and a meaningless world, leading to the Satanic-Nietzschean rivalling of the Deity)[1093] Camus makes his way towards what he calls a "middle way (*un moyen terme*)".[1094] One by one, all the key affirmative terms of his later philosophical claims that human beings are not solely historical beings emerge amidst hesitations, back-trackings, tentative formulations and retractions: classicism and Greek thought,[1095] nature and beauty as opposed to History,[1096] the fact of our biological mortality and need to

---

1091 Camus, "Interview à '*Servir*'" OC II 659. By the late 1940s, Camus had come to see existentialism as something like an uneasy blend of both. On the one hand, historicism ("L'existentialisme a gardé du hégélianisme son erreur fondamentale qui consiste à réduire l'homme à l'histoire..." (C II 180 [c Sep. 1946]), and on the other hand, as per Chapter Six, the universalisation of guilt.
1092 C II 127; C II Eng 64; cf. also 78–9)) Compare: "For Kirilov, as for Nietzsche, to kill god is to become god oneself; it is to realize on this earth the eternal life of which the Gospel speaks." (MS 146; MSe, 98).
1093 C II 192; C II Eng 98.
1094 C II 202; C II Eng 104.
1095 C II 165, 172–174; C II Eng 84, 88–9.
1096 C II 160, 174, 184, 189, 193, 196, 201, 209; C II Eng 80; 83; 89; 92; 94; 97; 99, 103.

consciously confront this mortality and two of the key terms of Camus' political thought we have seen in Chapter Four: namely, dialogue[1097] and the other.[1098]

It is a key claim of this book that it is this other dimension in Camus, contesting or 'balancing' all historicisms' partial, exclusive emphases on our determination by cultural, linguistic, political or institutional forces that remains Camus' most original contribution to 20th century French thought. In a period of ecological crisis wherein our relations with non-human nature are becoming paramount, Camus' species of contemplative naturalism (paralleled in 20th century French philosophy perhaps only by Pierre Hadot)[1099] is also arguably his most prescient contribution to contemporary thought. As Bruce Ward has reflected, it is certainly one of his most unique.[1100] Perhaps Camus' most beautiful essay, "Helen's Exile" (alongside the much-maligned "*Pensée de midi*" at the culmination of *L'Homme Révolté*) puts Camus' position most clearly:

> We have exiled beauty; the Greeks took up arms for her. First difference, but one that has a history [sic.] … What imagination could we have left for that higher equilibrium in which nature balanced history, beauty, virtue, and which applied the music of numbers even to the blood of-tragedy? We turn our backs on nature; we are ashamed of beauty … This is why it is improper to proclaim today that we are the sons of Greece. Or else we are the renegade sons. Placing history on the throne of God, we are progressing toward theocracy like those whom the Greeks called Barbarians and whom they fought to death in the waters of Salamis. … Deliberately, the world has been cut from everything that constitutes its permanence: nature, the sea, hilltops, evening meditation. Consciousness is to be found only in the streets, because history is to be found only in the streets—this is the edict…[1101]

At stake in Camus' thought, to be clear, is the attempt to found a philosophy of human nature, precisely as human *nature*, in a period wherein nearly

---

1097 C II 160; II Eng 81.
1098 C II 164; C II Eng 83: "L. When the detail is a human life, it is the whole world and whole of history for me."
1099 Cf. esp. Pierre Hadot *"L'Homme Antique et La Nature"*, *Études de Philosophie Ancienne* (Paris: Les Belles Lettres, 2010), 307–318.
1100 Bruce Ward, "Christianity and the Modern Eclipse of Nature: Two Perspectives", *Journal of the American Academy of Religion* Vol. 63, No. 4 (Winter, 1995): 825. Bruce K. Ward, "The Recovery of Helen", *Dionysius* 14 (1990): 169–194.
1101 HE 148–149.

all theoretical recourse to the category of 'nature' in political thought had become *verboten*. In his *Carnets*, Camus notes how for Hegel, "nature" is found at a lower level of his system, to be quickly "sublated" in *Geist's* evolutionary search for self-consciousness.[1102] In the tradition of Marxian ideology critique (and its legatees in feminist and post-colonial cultural criticism),[1103] despite the younger Marx's clear naturalism,[1104] any and all claims to "nature" are deemed highly suspicious. Ruling groups, it is noted, have always tried to "naturalise" their political advantages by convincing themselves and the subservient classes that the present political condition reflects an unchangeable natural, or theologically-sanctioned, arrangement. For all of Michel Foucault's disagreements with the Marxian legacy,[1105] his genealogical work shares this scepticism about claims to speak concerning any human nature, and aims to track in extraordinary detail the social and political construction of modern subjects.[1106] Lacanian psychoanalysis, despite Freud's hope to ground psychoanalysis in the modern scientific paradigm, stresses the cultural and linguistic shaping of even our most intimate desires: "the unconscious is structured like a language".[1107] In Slavoj Žižek's politicisation of Lacan (and in Badiou's adaptation and mathematisation of his master's linguistic structuralism), we are invited to draw political norms from the radical symbolic rupture at the culmination of the psychoanalytic cure,[1108] or in Badiou, from similarly unheralded and totally transformative "Events" like falling in love, scientific paradigm

---

1102 C II 200; C II Eng 103: "Hegel contre la nature. Cf. *Grande Logique*, 36–40. Pourquoi la nature est abstraite.—Ce qui est concret, c'est l'esprit. C'est la grande aventure de l'intelligence—celle qui finit par tuer toute chose..." Cf. C II 160; C II Eng 80.

1103 This is a central claim, for instance, concerning Camus' naturalism in Haddour, *Colonial myths*, 48, drawing on Roland Barthes' work on mythology.

1104 See Karl Marx, *Economic & Philosophic Manuscripts of 1844* (Moscow: Progress Publishers, 1959); Cf. Eagleton, *Marx* (London: Phoenix, 1977).

1105 Cf. Michel Foucault, "Two Lectures" (1976) in *Power/Knowledge: Selected Interviews and Other Writings, 1972–1977* ed. Colin Gordon (Brighton: Harvester 1980), 76–108.

1106 See Chapter One above and notes.

1107 For introductory accounts, see Dominic Chiesa, *Subjectivity and Otherness A Philosophical Reading of Lacan* (Cambridge, MA: MIT Press, 2007); Joanne Faulkner et al., *Understanding Psychoanalysis* (London: Acumen, 2007), chapter 5 "Jacques Lacan: Reading Freud to the Letter".

1108 Cf. Slavoj Zizek, *Plague of Fantasies* (London: Verso, 1997), 223–4; *Sublime Object of Ideology* (London: Verso, 1989) 124–8; *Tarrying with the Negative* (USA: Duke University Press, 1993) 251–7; *Welcome to the Desert of the Real: Five Essays* (London and New York: Verso, 2002) 152–4. For criticism, see Matthew Sharpe & Geoffrey Boucher, *Žižek and Politics: A Critical Introduction* (Edinburgh: Edinburgh University Press, 2010), 83–84; 180–185.

shifts, or the May 1968 revolts.[1109] Emmanuel Levinas, as we have seen, wants to ground his ethics in an Other which would break wholly with the order of nature, governed by the alleged universality of the self-oriented *conatus essendi* closed to the infinity of the Other.[1110] Even Jürgen Habermas, whose universalist ethics of dialogue is anticipated by Camus' mature political philosophy in ways we examined in Chapter Four, grounds this ethics in a transcendental argument beginning from inter-subjective, linguistic exchange, rather than by recourse to any imputed human nature.[1111] Philosophical hermeneutics, beginning from Heidegger into Gadamer's work, bases its contributions upon the work of interpreting texts.[1112] In large measure, then, Camus' 1948 diagnosis of European thought applies to the central strands of that thought still today:

> 'Only the modern city,' Hegel dares write, 'offers the mind a field in which it can become aware of itself.' We are thus living in the period of big cities.... Our most significant works [of literature] show the same bias. Landscapes are not to be found in great European literature since Dostoevsky. History explains neither the natural universe that existed before it nor the beauty that exists above it. Hence it chose to be ignorant of them. Whereas Plato contained everything—nonsense, reason, and myth—our philosophers contain nothing but nonsense or reason because they have closed their eyes to the rest. The mole is meditating...[1113]

Camus' point, we will try to show, is not that we should somehow simply disregard the undoubted insights of modern philosophical and social-scientific paradigms. These, by largely eschewing recourse to the category of 'human nature', have told us much about our determination by historical, cultural, political

---

1109   Alain Badiou, *Ethics; Manifesto for Philosophy* trans. Norman Madarasz (Albany: State University of New York Press, 1992). Politics has its Truth-Events, alongside art, love, and science: all completely rupture prior understandings of what is real and possible in the relevant "condition". See Alain Badiou, *Metapolitics*, trans. by Jason Barker; (New York: Verso, 2005).

1110   Levinas, *Totality and* Infinity; and *Otherwise than Being, or Beyond Essence*: and Chapter Four.

1111   Habermas, *Philosophical Discourse of Modernity*, 199–204, 206–209; 247–248, and esp. 311–326; *The Theory of Communicative Action*. Vol. 1: *Reason and the Rationalization of Society*, 3–23; *Justification and Application*, ch. 1; "Reflections on the linguistic foundations of sociology: The Christian Gauss Lectures (Princeton University, February–March 1971)", 1–103.

1112   Hans-Georg Gadamer, *Truth and Method* trans. Joel Weinsheimer, Donald G. Marshall (London: Continuum, 2006).

1113   HE 150–151; TL 492; "Ce soir le rideau se lève sur... René Char (1948)", OC II 764.

and economic forces. Such a disregard for human historicity, of course, is one charge levelled against Camus by Jeanson and Sartre in their fateful exchange following the appearance of *L'Homme Révolté*, and then after Camus' death by Edward Said and Azzedine Haddour.[1114] "Naturally, it is not a question of despising anything," Camus reflects in *The Rebel*, "... but of simply saying that it [a philosophy which tries to balance political history against recognition of those parts of our nature which resist political totalisation] is a thought which the world today cannot do without for very much longer."[1115] Contra Sartre et al., as he specifies in his response to Jeanson and the unpublished "Defence of *The Rebel*," Camus rightly distinguishes between historicism (the view that human nature and culture are wholly historically relative) and history or political life *per se*. He challenges the former: protesting against the idea that, as he put it ironically, even writing a "poem about a spring today would be to serve capitalism."[1116] He does not in any sense dream of escaping the latter, as we stressed in Chapter Four.[1117]

Camus' key terms for describing this other non-*historicist* side to his position turn directly around the key result of his arguments against attempts to rationalise murder: the idea of a limit circumscribing what is and is not legitimate. Contra Jorn Boisen's quite typical assertion, Camus' appeal to classical philosophy in Part V of the *Rebel* is not a "very personal vision" far from the critical spirit of Parts II-IV: offering rhetorical vagaries in place of "any real solution".[1118] As we shall see, this part of *L'Homme Révolté* completes Camus'

1114 Jeanson, "Soul in Revolt" 95–96; Sartre, "Reply to Albert Camus" 150–152; Haddour, *Colonial Myths* 31–33.
1115 HR 374; R 300. HR 374; R 300. See Camus' comments concerning Europe as both midday and midnight at Gay-Crosier, "De l'*Homo faber* à l'*Homo ludens*: défence et illustration de la pensée de midi", in *Albert Camus, Contemporain*, 41.
1116 At Aronson, *Camus and Sartre*, 58. Camus retorted that he would delight without shame in such a poem "if it was beautiful."
1117 As Jeanson has to note ("Soul in Revolt", 98), only to pass it by, as if this concession was not decisive: "I am certainly aware that this interpretation would seem to be challenged by certain passages in the book [*The Rebel*] in which Camus, on the contrary, forcibly insists on man's obligation not to ignore history because that would be 'to deny the real'..." See Camus, "Defence of *The Rebel*", in *Sartre and Camus: A Historic Confrontation*, 209–210, 214–216. Camus writes: "my book does not deny history (a negation of it would be senseless) but just examines the attitude that aims at making history into an absolute. So it isn't history that is rejected, but a frame of mind in relation to history". See Gay-Crosier, "De l'*Homo faber* à l'*Homo ludens*: défence et illustration de la pensée de midi", in *Albert Camus, Contemporain*, 42–44.
1118 Jorn Boisen, "Hedonisme et ethique: un paradoxe camusien?," 125.

'master argument' (see Introduction), giving positive form to the "Yes" Camus has argued is glimpsed in all genuine revolt in notions of balance or *mesure*, and a mode of thinking which excludes nothing. Understanding Camus' neo-Hellenism in this chapter will accordingly complete our recovery of Camus' 'master argument'.[1119] Camus wishes not simply to defend a limit within the political realm on the ability of any individual or institution to violate others' demands for dignity and a meaningful life. As we glimpsed at the end of the last Chapter, Camus also wants to limit the scope of 'the political' itself. He is one of the few philosophical voices in the European tradition, anticipating more recent ecological thought, who thinks our politics must today include a challenge to "twenty centuries of abortive struggle against nature, first in the name of a historic god and then of a deified history,"[1120] and that we need urgently to recover a sense of human belonging, as one limited species, within the natural order.

Two key forms of critique have constantly faced Camus' mature philosophical position. We will be addressing these criticisms, front and centre, in both this and the next Chapter.

The first such criticism, at the level of philosophical ideas, points to a deep tension which seems to rive Camus' thought, to the extent that after 1944 he increasingly seems to want to ground his political and wider commitments in a philosophical naturalism looking back to classical Greek thought. On the one hand, his philosophy is founded on the kind of modern metaphysical scepticism about any claim to philosophical or theological Rationalism we charted in Chapter Three. This scepticism is carried over into his conception of rebellion, which we saw began as an ethical matter (that of rebelling against false consolations against the absurd) before taking on its historical senses in *The Rebel*, as literary and philosophical outrage, then political revolt against natural evil and human injustice. Yet by the end of *L'Homme Révolté*, Camus is invoking the seemingly robust, 'essentialist' account of human nature he anticipates at the work's beginning:

> Analysis of rebellion leads at least to the suspicion that, contrary to the postulates of contemporary thought, a human nature does exist, as the Greeks believed. Why rebel if there is nothing permanent in oneself worth preserving?[1121]

1119 See Introduction, section "But Camus, a philosopher?" above.
1120 HR 373; R 299. Cf. C II 164; C II Eng 83.
1121 HR 30; R 16.

In "Helen's Exile" as elsewhere, Camus accordingly seems to ground his limit proscribing rationalised murder in a substantive account of nature he traces to Greek, notably presocratic, philosophy:

> The Greeks, who for centuries questioned themselves as to what is just, could understand nothing of our idea of justice. For them equity implied a limit, whereas our whole continent is convulsed in its search for a justice that must be total. At the dawn of Greek thought Heraclitus was already imagining that justice sets limits for the physical universe itself: "The sun will not overstep his measures; if he does, the Erinyes, the handmaids of justice, will find him out." We who have cast the universe and spirit out of our sphere laugh at that threat. In a drunken sky we light up the suns we want. But nonetheless the boundaries exist, and we know it.[1122]

The issue here, as has been argued by figures led by Alisdair Macintyre, is that moderns arguably no longer can 'know' any sense of normative boundaries rooted in the contemplation of nature.[1123] The reason is that any such form of culture seems militated against by the advent of the modern scientific project, and increasingly after Copernicus, the evolving sense of nature as spatiotemporally infinite, without any teleological or providential direction, inhabited by evolving species without a constant nature. How then, if at all, can we (or Camus) balance this seeming appeal to an ordered, classical sense of cosmos with Camus' modern scepticism, and the defence of modern science we have encountered in Chapter One (where science was defended as a source of rationality opposed to totalitarian madness) and Chapter Three (where science was defended as a descriptive and tentative, not explanatory and Rationalistic, way of thinking)? In one of the best diagnoses of this vital tension in Camus' thought, "Camus, God, and Process Thought," process theologian James Goss puts the dilemma precisely:

1122 HE 149. Cf. C II 174, C II Eng 89: "Tout l'effort de la pensée allemande a été de substituer à la notion de nature humaine celle de situation humaine et donc l'histoire à Dieu et la tragédie moderne à l'équilibre ancien. L'existentialisme moderne pousse cet effort encore plus loin et introduit dans l'idée de situation la même incertitude que dans celle de nature. Il ne reste plus rien qu'un mouvement. Mais comme les Grecs je crois à la nature."

1123 Alisdair Macintyre, *After Virtue* (Notre Dame: University of Notre Dame Press; 3rd edition: 2007) seemingly in Leo Strauss, *Natural Right and History* ch. 1; compare Thorson, "Albert Camus and the rights of man", *Ethics* 74: 4 (July 1974), 282–3 for a classic statement of this post-theological dilemma, influenced by Strauss.

If nature is indifferent and moves blindly through time, its purposelessness could hardly provide an 'example' for human purpose. This 'crisis' in Camus' position is characterized by Hans Jonas who, comparing the nihilism of existentialist thought to that of Gnosticism, states: 'A universe without an intrinsic hierarchy of being, as the Copernican universe is, leaves values ontologically unsupported, and the self is thrown back entirely upon itself in its quest for meaning and value. Meaning is no longer found but is 'conferred.' Values are no longer beheld in the vision of objective reality, but are posited as feats of valuation.' After World War II, Camus sought to escape from this reduction of all value to something conferred by men in history. To avoid purely 'subjectivistic' values, Camus, via the Greeks, posited the limits and beauty of 'objective' nature as man's sure guide. Yet, he never abandoned the dualism of his earlier writings; he continued to hold to a 'blind' universe. The inconsistency of his position results from his maintaining two mutually incompatible philosophical positions: a godless Cartesianism that portrays the physical universe without quality and the Greek notion that value is grounded in *physis*.[1124]

The second criticism is political, before it is philosophical. Jeanson and Sartre in response to *The Rebel* were quick to 'call' Camus on the book's appeal to a Mediterranean or Greek philosophical heritage, supposedly vindicating the limitation of the demands of "the political." As if, for one thing, any attempt from within political life to decree what is and is not political is not *itself* a politically contestable, in truth politically resigned or conservative assertion... The substance of their famous criticisms of *The Rebel*, beyond the polemical and sometimes highly personal dimensions of these texts, is to argue that Camus' book indicated the author's deep longing, fully clear in the last Part on "Midday Thought," to have done with 'history' or political life altogether. In Sartre's incisive formulations, Camus was drawn into politics and the resistance involuntarily. His actions against the Nazis were admirable. But they impressed upon Camus that "history," first experienced through the barbarism of the National Socialists, was an unremittingly bleak "Hell" or "whore" won over wholly to insolence, deception and violence.[1125] This sense of history explains the presentation in *The Plague* of fascism as a natural, not human, evil: and indeed, its and *The Rebel*'s focus on the old metaphysical problem

---

1124 James Goss, "Camus, God, and Process Thought", *Process Theology*, Vol. 4, Number 2 (Summer 1974), 114–128. At www-site http://www.religion-online.org/showarticle.asp?title=2375, last accessed October 2013.
1125 Sartre, "Reply to Albert Camus," 150–151; Jeanson, "Soul in Revolt," 94–95.

of evil we saw in Chapter Two (*La Peste* is "already a transcendental chronicle," in Jeanson's gloss).[1126] It also motivates Camus' desire to pit "historical absolutism" against "an irrepressible demand of human nature, of which the Mediterranean, where intelligence is intimately related to the blinding light of the sun, guards the secret."[1127]

Post-colonial criticism in the lineage of Albert Memmi's *The Coloniser and the Colonised* (1957),[1128] Conor Cruise O'Brien's *Albert Camus* and Edward Said's *Culture and Imperialism*,[1129] has radicalised Sartre and Jeanson's criticism.[1130] After the outbreak of the Algerian war in November 1954, Camus found himself increasingly isolated between the French Right and Left, in his continuing attempts to imagine a post-colonial Algeria in which the *pied noirs* might live alongside the indigenous Arab and Berber populations. After Camus' death, the Evian accords, and the repatriation of the *pied noirs* to mainland France, post-colonial critics in effect radicalised Sartre's and Jeanson's accusation against Camus fleeing European History into an idealised "Mediterranean" culture of somnolent beaches, azure evenings and blazing sunshine, far from Northerners' messianic fervours. It is not simply that Camus fled a Europe in which he never felt at home back to an idealised Mediterranean which he had experienced in his youth. This "indigenous" "Mediterranean" culture Camus had been celebrating since the mid-1930s was already a mystifying escape from the political realities of his *homeland*, French Algeria. Camus could not flee to an ahistorical Mediterranean from absolutist Europe, these critics claim.

1126 Jeanson, "Soul in Revolt", 82.
1127 HR 374; R 300.
1128 Cf. Neil Foxlee, "Mediterranean Humanism or Colonialism with a Human Face? Contextualizing Albert Camus' 'The New Mediterranean Culture'" *Mediterranean Historical Review* Vol. 21, No. 1, June 2006: 75–94: 80.
1129 Conor Cruise O'Brien, *Albert Camus*; Edward Said, *Culture and Imperialism*. Cf. also Peter Dunwoodie, "Negotiation of Confrontation? Camus, Memory and the Colonial Chronotype", in in Christine Margerrison, Mark Orme, Lissa Lincoln eds., *Albert Camus in the 21st Century: A Reassessment of His Thinking at the Dawn of the New Millennium*, 47–59.
1130 It is in fact remarkable, looking back at the 1952 exchange in *Les Temps Modernes*, how little attention is paid to the colonial issue, not only by Camus, but also by his *Marxissant* critics... *L'Homme Révolté* remains an almost completely European book, in terms of its critical targets (except in Part V's appeal to Greek and 'Mediterranean' culture). European colonialism is absent in *L'Homme Révolté* as an object of critique, although in "The Artist and His Time" of one year later, Camus would declaim the Marxist postulate of an end of history as "the object of a faith and of a new mystification... no less great than that which based colonial oppression on the necessity of saving the souls of infidels. (Camus, "The Artist and his Times" MSe, 209). In this light, Aronson's comments seem unjust at *Camus and Sartre*, 122.

A colonial possession of the French Empire (the "African Alsace" of Louis Bertrand et al.),[1131] Algeria had since 1830 been well and truly 'historicised' by the colonising French. History bore the face of invasion, forcible expropriations, and the systematic oppression to which the French had subjected the Arab and Berber populations. In this light, Camus' celebration of a philosophical naturalism which is very pointedly 'located' as 'Mediterranean' in *L'Homme Révolté* and elsewhere seems a prize exercise in colonialist ideology, legitimising France's violent possession of the colony. In Haddour's powerful statement of this position in his "Mythopoetics and Politics: Colonial Algeria in Myths and Counter-Myths":

> From the very beginning, ... the French Algerians put history on hold; yet they were playing a losing game ... They established a compartmentalised society which kept them separate from the colonised. There was an obvious gap: a distance between two images of Algeria, a French Algeria and a native one; a gap between an image of an historical Algeria marked by the scar of colonialism and Camus's mythic one, untainted by this history of oppression. These two images sit together uncomfortably. The French Algerians spent time dressing up this history by covering up its scars: they attempted to abolish the contradiction at the core of these two conflicting images of Algeria, by taking a holiday from history. The generous vision of Algeria with its sunny side intervened to compensate for the agony of a compartmentalised and sclerosed society ... The Camusian metaphor of 'nuptials' (*noces*) stands as a trope not for the colonised's assimilation but as a trope dissimulating the history of a divided society.[1132]

In order to adequately weigh these influential criticisms, as well as to complete our understanding of Camus' philosophical discourse, in this Chapter we will recount the features of what we will call Camus' philosophical neoHellenism. Our full response to the post-colonial criticism, including a consideration of what Camus aimed at in *Le Premier Homme*, will be undertaken in the final Chapter. Nevertheless, by recounting in this Chapter Camus' engagement with the West's classical Greek heritage, and thereby completing our reconstruction of Camus' philosophical discourse, we will in a preliminary way also be answering these criticisms. For we can accept the psychological and political cogency of Haddour et al.'s claims that Camus' images of the

---

1131 See Haddour, *Colonial Myths*, chapter 1 "Assimilation: A colonist stratagem in writing", 4–21, also 24–25.
1132 Haddour, *Colonial Myths*, 33.

'Mediterranean', or of his 'Greeks', was partly *motivated* by his own increasingly agonising attempts to come to terms with his doubly-displaced identity (*pied noir* in Paris, Frenchman in Africa) and the colonial crimes of the French: a struggle whose strains (amongst other things) shows itself, beneath the irony, in the semi-confessional dimension of *La Chute*.[1133] Yet what Camus, however motivated, *found* in classical art, literature and philosophy (to the extent that it can be shown to be true to the originals, and coherent on its own terms) is another matter. Camus' neoclassicism, we will show, has a validity and cogency which transcends the conditions of its genesis, and which can be read in relative independence of Camus' political biography. The popularity of Camus' philosophically-informed fictions, and to a lesser extent his philosophical essays amongst readers largely ignorant of their French-Algerian origins attests to this relative autonomy.[1134] Certainly, we should not prejudge the issue without looking to the relevant texts, instead accepting pre-emptively that Camus' "midday thought" can only be the mystifications of a liberal coloniser with a bad conscience,[1135] trying to escape his historical guilt by imagining what Davison, echoing Sartre and Jeanson, has called "a utopia outside of history and politics".[1136] Camus' position is, without question, not wholly historically innocent, as *The Rebel*, incidentally, would advise. Notably, to the extent that Camus identifies his neoclassical challenge to European historicisms with the wordless *ethos* of the *pied noirs* in the affectionately ironic portraits of

---

1133 Haddour *Colonial Myths*, 60–78.
1134 This is not to sponsor or celebrate such ignorance. Camus' presentation as a "universal" or "humanistic" author is *itself* seen as a function of the colonialist erasure of his works' Algerian origins. See Jean Déjoux's charge that "this transition to the universal appears to be a way of distancing oneself from immediate political realities…" cited at Foxlee, "Mediterranean Humanism or Colonialism with a Human Face?", 84. See below Chapter Six.
1135 See Albert Memmi's *The Colonizer and the Colonized*, originally published in French in 1957, for an analysis of the paradoxical situation of the "colonizer who refuses": the type of colonizer who opposes colonialism in "the impossible historical situation" (39) of being considered a traitor by other colonizers and yet who "places conditions" for his cooperation with the colonized in their struggle for justice (35). This is what leads to his "political ineffectiveness". Compare David Carroll, "Camus's Algeria: Birthrights, Colonial Injustice, and the Fiction of a French-Algerian People", MLN, Vol. 112, No. 4, French Issue (Sep., 1997), pp. 517–549: at 520, n. 4. As we will see, much of this accurately depicts Camus' awareness after 1954, culminating in the famous silence following January 1956.
1136 Haddour at Foxlee, "Mediterranean Humanism or Colonialism with a Human Face?", 84 bottom; cf. Davison's charge of Camus' "evasion of flight into unreality" at Ray Davison, 'Mythologizing the Mediterranean: The Case of Albert Camus', *Journal of Mediterranean Studies* 10 (2000): 77–92, at 80. Also Haddour *Colonial myths*, 29.

"Summer in Algiers" and "Minotaur, or the Halt at Oran," he invites criticism for obviating the *pied noirs*' colonial location.[1137] Yet Camus' thought, we will argue, is also not wholly bound to the markers of place which Camus assigns to it, based upon his own experiences.

Post-colonialist readings of Camus' *oeuvre* can certainly be questioned, in Foxlee's phrase, for being "reductive in [their] focus on colonialism as the only relevant context...," as well as on grounds of historical and textual accuracy.[1138] On the one hand, as we will see, Camus does not uncritically identify with the culture of his birth: certainly not the self-satisfied, threatened, racist culture of Marcel in "La Femme Adultère"[1139] which he attacks in the *Algerian Chronicles*, and whose courts absurdly hang Meursault for not crying at his mother's funeral. On the other hand, this is because, from the very beginning of his writing career (and not, contra Haddour, only after November 1954, when the Algerian war broke out),[1140] it was specifically to ancient Hellenic classicism and culture (rather than an idealised, modern French Algeria) that Camus looked for philosophical orientation and literary inspiration.

With this much said, let us proceed.

1.2 *A Greece of the Flesh* (la chair)

What one collection calls lyrically the "persistent voice" of Greek and Roman antiquity never ceased speaking in modern French letters. Camus is far from alone amongst modern French authors in dotting his literary and philosophical *oeuvres* with classical *motifs*.[1141] Notably, during the years surrounding the Vichy occupation, over a dozen leading playwrights produced dramas on classical themes. In this time, one critic has commented, "the Parisian stage became a virtual reincarnation of the theatre of Dionysus in 5th-century Athens..."[1142] As Paul Allen Miller has examined, Camus' *Caligula* (written

---

1137 Camus, "Summer in Algiers"; "Minotaur, or stopping at Oran."
1138 Foxlee, "Mediterranean Humanism or Colonialism with a Human Face?", 78. Compare David Carroll's bolder claim in *Albert Camus the Algerian* 15. See also Chapter Six below.
1139 Camus, "La Femme Adultère", *Exile and the Kingdom*; see Tarrow, *Exile from the Kingdom*, 175–177. Or of Raymond in *L'Étranger*, on whom see Tarrow, *Exile from the Kingdom*, 72–73, a typical *petit blanc* longing for domination and power.
1140 Haddour, *Colonial Myths*, 63, 75.
1141 Walter G. Langlois ed. *The Persistent Voice; Essays on Hellenism in French Literature Since the 18th Century in Honor of Professor Henri M. Peyre* (New York: New York University Press, 1971).
1142 Paul-Allen Miller, *Postmodern Spiritual Practices: The Construction of the Subject and the Reception of Plato in Lacan, Derrida and Foucault* (Ohio State University Press: Ohio, 2007), 31.

1938, first shown 1945) belongs alongside Annouilh's *Antigone*, Sartre's *Les Mouches*, and Brassilach's *Bérénice* in a generation of French, modernist theatre drawing on ancient paradigms to allegorically dramatise and "re-present" the wartime situation of the resistance generation.[1143] As works by Miriam Leonard and Allen Miller in particular have also emphasised, engagements with classical Greek thinkers (notably Plato, Aristotle, and the Stoics) and Greek dramatists (notably Sophocles and his *Antigone*) are similarly central to the *oeuvres* of France's great, post-1960 theorists' work (at least as mediated by Hegel, Nietzsche, and Heidegger): whether Lacan on Sophocles and Aristotle in *The Ethics of Psychoanalysis*, Derrida on Plato, Deleuze or the later Foucault on the Stoics, Lyotard on the sophists, and differently Pierre Hadot's works.[1144]

Yet the neoclassicism of Camus, precisely as an Algerian-French *pied noir* in many respects stands out both from the classical receptions of his continental, Parisian (and German) contemporaries, and that of the succeeding, structuralist and post-structuralist generations.[1145] Like many of these thinkers, to be sure, Camus was concerned to challenge the Right's ideological possession of the West's classical heritage, as we shall see. Yet for Camus in arguable contrast to, for instance, Lacan or Derrida, interest in the ancients was never restricted to examining particular, liminal moments (Antigone's "no!" to Creon, Socrates' *atopia*, the Platonic *pharmakon* etc.) anticipating or exemplifying his own projects (a psychoanalytic ethics "beyond the good", a post-Heideggerian deconstruction of Western metaphysics, etc.) Rather, from his earliest recorded writings, Camus much more directly identified himself, and expressly *shaped* his literary and philosophical work as involving a "return to the Greeks." Although we have so far skirted this, even a cursory acquaintance with Camus' work bears out this "constitutive" importance of classical literature and philosophy within it. His early essay collection *Noces*' title refers to the *hieros gamos* at the heart of pagan myth; and two of its lyrical meditations recall Camus' visits to classical ruins at Tipasa and Djemila in Algeria. Camus' first philosophical book is entitled *The Myth of Sisyphus*. His major philosophical work, *L'Homme Révolté*, recurs centrally to the myth of Prometheus in ways we have documented. Camus' *Carnets* are dotted with reflections on Plato, the Stoics, the classical tragedians, Greek and Roman historians.[1146] These notebooks

---

1143 Miller, *Postmodern Spiritual Practices*, 27–60.
1144 Cf. Miriam Leonard, *Athens in Paris: Ancient Greek Thought in Post-War French Thought* (Oxford: Oxford University Press, 2009); Miller, *Postmodern Spiritual Practices*, 61–226.
1145 Cf. Chapter Six below, especially the sections on *The First Man*; also EE Pref, 5–18.
1146 See the extremely helpful "Note Annex" in François Bousquet, *Camus le Méditerranéen, Camus L'Ancien* (Sherbrooke, Quebec: Éditions Naaman, 1977), 112–113.

make it clear that, at the time of his death, he was planning a third philosophical work, *The Myth of Nemesis*.[1147] Camus' 1954 collection *L'Été* contains lyrical essays on "The Minotaur, or the Halt at Oran" and "Helen's Exile", as well as "Prometheus in the Underworld". Although Camus never pursued a career as an academic philosopher, as we have said, we know that he wrote his *Diplôme des Hautes Études* on "Christian Metaphysics and Neoplatonism", including chapters on Gnosticism and Plotinus. With no small ambition, as we skirted in Chapter Two, the thesis set out to examine what Camus would later call the "true and only turning-point (*véritable et seul tournant*)" in Western history (between pagan antiquity and monotheistic Christendom) and promised himself in the 1950s that he would reconsider.[1148]

"My colleagues follow the path of German philosophers of the 19th century," Camus could announce to jubilant reception in Athens in April 1955, "but me, I was nourished by Greek philosophy ... I am the son of Greek philosophy."[1149] This statement is far from one of a kind. Receiving the Nobel Prize for Literature in 1957 in Stockholm, Camus again explained: "I have Christian preoccupations, but my nature is pagan. The sun ... I feel at ease amongst the Greeks ... the presocratics, Heraclitus, Empedocles, Parmenides ... I have faith in the ancient values, however much they have been badly represented since Hegel."[1150] One of Camus' two public addresses in Athens in 1955, two years prior, was a passionate argument for a return to tragic drama on the Greek paradigm, as modern men and women face the increasingly fate-like realities of technological and historical developments.[1151] "The truth is that it is a hard fate to be born in a pagan land in Christian times. This is my case," Camus genuflected in the same year as *L'Homme Révolté* appeared: "I feel closer to the values of the classical world than to those of Christianity. Unfortunately, I cannot go to Delphi to be initiated!"[1152]

1147 Cf. Bousquet, *Camus le Méditerranéen, Camus l'Ancien*, 98; on the importance of the Nemesis myth in Camus, see especially Laurence Viglieno, "Némésis: Déesse Inspiratrice du Dernier Camus?", in *Albert Camus et la Grèce* (Rencontres méditerranéens Albert Camus: Éditions du Sud, 2007), 49–66.

1148 C II 342; C II Eng 176.

1149 Camus, "Albert Camus à Athènes, *To Vina*, Athènes: 29 April 1955", at Barbara Papastavrou, "Albert Camus: De l'Amour Platon à son Engagement envers les Grecs", in *Camus et la Grèce*, 107.

1150 Camus at Bousquet, *Camus le Méditerranéen, Camus l'Ancien*, 101. See Henri Peyre, "Camus the Pagan" in *Camus, A collection of Critical essasys*, 65–70.

1151 Albert Camus, "On the Future of Tragedy", in *Lyrical and Critical Essays*, 295–310.

1152 Albert Camus, "Interview with Gabriel d'Aubarède in *Les Nouveles Littéraire*, May 10, 1951", LCE 357.

Nevertheless, as Ward has again reflected, Camus' "neoclassicism" was not that of a philologist or academician: "but neither was his purpose. His primary concern was not 'the sources in themselves,' but the sources insofar as they contain a teaching which might be of help in his own attempt to find a way out of modern nihilism."[1153] More basically than this, in a way which makes Haddour and the postcolonial critiques so potentially devastating in his case, Camus turned to these sources in light of his own continuing attempts at cultivating his own literary and philosophical identity.[1154] His Greeks reflect, and shape, his personal and political experiences. François Bousquet's observations in *Camus Le Méditerranéen, Camus L'Ancien* that "all of Camus' philosophy commences with a certain sensibility," and that "at its origin, Camus' philosophy is a lived philosophy"[1155] seem to us to be completely accurate.[1156] We have already seen how Camus' thought always responded to what he experienced as the pressing problems of the times: first, nihilism and suicide (Chapter Three); after 1942, totalitarianism and rationalised murder (Chapters One, Two, Four); earlier and right up to his premature end, the growing Algerian crisis (Chapter Six). In all these responses, as in his creative work up to *Le Premier Homme*, Camus would avow that he was searching to recover or articulate a truth or sense of existence he had first experienced growing up beneath *un ciel heureux* in the poor quarters of French Algiers, with his near-mute mother, overbearing *grandmère*, illiterate uncle and their mangy dog.[1157] In "The Minotaur, or the Halt at Oran," Camus goes close to identifying his own, famous post-Cartesian *skepsis* (Chapters Three, Four) with his experience of living in the European outposts of Oran or Algiers, set against the silent, searing backing of the North African deserts. His explicit contrast is with Descartes who, "for his meditations, chose as his desert the busiest commercial town of his time."[1158]

1153 Ward, "Recovery", 179.
1154 Cf. Carroll, *Camus the Algerian*, 8–9, 155–156.
1155 Bousquet, *Camus le Méditerranéen, Camus l'Ancien*, 103, 104.
1156 Cf. Michel Onfray, *L'Ordre Libertaire. La Vie Philosophique d'Albert Camus* Paris: Flammarion, 2013; in English language, Matthew Sharpe, "Camus' *Askesis*: Reading Camus, in Light of the *Carnets* (and his *L'Impromptu des Philosophes*)", *Philosophical Practice* March 2013, 8.1: 1149–1164.
1157 Cf. Camus, "Preface" to *L'envers et L'endroit*, LCE 13–17.
1158 MSO 111; cf. 118, 131; also Carroll, *Camus the Algerian*, 8: "The Algerian in Camus is also an important component of his agnosticism, of his determined resistance to political and religious doctrines, systems, and ideas, the side of him that maintains a distance from [...] national, religious, cultural, ethnic, and political identities, the side that resists oneness, sameness, uniformity, and all expressions of absolute truth ..." See below on the symbolism of the desert.

"To correct for a certain natural indifference, I was placed half-way between misery and sunlight," Camus reflected in 1957 of his Algerian beginnings:

> Misery prevented me from believing that all is well under the sun and in history, while the sunlight taught me that history is not everything. To change life, yes, but not this world, which was my divinity.[1159]

This fundamental sense of natural "plenitude"[1160] which Camus received in his formative experiences growing up bathing on the Mediterranean coasts, basking in the sun, admiring the half-naked beauties, keeping goal in the local football team, and tasting for the first time the joys of sensual love, lies at the heart of his lifelong resistance to being dubbed an "existentialist",[1161] and more besides. The same sensibility, rooted deeply in Camus' sense of place, shapes the marvellous opening of *"L'Exil de Helen,"* written in 1948 at the height of Camus' post-war political activism and dedicated to his friend, the poet René Char:

> The Mediterranean has its sunlit tragedy which is not that of the mists. On certain evenings on the sea, at the foot of the mountains, night falls on the perfect curve of a little bay, and an anguished fullness rises from the silent waters. We realise in such places that if the Greeks experienced despair, it was always through beauty and its oppressive quality. Tragedy, in this golden sadness, reaches its highest point. Our own time, on the contrary, has nourished its despair in ugliness and in convulsions. That is why Europe would be ignoble, if grief could ever have this quality...[1162]

The most famous articulation of Camus' youthful worship of the sea, sun, and beauty of the Mediterranean however is found in the opening essay of the 1937 *Noces*, "Nuptials at Tipasa". The essay documents the young Camus' visit, with an unnamed lover, to the classical ruins on the coast at Tipasa. Here, the young initiate hymns:

1159 EE Pref, 6–7.
1160 Camus, *Essais*, 380.
1161 Cf. *"Non, je ne suis pas* existentialiste..." (15 Novembre 1945) OC II, 655–656; with Albert Camus, "Pessimism and Courage": "I do not much relish the all too celebrated existentialism and to be honest, I find its conclusions false," PC 58.
1162 HE 148. Note that I have followed here the, in the author's opinion, superior translation by Thody in Philip Thody ed. *Albert Camus, Selected Essays and Notebooks* (London: Penguin, 1979), 136.

> I understand what is meant by 'glory': the right to love without limits. There is only one love in the world. To hold a woman's body is to hold in one's arms the strange joy that falls from the sky to the sea... In a sense, it is truly my life that I'm playing here, a life that tastes of warm stone, full of the sighs of the sea and the cicadas who are starting to sing now. The breeze is cool and the sky blue. I love this life with abandon and want to speak of it with liberty: it makes me proud of my human condition. True, others have often told me there is nothing to be proud of. And yet, there is: this Sun, this sea, my heart leaping with youth, my body tasting of salt and the vast setting where tenderness and glory merge in the yellow and the blue...[1163]

It is this sensibility (and this sensuality) that first shaped Camus' philhellenism, and continued to inform his work and life, as he confronted the darkest realities of the 20th century.[1164] Rather than coming to love the Greeks through the classical literature, Gide, Nietzsche and Schopenhauer we know Camus was being introduced to first by Jean Grenier, then René Poirier,[1165] Camus responded in classical literature to what he sensed was a 'Mediterranean' sensibility rooted in his own Algerian experiences. Camus' important journalistic articles of July 1939 on the misery of the indigenous population of Kabylie in the Algerian highlands (and indicting the colonial authorities as the agents and beneficiaries of this misery) is thus pointedly called "Greece in rags." It opens with a reflection on the common landscape shared by Algeria and the Greeks of his imaginings.[1166] Camus' presentation the previous year at the *Revue Rivages* likewise appeals with evident imaginative identification to that episode in Xenophon's *Anabasis* when:

> ... the soldiers of whom Xenophon speaks, returning from Persia to Greece after an interminable retreat, exhausted with hunger, thirst and fatigue, drunken with bitterness and humiliation... arrive at the summit of a hill overlooking the sea. And there, throwing up their arms, forgetful of their fatigue and defeat, far from the war [and] with blank eyes,

---

1163 NT 68–69.
1164 Cf. Bousquet, *Camus le méditerranéen*, 22–28; Planeille, "L'Hellade, 'Rivage déployé d'une mer genial", esp. 41–43.
1165 On Camus' early *paideia*, see Monique Crochet, *Les Mythes dans L'Oeuvre d'Albert Camus*, 18–43; also Herbert R. Lottman, *Albert Camus: A Biography* (New York: George Braziller, 1981), 38–76.
1166 Albert Camus, "La Grèce en haillons (5 juin 1939)" OC I, 653–656.

they started to dance before the shimmering waves wherein their gods were smiling.[1167]

Drawing on one of Camus' own favoured classical myths, Abbou has described Camus' philhellenism as the Ariadne's thread running through Camus' life, touching all of his literary, philosophical and political pursuits.[1168] Doubtlessly, as Richardson has rejoined, as the political situation continued to escalate in Algeria, Camus could "declare himself a son of Greece with a sense of simplicity with which he could never have declared himself a son of France."[1169] This is close to conceding on more favourable terms the post-colonialist charge that Camus' 'Mediterranean' was a universalising idealisation enabling Camus the man to avoid the very particular injustices visited by his French republic upon the Algerian "Greece in rags".

In order to assess the justice of the post-colonial claims, which threaten to discredit Camus' neoclassicism at its very beginnings, we need now to look at the two documents the young Camus wrote while still in Algeria. In these pieces, he gives his first, systematic expressions to his emerging sense of his neoHellenistic philosophy. The first, chronologically, is Camus' *Diplôme* thesis of 1936 on *Christian Metaphysics and Neoplatonism*. The second, from one year later, is Camus' public address at the *Maison de la Culture* on "The New Mediterranean Culture". Since this latter text has been more central to post-colonial critiques of Camus' sense of Greek thought; and since, as Woelfel has observed, Camus often used "the closely related symbols 'Greek' and 'Mediterranean' interchangeably,"[1170] we will address this text first. Having acknowledged the contextual politics and historical ambiguities of Camus' attempt in this important lecture to propose a progressive conception of the "Mediterranean", attending to the *Diplôme* thesis will then allow us to see how Camus' conception of Greek thought transcends its political conditions of genesis, reaching out towards a distinct understanding of the classical heritage, and his own mature philosophical position.

1167 Cited at Bousquet, *Camus le méditerranéen, Camus l'ancien*, 23. Cf. the slight variation in "New Mediterranean Culture" LCE 196.
1168 André Abbou, "Albert Camus: le retour à Ithaque", in A. Fosty (ed.), *Albert Camus et la Grèce* (Aix-en-Provence: Écritures du Sud, 2007), pp. 81–94; Cf. Luke Richardson, "Sisyphus and Caesar: the opposition of Greece and Rome in Albert Camus' absurd cycle", *Classical Receptions Journal* Vol. 4:1 (2012), 85. Ariadne and the Minotaur structures "Minotaur, or stopping at Oran" in LCE, 109–133.
1169 Richardson, "Sisyphus and Caesar", 85. Cf. Haddour, *Colonial myths*, 30–33, 48–49.
1170 Richardson, "Sisyphus and Caesar: the opposition of Greece and Rome in Albert Camus' absurd cycle", 83.

1.3   The Two Sides of Camus' "New Mediterranean Culture", and of His Greeks

"The New Mediterranean Culture" is a lecture Camus gave at the *Maison de la Culture* in Algiers in February 1937. Unquestionably, it looks forward to the kind of "Mediterranean humanism"[1171] Camus would later oppose to the secularised eschatologies of fascism and Stalinism in *L'Homme Révolté*. It is thus a highly important and revealing, if lesser known, Camusian text. In it, Camus argues for the existence of a distinctly Mediterranean culture. This argument is based on what he asserts are "obvious facts".[1172] These are, firstly, that:

> There is a Mediterranean sea, a basin linking about ten different countries (sic.). Those whose voices boom in the singing cafés of Spain, who wander in the port of Genoa, along the docks in Marseilles, the strange, strong race that lives along our coasts, all belong to the same family…[1173]

Secondly, Camus contends that this culture is united above all by a certain style of life rooted in the geographical setting, in which we recognise Camus' profile from *Noces*:

> Country is not the abstraction that sends men off to be massacred, but a certain way of appreciating life which is shared by certain people, through which we [in Algiers or Algeria] can feel ourselves closer to someone from Genoa or Majorca than to someone from Normandy or Alsace. This is what the Mediterranean is—a certain smell or scent that we do not need to express: we all feel it through our skin…[1174]

1171   This term is from David Ohana, *Mediterranean Historical Review*, Vol. 18, No. 1, June 2003, 59–75: cf. Foxlee, "Mediterranean humanism…", 78–79. Ohana gives the following definition of this school at 59: "Although they do not constitute a formal school of thought, they share an opposition to violence, integral nationalism, dictatorship, and ideological radicalism, an anti-racism stemming from their tolerance of the 'other' and their acceptance of the foreign and the different, a multicultural outlook that foreshadows postmodernist discourse, and an affirmation of dialogue as a form of human activity. They valued the warm, unmediated contact of dialogue between peoples and cultures. Rather than dreaming of a 'new man' they considered the problems of existing human beings in Mediterranean societies…"
1172   NMC 191.
1173   NMC 191.
1174   NMC 191.

Thirdly and most controversially, this culture is unquestionably identified with the Latin-speaking countries: "This culture, this Mediterranean truth, exists and shows itself all along the line: (1) In linguistic unity—the ease with which a Latin language can be learned when another is already known..." Indeed, it is this passage that O'Brien (alongside Dunwoodie and Lorcin)[1175] singles out as proving that Camus is "incapable of thinking in any other categories than as a Frenchman... It is quite clear that his Mediterranean culture is a European one and in Algeria a French one, and that the Arabs who have a part in this culture will have become French Arabs."[1176]

As Foxlee and Carroll have done most to point out, however, the text of Camus' "The New Mediterranean Culture" is not so clear-cut.[1177] For the same part of the lecture as we have just cited also asserts, in the immediately preceding paragraph to this identification of the Mediterranean with the Latin languages imposed by Roman conquest, that:

> The Mediterranean, an international basin traversed by every current, is perhaps the only land linked to the great ideas from the East. For it is not classical and well ordered, but diffuse and turbulent, like the Arab districts in our towns or the Genoan and Tunisian harbors. The triumphant taste for life, the sense of boredom and the weight of the sun, the empty squares at noon in Spain, the siesta, this is the true Mediterranean, and it is to the East that it is closest. Not to the Latin West. North Africa is one of the few countries where East and West live close together. And there is, at this junction, little difference between the way a Spaniard or an Italian lives on the quays of Algiers, and the way Arabs live around them. The most basic aspect of Mediterranean genius springs perhaps from this historically and geographically unique encounter between East and West.[1178]

This passage, more than any other, captures the ambiguities of Camus' position in terms of the colonial realities amidst which he was speaking. On the one hand, as critics have noted, Camus' claim that indigenous Arabs and colonisers living side by side in nearly the same conditions seems questionable, given

---

1175 See Richardson, "Sisyphus and Caesar", 83.
1176 At Foxlee, "Mediterranean Humanism...", 82.
1177 Foxlee, "Mediterranean Humanism..."; David Carroll, "Camus' Algeria: Birthrights, Colonial Injustice, and the Fiction of a French-Algerian People", *MLN*, Vol. 112, No. 4, French Issue (Sep., 1997), pp. 517–549, esp. 522–3.
1178 NMC 194–5.

the vastly inferior economic, political, social and legal conditions of native Algerians in February 1937 (which his near-contemporary journalism shows he was acutely aware of).[1179] On the other hand, Camus here clearly associates the vitality and distinctness of the "new Mediterranean culture" with its geographical and cultural locale at the crossroads between East and West.[1180] Thierry Fabre has placed Camus' valorisation of the "encounter" between East (meaning the middle Eastern, "Arabian" or "semitic" nations) and West in a line of progressive French discourses on the Mediterranean hearkening back to 19th century Saint-Simonians.[1181] As Foxlee has more recently stressed, the more immediate political context of Camus' lecture (which Foxlee argues postcolonial criticisms obviate, looking back at the speech post-1962)[1182] is just as important. It lies in Camus' attempts to wrest back a sense of Mediterranean culture from reactionary appeals by Louis Bertrand, Charles Maurras, the Algerian far Right (alongside Mussolini's fascists) to a conception of "Latin North Africa" to justify European colonialism.[1183] Camus does nothing if not foreground this political intent. "Perhaps there is something surprising in the fact that left-wing intellectuals can put themselves to work for a culture that seems irrelevant to their cause, and that can even, as has happened in the case of Maurras, be monopolized by politicians of the Right," the Lecture opens by reflecting.[1184] The entire speech is an attempt to wrest back a more inclusive conception of the Mediterranean, embracing indigenous authors and culture, from the anti-semitic "Latin Leagues" and organisations like *Le Croix de Feu*, who at that time were rallying to oppose the Blum-Violette reforms

---

1179 Richardson, "Caesar and Sisyphus", 81.
1180 Carroll, "Camus' Algeria", 522.
1181 Richardson, "Caesar and Sisyphus", 83–84.
1182 "They, however, can be accused in turn of what might be called 'chronocentrism': the inability, to adapt O'Brien's comment on Camus, to think of the past in any other categories than those of the present—or in this case, other than from the perspective of Algerian independence in 1962. Memmi's concept of the 'well-meaning colonizer', it should be remembered, did not emerge until 1957, when the Algerian War had already been underway for three years. In 1937, however, it was possible to be both a humanist and a 'well-meaning colonizer', although in Camus' case it is important to emphasize that this extended to supporting equal rights and the principle of one man, one vote." Foxlee, "Mediterranean Humanism", 89; cf. 87–88, especially the quote from Patrick McCarthy; also Susan Tarrow, *Exile From the Kingdom*, 95.
1183 See Foxlee, "Mediterranean Humanism...", 76, 80–81; Richardson, "Sisyphus and Caesar", 80–81.
1184 NMC 189–190.

championed by the *Maison de la Culture*.[1185] These reforms, which Camus passionately supported, would have seen partial Moslem enfranchisement. They were more or less shouted down by the Right.

The *Maison* itself aimed to bring together various Algerian organisations, including the Franco-Moslem Union. In the edition of the *Maison*'s journal following that in which Camus' "Mediterranean" lecture was published, the group published a manifesto (co-authored or perhaps sole-authored by Camus) demanding radical progressive reforms in Algeria, since "one cannot for example talk of culture in a country where 900,000 inhabitants [Muslim children] are deprived of schools, or of civilisation, when one is talking of a people diminished by unprecedented poverty and bullied by special laws and inhuman regulations."[1186] While this manifesto stops short of calling for Algerian independence, it is fair to recall that *no* French Algerians at this time were broaching this possibility. Moreover, as Camus would often lament, no one on the French mainland (including the PCF after 1936)[1187] was concerning themselves with the plight of the Algerian indigenous population under colonial rule.

The politics of Camus' position in the Algeria of 1937, including his staunch opposition to the colonialist Right, is also clear in the way that Camus' speech frames the cultural history of his progressive, anti-fascist conception of the new Mediterranean culture. It was to Rome that Mussolini was appealing to justify his conquest of Ethiopia in 1936, alongside his French colonialist admirers.[1188] To distinguish his Leftist conception of the Mediterranean, and defend the very idea of such a thing, Camus thus also sets out in this piece to sever his classical genealogy from the imperial Rome of the Right's political imagination. "The whole error lies in the confusion between Mediterranean and Latin, and in attributing to Rome what began in Athens," Camus contends.[1189] He then trenchantly elaborates this distinction between Greek and Roman antiquity, which Luke Richardson has shown runs throughout Camus' work[1190] and is a key component of Camus' cultural politics:

1185   See Foxlee, "Mediterranean Humanism…", 84–85.
1186   Camus, cited at Foxlee, "Mediterranean Humanism…", 88–89.
1187   Cf. Haddour, *Colonial Myths*, 28; Foxlee, "Mediterranean Culture", 87–88.
1188   NMC 293; Foxlee, "Mediterranean Humanism…", 76, 80–81; Richardson, "Sisyphus and Caesar", 80–81
1189   NMC 190.
1190   Richardson, "Caesar and Sisyphus", 66–89.

> But no. This is not the Mediterranean our *Maison de la Culture* lays claim to. For this is not the true Mediterranean. It is the abstract and conventional Mediterranean represented by Rome and the Romans. These imitative and unimaginative people had nevertheless the imagination to substitute for the artistic genius and feeling for life they lacked a genius for war. And this order whose praises we so often hear sung was one imposed by force and not one created by the mind. Even when they copied, the Romans lost the savour of the original..... It was not life that Rome took from Greece, but puerile, over-intellectualized abstractions. The Mediterranean lies elsewhere. It is the very denial of Rome and Latin genius. It is alive, and wants no truck with abstractions. And it is easy to acknowledge Mussolini as the worthy descendant of the Caesars and Augustus of Imperial Rome, if we mean by this that he, like them, sacrifices truth and greatness to a violence that has no soul.[1191]

While Haddour and others are thus certainly right to discern a political dimension to Camus' 1930s Algerian writings, the most directly political of these texts should put us on our guard against too quickly, retrospectively "writing Camus' position off" as the dream-bound rationalisations of a well-meaning coloniser. Camus does not indiscriminately idealise an ahistorical Mediterranean, blind to the way that this trope had been politically used and abused in the long history of Europe's colonisations of the African continent. From the start, he sharply distinguishes Greece from Rome. And in his Algerian context, Camus' attempt to disinter an image of Greece, opposed to the "soulless violence" of Roman imperium, from the start belongs with Camus' continuing resistance to fascism. To underline, we cannot therefore too simply oppose Camus' "Letters to a German Friend" or *The Plague* to Camus' *Algerian Chronicles*, as if in the latter he selectively forgets his hostility to the nationalist Right, although this is what Haddour claims and other post-colonialist critics, led by O'Brien, suggest.[1192]

1191 NMC 193.
1192 Haddour, *Colonial myths*, 82. "There were Arabs," O'Brien (at *Albert Camus*, 54–55) asserts, "for whom 'French Algeria' was a fiction quite as repugnant as the fiction of Hitler's new European order was for Camus and his friends. For such Arabs, the French were in Algeria by virtue of the same right of conquest." O'Brien concedes that "Camus would, of course, never have accepted this analogy as just", and his own qualified existential quantifier in the preceding is noteworthy. For counter-argument, see Carroll, *Albert Camus the Algerian*, 52–53, 57.

In this political context, Camus' 1936 *Diplôme* thesis on *Christian Metaphysics and Neoplatonism*, which we met in Chapter Two, also has great importance. There, we saw Camus' attempt to delineate the key features of evangelical Christianity: its eschatological sense of the imminent end of history, its hostility to the body, its imaginary of a post-humous fulfilment, and the deep sense of sin which the early Church shared both with Gnosticism and the later antique mystery cults. This characterisation of Christianity, so deeply important for all of Camus' work, emerges against the background of his attempt to comprehend the specific features of the "Greek" culture Christianity came to decisively supersede. It is undoubtedly important to repeat that, in *Christian Metaphysics and Neoplatonism* and throughout his *oeuvre*, Camus' "Greeks" are close to a Weberian "ideal type."[1193] Camus himself avows in the thesis' Introduction that it is in one sense "always arbitrary to speak of a 'Greek spirit' " *simpliciter*.[1194] Nevertheless, Camus proposes that it is possible to speak of "civilizations" and to discern within each certain "favoured themes," which become even more pronounced in the light of comparison with other civilizations. On this basis, Camus argues that "Hellenism" implies (contra the evangels and gnostics) "that man can be self-sufficient and that he has within himself the means to explain the universe and destiny":

> [Hellenism's] temples are constructed to its measure. In a certain sense, the Greeks accepted a sportive and aesthetic justification of existence. The line of their hills, or the run of a young man on a beach, provided them with the whole secret of the world. Their gospel said: our Kingdom is of this world. Think of Marcus Aurelius': "Everything is fitting for me, O cosmos, which fits thy purpose."[1195]

This Hellenic culture Camus positions as opposed to both Roman imperialism (with its "puerile, over-intellectualized abstractions") and early Christianity. In contrast to these competing forms of abstraction, Camus' Greek classical culture celebrated the concrete, and the body. It did so in ways the young writer, characteristically, associates with the Mediterranean youths of his time:

> For the first time in two thousand years the body has been shown naked on the beaches. For twenty centuries, men have strived to impose

---

1193 Cf. Bousquet, *Camus L'Ancien*, 108–109 on Camus' Greeks as comparable to a Weberian 'ideal type'.
1194 CMN 40.
1195 CMN 40.

decency on the insolence and simplicity of the Greeks, to diminish the flesh and elevate our dress. Today, reaching back over this history, young men sprinting on Mediterranean beaches are rediscovering the magnificent motions of the athletes of Delos...[1196]

For Camus' Greeks, importantly, evil hails from error or ignorance: a false conception of what is good or needful in any given situation, rather than an irrevocable flaw in our nature, or untameable compulsion to choose the worse.[1197] From Socrates forward, the remarkable "intellectualist" teaching that virtue is a kind of knowledge, necessary and (in Stoicism) sufficient for happiness, sets classical Greek thought apart from that of its successor Christian culture, as it pulls against the imperial drive for material conquest.[1198] The ideal in this culture, in its most elevated forms, was thus the sage, not the Saint. As the young author comments, the Greek philosophers, "[w]ithout always acknowledging it, ... made their sages God's equals [sic.]."[1199]

It is of course possible to pose counter-examples to any set of descriptions aiming to describe a civilisation spanning nearly 1500 years, and taking in everyone from Pyrrho to Iamblichus—not to mention poets as well as philosophers and statesman, Sparta as well as Athens, oligarchs and demagogues, and a host of other differentia. Yet Camus' delineation of basic features of Hellenism, aiming at once at doctrinal differences and what Camus calls "the affective plane", compares respectably with other such accounts.[1200]

1196 SA 82.
1197 With that said, Camus' "On the Future of Tragedy" LCE 295–31 turns on the distinction between preSocratic or pretragic Greek thought, which remained predominantly pious, and the culturally fertile moments when the world of the sacred was challenged by emergent secular human inquiry, notably in 5th century Athens. Differently, Camus in *L'Homme Révolté* notes that Epicurean thought, particularly in Lucretius' poem in "late antiquity", positions Epicurus almost in an almost "unGreek" messianic or salvific register (HR 48–52; R 30–31), as *Christian Metaphysics and Neoplatonism* likewise notes (CMN 42–43) the unparalleled "distress" of the later, syncretic Roman world in which "the desire for god is getting stronger." (CMN 42) Camus argues in both works that Gnosticism represents a late antique marriage of Greek (initiatory) and Christian (salvific) motifs (HR 52–53; R 31–32; CMN 68, 83–87), and that neoPlatonism's conception of philosophical reason as leading up to contemplative unity with the One, alongside the metaphysics of precession, prepares the way for Augustine's "second revelation" (CMN, 89–90, 102–3, and esp. 110–114).
1198 See Chapter Six on the riches in poverty, one of several Stoicising notion in Camus.
1199 CMN 41; C II 192; C II Eng 98.
1200 CMN 39.

TABLE 5.1 *Camus' understanding of the fundamental oppositions between pagan Greek and evangelical Christian cultures*

	Hellenism		Evangelical Christianity
i.	no creation *ex nihilo*, nor miracles	i.	creation *ex nihilo*, miracles
ii.	fundamental self-sufficiency of human condition	ii.	radical insufficiency (fall) of human condition: prevalence of suffering, natural and human evil (parallel Gnosticism).
iii.	this-worldliness (all is well, nature is beautiful)	iii.	Other-worldliness (this world is radically flawed)
iv.	the ideal of the sage (perfected human being (p. 41))	iv.	Christ as incarnated suffering God
v.	Virtue, knowledge and initiation (not grace) as means of perfection of nature (not salvation, redemption)	v.	Grace, love, faith as means of redemption from our nature, not its perfection (virtue & knowledge insufficient, manifestations of pride).
vi.	evil as error, ignorance, or *hybris*, not sin.	vi.	Evil as sin, rooted in human nature (and/or inherited from the first man).
vii.	history as cyclical, no last judgment or "end of history" (p. 41)	vii.	History as linear, including last judgment at end of history, eternal punishment of wrongdoers (p. 52)
viii.	(non-human) nature as inscribing limits to human capacity and right, beyond and indifferent to events of human history	viii.	Nature will be destroyed at end of history: setting for human drama of sin, incarnation, redemption
ix.	The heavens as *imitatio dei*, not human beings	ix.	Christ as incarnated god, man made in image of God.
x.	Either popular civic gods, enforcing justice and civic virtue, but having all-too-human characteristics (including vices), or "god of the philosophers", unconcerned with human affairs.	x.	One God, a creator God who loves his creatures, punishes wrongdoers, and suffers Himself in 2nd person of Trinity to redeem our sins.
xi.	"For a Greek, these conflicts [of faith and reason] are less acute, because Beauty which is both order and sensitivity, economy and the object of passion remains a ground of agreement [and reason]" (p. 91).	xi.	Reason as legislator (potential conflict with faith, "on certain points, irreconcilable" (p. 109)).
			Page references here from CMN

Furthermore, as the thesis stipulates from the beginning, for Camus as for Nietzsche (who we know is one of Camus' sources at this time), the Greece of Camus' ideal type was not one-sided: a kind of Schillerian or Goethean culture of light, life and form alone. It also had a darker side, carried in the myths of nocturnal and chthonic Gods and sublimated in the classical tragedies:

> Aeschylus along with Sophocles, the primitive masks and the Panathénées, the lecythes of the fifth century alongside the metopes of the Parthenon, and finally the mysteries as well as Socrates, all incline us to emphasize, next to the Greece of light, a Greece of darkness, ... just as real.[1201]

Again, Camus' appreciation of this two-sidedness of Greek thought, which is clearly reflective of Nietzsche's famous Apollonian-Dionysean opposition, is certainly rooted in his own, biographical experiences.[1202] But here, we need clearly to distinguish between Camus' more personal and existential experiences as the young, sun-loving man diagnosed with Tuberculosis, and his colonial political setting. For Camus, as we shall see, Algeria's startling and varied landscapes (on the one hand, its crystal blue waters and sharply defined coasts, on the other its deserts, rocky highlands and ever-present sunlight) spoke to him at once of "measure and excess [démesure]. Measure in its lines, excess in its light," and formed an ongoing basis for his core imagery.[1203] Camus' brush with death, as even the Sartre of 1952 could concede[1204] also left the young author with a profound sense of the imminence of mortality and as such,

---

1201 CMN 40; cf. HE 151. Cf. "*August [1939]*. Oedipus puts an end to the Sphinx, and casts out mystery by his knowledge of man. The whole universe of the Greeks is clear. But it is the same man who is savagely destroyed by destiny, by the implacable destiny of blind logic. The unshadowed light of tragic and mortal things." C I 161–162; C I Eng 75 CMN 40; cf. HE 151.

1202 As Camus would comment wryly in a later interview, aligning the two-sided "Greece" already present in *Christian Metaphysics and Neoplatonism*, in contrast both to Roman imperial culture and Christian theology, directly with his own sense of the Mediterranean: "The right explanation is always double, at least. Greece teaches us this, Greece to which we must always return. Greece is both shadow and light. We are well aware, aren't we, if we come from the South, that the sun has its black side?" Camus, "Three Interviews", LCE 357.

1203 C I 146; C I Eng 68; cf. Jacqueline Levi-Valensi, "Romans, Mesure et démesure", in David H. Walker réunis et présentés par *Albert Camus: Les Extremes et L'Equilibre* (Amsterdam: Editions Rodopi B.V., 1993); S. Brynon John, "Image and Symbol in the Work of Albert Camus", *Camus: A Collection of critical essays*, 132–144.

1204 Sartre, "Reply to Albert Camus," 153–4.

the transience of the sensual *noces* he so savoured.[1205] *Noces'* second essay "The Wind at Djemila", immediately following the joyous "Nuptials at Tipasa," explores this darker side to Camus' thought. It opens out to his sense of the two-sidedness of the classical world, "balancing shadow with light."[1206] Amidst the "violent bath" of sun, in the Algerian highlands near the decaying Roman ruins at Djemila, Camus reports feeling "defenceless against all the forces within me that were saying No"; gripped by the "physical terror of the animal that loves the sun."[1207] Yet it is implausibly reductive, if ingeniously speculative, to assign this to a lingering sense of guilt at his implication in the crimes of colonialism.[1208] As Richardson has stressed, the closing paragraph of "Wind at Djemila," picturing the return of the Roman ruins to nature, instead reinforces the critique of Romanism of "New Mediterranean Culture."[1209] It ties Camus' sense of the natural world, including our mortality, to the futility of a conception of culture which would assign greatness to imperial conquest:

> Towards evening, we were climbing the slopes leading to the village and retracing our steps, listening to explanations: 'Here is the pagan town; this area outside the field is where the Christians lived. Later on …' Yes, it is true. Men and societies have succeeded one another in this place, conquerors have marked this country with their non-commissioned officer's civilisation. They had a vulgar and ridiculous idea of greatness, measuring the grandeur of their empire by the surface it covered. The miracle is that the ruin of that civilisation is the very negation of that ideal. For this skeleton town, seen from high above as evening closes in and white flights of pigeons circle around the triumphal arch, engraved no signs of conquest or ambition on the sky. The world always conquers history in the end.[1210]

Throughout Camus' work, most famously in *L'Étranger*, readers are confronted with evocations either of the African desert or of the blinding darkness at the heart of the searing Mediterranean sun. These echo the sentiments Camus

---

1205   See Phillipe Forest, "Albert Camus et l'infanticide", in Lyotard ed. *Albert Camus, Contemporain*, 77–90.
1206   HE 149.
1207   WD 75, 77.
1208   Haddour, *Colonial Myths*, 31–33.
1209   Richardson, "Caesar and Sisyphus", 81.
1210   WD 79.

expresses in "Wind at Djemila."[1211] Such natural phenomena for Camus epitomise the inhuman dimension of the natural world, destructively manifest in such natural evils as the plague around which we have seen that both *La Peste* (1947) and *L'État de Siège* (1948) turns.[1212] As in Meursault's case, they also give figure to the "evil in men's hearts" Camus associated with excessive metaphysical or salvific ambitions: the kind of righteous ardour which animates the nameless "garrulous slave" in "The Renegade" to try to bring the One True Faith to the Sahara, only to find himself converted to a ghastly Fetishism.[1213] This is nature as it resists our best efforts at comprehension and control: "... not a world made to the measure of man—but which is closed to us";[1214] yet whose majesty, as we will stress below, resides *in this transcendence of humanity*. Camus stresses this, amongst other places, in the context of describing his response to the hillscapes of Tuscany:

> The human scale? ... When a mind faces landscapes whose grandeur clutches him by the throat, each movement of his mind is a scratch on his perfection. And soon, crossed out, scarred and re-scarred by so many overwhelming certainties, man ceases to be anything at all but a formless stain knowing only passive truths, the world's colour or its sun. Landscapes as pure as this dry up the soul and their beauty is unbearable...[1215]

The point for now is to have established the parameters of Camus' neoclassicism as it has emerged in his Algerian work in 1936 and 1937. This early work points clearly towards the key elements of Camus' mature philosophical neoclassicism in the 1940s and 1950s. Camus sets up a conception of the Greeks associated with this-worldly beauty, the pursuit of knowledge, the virtues (see Chapter Six) and a tragic, "darker" sense of human finitude and the impermanence of human endeavour. He poses this Greece against both Christian evangelism and theology, and (more decisively in his colonial political setting) against Roman imperialism, with its deified God-emperors: the latter of which,

---

1211 Cf. e.g. Albert Camus, "Three Interviews", in *Lyrical and Critical Essays*, 357; also "The Enigma", LCE 155: "I could tell them that it was the sun that helped me, and that the very thickness of its light coagulates the universe and its forms into a dazzling darkness."
1212 Consider the setting of Camus, "The Host" in EK, and Tarrow's "Exile from the Kingdom" in her book of that title, 172–193, which is invaluable on the elemental settings of the *récits* in this late collection.
1213 Camus, "The Renegade", EK, 33–61.
1214 Albert Camus, "Love of Life", 56; cf. Bousquet, *Camus le Méditerranéen, Camus L'Ancien*, 31.
1215 D 102, 101.

per Richardson, lastingly stands in Camus' thought for the kinds of mindless, *hybristic* excesses he dramatises in his most successful play, *Caligula*.[1216]

It is to Camus' mature philosophy, as it hearkens back to this fundamental neoHellenic sense that "one serves nothing in man if one does not serve the whole of man",[1217] that we turn now.

1.4 Contra *Philosophies of History*, Pace *Secular Messianisms*

"But there was darkness also in men's hearts," the neoStoic Doctor and diarist, Rieux, reflects at one point in the annals of the plague that decimated Camus' fictional Oran for the round of a year in 194–. And so it was that Camus' plans to follow his own Homeric dreams and visit *mētera Helláda* in late 1939 were cut short by the advent of European war. Soon enough, the conflict would instead make of him an Odyssean exile, far from his wife and Algerian homeland, marooned on the European continent:

> The year the war began I was to board a ship and follow the voyage of Ulysses. At that time, even a young man without money could entertain the extravagant notion of crossing the sea in search of sunlight. But I did what everyone else did. I did not get on that ship. I took my place in the queue shuffling towards the open mouth of hell. Little by little, we entered. At the first cry of murdered innocence, the door slammed shut behind us.[1218]

From 1942 onwards, as we examined in Chapter Four, Camus' philosophical work turns from the more individual focus of *The Myth of Sisyphus* (already opposed, as we have seen, to his Algerian political writings) towards a philosophical conception of "the recognition of a community whose struggles are shared."[1219] Camus' continuing recourse to classical Greek thought, alongside his horrified response to fascist and Stalinist regimes, has led some critics to see in his work, at the same time, a totalising repudiation of a singular "modernity",[1220]

1216 Richardson, "Caesar and Sisyphus", 68–70, 74–80.
1217 Albert Camus, "Prometheus in the Underworld", LCE 142.
1218 PU 139.
1219 Camus, "Letter to Roland Barthes on *The Plague*", LCE 339.
1220 Notably, Srigley, *Albert Camus' Critique of Modernity*; but also Samantha Novello, "La liberté de ne pas être moderne: le paradigm tragique de l'action politique dans l'oeuvre d'Albert Camus", in *Albert Camus et la Grèce*, 125–142. Both place great weight on Camus' comment, in light of a contrast between Greek thought as beginning in a sense of beauty while for "Europeans," beauty is at most a goal, "Je ne suis pas moderne," at C II 240; C II Eng 123–124. This quote needs to be balanced against the near contemporary avowals

in ways we have argued against in Chapters One through Four. As Novello has argued, Camus clearly ties his own experiences of solidarity and revolt in the resistance to fascism with his evolving sense of the meaning of classical Greek culture. In an important article on Camus' relations with the poet René Char, Novello stresses the representative nature of Camus' claims in his "Preface" to the German edition of Char's work. Here, Camus distinguishes two kinds of revolt: one, called "revolutionary" in *L'Homme Révolté*, that ends by enshrining a new appetite for totality and servitude; and the second, modelled on Camus' and Char's experiences with the French resistance, which "desperately defends a free order", and about which Novello comments: "The heritage which the resistants offer to posterity is the 'treasure' of liberty and of public happiness... it is a matter of an an-archic principle, which strikes the... relation of power/domination and replaces it with a horizontal relation...": that of the solidarity we highlighted in Chapter Four.[1221] It is this unique modern-ancient synthesis which shapes *L'Homme Révolté*'s closing advocacy of what he calls "Mediterranean" or "midday thought" against the legacy of modern German philosophy: not the kind of impossible nostalgia for past cultures Camus felt, but knew to be its own *tentation* or evasion.[1222]

Chapter Two detailed the genealogical claims of Camus' critique of modern totalitarianism. He contends that these regimes' ideological rationalisations, indebted in modern thought to the legacies of Rousseau, Nietzsche, Marx, and Hegel, involve effective "reoccupations" of pre-modern, theological modes of thought. In particular, as we saw in Camus' critique of Marx, Camus questions how each of these regimes stakes an ideological claim to having discerned the hidden Meaning of Human History: whether in the forms of a hitherto-unrecognised biological struggle between races, or the struggle between socio-economic classes. The Party in each regime presents itself as the agent or angel of History itself, charged with "immanentising the eschaton" by bringing

---

that "I will answer Yes to the challenges of my century", and rejection of Saint-Exupery's despairing "I hate my time", respectively in PU, 141 and HE 151–152, as we have said. Camus' sympathetic reading of the early modern revolts against theologically-sanctioned monarchies in *L'Homme Révolté* (Chapter Two); and Camus' avowal of the need to ground an ethics in the "fixed and radiant point of the present" (HR 381; R 305) are also to be weighed here, excluding nothing.

1221 Novello, "La liberté de ne pas être moderne: le paradigm tragique de l'action politique dans l'oeuvre d'Albert Camus", 132–133.

1222 Camus, "Artist and his Time", MSe 210: "I have not taken part in common struggles because I desire the world to be covered with Greek statues and masterpieces. The man who has such a desire does exist in me..."

about the salvific end of historical struggle or the millennial Reich.[1223] And it is this prophetically-framed, "world-Historical" vocation that, paradoxically, allows its progenitors in good conscience to practice the most "realist" forms of politics: forcing into compliance or physically killing all those people or parties who "make the mistake of getting in the way of the magnificent road to progress," to adopt Camus' phrase concerning Kadir's suppression of revolt in Hungary, 1956.[1224]

It is at this point that Camus' critical analysis of "Historical rebellion" in *The Rebel* looks back directly to his 1936 *Diplôme* thesis. One feature differentiating evangelical Christian from Greek thought, Camus stipulates in *Christian Metaphysics and Neoplatonism*, concerns competing notions of history. The Greeks imagined human history on the cycle of the natural seasons, as circular. "Aristotle, to give a definite example, did not believe that the time in which he was living was subsequent to the Trojan War," Camus comments in *The Rebel*.[1225] Historical writing emerged at the same time and place as natural philosophical inquiry in Greek Ionia in the 6th century. But the classical historians position great events (like Thucydides' Peloponnesian war) as almost like mythical episodes. They embody movements and patterns likely to be repeated by later peoples, and hence worth recording as vehicles of guidance and edification.[1226] By contrast, the young Camus already argued in *Christian Metaphysics and Neoplatonism* that the evangelicals' notion of history as moving in one direction from creation through fall, incarnation, towards redemption, is foreign to Hellenistic culture. "The philosophy of history, a notion foreign to the Greek spirit, is a Judaic invention."[1227] Camus takes up this thought exactly at the

---

1223   I use this term here from Eric Voegelin, *New Science of Politics* (Chicago: Chicago University Press, 1957, 1981). Compare here as elsewhere with Camus the 1949 study: Karl Löwith, *Meaning in History: The Theological Implications of the Philosophy of History* (Chicago: University of Chicago Ptess, 1957).

1224   Camus, "Kadar has his day of fear", RRD 159.

1225   HR 241; R 190.

1226   See for instance Thucydides' rationale at the end of Chapter One of his great work: "The absence of romance in my history will, I fear, detract somewhat from its interest; but if it be judged useful by those inquirers who desire an exact knowledge of the past *as an aid to the interpretation of the future, which in the course of human things must resemble if it does not reflect it,* I shall be content. In fine, I have written my work, not as an essay which is to win the applause of the moment, but as a possession for all time." Thucydides, *History of the Peloponnesian War* Book 1, Chapter 1. Translated by Richard Crawley at www-site http://www.gutenberg.org/files/7142/7142-h/7142-h.htm, last accessed January 2015 (italics ours).

1227   CMN 52.

beginning of his section of *L'Homme Révolté* on Marxism, recurring back to the end of antiquity, and to his youthful analyses:

> Christianity was obliged, in order to penetrate the Mediterranean world, to Hellenize itself, and its doctrine then became more flexible. But its originality lay in introducing into the ancient world two ideas that had never before been associated: the idea of history and the idea of punishment. In its concept of mediation, Christianity is Greek. In its idea of history, Christianity is Judaic, and this idea will be found again in German ideology...[1228]

Here, then, is the decisive link between Camus' earliest analysis of the supersession of the pagan by Christian culture and the modern world, including his critique of modern totalitarian thinking. These are two periods whose monumental cultural shifts Camus compares in his "*Intervention à la Table Ronde de 'Civilisation'*" in 1946.[1229] Camus sees Marxism as indeed the modern legatee of the eschatological Christian philosophy of history. "In contrast to the ancient world, the unity of the Christian and Marxist world is astonishing," Camus stakes a claim which he will develop in *La Chute*:

> The two doctrines have in common a vision of the world which completely separates them from the Greek attitude. Jaspers defines this very well: 'It is a Christian way of thinking to consider that the history of man is strictly unique.' The Christians were the first to consider human life and the course of events as a history that is unfolding from a fixed beginning toward a definite end, in the course of which man achieves his salvation or earns his punishment. The philosophy of history springs from a Christian representation, which is surprising to a Greek mind (*esprit*)...[1230]

Camus immediately specifies that he in no way means to suggest, by highlighting this comparison or common legacy, that Marxism is or was a theology: another position that has of course reemerged in recent times. It is a question of "reinstating" (*reştituant*) theological aspirations and predicates, now attached to the human "species being":

1228 HR 241; R 190.
1229 Camus, "Interventions à la table ronde de 'Civilisation' " OC II, 680.
1230 HR 241; R 190. Cf. HE 151 (on the contrast of Christian and Greek thought, this time with a view to nature); CMN 107–110, on the neoPlatonicians' opposition to Gnosticism and eschatology.

> Marxist atheism is absolute. But nevertheless it does reinstate (*reştitue*) the supreme being on the level of humanity. 'Criticism of religion leads to this doctrine that man is for man the supreme being.' [Marx] From this angle, socialism is an enterprise for the deification of man and has assumed some of the characteristics of traditional religions.[1231]

What is at stake in Marx, as Camus continues, is the secular "reoccupation" of another lineage of ideas foreign to classical Greek culture (about which, he notes, Marx was extremely ambivalent).[1232] This is the specifically messianic heritage derived from the West's Judaic and Christian past: a heritage which, in the works of figures as different as Derrida, Levinas or Lyotard, Walter Benjamin, Giorgio Agamben, Slavoj Žižek or Alain Badiou, has been revalorised in the search for alternatives to the present dispensation:

> This reconciliation [of Marxism and theology], in any case, is instructive as concerns the Christian origins of all types of historic Messianism, even revolutionary Messianism. The only difference lies in a change of register (*changement d'indice*)...[1233]

It is fair to say that Camus' greatest distance from most more recent Theory lies in his deep scepticism concerning this Judaic and Christian, messianic or eschatological legacy. This diagnosis is most directly stated in a note in the *Carnets* from Camus' 1945 visit to North America, where Camus ties messianism not to Marxism, but (intriguingly) to existentialism: "The idea of messianism is at the origin of all fanaticisms. Messianism [is] hostile (*contre*) to man. Greek reflection is not historical. Values are pre-existent. Contra modern existentialism."[1234] This assessment reflects Camus' statement of aims in "Neither Victims nor Executioners" of 1947, amongst the first of Camus' texts to provoke strong criticism from the French Marxists.[1235] In it, Camus attempted the untimely task "to define the conditions for a political position that is modest—i.e. free of messianism and disencumbered of nostalgia for an earthly paradise."[1236]

Chapter Three saw us situating Camus' critique of Western rationalism, and the kinds of fideism he associated with existentialism after *Le Mythe de Sisyphe*,

---

1231 HR 244; R 192.
1232 HR 245; R 193.
1233 HR 244–245; R 192–193.
1234 At OC II 1061.
1235 Camus, "Deux réponses à Emmanuel d'Astier de La Vigerie" OC II, 457–474.
1236 NVE 261 (end of second instalment, "November 20, 1946: Saving our Skins").

with and against Jacques Derrida's post-Heideggerian deconstruction of metaphysics. There, we argued, Camus' defence of an elementary, unrelativisable desire for unity pushes his thought in a different direction than Derrida's. At this point, we can specify a second, in many ways more decisive register of Camus' difference both from Derrida, and from other post-structuralist (or, as is sometimes today said of a figure like Badiou, post-post-structuralist) thinkers. Derrida's deconstruction of metaphysical philosophy, following Heidegger, targets what he calls the "metaphysics of presence."[1237] At times, in a way which reflects his master's ambiguous term "ontotheology" (which Heidegger applies equally to the Gods of the philosophers and the Christian *theos*),[1238] Derrida locates Judaic and Christian eschatology alongside the "Greek" conceptions of *logos, archē,* and *telos.* All these, he claims, exemplify the "metaphysical" longing for a stable point of identity, substance or presence (*parousia*), outside of the vicissitudes of historical becoming and difference.

Nevertheless, from the beginning, Derrida's deconstruction of Western conceptuality pointed his thought towards forms of thinking hitherto associated with apophaticism: the long theological tradition of challenging the limits of language in the name of other ineffable realities that Derrida was duly called upon to clarify his distance from.[1239] In particular, in ways that historian of ideas Ian Hunter (reprising one of Habermas' observations)[1240] has noted align Derrida with later French figures like Badiou, from Derrida's founding deconstruction of Husserl forward, he is attracted to uncovering what might

---

1237 For a good general account, see Christopher Norris, "Chapter Three: Metaphysics" in Jack Reynolds and John Roffe eds. *Understanding Derrida* (London: Continuum, 2004), 14–25. "Metaphysics of presence", alongside logocentrism or phonocentrism, is a continuous critical term in Derrida's work. See for instance Derrida's claim in the "Afterword" to *Limited Inc.*: "The enterprise of returning 'strategically', 'ideally', to an origin or to a priority thought to be simple, intact, normal, pure, standard, self-identical, in order then to think in terms of derivation, complication, deterioration, accident, etc. All metaphysicians, from Plato to Rousseau, Descartes to Husserl, have proceeded in this way, conceiving good to be before evil, the positive before the negative, the pure before the impure, the simple before the complex, the essential before the accidental, the imitated before the imitation, etc. And this is not just one metaphysical gesture among others, it is the metaphysical exigency, that which has been the most constant, most profound and most potent". Jacques Derrida, *Limited Inc.* ed. Graff, trans. Weber (Evanston: Northwestern University Press, 1998), 236.

1238 See Martin Heidegger, "The Onto-theo-logical Constitution of Metaphysics", in *Identity and Difference* trans. Joan Stambough (New York: Harper and Row, 1969), 42–74.

1239 Cf. Coward et al. ed. *Derrida and Negative Theology* (New York: SUNY 1992), especially Jacques Derrida, "How to Avoid Speaking", 73–142.

1240 Ian Hunter, "The History of Theory", *Critical Inquiry*, Vol. 33, No. 1 (Autumn 2006), 78–112.

be termed the "ultra-transcendental" conditions for the possibility of the linguistic and conceptual categories shaping subjects' experiences.[1241] Derrida calls these ultra-transcendental conditions "conditions of (im)possibility." In a way which reflects Heidegger's famous definition of truth as unconcealment or *alētheia*, they embody non- or (pre-)substantial, asignifying preconditions for the emergence of stable or "substantial" sense or signification. As Derrida writes of these ultra-transcendental (non-)objects or (non-)processes, paradigmatically, in his deconstruction of Husserl's *The Origins of Geometry*:

> This real non-appurtenance to any region at all, even to the archi-region, this anarchy of the noema is the root and very possibility of objectivity and of meaning.... In any event, the transcendentality of the opening is simultaneously the origin and the undoing, the condition of possibility and a certain impossibility of every structure and of every systematic structuralism...[1242]

Doubtlessly, this kind of deconstructive, transcendental theorising (which pushes thought back to recognising "an irruptive event," alterity or difference which would always-already underlie all linguistic sense)[1243] is a very different path to travel to arrive at secular reinstatements of messianism than that which Camus sees operating in Marx. Marx still posits a relatively continuous historical sequence, in which the transformations between different modes and relations of production, although violent and revolutionary, are both (a) the over-determined results of the unfolding of immanent historical contradictions within each historical social order, and (b) subordinate to the final proletarian revolution ending all history hitherto known. While Marx's vision of the *post-histoire* which awaits us after the final proletarian struggle is thus arguably under-determined, Marx's anthropology and political economics allow him to provide *some* concrete political promises and proposals. Post-structuralist theorising, like Camus', is deeply sceptical of the "bourgeois" sense of progress which Marx's philosophy of history inherits and transforms,[1244] but on its own grounds. Born out of phenomenology and structuralism (as we have seen with

---

1241 The term comes from Derrida, *Of Grammatology*, 62.
1242 Jacques Derrida, "'Genesis and Structure' and Phenomenology," *Writing and Difference*, trans. Alan Bass (Chicago, 1978), 163; cf. Hunter, "History of Theory", 81–87.
1243 Hunter, "History of Theory" 95, see 87.
1244 Cf. HR 240–250; R 189–197, on Marx's "bourgeois prophecy", comparable as a "metanarrative" to versions in Comte, de Maistre and Turgot: a point also famously central to Lyotard's *The Postmodern Condition*.

Derrida), this Theory tends to equate political orders with the transcendental structures which make linguistic sense, or what Kant had called "empirical experience," possible. As such, post-structuralist theories characteristically prompt us to read history very differently than Marx.[1245] After the discrediting of modern ideals of progress by the two world wars and the emergence of colonial struggles, history comes to be seen as the a-progressive succession of more or less incommensurable orders or structures (whether "epistemes" in the earlier Foucault, "states" in Badiou, or Derrida's or Althusser's "structures"...), punctuated by unheralded Events like to the 'non-appurtenance' evoked by Derrida's "Introduction" to *The Origins of Geometry* above. The model is what Hunter well describes as one of "... hermeneutic revelation involving the sudden eclipse of structures of thought under the impact of a novel phenomenon..."[1246] Since the operative sense of the historical order to be contested is a more or less closed structural totality making signification *per se* possible, while one can point out "symptomatic" points attesting to the finitude of the structure as a whole, there can be no sense in which the immanent logics of any given totality point beyond itself to a succeeding, continuous but different (let alone progressive) dispensation.

The result of this kind of theorising has thus been, since around 1975, a series of more and more openly messianic positions. These are, indeed, in several senses a good deal 'purer,' as forms of messianism, than that against which Camus in 1951 protested in Marx. If anything really new is to appear, to adopt Badiou's terms, it must be "indiscernible" in advance, for subjects living

---

[1245] There are always risks of over-generalising: whenever one generalises, this is unavoidable. The question is whether the particulars grouped together in any such conceptualisation remain saliently similar, set against a meaningful other. Here, that is, there are differences between the forms of messianism in Badiou and Zizek (who avow Christian precedents) and Agamben (who, via Benjamin, pushes Paul in a different direction) or Benjamin, within the Jewish heritage. But these species-differences within the genus of political messianism are of a different order to the genus-differences between forms of messianic thinking and those, like Camus', that argue against messianism for epistemic reasons (we cannot adjudge the truth of these predictive positions) and ethical grounds (they speak to unbalanced passions within us, and can license forms of illegitimate violence). Here as elsewhere, amongst this generation of French thinkers, Foucault is arguably the exception in his genealogical studies in the 1970s and early 1980s. These bring a kind of Nietzschean positivism, open to plurality and contingency, to the study of history which is absent in Derrida's, Althusser's, or Badiou's more simply transcendental renderings of history or 'the political' through the lens of formal structures or set-theretical 'states'.

[1246] Hunter, "History of Theory," 95.

or thinking within the given structure or "state of the situation."[1247] As Badiou adapts a Derridean trope, it will be "undecidable" in terms of its significance, pending a "decision" by an Evental subject who will "name" the indiscernible Event.[1248] The reason for this "undecidability" is that, for an Event to count as a potential pivot of structural change, it must completely break with the previously given regime of sense. It cannot develop out of the kinds of immanent contradictions within socioeconomic totalities Marx asked us to discern, and out of which he foresaw new modes of social regulation emerging. Instead, in Badiou's case, a decisionistic "fidelity" to this Event, uniting a new voluntaristic revolutionary Subject or vanguard, is needed.

And so we arrive, albeit via this very different, very refined intellectual path at the kind of configuration Gershom Scholem documents in Jewish messianism. This is one wherein the messiah is as "a transcendence breaking in upon history, an intrusion in which history itself perishes, transformed in its ruin because it is struck by a beam of light shining into it from an outside source..."[1249] We hasten to underline that such a claim concerning a messianic turn in Theory is anything but outlandish. Badiou and Žižek have vied since the turn of the millennium in reclaiming Saint Paul as a precursor or model for the kind of radically Evental, distinctly post-Christian revolutionary politics each aims to animate.[1250] Agamben, differently, has sought in Paul

---

1247 Badiou, *Metapolitics* 147 ("the state of the situation... supposedly controls all the sets and subsets of the situations"), 150; see Jason Barker, *Alain Badiou: A Critical Introduction* (London: Pluto, 2002), 11–12, 69.

1248 Here for example Alain Badiou, "Philosophy and Truth" in *Infinite Thought* trans. J. Clements et al. (London: Continuum, 2006), 46: "If it is possible to decide, using the rules of established knowledge, whether this statement is true or false, then the so-called event is not an event. Its occurrence would be calculable within the situation.... On the basis of the undecidability of an event's belonging to a situation a wager has to be made. This is why a truth begins with an axiom of truth. It begins with a groundless decision— the decision to say that the event has taken place"; cf. Quentin Meillassoux, "Decision and undecidability of the Event in *Being and Event* I and II", translated by Alyosha Edlebi, *Parrhesia* 19 (2014), 22–35. As Hunter's account stresses, the family resemblances, Badiou's more militant activist rhetoric aside, between this position and Derrida et al.'s post-structuralism, otherwise the objects of Badiou's polemical attacks, is clear. This was recognised by Terry Eagleton, *Figures of Dissent: Reviewing Fish, Spivak, Žižek and Others* (London: Verso 2003), 246–253; cf. Alex Callinacos, *Resources of Critique* (London: Wiley, 2006), 83–111.

1249 Scholem, *The Messianic Idea in Judaism, and Other Essays on Jewish Spirituality*, 10.

1250 Badiou, *Saint Paul The Foundation of Universalism*; Žižek, *Fragile Absolute* (London: Verso, 2002); Žižek, *The Puppet and the Dwarf: The Perverse Core of Christianity* (Massachussetts: MIT Press, 2003).

(alongside other messianic and gnostic figures)[1251] a harbinger of the kind of antinomic, post-historical dispensation in which the present, permanent 'state of siege' will allegedly be suspended or overcome.[1252] Derrida, after his decisive encounter with Levinas' work and his own 'ethical turn', began from the middle-1970s to evoke what he termed a "messianism without messianism," or a democracy or internationalism "to come", whose positive features nevertheless cannot be discerned...[1253]

According to Camus, such political messianisms' positings of a radically Other, redemptive dispensation are every bit as contestably "metaphysical" as the kinds of Rationalist claims to timeless, ahistorical essences Derrida and other post-structuralist theorists had begun by deconstructing. This kind of position places demands on our cognitive budgets that cannot be paid by experiential or critical rationality, as opposed to forms of fideism, "fidelity" or expectant openness to the gracious arrival of an unspeakable Otherness.[1254] Camus' epistemic ethics, the basis for his wider normative position (Chapter Three), however opposes all such willed suspensions of the principle of "living solely with what [we] know."[1255] This principle, as we saw (Chapter Four), underlies his notion of a post-metaphysical limit prohibiting murder and circumscribing the community of presently living human beings. In contrast to all messianisms, Camus' position involves what we might term a 'non-metaphysics of presence', or non-metaphysics of the present 'we are" opposed to

---

1251 Giorgio Agamben's *The Open* closes, remarkably, by recovering the gnostic Basilides (at Giorgio Agamben, *The Open* (Stanford: Stanford University Press, 2004), 90–92). For Camus' more critical approach to Basilides, see CMN 68, 70–72, 75, 80, 84.
1252 Giorgio Agamben, *The Time That Remains. A Commentary on the Letter to the Romans.* Translated by Patricia Dailey (Stanford: Stanford University Press, 2005).
1253 Jacques Derrida, *Spectres of Marx*, translated by Peggy Kamuf (New York: Routledge 1994), 165–170; "it is clear to anyone with a Jewish ear, for anyone with half an ear to the Jewish and Christian scriptures, that this whole thing called 'deconstruction' turns out to have a messianic ring..." Jacques Derrida, *Deconstruction in a Nutshell: A Conversation with Jacques Derrida*, edited with a commentary by John D. Caputo (New York: Fordham, 1997), 156. See on the messianic dimension in Derrida, Martin Srajek, "Connections between Cohen, Benjamin, and Derrida", in *Journal of Textual Reasoning* 2:2 (2015) at www-site http://jtr.lib.virginia.edu/textual-reasoning-vol-2-2-february-1993, last accessed February 2015; and John D. Caputo, *The Prayers and Tears of Jacques Derrida* (Indiana: Indiana University Press, 1997), esp. "Part III: The Messianic", pp. 118–159.
1254 Compare Habermas, *Philosophical Discourse of Modernity*, 181.
1255 MS 77–78; MSe 53.

all messianic promises that 'we shall be'.[1256] As the concluding passages of *The Rebel* declaim:

> The men of Europe, abandoned to the shadows, have turned their backs upon the fixed and radiant point of the present. They forget the present for the future, the fate of humanity for the delusion of power, the misery of the slums for the mirage of the eternal city, ordinary justice for an empty promised land.... They no longer believe in the things that exist in the world and in living man; the secret of Europe is that it no longer loves life.[1257]

2 *Mesure* and Nature

2.1 Camusian Mesure, *a Thought that Excludes Nothing*

For Camus, the most basic philosophical problem with totalitarian ideologies, vindicating their proponents' assumption of the rights to kill and enslave others (including people innocent of any crimes) is epistemic: they base their authority on false, pseudo-scientific or pseudo-logical claims to higher knowledge. As we have seen by looking at *The Myth of Sisyphus* and the opening moves in *The Rebel*, Camus thinks that, accordingly, in order to guarantee Adorno et al.'s "never again" concerning these regimes, Western culture needs to relearn the virtue of withholding assent to what is not certainly given. We must recognise when what we claim to know is only conjectural, or less than that. Certainly, we should withhold making mortal or 'existential' decisions on the basis of speculative claims. All claims like those of prophetic Nietzscheanisms, Marxisms or fascisms to know, speak or act in the name of the providential Meaning of History for Camus involve forms of epistemic "leap," as well as simply fallacious forms of argumentation, as we have seen. "In reality, the purely historical absolute is not even conceivable," Camus underlines in *The Rebel*:

> Jaspers's thought, for example ... underlines the impossibility of man's grasping totality, since he lives in the midst of this totality. History, as an entirety, could exist only in the eyes of an observer outside it and outside the world.[1258]

1256 HR 173–192, 25–265, 284–291; R 133–148, 197–210, 226–232.
1257 HR 281; R 305.
1258 HR 361; R 289.

A critical reason recognising its own limits, by contrast, far from leading to an embrace of Irrationalism, licenses exactly the kind of lucid, reflective monitoring of one's judgments advocated in the ancient world by the academic and Pyrrhonian sceptics, and as an ethical practice by the Stoics.[1259] After 1943, as Camus begins to write against the fascist and Stalinist realities, he accordingly adds to the profile of his Greeks from *Christian Metaphysics and Neoplatonism* the kind of sage Socratic scepticism and reflective awareness of the limits of human understanding he has advocated for in *The Myth of Sisyphus*. Here as elsewhere, "Helen's Exile" is the indispensable text:

> A fragment attributed to ... Heraclitus states simply "Presumption, regression of progress." And centuries after the Ephesian, Socrates, threatened by the death penalty, granted himself no other superiority than this: he did not presume to know what he did not know. The most exemplary life and thought of these centuries ends in a proud avowal of ignorance. In forgetting this, we have forgotten our virility...[1260]

As we have remarked, it is these epistemic limits circumscribing what we know that for Camus underlie the ethico-political limit that should be inscribed heretofore in national and international prohibitions on the *peine de mort*.[1261] At this point of the argument, however, we encounter the full force of Camus' earlier-cited claim that rebellion, although it begins in struggle and scepticism, points towards the reality of pre-existing limits in human nature, and nature more widely. From the time of "Helen's Exile" (1948) onwards, Camus moves to align this sceptical epistemic humility with a different, seemingly more metaphysically contentious sense that the ethical and metaphysical limits circumscribing the human condition mirror the limits and larger order evident in the recurrences of the natural world:

> The Greeks, who for centuries questioned themselves as to what is just, could understand nothing of our idea of justice. For them equity implied a limit, whereas our whole continent is convulsed in its search for a justice that must be total. At the dawn of Greek thought Heraclitus was already imagining that justice sets limits for the physical universe itself:

1259 This is what the Stoics thought of as a 'discipline or assent', on which see especially Pierre Hadot, *Inner Citadel: The Meditations of Marcus Aurelius* trans. M. Chase (USA: Harvard University Press, 1998), 87–88, 101–127, 235–236.
1260 HE, 149–150.
1261 TM 361 and Chapter Four, "Political Suicide?" above.

"The sun will not overstep his measures; if he does, the Erinyes, the handmaids of justice, will find him out." We who have cast the universe and spirit out of our sphere laugh at that threat. In a drunken sky we light up the suns we want. But nonetheless the boundaries exist, and we know it... the Greeks never said that the limit could not he overstepped. They said it existed and that whoever dared to exceed it was mercilessly struck down. Nothing in present history can contradict them.[1262]

We will return in our concluding section to the questions raised by this move, and how Camus' epistemic scepticism can be tied with this more Stoic or neo-Platonic sense of cosmic order. Certainly, this sense responds to an aesthetic sensibility set deep in Camus' nature, reflected in his lifelong propensity for writing concerning natural landscapes, and his love of his North African birthland. This sensibility is present in his *Carnets* from 1935, wherein he soon has to chide himself to "Seek contacts. All contacts. If I want to write about men, should[n't] I stop talking about the countryside [*paysage*]?"[1263] To give just one illustrative instance, it is in contemplating the Florentine landscape that Camus, in the closing essay "The Desert" in *Noces*, tells us he glimpsed the *sagesse* he had been searching for through the arc of the four essays:

> At first the hilltops had been hidden in clouds. But a breeze had risen whose breath I could feel on my cheek. As it blew, the clouds behind the curtains drew apart like two sides of a curtain. At the same time, the cypress trees on the summit seemed to shoot up in a single jet against the sudden blue of the sky. With them, the whole hillside and landscape of stones and olive trees rose slowly back into sight. Other clouds appeared. The curtain closed... As that evening fell over Florence, I was moving towards a wisdom where everything had already been overcome...[1264]

If we consider synoptically what are called Camus' "lyrical essays", we see that nearly each of them takes as a meditative prompt a feature of the natural world, or a geographical locale: the seaside ruins at Tipasa, the highland ruins at Djemila, Algiers in high summer, Tuscan hills, the desert in Oran, almond trees and the return of spring, sunset on the Mediterranean coasts,

---

1262 HE, 149, 152.
1263 C I 28; C I Eng 8. Cf. Blanchard, "Camus' *Pudeur*", MLN 112: 4 (1997), 680–681; Alan Woolfolk, "The Artist as Cultural Guide: Camus' Post-Christian Asceticism", *Sociological Analysis* 47:2 (Summer 1986): 93–110.
1264 D 103.

the sea close by...[1265] Again, however, we can most clearly see the philosophical precedents for Camus' mature position, and the way it is closely tied to his reception of classical Greek thought, in Camus' *Christian Metaphysics and Neoplatonism*. Here, Camus' treatment of the neo-Platonic mystic Plotinus is vital. Images of Camus as a die-hard atheist and wholly immanent thinker close our eyes to how, despite his metaphysical scepticism, Camus' aesthetic sensibility was unmistakably moved by Plotinus' sense of the beautiful harmony of the Platonic Ideas, and the philosopher's inescapably poetic language as he tried to give voice to this transcendent order. Plotinus' contemplative *philosophia* is one in which the young Camus senses a kindred direction, albeit played out in his own case through responsiveness to what he terms "the beauty of the world" or of "nature," rather than the ordered Ideas of an other-worldly Intelligence:

> To a certain extent, Plotinian reason is already the 'heart' of Pascal. But this does not mean we can equate it with Christian thought, because this concept of reason, being based on contemplation, is inscribed in the aesthetic: as well as a form of religious thought, Plotinus' is an aesthetic point of view. If things are explained, it is because things are beautiful. But Plotinus carries over into the intelligible world this extreme emotion that seizes the artist confronted with the beauty of the world. He admires the cosmos to the detriment of nature... This is why Plotinus describes reason in a sensual way. His reason is alive, fleshed out, stirring like a mixture of water and light...[1266]

The third dimension to Camus' philosophical neoclassicism, alongside epistemic scepticism and advocacy of ethical limits rooted in a contemplative sense of natural beauty, is what Camus calls *'mesure'*, a term most often translated as "moderation". As we have commented *en passant*, Camus was more than aware of how this term would be, and duly was, taken in Parisian circles. Speaking in Greece in 1955, Camus humorously commented that:

> If today, in a Parisian gathering, you were to evoke the notion of *mesure*, a thousand pairs of romantic arms would hit the roof. For them, *mesure* is nothing other than the diabolical moderation of the bourgeoisie...[1267]

1265 Respectively, NT, WD, SA, D, MSO, AT, HE; "The Sea Close by..." LCE 172–181.
1266 CMN 90.
1267 Camus, "L'Avenir de la civilization européenne" OC III 999.

However, as Camus immediately goes on to protest, this sense of a moderate "playing for safety"[1268] and avoiding all risk is not what he intends: "it being well understood that the equilibrium in question is not a comfort. Today one says of a man that he is "a well-balanced man" with a nuance of disdain. In fact, equilibrium requires effort and courage at every moment."[1269] Camus, however, could already in 1950 use a nearly-literal recourse to Plato's *Republic* to highlight how his thought looked out or back to different sources, outside of this Parisian cave:

> Paris is a marvellous cave and its inhabitants, seeing their own shadows reflected on the far wall, take them for the only reality that there is ... But we have learned, far from Paris, that there is a light behind us, that we must turn around and cast off our chains in order to face it directly, and that our task before we die is to seek, through any words, to identify it.[1270]

As Thomas Warren has argued, indeed, Camus' thought here again is deeply indebted to classical ethical philosophy and tragic poetry, whence the thought it aims at is the Greek *sophrosyne*. This term, so deeply inscribed in the philosophical heritage (and in contrast to the French *modération*, which Camus could have used but avoids) looks back to the proverbial Delphic *mēdan agan* (nothing too much). It carries the senses of a 'measuredness,' 'harmony,' 'limitedness,' 'proportion,' or 'rule' "implying a moral [and epistemological] interest in the very criteria, standards, forms, or proportions of nature or reality themselves," rather than a subjective or psychological phenomenon.[1271] Helen North, in terms directly evocative of Camus' "Helen's Exile", explains that "at the deepest level, *sophrosyne* is related to the Greek tendency to interpret all kinds of experience—whether moral, political, aesthetic, physical or metaphysical—in terms of harmony and proportion."[1272] Perhaps *sophrosyne*'s best known classical avatar comes in Aristotle's *Nicomachean Ethics*. Here *sophrosyne* names the specific virtue of reason moderating the body's (notably tactile) pleasures, although since such pleasures are a constant component of our psychic lives,

---

1268 Ross at p. 128 of Thomas Warren, "On the Mistranslation of *La Mesure* in Camus' Political Thought," *Journal of the History of Philosophy*, vol. 30, no. 1 (January 1992): 123–130.
1269 Camus, "L'Avenir de la civilization européenne" OC III, 1001.
1270 E 161; cf. Warren, "On the Mistranslation of *La Mesure* in Camus' Political Thought", 127.
1271 Warren, "On the Mistranslation of *La Mesure* in Camus' Political Thought", 128; cf. 124, 126.
1272 Helen North, *Sophrosyne* (Ithaca: Cornell University Press, 1966), 258; cf. Warren, "On the Mistranslation of *La Mesure* in Camus' Political Thought", 128.

in this way *sophrosyne* stands at the emblematic head of Aristotle's catalogue.[1273] It is to exactly this virtue, certainly, that Camus appeals in arguably the key passage of "Helen's Exile", opposing classical *mesure* to the modern messianisms sprung from Hegel and Nietzsche:[1274]

> Whereas the Greeks used reason to restrain the will, we have come to put the will's impulse at the very heart of reason, and reason has therefore become deadly. For the Greeks, values pre-existed all action, of which they definitely set the limits. Modern philosophy places its values at the end of action. They are not but are becoming, and we shall know them fully only at the completion of history. With values, all limit disappears, and since conceptions differ as to what they will be, since all struggles, without the brake of those same values, spread indefinitely, today's messianisms confront one another and their clamours mingle in the clash of empires. Excess (*démesure*) is a fire, according to Heraclitus. The fire is gaining ground. Nietzsche has been overtaken. It is no longer with hammer blows but with ammunitions that Europe philosophises.[1275]

Nevertheless, what is arguably most remarkable about Camus' rearticulation of this Greek virtue is the way that he frames it less around the psychological contest of reason and passion, than in light of competing, plural, or even contradictory claims to truth and right which solicit our attention or allegiance.[1276] "If my understanding on this point is adequate," Camus elaborated to his 1955 Athenian audience:

> ...*mesure* is not the refusal of contradictions, nor their solution. *Mesure*, in Hellenism...has always involved the recognition of the contradiction, and the decision to maintain it, whatever may come...It in any case...offers us not a solution, which is not what we await, but a method for confronting the problems which are posed to us and for moving towards a sustainable future.[1277]

1273 Aristotle, *Nicomachean Ethics* II.3 or III.10–1 with II.8–9.
1274 HE 151.
1275 HE 151.
1276 Indeed, as Zaretsky notes in *A Life Worth Living* 111, Camus does not cite Aristotle on the mean: but whether this follows from, or in any way vindicates, the assessment that Camus was not a philosopher we dispute.
1277 Camus, "L'Avenir de la civilization européenne" OC III 999.

This side of the epistemic and natural "limit", Camus depicts Greek thought as calling upon us to refuse to totalise as "the one thing needful" any one component of human experience: reason or passion, vulnerability or power, nature or history, innocence or culpability, the gods or human independence, justice or mercy, political life or contemplative creation. It is such mono-logical (and monologue-ic, as it were) 'totalisations' or 'all or nothing' positions which we have met often enough, in the forms of thinking behind theocracies and total modern states. Camus identifies them with "excess" or *démesure* and solitude, as opposed to solidarity, *mesure* or fraternity:

> Whatever we may do, excess will always keep its place in the heart of man, in the place where solitude is found. We all carry within us our places of exile, our crimes and our ravages. But our task is not to unleash them on the world; it is to fight them in ourselves and in others...[1278]

This, in fact, is Camus' rearticulation of the Greek *harmatology* he identified as a young man, in contrast to the idea that evil hails from sin. For Camus as for classical Greeks, evil hails from a form of blindness or error. It involves hypostasising a single demand as "the one thing needful"—the nation, the economy, the working class—when ethical and political issues are seldom so simple. As we saw in Chapter Four, one generous implication of this view is that there is no human pursuit, however callow (even, as we saw, the opening of gulags or camps, or terrorist violence) that does not express, however partially and perversely, the human desire for unity: "Terror is the homage the malignant recluse finally pays to the brotherhood of man..."[1279]

Camus instead asks us to embrace, alongside the "society of dialogue" we saw him defending in Chapter Four, a mode or thinking which would "exclude nothing."[1280] This logic is at the basis of the ideas he admires very much in Pascal, that "nothing is true that compels us to exclude"[1281] or indeed that "[w]e do not display greatness by going to one or other extreme, but in touching both at once."[1282] Camusian *mesure* involves the same, lucid openness to the two-sidedness of our condition that we saw the young Camus recognising in classical thought in his *Diplôme* thesis and earliest writings, mirrored in his

---

1278 HR 376; R 301.
1279 HR 308–309; R 248.
1280 The key statements of this idea, which Camus associates especially with Pascal, come in C II 54; PU 142; RT 165, 169.
1281 RT, 165.
1282 Pascal *Pensées*, #353.

own experiences. "Greek thought... never carried anything to extremes, neither the sacred nor reason, because it negated nothing, neither the sacred nor reason. It took everything into consideration, balancing shadow with light," "Helen's Exile" affirms.[1283] An important passage in *L'Homme Révolté* elaborates this neoclassical "law of *mesure*" as Camus sees it operating above all at the level of the forms of theoretical reason which have been summoned to vindicate the great historical excesses of the first half of the 20th century:

> This law of *mesure* equally well extends to all the contradictions of rebellious thought. The real is not entirely rational, nor is the rational entirely real. As we have seen in regard to surrealism, the desire for unity not only demands that everything should be rational. It also wishes that the irrational should not be sacrificed. One cannot say that nothing has any meaning, because in doing so one affirms a value sanctified by this opinion; nor that everything has a meaning, because the word 'everything' has no meaning for us. The irrational imposes limits on the rational, which, in its turn, gives it its *mesure*... In the same way, ... where could one perceive essence except on the level of existence and evolution?... Something that is always in the process of development could not exist—... [yet] being can only prove itself in development... The historical dialectic, for example, is not in continuous pursuit of an unknown value. It revolves around the limit, which is its prime value...[1284]

2.2   *Prometheus Reclaimed: From the Philosophers to the Poets*

We see then that Camus' model of *sophrosyne* is not exactly Aristotle's. In fact, Camus' expressed debts to the Greek philosophers are eclectic and change over time. (Aristotle is never foregrounded.)[1285] If we ask: from where exactly

---

1283   HE 148–149.
1284   HR 369; R 296.
1285   Again, see Zaresky, *Life Worth Living*, 111–113, on Camus' reference to the poets over 'the philosopher' on *mesure*. While Camus never specifies his view on the Platonic question of the relation between Greek philosophical thought and its epic, mythological and tragic poetry, his stated primary classical philosophic loyalties equivocate: from a stress on Socrates around 1945 (cf. OC II, 746; cf. OC III 364), to Plato in 1955 (cf. Barbara Papastavrou, "Abert Camus: De L'Amour Platon...", 107, where she quotes Camus in Athens proclaiming "Plato as the most important of all"), to the preSocratics, notably Heraclitus in the closing paeans to "La pensée de midi" in HR 369–370 (R 296), "Helen's Exile"; and in his attestation at Stockholm (in *Le Figaro littéraire* du 21 décembre 1957). Camus' conception of *mesure* draws as much, or more, on his understanding of the tragic poets as on any single ancient philosophical source.

in the Greek heritage Camus draws this sense of *mesure*, the answer is that Camus overwhelmingly takes his orientation from his reading of the classical poets, and after 1948 (through his friendship with Char) Heraclitus and the preSocratic thinkers. We know that Camus was from a very young age fascinated with classical Greek poets, notably the tragedians, which he read in translation. In 1936, with the Algerian *theatre d'équipe*, Camus produced a version of Aeschylus' *Prometheus Unbound*.[1286] His *Carnets* record at what points in his life (notably during the war) that Camus was reading his way through the classical historians and dramatists.[1287] Camus' *Caligula*, arguably his most successful play, drew directly from Suetonius, whom he had studied under Jean Grenier.[1288] Like *Le Malentendu* and *Les Justes*, Camus clearly hoped his dramas would answer that call he made in 1955 in Athens, in a vitally important text, for a regenerated classical theatre.[1289] As his literary writing attests, Camus was always attracted to "an ideal of simplicity"[1290]—indeed, an "Apollonian perfection of form"[1291]—which he admired in the ancients: a style in which nothing is overstated or belaboured, but "everything is reduced to its essentials".[1292] In a late interview, Camus avowed again the literary classicism given its clearest expression in 1942's "Intelligence and the Scaffold": if by that label we mean "a romanticism brought under control."[1293] In addition, we commented in Chapter Three that Camus, from around 1938, increasingly began to integrate the Greek myths with which the epic and tragic poets worked into his writing: "[t]he world in which I feel most at ease … [is] Greek myth."[1294]

1286 Lottman, *Albert Camus*, Ch. 13 ("Theatre d'Équipe"); Todd, *Albert Camus* 51–53; Zaretsky, *A Life Worth Living*, 65–67.
1287 Cf. Bousquet, *Camus le méditerranéen, Camus l'ancien*, "Note Annex" at 112–113, which lists all entries on classical thought and literature in the *Carnets*.
1288 On Caligula's classical setting, and Camus' opposition of Rome (excess, tyranny, martial valour) with the Greeks, see Luke Richardson, "Sisyphus and Caesar: the opposition of Greece and Rome in Albert Camus' absurd cycle", *Classical Receptions Journal* Vol. 4. Iss. 1 (2012), 66–89.
1289 Camus, "Lecture in Athens on the Future of Tragedy", LCE 295–310. On this text, see especially Mustapha Teubelsi, "Albert Camus, lecteur au tragédie grecque", in *Camus et la Grèce*, 95–105. As we saw in Chapter One, in the case of *La Peste*, as Archambault has stressed, Camus took as his classical model for Rieux's dispassionate chronicle Thucydides' *History of the Peloponnesian War*: in particular, the latter's account of the ravages of the Athenian plague. Cf. Archambault, *Camus' Hellenic Sources*, 54–62.
1290 Camus, "Intelligence and the Scaffold", LCE 211.
1291 Camus, "Intelligence and the Scaffold", LCE 213.
1292 Camus, "Intelligence and the Scaffold", LCE 211.
1293 Camus, "Three Interviews", LCE 353.
1294 C II 224; C II Eng, 317.

Camus' mature view of tragedy, in some ways, allows us to see very precisely the distinctness of Camus' claims concerning classical *mesure*. What is striking about the "Lecture in Athens on the Future of Tragedy," as opposed to other important accounts of this "rarest of flowers,"[1295] is Camus' emphasis on tragedy as *not* a wholly religious form of art, even in the form of balancing the competing demands of the two Gods, Dionysus and Apollo.[1296] Nor indeed, as in Hegel's account, is classical tragedy understood by Camus as a genre which (as in Hegel's reading of the *Antigone*) stages the conflict between two established cultural forms: divine and civic laws.[1297] For Camus, the dates are wrong for either of these accounts. Tragedy, as Cornelius Castoriadis has also noted, arises in democratic Athens, reaching its peak after the Kleisthenic reforms and dying as rapidly with the eclipse of the city's Periclean golden age.[1298] For Camus, more specifically, it arises at the point wherein, in Attic culture, the world of old gods had been challenged by the emergence of rational, historical and philosophical cultures. As in the re-emergence of forms of tragedy in Britain, Spain and France in the early modern period (the only other period in history in which new tragedies were produced),[1299] Camus contends, "each time the tragic age always seems to coincide with an evolution in which man, consciously or not, frees himself from an older civilisation and finds that he has broken away from it without having found a new form which satisfies him."[1300] Tragedy, that is, is a literature of revolt. It occurs each time "when man, through pride (or even through stupidity, as in the case of Ajax), enters into conflict with the divine order, personified by god or incarnated in society."[1301] When a wholly secular culture prevails, the conditions for tragedy are compromised every bit as much as in a still-wholly sacral society. In the former case, "man ceases to be a tragic figure, and becomes an adventurer"; as in the latter case,

---

1295 LFT 295–298.
1296 Friedrich Nietzsche, *Birth of Tragedy* edited by Raymond Geuss and Ronald Speirs (Cambridge: Cambridge University Press, 2007).
1297 Hegel, *Phenomenology of Spirit*, "VI. Spirit A.b. Ethical Action. Knowledge, Human and Divine. Guilt and Destiny".
1298 Cornelius Castoriadis, "The Greek Polis and the Creation of Democracy", in Cornelius Castoriadis, *The Castoriadis Reader* (Oxford: Basil Blackwell Publishers, 1997). On the comparison of Camus' with Castoriadis' views on democracy and tragedy, see my "Autonomy, Reflexivity, Tragedy: Notions of Democracy in Camus and Castoriadis" *Critical Horizons* 3: 1 (2002).
1299 LFT 296–297.
1300 LFT 194.
1301 LFT 302.

only forms of morality play or mysteries are possible.[1302] Not simply a creature of "light and shade," tragedy specifically requires a culture capable of recognising the metaphysical *denouement* Camus' philosophy has been describing since *Le Mythe de Sisyphe*. Both human self-assertion and revolt, which has its own legitimacy, and a larger order, limiting the legitimate scope of the rebellion, are required. Oedipus' tragedy would be impossible without the oracle preceding his birth; but equally, "this destiny would not have all its fatality if Oedipus did not resist it."[1303] Tragedy, that is, is metaphysically complex. It is a genre which dramatizes the two basic, conflicting demands Camus sees human beings as such as subject to: "the more justified the revolt, and the more necessary the [divinely or civilly sanctioned] order, the greater the tragedy."[1304] As a result of this framing two-sidedness:

> …in tragedy, each force is at one and the same time both good and bad… it wears the double mask of good and evil… Antigone is right, but Creon is not wrong. Similarly, Prometheus is both just and unjust, and Zeus, who pitilessly oppresses him, has right on his side… the perfect tragic formula would be 'All can be justified, no one is just.'[1305]

In the light of the Athenian tragedy lecture, Camus' decisive paragraphs early in *L'Homme Révolté* (left untranslated in the first English editions) on the Greeks and their place in the history of Western metaphysical and political rebellion take on their decisive sense. As we commented in Chapter Two, Camus' *L'Homme Révolté*, like *The Myth of Sisyphus*, is structured around Camus' reflections on a classical myth: that of Prometheus. Prometheus was the first rebel against Zeus and the Olympian Gods, on behalf of the human species. The titanic rebel could thus (seemingly) be compared to Satan, dear to Milton, the romantics, and the surrealists.[1306] Yet comparison of the two divine rebels highlights the great shift between Christian and classical thought which Camus frames in *The Rebel* in the terms which will later shape the Athenian lecture. "Beyond a doubt," Camus reflects on what he had made the theme of a 1943 essay "Prometheus in the Underworld (*enfers*)":[1307]

1302 LFT 306.
1303 LFT 304.
1304 LFT 302.
1305 LFT 301.
1306 Cf. HR 70–78, 110–117; and Chapter Three above.
1307 PU 138–142.

... certain characteristics of the Promethean myth still survive in the history of rebellion as we are living it: the fight against death ("I have delivered men from being obsessed by death"), messianism ("I have instilled blind hopes into men's minds"), philanthropy ("Enemy of Zeus... for having loved mankind too much").[1308]

Yet, Camus stresses, it is decisive that in the Greek orbit, Prometheus rebelled against only one God, albeit the tyrannical leader of the Olympians. He does not, like Satan, set himself *versus* Creation *per se*: "It is a question of settling a particular account, of a dispute about what is good, and not of a universal struggle between good and evil."[1309] For Camus' Greeks, to repudiate all of Nature and Destiny itself—as, in the case of modern revolutionary thought, to deny any meaning except what we create through the political or historical process—is to deny ourselves. Such absolutism is, for him, an exercise in "barbaric" futility emblematised by the Great King Darius' striking with rods at the sea at Salamis:[1310] "but the limits exist and we know it."[1311] Any "metaphysical rebellion" which as such claims to deny all meaning to reality or human life, outside of the blind play of force, class war or race struggle, "presupposes a simplified view of creation—which was inconceivable to the Greeks," Camus argues.[1312] Greek polytheism mythically expresses, for Camus, a sagely balanced sense of the place of human reality in the larger, plural order of the world. We are neither at its providential centre nor, because of that, bereft of our own limited place and intrinsic dignity.[1313] Ditto the divine: "The Greeks

---

1308 HR 46; R 26–27.
1309 HR 46; R 27.
1310 HE, 150.
1311 HE 149.
1312 HE 47; R 28.
1313 Compare the quote which Camus uses to introduce "Prometheus in the Underworld" from Lucian: "I felt that the gods were lacking as long as there was nothing to oppose them"; cf. also Camus' note in his *American Notebooks*: "Remake and recreate Greek reflection as a revolt against the sacred. But not the revolt contra the sacred of the romantics—itself another form of the sacred—but a revolt as a putting in its place of the sacred..." Camus in *Oeuvres Complètes II*, 1061; and this from "Trois Interviews": "And what is it in the Greek spirit that Christianity cannot admit? Many things, but this in particular: the Greeks do not deny the gods, but they assigned the gods [also] their part (*ils leur measuraient leur part*). Christianity which is a total religion, to use a word which is *à la mode*, could not admit this spirit which gives to [God] solely a place when He must, in their sense, possess all (*avoir toute la place*). But this [Greek] spirit can perhaps very well admit, on the contrary, the existence of Christianity..." *Oeuvres Complètes II*, 476.

gave [the gods] their place. But the gods were not everything."[1314] "The idea of innocence opposed to guilt, the concept of all of history summed up in the struggle between good and evil, was foreign to [the Greeks]," Camus argues, with an eye forward to his argument concerning Christian then modern messianisms: "In their [the Greek] universe there were more mistakes than crimes, and the only definitive crime was excess...":

> Of course, the Greeks described excess, since it exists, but they gave it its proper place and, by doing so, also defined its limits. Achilles' defiance after the death of Patroclus, the imprecations of the Greek tragic heroes cursing their fate, do not imply complete condemnation. Oedipus knows that he is not innocent. He is guilty in spite of himself; he is also part of destiny... Antigone rebels, but she does so in the name of tradition, in order that her brothers may find rest in the tomb and that the appropriate rites may be observed.... The Greek mind has two aspects and in its meditations almost always re-echoes, as counterpoint to its most tragic melodies, the eternal words of Oedipus, who, blind and desperate, recognizes that all is for the best....[1315]

The only corrective for tragic violence, then, is that each party recognise the limit to their claims; a limit circumscribed, in each case, by the legitimate, but equally limited claims of the other. This is why the advice given by the tragic choruses to the heroes and heroines, and to the audience, is almost always that of *mesure*. Or so Camus claims, evoking his central philosophical notions one by one: "the constant theme of classical tragedy is... that of the limit which must not be transgressed."[1316] More than this, recognising the limit amounts to not denying the other's claims, or what Camus will call in his Algerian texts "the reasons of the adversary."[1317] And herein lies the secret, Camus argues, to what Aristotle correctly saw as the cathartic, civilly therapeutic function of tragedy, albeit on Camus' different bases.[1318] The tragedies stage the destruction of the hero who ("through blindness or passion")[1319] goes too far, beyond blasphemy

---

1314   C II 165; C II Eng 84.
1315   HR 46–47; R 27. On this "all is well" of Oedipus, a recurring figure in Camus, cf. LFT 304-3-5, 307; and MS 166–167; MSe 122.
1316   LFT 302.
1317   AC 133, 135, 137.
1318   Aristotle, *Poetics* ch. 6, 1149b20.
1319   LFT 301.

to arrogance, from justified rebellion towards self-deifying revolution. They thereby show how:

> The only purification lies in denying and excluding nothing, in thus accepting the mystery of existence, the limitations of man, in short the order where man knows without knowing. Oedipus then says 'all is well', when his eyes have been torn out. Henceforth, he knows, although he never sees again... and this face with its dead eyes shines with the highest lesson of the tragic universe.[1320]

2.3   All is Well? The Consent within Revolt and the Black Side of the Sun

We have now reached the end of our Platonic itinerary of reconstructing Camus' philosophical discourse beginning from the "cave" in which his thought began, conceived as a response to the problems of his times—at the same time, placing his work in ongoing dialogue with more recent, better known theoretical and philosophical authorities. In this Chapter, indeed, we have also completed what is one further aim of this study: the pointed differentiation of Camus from the more recent post-structuralist and critical theorists we have been reading him alongside. Camus' neoHellenism points beyond the forms of philosophical grounding operative in all the more recent European philosophies we have met: each of which base their claims on what Camus' position suggests are wholly historical or political factors (a theory of power, language, signification, textual interpretation, even human dialogue, taken alone). In this light, Camus would not be surprised by today's widespread messianic turn in Theory. Already from the late 1940s, he interpreted the existentialism in his own time, moving into alliance with Marxism, as a mode of messianic thought looking back to Saint Augustine: one which can counter-pose to present injustices only the promise of a utopian historical or post-historical dispensation.[1321] Outside of the historicist cave (closed over by the assumption that human

---

1320 LFT 305.

1321 Camus never speaks systematically on the connection between existentialism and Marxism, except to note a common historicism which seems to push against the existentialist stress on freedom, as in: "Tout l'effort de la pensée allemande a été de substituer à la notion de nature humaine celle de situation humaine et donc l'histoire à Dieu et la tragédie moderne à l'équilibre ancien. L'existentialisme moderne pousse cet effort encore plus loin et introduit dans l'idée de situation la même incertitude que dans celle de nature. Il ne reste plus rien qu'un movement..." C II 174 (cf. C II 180; C II Eng 92) In Chapter Six, we will see his psychological critique of existentialism as a philosophy of universalised guilt, which provides a different avenue towards a secularised Augustinian position.

nature is wholly politically shaped, so the question of our place in larger nature can be sidelined), Camus' thought from its beginning moves towards a distinct form of tragic, aesthetic or contemplative naturalism. The real demands of political life, Camus argues, need to be balanced against those given to us by our nature as finite, mortal, natural beings inhabiting an order we did not create. "Far from … the glittering Parisian cave"[1322] as he writes in "The Enigma" (and Paris is here standing, philosophically and biographically, for the kind of historicisms Camus opposed) Camus' philosophical trajectory urges us to look again at the natural landscapes surrounding our expanding metropoles.[1323] He challenges us to recover a neoHellenic sense of limits rooted in the eternal, structured recurrences of the natural world of which we form one small part. Despite images of his work which will always abide (since they measure him against the abiding theological presuppositions Camus contested), Camus is never tempted by "absolute negation" or "nihilism." "These antinomies only exist in the absolute. They suppose a world and a method of thought without mediations."[1324] Camus' image of humanity is instead 'tragic,' in the precise sense we've now seen. We are beings with an inalienable dignity in a larger order which circumscribes boundaries to what we can legitimately attempt, this side of the kinds of murderous or suicidal *hybris* and blindness Camus depicts for us in his Meursault, his Cottard, his Stefan or his Caligula; opposes in his 'German friend' and systematically attacks in the different Hegelian and Nietzschean incarnations of modern German philosophy.

Nevertheless, alongside Camus' own Algerian tragedy (which we will consider in detail in the next Chapter), we raised at the beginning of this Chapter a seemingly crippling criticism of anything like a Camusian appeal to reanimate classical, contemplative modes of thinking. As we saw Goss putting this criticism very clearly, Camus seems to want to have his modern cake and eat it too. Clearly, in contrast to critical theory at its darkest and post-Heideggerian thought, Camus accepts the post-Baconian or post-Newtonian sciences. Indeed, as we have stressed, Camus sets descriptive scientific rationality up against the prophetic sides to modern ideologies, as a modern intellectual legacy worth defending (Chapters One and Two). He embraces the post-providential image of the world these sciences have delivered us. But Camus wants to eat this modern, naturalistic cake too.[1325] For he asks us, when we ascend

---

1322 E 161.
1323 HE 150–151; TL 492; "Ce soir le rideau se lève sur… René Char (1948)", OC II 764.
1324 HR 360; R 288.
1325 "Naturalism" is used here and in what follows not to indicate an epistemological position for which only the natural sciences can disclose truths, but to describe an ontological

beyond our Parisian caves, to somehow look to nature's ordered recurrences as the source of a renewed sense of humane ethical and political limits. Yet this is impossible: or so Goss claims, echoing a kind of argument about modern thinking which has been contended many times by other figures.[1326] Premodern Western thought (this kind of position goes) whether in its classical or Catholic forms, accepted an ordered, teleological cosmos in which each thing was assigned its natural or God-borne purpose. The modern natural sciences explain the material and efficient causes of things. They deny we can know their final causes (ends or purposes). This leaves all the world, and we within it, without orienting ends. We are left with a kind of cosmic abandonment writ large in the spatiotemporally infinite universe posited since Copernicus in which the earth is not at the centre, since there seems no longer to *be any* such centre.

This seeming contradiction in Camus, it can be argued, is reflected in a series of uneasy oscillations into which his thought seems to push him. On the one 'modernist' hand, he is the thinker of metaphysical *skepsis* and rebellion. His position thus ends by setting up a kind of tragic human "we are," set against the backdrop of an indifferent universe which periodically visits earthquakes, plagues, ebola epidemics and numberless infant deaths upon us (as a "black side to the sun," in one of his expressions.)[1327] This all at the same time as human beings continue to assume for themselves the happy right or need to "suspend the ethical," kill, torture, write metaphysical vindications for these exactions, and wage war. On the other "neoHellenic" hand, as Camus tells us in "The Desert", the highest truth of his philosophy is that, somehow, "in my revolt a consent lay dormant."[1328] This consent, truly indeed a "flourish of affirmations"[1329] by the time of "Helen's Exile" ten years later, has grown in to a fully-fledged paean to a beautiful, seemingly wholly benign natural order, emblematised by the sharp lines of Mediterranean coasts gilded by the evening sun.[1330] In this neoHellenic mood that finds expression also in *The Rebel*'s closing pages, the human "we are" Camus sets up in *The Rebel*

---

position which holds (minimally) that (a) there are no *knowable* supernatural entities or causes that people can universally agree about, (b) that the natural world is nevertheless intelligibly ordered, and (c) that we are a reflective, finite part of it.

1326 Goss, "Camus, God, and Process Thought", *Process Theology*, Vol. 4, Number 2 (Summer 1974), 114–128, as cited above.
1327 LCE 357.
1328 D 105, cf. 104: "every truth carries its bitterness within … every denial contains a flourish of affirmations …".
1329 D 104.
1330 HE 148.

seems less set tragically against a remorseless universe than always-already, classically at home ("in springtime Tipasa is full of gods...").[1331] We need only sweep the accumulated cultural illusions of 2000 years from our puzzled eyes: "to change life, yes, but not the world, which was my divinity."[1332] Revolt seems less in order in such a *kosmos* than speechless admiration, as Camus chastises his more political self in "Return to Tipasa": "But this still resembles a moral code, and we live for something that goes farther than morality. If we could only name it, what silence!"[1333]

We have been arguing that Camus is, if not a systematic then a highly original, highly coherent and well-informed thinker, although he never presented "the System" "in 1500 pages" we know he at one point envisaged,[1334] instead shaping his writings to different, predominantly extra-academic audiences and ends. So it seems unlikely that Camus could have failed to consider this kind of criticism, drawing attention to the relations between his simultaneous defences of a modern, post-scientific, post-providential sense of the world and a neoHellenic classicism. We are left to assume that Camus thought that his acceptance of something like the modern scientific worldview was in no way truly inconsistent with a contemplative, normatively orienting sense of natural order and beauty that might answer the modern West's cultural angst. What grounds for such an opinion are there, in Camus' thought as we have reconstructed it? And what sense, more widely, can be made of such a seeming squaring of the circle?

Let us consider Srigley's charge of inconsistency in *The Rebel* on this score first. Srigley suggests that there is no reconciliation possible between Camus' closing paeans to Mediterranean, neoHellenic naturalism in Part V with Part I's modern-sounding, epistemological language (culminating in the famous para-Cartesian "I rebel, therefore we are").[1335] But this conclusion is evitable. In the early part of *L'Homme Révolté*, as we saw, Camus wants methodologically, in light of the modern crisis, to assume nothing until he can build a larger perspective on the basis of his phenomenological analyses, and analyses of the history of modern rebellion. After his critique of modern metaphysical and historical revolt in *L'Homme Révolté* Parts II and III, and the defence these analyses suggest of the primary value of human solidarity (per the section "Rebellion and Murder" of Part V), Camus evidently felt that the

---

1331 NT 65.
1332 EE Pref, 7.
1333 RT 170.
1334 C II 193, 201; C II Eng 99–103–104.
1335 Srigley, *Camus' Critique* 8–9, 51.

book's argumentative achievements had licensed him to speak more affirmatively. To the question implied in his early statement that perhaps "contrary to the postulates of contemporary thought, a human nature does exist, as the Greeks believed...," Camus in *The Rebel's* closing sections of Part v on "Midday Thought" feels able to answer 'yes'.[1336]

Certainly, *The Rebel* has argued powerfully against the fascist and Stalinist avatars of the contrary supposition that no such nature exists, so human beings are only the creatures of historical struggle, variously conceived. Yet such an argument against the contrary by itself is insufficient: just as, for instance, an argument against the normative credentials of modern liberalism can license indifferently a Marxist, Moslem, Christian, or postmodern conclusion. If we are to comprehend Camus' positive argument here, we need to return one more time to his philosophical premises. In particular, we need to specify (in ways Camus does not always systematically do) the nature of the inalienable desire for unity to which he appeals to ground human revolt and dignity, *pereat mundus*. In *Le Mythe de Sisyphe*, as we commented in Chapter Three, Camus importantly specifies that this is above all a near-erotic desire not simply for order. It is a longing for *a specific kind of anthropocentric, or 'anthropophilic,' order*. To cite again this crucial passage:

> The mind's deepest desire, even in its most elaborate operations, parallels man's unconscious feeling in the face of his universe: it is an insistence upon familiarity, an appetite for clarity. Understanding the world for a man is reducing it to the human, stamping it with his seal..... The truism "All thought is anthropomorphic" has no other meaning... If man realized that the universe like him can love and suffer, he would be reconciled....[1337]

It is this specifically anthropomorphic register of the desire for unity that Camus thinks cannot be sustained before the realities of useless suffering, the death of innocents and natural catastrophes: all of which he will call "irrational", to indicate how they dash such a 'first-order' human longing to be wholly, unchangingly, at home in the cosmos. Nevertheless, we know that Camus does not think that descriptively, lucidly confronting these limits to our rational aspirations licenses Irrationalism: the fond, performatively contradictory doctrine that 'nothing has any order or meaning'. According to his "law of *mesure*", the desire for unity, confronted with its first order disappointments,

---

1336 HR 30; R 16.
1337 MS 34; MSe 17.

as it were recurs at a 'second-level,' reflective order: "the desire for unity not only demands that everything should be rational. It also wishes that the irrational should not be sacrificed..."[1338] Since we cannot legitimately explain (or explain away) the kinds of phenomena which make human beings curse the gods or despair, we must 'change the frame' of our considerations.

Scientific rationality, Camus accepts, tries scrupulously to suspend metaphysical claims. It aims instead to treat them as hypotheses, testable against an external reality which is given authoritative right of reply. Like Camus' sparsely classical, descriptive prose, it thus aims at what Camus above calls "not sacrificing," but trying lucidly to describe "the irrational": here, the kinds of astronomical, geological, cultural, biological, psychological and evolutionary truths which have compromised the Christian West's sense of the human species' cosmic centrality since 1600. Of course, measured against a presupposed 'sacred canopy' of a posited teleological, created, anthropocentric universe, much of what science has discovered can only appear tendentially 'meaningless' or even 'chaotic'. Yet, if we bracket such an inherited cultural frame, the suppressed 'All or Nothing' disjunctive premise operating here (which still at times excites Nietzsche, a preacher's son),[1339] is no longer sound. The natural regularities and systems discovered by the sciences (including those uncovered in the ecological sciences) do not bespeak a creation set to order for the mind and purposes of human beings. But science does nothing if not continue to discover forms of order and rationality in nature, allowing us, in applied technologies, to harness these regularities in new ways to our ends. And if, at its outer edges (at the quantum level, for instance), the sciences do confront seemingly abyssal uncertainties, these uncertainties do not at any point 'impact backwards', somehow rendering nugatory all the theoretical postulates required to even *see* such limits to human understanding which previous cultures could not even dream of. These limits, to use Camus' terms, set boundaries to our capacities to understand.[1340] They do not destroy it, let alone decimating the

---

1338 HR 369; R 296.
1339 I.e. 'Either a providential universe with a knowable Creator-Soter God exists (A), or there is no meaning in life (B)'. 'But not A', 'therefore...'
1340 "The quantum theory, relativity, the uncertainty of interrelationships, define a world that has no definable reality except on the scale of average greatness that is our own. The ideologies which guide our world were born in the time of absolute scientific discoveries. Our real knowledge, on the other hand, justifies a system of thought based on relative discoveries. 'Intelligence,' says Lazare Bickel, 'is our faculty for not developing what we think to the very end, so that we still believe in reality.' Approximative thought is the only creator of reality." HR 368; R 294–295.

cumulative body of accepted naturalistic understandings gathered across generations of inquirers since the 17th century.

So science does not rob the world of order: a profoundly idealistic fallacy, related to what the recently-passed critical realist Roy Bhaskar called the "epistemic fallacy."[1341] Science attempts to plumb and mirror this order in ever more exact ways, rather than assuming in advance that we are in possession of its comprehension. In doing so, the sciences have discovered that the natural order is not anthropocentric. The earth is older than we thought it was, not at the centre of the universe; and the *homo sapiens*, far from being unique in an order where all species were created all at once *per Genesis*, has evolved like these other species over spacious aeons to have its present capacities and limits.

Faced with this scenario, we can continue to measure what we know against the inherited Christian-providential, cultural frameworks it challenges. The result will be, more or less inevitably, forms of despair and powerful motivations pushing towards defiant forms of Irrationalism or fundamentalism: "[b]ack to the Middle Ages, back to primitive mentality, back to the land, back to religion, to the arsenal of old solutions."[1342] Or, in what is Camus' option, we can accept that, given the modern scientific revolutions, our very framework for understanding ourselves and the world, including our ideas of God, must change. There is still order in the world: "ever the same sky throughout the years, unfailing in strength and light, itself insatiable…"[1343] The same sun greets us each morning as greeted Aristarchus, Democritus, Moses, Aristotle or Aquinas; just as the same physical laws apply, independently of what humans happen to think about them. What must be overcome is the supposition that for the world's order to be beautiful, inspiring, or normatively directive, it would have to be anthropocentric: created for us by a God in whose image we take ourselves as having been created.

In the several ways we have recounted, Camus challenges this monotheistic premise. And however rhetorical are the texts in which Camus has bequeathed it to us, his challenge to this assumption is Camus' most profound ontological

---

1341 I mean to say that it tacitly supposes that human categories shape the world they set out to understand; hence if humans decide the world is without order, it must *be* without such order. For Bhaskar, the epistemic fallacy likewise supposes that we cannot describe the world except by describing our understandings of the world ("Since we only know the world through our categories, the only thing we can know are our categories…") See Roy Bhaskar, *Reclaiming Reality* (London & New York: Verso, 1989).

1342 C II 26; C II Eng 9.

1343 RT 166.

legacy in a world facing ecological collapse, and the impossibility of the West's retreating back into its former, sacred canopy. "At the heart of all beauty there lies something inhuman," we recall Camus arguing in *Le Mythe de Sisyphe* (Chapter Three).[1344] Already the seeming paradox is clear, relative to the idea that what pleases us (*ergo* the beautiful) must be useful, beneficial or at least referable to our ends. But nature's beauty only emerges for Camus, as of course Kant and modern aestheticians agree on their own idealist terms, when we put aside "the images and designs that we had attributed to [nature] beforehand."[1345] It is when nature thus "becomes itself again" that we are capable of discerning and responding affectively to that 'purposiveness without purpose' Kant described.[1346] But epistemically a realist, Camus talks (in contrast to Kant) of a nature independent of us: "inhuman" or "not made to our scale". This is the order of that "benign indifference" that Meursault is finally able to sense in the night sky, after his cathartic exchange with the Priest in *L'Étranger*, asking him to embrace the prospect of another life.[1347] Just as human beings can visit exile upon their fellows and invite them to forms of communion, so too nature, far from being an Edenic paradise and simple refuge from history in Camus, is to be affirmed *precisely insofar as it transcends human control and bespeaks an order serenely beyond our measure*. This order is literally fatal for us (as well as fecund). It is the desert, as well as the cooling waters in which Rieux and Tarrow bathe:[1348] "and in the desert, all men, both he and the guest, were nothing".[1349] Particularly in "The Minotaur, or the Halt at Oran," Camus associates the ages-old longing of some human beings to withdraw ascetically into the desert to this extra-human dimension to nature, whose only political corollary can be murderous. "Oh, to be nothing!," Camus exclaims:

1344 M 30; MSe 14.

1345 MS 30; MSe 14.

1346 Immanuel Kant, *Critique of Judgment*, trans. Paul Guyer (Cambridge: Cambridge University Press, 2002), sec. 10, 15.

1347 S 76.

1348 See on the role of flowing water in "The Growing Stone", the most affirmative, culminating story in *Exile and the Kingdom*, Tarrow, *Exile from the Kingdom*, 193. But as the desert is at once a place of annihilation, as well as of higher epiphanies; so too the water can drown and corrode, and needs the works of an engineer like D'Arrast to be channelled and brought to heal... In short, here again, we see the complexity of Camus' thought: which does not simply pit nature (positive) versus history (negative), but preserves a two-sided sense of nature herself.

1349 At Tarrow, *Exile from* the Kingdom, 179. Cf. EK 92: "the solitary expanse where nothing had any connection with man."

> For thousands of years this great cry has roused millions of men to revolt against desire and pain. Its dying echoes have reached this far, across centuries and oceans, to the oldest sea in the world. They still reverberate dully against the compact cliffs of Oran. Everybody in this country follows this advice without knowing it. Of course, it is almost futile. Nothingness cannot be achieved any more than the absolute can. But since we receive as favours the eternal signs brought us by roses or by human suffering, let us not refuse either the rare invitations to sleep that the earth addresses us. These have as much truth as the others...[1350]

The "truth" here is that this inhuman order has a magnificence which, seen aright, calls forth the kind of self-forgetting or self-transcending admiration that Camus powerfully felt and aimed to convey in his lyrical writings.[1351] The following passage from his early *Carnets*, the basis for the final Florentine *epopteia* in "The Desert" cited above, puts the thought in play here:

> Millions of eyes have looked at this landscape, and for me it is like the first smile of the world. It takes me out of myself, in the deepest meaning of the expression ... it denies me a personality, and deprives my suffering of its echo. The world is beautiful, and that is everything. The great truth which it patiently teaches me is that neither the mind nor the heart has any importance. And that the stone warmed by the sun and the cypress tree swelling against the empty sky set a boundary to the only world in which to be right has any meaning: nature without men. This world reduces me to nothing. It carries me to the very end. Without anger, it denies that I exist. And, agreeing to my defeat, I move towards a wisdom where everything has already been conquered—except that tears come into my eyes, and this great sob of poetry makes me forget the truth of the world.[1352]

So we return to a thought touched upon in Chapter Three. This is that, as Camus enigmatically says in *Le Mythe de Sisyphe*, the systems of thought which claim to explain everything in terms referring to human purposes, rob

---

1350 MSO 131; Cf. RG. 191 where Camus posits a "desire for death", sounding almost like the later Freud.
1351 C I 89; C I 39: Camus here as elsewhere attests his own ascetic "desire to be stripped bare of everything" ('cet immense désir de dépouillement...'). See Chapter Six below, "Literature and Philosophy as a Way of Life".
1352 C I 73–74; I 31 Eng.

life of the dimensions which enable its wonder to be most fully experienced. They "impoverish that reality whose inhumanity constitutes man's majesty."[1353] According to what Camus at several points calls a "secret" he continues seeking to express,[1354] it is the factually limited place of man in the non-anthropocentric, non-providential "inhuman" universe ("the scale of relative greatness that is our own")[1355] that gives, or ought to give us, normative orientation and a sense of ineluctable limits.

In this light, Camus can accept with Sophocles' blinded Oedipus at Colonus that "all is well," even in a world in which the innocent will continue to suffer and nature visit catastrophes upon us; sublimely showing its independence from our aspirations by levelling cities as a giant might swat a fly, and sending epidemics which destroy *en masse* the lives of innocents. If you like, what Camus' thought at this point suggests is that it is our limited place in this cosmos *to be that creature who can understand how we are part of an order almost infinitely larger and more complex than we had hitherto imagined: and also, with intelligence and courage, to accept these natural truths and limitations.* It is then, as it were, our right and place in this order to resist, when we can, the senseless slaughter of innocents at the hands of natural and human causes; so long as we "consent" in advance to the limits our nature (and wider nature) sets for us which mean that, as Camus writes in the *Rebel*, "children will still die unjustly even in a perfect society."[1356]

"[I]f man were capable of introducing unity into the world entirely on his own, if he could establish the reign, by his own decree, of sincerity, innocence, and justice, he would be God Himself,"[1357] Camus reflects. But, contra the messianic experiments of the last century and the long history of human projects in self-deification, we are not. Oedipus must strike out his eyes, and even for his unwilled excesses, leave the city of Thebes. We cannot practically assent, finite and vulnerable as we are, to everything an order not made to our scale visits upon us and our kind. By human standards of justice (and parental love), the death of a helpless child by natural causes is as outrageous as the systematically-engendered, and politically chosen atrocities of fascism, Stalinism, or colonialism. But we can theoretically attempt to comprehend as much of this natural order as we can, humbly attentive to the way it operates indifferently to human hopes and fears. Moreover, aesthetically and reflectively, we can be

---

1353 MS 80; MSe 55.
1354 Eg RT 170; Cf. egs C I 76; C II 138; C III 65, 81, 179.
1355 HR 368; R 294–295.
1356 HR 378; R 303.
1357 HR 356; R 285.

moved by its inhuman scale and majesty, of which human history and civilization is itself only a tiny passing part, to a renewed humility and sense of our own limits. This in any case seems to be something like the heart of what Camus' philosophical discourse aimed at finding words for:

> No possible form of wisdom today can claim to give more. Rebellion indefatigably confronts evil, from which it can only derive a new impetus. Man can master in himself everything that should be mastered. He should rectify in creation everything that can be rectified. And after he has done so,...[e]ven by his greatest effort man can only propose to diminish arithmetically the sufferings of the world. But the injustice and the suffering of the world will remain and, no matter how limited they are, they will not cease to be an outrage. Dimitri Karamazov's cry of "Why?" will continue to resound; art and rebellion will die only with the last man.[1358]

1358 HR 378; R 303.

CHAPTER 6

After the Fall, the First Man

1   Judgment, *The Fall*, and the Post-Prophetic Philosopher

1.1   *Exile and Algeria: The Post-Colonial Case against Albert Camus*
In his 1958 "Preface" to the republication of his first collection of essays, *L'Envers et L'endroit*, Camus concludes with a disarming statement, prompted by his returning to these aesthetically unbalanced, semi-autobiographical pieces. This statement reflects what we have been arguing about Camus' philosophical discourse: that it turns around a single set of claims that Camus continues to develop and unfold across the different genres of his writing, beneath their apparently disordered appearances. "Nothing prevents me from dreaming, even in the very hour of exile," Camus reflects:

> ...since at least I know this, with sure and certain knowledge: a man's work is nothing but this slow task to recover, through the detours of art, those two or three great and simple images in whose presence his heart first opened. This is why, perhaps, after working and producing for twenty years, I still live with the idea that my work has not even begun.[1359]

The statement calls to readers' minds Camus' earlier claim, concluding the "The Enigma" of 1950, to the effect that every artist "pursues his truth". "[I]f he is a great artist, every work brings him closer to it...if he is mediocre, every work takes him further from it, the centre is then everywhere, the light disintegrates."[1360] For Camus, as the manuscript of *Le Premier Homme* finally published by his family in 1994 would show, this "truth" to which he felt compelled to return involved "that old woman, a silent mother, poverty, ... the populated loneliness of love..." he experienced in his childhood and youth growing up in Belcourt, a suburb of *pied noir* Algiers.[1361]

'But this is just the point,' the postcolonial critics of Camus' work rejoin. 'If the 'truth' of Camus' work resides somehow in his Algerian identity, or rather his identity as a *pied noir* settler in French Algeria on the eve of its demise, then this truth is not the 'light' he claims for it. At the very least, this light is haunted

---

1359   EE Pref, 17.
1360   E 161.
1361   EE Pref, 13.

by a black side which is not simply that of the blinding North African sun. Much more human, all-too-human, this darkness, which Camus was never able "to come to terms with,"[1362] was the irreparable, continuing violence and injustice of French colonisation in Algeria, of which Camus was one more, if perhaps well-meaning, beneficiary.' There is a moment in Camus' *Le Premier Homme* which in a way dramatizes how post-colonial critics ask us to reenvisage Camus' work after his death in 1960, and the Evian accords and forced emigration of his *pied noir* community after 1962. The novel, whose protagonist Jacques Cormery is transparently based on Camus' own life, has begun in grand mythopoetic style: by narrating what we soon come to realise is the author's own birth in the Algerian hinterland. We then jump ahead to a present, around the time of Camus' writing (1957 or 1958). Cormery, a grown man, visits his father's grave at Saint Brieuc cemetery, where he has been buried on the French mainland after dying in the Marne in 1914. He then commutes by steamship, absorbed in somnolent reverie of his childhood, to visit his family. He has just been reunited with his illiterate, nearly deaf and mute mother. The mother had gone to the kitchen to prepare stew, and Jacques had "taken her place", contemplating the Belcourt street below "in the liveliness of a Sunday morning." Then, the real of history returns like the proverbial repressed to trouble his self-concerned reveries:

> The explosion resounded at the very moment Lucie Cormery came back to the room. / It sounded very close, enormous, as if it would never stop reverberating. It seemed that they had long since stopped hearing it, but the bulb in the dining-room was still shaking behind the glass shell. His mother had recoiled to the back of the room, pale, her dark eyes full of a fear she could not control, and she was unsteady on her feet. / 'It's here. It's here,' she was saying...[1363]

What was "here" was the war for Algerian independence, spearheaded by the *Front de Libération Nationale* (FLN), who after August 1955 began using terrorist violence against civilian *pied noir* targets (in this case, a crowded bus-stop) in order to prosecute their cause. Its rude and bloody interruption of Camus/Cormery's "search for the father," the animating motive of the novel's action, says nearly everything we need to know, according to Camus' harshest contemporary and posthumous critics on the Algerian issue. As we began to see in Chapter Five, according to these critics, Camus' famed political universalism

---
1362 O'Brien, *Albert Camus*, 26.
1363 Albert Camus, *The First Man* translated David Hapgood (London: Penguin, 1996), 58.

was a universalising, ideological fiction serving to render invisible the very particular, very located, injustices associated with Camus' *pied noir* heritage. Camus' philosophical stress on the "fixed and radiant point of the present" may or may not serve as a countervailing argument against modern secularised political messianisms. It may or may not reflect Camus' deep immersion in classical philosophical culture. Looked at with an exclusive eye to the Algerian context, it reappears as another incarnation of the French Algerians' desire to "put history on hold... play a trick on history," in order to "obviate colonial tensions... Camus reflects a society that dreams in an 'absolute now'... a flight from history..., haunted by their historical crimes perpetrated against the Arabs."[1364] As for Camus' lyrical invocations of 'noces' with the Algerian landscape, from this early essay collection through to "La Femme Adultère" in 1957's *Exile and the Kingdom*, Azzedine Haddour diagnoses these as the manic compensations for a deepset melancholia occasioned by Camus' awareness, and attempts to disavow, these founding violences:

> One must interpret the mythology of the Mediterranean constructed by Camus, the jubilant language evoking happiness, joy and exuberance in the light of economic conditions of a mania which endeavours to overcome a complex threatening the colonial ego...[1365]

There is no question that, by the time of his death in January 1960, Camus cut a lonely figure concerning the Algerian war.[1366] His 1958 "Preface" to *Actuelles III* (*The Algerian Chronicles*) acknowledges that the writings collected there from over two decades on Algeria record "the history of a failure."[1367] Camus' general position on Algeria, always advocating for the peacable coexistence of Arabic and European populations, rather than the expulsion of the French settlers, is well known. It has been copiously documented and debated.[1368] In the 1930s and during the war, Camus defended a particular conception of Arab "assimilation". He advocated unsuccessfully for the 1936 Blum-Violette plan (granting limited franchise to the Arabs) and, in 1938–'39, wrote a series of articles

---

1364 Haddour, *Colonial Mythology*, 32; cf. Said, *Culture and Imperialism*, 184.
1365 Haddour, *Colonial Mythology*, 70.
1366 See the comments by Catherine Camus, in "Preface" to Camus, *The First Man*, vi.
1367 Albert Camus, *Algerian Chronicles* translated Arthur Goldhammer with an Introduction by Alice Kaplan (Cambridge, Massachusetts: Belknap Press, 2013), 32.
1368 For a valuable recent account, placing Camus' positions alongside his contemporaries, see Guy Dugas, "Camus, Sénac, Roblès: les écrivains de l'École d'Alger face au terrorisme", *Camus in the 21st century*, 189–205.

strongly condemning the treatment and conditions of the indigenous populations in *Alger Republicain*, proposing a host of economic, educational, and social reforms. In 1945, in a series of articles published in *Combat* after the Sétif massacres on V-E-day (involving firstly Arab violence against the French, then disproportionately brutal French reprisals), Camus admitted that assimilation was now impossible, and no longer desired by most Arabs.[1369] Instead, he endorsed then-Arab moderate Ferhat Abbas's Manifesto calling for an Algerian constitution guaranteeing immediate and effective political participation and legal equality for Muslims.[1370] (Abbas and the "Friends of the Manifesto" were duly arrested by the colonial authorities).

Over the next decade of rigged elections, legal and political reforms blocked piece by piece by the *colon* ultras, the anti-colonial struggles in Indochina and Tunisia, Camus published little on his homeland.[1371] He broke his silence in 1955 and 1956, trying in the immediate aftermath of the Phillippeville terrorist actions of the FLN to broker a civilian truce. Never would Camus give ground on his basic commitment to the idea that both the 1 million French and 8 million Arab and Berber Algerians were "condemned to live together":[1372] and that the "French reality" of a community settled in Algeria for over 100 years "can never be eliminated",[1373] and "should not be sacrificed to the immense sins of French colonisation."[1374]

1958 saw Camus publish the *Algerian Chronicles*. Camus now added a Preface to his articles of 1938–1939, 1945, 1955–1956, and a short "note" in response to "those who ask me what future one may hope for in Algeria."[1375] In it, Camus propounded his final vision: that of an Algerian-French Federation based on the Lauriol Plan, responding to a recognition that "the era of colonialism is over", and aiming at a "union of differences".[1376] In a first phase, this Plan envisaged the French National Assembly being divided, from hereon to include a Moslem section with authority on all matters concerning Moslems; and then,

---

1369 AC, 130; David Carroll, *Albert Camus the Algerian: Colonialism, Terrorism, Justice.* (New York: Columbia University Press, 2007), 142.

1370 AC 128–9.

1371 See Tarrow, *Exile from the Kingdom*, 172–173.

1372 AC 114, 123; cf. 153–154, where Camus describes the conflict as akin to a tragic family quarrel.

1373 AC 114; cf. 145.

1374 AC 126.

1375 AC 175.

1376 AC 180, 181. For the deep proximities between this and Jacques Derrida's vision (and criticism of Nora's position), see Baring, "Liberalism and the Algerian War: The Case of Jacques Derrida", esp. 240–244. Cf. AC 180, 181.

in a second phase, the institution of an Algerian regional assembly to "represent the distinctive views of Algeria" (coupled with a federal, metropolitan-Algerian senate).[1377] In this way, "two categories of equal but distinct citizens" would be created: "a sort of revolution against the regime of centralisation and abstract individualism created in 1789..."[1378] In addition, reparations should be paid to "eight million Arabs who have hitherto lived under a particular form of repression" and it should be made incumbent upon the French government to avow that it would heretofore "treat the Arab people of Algeria justly and free them from the colonial system."[1379] Nevertheless, Camus now also warned against what he called a "new Arab imperialism", "an Algeria linked to an Islamic empire that would subject the Arab peoples to additional misery and suffering and tear the French people of Algeria from their natural homeland"[1380], amplifying suspicions he had been expressing since 1945 that behind the FLN's push for Algerian independence was the agency of Nassar's Egypt.[1381] Egypt, Camus in turn suggested, was as a puppet "used by Russia for the moment as part of its global strategy... to encircle Europe from the South."[1382] "There has never been an Algerian nation," Camus claimed[1383] in an uncharacteristically strident and provocative, only technically defencible, proposition.[1384]

By 1958, Camus however knew his opinion was marginal both within Algeria and in France, wherein "one segment of... public opinion vaguely believes that the Arabs have somehow acquired the right to kill and mutilate, while the other is prepared to justify every excess."[1385] His campaign for a Civilian Truce, suspending violence against civilians in order to bring the feuding parties together in January 1956 had been shouted down by Ultras in the audience, with Camus needing to be ushered to and from the stage by a bodyguard of friends.[1386] Despite winning the Nobel Prize for Literature the previous year, *Actuelles III* fell nearly dead from the presses. In France, Sartre and de Beauvoir led a chorus of voices on the Left, echoed by the nationalists in Algeria, condemning Camus'

1377 AC 180.
1378 AC 181; cf. 127 (for Camus' claim that the French owe the Berbers and Arabs "a stunning reparation", hardly an unrepentant colonialists' denial; cf. Carroll, *Camus the Algerian*, 52).
1379 AC 179.
1380 AC 35.
1381 AC 130, 134–135, 146.
1382 AC 178. See Aronson, *Camus and Sartre*, 213
1383 Cf. Said, *Culture and Imperialism*, 183.
1384 Previously, the territory of what became after French invasion "Algeria" had been a regency within the Ottoman empire, ruled by the deys out of Algiers, not a modern nation-state.
1385 AC 18.
1386 Zaretsksy, *A Life Worth Living*, 82–3; Parker, *Artist in the Arena*, 155–157.

"tender-hearted realism [sic.]";[1387] "the fraud... in the fact that he posed at the same time as a man above the battle, thus providing a warning for those who wanted to reconcile this war and its methods with bourgeois humanism."[1388] Like the character Daru Camus pictures in the story "L'Hôte" (both "host" and "guest") who neither delivers the Arab accused of murder in his care up to French Law nor unequivocally frees him, thereby pleasing no one,[1389] Camus knew that his 1958 volume would "satisfy no one, and I know in advance how it will be received on both sides."[1390] At the close of the 1958 "Preface", Camus in effect "signs off" ("this is my testimony, and I shall have nothing more to say"),[1391] vowing a public silence that would become definitive: "in order to add neither to [Algeria's] misfortune nor to the stupidities that have been written with respect to the subject."[1392] On the public record, Camus' famous final remark to a young Algerian agitator at the Stockholm reception of his Nobel prize: "I believe in justice, but I will defend my mother before justice" has been pointed to by critics as proof positive of the collapse of Camus' moral authority in this issue so closely touching himself and his family.[1393]

It was Michael Walzer, in the context of an unlikely defence of Camus for this alleged partiality[1394] who commented that Camus' silence after 1958 "was eloquent in its hopelessness."[1395] For Nora, O'Brien, Said and others, if Walzer had learnt how to read Camus' fictional works from the 1940s "contrapuntally" (in Said's term),[1396] he needn't have pointed only to Camus' final silence to understand how his works, from the very beginning, "very precisely distill

---

1387 At Aronson, *Sartre and* Camus, 210; cf. 190–192, for Sartre's Salle Wagam speech on January 27, 1956; Zaretsky "Silence Follows: Albert Camus in Algeria", *Critical Insights: Albert Camus*, 126.
1388 De Beauvoir, at Zaretsky "Silence Follows", 121.
1389 Camus, "The Host" in *EK*, 28–35.
1390 AC 23. See Carroll, *Camus the Algerian* 108: "[Camus's] refusal to support either the French or Arab side in the war, to be one of "us" or one of "them," left him in a political no-man's land, as isolated as the schoolteacher Daru at the end of "The Guest/Host." This point is also made by Tarrow, *Exile from the kingdom*, 183–4.
1391 AC 35.
1392 Letter to Jean Sénac of Feb. 1957, at Roger Quilliot, *Sea and Prisons: A Commentary on the Life and Works of Albert Camus* (USA: University of Alabama Press, 1976), 228.
1393 O'Brien, *Albert Camus*, 81; see James Le Sueur, *Uncivil War: Intellectuals and Identity Politics During the Decolonization* (US: University of Pennsylvania Press, 2001), 123–131.
1394 Michael Walzer, "Commitment and social criticism: Camus's Algerian war," *Dissent* (Fall 1984), pp. 424–432.
1395 At Robert Zaretsky, "Silence Follows: Albert Camus in Algeria" in Stephen G. Kellman ed. *Critical Insights: Albert Camus* (Pasadena, California: Salem Press, 2012), 117–131, at 130.
1396 Said, *Culture and Imperialism*, 166–67.

the traditions, idioms, and discursive strategies of France's appropriation of Algeria. He gives its most exquisite articulation, its final evolution to this massive 'structure of feeling' ":[1397]

> His clean style, the anguished moral dilemmas he lays bare, the harrowing personal fates of his characters, which he treats with such fineness and regulated irony: all these draw on and in fact revive the history of French domination in Algeria, with a circumspect precision and a remarkable lack of remorse or compassion.[1398]

The *loci classici* of this post-colonial criticism are well-established. Camus' *Outsider*, it is argued, "outs" the murderous unconscious of the *pied noir colon*'s occupation of Algeria: with Meursault callously killing an Arab on the beach.[1399] This Arab, unlike the whites in the story (Raymond, Celeste, Marie...), bears no name: as if he were "not quite a man... The reader does not quite feel that Meursault has killed a man. He has killed an Arab."[1400] The conceit that a European man should be tried and executed for killing an Arab paints the colonial legal system with a justice which it never practiced towards the colonised populations;[1401] or else the trial itself, truly a farce which sees Meursault's advocate having to remind the court that he is not on trial for his way of life or morality in general but for killing a man,[1402] redoubles the violent exclusion of the true stranger, the Arab, already perpetrated by Camus in withholding from him any name.[1403] Neither is *The Plague*, so often celebrated as the pinnacle of Camus' ethical writing, innocent of implication in colonial crime. Allegory though it may be (and an allegory for European fascism), it is after all set in the Algerian city of Oran, dated in the 1940s: and one of the characters, Rambert, is isolated in the quarantined city after being sent, as Camus was by *Combat*

1397 Said, *Culture and Imperialism*, 184.
1398 Said, *Culture and Imperialism*, 181.
1399 Cf. Carroll, *Camus, The Algerian*, 24.
1400 O'Brien, *Albert Camus*, 25–26.
1401 O'Brien, *Albert Camus*, 23: "[...] the presentation in this way of a court in Algeria trying a crime of this kind involves the novelist in the presentation of a myth: the myth of French Algeria. What appears to the casual reader as a contemptuous attack on the court is not in fact an attack at all: on the contrary, by suggesting that the court is impartial between Arab and Frenchman, it implicitly denies the colonial reality and sustains the colonial fiction."
1402 "'Is my client on trial for having buried his mother, or for killing a man?', he asked", S 60; cf. Carroll, *Camus the Algerian*, 28.
1403 Haddour, *Colonial myths*, 42–46.

in 1945, to report on the conditions of the Arabs in the city. No sooner has their plight been raised, however, than Camus repeats the kind of exclusion—O'Brien even goes so far as to say "final solution"[1404]—of the Arabs that he had practiced in *L'Étranger*:

> Now the curious thing is that, after having provided the occasion for this demonstration of integrity, the Arabs of Oran absolutely cease to exist. Their problems, including their health problems, had been sufficiently large and distinct to attract the visit of a reporter from 'a large Paris newspaper' but at that point they disappear.[1405]

The post-colonial criticism even provides us with a reading of Camus' darkest, most wilfully ambiguous text, *La Chute* of 1956, which promises to "put everything in its proper place,"[1406] like the uncanny laughter that the monologic protagonist Jean-Baptiste Clamence hears one night near the Pont des Arts. "It is not, I think, fanciful to relate [the] concept of limbo" which Clamence evokes to describe the fogs and canals of Amsterdam to "Camus's position on the struggle in his native Algeria." After all, as O'Brien continues:

> Torn between justice and his mother, Camus was drawn into a long hesitation which seemed to many like neutrality. Eventually, with the decision to put his mother first, he came by 1958 to support everything that was fundamental in the French Government's position [...] Clamence's paralysis on the bridge [in *The Fall* of 1956 thus] corresponds to that of his creator, before the conflicting call of what he had thought of as his country. The laughter which follows him, which 'put things in their proper places', is provoked by the discrepancy between what he has been saying [always talking of justice, as Clamence, a former defence lawyer, had so often done] and how he behaves ... He who had talked so much of justice must now abjure such language, since there is something he prefers to justice [his mother, per 1957s avowal]. The emergence of the ironical judge penitent prepared the way for a different view of life, more conservative and organic. Essentially Camus is beginning to take the side of his own tribe against abstract entities.[1407]

1404 O'Brien, *Albert Camus*, 48.
1405 O'Brien, *Albert Camus*, 45–46.
1406 F 39. "[I]t was a good, hearty, almost friendly laugh, which re-established the proper proportions"; cf. O'Brien, *Albert Camus*, 82.
1407 O'Brien, *Albert Camus*, 81–82.

Haddour's post-colonial reading of *La Chute* differs from O'Brien's in the letter, but neither in its spirit, nor its verdict of Camus' colonial guilt. If the novella (uniquely amongst Camus' work) is set in Northern Europe, this is because Camus is both wrestling with, and desperately trying to evade, his repressed colonialist's guilt concerning Algeria, after the outbreak of war: "The Algerian war which broke out on 1 November 1954 (a month after his visit to Holland) necessitated an exile in his fiction to the mire of Amsterdam."[1408] True, the novel contains an acerbic critique of bourgeois mendacity, hypocrisy, and egocentrism. It couples this with pointed commentary on Holland's colonial "whoring" in the Indonesian archipelago.[1409] But this alibi does not persuade Haddour: "Camus does not hesitate to attempt a critique of Dutch colonialism, yet the Algerian conflict is suppressed in his treatment of Holland and Java: the specificity of colonial difference is subsumed in the universality of a bourgeois sameness."[1410] For Haddour, *pace* O'Brien's prosecution, it is not the limbo of *La Chute*'s setting that speaks most loudly of Camus' well-meaning, but nonetheless fundamental political guilt. It is the novella's singular darkness: "... the darkness of *La Chute* can be attributed to Camus' realisation of the untenability of his own position [concerning Algeria]—his bitter awakening to his own hypocrisy..."[1411] The apparent biblical motif or motifs that lace the text, that is, should be read as one more false, ideological universalisation, alongside Camus' philosophical appeals to justice and solidarity, and his lyrical evocations of love or natural beauty. Beneath the enchanting, duplicitous surfaces, we should seek out the particular traumatic cause or crime. In truth, despite the appearances—and *in* the very absence of Algeria from Clamence's discourse (barring, arguably, one sentence)[1412]—*The Fall*'s mythology, philosophy or psychology when seen aright are all "... bound up with a narrative which is announcing the demise of French colonialism and the attendant political suicide of the *pied noirs*..."[1413]

1.2   Camus' Fall, *the Judge-Penitents, and the Mandarins*

It is not our task here to undertake the kind of point-for-point rebuttal of the post-colonial criticisms of Camus that has been undertaken by David Carroll in his important work *Albert Camus the Algerian*. Suffice it to say on this score,

---

1408 Haddour, *Colonial myths*, 70, 72.
1409 F 13–14.
1410 Haddour, *Colonial myths*, 76.
1411 Haddour, *Colonial myths*, 77.
1412 Cf. Haddour, *Colonial myths*, 76.
1413 Haddot, *Colonial Myths*, 77.

with Carroll, Margerrison and others, that the case for the prosecution is not as clear-cut as its advocates would have us believe. Here as elsewhere, Camus' identity as a Frenchman born to a poor *pied noir* family was fraught and his commitments divided: just as, as a thinker and a writer, his views were not simply assimilable to the absolute, all or nothing dichotomy of coloniser-colonised. "Camus's most severe postcolonial critics find nothing contradictory or impossible about his situation, however, and therefore do not just criticize the political inefficacy of his position but also treat it as a defence of colonialism itself."[1414] As Carroll stresses, from the start, Camus never questioned *whether* French colonialism should be opposed. He "tried in vain to sound the alarm" from 1939[1415] about France's legal, political, and economic "crimes" against "a people of impressive traditions, whose virtues are eminently clear to anyone willing to approach them without prejudice."[1416] The question for him was *how* this colonialism should be opposed: whether by reform and reparations, or revolution and collective expiation.[1417] Certainly, despite O'Brien et al.'s uncharitable suggestions, one cannot find anything like the bellicose or openly racist statements of a pro-fascist thinker like Heidegger in Camus. Consistently decrying "the general contempt in which the colonist holds the unhappy people of this country,"[1418] Camus praises at different points the courage, conscientiousness, friendliness, "legendary... thirst for learning and taste for study" of the native Algerians. In turn, he urges the French to ask "pardon for our feverish need for power, the natural bent of a mediocre people." The French can learn "lessons in dignity and justice" from this "wiser people".[1419] Camus' "*Message lu par Jean Amrouche à la Maison de la Chimie, le 18 Novembre 1946*" underscores what Camus' critique of the Western penchant for political messianisms (Chapter Two) would lead us to expect. Far from reproducing orientalist imputations concerning the "mystic East", Camus ironically assures his hearers that, just as he could not become a Moslem:

> ...I doubt that any amongst you assembled here could ever become this strange animal, unstable and unhinged (*démesuré*), avid to know and

---

1414 Carroll, *Albert Camus the Algerian*, 108–109.
1415 AC 23.
1416 AC 90.
1417 AC 31; cf. AC 27, 176
1418 AC 56.
1419 On the virtues of Arab and Berber populations, see Camus' testimony at AC 56, 59, 65, 70, 71, 82, 83, 90–91, 99, 103–4, 127, 157, 176, 182.

taste all, living off his contradictions and mad for an impossible knowledge that we call a European.[1420]

Equally, Said's attempt to position Camus' fiction as continuous with the French "schoolbooks from World War One to the period right after World War Two" as surveyed by Manuela Semidei wants clemency, to say the least.[1421] The presentation of the colonial legal system in the unusual case of Monsieur Meursault in *L'Étranger* is hardly a glowing advertisement for French colonial justice.[1422] Equally, even if we accept O'Brien et al.'s emphasis on Oran as the location of *La Peste*'s allegorical action, we saw in Chapter One that the "plague" in this novel lay as much, or more, in the regime's responses to the disease as in the disease itself.[1423] Finally, as we commented in Chapter Five, post-1962 criticisms of Camus' support for assimilation in the 1930s in light of the Evian accords run the risk of artificially reading our own standards back into a very different historical conjuncture. In an irony of history, Camus took fire from the French Right for over two decades after 1936 for the same positions

---

1420 Camus, "Message lu par Jean Amrouche à la Maison de la Chimie, le 18 Novembre 1946" OC II 689.
1421 Said, *Culture and Imperialism*, 179. Per Said's gloss of these schoolbooks: "Her findings show a steadily mounting insistence on France's colonial role after World War One, the 'glorious episodes' in its history as 'a world power,' as well as lyrical descriptions of France's colonial achievements, its establishment of peace and prosperity, the various schools and hospitals benefitting the natives, and so forth ... these interwar school texts favourably contrast France's superior colonial rule with Britain's, suggesting that French dominions are ruled without the prejudice and racialism of their British counterparts. By the 1930s this motif is endlessly repeated. When references are made to violence in Algeria, for example, they are couched in such a way as to render French forces having to take such disagreeable measures because of the natives' '*ardeur religieuse et par l'attrait du pillage*.'" It beggars credulity as well as clemency to associate Camus' fiction or journalism with such ideological documents: cf. Foley, *Camus, From the Absurd to Revolt*, 143–144. See esp. AC 59–64 for Camus' views on the glory, or rather the poverty, of the schools of the Kabylia region; AC 72–80 and 93–99 concerning France's 'benevolent' economic management and the colonial regime's responsibility for the famine of 1945.
1422 Carroll, *Albert Camus the Algerian*, 28–33. Cf. Tarrow, *Exile from the Kingdom*, 69–77: Meursault, Tarrow argues, this man as nearly-silent and inscrutable as the arabs that threateningly surround his circles of concern (if that is the word), is 'othered' or 'arabed' by his own society, a fact represented by his initial imprisonment amongst the arabs, who help him sympathetically. See esp. 76, 79–80.
1423 This suggests that the colonial regime is being targeted in *La Peste*, if we follow this line of reasoning.

that, after 1962, he would be condemned by post-colonial critics. As Carroll reminds us:

> Camus' view [from 1936 to circa-1945] is that only a noble, independent, self-aware people could be freely assimilated into the French people; only by remaining itself could it become other. [...] Today, this would be considered a multiculturalist position. In Algeria in 1939, it was considered a subversively anti-colonialist position [...][1424]

There can be no doubt that the 1950s were an extraordinarily difficult period for Albert Camus. Reading Camus' *Carnets* from around the end of 1951 onwards, for the first time one encounters what Spinoza called the sad passions: melancholia ("even my death will be contested ... yet what I most desire today is a quiet death, which would bring peace to those whom I love...");[1425] loneliness ("today,... my solitude overflows with shadows and works that belong only to me..."; "indeed, solitary from now on....");[1426] guilt ("I have the most dreadful opinion of myself, for days on end"); an acute sense of exile ("*Medea*: 'what a misfortune is the one of the man without a city!' ... I am without a city");[1427] and harrowing despair.[1428] A deeply important, revelatory note in April–May 1959 shows the extent of Camus' soul-searching, and longing for a personal renaissance:

> For almost five years (*sic.*) I have been critical of myself, of what I believed, of what I lived. This is why those who share the same ideas believe themselves to be the target, and bear such an immense grudge against me; but no, I wage war with myself and I will destroy myself, or I will be reborn, that is all.[1429]

The dating of this note is itself eloquent. There is no question that the war in Algeria, beginning 1 November 1954, was a prime cause of Camus' *malaise*. As he appealed to Azziz Kessous in his October 1955 open Letter, after nearly a

---

[1424] Carroll, *Albert Camus the Algerian*, 136. Compare Aronson on Camus' reportage of Sétif, at Ronald Aronson, *Camus and Sartre: The story of a friendship and the quarrel that ended it* (Chicago: Chicago University Press, 2004), 62.
[1425] C III 42; C III Eng 31.
[1426] C III 30; C III Eng 30.
[1427] C III 44; C III Eng 32.
[1428] See C III 62; C III Eng 49, examined below.
[1429] C III 267; C III Eng 247. Cf. Audi, *Qui témoignera*, 49.

decade of silence concerning his homeland: "Believe me when I tell you that Algeria is where I hurt at this moment, as others feel pain in their lungs."[1430] As Haddour rightly points out, it cannot be contingent that Clamence in *The Fall* recalls that the woman committing suicide on the Seine (whose cries he did not respond to, and whose memory Clamence repressed until a second, uncannily similar episode) fell from the Pont des Arts "one particular night in November":[1431]

> I was trembling, I believe from cold and shock. I told myself that I had to be quick and I felt an irresistible weakness steal over me. I have forgotten what I thought then. "Too late, too far…", or something of the sort. I was still listening as I stood motionless. Then, slowly under the rain, I went away. I informed no one.[1432]

The critical question is whether the post-colonial readings of Camus, with their exclusive focus on Camus' Algerian identity, do not represent an unjust judgment on his work. Carroll's verdict is perhaps hyperbolic when he writes: "I would even say that to judge and indict Camus for his 'colonialist ideology' is not to read him."[1433] Yet it raises a genuine concern about politicising reductionism here: particularly faced with such an over-determined, multi-layered text as *La Chute* of 1956, if not about all of Camus' literary and philosophical writings: "… it is not to treat [Camus'] … texts in terms of the specific questions they actually raise, the contradictions they confront, and the uncertainties they express."[1434]

In the specific case of *The Fall*, others of Camus' personal, spiritual and philosophical preoccupations can, quite simply, be shown to shape the text. These wider preoccupations intersect biographically and psychologically with Camus' Algerian "*angoisse*"[1435] following November 1954 (we know, in fact, that he wrote this text after his October 1954 visit to Amsterdam). But they are not reducible to its symptoms or veils. Without these preoccupations, the novella would be nothing like the extraordinarily rich, unsettling text we know which continues to speak to, entertain and trouble audiences ignorant of the Algerian *malaise* of its author. In particular, we will argue, *La Chute* speaks more directly

---

1430 AC 113.
1431 F 69. See Haddour, *Colonialist Mythology* 72.
1432 F 70.
1433 Carroll, *Albert Camus the Algerian*, 15.
1434 Carroll, *Albert Camus the Algerian*, 15.
1435 AC 151.

than any of Camus' literary texts since his unpublished first novel *La Mort Heureuse* to what we called in our Introduction the "second pillar" of Camus' identity as a *philosophe*: *viz*. Camus' concern with the Socratic question of how to live, and his own attempt to live an examined life, and assist others in their like attempts to live well.[1436]

We have skirted this second pillar of Camus' neoHellenic philosophical persona hitherto: most notably, in Chapter Four's stress on the biographical, passionate genesis of Camus' philosophical 'research program,' moving from questions concerning the absurd (and suicide) to the study of rebellion (and murder) after 1942. Above all, we approached its heart in the Concluding Remarks to Chapter Three, with the idea of Camus' thought "returning to its beginnings" in self-examination. Having now dialectically unfolded the key tenets of Camus' philosophical discourse, however, it is time to give its due to Camus' abiding concern with the formation of the self, and the persona and roles of the intellectual. To recall our structuring recourse to the Platonic cave allegory, in this *eikon* in the *Republic* the philosopher must "go back down" into her city to bring the Truths she has seen to her fellows, and the benefits therefrom. Just so, if it is asked what is the prescriptive corollary of Camus' philosophical neoHellenism unfolded in Chapter Five, we will answer that Camus believed reformed political laws and institutions (centring around the three-fold prohibition of rationalised killing, deceit and servitude (Chapter Four)) are necessary but insufficient for the second "renaissance" for which he hoped. Camus also believed that the West would need men and women of renewed, neoclassical virtues, culture, and "style[s] of life".[1437] At stake is what Camus called in his later *Carnets* an "everyday aristocracy (*aristocratie quotidienne*)"; models for which he sought in the lives and achievements of the artists and thinkers he admired; and whose excellences he aspired to cultivate in himself and inspire in his readers.[1438] In the 1950s, as Audi has invaluably examined, Camus felt compelled to return to this earliest and most abiding of his concerns after the greatest professional shock of his life, the bitter polemics surrounding *L'Homme Révolté*. *The Fall* and what we have of *The First Man* are the

---

1436 Unfortunately, we cannot deal with this novel here, and its anticipations and contributions to Camus' philosophical development. See for an excellent recent examination touching on these issues, George Strauss, "A Reading of Albert Camus' *Le Mort Heureuse*", in *Camus, Albert Critical Insights*, 147–169.
1437 Camus, "Un Style de Vie", OC II 673.
1438 C III 64; C III Eng 51.

fruits of this "war with myself,"[1439] goaded in particular by his bitter exchange with Sartre and *Les Temps Modernes* in 1952, as we will presently see.

The originality and complexity of Camus' *La Chute*, challenging any too-single minded hermeneutic, is attested by the divisions in the text's receptions. Camus' novella, alongside "The Renegade" in *Exile and the Kingdom*, foregrounds its own duplicity. It is set amidst the fogs of Amsterdam and the Zuider Zee, in pointed contrast to the clarity of Mediterranean light that fills nearly all of Camus' other pages.[1440] On the sixth and final day of our liaisons with the protagonist (there will be no Sabbath), this "Jean-Baptiste Clamence" disarmingly confesses to his longstanding practice of dissemblance:

> I know what you're thinking: it's very hard to disentangle the true from the false in what I'm saying. I admit you are right. I myself... But what do I care? Don't lies eventually lead to the truth? And don't all my stories, true or false, tend toward the same conclusion? Don't they all have the same meaning? So what does it matter whether they are true or false if, in both cases, they are significant of what I have been and of what I am? Sometimes it is easier to see clearly into the liar than into the man who tells the truth. Truth, like light, blinds. Falsehood, on the contrary, is a beautiful twilight that enhances every object...[1441]

The Fall's "abandonment of linearity and omniscience, but also the adoption of an interrogative and the allocation of a heightened role for the reader"[1442] has prompted some critics to see in the text a harbinger of later, postmodern literary experiments in the infinite dissemination of the signifier, without determinate final meaning. For Anne Varbonne, for example: "The text [of *La*

1439   C III 267; C III Eng 247.
1440   See F 12–15, 97–98.
1441   F 121. Truth, Clamence has elsewhere reflected, "is a colossal bore". F 101.
1442   Edmund J. Smyth, "Camus, the *Nouveau Roman* and the Postmodern" in *Originality and Complexity of Albert Camus' Writing*, 12. Cf. p. 14: "In *The Fall*, the playfully digressive structure of the dramatic monologue and direct interpellation of the reader brings the novel into line with some of the most formally radical contemporary novels." Contrast this with Said's criticism of Camus' alleged "realism", at *Culture and Imperialism*, 176: "Camus's writing is informed by an extraordinarily belated, in some ways incapacitated colonial sensibility, which enacts an imperial gesture within and by means of a form, the realistic novel, well past its greatest achievements in Europe." See for a comparable critique of the idea of Camus as an unrepentant realist (contested of course by Camus himself in "Rebellion and Art" in *The Rebel*), Aurélie Palud, "The Complexity and Modernity of *The Plague*", *Originality and Complexity of Albert Camus' Writing*, 19–34.

Chute] ... appears as a hybrid text that blends genres and discourses in order to unravel the functioning of the construction of the meaning of the subject and of the text."[1443] For other postmodern or post-structuralist critics, the text is self-reflexive, not simply in an autobiographical sense, but in the sense of a literary reflection upon (and enacting of) the impossibility of veridically representing the self, the world, or an historical calamity like the *Shoah*, indexed in the text by the location of Clamence's house in the Jewish quarter of Amsterdam, "cleaned out" by the Nazis in World War II.[1444] "*La Chute* is, among other things, a *mise en abyme* of the act of reading, a meditation on the potential and limitations of the written word."[1445]

At the opposite end of the hermeneutic spectrum, Christian authors have looked to *La Chute* above all to support their claims that, in the later 1950s, Camus was not far from awakening to grace. Far from flirting with a postmodern *délire* or sense of the impossibility of truthfully bearing witness, Camus' *The Fall* attests clearly the author's proximity to converting to Christianity.[1446] These critics, beginning from the novella's biblical title, can point to a host of evidences attesting to the depth of Camus' engagement with the Christian faith in this text. Do not the circular canals of Amsterdam, Clamence taunts us, call to mind the seven circles of Dante's Hell?[1447] This uncanny protagonist's very name, meanwhile, "Jean-Baptiste Clamence" calls to mind the voice in the wilderness announcing the arrival of the incarnated truth. Although the theme of guilt and innocence is a key register in *L'Homme Révolté* (recall that totalitarian regimes institute a total, 'objective' guilt in their populaces), this Augustinian preoccupation dominates *La Chute*. Guilt, for Augustine, accrues to human beings to extent that, after the fall, we cannot

---

1443 Emmanuelle Anne Varbonne, "Albert Camus's *The Fall*: The Vertiginous Fall into Language, Representation and Reality", in *Originality and Complexity*, 38.
1444 F 10–11: "Your hotel is on one of them, the Damrak. You first, please. I live in the Jewish quarter or what was called so until our Hitlerian brethren made room. What a cleanup! Seventy-five thousand Jews deported or assassinated; that's real vacuum-cleaning. I admire that diligence, that methodical patience! When one *has* no character one has to apply a method. Here it did wonders incontrovertibly, and I am living on the site of one of the greatest crimes in history."
1445 David R. Ellison, "Camus and the Rhetoric of Dizziness: *La Chute*," *Contemporary Literature* 24, no. 3 (1983): 325–26.
1446 Father Bernard C. Murchland, "The Dark Night before the Coming of Grace?", *Camus: A Collection of Critical Essays*; Richard H. Akeroyd, *Spiritual Quest of Albert Camus* (Alabama: Portals Press, 1976), 124. Cf. Alfred Cordes, *The Descent of the Doves: Camus' Journey of the Spirit* (Washington: University Press of America, 1980), esp. "The Ascent", 133–197.
1447 F 14–15.

help but sinfully love ourselves in place of God, as Camus had examined in his *Diplôme* thesis.[1448] But it is his own hidden duplicity and selfishness behind his apparent "glittering virtues" ("no one has anything of his own, except falsehood and sin" (Augustine))[1449] which Clamence discovers after his own "fall": " 'I, I, I' was my constant refrain".[1450] Despite avowing at the start of the fourth day that "I have no friends … only accomplices,[1451]" on the fifth day, Clamence calls Jesus "my friend." This part of *The Fall* contains Camus' most sympathetic passages concerning the "clemency" (viz. *clémence*) of the founder of Christianity, albeit couched like everything else, in "Clamence"'s squid ink of black irony: "He spoke softly to the adulteress: 'Neither do I condemn thee!' … He simply wanted to be loved, nothing more. Of course, there are those who love him, even among Christians. But they are not numerous…"[1452] Prompted by all this evidence, some Christian critics have asked, can we not hear the softening of Camus' own opposition to Christianity as a "religion of injustice" in Clamence's confessions?[1453] Who else could Clamence by referring to but Camus himself, when he declaims *en passant* about:

> … our moral philosophers, for instance, so serious, loving their neighbour and all the rest—nothing distinguishes them from Christians, except that they don't preach in churches. What, in your opinion, keeps them from becoming converted? Respect perhaps, respect for men; yes, human respect. They don't want to start a scandal, so they keep their feelings to themselves…[1454]?

Indeed, isn't Clamence's final recognition that "it's too late, it's always too late" to save the girl who jumped from the Pont des Arts[1455] not evidence that Camus' philosophical humility has given way to faith, more humble still?:

1448 CMN 120–123.
1449 At CMN 120.
1450 F 48.
1451 F 73.
1452 F 115.
1453 Alfred Cordes, *The Descent of the Doves: Camus' Journey of the Spirit* (Washington: University Press of America, 1980), esp. "The Ascent", 133–197; Akeroyd, *The Spiritual Quest of Albert Camus*; James W. Woelfel, *Camus: A Theological Perpsctieve* (Nashville, New York: Abingdon Press, 1975). Cf. Srigley, *Camus' Critique of Modernity*, 64.
1454 F 133–134.
1455 F 147. These are Clamence's last words in the bating monologue, whose irony, I suggest, we should remain on our guards about: "A second time, eh, what a risky suggestion! Just suppose, *cher maître*, that we should be taken literally? We'd have to go through with it.

There is a kind of rest possible when a situation has been accepted and defeat admitted: indeed this gives a kind of superiority... Saint-Exupéry spoke of the same principle: 'I thought myself to be lost, I believe I'd plumbed the very depths of despair but, once I'd resigned myself, experienced peace'.[1456]

Yet a third genus of interpretation of *The Fall* accepts many of the premises of these Christian analyses, but draw opposite conclusions.[1457] Robert Solomon recognised in the monologue's two halves, punctuated by Clamence's "fall" after the two uncanny episodes on the Seine, a near-Christian trajectory. He sees the Clamence of the first half of the story ("But just imagine, I beg you, a man at the height of his powers, in perfect health, generously gifted,... and fundamentally pleased with himself without showing this otherwise than by a felicitous sociability...")[1458] as a kind of Greek, pagan overman, uncorrupted by Christian self-mortification. After his 'fall', he begins to see himself through Christian eyes: as despicable.[1459] Ronald Srigley occupies a different, although similarly non-Christian position again. For him, *The Fall* responds in Camus' life to the trauma of his encounter with Sartre: for although "he had already won the debate with Sartre on the level of principle, there was something in his writings that justified Sartre's criticism nonetheless."[1460] According to Srigley, Camus had ceded too much ground to "modernity" still in *The Rebel*. So although that text (per Chapters Two and Five) traces the origins of totalitarian messianisms to the historical dimension introduced by the JudaeoChristian legacy, this critique left the foundations of such thinking untouched. *The Fall* then, interposed between the second cycle on revolt and the third cycle on love completes Camus' supposed double-critique of modernity and Christianity: "he explores this metaphysical unrest and its apocalyptic expressions as manifestations of a self-love that becomes deadly because it has been loosed from all forms of restraint."[1461] Contesting Solomon's reading, Srigley notes that

---

    Brr...! The water's so cold! But let's not worry! It's too late now. It will always be too late. Fortunately!"

1456 Akeroyd, *Spiritual Quest*, 58.
1457 And can cite several Camusian denials, for instance that in *Le Mode* of August 31 1956, rebutting suggestions he was rallying to the church: "rien vraiment ne les y authorise", at Pascal, "Camus, Philosophe malgré lui", 176.
1458 F 27.
1459 Robert Solomon, *Dark Feelings, Grim Thoughts: Experience and Reflection in Camus and Sartre* (Oford: Oxford University Press, 2006), 207–209. Cf. Srigley, *Camus' Critique*, 84–85.
1460 Srigley, *Camus' Critique*, 81.
1461 Srigley, *Camus' Critique*, 65.

Clamence does not give up on his self-love, when he discovers his new vocation as "judge-penitent" after his fall and his trials and tribulations attempting to come to terms with it (see anon). Instead, this singular new vocation sees him assuming a perversely gratifying sense of superiority over others, based on a claimed para-Augustinian insight into the universal, measureless guilt of all human beings:

> Believe me, religions are on the wrong track the moment they moralize and fulminate commandments. God is not needed to create guilt or to punish. Our fellow men suffice, aided by ourselves. You were speaking of the Last Judgment. Allow me to laugh respectfully. I shall wait for it resolutely, for I have known what is worse, the judgment of men. For them, no extenuating circumstances; even the good intention is ascribed to crime... Fortunately, *I* arrived! I am the end and the beginning: I announce the law. In short, I am a judge-penitent...[1462]

Srigley is at pains to contest the autobiographical dimension to *La Chute* which "most commentators," as he argues, have asserted.[1463] Srigley is certainly right that Clamence is *not* Camus, despite the propensity of critics, even in Camus' lifetime, to identify the two. Their lives, in many respects, seem pointedly opposed. In 1939–'45, for instance, Camus left Algeria, going to France and joining the resistance; Jean-Baptiste at this time fled Paris via the Southern Zone into North Africa (after rejecting the idea of joining the resistance as "a little mad") where he is imprisoned.[1464] Again, Clamence boasts of writing, in some of his darker hours, an *Apotheosis of the Guillotine*.[1465] Camus was soon to write "Reflections on the Guillotine", and resolutely argued against capital punishment from 1945 until his death.

If the *Carnets* are to be believed, Srigley is also correct to point to Camus' bruising encounter with Sartre and Jeanson concerning *L'Homme Révolté*, in locating the conception of Camus' darkest character of all, Jean-Baptiste Clamence. He goes too far, however, in opposing any autobiographical dimension to the text beyond this observation. For the personal, biographical effect of this event on Camus can scarcely be overstated: rather than its effect on Camus' philosophical discourse. Camus' shock at Jeanson's then Sartre's bold attacks motivates many of the comments from the *Carnets* cited above (which

---

1462 F 81, 87.
1463 Srigley, *Camus' Critique of Modernity*, 84–84.
1464 F 120–123.
1465 F 92–93.

date from 1951–1952), attesting to Camus' psychological anguish in this last decade of his life: "Polemic with *Temps Modernes*. Attacks 'Arts', 'Carrefour', 'Rivarol'. Paris is a jungle, and all the hounds are mangy," reads one note.[1466] Camus indeed attests at this time to a vivid sense of persecution, as if he were being run out of the city, or asked to strike out his eyes:

> ...every man and woman on me, to destroy me, seeking their share without respite, without ever lending a hand, coming to my aid, loving me finally for what I am so that I may remain what I am. They think my energy has no limits... but I have put all my strength in the exhausting passion to create, and for the rest, I am the most depraved and needy of beings.[1467]

The page preceding Camus' mention of Jeanson's (and kindred) attacks, we read, very significantly in terms of *The Fall*: "hell is here, to be lived. Only those who remove themselves from life escape."[1468] Such sentiments are extraordinary coming from the celebrated author of *L'Étranger* and *La Peste* (which sold around 100000 copies within 1947 alone), the celebrated editor of *Combat*, the glamorous Humphrey Bogart-lookalike, seducer and man of the theatre; the leading *gauche* intellectual and *littérateur* of post-war Paris; the man of whom the Sartre of 1952 could still write, amidst the most extraordinary public attack:

> You have been for us—and tomorrow you could be again—the admirable union of a person, an action, and a work...you were a *person*, the most complex and the richest, the last and most welcome heir of Chateaubriand, and the conscientious defender of a social cause...[1469]

Nevertheless, as we have challenged Srigley's reading of *L'Homme Révolté*,[1470] we think the *Carnets* also contest Srigley's argument for a break between this decisive philosophical text and the novella of 1956. In his invaluable work *Qui Témoignera pour nous? Albert Camus face à lui-meme*, Paul Audi has argued that, if we ask what exactly it *was* about Sartre and Jeanson's criticism of *The Rebel* that deeply hurt Camus, despite the arguable intellectual poverty

---

1466   C III 63; C III Eng 50.
1467   C III 38.
1468   C III 62; C III Eng 49.
1469   Sartre, "Reply to Albert Camus," in *Camus and Sartre: A Historic Confrontation*, 147. Cf. Aronson, *Camus and Sartre*, 183–185.
1470   See Chapter Two above.

of their criticisms, this answer lies in nothing so abstract as Srigley's 'incomplete critique of modernity.' First of all, it was the simple, personal betrayal Camus felt: that *Les Temps Modernes* could delay so long its reply and then that his friend Sartre could assign the case for the effective prosecution of his book to Francis Jeanson. "Pharisees of justice", the rawest note in the *Carnets* reads, announcing a biblical term with which Clamence will conjure.[1471] It ends: "Sartre, the man and the mind, betrayal (*déloyal*)."[1472] Second, after having soared above the judgment or condemnation of his contemporaries, for the first time Camus learnt palpably that people (even those he loved) would not laud each of his achievements or treat them with sympathy. As Audi comments, when Camus' anti-hero in *La Chute* reflects in the following terms after being "called" by the laughter on the Seine,[1473] we can also hear the angst of Clamence's creator after *Les Temps Modernes'* polemical prosecution of 1952:

> For a long time I had lived in the illusion of a general agreement, whereas, from all sides, judgments, arrows, mockeries rained upon me, inattentive and smiling. The day I was alerted I became lucid; I received all the wounds at the same time and lost my strength all at once. The whole universe then began to laugh at me.[1474]

Thirdly and taking all, Audi contends, Sartre's remarkable accusation: "you may have been poor, but you are no longer poor. You are a bourgeois, like Jeanson and I ..." had an effect on Camus that Sartre could scarcely have imagined.[1475]

1471 Cf. F 9: "Do you have any possessions? Some? Good. Have you shared them with the poor? No? Then you are what I call a Sadducee. If you are not familiar with the Scriptures, I admit that this won't help you. But it does help you? So you know the Scriptures? Decidedly, you interest me".

1472 C III 63; C III Eng 50.

1473 F 84 "From the evening when I was called—for I was really called—I had to answer or at least seek an answer ..."

1474 F 81. Cf. F 78, also adduced by Audi at *Qui Témoignera pour nous?*, 64: "My relations with my contemporaries were apparently the same and yet subtly out of tune. My friends hadn't changed. On occasion, they still extolled the harmony and security they found in my company. But I was aware only of the dissonances and disorder that filled me; I felt vulnerable and open to public accusation. In my eyes my fellows ceased to be the respectful public to which I was accustomed. The circle of which I was the centre broke and they lined up in a row as on the judge's bench. In short, the moment I grasped that there was something to judge in me, I realized that there was in them an irresistible vocation for judgment. Yes, they were there as before, but they were laughing ..."

1475 Sartre, "Reply to Albert Camus", 134.

This public interpellation as "bourgeois", amongst all of Sartre's invective ("you have become a counter-revolutionary,"[1476] etc.), touched Camus to the quick. For Camus—the son of a poor, illiterate, near-silent war widow, the first of his family to be schooled, let alone everything else—*had* indeed 'become who he was' only by coming "to incarnate the contrary of what his mother was... [:] a master of discourse."[1477] Like Clamence, then, who after hearing the *unheimlich* laugh, came for the first time to see himself as "double,"[1478] faced with Sartre's charges, Camus felt himself a little of his own "traitor,... philistine,... pharisee": someone who had indeed come close to betraying that "truth" of his origins we begun this last Chapter by invoking.[1479] Sartre again hit closer to his former friend's quick than he probably cared to imagine, when he derisively mocked Camus' alleged, self-perceived "mandate" in *L'Homme Révolté* and elsewhere: "if it's true that poverty sought you out and said: 'Go and speak in my name'..."[1480]

How was Camus to respond? His probity and brilliance, as Audi sees it, was to realise that to return fire with Sartre (as he had already replied to Jeanson), using the same medium of the polemical riposte was unlikely to have any effect, beyond escalating the histrionics. We know that Camus did draft (but not publish) a highly cogent "Defence of *The Rebel*" which contains some of the clearest statements of the philosophy of *mesure*, and an almost point-for-point rebuttal of his former friend's 'accusations'.[1481] Yet what Camus came acutely to see, reading and rereading Sartre's 'charges against him,' was how much academic writing, certainly in the Parisian milieu, participates in the same species of language game or "idiom"[1482] as the law-courts. It is a matter of passing *judgment*, naming friend and enemy, and on political matters, assigning innocence and guilt:

> Camus had very quickly understood—or at least, he had sensed—that to trade fire with his antagonists would be to do nothing more than participate (*partager*) in the same language: that is, a *judicial* language, that of the courtroom, the requisition, of pleading, sentencing, passing

---

1476 Sartre, "Reply", 132.
1477 Audi, *Qui Témoignera*, 49.
1478 F 9, 12, 40, 47,88 (in fact, double" is one of Jean-Baptiste's favorite words).
1479 Audi, *Qui Témoignera*, 48. See Camus, *First Man*, 228 (in an accompanying note): "O mother, forgive your son for having fled the night of your truth...."
1480 Satre, "Reply", 133.
1481 Camus, "Defence of *The Rebel*", in *Sartre and Camus: A Historic Confrontation*, 205–223.
1482 Audi, *Qui Témoignera* 64.

judgment, condemnation and acquittal... the intellectual trial (*procès intellectuelle*): that is, the trial of one intellectual by another intellectual.[1483]

The Fall, alongside "The Renegade," Audi argues, represents Camus' remarkable attempt to "change the terrain," rather than perpetuate the trial or counter-trial of his alleged, hopelessly complicit *"belle âme"*. The irony which had always been an essential element of his work would now take on a new, darker edge, verging into blank, black cynicism. It is as if, with *The Fall*, Camus responded to Sartre et al. in a way these others could never have anticipated, saying: *'so you would like to place me and my life on public trial, assign guilt and blame, and present me derisively as a 'divinely-mandated'*[1484] *Christian manqué;*[1485] *a "lawyer who says 'these are my brothers' "*[1486] *to the poor and deserving, "because these words stand the best chance of making the jury weep";*[1487] *or even "the Chief Prosecutor" in "the Republic of Beautiful Souls"*[1488] ... *Well then! Let me introduce you to Jean-Baptiste Clamence, a man almost too perfectly "in harmony" with himself, to paraphrase your collaborator;*[1489] *if not the Chief Prosecutor then an heroic defence Lawyer for "widows and orphans";*[1490] *a model of seeming charity, humility, courtesy, liberality and virile natural sensuality who, in truth (and just as you say), has "other motivations":*[1491] *a figure who, like the portrait you paint in your Prosecution of the author of* The Rebel, *is at once me and not me; like a moving image that goes in and out of focus, passing from truth to parody almost imperceptibly, with the seeming aim of blending the two vertiginously in the minds of readers...'*[1492]

Despite Srigley's protestations, there can be no doubt that there is in *The Fall* an autobiographical strata or stratas: Camus' guilt concerning his marital infidelities and almost-compulsive Don Juanism; his sense of duplicity and of not being the wholly-noble, upright man he had widely been taken to be (Camus reports losing faith in his "star" after *The Rebel* controversies: "Each

---

1483 Audi, *Qui Témoignera*, 63–64.
1484 Sartre, "Reply", 133.
1485 Sartre, "Reply", 134.
1486 Sartre, "Reply", 133–134.
1487 Sartre, "Reply," 134.
1488 Sartre, "Reply," 137.
1489 Jeanson, "The Soul in Revolt", 82.
1490 F 17.
1491 Sartre, "Reply," 134.
1492 Cf. Aronson, *Camus and Sartre*, 192–198; also Tony Judt, *The Burden of Responsibility: Blum, Camus, Aron, and the French Twentieth Century* (Chicago: Chicago University Press, 1998), 104.

time someone tells me that they admire the man in me, I have the impression of having lied all my life.")[1493] This is in no way to deny the mythical or religious registers we have already mentioned in this novella set in the seventh circle of a secular hell;[1494] in a bar peopled by a virtual Darwinian "first man", the proprietor-'gorilla';[1495] spoken by a self-chosen-prophet without clemency whose patronym is "Clamence", the confessed thief of *The Just Judges* by Van Eyck[1496] who, by the end, seems to be almost begging us to condemn him or hand him over to the police.[1497] Nor is it to deny the Algerian referent behind the uneven Dutch facades of *The Fall*; and Camus' growing anguish concerning the escalating violence and disappearance of all prospect of a federal, multi-cultural solution in his homeland. Yet Clamence's disarming power, of all of Camus' protagonists, comes from how Camus the man was wrestling in this book, very intimately, with (Sartre *dixit*) his own sense of "mandate" as a thinker and as a writer: and pitting his own sense of this task against his disillusioned sense of the Parisian intellectual cave, and the persona of the kind of philosopher embodied by his former friend, Jean-Paul Sartre. Clamence, that is, is not simply a double of Camus, as he saw himself in his darkest hours. He is also, even more so, an uneven mirror-image of how Camus came to see Sartre and the contemporary Parisian intellectual mandarins.

Again, the *Carnets* are the indispensable guide here. For it is again not first in *The Fall* itself, but in Camus' notebooks in the weeks and months surrounding *The Rebel* polemics, that we find *La Chute*'s key claims concerning Clamence's secularised prophetism emerging. "T.M. [*Temps Modernes*] they

---

1493 C III 81; C III Eng 67.
1494 F 14.
1495 F 3–4. "There, I dare hope he understood me; that nod must mean that he yields to my arguments. He is taking steps; indeed, he is making haste with prudent deliberation. You are lucky; he didn't grunt. When he refuses to serve someone, he merely grunts. No one insists. Being master of one's moods is the privilege of the larger animals.... You are right. His silence is deafening. It's the silence of the primeval forest, heavy with threats. At times I am amazed by his obstinacy in snubbing [4] civilized languages. His business consists in entertaining sailors of all nationalities in this Amsterdam bar, which for that matter he named—no one knows why—Mexico City. With such duties wouldn't you think there might be some fear that his ignorance would be awkward? Fancy the Cro-Magnon man lodged in the Tower of Babel! He would certainly feel out of his element. Yet this one is not aware of his exile..." See Haddour, *Colonial Myths*, 66–67.
1496 F 128–9. See Burton W. Wheeler, "Beyond Despair: Camus' *The Fall* and Van Eyck's 'Adoration of the Lamb'", *Contemporary Literature* vol. 23, no. 3 (Summer 1982), 343–364.
1497 F 146. See the alternative endings, where this *fin* in fact is entertained by Camus, at OC III 768–770.

admit sin and refuse grace. Thirst for martyrdom," Camus notes.[1498] Here, we can see the genesis of Clamence's symptomatic generalisation of his own sense of guilt (see below) into the strident enunciation of an Augustinianism without grace:[1499]

> For it cannot be said there is no more pity; no, good Lord, we never stop talking of it. Simply, no one is ever acquitted any more. On dead innocence the judges swarm, the judges of all species, those of Christ and those of the Antichrist, who are the same anyway... For one mustn't blame everything exclusively on the Christians. The others are involved too.[1500]

Again: "T.M. [*Temps Modernes*] polemic—knavery. Their sole excuse is in this terrible time. Finally, in them something aspires to servitude. They dream of going there by some noble pathway, full of thoughts. But there is no royal path to servitude. There is cheating, insult, denunciation of the brother. After that, the sound of thirty derniers."[1501] Here, again, we recognise the antecedence of Clamence's "Copernican turn" in *La Chute*: the notion, giving expression to a near-unconscious self-loathing,[1502] that "to get everyone involved in order to have the right to sit calmly on the outside oneself [sic.]," one should not simply declaim others' sins from on high (risking being rightfully denounced oneself):

> Well, here's the stroke of genius. I discovered that while waiting for the masters with their rods, we should, like Copernicus, reverse the reasoning to win out. Inasmuch as one couldn't condemn others without immediately judging oneself, one had to overwhelm oneself to have the right to judge others. Inasmuch as every judge some day ends up as a penitent, one had to travel the road in the opposite direction and practice the profession of penitent to be able to end up as a judge...[1503]

1498   C III 62; C III Eng 49.
1499   See Camus, "Defence of *The Rebel*", 217: "nor, on the contrary, like others—Jansenists without God—by restoring universal sin without the compensation of grace, and in an excess of penitence without charity, mortifying themselves by adhering to that which denies them..."
1500   F 116.
1501   C III 64; C III Eng 51.
1502   C II 226 ("L'impression de culpabilité chez les intellectuels séparés du peuple. Le 'gentilhomme repentant' (du péché social)." (C II Eng 116).
1503   F 137–138.

Upon reading de Beauvoir's *Mandarins* in December 1955, the *Carnets* show how the ultimate term was added: "Existentialism. When they accuse themselves, one can be sure that it is always to crush others. Judge-penitents." (We recall Sartre's "You are a bourgeois, *like Jeanson and I*")[1504] *Incipiat Jean-Baptiste Clamence*:

> Covered with ashes, tearing my hair, my face scored by clawing, but with piercing eyes, I stand before all humanity recapitulating my shames without losing sight of the effect I am producing, and saying: 'I was the lowest of the low.' Then imperceptibly I pass from the 'I' to the 'we.' When I get to 'This is what we are,' the trick has been played and I can tell them off. I am like them, to be sure; we are in the soup together. However, I have a superiority in that I know it and this gives me the right to speak. You see the advantage, I am sure. The more I accuse myself, the more I have a right to judge you. Even better, I provoke you into judging yourself, and this relieves me of that much of the burden. Ah, *mon cher*, we are odd, wretched creatures, and if we merely look back over our lives, there's no lack of occasions to amaze and horrify ourselves. Just try. I shall listen, you may be sure, to your own confession with a great feeling of fraternity.[1505]

Srigley is thus right to stress Camus' arguing here, very clearly, for the "secularising" link between Augustinian Christianity ("They have hoisted him [Jesus] onto a judge's bench, in the secret of their hearts, and they smite, they judge above all, they judge in his name")[1506] and a species of modern philosophy: in this case, a Sartrean existentialism making its peace first with Stalinism, and soon enough with Maoism. Yet, at the same time as we cannot accept any interpretation which suggests that Clamence's blanket decrial of universal guilt should be read as Camus' own; neither do we agree that Camus' plumbing of Clamence's knavery bespeaks a break between *La Chute* and *L'Homme Révolté*'s key claims. Recall that in Chapter Two we argued that, given Camus' critiques of the modern total ideologies, these could be systematically presented as so many, paralogical responses to the protasis: "If natural and human evil seem necessary to God or in nature, His creation, *then* ... " Each, in response to this protasis, was drawn to accept the legitimacy of murder on the basis of casting, indefensibly, an "all or nothing" judgment on the world: "then God is dead ... historical struggle alone is real ... the world is will to power and

---

1504 C III 147; C III Eng 131. See Aronson, *Camus and Sartre*, 179.
1505 F 140.
1506 F 115.

nothing else...," etc. At stake, that is, was the kind of longing for absolution that the "confused spirit" of "The Renegade" professes in a moment of lucidity, in the story Camus confided to Grenier aimed to represent "... the intellectual turned communist... who ends up adoring the religion of evil".[1507] According to this kind of logic, the (merely) 'better' is truly the enemy of the Good: a situation which makes the decisive clarity of opting for "diabolical evil"[1508] alone seem authentic, and all mediation, moderation and compromise a hopelessly "bourgeois" betrayal:

> I had been misled, solely the reign of malice was devoid of defects, I had been misled, truth is square, heavy, thick, it does not admit distinctions, good is an idle dream, an intention constantly postponed and pursued with exhausting effort, a limit never reached, its reign is impossible. Only evil can reach its limits and reign absolutely, it must be served to establish its visible kingdom, then we shall see, but what does 'then' mean, only evil is present, down with Europe, reason, honour, and the cross...[1509]

In the same way, Clamence's villainy in *The Fall* lies in his absolutising response to the protasis delivered to him by the laughter on the Seine, undermining his pretentions of being a truly *honnête homme*: "if I am guilty/hypocritical/'fallen', then..." Nobody if not an "all or nothing" thinker, Clamence infers improbably: "if I am guilty, then all are guilty." The "leap" here, foregrounded by Clamence's own attention to his pronouns,[1510] is from "I" to "we": a more personal, pronominal affair than the kinds of paralogism we saw operating in *The Rebel*'s forms of absolute, violent affirmation and negation. "I didn't want their esteem because it wasn't general...," Clamence tells us at one point:[1511] as if, despite

---

1507 Quoted in Orme, *Development of Albert Camus' Concern*, 262, n. 4; Parker, *Artist in the Arena*, 160. See Newmark, "What Camus' Fiction couldn't teach us", 119, and the brilliant observation that the wholly angular city of salt the 'Confused Spirit' is sent to convert "resembles nothing so much as Paris or New York..."
1508 Cf. Slavoj Žižek, *Plague of Fantasies* (London: Verso, 1997); cf. my "Of Diabolical Evil and Related Matters", *Journal of Žižek Studies* 3: 3 (2009), 1–24; Sharpe & Boucher, *Žižek and Politics*, 105, 121–2, 125–127.
1509 Albert Camus, "The Renegade", in *Exile and the Kingdom* trans. Justin O'Brien (New York: Random House, 195), 54.
1510 And of course, the vocatives: Clamence artfully, subtly changes the way he addresses his interlocutor and us as we go, until the 6th day: *Monsieur* (I), *cher monseiur* (II), *mon cher compatriote* (III), *cher ami* (IV), *cher ami, trés cher, mon ami* (V), to a final *cher maître* (day VI, towards the end)—at which point, as it were, the trap is sprung.
1511 F 93.

Kojeve's comparable leap, a non-universal satisfying esteem was not both possible and itself a general thing. "In order to forestall the laughter" at his shortcomings, Jean-Baptiste confesses: "I dreamed of hurling myself into the general derision":[1512] as if there was no other, less melodramatic or "adolescent"[1513] way of confronting one's imperfections. "After prolonged research on myself," Clamence announces his 'method': "I brought out the fundamental duplicity of the human being": as if a sample of one, looked at in the light of a wounded narcissism, were a valid basis to infer concerning human nature *per se*.[1514] The result of all these flattering paralogisms is a kind of perversion of Camus' ideal of solidarity in *The Rebel*: a "we are," but the "we are" of universal guilt or slavery: "I have no more friends; I have nothing but accomplices. To make up for this, their number has increased; they are the whole human race."[1515] In fact, Clamence's universe, the universe of the Judge-Penitent, is the "universe of the trial" we saw for Camus adequately described the totalitarian universe: "when we are all guilty, there will be democracy":[1516] "the others get theirs too, and at the same time as we—that's what counts. All together at last, but on our knees and with our heads bowed":[1517] Clamence alone soaring high above, since he at least knows his own guilt, and shouts it from his later modern mountaintop, perched on his bar-stool at the *Mexico City*. Clamence is, par excellence, the new kind of European philosopher who philosophises not with a hammer, but (given half the chance) with the "ammunitions" of "Helen's Exile":

> For instance, you must have noticed that our old Europe at last philosophizes in the right way. We no longer say, as in simple times: "This is the way I think. What are your objections?" We have become lucid. For the dialogue we have substituted the communiqué: "This is the truth," we say. "You can discuss it as much as you want; we aren't interested. But in a few years there'll be the police who will show you we are right."[1518]

The Fall, in and beneath its many layers, is a continuous development and psychological deepening of Camus' 'master argument' in *The Myth of Sisyphus* and

---

1512 F 91.
1513 HR 382; R 306; see Jeanson, "To tell you everything", *Sartre and Camus, An Historic Confrontation*, 197.
1514 F 84. See Jean Sarrochi, "Les Fureurs adolescents", in *Les Extrêmes et l'équilibre*, 3–17.
1515 F 73.
1516 F 136.
1517 F 136.
1518 HE 151; F 45.

The Rebel. It gives all the weight and colour of a fictional, semi-autobiographical life to Camus' claim that "there is undoubtedly an evil which men accumulate in the desire for unity," and that this evil is a particular vocational hazard of the life of the mind.[1519] Of course, Clamence indicates by the end that his is far from the "perfect solution",[1520] as against for instance hearing the oddly "benevolent" call of the mocking laughter to greater, genuinely repentant self-awareness.[1521] He too is a philosophical suicide and a 'leaper', who wants to take as many others down with him as he can. "I am happy—," he thus in effect *warns* us, protesting too much: "I am happy, I tell you, I won't let you think I'm not happy, I am happy unto death!"[1522] Or, to quote Camus in *The Rebel* again:

> 'The human being needs happiness, and when he is unhappy, he needs another human being'. Those who reject the agony of living and dying wish to dominate. 'Solitude is power,' says Sade. Power, today, because for thousands of solitary people it signifies the suffering of others, bears witness to the need for others. Terror is the homage that the malignant recluse finally pays to the brotherhood of man...[1523]

1.3 For a Civil Truce: The Post-Prophetic Philosopher as Stand-in and Mediator

The long history of Western philosophy has seen many *personae*, social and political roles assigned to its philosophers: from Heraclitus leaving his gnomic utterances on the steps of the Temple in Ephesus to today's conference-going and multi-publishing professional. Martha Nussbaum, in an article from the turn of the millennium, has argued for four paradigms of the philosopher in politics, drawn from the ancient schools and the modern liberal tradition. These are, respectively, the Platonic philosopher who, ideally, would bring his recondite knowledge to the levers of government itself (the philosopher-King); the Aristotelian philosopher, more grounded in empirical researches, who presents himself and his proposals as an advisor to existing rulers, and educator of the future governing classes; the Stoic philosopher counsellor, bringing a new moral universalism, sophisticated moral psychology and therapeutic metaphilosophy to the poleis; and the liberal philosopher, formulating

---

[1519] HR 378; R 303.
[1520] F 144 (or "ideal").
[1521] F 96: "its benevolent, almost tender quality that hurt me..."
[1522] F 144.
[1523] HR 308–309; R 248. Compare: " 'Obey', said Frederick the Great to his subjects, but when he died his words were: 'I am tired of ruling slaves.' ", at HR 313; R 251.

and advocating policy proposals in a multi-cultural public sphere, awake to the irreducible plurality of ways of life, and "without claiming for [her proposals] the backing of a comprehensive view of ethical or cosmological truth."[1524]

Nussbaum's categorisation is probably not intended to be exhaustive, and its schematisation can be questioned. Already in Plato and Xenophon, we find in the "eleatic stranger" (or the Simonides of the *Hiero*) instances of the wise "Aristotelian" advisor to would-be princes or tyrants. More importantly for us here, with an eye to Jean-Baptiste Clamence and the quasi-prophetic figure of the "judge-penitent," Plato and the Greeks were already familiar with a further, august model of the philosopher as Lycurgian regime-founder or Solonic Law-giver: a political role many philosophers up to Rousseau and beyond have continued to eye with *envie*. Plato's disputes with the poets and sophists equally reflect his lively, post-Gorgianic awareness of the power of persuasive speech to found and shape public opinion, like a political architect or prophet. Philosophy, like the Western theological tradition to which it contributed many categories, long claimed a privileged epistemic status as 'queen of the sciences' or 'science of sciences'. As Nussbaum's Rawlsian qualification concerning the contemporary philosopher's claiming any "comprehensive" perspective reflects, however, in the modern period the natural sciences' increasing separation from philosophical or theological supervision, together with the proliferation of social sciences primed to take on Nussbaum's "Aristotelian" role of formulating concrete policy to power, has engendered a continuing crisis of philosophy's public and private roles.

The angloamerican, analytic tradition of the 20th century has tried, in large measure, to operate on the basis of the unquestioned authority of the natural sciences: seeking to address, using reason alone, whatever questions recalcitrant to scientific inquiry remain; to clarify the sciences' conceptual and other presuppositions; and to critically expose the erroneous sources of human beings' continuing propensities to ask and try to answer undecidable questions. One style of continental theorising represented pre-eminently by Martin Heidegger (but continued today by Agamben, Badiou, Žižek and others), by contrast, has challenged the sciences' claims to absolute or relative epistemic authority. In the same breath, it more or less totally critiques the social sciences' worth and regnancy in shaping public policy, and calibrating intellectual inquiry to the apparati and demands of modern government. In lieu of its traditional functions of understanding the whole, including nature; or of prescribing norms or educating the next generations of the best and brightest, the point is, this philosophising has gravitated repetitively

---

1524 Martha Nussbaum, "Four Paradigms of Philosophical Politics", *Monist* (2000), 487.

towards fascination with the kinds of transcendental messianic Acts, Events, Destinings or Revolutions which would entirely overthrow existing modes and orders (see Chapter Five). Contemporary regimes, with equal inevitability, are presented as more or less wholly moribund, world-less; and founded on and sustained by illegitimate violences rationalised by appeals to high-sounding ideals. No more than Camus' Jean-Baptiste Clamence (less gadfly than barfly at the *Mexico City*) have such philosophers or their students withdrawn into the desert. Accelerating confusion about the functions of the University and humanities, and the dethroning of philosophy and theology, have threatened to turn these disciplines into their own kinds of extramural deserts, relative to the shaping of public life. In such transcendental isolation, the temptation to take on the mantle of prophet, casting down imbrications upon the "thoughtless" later modern "nest of vipers" ("animals of the city",[1525] "society of the spectacle",[1526] etc.), while awaiting "the masters with their rods," as Jean-Baptiste would rejoin, is less inspired than all-too-human.[1527]

Camus' critics have widely noted the significance of the fact the *La Chute* and "The Renegade" are Camus' only two fictions presented in the form of a monologue. This, before anything else, is an unmistakable index that these "confessions" are to be read critically or ironically. "Plato is right and not Moses and Nietzsche," we recall *The Rebel* critiquing the form of prophetic, monologuic utterance (Chapter Four); just as *The Fall* dramatises the kind of spiritual-psychological *malaise* underlying the longing to lay down or seek out such discourses of the master.[1528] What then is the role of the philosopher in a post-metaphysical dispensation, and a world wherein powerful epistemic, ethical and political reasons speak against the prospects of voices crying in the wilderness, conjuring with wholesale messianic redemption?

We have seen how Camus' critics in the post-colonial literature have, in their manner, posthumously tried and found him guilty of complicity in the colonial crimes of the French nation in Algeria.[1529] This condemnation is as much a collective as an individual judgment. For these critics, the post-Evian expulsion of over one million French *pied noirs, en masse*, from Algeria was

---

[1525] Alain Badiou, *Ethics: An Essay on the Understanding of Evil*, trans. P. Hallward (London, Verso, 2002), 51.
[1526] Agamben, *Homo Sacer*, 11–13, 52, 120–121, 187–188.
[1527] F 138.
[1528] HR 354; R 283–4.
[1529] For a recent assessment of this kind, see Orme's section "Dialogue of the Deaf: Camus' Algerian Monologue" in *The Development of Albert Camus' Concerns*, 185–196, whose title indicates Orme's judgment.

the only and evident way to restore justice to the Arab and Berber populations of North Africa. Every member of this French Algerian population, by virtue of their birth, shared in the objective colonial guilt: even if we can admit that some were "well intentioned colonisers," in Memmi's phrase, and that many of them (as Camus protested) were amongst the most disadvantaged of French subjects, not "whip-wielding, cigar-chomping colonists driving around in Cadillacs".[1530] Equally, only advocacy for such a European depopulation of Algeria and complete support for whatever means were necessary to bring this about could have been legitimate, in 1935 as in 1960:

> ...there was always the more difficult and challenging alternative of first judging, then refusing France's territorial seizure and political sovereignty, blocking as it did a compassionate, shared understanding of Algerian nationalism, [so] Camus's limitations seem unacceptably paralysing...[c]ounterpoised with the decolonizing literature of the time, whether French or Arab—Germaine Tillion, Kateb Yacine, Fanon, or Genet....[1531]

We saw previously Camus' political position: increasingly aware of political defeat, Camus moved from advocating full republican assimilation (in the 1930s) of the Arab population, to recommendations (in the 1940s and 1950s) for a federal French-Arab Algeria, eventually on the model of the Lauriol plan. "I, for one, believe only in differences, not uniformity," Camus wrote, sounding in advance the keynote of liberal forms of postmodernism: "because differences are the roots without which the tree of liberty withers and the sap of creation and civilisation dry up."[1532] At no point, we saw, did Camus question France's culpability and the systematic injustice of colonial super-exploitation: "the era of colonialism is over, and the only problem now is to draw the appropriate consequences."[1533] No one questions that, in the court of historical outcomes, Camus' 1950s attempts to influence affairs, and to mediate between the

---

1530 AC 115; Albert Memmi, *The Colonizer and the Colonized* with an Introduction by Jean-Paul Sartre (USA: Beacon Press, 1991).
1531 Said, *Culture and Imperialism*, 185.
1532 AC 153.
1533 AC 31. In 1945, indeed, he felt it necessary to remind his continental French readers in *Combat* "that Algeria exists"; and that present French policy was contributing to the political and economic immiseration of a people "that too many French people in Algeria and elsewhere imagine as a shapeless mass without interests." (AC 90–91, compare bottom of AC 126). In the light of these statements, the repeated claims of critics that Camus did not recognise the realities of colonialist, structural oppression seem invalid. See e.g.

colonialist ultras and the growing Algerian independence movement, backed after 1954 by the Parisian *Marxissant* Left, roundly failed:

> ... finding it impossible to join either of the camps, recognising the gradual disappearance of the third camp in which it was still possible to keep a clear head, doubtful of my own certitudes and knowledge, and convinced that the true cause of our follies is to be found in the way in which our intellectual and political society habitually operates.[1534]

What concerns us here is what Camus' attempts at political engagement reveal about his conception of what we might call the "post-prophetic" public intellectual. The first point here again, as with *La Chute*, is to contest claims that Camus gave up on the political principles of *L'Homme Révolté*, in this case due to his partisan commitment to the *pied noirs*. Camus opposed the kinds of Manichean declamations of the "historic state of sin" accruing to the entire *pied noir* population, according to the same conceptions that pitted him against the totalitarian "universe of the trial," with its Orwellian notion of the 'objective guilt' of classes, populations, minorities... "The idea of acknowledging guilt as our judge-penitents do, *by beating the breasts of others*, revolts me," Camus writes in his 1958 "Preface" to his *Algerian Chronicles*, again with the Parisian intellectual milieu squarely in his sights: "they would do better to offer themselves up."[1535] Given a comprehensive enough view of history, Camus notes, no nation is "holy and pure": which robs France's critics of reasons to single out her crimes alone as demanding total expiation.[1536] Here as elsewhere, though, it is necessary to immediately add to this the *envers*. For Camus at the same time categorically condemned the murderous barbarism of French reprisals for FLN attacks and the use of torture, in words of uncanny contemporaneity:

> The reprisals against the civilian population of Algeria and the use of torture against the rebels are crimes, for which we all bear a share of responsibility. That we have been able to do such things is a humiliating reality that we must henceforth face. Meanwhile, we must refuse to justify these methods on any grounds whatsoever, including effectiveness. Once one

---

Aronson's claims at *Camus and Sartre*, 188–190, 219 (for only one, more moderate critic on this issue). AC 90–91. Or compare bottom of AC 126.

1534 AC 24.
1535 AC 31.
1536 AC 31.

begins to justify them, directly or indirectly, no rules or values remain. One cause is as good as another, and pointless warfare, unrestrained by the rule of law, consecrates the triumph of nihilism... Can a method really be 'effective' if its result is to justify the very crimes that we seek to fight?... 'It may have cost us something in the way of honour,' they say, 'but it saved lives by leading to the discovery of 30 bombs.' But it also created 30 new terrorists, who will employ different tactics in different places and cause the deaths of still more innocents...[1537]

As Carroll has stressed, it was Camus' principled argument against any political, philosophical or theological vindications of murder that prevented him from being able to condone the actions of the FLN. This remained so, even as he increasingly saw their revolt as vindicated (if not their conception of its goals)[1538]—and vindicated precisely by the injustices, intransigence and increasing inhumanity of the French powers. In Carroll's words: "it was primarily his disgust at and refusal to accept all justifications for the murder of civilians during the Algerian War that made it impossible for him to support either side, even the side that had justice on its side."[1539] In Camus' words in *The Rebel*: "Does the end justify the means? That is possible. But what will justify the end? To that question, which historical thought leaves pending, rebellion replies: the means."[1540] Camus' infamous remark "I believe in justice, but I will defend my mother before justice," in this light, represents (contra Waltzer or O'Brien) no shift in Camus' position towards a passionate, prerational parochialism.[1541] As Camus' preceding comments which frame this statement make very clear, the "justice" Camus was considering here was one which licensed killing civilians in spectacular attacks. As such, the author of *L'Homme Révolté* could not support its kind anywhere: "I have always condemned terror. I must also condemn the blind terrorism that can be seen in the streets of Algiers, for example, which someday might strike my mother or family." Camus believed in and fought for "the infinite force of justice" as he saw it.[1542] But he would also

---

1537 AC 26.
1538 Orme quotes Camus, reported by Herbert Lottman: "It's true I wasn't shocked by the resistance to the Nazis, because I was French and my country was occupied. I should accept the Algerian resistance, too, but I'm French", at *Development of Camus' Concerns*, 190.
1539 Carroll, *Albert Camus the Algerian*, 89–90. Compare Foley, *Camus: From the Absurd to Revolt*, 171–172; Zaretsky, *Elements of a Life*, 6.
1540 HR 365; R 292.
1541 Cf. Walzer, "Commitment and social criticism: Camus's Algerian war," *Dissent* (Fall 1984), 424–432; O'Brien, *Albert Camus*, 82.
1542 AC 112.

always insist after 1945 that "no cause justifies the killing of innocent people," whether in Algeria, Hungary, or France.[1543] Evoking Socrates, he maintained that "even when it comes to winning wars, it is better to suffer certain injustices than to commit them."[1544]

In an important series of articles of late 1955 in *L'Express*, Camus accordingly appeals to what he terms a "law of the intellect" to oppose the "casuistry of blood" increasingly reigning in Algeria: the "infernal dialectic"[1545] wherein each side to the conflict justified its crimes by pointing to the wrongs of its foes.[1546] This law of the intellect, beyond historicism:

> ... dictates that, although one must never cease to demand justice for the oppressed, there are limits beyond which one cannot approve of injustice committed in their name ... Otherwise, the relative notions of innocence and guilt that guide our action would disappear in the confusion of general criminality.[1547]

It is therefore with Camus' philosophy of limits from *The Rebel* squarely in mind (licensing violence only in cases of self-defence, when all peaceable means are exhausted, and never targeting non-combatants (Chapter Four)) that his much-maligned attempt to sue for a "civilian truce" between the two sides needs to be understood. Camus confided in October 1955's open Letter to Aziz Kessous that he was fully aware of the prospect of receiving "only laughter and the din of the battlefield" in reply for this plea, after the battle of Philippeville in August 1955 (and massive French reprisals) had irreversibly escalated the violence.[1548] Yet at this point, what we might term a self-reflective register of Camus' notion of *mesure* intervenes: one touching on what can be asked and expected of the post-metaphysical intellectual in the political arena. Such a thinker can no longer present themselves as a prophetic figure, whether armed or unarmed: the luminous 'great thinker' or 'master of conscience' who 'has all the answers,' capable of categorically assigning innocence and guilt, and calling down assassinations or mass expropriations. In a situation of violent,

---

1543 AC 152; AC 215.
1544 AC 26. For the Socratic (and Montaignian) precedent in Camus' Algerian attempts, see Roger Quilliot, "Albert Camus' Algeria", in *Camus: A Collection of Critical Essays*, 44. Cf. AC 26.
1545 AC 28, 153; "a bloody marriage of terrorism and repression", AC 153; cf. AC 27–28, 115.
1546 AC 28.
1547 AC 134.
1548 AC 115.

passionate conflict like Algeria 1955, the most that he can do—to adapt a phrase from Jürgen Habermas—is present himself as a "stand-in and interpreter" between the opposing parties,[1549] and the broker of dialogue between them. "If the intellectual does not join the combatants themselves," Camus challenges his metropolitan contemporaries in 1958, "then his (admittedly less glorious) role must simply be to calm things down to the point where reason might again play its part..."[1550]

The first thing Camus proposes on these bases in the 1955 *L'Express* articles reflects his wider philosophical assessment of the importance of sympathetic imagination in ethical life (Chapter Four). He advocates for the importance of adversaries being made to sit down together, face-to-face: "the world today is one in which the enemy is invisible. The fight is abstract... to see and hear the other can... give meaning to the combat and just possibly make it unnecessary..."[1551]

Secondly, and more specifically touching his own role as an intellectual, Camus argues that thinkers can use their analytic abilities to critically challenge the mirroring simplifications and misunderstandings each of the adversaries harbours concerning the other, bred of anger, hatred, and the desire for revenge: "I will therefore devote several articles to the[se] simplifications, explaining to each party to the talks the reasoning of its adversaries."[1552] This Camusian phrase, "the reasons of the adversary" recurs as a *leitmotif* throughout the following articles, and the entire *Algerian Chronicles*.[1553] Although the intellectual cannot dictate final solutions, this being the third thing, he can work to facilitate mutual understanding, thereby giving non-violent solutions a chance. He can do this by prompting each party to the conflict "to recognise what is just in the cause of your adversaries."[1554] The first *L'Express* article, in this vein, tackles metropolitan French illusions about the *pied noirs*, reminding them that "all of France battened themselves on the hunger of the Arabs." The responsibility

---

1549 Jürgen Habermas, "Philosophy as Stand-In and Interpreter," in *Moral Consciousness and Communicative Action* (USA: Polity, 1992). We hasten to add that in this piece, Habermas depicts philosophy as standing in and interpreting between different specialised positive and social sciences, not between political positions in the public sphere. With that reservation noted, the term and the concept still applies to Camus' post-prophetic conception of the intellectual's role, as played out in Algeria after 1954, without transcendent or final success.
1550 AC 28.
1551 AC 114.
1552 AC 124.
1553 AC 133, 135, 137.
1554 AC 143; cf. AC 32.

for the present "disaster" lies "with a series of French governments, backed by the comfortable indifference of the press and public opinion and supported by the complacency of lawmakers" on the mainland, as well as in the colony.[1555] The following piece is addressed to the *pied noirs* themselves. It argues that no French Algerian can legitimately condemn Arab violence who does not oppose, at the same time, "the excesses of the repression."[1556] Camus urges the need to recognise the Arabs' independent culture, and opposes the idea that progressive reform within a federated French-Algerian framework must mean surrender: "for a nation like France, the ultimate form of surrender is called injustice."[1557] The third article, specifically entitled "The Adversary's Reasons", addresses Algerian militants. It urges them to recognise that "the massacre of civilians, in addition to reviving the forces of oppression, exceeded limits." Camus appeals to moderate "militants of the North African movement" to oppose the pan-Islamic, extreme wing of the FLN.[1558] It was on the basis of these appeals that he made his ill-famed appearance in Algiers on January 22 1956, at the head of a fast-dissolving "party of truce".[1559] Camus' aim was to call for a cessation in the violences of both sides directed against non-combatants: to "not only save precious lives but to restore a climate that could lead to healthy debate..."[1560]

Critics are right to suggest that Camus' attempt to stand "in no-man's land," impartially outside or above the growing conflict was contestable. Camus made clear enough his opposition to the expropriation and expatriation of the *pied noirs*, and the idea of a wholly independent Algeria. At times, moved by his sorrow, anger and fear for this prospect, he calls those antagonists "purely emotional"[1561] (or victims of a "fanatical intransigence")[1562] who would soon enough preside over the very real, very historical expropriation of the *pied noirs*, and the end of French Algeria. With the benefit of hindsight, we know that Camus was wrong to see Stalin's hands, columns and tanks behind the North African independence movements with a view to encircling and "Kadarising" Europe.[1563] Camus' anxieties about the kinds of non-democratic government

---

1555 AC 127.
1556 AC 129.
1557 AC 130.
1558 AC 134.
1559 AC 147.
1560 AC 155.
1561 AC 177.
1562 AC 207.
1563 AC 178.

the FLN, if successful, would institute ("the rule of the most uncompromising leaders of the armed insurrection..."),[1564] however, were more prescient, with the military quickly assuming dictatorial powers in Algeria after the revolution.[1565] These things considered, our point here is that Camus' larger metaphilosophical and political position—his refusal to assume the mantle of an infallible prophetism and attempt instead to create "room for whatever dialogue is possible"[1566]—allows the possibility that he, too, might have been corrected in *his* simplifications and prejudices at the roundtable for which he called. There is no question, as we know from Camus' private letters to René Cory (the President of the Fourth Republic) asking for the pardon of condemned FLN militants in September–October 1957, that he made real and continuing efforts to respect the humanity of the other, even as he opposed their means and ends. Only if we then "worship at the altar of the fait accompli",[1567] and pass over the gravity of Camus' arguments against terrorist violence, does it seem possible to condemn as wholly guilty and unforgivable Albert Camus' advocacy first of a federal French-Algeria, and then for a peaceful solution to the Algerian crisis after November 1 1954.

2   Philosophy, the Virtues, Love and Wonder

2.1   *Literature and Philosophy as a Way of Life, the Camusian Virtues*

Nevertheless, historically, Camus did fail in Algeria. As for Clamence in *The Fall*, it was "too late" and too much.[1568] There was "stunning" historical justice in the Arab cause,[1569] rebelling against the "vast, tragic, and ... irreparable" crimes of the French colonisers against the colonised North African peoples.[1570] And, as Camus came to realise after 1945, any chance of producing a culture of mutual respect and equality between European and Arabs was quashed by the colonial Right in the 1930s (coupled with the Communists' retreat): a fact violently brought home by the V-E-day massacre and reprisals at Sétif. When we ask, however, of a philosopher and of Camus: 'what does he practically propose, having 'gone back down' from the heights of her theoretical reflections?', it is

---

1564   AC 33, 35.
1565   See Carroll, *Camus the Algerian*, 111–113.
1566   AC 115.
1567   AC 32.
1568   F 70.
1569   AC 127.
1570   AC 207.

interesting to reflect upon how easily we assume that the philosopher must come back down from a mountain, as it were (or from outside the cave) with a single, all purpose tablet, prescribing a single revolutionary Act or Actions. In Camus' case, it thus rolls off the pens and word processors that Camus' philosophical value was 'shown up' by his Algerian failure, despite the long, bloody history of that tragic and violent colonial situation (and, in Camus' case, despite the more favourable report we are likely to deliver on his resistance activities, the existential origins of the post-war philosophy of revolt). There is a fragment in Nietzsche where he remarks that the notion of a single, decisive Act or conversion, as against the prolonged cultivation of deepset, habitual dispositions of character (the virtues) beginning in earliest life, is a decisive marker of the transition between classical and monotheistic cultures.[1571] Camus, in his *Diplôme* thesis, had noted that, even in late antique Gnosticism, neoPlatonism, and the mystery cults, pagan initiation (implying the active acquisition of knowledge) differed from the Christian sense of salvation: which, as we know, is a gift delivered by grace from above.[1572] The early evangels' hostility to knowledge, Paul's emphasis on faith over works, and Augustine's critique of the pagan cultivation of virtues as rooted in pride[1573] all mark out this decisive cultural shift, "folly to the Greeks." For conversion is indeed presented as a one-off event, on the paradigmatic model of Paul's Damascene moment. This is the existential corollary of a revolutionary overthrow of existing modes and orders, and the institution all at once of something wholly New presently being appealed to by new *maîtres penseurs* as the model for the kind of neo-revolutionary militancy Camus consistently opposed from the early 1940s.

In fact, he opposed it already in his political writings of the late 1930s on the injustices of colonial Algeria.[1574] It is, as we saw in Chapter Five, a new Mediterranean "culture' with which the young Camus of 1937 was already concerned; as his Kabylie articles advocate for economic, legal, and educational reforms, if dignity is to be restored to the indigenous people.[1575] A 'culture', the issue is, while it may presuppose or engender changed political institutions, is a larger, more holistic thing than a set of political or legal institutions. Just so, we want to argue, Camus' recommendations concerning "what is to

---

1571 Friedrich Nietzsche, *Beyond Good and Evil*, translated R.J. Hollingdale (London: Penguin, 2003), #47.
1572 CMN 52–53, 68–69.
1573 CMN 120.
1574 AC 65: 'In the face of such an urgent situation, we must act quickly, and it would be foolish to contemplate a utopian scheme or advocate impossible solutions."
1575 AC 53–83.

be done?" are as little exhausted in his wholly political proposals in *The Rebel* or the *Algerian Chronicles*, as his *oeuvre* (or even his practical philosophy) can be judged, without reductivism, according to assessments of *ta politika* alone. The point can be made, by asking what might the preconditions be, not to resolve a situation like that in Algeria, but to prevent its "infernal dialectic" of crimes and grievances developing?[1576] Camus' answer, again reflecting his native and acquired neoHellenism is: only by engendering entire, renewed "style[s] of life" in the next generations, rooted in the cultivation of a profile of neoclassical virtues.[1577]

We have several times approached Camus' interest in philosophical and ethical self-formation. Recall from the Introduction Camus' remarkable argument that he was not a (modern, academic) philosopher: since "what interests me is to know how one must conduct oneself."[1578] This, it is necessary to underline, represents the deepest basis for Camus' respect for true forms of Christianity: that Christianity demands of adherents an entire way of life, not simply a doctrine—and, in the call to "grace" heard by Paneloux after the death of the Othon boy in *La Peste*, a willingness to take on the burden of the suffering of others.[1579] In Chapter Three, in fact, we saw that the culmination of Camus' reflections on "philosophical suicide" in *Le Mythe de Sisyphe* is the assertion: "now, the point is to live":[1580] a point which, at that stage of the argument, we allowed to lead into Camus' notion of political responsibility, beginning in the virtuous honesty to 'count oneself in' the judgments to which one accedes about the world and other people. Yet the second half of that text itself, with its exemplars of Don Juan, the actor and the conqueror (alongside Camus' Sisyphus himself) each represent attempts to give imaginative 'flesh' or "breath" to forms of living which remain faithful to the truth(s) of the absurd.[1581] Even when 'philosophy' is treated in this fecund text, Camus takes another leaf from Nietzsche's books, and proposes that we read the most systematic, apparently impersonal texts as indirect confessions or biographies

---

1576 AC 153.
1577 See Camus, "Un Style de Vie (26 janvier 1946)", OC II 672–674.
1578 Camus, "Interview à 'Servir'", OC II, 659.
1579 P 87–191; Merton, "*The Plague* of Albert Camus: An Introduction and Commentary", 208–211. See C II 116: "Les Grecs n'auraient rien compris à l'existentialisme—alors que, malgré le scandale, ils ont pu entrer dans le Christianisme. C'est que l'existentialisme ne suppose pas de conduite."
1580 MS 92; MSe 65. Cf. D 97.
1581 MS 98; MSe 68; Cf. Levi-Valensi, "Si tu veux être philosophe...", 27–31.

of their author, complete with their own conceptual dramas, narratives, if not heroes and villains.[1582]

Arguably the most biographically revealing section in *Le Mythe* itself, though, comes in the section on "Absurd Creation." While we have examined the model of 'testimony' to the diverse, extrahuman density of reality Camus develops here, the framing concern of the section is with the *persona* of the artist, as much as their objectified creations. If art exerts such a fascination for Camus, and seems to him so well to answer to the exigencies of the absurd, it is because:

> Of all the schools of patience and lucidity, creation is the most effective. It is also the staggering evidence of man's sole dignity: the dogged revolt against his condition, perseverance in an effort considered sterile. It calls for a daily effort, self-mastery, a precise estimate of the limits of truth, measure, and strength. It constitutes an ascesis... perhaps the great work of art has less importance in itself than in the ordeal it demands of a man and the opportunity it provides him of overcoming his phantoms and approaching a little closer to his naked reality...[1583]

Camus' definitive statement concerning art and style, alongside the section "Revolt and Art" in *L'Homme Révolté*, however comes in another 1942 piece we met above, "Intelligence and the Scaffold." What concerns us is how Camus here conceives of that Apollonian "ideal of simplicity"[1584] he so admires in the French classicists—"the stubborn clinging to a certain tone" while documenting even the most extreme events of life[1585]—in ethical terms. Such restrained style, he argues, reflects "a studied art that owes everything to intelligence and its attempts to dominate" the passions, the "dispersion" of life, and the medium of language.[1586] In other words, as in *Le Mythe*, in admiring the style of Stendhal, Madame de Lafayette or Gide, Camus admires the artist *lui-même* (to inevitably evoke Bossuet). Artistic creation not only produces works. Creation is *itself* a formative ethical practice:

> ...a school for life,... precisely because it is a school of art. To be more accurate, the lesson of these lives and these works of art is no longer

---

1582 MS 137–138; MSe 100.
1583 MS 155–156; MSe 115.
1584 Camus, "Intelligence and the Scaffold", LCE 210, 213.
1585 IS, 217.
1586 IS, 215.

simply one of art, but one of style. We learn from them to give our behaviour a certain form.[1587]

It is this admiration for the attempt to reflectively "give behaviour a certain form" that brings Camus closest to what is today in the academy called 'virtue ethics'. As per Chapter Five, it is questionable whether we should understand Camus' thoughts to have been shaped by his encounter with classical authors. In the *Carnets*, he shows his reading of Marcus Aurelius, Plato, and Montaigne (who is steeped in classical authors, led by his beloved Seneca and Plutarch). We also know Camus read Epictetus while in hospital facing death as a young man, and that Camus drew philosophical solace from the Stoic.[1588] Yet it seems as true to say that Camus' reading of these authors was shaped by the formative experiences we will return to presently, as they are represented in *Le Premier Homme*. Whichever the case, there is no doubt that Camus found his way to, and accepted the three or four definitive parameters of the classical authors' conception of the virtues: first, that the virtues are lasting, beneficent dispositions to think, feel, and act in certain ways, set deep in a person's character over a span of time, rather than 'once-off' occurrences; secondly, that they involve the mastery of the untethered passions, which by themselves tend to epistemic blindness and behavioural excess; thirdly, that this mastery is achieved through education, the imitation of admirable exemplars ("the globe of precepts")[1589] and through the repetitive habituation of these excellent modes of thinking, feeling and action (in what Camus above terms an "ascesis" or elsewhere "a difficult science of living").[1590] For all of the classical Hellenic and Roman schools, finally, the virtues are not exercises in self-denial or ascetic abnegation (neoPlatonism is an arguable exception). Rather, they are necessary (and for the Stoics, sufficient) accomplishments if a person or people are to live happily and well.[1591]

1587 IS, 216.
1588 See "Annex" in Bousquet, *Camus le Méditerranéen*, 112–113; on Camus' reading of Epictetus in hospital, see the same text, page 35.
1589 Francis Bacon, "Of Great Place", *Essays, Civil and Moral. The Harvard Classics, 1909–14*. Found online at www-site http://www.bartleby.com/3/1/11.html, last accessed December 24, 2014.
1590 Camus, "Nuptials at Tipasa", 69 (translation mine: "la difficile science de vivre"... at Camus, *Noces suivi de l'été* (Paris: Gallimard, 1958), 17.
1591 With that said, again care is needed. Hadot notes how to live fully well as a human being, in all the schools in different ways, positions the sage as in effect, by this fulfilment, almost more-than-merely-human, and participating in something divine. See e.g. Pierre

It is with exactly this classical framework in hand that Camus, as he became more politically engaged, came to call for the cultivation of what he calls in "The Almond Trees" of 1942 certain "conquering virtues" as needful for a rejuvenated European culture.[1592] We have already seen in Chapter Four the role Camus assigns to modesty in democratic culture, and the toleration of adversarial opinions; and in Chapter Five, the epistemic and ontological grounds of Camus' notion of *mesure*, which is also a virtue of character, taming our passionate tendencies to excess. Each of the key lyrical essays in the 1954 collection *L'Été*, in this vein, defends one or more such virtues: strength of character ("Almond Trees"); courage wed to intelligence ("Prometheus in the Underworld"); humility and friendship ("Helen's Exile"); humility and fidelity to self, despite the vicissitudes of fame ("The Enigma"); and the love of beauty and a chastened *philanthropia* everywhere.

Here as everywhere else with Camus, we need to be careful to honour each side of his complex position, and not project our own preferences onto selective citations. Certainly, Camus' scepticism operates in this field, as it does in Montaigne, about the possibility of a pure virtue, or the Greek ideal of the Godlike sage.[1593] On one hand, Camus reflects characteristically that "I know myself too well to believe in pure virtue."[1594] On the other hand, like Montaigne or Voltaire before him, both of whom associated the cruelty of Europe's religious wars not with a recursion to animal barbarity, but with agents fanatically convinced of their own righteousness,[1595] Camus can write in the mid-1940s that "[p]ractically, and for the moment, I prefer a debauchee (*un débauché*) who does not kill anyone to a puritan who kills everybody..."[1596] Camus is only too aware of the "madness of virtue which has shaken this century," prosecuted

---

       Hadot, "Models of Happiness Proposed by the Ancient Philosophers," in P. Hadot, *Etudes de Philosophie Ancienne*, Paris: Belles Lettres, 2010), 327–338.

1592 Albert Camus, "The Almond Trees," 137.

1593 CMN 41. See Albert Camus, "Le Témoin de la liberté", *Oeuvres Complètes II*, 494. For Montaigne's critique of the Hellenistic notion of the perfected sage, in the context of Montaigne's response to the religious strife of his times, see David. Schaeffer, *The Political Philosophy of Montaigne* (USA: Cornell University Press, 1990), 227–250.

1594 C II 203, 172; C II Eng, 105; 88, 141.

1595 See Matthew Sharpe, "On a Forgotten Argument in French Philosophy: Sceptical Humanism in Montaigne, Voltaire, Camus", *Critical Horizons* (Feb. 2015). Camus repeats Montaigne's argument concerning the 20th century at Albert Camus, "Projet de preface", *Oeuvres Complètes II*, 500. See also the "Concluding Remarks" to Chapter Four above.

1596 C II 212; C II Eng 109. Again, cf. Schaeffer, *Political Philosophy of Montaigne*, 227–250.

by the agents of competing total ideologies[1597] who have "chosen to call 'virtue' what serves the advent of the society they desire."[1598] By the same token, Camus does not see the abuse of appeals to the virtues as valid arguments against trying to conceive and cultivate the virtues *per se* in genuinely beneficent forms—any more than failed physical theories might render physics a nugatory endeavour. Indeed, tracing out what we might term the particular 'physiognomy' of Camus' conception of the virtues (at once highly classical and markedly his own) will recall to our mind not simply Camus' founding scepticism, but also Camus' distinct appeals to balance, *mesure*, and excluding nothing.

The principal object to be worked upon, if Camusian virtues are to be cultivated, are the passions. These, as in the classical philosophers, we have seen for Camus are imbricated in our judgments of the world (most notably, in our *desire* for unity). Characteristically, Camus does not advocate for the complete eradication of the passions, as per the Stoic *apatheia*. Like the peripatetics, and renaissance figures like Francis Bacon or Montaigne, he opposes any of idea of "an extreme virtue consisting in killing the passions," recommending instead "a more profound virtue that consists in balancing them (*à les équilibrer*)."[1599] The passions, by themselves, are natural constituents of human life and flourishing (each must *"vivre avec ses passions"*).[1600] This is not a theory of fallen, innate sinfulness or 'objective guilt' in any form, as we know. Besides, "our world does not need tepid souls. It requires ardent hearts who strive to give moderation its just place."[1601] We have of course seen in Chapter Four the place of the "moral sentiments," rooted in sympathetic imagination, in Camus' political make-up: and "[l]a fièvre de la justice" of which Camus spoke in *Combat* as underlying the resistance.[1602] Camus spoke candidly, although always with a *pudeur*,[1603] about his own passions and their disorder[1604] and of his own experience of "the two thirsts one cannot long neglect without drying up—I mean loving

---

1597 C II 250; C II Eng 128. Cf. "I have tried with all my strength, knowing my weakness, to be a moral person. Morality kills." C II Eng 131.
1598 C II 202; C II Eng 104.
1599 C II 238; C II Eng 123.
1600 C II 57; C II Eng 26.
1601 Camus *Combat*, novembre 1944, cited at Marcel J. Melançon, *Albert Camus. Analyse de sa pensée* (Suisse: Les Éditions universitaire Fribourg, 1976), 134.
1602 Camus, *Combat*, november 24 1944, at CAC 122.
1603 Marc Blanchard, "Before Ethics: Camus's *Pudeur*," *MLN* 112: 4(1997).
1604 "In order to be created, a work of art must first of all make use of the dark forces of the soul. But not without channelling them, surrounding them with dikes, so that the water in them rises..." (EE Pref 15).

and admiring."[1605] His literary works stage characters predominantly moved by different passions: despair (*Caligula*), the longing for happiness (Cherea in *Caligula* or Rambert in *La Peste*) or for money (Cottard), romantic love (Victoria in *State of Siege*), the desire for power (Clamence in *La Chute* or the eponymous "renegade"), and longing for communion (Janine in "The adulterous woman," d'Arrast in "The Growing Stone").

Nevertheless (*l'envers et l'endroit*), Camus does not thereby maintain that the passions do not need education and edification. "Unless a man has dominated their desire, they can master nothing. And we almost never master desire," Camus comments.[1606] Here is the thing: "each passion, noble enough in itself, becomes murderous if it is not limited by other passions and relativised," Camus contends.[1607] This is an exact figuring of the philosophy of *mesure* in the area of moral psychology. If the love of truth (good in its place) is pursued, proverbially, '*pereat mundus*,' Camus reflects, this speaks against it.[1608] Despair at the loss of a loved one is natural: if it becomes an 'all or nothing' despair at creation itself *à la* Caligula, this is excessive. Fear of death, short of philosophical reflection or religious consolation (and despite these) is natural:[1609] if it prevents one from living with dignity and minimal respect for others, it is too much. The premier example of Camus' 'measured' moral psychology—one which divides Camus' entire life—is the tension or "balance" that he sees as necessary between the love of justice, calling for political action, and the desire for beauty, suggesting contemplative and creative withdrawal. Its definitive statement comes in "Return to Tipasa," as Camus reflects upon his own division between these conflicting desires:

> But, after all, nothing is true that compels us to exclude. Isolated beauty ends up simpering; solitary justice ends in oppression. Whoever aims to serve one exclusive of the other serves no one, not even himself and eventually serves injustice twice.[1610]

1605 RT 168. See the final section below.
1606 C II 266; C II Eng 137.
1607 To use the words of Melançon, in *Albert Camus. Analyse de sa pensée*, 172: one of few authors to attend specifically to the virtues in Camus, and to whom I am indebted in this section.
1608 "C. and P.G.: the passion for truth. Around them everyone is crucified." C II 135; C II Eng 69.
1609 "One cannot deny that men fear death. The privation of life is indeed the supreme penalty and ought to incite in them a decisive fear. The fear of death, arising from the most obscure depths of the individual, ravages him; the instinct to live, when it is threatened, panics and struggles in the worse distress (*angoise*)..." RG 189.
1610 RT 165.

> For there is merely bad luck in not being loved; there is misfortune in not loving. All of us, today, are dying of this misfortune. For violence and hatred dry up the heart itself; the long fight for justice exhausts the love that nevertheless gave birth to it. In the clamour in which we live, love is impossible and justice does not suffice...[1611]

Here then we see the reason why the Camusian philosophy of 'balance' does not lead him to posit any kind of *tranquilitas* as the possible or desirable psychological goal, all his other proximities to the Hellenistic philosophers notwithstanding. Camus talks instead of "tension" which comes from weighing, feeling and recalling, and simultaneously trying to honour the competing demands and passions of life. If there is any "serenity" in play here, it is one of "an interminable tension and [the] agonised serenity (*sérénité crispée*) of which Char speaks... the true life is present at the heart of this tearing apart (*ce déchirement*). It is this tearing itself, the mind soaring over volcanoes of light, the madness of justice, the extenuating intransigence of moderation."[1612] Jeanson and Sartre notwithstanding, we are far from the bourgeois shop steward or self-satisfied financier, complacently planning their next affair, promotion or holiday as the world lurches between catastrophes.[1613]

If we ask then what the primary Camusian virtue could be, given this moral psychology, the answer again is deeply redolent with the classical Greek philosophers, although given its own, distinctly Camusian spin. It was their reflections on the unity and apparent divisions of the virtues that led the classical philosophers after Socrates to consistently accord the highest value to the virtue of wisdom (*sophia* or *phronēsis*). Socrates famously taunted that "virtue *is* knowledge," and the Stoics accepted the claim: arguing that virtue (the only true good) consists in knowing how to comport oneself towards things, beyond our control, which are in themselves neither good nor evil. As much as Aristotle tried to contest Socrates' apparently counter-sensical "intellectualist" notion, by the end of *Nicomachean Ethics* VI, he too has argued that, if one has *phronēsis*, one will by that fact have all the other virtues.[1614] The reasoning here is exoteric. If courage is not tied to practical know-how, it will be exercised at the wrong times, with the wrong objects, for the sake of the wrong causes.

1611 RT 168.
1612 HR 378; R 302–303. See Orme, *Development of Camus' Concerns*, 251 n. 19.
1613 Maurice Weyembergh, "La tentation du 'tout est permis': Camus entre 'détour' et 'retour' ", in D. Lyotard ed. *Camus, Contemporain*, 71–72, 76; Pascal, "Camus, Philosophe malgré lui", 187–188.
1614 Aristotle, *Nicomachean Ethics*, VI.13.

Likewise, each of the other virtues has its appropriate times, means and places, and it is the wisdom of the virtuous man to know these occasions to respond and act well. Without citing, and probably without needing these texts, Camus found his own observational way to the same arguments concerning what is, for him, the highest virtue: one which he variously calls "lucidity", "clear-sightedness", or simply "intelligence". We can illustrate Camus' conception of lucidity by looking at Camus' typically two-sided, nuanced statements concerning the virtue of courage.

On one hand, courage, alongside heroism and fidelity, for Camus, is a virtue: admirable and necessary in itself for individuals and groups. As Melançon has astutely observed, in his "Letters to a German Friend", Camus comes close to defining human beings according to their capacities for courageously opposing all natural and human forces which destroy or demean them: "What is the human being?...He is the force that always ends by balancing tyrants and gods."[1615] "The renaissance today depends on our courage and our will to clear-sightedness," Camus could claim in 1957, in words echoing "Prometheus in the Underworld" of nearly two decades before.[1616]

On the other hand, in notable contrast to Nietzsche, the younger Heidegger and their epigones, Camus insists that it is the continuing fascination with ideals of "heroism," "fidelity" or "authenticity" that needs to be cooled in modern Europe, not fanned. This is because, if we consider the classical question concerning the relation between different desirable traits, they are what Camus calls "secondary values." And why secondary? Simply: because the guards of concentration or extermination camps, no less than the founders of houses of mercy, can be courageous and faithful to their causes in face of all opposition, benevolent or malign. "One cannot justify just any type of heroism, any more than any type of love," Camus observes: for excessive or misguided forms of romantic love can of course become self- (and other-) destructive, as Lucretius amongst the ancients in particular explored.[1617] "Heroism and courage should be considered as secondary values—after having given proof of courage," Camus thus writes, seemingly again with chicken-hawkish

---

[1615]   LGF 14.

[1616]   Albert Camus, *Conférence*, décembre 1957, cited at Melançon, *Camus: Analyse de sa pensée*, 177. Cf. PU 141.

[1617]   Camus, "Entretien sur la révolte", OC III, 401. See Martha Nussbaum, "Chapter Five. Beyond Obsession and Disgust: Lucretius on the Therapy of Love", in *Therapy of Desire*, 140–191.

'judge-penitents' in his crosshairs.[1618] Moreover, as Camus commented in his "Preface" to the *Algerian Chronicles*, in a formulation as timely in a period of renewed academic fascination with Schmitt and Kojeve as it was in 1958:

> Although it is historically true that values such as the nation and humanity cannot survive unless one fights for them, fighting alone cannot justify them (nor can force). The fight must itself be justified...[1619]

What then decides when and which forms of courage, this 'secondary virtue', are admirable? It is a question of which *ends* all 'secondary virtues', including even the temperate control of one's passions, go to serve. And such ends can only be assigned (and maintained in mind) by a lucid, reflective intelligence which excludes nothing of pertinence to the given situations. Here then it is invaluable to recall Doctor Rieux's reflections on the virtues of the sanitary teams in *La Peste*, which are definitively Socratic or neoStoic, and certainly speak for Camus:

> The evil that is in the world always comes of ignorance, and good intentions may do as much harm as malevolence, if they lack understanding. On the whole, men are more good than bad; that, however, isn't the real point. They are more or less ignorant, and it is this that we call vice or virtue; the most incorrigible vice being that of an ignorance that fancies it knows everything and therefore claims for itself the right to kill. The soul of the murderer is blind; and there can be no true goodness nor true love without the utmost clear-sightedness...[1620]

Almost always, then, when Camus mentions courage positively, as here when Rieux talks of "true" goodness or "true" love, it is to couple courage with intelligence. Culture itself for him in 1957 is "the force of the heart, intelligence [and] courage, sufficient to hold in check our destiny..."[1621] Above all, in "Prometheus in the Underworld," Camus tells us that:

1618 C II 123–124; C II Eng 62. Cf. "We do not want just any kind of hero. The reasons for heroism are more important than heroism itself. The more important value (*la valeur de conséquence*) therefore comes before the heroic value." C II 190; C II Eng 97. See P 115, where Rieux reports exactly these convictions.
1619 AC 32.
1620 P 110.
1621 Camus, "*Conférence*, janvier 1956", at Melançon, *Camus: Analyse de sa pensée*, 179. Cf C I, 105 and "Culture: cri des hommes devant leur destin," at C I, 50; C I Eng 19.

I will answer Yes to the question of the century, because of the thoughtful strength and the intelligent courage I still feel in some people who I know...[1622]

The 'propositional content' of this lucid intelligence, as Camus saw it, we have also by now seen: at least at the theoretical level. It is Camus' discourse of *mesure* and of excluding nothing: giving to each passion and real exigency we face, as far as we possibly can, its time and place. And here is where our 'second pillar' of Camus as a *philosophe* interested "in how one must conduct oneself" needs most to be weighed. To the extent that (urged by contemporary academic and institutional incentives) we 'reify' written philosophical discourse as the self-standing end of philosophising, we assume that philosophising ends with the 'once-off' discovery or justification of arguments or positions. Yet, for Camus from the start, the recognition of the absurd, for example, is never a one-off. The 'stage-sets' (*les décors*) of mundane life collapse one fine day, in the kinds of experiences we saw that Camus thinks awaken consciousness to our mortality, the inhumanity of nature, and our limitedness within it.[1623] But "the mechanical aspect of things and people"[1624] soon enough returns. And with it comes the simple tendency to elude or forget the challenging truths one has affirmed, in the moment of philosophical clear-sightedness: "...as everything finally becomes a matter of habit, we can be certain that [even] great thoughts and great actions become insignificant..."[1625] An important note from early 1942 describes the dilemma. The note reflects on the situation of a man who "tries to live continuously with his views". Such a man realises that the "most difficult thing in the world" is to maintain such an awareness: "Circumstances almost always stand in his way. He has to live lucidly in a world where dispersion is the rule. He thus realises that the real problem, even without God, is the problem of psychological unity..."[1626] How, that is, is a person to integrate the truths he has theoretically assented to, so they become the psychologically-determinative shaping beliefs that can structure his life, loves, passions, and struggles, over the course of an entire life? How, in another key Camusian term, is a person to keep these truths "present", so that she can act and choose in full consciousness of the significance of her actions? A soul "conscious without cease" remains Camus' ideal ("a continued presence of

---

1622 PU 141.
1623 MS 29; MSe 12.
1624 C II 86; C II Eng 43. Camus was dreaming at this time of an "Anthologie de l'insignifiance".
1625 C II 86; C II Eng 43.
1626 C II 19; C II Eng 6.

self with self... not happiness, but awareness"),[1627] from before the time of *Le Mythe*: "the present and the succession of presents before a constantly conscious soul..."[1628] In "The Wind at Djemila", he goes as far as to hold that the goal of civilization is to form people capable of consciously, with clear eyes, confronting the reality of their own deaths without illusions.[1629] Happiness itself, Camus says, is "a long patience."[1630]

It might perhaps, in some alternate universe, be desirable that things were so simple that taking an undergraduate course in ethics would make each student a *phronimos* or sage (as against being able to hopefully write a sound term paper). But as Aristotle and the other Greeks knew, more is required. Plutarch's "On the Education of Children" lists nature, nurture or habituation, and education as the three components of a well-formed young man or woman.[1631] Camus will rejoin that a life lived lucidly and well requires three or four things, each of which again draw from and evoke ancient and renaissance precedents. There is first, as per the Stoics or Epicureans, forms of "ascesis" or self-discipline. Second, there is the cultivation of memory to keep clearly in mind over time, despite all temptation and distractions,[1632] everything one has assented to as true, right or real. Thirdly, there is Camus' own version, born of poverty, sea and sunshine, of what the Stoics called *megalopsychia*, "the

---

1627 C I 23; C I Eng 5; cf. "that constant presence of man in his own eyes" of MS 78; MSe 54: "being faced with the world as often as possible", MS 88; MSe 62.

1628 MS 90; MSe 63.

1629 WD 77.

1630 C I 97; C I Eng 43.

1631 Plutarch, "Education of Children", para. 4 ("As a general statement, the same assertion may be made in regard to moral excellence that we are in the habit of making in regard to the arts and sciences, namely, that there must be a concurrence of three things in order to produce perfectly right action, and these are: nature, reason, and habit. By reason I mean the act of learning, and by habit constant practice. The first beginnings come from nature, advancement from learning, the practical use from continued repetition, and the culmination from all combined; but so far as any one of these is wanting, the moral excellence must, to this extent, be crippled...", at www-site http://penelope.uchicago.edu/Thayer/E/Roman/Texts/Plutarch/Moralia/De_liberis_educandis*.html last accessed January 2015); cf. Aristotle, *Nicomachean Ethics*, II.1–5.

1632 "It is the pleasure of living that disperses, abolishes concentration, halts any upsurge towards greatness. But without the pleasure of living... No, there is no solution." (C II 251; C II Eng 129). Sexuality was given to man to divert him from his true path. It is his opium." (C II 49; C II Eng 22) "See C III 41, 79–80; C III 30, 66; with C II 50–52–53; C II Eng 23, 25; and see also Alan Woolfolk, "The Artist as Cultural Guide: Camus' Post-Christian Asceticism", *Sociological Analysis* 47: 2 (Summer 1986): 93–110.

epistēmē of being above what befalls both good and bad men alike."[1633] Lastly and above all, Camus speaks of a "will to happiness" and "a strange form of love" in face of all the horrors and beauties of our lives which he sought to reactivate in himself by writing *Le Premier Homme* as the Algerian war raged, as we will see in our last section.[1634]

We saw above how Camus is drawn to art as a practice, discipline, or way of life. His *Carnets*, featuring notes on the lives of Tolstoy and other great authors,[1635] reflect this sense that art (like *philosophie*) is "a discipline a man sets himself for understanding and loving."[1636] "The great souls interest me—and they alone", Camus reflected on his own search to give himself examples to sate his "thirst for admiration" and direct his attempts to live well.[1637] The issue, as Camus put it acerbically, is that virtue "is not learnt as quickly as how to manipulate a machine gun. The combat is unequal":[1638] any more than Camus conceived of personal and collective liberty or justice to be "sprint races", as against exhausting "long-distance" affairs.[1639] Camus instead argues for the need, beyond institutional changes, to "forge an art of life in our times of catastrophe in order to be reborn and to fight then, openly, against the instinct of death at work

---

1633 Stobaeus, *Anthologion Ioannis Stobæi Florilegium* 2.59.4–62.6 Cf. Diogenes Laertius' "to despise the things that seem to cause trouble" at *Lives of the Eminent Philosophers* VII 128. See Christoph Jedan, "Stoic Virtues" (Habilitationsschrift zur Erlangung der Lehrbefähigung für das Fach Philosophie, Berlin 1970).

1634 C I 96–97; C I Eng 43; HR 379; R 304. Compare the "experience of love which still has to be defined" that arises beginning from the absurd at C II 177; C II Eng 91 and see next section.

1635 To take the case of Tolstoy, Camus recurs to his life throughout the *Carnets*: C I, 241, 242; C II, 11, 12, 225, 238, 246, 271, 287, 288, 292; C III, 26, 27, 34, 75, 82–83, 84, 86, 92, 94, 102, 103, 192, 193, 206.

1636 MS 133; MSe, 96–97.

1637 C II, 267; C II Eng 137; cf. RT 168.

1638 C II, 265; C II Eng 136.

1639 F 132–3: "Oh, no! It's a chore, on the contrary, and a long-distance race, quite solitary and very exhausting." Cf. "Liberty is a cry, followed by a long struggle, not a comfort or an alibi" (Camus, *L'Express* 1955); "Men are more lazy than cowardly, and often prefer peace and servitude to freedom"; for freedom is "a perpetual risk and an exhausting adventure... that is why people flee from... the demands of freedom to rush towards all kinds of servitude to obtain at least comfort for the soul". We must 'payer' the 'sang de la liberté' if liberty is to be protected. Likewise for the other principal political virtue: "justice must be achieved with the blood of men and women"; "the obstinacy of injustice can only be conquered by an obstinacy of justice." Indeed, "justice dies the moment when it becomes a comfort, when it ceases to be a burn, and an effort on oneself..." The preceding quotes come from Melancon, *Camus, Analyse de sa pensée*, 171 and 167.

in our history."¹⁶⁴⁰ The highest dignity of human beings, we have seen Camus argue (Chapter Three), comes from a kind of clear-sighted perseverance in face of the inhumanities of the world. Here as elsewhere, Camus first and foremost 'counts himself in'. He tells us of his own efforts to avow and confront his own excesses and disorders, and "to cure them by the exercise of will."¹⁶⁴¹ Camus' *Carnets* of course contain sketches and drafts for many ideas and images to duly appear in his published literary and theoretical writings: they are one of the writer's workshops.¹⁶⁴² Nevertheless, there are entire strata of these remarkable reflections that can only be read as the documents in Camus' own attempts at his own self-curing. A long entry of September 15, 1936, for instance, describes Camus' efforts at self-transformation in these terms:

> My effort now is to carry this presence of myself to myself through to the very end, to maintain it whatever aspect my life takes on—even at the price of the loneliness that I know it is so difficult to bear. Not to give way—that is the whole secret. Not to surrender, not to betray.¹⁶⁴³

Or there is this remarkable set of injunctions to himself, every bit like Marcus Aurelius', from April or May 1958:

> Remain close to the reality of beings and things.
>   Return as often as possible to personal happiness . . . Recover energy—as the central force.
>   Recognise the need for enemies. Love that they exist . . .
>   Recover the greatest strength, not to dominate but to give.¹⁶⁴⁴

It is this decision, as well as the (for him intersecting) wish to be the best artist he could be, that underlay Camus' resolve from at least April 1938 to "every day,

---

1640 Albert Camus, "Albert Camus's Nobel Prize Reception Speech", with French and parallel-text translation by Joseph Gruenbaum, at www-site http://josephpg.com/2014/04/19/albert-camuss-nobel-prize-reception-speech/, last accessed January 2015. (Camus, "Discourse de 10 decembre 1957", OC IV, 241). Compare: a life well lived "is not possible without a discipline which is difficult to reconcile with the world. Here lies the problem, for it must be reconciled with the world. What must be achieved is living by a Rule in the world." (C II 19; C II Eng 6)
1641 C II 261; C II Eng 134.
1642 Philip Thody "Introduction", to Albert Camus, *Carnets 1935–1942* trans. with Introduction and notes by Philip Thody. (London: Hamish Hamilton, 1963), pp. vii–xi, viii–x, xi.
1643 C I 76; C I Eng 32–33.
1644 C III 221; C III Eng 204.

write (*noter*) in this notebook."[1645] Secondly, then, we see how the cultivation in particular of a kind of embodied memory is in play in Camus' lived sense of philosophy, including in this form of self-writing:[1646] remembering that it is a "fidelity" to the absurd that "revolt" aspires to honour in *Le Mythe*; and how (decisively) in *L'Homme Révolté* it is revolutionaries' passionate, tragic tendencies to *forget* or *break faith with* the noble, originary promises of their own political and metaphysical revolts that sees them betraying self and other, and becoming the active agents of the forms of insult and violence they initially opposed.[1647] In Duvall's words, "the call to memory is at the heart of Camus' work."[1648] The "ruthlessness" of the kind of ascesis Camus at times demanded of himself, to attain to this conscious lucidity and recall and maintain it over time, is evident in the program he formulated for himself in November 1939 ("to prevent one's desires from straying, one's thoughts from wandering"):

> One single, unchanging subject for meditation. Reject everything else.
> Work continuously, at a definite time, with no falling off etc. (Moral training and asceticism too).
> A single moment of weakness and everything collapses, both practice and theory.[1649]

Central in all of Camus' efforts, formed by his brush with youthful death by Tuberculosis and the recurrence of symptoms throughout his life, is one "spiritual exercise"[1650] the ancient schools also enjoined:[1651] the *memento mori* or

---

1645 C I 107; C I Eng 48.
1646 Here again, see on the ancient practices of writing as a spiritual exercise or 'technique of the self', Foucault, "Self-Writing", at www-site http://foucault.info/documents/foucault.hypomnemata.en.html, last accessed February 2015; and Hadot, *Inner Citadel*, 26–29, 31, 33–34, 50–51.
1647 HR 367; R 294. "The primary faculty of man is forgetfulness". (C II 36) "My immense ability for forgetfulness", reads one note in the *Carnets* from early 1951. (C II 344; C II Eng 177). A note from 1950 cites Max Jacob's 'With a strong memory, you can create a precocious experience.' Camus responds in the imperative: "Cultivate one's memory, immediately." (C II 262; C II Eng 134).
1648 William E. Duvall, "Albert Camus against history", *The European Legacy* 10: 2, 139–147, at 143. See Maurice Weyembergh, "La tentation du 'tout est permis': Camus entre 'détour' et 'rétour'", in D. Lyotard ed. *Camus, Contemporain*, 72–73.
1649 C I 193; C I Eng 91.
1650 Cf. Hadot *Philosophy as a Way of Life*, 58; 68–69; 93–101 (on the spiritual exercise of *memento mori* in different philosophical schools, then as adopted and adapted in Christian monasticism).
1651 Camus registers his admiration of Montaigne's "Philosophy as Prepration for Death" (*Essays* I.20), itself a collection of the ancient opinions on this topic, at C II 197; C II Eng 101.

recollection of our mortality, not from morbidity, but out of the desire to mindfully stay "awake"[1652] to the transience of time and the need to 'seize the day' (*carpe diem*):

> The sensation of death which from now on is so familiar to me... to have a foreboding of death simply at the sight of a pocket handkerchief filled with blood is to be effortlessly plunged back into time in the most breathtaking manner: it is the terror of becoming.[1653]
>
> The degradation involved in all forms of suffering. One must not give in to emptiness. Try to conquer and 'fulfil' time. Time—don't waste it.[1654]
>
> Don't forget: illness and the decay it brings. There is not a minute to lose—which is perhaps the opposite of 'we must hurry.'[1655]

For Camus, significantly, the fact that we each must die our own deaths shows definitively the falsity of constructivist or culturalist claims that human beings are solely social or historical creatures: death recalls to each of us, soon enough, that we are also parts of the natural world.[1656] In this way, interestingly, its recollection for Camus points in an almost opposed direction to the signification accorded the *memento mori* in Heidegger, wherein confronting our finitude "calls" us to the recognition of our allegedly authentic, culturally-particular historicity.[1657] It is however the specific ethical signification that Camus assigns to the recognition of death, not existentialist and highly neoStoic, that leads to the third dimension of his philosophical way of living (alongside ascesis and the cultivation of memory). This is Camus' almost innate sense of "indifference" or "detachment from human concerns",[1658] reflected (as ever, cynically and in a distorted form) in his Clamence's inability "to believe that human affairs were serious matters. I had no idea where the serious might lie, except

---

1652 On wakefulness versus sleep as metaphor for states of attention, see esp. MS 29; MSe 13; MS 65; MSe 44–45; MS 131; MSe 94–95.
1653 C II 89; C II Eng 45.
1654 C I 118; C I Eng 54.
1655 C II 104; C II Eng 52.
1656 C II 157; C II Eng 80.
1657 C II 89; C II Eng 45. With that said, for Camus as in *Sein und Zeit*, and as for the ancient Stoics, the lucid recognition of one's mortality "gives form to love as it does to life—by transforming it into destiny..." (C II 89; C II Eng 45; cf. Heidegger, *Being and* Time, sec. 53) Camus, however, immediately follows this up with a stronger ontological claim, reflecting his philosophy of *mesure* (here life is 'balanced' by death): "What would this world be without death, but a succession of forms fading away and being reborn, an anguished flight, an uncompletable world. But happily death, the stable one, is here." (C II 89; C II Eng 45)
1658 EE Pref 9.

that it was not in all this I saw around me—which seemed to me merely an amusing game, or tiresome."[1659] "There is only one liberty: in coming to terms with death." Camus reflects in the *Carnets*, echoing the famous *bon mot* of Seneca's: "the person who has learned how to die has unlearned how to be a slave."[1660] *Le Mythe* concurs about the importance of "feeling henceforth sufficiently remote from one's own life to increase it and take a broad view of it…"[1661]

The psychological or spiritual reason for such detached *megalopsychia*, Camus makes clear in *Le Mythe*'s conception of "absurd freedom" by recourse to monastic forms of *kenosis*: the emptying out of all attachments to worldly things to make room for God.[1662] Epictetus' Stoic *Handbook* lays the rationale for such a liberating *kenosis* out with the freed slave's characteristic, punchy clarity: "Of things some are in our power [*eph'ēmin*], and others are not," he begins: "In our power are opinion, impulse, desire, aversion and in a word, whatever are our own acts. Not in our power are the body, property, reputation, offices, and in a word, whatever are not our own acts." It follows, as night follows day, that if we take these "externals" as necessary to our happiness, this most prized goal is ceded to the hazards of chance, opinion, and the passing good graces of others. In time, with certainty, they and our happiness will thus be lost, as Clamence discovered: "you will be hindered, you will lament, you will be disturbed, you will blame both gods and men"; "… perhaps you will not gain even these very things (power and wealth)…: certainly you will fail in those things through which alone happiness and freedom are secured."[1663] It is for operating just such an Epictetan *kenosis* of attachment to 'externals' upon him, Camus would reflect in his autobiographical "Preface" to *L'Envers et Endroit*, that he came to see his bodily illness as its own spiritual and philosophical boon:

1659 F 86–87. Cf. Srigley, *Camus' Crtique of Modernity* 107–108, who makes an interesting parallel with Plato's *Laws* here: his reasoning closely approaches what Pierre Hadot has argued for the "view from above" in ancient philosophy: philosophical reflection, and ascent to theoretical insight, ideally allows people to distance ourselves somewhat from our egoistic conceits, an ideal that runs through into Petrarch and Bacon in the renaissance, and Hadot locates in later moderns like Goethe. (Pierre Hadot, "The view from above", in *Philosophy as a way of life*, 138–149).

1660 C II 192; C II Eng 98. See Seneca, *Letters to Lucilius*, "XXVI. On Old Age and Death", translated by Richard Mott Gummere (A Loeb Classical Library edition; volume 1 published 1917), digitalised at www-site http://en.wikisource.org/wiki/Moral_letters_to_Lucilius/Letter_26, last accessed January 2015.

1661 MS 85; MSe 59.

1662 See MS 84 MSe 58–59; D 99–100. See Chapter Three, section "Je suis revenu à mon commencement: the Irreducibility of the Subject and the Primacy of Ethics" above.

1663 Epictetus, *Handbook* I.1–4.

> The illness surely added new limitations, the hardest ones, to those I had already. In the end [though] it encouraged freedom of the heart, that slight detachment from human concerns, which has always saved me from resentment. Since living in Paris I have realised this is a royal privilege. I've enjoyed it without restrictions or remorse, and until now at any rate, it has illuminated my whole life.[1664]

As Audi again has stressed,[1665] it is impossible to overvalue this 1958 "Preface", for the reedition of Camus' first, youthful publications: themselves a collection of lyrical meditations with an intimately autobiographical component, especially "Between Yes and No"'s portrait of his silent mother and his childhood in Algiers.[1666] It is in this "Preface" that Camus announces the dream of trying somehow to rewrite these early stories (as he would do in part in *Le Premier Homme*); in order to "draw closer to his own centre... the two or three great and simple images in whose presence his heart first opened..."[1667] and regenerate himself as an artist and a man (see below). It is in this "Preface" also that, alongside his own illness, Camus credits his material poverty as the son of an illiterate working class *pied noir* widow with a formative ethical impact on his life. It shaped his deepest conceptions of happiness, love, and the pursuits of the mind. In particular, it enabled him to look down upon the riches that others envy, kill and die for, as if these were the truly necessary or sufficient constituents of a good life. On the contrary, Camus reflects, "for me the greatest luxury has coincided with a certain bareness":[1668] "I still have to make an effort to realise that others can feel envious of such [material, monetary] wealth."[1669] If there is a "secret" to Camus' universe, we thus see how close it lies to the much-maligned 'paradoxes of the Stoics' of antiquity: that, if the true, highest riches are virtue or a certain wisdom or wakeful "lucidity", then "poverty does not necessarily involve envy" or unhappiness.[1670] Indeed, "the under worker at the Post office can be the equivalent of the conqueror", as Diogenes in his barrel could mock the regnant Alexander, asking him to move aside since he

---

1664 Pref EE 10. See C II 57: "La maladie est un couvent qui a sa règle, son ascèse, ses silences et ses inspirations..."
1665 Audi, *Qui Témoignera...*, 52–54.
1666 EE 30–39; cf. also the final of the three scenarios in "Irony", at EE 26–29.
1667 EE Pref 16–17.
1668 EE Pref 9.
1669 EE Pref 8.
1670 EE Pref 9.

was blocking the Cynic's Athenian sun.[1671] Material poverty, if it can be (as it was for the boy Camus) innocent of concerns for the morrow and the grinding miseries of enslaving labour, can be the nursemaid of this higher happiness: what Camus calls a kind of "spiritual snobbery" which consists in being free from excessive dependency on material things, and thereby money[1672]—*megalopsychia* in the true sense, the Stoics rejoin. This is why Camus can even ask himself and us, just as if he were a cynicising Stoic:

> What could a man want that is better than poverty? I do not say misery, any more than I mean the work without hope of the modern proletarian. But I do not see that one could desire more than poverty with an active leisure.[1673]

As Geraldine Montgomery has commented, Camus' philosophy—however much people direct the charge of 'moralist' at him—aims at something "far beyond the moral." Indeed, it aims at cultivating a certain lasting disposition, "to accede to a beyond the ethical which is manifested in a spiritual transformation."[1674] "Any life directed towards money is a death. The renaissance lies in disinterestedness," Camus reflects, soon after penning the preceding paradoxical reflection in the *Carnets*.[1675] "It is legitimate to glory in the diversity and quantity of experience … only if one is completely disinterested in the object of one's desires …"[1676] Or again, concerning solidarity with oth-

---

1671 MS 150; MSe 68.
1672 C I 97; C I Eng 43.
1673 C II 88; C II Eng 43. Cf. C I 15; C I Eng 1: Camus' wish to speak of a "nostalgia for poverty" in the very opening entry of the *Carnets*.
1674 Geraldine F. Montgomery, "Plus loin que la morale", in *Camus in the 21st Century*, 134.
1675 C II 92; C II Eng 46. Of course, here as elsewhere, Camus' meaning needs to be qualified, as his work amply documents 'excessive' or 'unbalanced' forms of 'indifference' too: the cynical active nihilisms of Caligula or Cottard, or the more passive forms—often equally murderous—of Meursault (see Chapter Three: 'Excursus: Aburd Heroes?"). I am arguing that Camus' meaning here, in valorising a species of elevated indifference is closer by disposition and cultivation to the classical Stoics, when they describe external things as 'undifferentiated' (*ta adiaphora*): not by themselves, but in relation to the expectations and fears of happiness and perdition we place in them. They can provide neither. Happiness depends primarily on the state of our psyches, and hence we should treat these 'externals' with a minimal cognitive, desiderative and affective 'reservation' (*hypexairēsis*) so we are not, like Romeo, fortune's fools. The different forms of indifference documented by Camus have been ably delineated in Claude Treil's important study, *L'indifference dans l'oeuvre d'Albert Camus* (Paris: Cosmos, 1971). Cf. C II 92; C II Eng 46.
1676 C I 91; C I 193.

ers: "now I have learned to expect less of [people] than they can give—a silent companionship. And their emotions, their friendship, and noble gestures keep their full miraculous value in my eyes: wholly the fruit of grace."[1677]

As for Camus' own renaissance after the debilitating polemics following *The Rebel* and his political failures in the Algerian political arena, Camus had realised by 1958 that it was imperative for him now, more than ever, to return to himself: or rather, through the kind of spiritual exercise of a controlled anamnesis, to try to recover his mnemic sense of the material poverty of his childhood and what it had spiritually delivered him: the "single source ... within himself which nourishes during his lifetime what he is and what he says."[1678] Camus would now take on just that "mandate" Sartre had derisively assigned him in 1952, in another irony Camus' former friend could scarcely have imagined. He would undertake the personal and aesthetic challenge of trying to give mature art and story to what the "awkward pages" of *L'envers et l'endroit* had tried to explore way back in 1937, since there was "more love in these awkward pages than in all those that have followed," as Camus' friend the philosopher Brice Parain had seen.[1679]

It is with these philosophical reflections in mind, we believe, that the genesis, power and meaning of what exists of *Le Premier Homme*, Camus' last work, is to be sought. We are in the presence of one more document in Camus' Socratic "return to his beginnings," and an extraordinary testament to Camus' continuing attempts to cultivate his own memory. It is to what this incomplete masterpiece reveals concerning Camus' conceptions of love and *bonheur*, the fourth dimension to his conception of the examined life that we now finally turn.

2.2 The First Man as Algerian Text: Camus' Fictional True Algeria

The incomplete, handwritten manuscript and folio pages of *Le Premier Homme* were in the car when Camus died on January 4, 1960, not yet 47 years old. His most transparently autobiographical work (although the protagonists' and other names are changed), Camus' family withheld its manuscript from publication until 1994. They did so out of love for Camus and a concern that its publication in the early 1960s would have added fuel to Camus' *Marxissant* and Algerian critics' fires. The novel, we also know, was to form the centrepiece of a third or fourth cycle of works. This cycle was being built, when Camus died, around the myth of Nemesis and the subject of love: after the cycle or intervening 'half-cycle' on judgment and exile represented by *La Chute* (1956), the

---

1677 C I 191; C I Eng 77.
1678 EE Pref 6.
1679 EE Pref 6.

stories of *Exil et Royaume* (1957), and perhaps *The Algerian Chronicles* (1958). The figure of Nemesis, absent from the extant pages of *Le Premier Homme*, would not have been new to Camus' writings. She appeared both in "Helen's Exile" and the closing pages of *The Rebel*. There, the pagan goddess stood as the goddess of *mesure*, not of vengeance: "all those who transgress the limits are by her pitilessly chastised."[1680] Alongside the novel, Camus planned a poetic-philosophical work in aphoristic style around the theme of love. Several designated fragments (under the header "Nemesis") remain, including the following mesmerising fragment in the last *Carnets*. Dated December 1959, this note gives us some sense of what the work's tone, and its content, might have been. It is seemingly a development in new depth, on new topics, in a new aphoristic form of Camus' "midday thought," exploring the interlacing of oppositions according to relations of balance and *démesure*:

> *For Nemesis* (at Lourmarin, December '59). / Black horse, white horse, a single hand of man controls the two passions. At breakneck speed, the race is joyous. Truth lies, frankness hides. Hide yourself in the light. / The world fills you and you are empty: plenitude. /Soft sound of foam on the morning beach; it fills the world as much as the clatter of fame. Both come from silence. / The one who refuses chooses himself, who covets prefers himself. Do not ask nor refuse. Accept surrender. / Flames of ice crown the days; sleep in the motionless fire. / Equally hard, equally soft, the slope, the slope of the day. Back at the summit? A single mountain. / The night burns, the sun creates darkness. O earth, that suffices at everything. Freed of everything, enslaved to yourself. Enslaved to others, freed of nothing. Select your servitude. / Behind the cross, the devil. Leave them together. You empty altar is elsewhere. / The waters of pleasure and of sea are equally salty. Even within the wave. / The exiled individual reigns, the king is on his knees. In the desert, solitude ceases. / On the sea, without truce, from port to island, running in the light, above the liquid abyss, joy, as long as very long life. / You mask yourself, here they were naked. / In the brief day that is given to you, warm and illuminate, without deviating from your course. / Millions of other suns will come for your rest. / On the flagstones of joy, the first slumber. / Sowed by the wind, reaped by the wind, and creative nonetheless, and proud to live a single instant.[1681]

1680 HE 149; HR 369–370; R 296.
1681 C III 276–277; C III Eng 255–256. See for references to Nemesis, and a series of similar reflections from the late 1940s onwards, C II, 198, 328, 342; C III, 44, 78, 81, 187, 190, 207, 274.

By contrast with *The Myth of Nemesis*, there were 144 pages of the manuscript of *The First Man* recovered from the wreckage in 1960, alongside pages of notes, projected passages, character sketches, dialogues and episodes, and a three part plan (of which we have only drafts from the first two, ending before 'Jacques Cormery"s adolescence and experiments in romantic love). So it is more possible for readers and critics to form meaningful interpretations of what Camus was attempting in this remarkable book. That said, it is impossible for anyone to know how the work would finally have taken shape, and all it would have been, said and shown.

Catherine Camus' decision to publish her father's *Le Premier Homme* in 1994 has understandably generated a sizable critical response. Much of this response, certainly in academic venues, has turned around "the Algerian" in the work: as Catherine and her mother had anticipated when holding the manuscript back from the public.[1682] Certainly, what we have of the incomplete novel is set squarely in the Algeria of Camus' childhood, youth, and political activism. Moreover, as we began this last chapter by foregrounding, no one can argue that *The First Man* was going to turn away *à la The Plague* from the Algerian troubles, the violent colonial history of Camus' homeland and the deepset hostilities between the Arab and Berber peoples and their *pied noir* occupiers. In the third chapter, the protagonist's failing attempts to solicit any meaningful information from his mother about who his father was is interrupted by the bombing of the bus station; then Cormery's attempt to shelter or protect a fleeing Arab, in whose attested innocence he instantly believes.[1683] This episode, however, is only the first of many moments and ways in which the political troubles and violence encircle and disrupt Jacques Cormery's attempts to find out anything at all about that "first man",[1684] his father, who had died in a straw hat on the Marne for a French homeland he would see only once.[1685] From the school principal Levesque, Jacques learns of his father's reaction, in the Moroccan war, to finding a comrade with his throat slit, and his severed genitals grotesquely stuffed in the dead Frenchman's gaping mouth: "'... a man doesn't do that,' [Cormery had exclaimed] ... '[but] there are Frenchman who do do it [also]', said Levesque. 'Then they too aren't men.' And suddenly [Cormery] burst out: 'A filthy race! What a race! All of them, all of them ...'"[1686]

1682 Catherine Camus, "Editor's Note", FM, vi.
1683 FM 58–60.
1684 See Raylene Ramsay, "Colonial/Postcolonial Hybridity", in *Albert Camus in the 21st Century*, 78–80.
1685 FM 52–56.
1686 FM 51, 52.

When Jacques accompanies the old settler 'Veillard' to the Arab caretaker Tamzal's house at Mondovi, their visit is watched by Arabs, whose invisible, threatening presence is announced by the barking of the dog and by the careful locking of doors ('They're there, but they're waiting'). The men then reflect on the war. "*Mektoub*," said Tamzal, 'but war is bad'. 'There's always been war,' said Veillard. 'But people quickly get accustomed to peace. So they think it's normal. No, war is what's natural.' "[1687] Veillard tells of a *pied noir* farmer, who having been told at the town meeting that "they would have to reconsider colonial issues," bitterly sowed his crops with salt: 'young man, since what we made here is a crime, it has to be wiped out.' "[1688] Camus had projected an Arab character, Saddock, a childhood friend with Jacques, who would become an FLN guerrilla and debate with him the justice of terrorist violence, and the notion of "objective guilt". Jacques, who was not going to betray his Arab friend, was to be arrested by the French for harbouring the enemy.[1689]

Camus likewise in no way shrinks in this text from attesting to the deepset racism amongst the poor *pied noirs* of his upbringing:

> Unemployment, for which there was no insurance at all, was the calamity most dreaded. This explained why these workers, in Pierre's home as in Jacques's, who in their daily lives were the most tolerant of men, were always xenophobes when it came to work, accusing in turn the Italians, the Spaniards, the Jews, the Arabs, and finally the whole world of stealing their work-an attitude that is certainly disconcerting to those intellectuals who theorize about the proletariat, and yet very human and surely excusable. It was not for mastery of the earth or the privileges of wealth and leisure that these unexpected nationalists were contending against other nationalities; it was for the privilege of servitude. Work in this neighborhood was not a virtue but a necessity, that, to provide a living, led to death.[1690]

Even the extraordinary lyrical reflection (entitled "A mystery to himself")[1691] which death made Camus' last, relatively completed literary passage is not insulated from its historical setting. Instead, we find in the midst of Jacques' poetic meditations upon "the secret part of himself... this blind stirring in

---

1687 FM 141.
1688 FM 149, 141.
1689 FM 250–251.
1690 FM 200.
1691 FM 215–221.

him... matched by this enormous country around him," the ensuing clear-sighted reflection on the *pied noirs'* threatened, violence-haunted reality:

> ...this was the very country into which he felt he had been tossed, as if he were the first inhabitant, or the first conqueror, landing where the law of the jungle still prevailed, where justice was intended to punish without mercy, what custom had failed to prevent—around him these people, alluring yet disturbing, near and separate, you were around them all day long, and sometimes friendship was born, or comraderie, and at evening they still withdrew in their closed houses, where you never entered, barricaded also with their women you never saw, or if you see them on the street you did not know who they were, with faces half veiled and their beautiful eyes sensual and soft above the white cloth, and they were so numerous in the neighbourhoods where they were concentrated, so many of them that by their sheer numbers, even though they were exhausted and submissive, they caused an invisible menace that you could feel in the air some evenings when a fight would break out between a Frenchman and an Arab, just as it might have broken out between two Frenchmen or two Arabs, but it was not viewed the same way...[1692]

There is then no doubt that *The First Man* would have been Camus' most extended, literary depiction of the colonial situation, and one which would have made clearest "the Algerian in him."[1693] The text also gives us fertile glimpses of what Dunwoodie and others[1694] have rightly suggested was for Camus his own "imagined community," to evoke Benedict Anderson's celebrated definition of the modern nation-state: "the fiction of a French-Algerian people."[1695] This "fiction" was just that, a fiction: as history was to prove, given the deep historical scars *The First Man* registers.[1696] Yet it remains to ask, as Carroll does, whether Camus' multi-cultural vision whose political form we

---

1692 FM 216–217.
1693 FM 253 (note by Camus, presumably of Cormery as an adult in Paris): "what they did not like in him was the Algerian"; see Carroll, *Camus the Algerian*, 4–7.
1694 Peter Dunwoodie, "Negotiation or Confrontation? Camus, Memory, and the Colonial Chronotype" in Christine Margerrison, Mark Orme, Lissa Lincoln eds., *Albert Camus in the 21st Century*, 47–60.
1695 Cf. David Carroll, "Camus's Algeria: Birthrights, Colonial Injustice, and the Fiction of a French-Algerian People," MLN, Vol. 112, No. 4, French Issue (Sep., 1997), pp. 517–549. Cf. Tarrow on the divided identity of the teacher Daru, geographically and culturally, in "The Guest", at *Exile from the Kingdom*, 181–183.
1696 See esp. FM 145–145 and below.

have seen was not the worst in a situation wherein what many have argued was the simply best solution involved expatriating over a million *pied noirs* after eight years of escalating violence, and the installation of a highly militarised regime in Algeria:[1697]

> It would even be possible to make the argument that [Camus' solution] might even have been one of the best, although, given the harsh and deeply-rooted realities of colonial privileges, racial and cultural prejudices, and economic and political injustices and inequalities, it was undoubtedly the least likely ever to be actualized, especially once armed insurrection, terrorism, severe military repression, deportations, and the systematic torturing of prisoners had begun.[1698]

What remains so singular about Camus' imagined Algerian community in *Le Premier Homme*, not least given Camus' repudiation by Marxist critics, is that it is so resolutely a "classed" imaginary community.[1699] For reasons whose philosophical motivations we have now seen, and which political critics have been quick to decry,[1700] Camus valorised the materially poor *pied noirs* amongst whose houses, streets, factories, workshops, tramways, buses and bustling streets he had grown up. "For me honour in the world is found among the oppressed, not those who hold power," one of Camus' notes assigns to Cormery: "and it is from that alone [wielding power] that dishonour arises."[1701] *The First Man*'s 'true Algerians' thus find their place in a long lineage of Camusian, ordinary heroes or non-heroes (doctors, workers, teachers, engineers, an overweight, aging woman...) Their eminent representative is perhaps the ironically-named "Grand" in *La Peste* who joins the sanitary teams out of a simple sense that it is the only thing to do, and spends his spare hours trying to craft a single, well-turned sentence.[1702] It is Camus' continuing search

---

1697 See Carroll, *Camus the Algerian*, 112–117 on this point: "there is sufficient evidence available to make a convincing argument that the cause of Algerian Independence was in fact more hurt by terrorism than helped by it" (113).
1698 Carroll, "Camus's Algerian Birthrights", 547.
1699 See FM 158.
1700 Dunwoodie, "Negotiation or Confrontation? Camus, Memory, and the Colonial Chronotype", 57. Here, as in Haddour, Sartre and Jeanson's charge of class-blindness is turned on its head: Camus is charged, with more justice arguably, of highlighting class over race in the Algerian setting, as a means to obviate the colonial realities. But see above.
1701 FM 230.
1702 P 39–42, 86–89.

for an "everyday aristocracy"[1703] to be found "among the oppressed" that forever keeps the door closed to any neoconservative appropriation of Camus' opposition to pan-Islamism. This opposition, we note, is to be weighed in the same scales as his like opposition to Western forms of theocracy, secular or transcendent: and his staunch opposition to all political appeals to religious passions and dogmata.[1704]

In many ways, Camus' archetypal, almost Christ-like model for his true Algeria is the ignorant, silent, unfathomable mother to whom we know Camus dreamed of addressing the manuscript of *Le Premier Homme*.[1705] An emerging idea of the book's final scene would have featured the prodigal Jacques confessing to her, and asking her forgiveness for words and actions she could scarcely have imagined.[1706] So in *The First Man*, indeed, as charged by Haddour and others, we seemingly do have a lyrical, inescapably escapist fantasy: that of an ahistorical, virtuous and poor *pied noir* community emblematised by this mother.[1707] Possessing nothing, not even collective memory, they become the kindred in poverty of the Arabs who menacingly surround them; and with whom they share all that they possess:[1708] namely, only their deep, pre-reflective sense of belonging to the same harsh country and increasing despair at the violence that was tearing Algeria apart.[1709] In the section of the notes entitled "End," we find perhaps Camus' rawest *cri de coeur* in this vein, and his last written words on the troubles, as fortune would dictate:

> Give back the land, the land that belongs to no one. Give back the land that is neither to be sold nor to be bought.... Give back the land to the poor, to those who have nothing and who are so poor that they never

---

1703 C III 64; C III Eng 51.
1704 Cf. Jason Doughart, "Neoconservatism in the Political Thought of Albert Camus: A Preliminary Inquiry", *Journal of Camus Studies*, 2012.
1705 FM 5. Cf. FM 232, 249, 250.
1706 FM 254–255.
1707 Dunwoodie, "Negotiation or Confrontation? Camus, Memory, and the Colonial Chronotype", 48–49: "a highly selective past, of *European* suffering, sacrifice and poverty... interpreted as a ground for an idealised future..." (at 48) For a contrasting, more sympathetic critical opinion, which goes so far as to suggest that Camus' *pied noirs*, by virtue of their hybridity and lack of historical roots, might presage the newly universal state of things in the later modern 'globalised' world, see Raylene Ramsay, "Colonial/Postcolonial Hybridity", in *Albert Camus for the 21st Century*, esp. 76–77, 83–85.
1708 FM 255: "The poor and ignorant Berber peasant. The settler. The soldier. The white with no land. He loves them, these people..."
1709 Carroll, "Camus's Algerian Birthrights", 528–530; cf. AC 151–153.

desired to have and to possess, to those in this land who are like her [his mother], the immense herd of the wretched, mostly Arab and a few French who live and survive here through stubbornness and endurance, with the only pride that is worth anything in the world, that of the poor, give them the land as one gives what is sacred to those who are sacred.[1710]

2.3 Childhood, Poverty, and Wonder: The First Man *as Literary-Philosophical Exercise*

There is then a very real as well as 'fictional' political register to Albert Camus' last, unpublished novel. The question for us reading *Le Premier Homme*, as for so much of Camus' work, is whether a solely-political interpretation remains one-sided, screening out literary, rhetorical, philosophical and psychological dimensions of the text. And here as elsewhere, we must agree with Carroll that this appears to be so. There is, first of all, the simple consideration that of the extant chapters, six of eleven deal with Jacques' childhood (and three others deal with his search for his father): his relations with his family, friends, school chums, teachers. All of these are recalled for us amidst the author's vivid, highly sensual evocations of:

> ...a series of obscure longings and powerful, indescribable sensations, the odours of the schools, of the neighbourhood stables, of laundry on his mother's hands, of jasmine and honeysuckle in the upper neighbourhoods, of the pages of the dictionary and the books he devoured, and the sour smell of the toilets at home and at the hardware store, the smell of the big, cold classrooms, the warmth of his favourite classmates, the odour of warm wool and faeces that Didier carried around with him, of the cologne big Marconi's mother doused him with and so profusely that Jacques, sitting on the bench in class, wanted to move still close to his friend, the scent of the lipstick Pierre took from one of his aunts and that several of them sniffed together, excited and uneasy, like dogs that enter a house where there has been a female in heat, imagining that this was what a woman was, this sweet-smelling chunk of bergamot and cosmetic cream that, in their rough world of sweating and dust, revealed to them a world refined and delicate and inexpressively seductive...[1711]

The political register granted, hermeneutic and wider charity suggests we need also to account for the vast majority of the text's pages and concerns: both

---

1710 FM 255.
1711 FM 218–9.

'in themselves', as well as, on that basis, in their uneasy relationship with the political violences that punctuate the extant manuscript.

In the case of *The First Man*, moreover, we know from Camus' own testimony that any exclusively politicising readings of the text run up against what the author himself took to be its principal subject: the psychological, spiritual or ethical reality of love, the theme of the new cycle.[1712] In what follows, we approach this subject from the perspective we have developed in this book. For within this perspective of Camus as a *philosophe* interested in how to live, Camus' anamnetic restaging of his own childhood represents one more—and in a very clear sense the most radical—instantiation of Camus' Socratic, self-reflective species of philosophising.[1713] The Socratic *gnôthi seauton* ('know thyself') could, indeed, scarcely go farther than the kind of richly evocative excavation of his own history and memory that *Le Premier Homme* undertakes in search of his absent father—or, in his place, of that "secret", "dark fire"[1714] within him which had underlain Camus'/Cormery's restless searchings, vices and strengths, and which remained so intimately bound up for him with the enigma of his mother's love and her impassive silence.[1715] In a remarkable note found with the manuscript, in fact, Camus gives us an insight into the kind of extraordinary spiritual exercise he seems to have undertaken upon himself, in order to so vividly anamnetically recover the world of his childhood. As in the self-formative passages from the *Carnets* cited above, so reminiscent of Hellenistic self-writing, we note the imperatives to himself and the quietly urgent tone:

> Free oneself from any concern with art and form. Regain direct contact, without intermediary, thus innocence. To give up art here is *to give up one's self.* Renouncing the self, not through virtuousness. On the contrary, accept one's hell. One who wants to be better prefers his self, one who wants to enjoy prefers his self. The only one who renounces his self, his I, is one who accepts *whatever happens* with its consequences. Then this

---

1712   See Victor Brombert, "Boyhood's Dark Fire", *New York Times* August 27, 1995, Sunday, Late Edition—Final, at www-site http://www.nytimes.com/books/97/12/14/home/camus-firstman.html, last accessed February 2015. It is notable that non-academic reviewers have tended to respond more to the affective dimension of the text, and less to its politics. In doing so, they have arguably come closer to honouring Camus' wider intentions, 'excluding nothing'.

1713   See above Chapter Three, "Concluding remarks: Camus' Socratism, between philosophy, autobiography, and literature".

1714   FM 218, 216.

1715   See Audi, *Qui Témoignera*, 23–44.

one is in direct contact. / Regain the greatness of the Greeks or the great Russians through this distanced innocence. Do not fear. Fear nothing. But who will help me?[1716]

It is at the heart of this extraordinary "discipline...for understanding and for loving" that writing *Le Premier Homme* represented for Camus, that *amor* emerges as of pivotal importance.[1717] Camus had previously skirted the subject of love in many places, as we know. A "love of life" tied to "despair of life" had already emerged in *L'envers et L'endroit*, and the opening meditation of the *Noces* tells us that "the right to love without measure" is what "is called glory".[1718] Again, we have been told in *L'Homme Révolté* that true rebellion "cannot exist without a strange sense of love...an insane generosity which consists of giving all to the present,"[1719] even to the point of sacrifice for the sake of human life and dignity. The *Carnets* of 1945 enigmatically promise that: "beginning from the absurd, it is not possible to live in revolt without arriving at some point at an experience of love which remains to be defined."[1720]

But in *Le Premier Homme* and the extant notes surrounding its remaining, unwritten parts, love—filial, romantic, the love between friends, "the marvellous complicity of those who have to fight and suffer together"[1721] —is present almost everywhere. "In short I wanted to speak of those I loved. And of that only. Intense joy," another of the *First Man*'s accompanying notes professes.[1722]

And just so, after the opening's imagining of Camus'/Cormery's birth at Mondovi, and the uncanny scene in which the grown Jacques (now a successful adult who has made his life in France) realises besides his father's grave at Saint Brieuc that he has outlived this 'first man',[1723] we are made privy to Cormery's reunion with the Grenier-figure Malan ("immensely cultivated...the one figure [Cormery knew] who had his own way of thinking, to the extent that this is possible...")[1724] Shortly into the ensuing exchange, Jacques tells his old teacher, without much diegetic motivation, that he is incapable of arrogance before Malan. And why is this? In a way which in the present state of the draft

---

1716 FM 241.
1717 MS 133; MSe, 96–97.
1718 NT 68–69.
1719 HR 379; R 304.
1720 C II 177; C II Eng 91.
1721 FM 240–241.
1722 FM 230.
1723 FM 19–22; see Salgado, "Memoir at Saint-Brieuc" *MLN*, Vol. 112, No. 4, French Issue (Sep., 1997), 588–589.
1724 FM 23.

comes almost as unexpectedly as Malan finds it within the diegesis, Jacques baldly states that this is:

> 'Because I love you,' Cormery said quietly ... 'because', Cormery went on, 'when I was very young, very foolish, and very much alone—you remember, in Algiers?—you paid attention to me and, without seeming to, you opened to me the door of everything I love in the world.' 'Oh, you were gifted.' 'Of course. But even the most gifted person needs someone to initiate him. The one that life puts in your path one day, that person must be loved and respected for ever, even if he's not responsible. That's my faith.'[1725]

Or again, consider the Chapter "6A: School" in which Camus recalls his relations with the Louis Germain figure, Camus' high school teacher: in the novel, 'M. Bernard'. "This man had never known his father, but he often spoke to Jacques of him in a rather mythological way," the Chapter begins: "and in any case, at a critical time he knew how to take the father's role."[1726] The Chapter's anamnesis crescendoes in the moving narration of the events surrounding young Jacques' ardent love for Dorgelè's novel about the war in which his father perished, *Les Croix des Bois*. This book, M. Bernard/Germain, a veteran himself, would read to the students at different times of the year as a special pedagogical treat:

> And on the day at the end of the year when, as they arrived at the end of the book, M. Bernard read them the death of D. in a subdued voice, when he closed the book in silence, facing his own memories and emotions, then raised his eyes to the silent, overwhelmed class, he saw Jacques in the first row staring at him with his face bathed in tears and shaking with sobs that seemed as if they would never end. 'Come come child,' M. Bernard said in a barely audible voice, and he stood up to return the book to the case, his back to the class.

The narrative then cuts back to the present. The retired teacher now makes a gift of the very same copy of *Les Croix des Bois* to his remarkable student, the mature Jacques Cormery who has come to visit him in his continuing search for his origins:

1725 FM 25–26.
1726 FM 106.

'Here, this is for you'. Jacques received a book bound in grocery-store paper with no writing on its cover. Before he even opened it, he knew it was Dorgelè's *Les Croix des Bois*, the very copy M. Bernard had read in class. 'No, no,' he said, 'it's...' He want to say: 'It's too beautiful.' He could not find the words. M. Bernard shook his old head. 'You cried that last day, you remember? Since that day, the book's belonged to you.'[1727]

In an important note, Camus seems to explain what is at stake in these depictions of Jacques' relations to his teachers. "At age 40, he [Jacques] realises he needs someone to show him the way and to give him praise or censure, like a father. Authority and not power."[1728] It is the same distinction that Camus stresses in his essay "On Jean Grenier's *Les Isles*", contrasting the relationship of authority between a master and disciple with "the half-truth [sic.] that delight[s] our intellectual society[:] this stimulating thought—that each conscience seeks the death of the other. At once we all become masters and slaves..."[1729] But when it is a matter of relations of authority rooted in respect, the word "master" takes on a different meaning which is lost in the Kojevian species of Hegelianism Camus is targeting here, so famously influential then and since. This different sense of 'mastery' is "one tied to the word 'disciple' in respect and gratitude... Mind thus engenders mind, from one generation to another, and human history, fortunately, is built as much on admiration as on hatred."[1730] In the 1958 "Preface" to *L'Envers et L'Endroit* which virtually announces the project of *The First Man*, Camus tells us that his literary and philosophical life "began by admiring others, which is heaven on earth."[1731] To recapture and to convey this sense of loving admiration, and to depict its 'heaven on earth' clear-sightedly amidst the surrounding violences of colonial Algeria: this pursuit, alongside any and all the political registers, is surely the heart of *Le Premier Homme*, "at the same time [as] it should be [read as] the history of the end of a world."[1732] "There always comes a moment when people give up struggling and tearing each other apart: willing at last to like each other for what they are. It's the kingdom of heaven," as Camus had reflected in April 1950.[1733] But there is more.

1727 FM 116.
1728 FM 235.
1729 Camus, "Jean Grenier's *Les Isles*" LCE 329.
1730 Camus, "Jean Grenier's *Les Isles*" LCE 330.
1731 EE Pref 10.
1732 FM 232.
1733 C II 323; C II Eng 253. Cf. Willhoite, *Beyond Nihilism*, 68.

As critics have noted, the pall of forgetfulness hangs heavy over the text from near to its opening pages: "the result of specific social conditions and a means of self-defence and survival therein".[1734] After the almost-epic beginning recasting Cormery's birth, Jacques' search for his father consistently yields very little: "an impalpable memory—the light ash of a butterfly wing incinerated in a forest fire."[1735] At Saint Brieuc, there is the grave site and its revelation etched in the stone: one received with "tenderness and pity," that Jacques was now older than this man who had engendered him, *contra* "the natural order of the world."[1736] His mother recollects almost nothing ('Papa?' She looked at him, and now she was paying attention. 'Yes'. 'His name was Henri, and what else?' 'I don't know.')[1737] Jacques can only garner the violent fragments concerning his father's Morrocan war service we recounted in the previous section from his School Principal. He is warned against the search itself by Malan/Grenier. Even the house where he was born in Mondovi has disappeared without a trace, surrounded by fields sowed with the salt of the gathering Arab-French war.[1738] Cormery's attempts to *reimagine* his father back into the trials and perils of the first European settlers, likewise, is broken and partial:[1739] "where was his father in all this? Nowhere, and yet these barges hauled one hundred years ago along the canals at the end of autumn … taught him more about the young dead man at Saint Brieuc than the [senile] and disordered recollections he had gone to seek."[1740] It is as if in the French North Africa of these "persecuted-persecutors from whom his father descended",[1741] as Camus reflects:

1734 Dunwoodie, "Negotiation of Confrontation? Camus, Memory and the Colonial Chronotype", 49. See Pierre-Louis Rey, "Les stratas de la mémoire dans *Le Premier Homme*", in *Albert Camus, Contemporain*, 123–124 on the sense of "immobility" that pervades the novel: nothing changes, all is forgotten or, in the case of violence, timelessly repeated, going back to Cain ("Let's be fair," added the old doctor, "we shut them up in caves with their whole brood, yes indeed, and they cut the balls off the first Berbers, who themselves … and so on all the way back to the first criminal—you know, his name was Cain—and since then it's been war; men are abominable, especially under a ferocious sun…"

1735 FM 251.
1736 FM 20.
1737 FM 48.
1738 FM 24.
1739 On the necessity of imagination, and the significance of this superimposition of the father back amidst the first settlers (which identifies Cormery *with* the *pied noirs* collectively, see Dunwoodie, "Negotiation of Confrontation?", 53–54; Salgado, "Memoir at Saint-Brieuc", 289, 593; Rey, "Les stratas de la mémoire dans *Le Premier Homme*", 128–9.
1740 FM 141. Cf. "In most case, the town halls of Algeria *have no archives*." FM 226.
1741 FM 149.

> The history of men, that history that kept on plodding across one of its oldest territories, while leaving so few traces on it, was evaporating under a constant sun with the memory of those who made it, reduced to paroxysms of violence and murder, to blazes of hatred, to torrents of blood, quickly swollen and quickly dried up, like the seasonal rains of the country...[1742]

Set amidst this land of violence and forgetfulness, what Camus clearly wanted to do in *Le Premier Homme* was to "rescue this poor family [his own] from the fate of the poor, which is to disappear without a trace", moved by his love for his people: "the Speechless Ones. They were and are greater than I."[1743] Camus' contrast of this autobiographical project with Proust's *Remembrance of Things Past*, as Jacques tries in vain to draw information from his mother, hence speaks eloquently to the novel's wider goals:

> To begin with, poor people's memory is less nourished than that of the rich, it has fewer landmarks in space becayse they seldom leave the place where they live, and fewer reference points in time throughout lives that are grey and featureless... remembrance of things past is just for the rich. For the poor, it only marks the faint traces on the path to death. And besides, in order to bear up well, one must not remember too much, but rather stick close to the passing day, hour by hour, as his mother did...[1744]

The First Man was to have recalled and quietly hymned the people who had made Albert Camus the man who he had become: the poor and semi-literate people whose world of sunlight, ignorance and poverty he had ardently wished to leave as a child, to which he nevertheless always longed to return, and which he knew all too well was soon to pass away forever.[1745] In this extraordinary incomplete novelic experiment, so different from those preceding it, populated by flowing, seemingly endless sentences as fluid and multi-colored

---

1742 FM 151. Cf. Louis Rey, "Les stratas de la mémoire dans *Le Premier Homme*", 127.
1743 FM 238.
1744 FM 62–63. See Dunwoodie, "Negotiation of Confrontation? Camus, Memory and the Colonial Chronotype", 51–52.
1745 See Maria Teresa Puleio, "Albert Camus lu par Assia Djebar: ou comment écrire 'ensemble' l'histoire des *pieds-noirs* et des colinisés", in *Albert Camus in the 21st Century*, 61–72, which documents Algerian novelist Assia Djebar's remarkable response to reading *The First Man* as speaking to the authenticity of Camus' identity as a specifically Algerian author, trying to write the history of a people threatened by an "immense forgetfulness".

as the memories Camus was able to salvage from his "immense talent for forgetfulness"[1746] and the collective amnesia that marked the *pied noir* settlers, Camus had wanted to offer up a love-borne tribute to his mother, uncle, childhood friends, and his teachers. *The First Man* sets out to shore up their names and memories against "that immense oblivion that was the ultimate homeland of his people, the final destination of a life which began without roots...": the historically so compromised, and soon indeed to be condemned world of the French Algerians.[1747] To be sure, Camus' elevation of his family to exemplary status allowed him "to sidestep the colonial ethos of acquisition and transformative destruction, the issue of capitalist exploitation and the process historically central thereto, namely expropriation."[1748] It also nevertheless allowed Camus to revisit his own personal and spiritual origins. It allowed him to try to return to the original, unprepossessing sources of the core virtues that emerge throughout his life's work: a predogmatic human solidarity, friendship, admiration, and a love of life not yet caught up in the joyless pursuits of conquest, status, power and fame he/Cormery would soon enough encounter on the European mainland amidst the bloodshed of an international war.

For all our criticism of his work, then, it seems to us that Ronald Srigley's suggestion is incisive that, if we are to reach the philosophical and mythopoetic core of *Le Premier Homme*, then we need to understand Camus' placing of a work entitled *The First Man* after *The Fall*. For Srigley, Camus' reversal of the order of these works' pointedly biblical titles suggests that, in his last work, Camus wanted to pass beyond the world of eschatological judgment and universal culpability of Augustinian and modern political theodicies: not 'in theory', as he had attempted in *L'Homme Révolté*, but performatively, in a new kind of literary text. The book's intense but non-judgmental, completely atheoretical descriptions of everything the boy Jacques sees and senses reflect Camus' own attempt to break through to a perspective wholly liberated from metaphysical categorisations of the human animal as innately 'fallen', or as the creature of grand 'objective' Historical processes which claim total explanatory, exculpatory or emancipatory power. If the Algerians whose passing world Camus documents so vividly in *Le Premier Homme* are "first men," it is to the extent that they were raised without religion, tradition, and memory:[1749] belonging neither with the Arabs whose world surrounded them; nor with the French

---

1746 C II 344; C II Eng 177.
1747 FM 151.
1748 Dunwoodie, "Negotiation of Confrontation?", 56.
1749 Jacques only learnt about religion at the *Lycée* because it was the 'done thing' there (or, per Camus' notes, when he visited Italy, by admiring the art). Camus' *pied noir* poor simply

of the mainland who characteristically treated them with scorn (these 'black feet' who would hardly be welcomed back into France after 1962); nor, least of all, with the Parisian critics who after 1954 would condemn them *en masse*. They were "children without God or father... we lived without legitimacy—Pride," as Camus writes in his notes for the book.[1750] It is in this sense that these unlikely *premiers hommes* were, for Camus, "not men on the wane as they shout in the newspapers, but men of a different and undefined dawn."[1751] *Le Premier Homme* would aim to undertake "two exaltations: the poor woman and the world of paganism (intelligence and happiness)."[1752]

So *The First Man*, its own very peculiar kind of *bildungsroman*, is overdetermined not simply by political, but also the 'erotological', 'donative,' spiritual or philosophical registers we have now recovered. To do the text justice, we must, like Van Eyck's judges ascending to pay obeisance to the West's emblematic embodiment of transpolitical *caritas*, put aside absolute political judgment a while: or at least, following Camus, place politics, one important component of the novel, alongside these other transpolitical dimensions. *The First Man* is above all the imaginative, near-autobiographical testimony of a remarkable philosopher and *litterateur* raised amidst silence and illiteracy, who had as such almost to 'father himself': aided only by the fortunate chances of being 'found' by good teachers, Germain and Grenier, and being educated to unassuming virtues amongst his childhood friends and family, the neighbourhood cats and dog catchers, chicken coups and games of soccer at recesses.[1753] And if Camus' writing in this book, as Srigley's analysis also suggests, is so purely a return to the kind of descriptive, restrained *témoignage* Camus had valorised in his earliest aesthetic essays after reading Richard's *La Douleur*,[1754] this is because it participates in an intensely cultivated, deliberate search for a new, post-eschatological "discipline.. for understanding and loving."[1755] We have seen that Camus did not want in this book (above all his others) to suppress the violence, bloodshed, grinding poverty and hateful prejudices that bordered the enchanted world of his formation. But Pierre Grouix is right, with Srigley, to stress Camus' last work's perfect absence of recondite theoretical jargon, as

---

had no real time, amidst their labours and difficulties for religion, beyond honouring its conventional rituals. See FM 152.
1750   FM 256; cf. FM 148, 152.
1751   FM 256.
1752   FM 256, 252.
1753   FM 152.
1754   Camus, "Encounters with André Gide", LCE 249.
1755   MS 133; MSe, 96–97.

Camus meditatively honors the humble, flawed people and inglorious settings amidst which his life had begun.[1756] To be sure, the narrative's reveric slowness is tinged everywhere with a certain melancholia and the author's reserved passion: in stylistic contrast alike to the blankness of Meursault's testimony, the dispassionate objectivity of Rieux's chronicling in *Le Peste*, or Clamence's duplicitous cynicism. Catherine Camus is right instead to say in her "Editor's Note" that "it seems to me that one can most clearly hear my father's voice in this text because of its very rawness."[1757] It seems to us, indeed, that this sensuous, renewed rawness so close to the sights, touches, sounds and smells of the world of a child and "the magnificent (*magnifique*) and childish world of the creator"[1758] also bespeaks something else: Camus' philosophical attempt to overcome, one more time, the worldly-wise cynicism that "dries up" our capacity for those experiences of love, admiration and gratitude without which the portals of happiness remain closed to any life.[1759] The classical sage, Pierre Hadot reminds us, sees the world as if for the first time, at the same time as his seasoned understanding reaches out to encompass the whole.[1760] Although not a 'philosophical' work in its form or in its language, likewise, *Le Premier Homme* asks its reader to return, with Camus, to that most fecund affect Plato had taught in the *Theaetetus* lay at the genealogical origin not only of art[1761] but of all philosophy:

1756 Pierre Grouix, "L'absence de la philosophie dans *Le Premier Homme*", in Anne-Marie Amiot & Jean-François Mattéi, *Albert Camus et la Philosophie*, 65–82.
1757 Catherine Camus, "Editor's Note," FM, vii.
1758 MS 131; MSe 95.
1759 RT 168.
1760 Pierre Hadot, "The Figure of the Sage", in P. Hadot, *L'Études de Philospohie Ancienne* (Paris: Les Belles Lettres, 2010), 233–257. At 251, to illustrate how the consciousness of the sage differs from "the unconsciousness in which people mostly live, or what one can call their blindness with regards to the universe, which allows us to suppose that only the Sage knows how to see the Cosmos", Hadot cites Lucretius, *De nat. rerum*, II, 1054: "...if the entire world today, for the first time, appeared to mortals, so brusquely, as if improvised, surging up before their eyes, can one picture anything more marvellous than this spectacle, far beyond anything which the imagination of human beings could conceive? And yet no one deigns any longer to raise their eyes towards the luminous regions of the sky, so that one is fatigued and blasé about this spectacle..."
1761 As Aristotle nevertheless avows, at *Poetics* XXIV: "the element of the wonderful is required in Tragedy. The irrational, on which the wonderful depends for its chief effects, has wider scope in Epic poetry, because there the person acting is not seen. Thus, the pursuit of Hector would be ludicrous if placed upon the stage—the Greeks standing still and not joining in the pursuit, and Achilles waving them back. But in the Epic poem the absurdity

Theodorus seems to be a pretty good guesser about your nature [Theaetetus]. For this feeling of wonder shows that you are a philosopher, since wonder is the only beginning of philosophy, and he who said that Iris [the messenger of heaven] was the child of Thaumas [wonder] made a good genealogy.[1762]

---

passes unnoticed. Now the wonderful is pleasing, as may be inferred from the fact that every one tells a story with some addition of his knowing that his hearers like it..."

1762 Plato, *Theaetetus*, 155d. Cf. Cf. Amiot & Mattei, "Avant Propos", 8: "...and what made Camus think, like the Socrates of the *Thaeatetus*, is admiring wonder, the *thamazein*, before the beauty of the world and its naked presence..."

Appendix One: *L'Homme Révolté* in 40 Premises

Given the persistence of claims that Camus' *The Rebel* was a "failed great work",[1763] and in particular that the conclusions in Part V either/both (a) don't follow from the critical analyses of Parts II and III; and/or (b) represent the triumph of rhetorical vagaries over a defined political philosophy, it is worthwhile delineating the book's key premises. As in Appendix Three and throughout the book, 'rhetoric versus clear thinking' is one opposition which Camus' humanism challenges.

L'Homme Révolté/The Rebel

Introduction

1. Age of organised state-based murder demands question: can murder be rationally justified, excused, adopted as instrument of policy?
2. Method: from *MS*, assume nothing, doubt everything—can't doubt desire for unity (which animates doubt, demands evidence), in its confrontation with a world not "made to our measure."
3. If suicide is thus prohibited (life and consciousness necessary for confrontation with absurd), murder is likewise prohibited.
4. Already, a primary value is indicated: "the first step of a mind overwhelmed by the strangeness of things is to realise that this feeling of strangeness is shared with all men and that the entire human race suffers from *the division between itself and the rest of the world*."[1764]
5. (from (3)) Confrontation with absurd involves revolt: against consolations which conceal it (like the picture in front of the man before the firing squad)
6. Assuming nothing beyond revolt, we can still study history of revolt as means of examining our question.

Part I

7. The rebel says 'no!' (denial, refusal) to particular action, policy, institution; but the 'no' supposes an affirmation ('yes') to

---

[1763] Orme, *Development of Camus' Concerns*, 152, 249 n. 4. Orme is citing McCarthy.
[1764] HR 38; R 22.

    a. some limit ('thus far, no farther')
    b. some reality/value 'this side' of this limit (something to be defended, come what may).

8. People can, have, do revolt for principles (eg: no deceit, justice), and for sake of others. Thus:
9. The value presupposed by rebellion is (confirming 4) one of solidarity, common dignity, shared suffering, justice in the face of a world 'beyond our measure', a demand for relative, humane unity and order in a world 'beyond human measure'.
10. Nb. This value does not await any end of history; it exists in the present, where it must be (re)created, and its primary objects are 'really-existing' people.

Parts II and III: History of Modern Metaphysical, then Historical Revolt

11. Strictly speaking, no revolt was possible in pre-modern societies where 'sacred canopy' is unquestioned (we note that this could certainly be questioned).
12. the modern age, age of revolt, "begins with the crash of falling ramparts":[1765] against
13. natural evil, as rationalised in Augustinian theodicy (metaphysical rebellion (HR Part II)), as:

    a. Just punishment for sinfulness
    b. Necessary in higher order (Christianised Stoic notion)
    c. Reflection of God's inscrutable justice (predestination: later theological nominalism, voluntarism)

14. political evil, as the assumption by human agents of the 'divine right' to kill, enslave, deceive, exile and expropriate (HR Part III).
15. For early modern rebels, (13) a &/or b &/or c may be true, but

    a. we can't know if they are, whether we can witness suffering and injustice;
    b. if (13) a, b, or c is true, they are unjust.

16. Hence, modern rebellion, even in its political forms (14), has metaphysical presuppositions and implications.

1765 HR 45; R 26.

- *L'Homme Revolté* is a response to the problem of evil (esp. rationalised homicide and genocide), as MS was a response to problem of metaphysical homelessness.

17. all modern revolution begins from premise: "if natural and human evil seem necessary to God, in Nature . . ." (revolt)

Absolute negation (revolution) then involves illegitimate, illogical "leaps" on the basis of this legitimate protasis:

17. *De Sade*: "then . . . God must wish for destruction

    - we must follow God (leap);
    - . . . and thus we must become his willing executioners.

18. *Romantics, surrealists*: ("sympathy for the devil") "then . . . we, like Milton's Satan, are the victim of injustice;

    - and we should make our lives (in dandyism) and our art a standing protest against His Order (leap). . .
    - Thus crime is justifiable, the criminal a martyr, excess the portal of higher revelations . . ."

19. *Ivan Karamazov*: "then . . . He does not deserve to exist;

    - thus He cannot Exist (leap 1);
    - Thus everything is permitted (leap 2)".

20. *Fascism (compare "Letter to German Friend")*: "then . . . there is no higher Meaning to this world:

    - the suffering of the weak must be an ineradicable part of the world order
    - Thus, the strong (those capable of seeing this without nostalgia) should do whatever they need to (murder, exploitation, deceit) to achieve rule (the fascists' leap)."

Absolute Affirmation (revolution) likewise makes "leaps" on the basis of the protasis of (16):

21. *Nietzsche:* "then... God's only excuse is that he does not exist...

    - any values that do exist cannot come from Him, or from any other Transcendent Other-worldly source;
    - *thus* this sad and suffering world alone is true (leap 1);
    - the highest value, which will be embodied by the Overman, must be to totally affirm this world, including hierarchy, exploitation, murder (leap 2)..."

22. *Rousseau:* "then morality must not come from, or depend upon, either a transcendent Deity, or be found in Nature;

    - It must come from the pact or General Will between citizens, which is in effect divinised (secularisation of God, political theology: the leap)
    - All factions, criminals against the General Will may be "compelled to be free";
    - *Thus* 'either virtues or the terror".

23. *Marx & Leninism (via Hegel):* "then... any values that do exist cannot come from Him, or from any other Transcendent Other-worldly source...;

    - indeed, theological and Formal, Transcendent principles have been used to rationalise and mystify real injustice...
    - *thus* human History alone, the long story of class struggle/struggle for recognition alone is true (leap 1)";
    - and so the highest value must be to do whatever it takes (including murder, hierarchy, vanguardism, deceit) to expedite the end of Historical struggle, with the advent of a classless society (leap 2)."

    ### Rebellion versus Revolution

24. rebellion, to be true to itself, requires memory, solidarity, and self-control. If we absolutise:

    a. *either* the 'yes' (*'all* or nothing', in defiance—'whatever we, the victims, do is right... the world must be affirmed, including in all its evils')...,
    b. ... or the 'no' ('all *or nothing*', in despair; 'since the world is unjust, who can blame us? the strong must do what they must... the poor will always be with us...'), we assume the right to kill.

25. (24) a and b are 'all or nothing' modes of thinking, replacing an illegitimate excessive claim to 'totality' for the legitimate, innate desire for 'unity':

- They are explicable, even 'understandable', but partial, one-sided, excessive and finally para-logical responses to the at least two-sided demands of rebellion;
- They are also 'nihilistic' since they assign no primary, inalienable value to human life (Camus' decisive definition of this polemical term).

26. a. If we accede to forms of absolute affirmation or negation (24 a and b), we betray the very value we started by affirming in our rebellion (performative self-contradiction);
    b. we do so by undertaking the indicated 'leaps' of logic, animated by desire or despair: laying illegitimate claim to an "all" (e.g.: a Meaning of History) or a "nothing" that experience, reason, and our demand for unity do not license.
    c. Our rebellion has 'come full circle'; and tragically, become a revolution: 'meet the new boss, same as the old boss'.

Part v: The Positive Philosophy, a Primary 'yes' ('Nihilistic Murder')

Given HR Part I and the *per via negativa* work of HR Parts II–III;

27. only the availability of an absolute meaning (such as those furnished in the secularised revolutionary theologies of (premises 17–23)) could license "the disturbance...to the order of things"[1766] involved in taking the life of another human being.
28. the limit ('yes') implicitly affirmed in revolt must be duplicated "everywhere that a human being is to be found—the limit being precisely that human being's power to rebel".[1767]
29. thus, the limit bounds a primary, inalienable value:

"in assigning oppression a limit within which begins the dignity common to all men, rebellion defined a primary value. It put in the first rank of its frame of reference an obvious mutual complicity between men, a common texture, the solidarity of chains..."[1768]

1766 HR 352; R 282.
1767 HR 355; R 284.
1768 HR 351; R 281.

Three Founding 'nos' (Sections 'Nihilistic Murder', 'Historical Murder')

Any truly rebellious, post-metaphysical order must accordingly be based on founding prohibitions:

30. *against murder*, since "he who does not know everything cannot [rightly] kill anyone..."[1769] without *in that act* perfomratively claiming a godlike warrant to which a metaphysical agnosticism shows he has no legitimate right:

    "Authentic arts of rebellion will only consent to take up arms for institutions that limit violence, not for those which codify it. A revolution is not worth dying for unless it assures the immediate suppression of the death penalty; not worth going to prison for unless it refuses in advance to pass sentence without fixed terms..."[1770]

31. *against calculated deceit*: "since in the same way... the man who lies shuts himself off from other men."[1771]

32. *against servitude and systematic exploitation*: since

    "there is in fact nothing in common between a master and a slave; it is impossible to speak and communicate with a person who has been reduced to servitude. Instead of the implicit and untrammelled dialogue through which we come to recognise our similarity and consecrate our destiny, servitude gives rise to the most terrible of silences."[1772]

30–32: AC's effective response to Ivan Karamazov and many others: *If there is no providential God or Order, then ethics must be defended*: viz.

    "If injustice is bad for the rebel, it is not because it contradicts an eternal idea of justice, but because it perpetuates the silent hostility that separates the oppressor and the oppressed. It destroys the small part of reality that can be realised on this earth through the mutual understanding of men."[1773]

1769 HR 361; R 289.
1770 HR 364; R 292.
1771 HR 354; R 283.
1772 HR 354; R 283.
1773 HR 354; R 283.

APPENDIX ONE

Yes and No: Science and Reason Critiqued, Not Totally Negated

33. From *The Myth of Sisyphus*, we know that: "If I recognise the limit of the reason I do not thereby negate it, recognising its relative powers. I merely want to remain in the middle path where the intelligence can remain clear...in the subtle instant that precedes the leap."[1774]

    → *The Rebel* corollary: 'If I recognise the role that ideological systems claiming absolute knowledge have played in sanctifying total regimes, I do not thereby totally question reason's powers...'

    In particular, reason still has positive value:

    a. *as critical*: to show fallacies of ideological uses of reason, in service of irrational or unchecked human demand for unity;
    b. *as descriptive*: "without being capable of explanation, it may still justify itself at the level of description":

"Nothing is less determined on conquest than reason. History is not made with scientific scruples, we are even conditioned to not making it from the moment when we claim to act with scientific objectivity. Reason does not preach, or if it does, it is no longer reason. That is why historic reason is an irrational and romantic form of reason, which sometimes recalls the false logic of the insane and the mystic affirmation of the Word of former times [rationalisation of metaphysical premises, granted on faith]..."[1775]

Yes and No: A Qualified Defence of Political Liberties

35. The real historical implication:

    - of nominal 'freedom' as an ideological value appealed to in mystifying concrete economic exploitation...;
    - and of nominal 'justice' as a value appealed to in suppressing freedoms...;

    in no way impugn freedom or justice as values and virtues *per se*.

36. On one hand, to call into question all norms and laws, is by itself problematic: "if absolute domination by the law does not represent liberty, [neither] does absolute freedom of choice. Chaos is also a form of servitude."[1776]

1774 MS 73–74; MSe 50.
1775 HR 278; R 221.
1776 HR 97–98; R 71.

37. Capitalist injustices license claim only that "bourgeois freedom is a hoax"; not "freedom is a bourgeois hoax".

"... in particular, the few democratic liberties we still enjoy are not unimportant illusions that we can allow to be taken from us without a protest. They represent exactly what remains to us of the great revolutionary conquests of the last two centuries."[1777]

38. Since freedom is necessary condition for:

   a. Criticism of existing injustices;
   b. Artistic and political creation, philosophical and scientific exploration;

"One might even have to fight a lie in the name of a quarter truth. That is our situation today. However, the quarter truth contained in Western society is called liberty... without liberty, heavy industry can be perfected, but not justice or truth." ("Wager of our Generation", RRD 248)

Institutional Prescriptions

39.

   a. *A free press*: "Not that the press is in itself an absolute good... a free press can of course be good or bad, but most certainly without freedom it will be bad... with freedom of the press, nations are not sure to go towards justice and peace. But without it, they are sure of not going there. For justice is done to peoples only when their rights are recognised, and there is no right without expression of that right..."[1778]
   b. *Multiple political parties*: "the first thing to define totalitarian society whether of the Right or Left is the single party, and the single party has no reason to destroy itself. This is why the only society capable of evolution and liberalisation and the only one that deserves both our critical and our active support is the society that involves a plurality of parties as part of its structure."
   c. *A state not bound by any single secular or theological ideology*: "Politics is not religion, or when it is, it is the inquisition. How could society define an absolute? But society and politics... still have the responsibility of arrang-

---

[1777] BF 93.
[1778] Camus, "Homage to an Exile", RRD 102.

ing everyone's affairs so that each will have the leisure and the freedom to pursue this common search."[1779]

d. An independent judiciary and rule of law, versus totalitarian 'state of siege': "the limit where freedom begins and ends is where its rights and duties come together, is called the Law, and the state must bow to the law".[1780]

e. Freedom from poverty: thus limitations of unlimited economic "freedoms" to accumulate wealth, for "it is quite true that there is no possible freedom for a man tied to his lathe all day long when the evening comes crowds into a single room with his family,... this fact condemns a class, a society and the slavery it assumes..."[1781]

Modes of Political Change: In Almost All Situations, Reformist Not Revolutionary

40. given (30–32), political change must involve the renunciation of murderous violence, terrorism, committed on principle, as well as systematic deceit: "uncompromising and limited action springing from rebellion upholds the reality [it has discovered, that of human dignity] and only tries to extend it farther and farther".[1782]

41. so change must be bottom-up, versus all vanguardism (top-down, "Caesarism", "intellectuals, wishing they were military"):

As for knowing if such an attitude can find political expression in the contemporary world, it is easy to evoke ... what is traditionally called revolutionary trade-unionism. Cannot it be said that even this trade-unionism is ineffectual? The answer is simple: it is this movement alone that, in one century, is responsible for the enormously improved condition of the workers from the sixteen-hour day" to the forty-hour week...[1783]

- rebellious progressive politics requires no final answers, but concrete policies and campaigns:

1779 HR 377; R 302.
1780 Camus, "Homage to an Exile," RRD 101.
1781 BF 90.
1782 HR 365; R 293.
1783 HR 371; R 297.

"... because trade-unionism started from a concrete basis, the basis of professional employment (which is to the economic order what the commune is to the political order), the living cell on which the organism build itself, while the Caesarian revolution starts from doctrine and forcibly introduces reality into it. Trade-unionism, like the commune, is the negation, to the benefit of reality, of bureaucratic and abstract centralism. The revolution of the twentieth century, on the contrary, claims to base itself on economics, but is primarily political and ideological. It cannot, by its very function, avoid tenor and violence done to the real."[1784]

[1784] HR 372; R 298.

Appendix Two: Camusian *Mesure*: Philosophic, Aesthetic, and Political

field	Excess / negation: No!		Moderation Yes and no		Excess (affirmation): Yes!
reason's capacity to understand totality (*MS*)	Irrationalism, mysticism (Kierkegaard, Chestov)		Absurd man and rule of life (stay awake; reason critical & descriptive)		Rationalism (Husserl, differently Hegel, Marx)
Response to divine, natural, divinely sanctioned injustice (*HR*)	Irrational, absolute negation (if we are victims, we may become/license crime: de Sade, romantics, surrealists, fascism)	L	The rebel, faithful to both "yes" to human solidarity, justice, inalienable dignity'; "no" to either natural or human injustice, senseless suffering	L	'Irrational Reason' (absolute affirmation) : of formal values (Rousseau) : of all creation as will-to-power (Nietzsche) : of History as struggle for recognition, classless society (Hegel, Marx)
Violence? Deceit? ("Nihilistic Murder", "Historic Murder")	Yogi/Saint/victims: absolute refusal of all violence oneself leaves injustice of others unopposed (inefficacy of abstention)	I	The rebel Prohibition against rationalised murder.	I	The executioners: Violence is way of "making History", "achieving the rule of the Master race"…
Justice, or Freedom? ("Historic Murder")	Absolute extolling Freedoms = "No" to justice; since absolute freedom is freedom to kill, harm, deceive; absolute freedom to trade → impoverishment of others as "unintended consequence"	M	Freedoms of press, expression, thought, religious conviction, assembly, political agitation, limited by… Justice in distribution of freedoms (which circumscribe Justice's limit), burdens and duties of political life, including controlled economy	M	Absolute extolling Justice = denying freedom, until Justice is achieved ("state of siege", "emergency"; order, over law, presumption of innocence before History/Truth, etc.).

(cont.)

field	Excess / negation: No!		Moderation Yes and no		Excess (affirmation): Yes!
History/ reality" or Virtue?	Virtue over History: the Jacobins, Rousseau, Kant: Terror against all unvirtuous individuals or "factions"	I	Virtues rooted in primary value of human solidarity: "the mutual recognition of a common destiny and the communication of men between themselves"	I	History, "Reality" over all formal principles: cynical realism, historical nihilism, the strong do as they can, the weak suffer as they must
Individual or collective	Individual over collective: solitude, deceit, chaos, enslavement of weak by strong	T	"we are" Versus "we shall bes" of messianisms, theological and secular; versus "I am" of excessive individualism/ liberalism	T	Collective over individual: killing plurality, initiative
Creation (and "reality", including political realities	Formal experimentation: non-representational art		"style": "spurns [reality] without escaping from it"		"realism" Either American style: reduces humans to automata (*L'Etranger* [?]): or "socialist", reduces art to propaganda
Creation and morality	Formal experimentation: non-representational art		Tragedy: between yes and no, two forces equally balanced: "all are justified, none is Just"		Morality plays, the mass as liturgical theatre reaffirming sacral dogmata.

field	Excess / negation: No!	Moderation Yes and no	Excess (affirmation): Yes!
All or nothing?	"Nothing (Nature, History, Reality, Truth...) is..." MONOLOGUE, PROPHECY	Sometimes..., mostly...., given particular circumstances... what we presently understand... pending investigation...: "the word 'everything' has no signification for us" DIALOGUE	All (Nature, History, Reality, Truth...) is... MONOLOGUE, PROPHECY

Appendix Three: Philosophy United to Rhetoric: The 'Master Argument' in "Letters to a German Friend"

"There is, after all, some justice in the claim [of Thomas Lanston Thorston] that whatever its merit as a rallying cry in the midst of moral crisis, *Letters to a German Friend* is a work written 'more from the heart than from the mind.'"[1785] Here again this thought of Orme's arguably stands as representative of an opposition, heart and mind, that can be shown to not simply apply. It is true that LGF, a series of fictive open letters to a clearly fictional "German friend" published in *Revue Libre, Cahiers de la Liberation, Liberté*, then *Combat* after liberation, are indeed a piece of political advocacy: "a document of the struggle against violence".[1786] We are meant to sympathise and side with the author, not the addressee—although some critics like Susan Neiman have argued, for characteristic Camusian reasons we will see, that Camus concedes far too much to his fascist interlocutor. (She accuses Camus of an "astonishingly mild" view of Nazism).[1787] Nevertheless, this rhetorical purpose does not speak against the way that almost all of the letters' contents, in Tarrow's words, "assume a knowledge of Camus' philosophical thought."[1788]

Here, we want to illustratively show that Camus' "Letters to a German Friend" indeed reflect, in condensed form, what we called in the "Introduction" the key premises of Camus' 'master argument': running from epistemic scepticism, via ethical life-affirmation towards political solidarity as a post-metaphysical primary value; the conception of *mesure* in a form of philosophical thinking which "excludes nothing"; and a conception of evil as hailing from partiality, excess and error, not total inhumanity, innate wickedness or inherited falleness. As in Appendix One, we will proceed here using note form to maximise analytic clarity.

1. *each letter either (1 and 2) responds to a specific, imagined charge that Camus assigns to his 'German friend', or defends a positive ideal (3 and 4):*

- Letter 1: response to the charge that "you [Camus, the French] do not love your country":

[1785] Orme, *Development of Camus' Concerns*, 125; he is quoting Thomas Lanston Thorson, "Albert Camus and the Rights of Man", *Ethics* 74 (1964): 288.
[1786] Camus, at Tarrow, *Exile from the Kingdom*, 95.
[1787] Neiman, *Evil in Modern Thought*, 297.
[1788] Tarrow, *Exile from the Kingdom*, 99.

You said to me: 'The greatness of my country is beyond price. Anything is good that contributes to its greatness. And in a world where everything has lost its meaning, those who, like us young Germans, are lucky enough to find meaning in the destiny of our nation must sacrifice everything else ... you just don't love your country.' (LGF 5)

- Letter II: response to charge that "in all her intelligence, France repudiates herself"

  Some of your intellectuals prefer despair to their country—others, the pursuit of an improbable truth. We put Germany before truth, and beyond despair." (LGF 13)

- Letter III: a defence of idea of "Europe" poisoned by Nazi ideal of German *lebensraum*.
- Letter IV: final defence against National Socialism on the positive basis of affirming human solidarity.

2. *Camus' recognition of the humanity of the other.*

- In the Introduction, we commented that a corollary of Camus' position is the classical sense that evil hails from partiality, excess, or error: as against assigning a wholly fallen, sinful or malign nature to others. LGF shows how this philosophical position extends even to the Nazis, in ways that have attracted Neiman's ire.
- Camus thus begins by affirming how much he had shared, in the beginning, with the German friend: both were products of the modern breakdown of inherited traditions. Nazism in such a cultural setting represented a temptation.
- In fact, such forms of extolling strength and efficacy alone are a permanent temptation to human beings, given the complexity of the human condition, and the difficulty of attaining virtue, intelligence or happiness.
- We italicise the relevant phrases in the citations that follow. Note again that Camus, far from exhausting himself in triumphantly declaiming the other, constantly 'returns to his beginnings', and questions "our" responses and attitudes:

  - Letter I: "*We had much to overcome*, first of all, *the constant temptation to emulate you*. For *there is always something in us* that yields to instinct, to contempt for intelligence, to the cult of efficiency. *Our great virtues* eventually become tiresome to us. *We become ashamed* of our intelligence, and *sometimes we imagine* some barbarous state where truth would be effortless..." (LGF 7)

- Letter II: "At this point, I see you smile. You always distrusted words. *So did I, but I mistrust myself more.*" (LGF 14)
- Letter IV: "For a long time *we both thought* that this world had no ultimate meaning and that consequently we were cheated. *I still think so in a way.* But I came to different conclusions from the ones you used to talk about, which, for so many years now, you have been trying to introduce into history." (LGF 27)
- "*I know that heaven*, which was indifferent to your horrible victories, will be equally indifferent to your just defeat…" (LGF IV, 32 (cf. LGF III on Christianity, and its divided responses to Hitlerism)).

- Letter IV thus culminates in an appeal for the French and allies to oppose the Nazis "in their power", respecting them in their humanity ("not mutilating your soul") they scorned in others. (LGF 30–31) (Here as elsewhere in Camus, a phrase from Marcus Aurelius, whom we know from the *Carnets* that he had read, resonates: "the best revenge is not to become like the one who harms you.")[1789]

3. *for a few "fine distinctions": a thought which excludes nothing*

- In a way that, absent a wider understanding of Camus' position does seem too forgiving by half, Camus claims that the long struggle against fascism represents the attempt to defend a few "fine distinctions" at the level of culture:

  - "We are fighting for the distinction between sacrifice [legitimate where necessary] and mysticism [Nazism], between energy [legitimate, necessary] and violence [Nazism], between strength [legitimate, necessary] and cruelty [Nazism], for that even finer distinction between the true and the false, between the man of the future and the cowardly gods you revere." (LGF 9–10)
  - Letter I goes on to pose

    - against the blind patriotism of fascism, not anti-patriotism, but a patriotism which (*excluding nothing*) can incorporate criticism of the government of the day and its actions....
    - ...against the mindless 'greatness' of 'resolutely' following orders, *true* greatness and strength of character...

[1789] Cf. the end of *Carnets* I: "Cf. Marc-Aurèle: 'Partout où l'on peut vivre, on y peut bien vivre.' 'Ce qui arrête un ouvrage projeté devient l'ouvrage même.' 'Ce qui barre la route fait faire du chemin'. *Terminé février 1942*." (C I 252; C I Eng 120)

- ○ ...against the defence of heroism as an end in itself, a heroism which (*excluding nothing*) realises that violence and cruelty is in itself empty and regrettable, and that private happiness is a legitimate human good.

- Letter II opposes to the fascist attack on "critical thinking" (e.g.: in Heidegger) in the name of patriotism alone a form of intelligence consistent with civic virtue: "we have formed an idea of our country which puts her in her proper place, *amid other great concepts* [*excluding nothing*]—friendship, mankind, happiness, our desire for justice." (LGF 14)

4. *Fascism as not wholly without any reason: but the product of all-or-nothing thinking which falsely totalises One Thing (the Leader, [as] the Nation), thereby excluding (and setting out to destroy) other legitimate values.*

- Nazism involves a series of passionate errors, collapsed distinctions, not complete madness (we recall that, by 1933, nearly one third of Germans had voted for the NSDAP): "you no longer distinguish anything: *you are nothing but a single impulse.*" (LGF II, 18)
- i.e. national unity, loyalty, order is *a* good; but National Socialism elevated it as *the Good*, to *the exclusion and subordination of all competing goods*: "you are fighting against everything in man that does not belong to the mother country" (LGF II, 14); "even the gods are mobilised in your country." (LGF II, 18)

5. *the price of acceding to such a blind 'all-or-nothing' form of excessive nationalism is a series of paralogical 'leaps'* (LGF IV, 27–28): *"Your logic was merely apparent"* (LGF IV, 28)

- Premise: "You never believed in the meaning of the world" ("in a way," we saw Camus agrees);
- False fascistic deduction 1: "and you therefore deduced the idea that everything was equivalent and that good and evil could be defined according to your [or the Fuhrer's] wishes."
- **Hidden disjunctive assumption 1: 'either divine Meaning *or* self/power of the strongest/'political realism''.**
- False fascistic deduction 2: "You supposed that in the absence of any human or divine code [premise], the only values were those of the animal world—in other words, violence and cunning."
- **Hidden disjunctive assumption 2: 'either divine Meaning or "animal...violence and cunning"'**
 → cf. Dostoevsky's Ivan: "if there is no God, everything is permitted."

6. *these paralogisms speak from, and reflect, the excessive, illogical 'logic' of the passions: in this case, the passions of despair and humiliation and hatred.*

- Recalling the excess that saw Caligula, in indignation and despair, take on the role of a human epidemic (Chapter Three), the fascists infers from the absence of divinely mandated justice their own 'divine right' to act with injustice and scorn for humanity.

  - "you saw the injustice of our condition *to the point of being willing to add to it*." (LGF IV, 27)
  - "in short, you chose injustice and *sided with the gods* ..." (LGF IV, 28)

- despair, by itself, can be a legitimate response, when it is balanced with other human affects and commitments: but by itself, 'excluding all others', it becomes excessive and potentially malign (i.e. another illustration *per via negativa* of Camus' defence of the 'thought that excludes nothing'):

  - "...your despair constituted your strength. The moment despair is alone, pure, sure of itself, pitiless in its consequences, it has a merciless power..." (LGF IV, 29)

7. *Camus response: a revolt of the heart, then the mind*:

- *Level of heart*: "... to tell the truth, I, believing I thought as you did, saw no valid argument to answer you except a fierce love of justice..." (LGF IV, 27: see (2) above)
- *Level of mind*: "if nothing had any meaning, you would be right. But there is something that still has meaning." (LGF II, 14) What is this?
- *The human power to resist divine or human imposition of senseless suffering*: "What is truth?', you used to ask. To be sure, but at least we know what falsehood is: that is just what you have taught us. 'What is spirit?' We know its contrary, which is murder. 'What is man?' There I stop you. Man is that force which cancels all tyrants and gods. He is the force of evidence. Human evidence is what we must preserve..." (LGF II, 14)
- *Letter IV thus gives one of Camus' clearest statements of the performative, inalienable and irreducible desire for unity, pereat mundus, which runs from <u>The Myth</u> into <u>The Rebel</u>*, "Introduction": "I continue to believe the world has no ultimate meaning [the absurd, side 1 (see (2) above)]. But I know that something in the world has a meaning and that is man, because he is the only creature to insist on

having one [the absurd, side 2]. The world has at least the truth of man, and our task is to provide its justification against fate itself." (LGF IV, 28)

8. *Rhetorical conclusion*: these are the reasons why Camus "chose justice in order to remain faithful to the world.... Refusing to accept that despair and that tortured world, I merely wanted men to discover their solidarity in order to wage war against their revolting fate...", rather than becoming active agents or servants of the inhuman dimensions of our condition. (LGF IV, 28)

Bibliography

"Camus, Albert and the anarchists", *Organise! Magazine*, at www-site https://libcom.org/library/albert-camus-anarchists, last accessed February 2015.

Aronson, Ronald. *Camus and Sartre: The story of a friendship and the quarrel that ended it* (Chicago: Chicago University Press, 2004).

———. "Camus and Sartre on Violence—the unresolved Conflict", *Journal of Romance Studies* Vol. 6, no. 1 & 2 (2006), 66–77.

Abbou, André. "Albert Camus: le retour à Ithaque", in A. Fosty (ed.), *Albert Camus et la Grèce* (Aix-en-Provence: Écritures du Sud, 2007), 81–94.

Adorno, Theodor. and Max Horkheimer, *The Dialectic of Enlightenment*, translated by John Cumming (NY: Continuum, 1989).

Agamben, Giorgio. *Homo Sacer: Sovereign Power and Bare Life*, translated by Daniel Heller-Roazen (USA: Stanford University Press, 1998).

———. *State of Exception* translated Keven Ateill (Chicago: University of Chicago Press, 2005).

———. *Time that remains: A commentary on the Letter to the Romans*, translated by Patricia Dailey (Stanford: Stanford University Press, 2005).

———. *The Open* (Stanford: Stanford University Press, 2004).

———. *The Kingdom and the Glory: For a Theological Genealogy of Economy and Government* trans. Lorenzo Chiesa (Stanford: Stanford University Press, 2011).

Ahluwalia, Pal. *Out of Africa: Post-Structuralism's Colonial Roots* (USA: Routledge, 2010).

Akeroyd, Richard H. *Spiritual Quest of Albert Camus* (Alabama: Portals Press, 1976).

Allen Miller, Paul. *Postmodern Spiritual Practices: The Construction of the Subject and the Reception of Plato in Lacan, Derrida and Foucault* (Ohio State University Press: Ohio, 2007).

Altman, William. *The Crisis of the Republic* (USA: Lexington, 2013).

———. *Leo Strauss: The German Stranger* (USA: Lexington, 2010).

———. *Martin Heidegger and the First World War: Being and Time as Funeral Oration* (USA: Lexington, 2012).

Arendt, Hannah. *Eichmann in Jerusalem: The Banality of Evil* (London: Penguin Classics, 2006).

Amiot, Anne-Marie & Mattei, Jean-François. "Avant-Propos," *Albert Camus et la Philosophie* (Paris: Presses Universitaires de France, 1997), 1–19.

Anderson-Gold, Sharon and Pablo Muchnik (eds). *Kant's Autonomy of Evil: Interpretive Essays and Contemporary Applications.* (New York: Cambridge University Press, 2010).

Archambault, Paul. *Camus' Hellenic Sources* (Chapel Hill: University of North Carolina Press, 1972).

Audi, Paul. *Qui témoignera pour nous? Albert Camus face à lui-même* (Paris: Éditions Verdier, 2013).

Arendt, Hannah. *Origins of Totalitarianism* (USA: Harvest, 1976).

———. "Tradition and the Modern Age", *Between Past and Future* (London: Penguin, 2006), 17–40.

Bacon, Francis. "On Death" (Essays, Civil and Moral. The Harvard Classics. 1909–14), at www-site http://www.bartleby.com/3/1/2.html, last accessed January 2015.

———. "Of Great Place", Essays, Civil and Moral. The Harvard Classics. 1909–14. online at www-site, last accessed December 24 2014.

Badiou, Alain. *Saint Paul: The Foundation of Universalism*, trans. R. Brassier (Stanford, Stanford University Press, 2003).

———. *Ethics; Manifesto for Philosophy* trans. Norman Madarasz (Albany: State University of New York Press, 1992).

———. *Metapolitics* trans. by Jason Barker; (New York: Verso, 2005).

Badiou, "Philosophy and Truth" in *Infinite Thought* trans. J. Cléments et al. (London: Continuum, 2006).

Baker, Keith Michael. "Transformations of Classical Republicanism in Eighteenth-Century France", *The Journal of Modern History*, Vol. 73, No. 1 (March 2001): 32–53.

Baring, Edward. *The Young Derrida and French Philosophy, 1945–1968* (Cambridge: Cambridge University Press, 2011).

———. "Liberalism and the Algerian War: The Case of Jacques Derrida", *Critical Inquiry* Vol. 36, No. 2 (Winter 2010), 239–261.

Barker, Jason. *Alain Badiou: A Critical Introduction* (London: Pluto, 2002).

Barthes, Roland. "Réflections sur le style de *L'Étranger*," *Oeuvres Complètes* Vol. 1 (Paris: Seuil, 1994), 60–63.

Bataille, George. "Le Temps de Révolte", reproduced at www-site http://www.pileface.com/sollers/article.php3?id_article=938, last accessed January 2015.

Bayle, Pierre. *Historical and Critical Dictionary*: Selections trans. R. Popkin (London: Hacket, 1991).

———. "A Philosophical commentary on these words of the Gospel, *Luke 14.23*: 'Compel them to come in, that my house may be full' " edited by John Kilcullen and Chandran Kukathas (Indianapolis: Liberty Fund, 2005).

Bernstein, Richard. *Radical Evil: a philosophical interrogation* (Malden, MA: Polity Press 2002).

Birchall, Ian H. *Sartre against Stalinism* (USA: Berghahn Press, 2004).

———. "The Labourism of Sisyphus: Albert Camus and Revolutionary Syndicalism", *Journal of European Studies* 20 (1990).

———. "Neither Washington nor Moscow? The rise and fall of the Rassemblement Démocratique Révolutionaire", *Journal of European Studies* 29 (1999): 365–404.

Blanchard, Marc. "Editor's Introduction", MLN Vol. 112, No. 4, French Issue (Sep., 1997), pp. 497–498.

———. "Camus' *Pudeur*", MLN 112: 4 (1997).

Blanchot, Maurice. "The Great Hoax", in *The Blanchot Reader* edited with an Introduction by Michael Holland, with translations by Susan Hanson, Leslie Hill, Michael Holland, Roland-François Lack, Ian Maclachlan, Ann Smock, Chris Stevens, and Michael Syrotinski (Oxford: Blackwell, 1995).

Blumenberg, Hans. *The Legitimacy of the Modern Age* translated by R.M. Wallace (USA: MIT Press 1997).

Boer, Roland. "The Apostasy of Terry Eagleton", in *Criticism of Heaven: On Marxism and Theology* (Leiden, Boston: Brill, 2007), 275–334.

Boisen, Jorn. "Hédonisme et éthique: un paradoxe camusien?" in Christine Margerrison, Mark Orme, Lissa Lincoln eds., *Albert Camus in the 21st Century: A Reassessment of His Thinking at the Dawn of the New Millennium* (Amsterdam, New York: Editions Rodopi B.V., 2008).

Bourg, Julian. *From Revolution to Ethics: May 1968 and Contemporary French Thought* (USA: McGill, Queen's University Press, 2007).

Bousquet, François. *Camus L'Ancien, Camus Le Mediterraneen* (Sherbrooke, Quebec, Canada: Éditions Naaman, 1977).

Brochier, Jean-Jacques. *Camus, Philosophe pour Classes Terminales* (Paris, La découverte, 1970/1979).

Brombert, Victor. "Boyhood's Dark Fire", *New York Times* August 27, 1995, Sunday, Late Edition—Final, at www-site http://www.nytimes.com/books/97/12/14/home/camus-firstman.html, last accessed February 2015.

Brooke, Christopher. *Philospohic Pride: Stoicism and Poilitical Thought from Lipsius to Rousseau* (Princeton: Princeton University Press, 2012).

Bronner, Stephen Eric. *Camus: Portrait of a Moralist* (Chicago: University of Chicago Press, 2009).

Brown, Jennifer Stafford. "Prison, Plague, and Piety: Medieval Dystopia in Albert Camus's *The Plague*", in The *Originality and Complexity of Albert Camus's Writings*, edited by Emmanuelle Anne Vanborre (Palgrave Macmillan, division of St. Martin's Press LCC, New York, NY, 2012), 94–110.

Calhoun, Craig ed. *Habermas and the Public Sphere* (USA: MIT Press, 1993).

Callinacos, *Resources of Critique* (London: Wiley, 2006).

Callinacos, Alex. *Against Postmodernism: A Marxist Critique* (London: Polity Press, 1990); Terr Eagleton. *The Illusions of Postmodernism* (London: Wiley-Blackwell, 1996).

Camus, Albert. *The First Camus: Youthful Writings* with an Introduction by Paul Viallaneix, translated by E.C. Kennedy. (New York: Vintage, 1977).
- "Essay on Music", FC 130–155.
- "Contradictions", FC 210.
- "Art in Communion", FC 215–223.

Camus, Albert. *Christian Metaphysics and Neoplatonism*. translated with Introduction by Ronald Srigley (Columbia & London: University of Missouri Press, 2007).

———. "Caligula," *Caligula and Other Plays*, translated Stuart Gilbert (London: Penguin, 2006).

———. "Author's Preface" to *Caligula and Three Other Plays* trans. Justin O'Brien (NewYork: Alfred A. Knopf, 1958).

———. *Albert Camus: Lyrical and Critical Essays*, edited by Phillip Thody, translated by Ellen Conroy Kennedy (Vintage: New York, 1987).
- "Between the Wrong Side and the Right Side" in LCE, 3–62.
- "Love of Life", in LCE 52–57.
- "Nuptials at Tipasa", LCE 65–72.
- "Wind at Djemila", LCE 73–79.
- "Summer in Algiers", LCE 80–92.
- "Desert", LCE 93–105.
- "Prometheus in the Underworld", LCE 138–141.
- "Helen's Exile", LCE 148–153.
- "The Enigma", LCE 154–161.
- "Return to Tipasa", LCE 162–171.
- "The Sea Close by...", LCE 172–181.
- "New Mediterranean Culture", LCE 189–198.
- "On Jean-Paul Sartre's *La Nausée*", LCE 199–202.
- "On Sartre's *Le Mur* and Other Stories", LCE 203–206.
- "On Ignazio Silone's Bread and Wine", LCE 207–209.
- "Intelligence and the Scaffold", LCE 210–218.
- "Portrait of a Chosen Man", LCE 219–227.
- "Encounters with André Gide", LCE 248–253.
- "Roger Martin du Gard", LCE 254–287.
- "Herman Melville", LCE 288–294.
- "Lecture on the Future of Tragedy", LCE 295–310.
- "On Jean Grenier's *Les Illes*", LCE 326–333.
- "Letter to Roland Barthes on *The Plague*", LCE 338–341.
- "Three Interviews", LCE 345–365.
- "Encounter with Albert Camus"/"Interview with Gabriel d'Auberède in *Les Nouvelles Littératres*, May 10, 1951", LCE 349–357.

———. *Le Mythe de Sisyphe* (Paris: Gallimard, 1942 [2008]).

———. *The Myth of Sisyphus*, translated by Justin O'Brien (New York: Vintage, 1991).

Camus, "The Artist and His Time", *The Myth of Sisyphus*, 205–212.

———, "Introduction aux *Maxims et anecdotes* de Chamfort", *Albert Camus Oeuvres Complètes I 1944–1948* (Gallimard Bibliothèque de la Pléiade, Paris: 2006), 923–932.

Camus, Albert. *Carnets I, mai 1935–février 1942* (Paris: Gallimard, 1962).

———. *Carnets 1935–1942*, translated with Introduction & notes by Philip Thody (London: Hamish Hamilton, 1963).

———. *Carnets II, janvier 1942–mars 1951* (Paris: Les Éditions Gallimard, 1964).

———. *Carnets 1942–1951*, translated with Introduction & notes by Philip Thody (London: Hamish Hamilton, 1966).

———. *The Plague* trans. S. Gilbert (London: Penguin, 1948).

———. "La Grèce en haillons (5 juin 1939)", OC I 653–656.

- Camus, Albert. "Tout ne s'arrange pas," in OC I 922–923.
- Camus, Albert. "Introduction aux *Maximes et anecdotes* de Chamfort" OC I 923–932.
- Camus, "Au service de l'homme", OC I 933–938.

Camus, Albert. *Oeuvres Complètes II* (Gallimard Bibliothèque de la Pléiade, Paris: 2006).

- "Commentaire de Stephan sur Thucydide et Lucrèce. Fragment du chapitre V, IIIeme partie", OC II 258–261.
- "Les Archives de *La Peste*", OC II 271–284.
- "Exhortation aux Medicins de la Peste", OC II 282–285.
- "Discours de la Peste à ses administers", 370–372
- "Démocratie et modestie", OC II 427–429.
- "Dialogue pour la dialogue (Défence de l'Homme, juillet 1949)", OC II 479–481.
- "Interview non publiée", OC II 481–2.
- "Le Témoin de la liberté", OC II 488–496.
- "Projet de preface", OC II 497–502.
- "Conférence au couvent de Latour-Marbourg", OC II 502–512.
- "Remarques sur la politique internationale", OC II 649–654.
- "'Non, je ne suis pas existentialiste", OC II 654–655.
- "Interview à *Servir*", OC II 659–661.
- "Un Style de Vie", OC II 672–673.
- "Message lu par Jean Amrouche à la Maison de la Chimie, le 18 Novembre 1946", OC II 688–690.
- "Intervention à la table ronde de 'civilization' ", OC II 677–686.
- "Nous autres meurtrieurs", OC II 686–688.
- "Réflexions sur une démocratie sans catéhisme", OC II 715–718.
- "Albert Camus parle avec Nocola Chiaramonte", OC II 718–720.
- "Lettre à Marcel Ayme," OC II 733–734.

- "La Crise de l'Homme", OC II 737–749.
- "Sommes-nous des pessimistes?", OC II 749–754.
- "Ce soir le rideau se lève sur... René Char (1948)", OC II 764–768.
- Albert Camus / 'Antoine Bailly', "*Impromptu des philosophes*", OC II 769–795.

Camus, Albert. "Révolte et conformisme (*Arts* 19 octobre 1951)", *Oeuvre Complètes III 1949–1956* (Gallimard Bibliothèque de la Pléiade, Paris: 2008).

- "Remarque dur la révolte", OC III 327–338.
- "Le meurtriurs délicats", OC III 338–345.
- "La Meurtre et l'Absurde", OC III 344–350.
- "Le Temps des Meurtrieurs", OC III 351–365.
- "Révolte et conformisme (*Arts* 19 octobre 1951)", OC III 393–394.
- Défence de *L'Homme Révolté*, OC III 366–379.
- "Les Pharisiens de la justice (*Caliban*, 1950)", OC III 385–6.
- "Révolte et conformisme (suite), (*Arts*, 18 novembre 1951)", OC III 394–397.
- "Entretien sur la révolte (*Gaxette des lettres* 15 fevrier 1952)", OC III 397–403.
- "Éparation des purs (28 mai 1952)", OC III 403–4.
- "La litérature et la travail (mai-juin 1954)", OC III 929–933.
- "Interview au *Diario* de Säo Paulo (6 août 1949)", OC III 866–868.
- "L'Avenir de la civilization européenne", OC III 995–1011.
- "La metier de l'homme (14 mai 1955)", OC III 1015–1018.
- "La vraie débat (4 juin 1955)", OC III 1018–1021.
- "La condition ouvriere (15 decembre 1955)", OC III 1058–1060.
- "Remerciement à Mozart" (2 fevrier 1956)", OC III 1078–1080.
- "Le dialogue et le vocabulaire" (decembre 1952-navier 1953)", OC III 1105–1108.

Camus, Albert. "A Letter to the editor of *Les Temps Modernes*" in Adrian Van der Hoven & Spritzen, David A. ed. and trans., *Sartre and Camus: A Historic Confrontation* (Amherst, NY: Humanity Books, 2004), 107–130.

———. "Defence of *The Rebel*", in *Sartre and Camus: A Historic Confrontation*, 205–223.

———. "State of Siege" in *Caligula & Three Other Plays* (USA: Knopf, 1958).

———. *L'Homme Révolté* (Paris: Gallimard, 1952).

———. Noces suivi de l'été (Paris: Gallimard, 1958).

———. *The Rebel* translated by Anthony Bower, with a Foreword by Sir Herbert Read (New York: Vintage Books, 1971).

———. *Essais*, Édition de Louis Faucon et Roger Quilliot. Introduction de Roger Quilliot (Collection Bibliothèque de la Pléiade (n° 183), Gallimard, 1965).

———. *Carnets II Carnets II, janvier 1942–mars 1951* (Paris: Les Éditions Gallimard, 1964), 146.

———. *Carnets 1942–1951*, translated with Introduction & notes by Philip Thody (London: Hamish Hamilton, 1966).

———. "Neither Victims nor Executioners", in *Camus at Combat*, 255–276.

———. "The Just", trans. H. Jones & J. O'Brien (London: Penguin 1970).

———. *Carnets III. mars 1951–décembre 1959* (Paris: Les Éditions Gallimard, 1989).

———. *Notebooks 1951–1959*, translated with Introduction & notes by Ryan Bloom (Chicago: Ivan R. Dee, 2008).

———. *Oeuvres Complètes IV, 1956–1959* (Gallimard Bibliothèque de la Pléiade, Paris: 2008).

- Camus, Albert. "Discourse de Suéde: Discourse de 10 decembre 1957", OC IV 237–244.
- Camus, Albert. "Pourquoi je fais du theatre", OC IV 603–609.

Camus, Albert. *Camus at Combat: Writing 1944–1947* ed. Jacqueline Lévi-Valensi, trans. Arthur Goldhammer, with a Foreword by David Carroll (Princeton: Princeton University Press, 2006).

———. "Pessimism and Courage", in *Resistance, Rebellion, Death*, translated with Introduction by Justin O'Brien (New York: Vintage, 1960).

- Camus, Albert. "Create Dangerously", in *Resistance, Rebellion, Death* trans. Justin O'Brien (New York: Vintage, 1960), 249–272.
- "Letters to a German Friend", RRD 5–32.
- "The Flesh", RRD, 41–53.
- "Pessimism and Courage", RRD 57–60.
- "Defence of Intelligence", RRD 61–66.
- "The Unbeliever and Christians", in RRD 67–74.
- "Bread and Freedom", RRD 87–97.
- "Homage to an Exile," RRD 98–108.
- "Kadar had his day of fear", RRD 157–164.
- "Socialism of the Guillotine", RRD 165–172.
- "Reflections on the Guillotine", RRD 173–233.
- "The Wager of Our Generation," in RRD 237–248.
- "Create Dangerously", RRD 249–272.

Camus, Albert. *Exile and the Kingdom* translated by Justin O'Brien (New York: Vintage 1958).

- "The adulterous woman", EK 3–32.
- The Renegade", EK 33–61.
- "The Guest", EK 86–109.
- "The Growing Stone", EK 159–213.

Camus, Albert. *The Fall* translated Justin O'Brien (New York: Vintage, 1956).

———. *The First Man* translated David Hapgood (London: Penguin, 1996).

———. *Algerian Chronicles* translated Arthur Goldhammer with an Introduction by Alice Kaplan (Cambridge, Massachusetts: Belknap Press, 2013).

Camus, "Albert Camus's Nobel Prize Reception Speech", with French and parallel-text translation by Jospeh Gruenbaum, at www-site http://josephpg.com/2014/04/19/albert-camuss-nobel-prize-reception-speech/, last accessed January 2015.

Camus, Albert & Jean Grenier. *Albert Camus & Jean Grenier, Correspondence 1932–1960* translated with an Introduction by Jan E. Rigaud (USA: University of Nebraska Press, 2003).

Camus, Catherine. "Editor's Note", in Albert Camus, *The First Man* translated David Hapgood (London: Penguin, 1996).

Caputo, John D. *The Prayers and Tears of Jacques Derrida* (Indiana: Indiana University Press, 1997)

Card, C. *Confronting Evils: Terrorism, Torture, Genocide* (Cambridge: Cambridge University Press, 2010).

Carroll, David. "Rethinking the Absurd: *Le Mythe de Sisyphe*" in *Cambrideg Companion to Camus*, edited by Edward J. Hughes (Cambridge: Cambridge University Press, 2007), 53–66.

———. *Albert Camus the Algerian: Colonialism, Terrorism, Justice* (USA: Columbia University Press, 2008).

———. "Camus's Algeria: Birthrights, Colonial Injustice, and the Fiction of a French-Algerian People", *MLN*, Vol. 112, No. 4, French Issue (Sep., 1997), pp. 517–549.

de Cassagne, Innes. "Tension et equailibre des extremes dans l'idéal classique de Camus", réunis et présentés par David H. Walker, *Albert Camus: Les Extremes et L'Equilibre* (Amsterdam: Editions Rodopi B.V., 1993), 171–188.

Castoriadis, Cornelius. "The Greek Polis and the Creation of Democracy", in Cornelius Castoriadis, *The Castoriadis Reader* (Oxford: Basil Blackwell Publishers, 1997).

Causset, Pierre. "La Prélude d'une pensée: Métaphysique chrétienne et néoplatonisme", *Albert Camus et la philosophie*, 223–240.

Chiaramonte, Nicola. "Sartre versus Camus: A Political Struggle", in *Camus: A Collection of Critical Essays* ed. Germaine Brée (Englewood Cliffs, N.J.: Prentice-Hall, 1962), 51–57.

Chiesa, Dominic. *Subjectivity and Otherness: A Philosophical Reading of Lacan* (Cambridge, MA: MIT Press, 2007).

Cordes, Alfred. *The Descent of the Doves: Camus' Journey of the Spirit* (Washington: University Press of America, 1980).

Coward, Harold & Toby Foshay ed. *Derrida and Negative Theology* (New York: SUNY 1992).

Cox, iHarvey. The Secular City: Secularisation and Urbanisation in Theological Perspective (New York: Macmillan CO, 1965)

Craiutu, Aurelian. *A Virtue for Courageous Minds: Moderation in French Political Thought, 1748–1830* (USA: Princeton University Press, 2012).

Crochet, Monique. *Les Mythes dans L'Oeuvre d'Albert Camus* (Paris: Éditions universitaires, 1973).

Crowley, "Camus and Social Justice", *Cambridge Companion to Camus*, 93–105.

Cruickshank, John. *Albert Camus and the Literature of Revolt* (New York: Oxford University Press, 1959).

Curtis, Jerry L. "Camus' Portrayal Of Women In 'State Of Siege': Exegesis and Explication", *Orbis Litterarum* 1998: 53, 42–64.

Davis, Colin. "Violence and Ethics in Camus", in *Cambridge Companion to Camus* (Cambridge: Cambridge University Press, 2007), 106–118.

Davison, Ray. 'Mythologizing the Mediterranean: The Case of Albert Camus', *Journal of Mediterranean Studies* 10 (2000): 77–92.

Dean, Mitchell. *Governmentality: Power and Rule in Modern Society* (London: Sage, 2010 [2nd ed.]).

Degenève, Jonathan. "*'Quelle absence!': Blanchot lecteur de Camus*," at www-site http://www.blanchot.fr/fr/index.php?option=com_content&task=view&id=134&Itemid=41, last accessed January 2015.

Derrida, Jacques. *Speech and Phenomena* (Evanston: The John Hopkins University Press, 1973).

———. *Edmund Husserl's 'Origin of Geometry': An Introduction* by trans. John P. Leavey (USA: University of Nebraska Press, 1989).

———. *Spectres of Marx*, translated by Peggy Kamuf (New York: Routledge 1994).

———. *Margins of Philosophy* trans. Alan Bass (Chicago: Chicago University Press 1982).

– "Signature, Event, Context", *Margins of Philosophy*, 307–330.

Derrida, Jacques. *Limited Inc.* ed. Graff, trans. Weber (Evanston: Northwestern University Press, 1998).

———. "How to Avoid Speaking", in Coward, Harold & Toby Foshay ed. *Derrida and Negative Theology* (New York: SUNY 1992), 73–142.

———. "Violence and Metaphysics" in *Writing and Difference* trans. Alan Bass (Chicago: Chicago University Press 1978), 79–153.

– "Violence and Metaphysics", 97–192.

– "From Restricted to General Economy: An Hegelianism without Reserve", *Writing and Difference*, 317–350.

– Derrida, "'Genesis and Structure' and Phenomenology," *Writing and Difference*, (Chicago, 1978), 183–211.

Derrida, Jacques. *Positions* translated and annotated by Alan Bass (London: Athlone Press, 1981).

———. *Dissemination*, translated, with an Introduction and additional notes by Barbara Johnson. (London: The Athlone Press, 1981).

———. *Of Spirit: Heidegger and the Question* trans. A. Bloomington and R. Bowlby (Chicago: Chicago University Press, 1989).

———. "Heidegger: The Philosopher's Hell," in *Points. Interviews 1974–1994*, edited by Elizabeth Weber, translated by Peggy Kamuf et al., 181–90, (Stanford, California: Stanford University Press, 1995).

———. "Adieu to Emmanuel Levinas" in *Adieu to Emmanuel Levinas* translated by Pascale-Anne Brault & Michael Naas (Stanford: Stanford University Press, 1999).

———. *Of Grammatology* trans Gayatry Chakravorty Spivak (Baltimore and London: John Hopkins University Press, 1976).

———. *The Death Penalty* translated by Peggy Kamuf (Chicago: University of Chicago Press, 2013).

———. "Ends of Man", *Margins of Philosophy* trans Alan Bass (Chicago: Chicago University Press, 1986).

———. "Principle of Reason: The University in the Eyes of its Pupils", *Diacritics* XIX (1983): 3–20.

———. "Autoimmunity: Real and Symbolic Suicides," trans. Pascale-Anne Brault and Michael B. Naas, *Philosophy in the Time of Terror: Dialogues with Jürgen Habermas and Jacques Derrida*, ed. Giovanna Borradori (Chicago: Chicago University Press, 2003), 85–136.

Derrida, Jacques in interview with Richard Kearney: "Deconstruction and the Other", in Richard Kearney ed., *Dialogues with Contemporary Continental Thinkers* (Manchester: University Press, 1984.

Derrida, Jacques with John D. Caputo. *Deconstruction in a Nutshell: A Conversation with Jacques Derrida*, edited with a commentary by John D. Caputo (New York: Fordham, 1997).

Dews, Peter. "The *Nouvelle Philosophie* and Foucault", *Economy and Society*, Volume 8, Issue 2 (1979), 127–171.

———. "The New Philosophy and the End of leftism", in *Radical Philosophy Reader*, ed. R. Edgley et al. (London: Verso, 1985), 361–384.

———. *Logics of Disintegration: Poststructuralist Thought and the Claims of Critical Theory* (London: Verso, 2006).

———. *The Idea of Evil* (Oxford: Blackwell, 2008).

Diogenes Laertius, *Lives of the Eminent Philosophers*, translated by C.D. Yonge, at www-site http://classicpersuasion.org/pw/diogenes/dlsocrates.htm, last accessed January 2015.

Doughart, Jason. "Neoconservatism in the Political Thought of Albert Camus: A Preliminary Inquiry", *Journal of Camu Studies*, 2012.

Dunn, Susan. "Camus and Louis XVI: An Elegy for the Martyred King", *French Review* 62 (1989).

Dunwoodie, Peter. "Albert Camus and the Anarchist Alternative", *Australian Journal of French Studies* 30 (1993), 84–103.

———. "Negotiation of Confrontation? Camus, Memory and the Colonial Chronotype", in in Christine Margerrison, Mark Orme, Lissa Lincoln eds., *Albert Camus in the*

21st Century: A Reassessment of His Thinking at the Dawn of the New Millennium, 47–59.

Durant, Will. *The Story of Philosophy* (USA: Simon & Schuster, 1937).

Durant, Will & Ariel. *The Age of Voltaire* (New York: Simon & Schuster, 1965).

Eagleton, Terry. "Where do postmodernists come from?" *Monthly Review* 47(3), July 1995: 59–70.

———. *After Theory* (London: Basic Books, 2003).

———. *Figures of Dissent: Reviewing Fish, Spivak, Žižek and Others* (London: Verso 2003), 246–253.

Ellison, David R. "Camus and the Rhetoric of Dizziness: *La Chute*," *Contemporary Literature* 24, no. 3 (1983).

Engberg-Pederson, Troel. "Discovering the Good: Oikeiosis and Kathekonta in Stoic Ethics", The Norms of Nature: Studies in Hellenistic Ethics, edited by Malcolm Schofield and Gisela Striker (Cambridge: Cambridge Uni. Press 1986), 145–184.

Faulkner, Joanne et al., *Understanding Psychoanalysis* (London: Acumen, 2007).

Faye, Emmanuel. *Heidegger: The Introduction of Nazism into Philosophy in Light of the Unpublished Seminars of 1933–1935*, Michael B. Smith (tr.), Yale University Press, 2009).

Ferrara, Alessandro. "The separation of religion and politics in a post-secular society", *Philosophy & Social Criticism* vol. 35. (2009),77–92.

Ferry, Luc. *Political Philosophy 1: Rights, the New Quarrel Between Ancients and Moderns* (Chicago: University of Chicago Press, 1990).

Ferry, Luc & Alain Renaut, *Heidegger and Modernity* (Chicago: Chicago University Press, 1990).

Foley, John. "Albert Camus and Political Violence" in Christine Margerrison, Mark Orme, Lissa Lincoln eds., *Albert Camus in the 21st Century: A Reassessment of His Thinking at the Dawn of the New Millennium* (Amsterdam, New York: Editions Rodopi B.V., 2008), 209–221.

———. *Albert Camus: From the Absurd to Revolt* (Stocksfield: Acumen, 2008).

Fosty, A. (ed.), *Albert Camus et la Grèce* (Paris: Broché, 2008).

Foucault, Michel. *The Order of Things: An Archaeology of the Human Sciences* (Oxford and New York: Routledge, 1989).

———. *Discipline and Punish*, translated by Alan Sheridan (New York: Vintage, 1977).

———. "Preface" to *Anti-Oedipus: Capitalism and Schizophrenia* Translated from the French by Robert Hurley, Mark Seem, and Helen R. Lane (Minneapolis: University of Minnesota Press, 1983).

———. *History of Sexuality: Volume 1, The Will to Knowledge* trans. R. Hurley (London: Penguin, 1998).

———. "The Subject and Power", in *Critical Inquiry*, Vol. 8, No. 4 (1982), 777–795.

———. "On the Genealogy of Ethics: An Overview of Work in Progress," in Hubert L. Dreyfus and Paul Rabinow, *Michel Foucault: Beyond Structuralism and Hermeneutics*, Second Edition With an Afterword by and an Interview with Michel Foucault (Chicago: The University of Chicago Press, 1983).

———. *The History of Sexuality, vol. 1. An Introduction* (London: Allen Lane, 1979).

———. "Two Lectures" (1976) in *Power/Knowledge: Selected Interviews and Other Writings, 1972–1977* ed. Colin Gordon (Brighton: Harvester 1980), 76–108.

———. "Nietzsche, Genealogy, History." *The Foucault Reader*, edited by Paul Rabinow (New York: Pantheon, 1984), 76–100.

———. *Power/Knowledge: Selected Interviews and Other Writings, 1972–1977*, ed. Colin Gordon (New York: Pantheon, 1980).

———. "Right of Death and Power over Life," in *The Foucault Reader* ed. P. Rabinow (London: Penguin, 1984).

———. "Self Writing" in *Dits et écrits*, pp. 415–430 at www-site http://foucault.info/documents/foucault.hypomnemata.en.html, last accessed February 2015.

Foxlee, Neil. *Albert Camus's "The New Mediterranean Culture": A Text and Its Contexts* (Bern: Peter Lang, 2010).

———. "Mediterranean Humanism or Colonialism with a Human Face? Contextualizing Albert Camus' 'The New Mediterranean Culture'" *Mediterranean Historical Review* Vol. 21, No. 1 (June 2006), 75–94.

Freeman, Edward. *The Theatre of Albert Camus* (London: Methuen & Co., 1971).

Fraser, Nancy. "Foucault on Modern Power: Empirical Insights and Normative Confusions," *Praxis International* 1 (October, 1981): 272–287.

Gadamer, Hans-Georg. *Truth and Method* trans. Joel Weinsheimer, Donald G. Marshall (London: Continuum, 2006).

Gay, Peter. *The Enlightenment: An Interpretation, Volume 1: The Rise of Modern Paganism* (London: W.W. Norton and co., 1966).

———. *Voltaire's Politics: The Poet as Realist* (USA: Yale University Press, 1988).

Gay-Crosier, Raymond. "De l'*Homo faber* à l'*Homo ludens*: defence et illustration de la pensée de midi", in *Albert Camus, Contemporain*, 29–44.

Glucksmann, André. *The Master Thinkers*, translated by Brian Pearce (New York: Harper & Row: 1980).

Golumb, Jacob. *In Search of Authenticity: Existentialism from Kierkegaard to Camus* (London: Routledge, 1995).

Gordon, Daniel ed. *Postmodernism and the Enlightenment: New Perspectives in Eighteenth-Century French Intellectual History* (London: Routledge, 2000).

Goss, James. "Camus, God, and Process Thought", Process Theology, Vol. 4, Number 2 (Summer 1974), 114–128. At www-site http://www.religion-online.org/showarticle.asp?title=2375, last accessed October 2013.

Grouix, Pierre. "L'absence de la philosophie dans *Le Premier Homme*", in Anne-Marie Amiot & Jean-François Mattéi, *Albert Camus et la Philosophie* (Paris: Presses Universitaires de France, 1997), 65–82.

Guérin, Jeanyves & Diane S. Wood, "Albert Camus: The First of the New Philosophers", *World Literature Today* Vol. 54, No. 3 (Summer, 1980), 363–367.

Guérin, Jeanyves. "Camus: Philosophe pour classes terminals?", in *Albert Camus et la philosophie* (Paris: Presses Universitaires de France, 1997), 85–100.

Gutting, Gary. *Thinking the Impossible: French Philosophy since 1960* (Oxford University Press, Oxford and New York, 2011).

Habermas, Jürgen. *The Philosophical Discourse of Modernity: Twelve Lectures* translated T. McCarthy (Massachusetts: MIT Press, 1990).

———. *The Structural Transformation of the Public Sphere* (USA: MIT Press, 1991).

———. "Philosophy as Stand-In and Interpreter," in *Moral Consciousness and Communicative Action* (USA: Polity, 1992).

———. "Secularism's Crisis of Faith: Notes on Post-Secular Society", *New perspectives quarterly*, vol. 25 (2008): 17–29.

———. "On systematically distorted communication", *Inquiry* Volume 13, Issue 1–4, 1970: 205–218.

———. *The Theory of Communicative Action. Vol. I: Reason and the Rationalization of Society*, T. McCarthy (trans.). (Boston: Beacon, 1984), 3–23.

———. *Justification and Application*, trans. C.P. Cronin (Cambridge, MA: MIT Press, 1993)

———. "Reflections on the linguistic foundations of sociology: The Christian Gauss Lectures (Princeton University, February-March 1971)", in J. Habermas, *On the Pragmatics of Social Interaction*, trans. B. Fultner (Cambridge, MA: MIT Press, 2001), 1–103.

Haddour, Azzedine. *Colonial Myths: History and Narrative* (UK: Manchester University Press, 2000).

Hadot, Pierre, "Forms of Life and Forms of Discourse in Ancient Philosophy" in *Philosophy as a Way of Life* translated M. Chase (London: Wiley-Blackwell, 1996), 49–70.

———. "The view from above", in *Philosophy as a way of life*, 138–149.

———. "La Physique Comme Manière de Vivre" in *Exercises Spirituels et Philosophie Antique* (Paris: Broché, 2002).

———. "Année 1979–1980", in Pierre Hadot, *Études de Patristique et D'Histoire des Concepts* (Paris: Le Belles Lettres, 2010), 162–167.

———. "Ancient Man and Nature", *Études de Philosophie Ancienne* (Paris: Les Belles Lettres, 2010), 307–318.

———. "The Figure of the Sage", in P. Hadot, *L'Études de Philospohie Ancienne* (Paris: Les Belles Lettres, 2010), pp. 233–257.

———. *The Inner Citadel: The Meditations of Marcus Aurelius*, translated by M. Chase (USA: Harvard University Press, 1998).

———. *What is Ancient Philosophy?*, trans. M. Chase (USA: Belknap Press, 2002).

Hanna, Thomas. *The Thought and Art of Albert Camus* (Chicago: Regnery, 1958).

Hanna, Thomas L. "Albert Camus and the Christian Faith", in Germaine Brée ed. *Camus: Critical Essays* (Englewood Cliffs, N.J.: Prentice-Hall, 1962), pp. 48–58.

Harding, Thomas. *Hans and Rudolf* (London: Random House, 2013).

Heffernan, George. " 'Mais personne ne parraissait comprendre': Atheism, Nihilism, and Hermeneutics in Albert Camus' *L'Étranger/The Stranger*" *Analecta Husserliana* CIX (2011), 133–152.

Hegel, W.G.F. *Phenomenology of Spirit*, Translated by J.B. Baillie, at www-site https://ebooks.adelaide.edu.au/h/hegel/phenomenology_of_mind/complete.html.

Heidegger, Martin. "Modern Science, Metaphysics and Mathematics", in David Farell Krell ed., *Martin Heidegger Basic Writings* (San Francisco: Harper, 1998), 296–305.

———. "Letter on Humanism", in David Krell ed. *Basic Writings* (New York: Harper and Row, 1977), 189–242.

———. *Being and Time* translated by J. Macquarie and E. Robinson (London: Blackwell, 1978).

———. "Self-Assertion of the German University" in Richard Wolin The Heidegger Controversy (USA: MIT Press, 1993), 29–39.

———. "The Onto-theo-logical Constitution of Metaphysics", in *Identity and Difference* trans. Joan Stambough (New York: Harper and Row, 1969) 42–74.

——— *Introduction to Metaphysics* trans. Gregory Fried and Richard Polt (Yale: Yale University Press 2000).

Hélein-Koss, Suzanne. "Albert Camus et le 'Contrat Social' ", *Studies on Voltaire and the Eighteenth Century* 161 [1976].

Henri-Lévy, Bernard. *Barbarism with a Human Face* translated by George Holoch (New York: Harper & Row, 1979

Herf, Jennifer L. *Reactionary Modernism: Technology, Culture, and Politics in Weimar and the Third Reich* (Cambridge: Cambridge University Press, 1986).

Hochberg, Herbert. "Albert Camus and the Ethics of Absurdity", *Ethics* 75 (1965), 87–102.

Holub, Robert C. *Crossing Borders: Reception Theory, Poststructuralism, Deconstruction* (USA: University of Wisconsin Press, 1992).

Horkheimer, Max. "Theism and Atheism", *The Critique of Instrumental Reason* (London: Continuum, 1974), at www-site https://www.marxists.org/reference/archive/horkheimer/1963/theism-atheism.htm, last accessed February 2015.

Hughes, Edward J. ed. *The Cambridge Companion to Camus* (Cambridge: Cambridge University Press, 2007)

Hunter, Ian. "The History of Theory", *Critical Inquiry*, Vol. 33, No. 1 (Autumn 2006), pp. 78–112.

Huysmans, Jef. "The Jargon of the Exception—on Schmitt, Agamben and the Absence of Political Society", International Political Socology (2008), 2: 165–183.

Isaac, Jeffrey C. *Arendt, Camus, and Modern Rebellion* (Yale: Yale University Press, 1994).

Israel, Jonathan. *The Democratic Enlightenment: Philosophy, Revolution and Human Rights 1750–1790* (Oxford: Oxford University Press, 2011).

———. *The Radical Enlightenment: Philosophy and the Making of Modernity, 1650–1750* (Oxford: Oxford University Press, 2001).

Jacobsen, Norman. *Pride and Solace: The Functions and Limits of Political Theory* (Berkeley: University of California Press, 1978).

Jameson, Fredric. *Fables of Aggression* (London and New York: Verso, 2008 [1979]).

Janicaud, Dominique. *Phenomenology and the 'Theological Turn': The French Debate* (USA: Fordham University Press, 2000).

Jeanson, Francis. "Albert Camus, or the Soul in Revolt", in *Sartre and Camus: A Historic Confrontation* edited and translated by David A. Spritzen (Humanity books, New York, 2004), 79–106.

Jedan, "Stoic Virtues" (Habilitationsschrift zur Erlangung der Lehrbefähigung für das Fach Philosophie, Berlin 1970).

Judt, Tony. *The Burden of Responsibility: Blum, Camus, Aron, and the French Twentieth Century* (Chicago: Chicago University Press, 1998).

Kassoul, Aicha and Mohamed Lakhdar Maougal, *The Algerian Destiny of Albert Camus* (Ann Arbor, MI: Academica Press, 2006).

Kant, Immanuel. *The Metaphysics of Morals* translated and edited by Mary Gregor (Cambridge: Cambridge University Press, 2003).

———. *Critique of Judgment*, trans. Paul Guyer (Cambridge: Cambridge University Press, 2002).

Kateb, George. *Utopia and Its Enemies* (New York: Free Press, 1963).

Kauppi, Niilo. *French Intellectual Nobility: Institutional and Symbolic Transformations in the Post-Sartrian Era* (USA: State University of New York Press, 1996).

———. *Radicalism in French Culture: A Sociology of French Theory in the 1960s* (Ashgate: Surrey, 2012).

Kellman, Stephen G. ed., *Critical Insights: Albert Camus* (Pasadena, California: Salem Press, 2012).

Kingston, Rebecca. "Religion" in *The Montesquieu Dictionary* at www-site http://dictionnaire-montesquieu.ens-lyon.fr/en/article/1377637039/en/, last accessed December 2014.

Kirchheimer, Otto. 'Criminal Law in National Socialist Germany' in W. Scheuermann (ed.) *The Rule of Law Under Siege* (Berkeley: University of California Press, 1996).

Kundera, Milan. *The Art of the Novel* (USA: Harper Perrenial Classics, 2003).

Lacan, Jacques. *Ecrits: The First Full Edition in English* translated by Bruce Fink et al. (New York, London: W.W. Norton and co., 2006).

Lamb, Matthew. "Reexamining Sartre's Reading of The Myth of Sisyphus", *Philosophy Today* 56, 1 (Feb. 2012).

———. "Philosophy as a Way of Life", *Sophia* 50: 4 (2011): 561–576.

Langlois ed. *The Persistent Voice; Essays on Hellenism in French Literature Since the 18th Century in Honor of Professor Henri M. Peyre* (New York: New York University Press, 1971).

Lara, Maria Pia ed. *Rethinking Evil: Contemporary Perspectives* (Berkeley: University of California Press, 2001).

———. *Narrating Evil: A Postmetaphysical Theory of Reflective Judgment* (Columbia: Columbia University Press, 2007).

Larson, J. "Albert Camus' *Caligula* and the Philosophy of the Marquis de Sade", *Philosophy and Literature*, Volume 37, Number 2, October 2013.

Laursen, John Christian. "Baylean Liberalism: tolerance requires nontolerance" in *Beyond the persecuting society: Religious toleration before the Enlightenment*, edited by John Christian Laursen and Cary J. Nederman, 197–215. Philadelphia: University of Pennsylvania Press, 1998).

Lazere, Donald. "Camus on Doublespeak" *The English Journal*, Vol. 66, No. 7 (Oct., 1977), 24–26.

Lecourt, Dominique. *The Mediocracy: French Philosophy Since the Mid-1970s*, translated Gregory Elliot (London: Verso, 2002).

Leibniz, G.W. *Theodicy: Essays on the Goodness of God, the Freedom of Man and the Origin of Evil*, edited with an Introduction by Austin Farrer, Fellow of Trinity College, Oxford, Translated by E.M. Huggard from C.J. Gerhardt's Edition of the Collected Philosophical Works, reproduced as Project Gutenberg EBook at www-site www.gutenberg.org/files/17147/17147-h/17147-h.htm, last accessed October 2014.

Leonard, Miriam. *Athens in Paris: Ancient Greek Thought in Post-War French Thought* (Oxford: Oxford University Press, 2009).

Levinas, Emmanuel. "Is Ontology Fundamental?" in *Basic Philosophical Writings* ed. S. Critchley et al. (Bloomington: Indiana University Press, 1996).

———. *Totality and Infinity: An Essay on Exteriority*, translated by Alphonso Lingis (Duquesne: Duquesne University Press, 2011).

———. "God and Philosophy", in *Of God Whom Comes to Mind* (Stanford: Stanford University Press., 1998), 55–78.

———. *Difficult Freedom: Essays on Judaism* (USA: John Hopkins University Press, 1997).

———. *Otherwise than Being or Beyond Essence* translated by Alphonso Lingis (Pittsbrgh: Duqesne University Press, 1998).

Levine, Alan. "The Prehistory of Toleration and the Varieties of Scepticism" (USA: Lexington, 1999).

Lévi-Valensi, Jacqueline. "'*Si tu veux être philosophe*...'", *Albert Camus et la philosophie* (Paris: Presses Universitaires de France, 1997), 21–34.

Levi-Valensi, "Romans, Mesure et démesure", in David H. Walker réunis et présentés par *Albert Camus: Les Extremes et L'Equilibre* (Amsterdam: Editions Rodopi B.V., 1993), 245–259.

Lilti, Antoine. "Private lives, public space: a new social history of the Enlightenment" in Daniel Brewer ed., *Cambridge Companion to the French Enlightenment* (Cambridge: Cambridge University Press, 2014).

Longstaffe, Moya. "'*Ces forces obscures de l'âme*': Women, Race and Origins in the Writings of Albert Camus (review)", *French Studies: A Quarterly Review* Volume 63, Number 2, April 2009.

Losurdo, Dominic. *Heidegger and the Ideology of War" Community, Death and the West* (USA: Humanity Books, 2001).

Lottman, Herbert R. *Albert Camus: A Biography* (London: Picador, 1979).

Lyotard, Dolorès. *Albert Camus Contemporain* (Lille: Septentrion Presses Universitaires, 2009).

Lyotard, Jean-François. *The Postmodern Condition: A Report on Knowledge* (US: University of Minnesota Press, 1984).

Macintyre, Alisdair. *After Virtue* (Notre Dame: University of Notre Dame Press; 3rd edition: 2007).

Margerrison, Christine, Mark Orme & Lissa Lincoln (eds), *Albert Camus in the 21st Century: A Reassessment of his Thinking at the Dawn of the New Millennium* (Amsterdam: Rodopi, 2008).

———. "Albert Camus: Elements of a Life (review)," *French Studies: A Quarterly Review*, Volume 65, Number 2 (April 2011).

———. "Algeria's Others" in Stephen G. Kellman ed. *Critical Insights: Albert Camus* (USA: Salem Press, 2012).

Marx, Karl. *Economic & Philosophic Manuscripts of 1844* (Moscow: Progress Publishers, 1959); Cf. Eagleton, *Marx* (London: Phoenix, 1977).

Matuštík, Martin Beck. *Radical Evil and the Scarcity of Hope* (Bloomington/Indianapolis: Indiana University Press, 2008).

McCarthy, Thomas. "The Critique of Impure Reason: Foucault and the Frankfurt School", *Political Theory* Vol. 18, No. 3, (Aug. 1990), 437–469.

———. "The Politics of the Ineffable: Derrida's Deconstructionism in Hermeneutics in Ethics and Social Theory," *Philosophical Forum* 21: 1–2 (1989): 146–168.

McGushin, Edward F. *Foucault's Askesis: An Introduction to the Philosophical Life* (USA: Northwestern University Press, 2007).

Mclure, Roger. "Autour de la vérité avec Camus, Ayer et le barman", in David H. Walker ed., *Albert Camus: Les Extremes et l'Equilibre*, 75–88.

Meillassoux, Quentin. "Decision and undecidability of the Event in *Being and Event* I and II", translated by Alyosha Edlebi, *Parrhesia* 19 (2014), 22–35.

Memmi, Albert. *The Colonizer and the Colonized* with Introduction Jean-Paul Sartre (USA: Beacon Press, 1991).

Merton, Thomas. "Seven Essays on Albert Camus" in *The Literary Essays of Thomas Merton*, edited by Brother Patrick Hart (USA: New Direction, 1995), 181–304.

– "*The Plague* of Albert Camus: A Commentary and Introduction", in *The Literary Essays of Thomas Merton* edited by Brother Patrick Hart (New York: New Directions Books 1981).

– "Camus: Journals of the Plague Years", in *Literary Essays of Thomas Merton*, 218–231.

Milbank, John. *Theology and Social Theory* (Oxford: Blackwell, 2006 [2nd edition]).

Milbank, John, Catherine Pickstock &Graham Ward eds. *Radical Orthodoxy: A New Theology* (London: Routledge, 1998).

Miller, James. "Carnivals of Cruelty: Foucault, Nietzsche, Cruelty", Political ThEORY Vol. 18, no. 3 (1990), 470–492.

Montaigne, Michel de. "Of Experience" in *The Complete Essays of Montaigne* translated Donald Frame (Stanford: Stanford University Press, 1971).

Montgomery, Geraldine F. "Plus loin que le morale", in *Camus in the Twenty First Century*, 132–142.

Mori, Gianluca. "Pierre Bayle, The rights of the conscience, the 'remedy' of toleration." *Ratio Juris* 10, no. 1 (1997): 45–60.

Murchland, Father Bernard. "The Dark Night before the Coming of Grace?", *Camus: A Collection of Critical Essays*, 59–64.

Neiman, Susan. *Evil in Modern Thought: An Alternative History of Philosophy* (Princeton: Princeton University Press, 2004).

Neumann, Franz. "Anxiety and Politics" in *The Democratic and Authoritarian State* (Glencoe: Free Press, 1957), 270–300.

———. "The Concept of Political Freedom", The Democratic and Authoritarian State (Glencoe: the Free Press, 1957), 160–200.

———. "The Changing Function of Modern Law", in *Democratic and Authoritarian State*, 23–68.

Nietzsche, Friedrich. *Birth of Tragedy* edited by Raymond Geuss and Ronald Speirs (Cambridge: Cambridge University Press, 2007).

———. *Beyond Good and Evil*. Translated R.J. Hollingdale. (London: Penguin, 2003).

———. *The Will to Power*: In *Science, Nature, Society and Art*. (USA: Random House, 1968).

———. *Twilight of the Idols* (*Die Götzen-Dämmerung*) Text prepared from the original German and the translations by Walter Kaufmann and R.J. Hollingdale, at www-site http://www.handprint.com/SC/NIE/GotDamer.html#sect4, last accessed January 2015.

Nora, Pierre. *Le Française d'Algérie* (Paris: René Julliard, 1961).

Norris, Christopher. "Chapter Three: Metaphysics" in Jack Reynolds and John Roffe eds. *Understanding Derrida* (London: Continuum, 2004), 14–25.

———. *Against Relativism: Philosophy of Science, Deconstruction and Critical Theory* (Oxford: Blackwell Publishers, 1997).

North, Helen. *Sophrosyne* (Ithaca: Cornell University Press, 1966).

Novello, Samantha. "La liberté de ne pas être moderne: le paradigm tragique de l'action politique dans l'oeuvre d'Albert Camus", in *Albert Camus et la Grèce*, 125–142.

Nussbaum, Martha. *Upheavals of Thought: The Intelligence of Emotions* (Cambridge: Cambridge University Press, 2003).

———. *Love's Knowledge* (Oxford: Oxford University Press, 1992).

———. *Therapy of Desire* (Princeton: Princeton University Press, 1993).

———. "Four Paradigms of Philosophical Politics", *Monist* (2000).

O'Brien, Conor Cruise. *Albert Camus* (Great Britain: Collins/Fontana, 1970).

Oake, Roger B. "Montesquieu's Religious Ideas", *Journal of the History of Ideas*, Vol. 14, No. 4 (Oct., 1953), pp. 548–560.

Onfray, Michel. *L'Ordre Libertaire. La Vie Philosophique d'Albert Camus* (Paris: Flammarion, 2013).

Orme, Mark. *The Development of Albert Camus's Concern for Social and Political Justice: "Justice pour un Juste"*. (Madison, NJ: Fairleigh Dickinson University Press, 2007).

Ott, Hugo. *Martin Heidegger: A Political Life* trans. Allan Blunden (New York: Basic, 1993).

Palud, Aurélie. "The Complexity and Modernity of *The Plague*", *Originality and Complexity of Albert Camus' Writing*, 19–34.

Papastavrou, Barbara. "Albert Camus: De l'Amour Platon à son Engagement envers les Grecs", in *Camus et la Grèce*, 107–116.

Pascal, Georges, "Camus ou le philosophie malgré lui", in *Albert Camus et la philosophie*, 173–188.

Patal, Daphne and Wilfrido Corrall eds. *Theory's Empire: An Anthology of Dissent* (USA: Columbia University Press, 2005).

Parker, Emmett. *Albert Camus, the Artist in the Arena* (USA: Wisconsin Press, 1966).

Pascal, Georges. "Albert Camus ou le philosophe malgré lui" in Anne Mari Arriot & Jean-François Mattéi dir. *Albert Camus et la philosophie* (Paris: Presses Universitaires de France, 1997), 173–185.

Pearson, Roger. *Fables of Reason: A Study Of Voltaire's Contes Philosophiques* (Oxford: Oxford Scholarship online, 1993).

Peyre, Henri. "Camus the Pagan" in *Camus, A collection of Critical essasys*, 65–70.

Phillips, Elizabeth. *Political Theology: A Guide for the Perplexed* (London: Bloomsbury, 2012).

Picketty, Thomas. *Capital in the Twenty-First Century* (USA: Harvard University Press, 2014).

Pisier, Évelyne & Pierre Bouretz "Camus et le marxisme" in Revue française de science politique, 35e année, no. 6 (1985) 1047–1063.

Plutarch, "Life of Pericles," *Parallel Lives* (from Vol. III of the Loeb Classical Library edition, 1916), at www-site http://penelope.uchicago.edu/Thayer/E/Roman/Texts/Plutarch/Lives/Pericles*.html, last accessed February 2015.

———, "The Education of Children", from *The Moralia* (Vol. I of the Loeb Classical Library, 1927) at www-site http://penelope.uchicago.edu/Thayer/E/Roman/Texts/Plutarch/Moralia/De_liberis_educandis*.html last accessed January 2015.

Podhoretz, Norman. "Camus and his critics", in *New Criterion* 1982, at www-site http://www.newcriterion.com/articles.cfm/Camus-and-his-critics-6546, last accessed January 2015.

Popkin, Henry. "Camus the Dramatist" in *Camus, A collection of critical essays*, 170–72.

Popkin, Richard. *The History of Scepticism from Savonarola to Bayle*, third enlarged edition (Oxford: Oxford University Press, 2003).

Quilliot, Roger. *Sea and Prisons: A Commentary on the Life and Works of Albert Camus* (USA: University of Alabama Press, 1976).

———. "Albert Camus' Algeria", in *Camus: A Collection of Critical Essays*, 38–47.

Quilliot, Roland. "Lumières et ambiguités de la trajectoire camusienne", *Albert Camus et la philosophie*, 198-2-4.

Ramsay, Raylene. "Colonial/Postcolonial hybridity", in Christine Margerrison, Mark Orme, Lissa Lincoln eds., *Albert Camus in the 21st Century: A Reassessment of His Thinking at the Dawn of the New Millennium* (Amsterdam, New York: Editions Rodopi B.V., 2008), 73–85.

Rasmussen, Dennis. *Pragmatic Enlightenment* (Cambridge: Cambridge University Press, 2013); Genevieve Lloyd, *Enlightenment Shadows* (Oxford: Oxford University Press, 2013).

———. "Contemporary Political Science as an Anti-Enlightenment Project" at www-site http://www.brown.edu/Research/ppw/files/Rasmussen_PPW.pdf, accessed November 2014.

Ratti, Manav. *The Postsecular Imagination: Postcolonialism, Religion, and Literature* (London and New York: Routledge, 2013).

Rey, Pierre-Louis. "Les stratas de la mémoire dans *Le Premier Homme*", in *Albert Camus, Contemporain*, 121–130.

Richardson, Luke. "Sisyphus and Caesar: the opposition of Greece and Rome in Albert Camus' absurd cycle", *Classical Receptions Journal* Vol. 4: 1 (2012): 66–89.

Riskin, Jennifer. *Science in the Age of Sensibility: The Sentimental Empiricists of the French Enlightenment* (Chicago: Chicago University Press, 2002).

Rockmore, Tom. *On Heidegger's Nazism and Philosophy* (Berkeley – Los Angeles – Oxford: University of Califiornia Press 1991).

Sabot, Phillipe. "Les Mésaventures de la dialectique: Camus critique de Kojève dans L'Homme Rèvoltè" in Dolorès Lyotard ed. (Paris: Les Presses Universitaires des Septentrion, 2009), 45–60.

Sagi, Agi. *Albert Camus and the Philosophy of the Absurd* (Rodopi, 2002).

Sagi, Avi. "Is the bsurd the problem or the solution? *The Myth of Sisyphus* reconsidered", in in Stephen G. Kellman ed. *Critical Insights: Albert Camus* (USA: Salem Press, 2012), 188–200.

Said, Edward. *Culture and Imperialism* (London: Vintage, Random House Group Limited, 1994).

Salgado, Raquel Scherr. "Memoir at Saint-Brieuc" *MLN*, Vol. 112, No. 4, French Issue (Sep., 1997), pp. 576–594.

Sarrochi, Jean. "Les Fureurs adolescents", in Les Extrêmes et l'eéquilibre, 3–17.

Sartre, Jean-Paul. "Tribute to Albert Camus," in *Camus: A Collection of Critical Essays*, ed. Germaine Brée (Englewood Cliffs, NJ: Prentice-Hall, Inc., 1962).

———. "Camus' '*The Outsider*' ", *Literary and Philosophical Essays* translated by Annette Michelson (London: Hutchinson & Co., 1968).

———. "Reply to Albert Camus," in *Sartre and Camus: A Historic Confrontation*, 131–162.

———. *Being and Nothingness: An Essay on Phenomenological Ontology*, translated by Hazel E. Barnes (New York: Washington Square Press, 1984).

———. "Existentialism is a Humanism", Existentialism from Dostoyevsky to Sartre, ed. Walter Kaufman (Meridian Publishing Company, 1989).

Sasso, Robert. "Camus et le refus du système", *Albert Camus et la philosophie*, 205–221.

Schaeffer, David. *The Political Philosophy of Montaigne* (USA: Cornell University Press, 1990).

Scherr, Arthur. "Marie Cardona. An Ambivalent Nature-Symbol in Albert Camus's L'étranger" *Orbis Litterarum*, vol. 66, no. 1 (Feb. 2011).

Schimdt, James. "The Legacy of the Enlightenment", *Philosophy and Literature* Vol. 26: 2 (October 2002), 432–442.

Schmitt, Carl. *Political Theology: Four Chapters on the Concept of Sovereignty*. Translated by Guy Oakes (Cambridge, Mass.: MIT Press, 1985).

Schmitt, *Concept of the Political* translated with a Introduction by George Schwab, Preface by Tracey Strong (Chicago: Chicago University Press, 1996).

Schmitt, Gary and A. Shulsky, 'The World of Intelligence (By Which We Do Not Mean *Nous*)', *Leo Strauss, the Straussians, and the American Regime* (USA, Rowman and Littlefield, 1999).

Scholem, Gershom. *The Messianic Idea in Judaism, and Other Essays on Jewish Spirituality* (London: Allen and Unwin, 1971).

Schosler, Jorn. "Rousseau, Camus et le nihilism: sur l'actualité de Rousseau", *Orbis Litterarum* 40 (1985): 97–110.

Seneca, *Letters to Lucilius*, "XXVI. On Old Age and Death", translated by Richard Mott Gummere (A Loeb Classical Library edition; volume 1 published 1917), digitalised at www-site http://en.wikisource.org/wiki/Moral_letters_to_Lucilius/Letter_26, last accessed January 2015.

Sessler, Tal. *Levinas and Camus: Humanism for the Twenty-First Century* (UK: Bloomsbury, 2008).

Sharpe, Matthew. "Autonomy, Reflexivity, Tragedy: Notions of Democracy in Camus and Castoriadis" *Critical Horizons* 3: 1 (2002).

———. "Of Diabolical Evil and Related Matters", *Journal of Žižek Studies* 3: 3 (2009), 1–24.

Sharpe, Matthew & Geoffrey Boucher, *Žižek and Politics: A Critical Introduction* (Edinburgh: Edinburgh University Press 2010).

Sharpe, Matthew. "Reading Camus with, or after, Levinas: rebellion and the primacy of ethics", *Philosophy today*, vol. 55, no. 1, (Spring 2011), 82–95.

———. "Only Agamben Can Save Us? Against a recent messianic turn in post-Heideggerian critical theory", *Bible and Critical Theory* 5: 3 (2011).

———. "Invincible Summer: Camus' Philosophical Neoclassicism", *Sophia*, Vol. 50, Issue 4 (Dec. 2011), 577–592.

——— "Camus' *Askēsis*: reading Camus in light of the *Carnets* (and his *L'Impromptu des philosophes*), *Philosophical practice*, vol. 8, no. 1 (2013), pp. 1149–1164.

———. "A Just Judgement? Considerations on Ronald Srigley's *Camus' Critique of Modernity*," *Thesis Eleven*, vol. 120, no. 1 (2014), pp. 43–58.

———. "The Black Side of the Sun: Camus, Theology, and the Problem of Evil," in *Political Theology*, 2014.

———. "Meursault (and Caligula) avec de Sade: On the relations between the Literary Absurds and Camus' Philosophical Discourse", *Journal of Camus Studies* (2014).

———. "On a Forgotten Argument in French Philosophy: Sceptical Humanism in Montaigne, Voltaire and Camus", *Critical Horizons*, Vol. 16, no. 1 (Feb. 2015).

Sherman, David. *Albert Camus* (London: Wiley-Blackwell, 2008).

Smyth, Edmund J. "Camus, the *Nouveau Roman*, And the Postmodern" in *Originality and Complexity of Albert Camus*, (Palgrave Macmillan, division of St. Martin's Press LCC, New York, NY, 2012), 7–18.

Solomon, Robert. *Dark Feelings, Grim Thoughts: Experience and Reflection in Camus and Sartre* (Oxford: Oxford University Press, 2006).
Spivak, Gayatri Chakravorty & Michael Ryan, "Anarchism Revisited: A New Philospohy. Contra le Nouvelle Philosophie", Diacritics Vol. 8, No. 2 (Summer 1978), 66–79.
Sprintzen, David. *Camus: A Critical Examination* (Philadelphia: Temple University Press, 1998).
Sprintzen, David A., Salam Hawa, Bernard Murchland, and Adrian van den Hoven, "Historical and Critical Introduction: From Freindship to Rivals", in *Sartre and Camus: An historic confrontation*, 31–78.
Srajek, Martin. "Connections between Cohen, Benjamin, and Derrida", in *Journal of Textual Reasoning* 2: 2 (2015) at www-site http://jtr.lib.virginia.edu/textual-reasoning-vol-2-2-february-1993, last accessed February 2015.
Srigley, Ronald. *Albert Camus' Critique of Modernity* (Missouri: Missouri University Press, 2011).
Stern, Daniel. "The Fellowship of Men that Die: The Legacy of Albert Camus", *Cordozo Studies in Law and Literature*, Vol. 10, No.2 (Winter, 1998), 183–198.
Strauss, George. "A Reading of Albert Camus' Le Mort Heureuse", in Camus, Albert Critical Insights, 147–169.
Strauss, Leo. *Natural Right and History* (Chicago: Chicago University Press, 1953).
———. *City and Man* (Chicago: Chicago University Press, 1963).
———. *Philosophy and Law* translated with Introduction by Eve Adler (USA: SUNY, 1995).
———. "Preface to the English Translation," *Spinoza's Critique of Religion* (Chicago: University of Chicago Press, 1997).
Le Sueur, James. *Uncivil War: Intellectuals and Identity Politics During the Decolonization* (US: University of Pennsylvania Press, 2001).
Tal, Uriel. *Religion, Ideology and Politics in the Third Reich: Selected Essays* (London: Taylor & Francis, 2004).
Tarifa, Fatos. "The Poverty of the 'New Philosophy'", *First principles ISI Web Journal*, at www-site http://www.firstprinciplesjournal.com/articles.aspx?article=1661&theme=home&page=4.
Tarrow, Susan. *Exile from the Kingdom* (USA: University of Alabama Press, 1985).
Taylor, Charles. *A Secular Age* (Cambridge, Massachusetts: Harvard, 2007).
Teubelsi, Mustapha. "Albert Camus, lecteur au tragédie grecque", in *Camus et la Grèce*, 95–105.
Thody, Phillip. *Albert Camus, 1913–1960* (New York: Macmillan, 1980).
———. "Introduction", to Albert Camus, *Carnets 1935–1942* trans. with Introduction & notes by P. Thody (London: Hamish Hamilton), pp. vii–xi.
Thorson, Thomas Lanston. "Albert Camus and the Rights of Man", *Ethics* 74 (1964).

Thucydides, *History of the Peloponnesian War*, translated by Richard Crawley at www-site http://www.gutenberg.org/files/7142/7142-h/7142-h.htm, last accessed January 2015.

Todd, Olivier. *Albert Camus: A Life* trans. B. Ivry (New York: Carroll & Graf, 2000).

Tomaselli, Sylvania. "Reason", in *The Blackwell Companion to the Enlightenment*, ed. John W. Yolton (Oxford: Blackwell, 1991).

Van der Hoven, Adrian & Spritzen, David A. ed. and trans., *Sartre and Camus: A Historic Confrontation* (Amherst, NY: Humanity Books, 2004).

Varbonne, Emmanuelle Anne. "Albert Camus's *The Fall*: The Vertiginous Fall Into Language, Representation and Reality, in *Originality and Complexity of Albert Camus" Writings*, 35–52.

Viallaneix, Paul. "The First Camus", in *Youthful Writings: The First Camus*, translated by Ellen Conroy Kennedy (New York: Alfred A. Knopf, 1970).

Viglieno, Laurence. "Némésus: Déesse Inspiratrice du Dernier Camus?", in *Albert Camus et la Grèce* (Rencontres méditerranéens Albert Camus: Éditions du Sud, 2007), 49–66.

Voegelin, Eric. *The New Science of Politics* (Chicago: University of Chicago Press, 1987).

Voltaire, "Poem on the Disaster at Lisbon," translated by Joseph McCabe, *Voltaire: Selected Texts* (London: Watts & Co., 1948).

———, *Philosophical Dictionary*, translated by William F. Fleming: at www-site https://ebooks.adelaide.edu.au/v/voltaire/dictionary/complete.html, last accessed December 2014.

Wallace, Robert M. "Translator's Foreword" to Hans Blumenberg, *The Legitimacy of the Modern Age* translated by R.M. Wallace (USA: MIT Press 1997).

Walker, David ed., *Albert Camus: Les Extremes et l'Equilibre* (Actes du colloque de Keele, 25–27 mars 1993. Amsterdam: Rodopi, 1994).

Walker, I.H. 'Camus, Plotinus, and *'Patrie'*: the Remaking of a Myth', *Modern Language Review*, 77: 4 (October 1982), 829–39.

Walzer, Michael. "Commitment and social criticism: Camus's Algerian war," *Dissent* (Fall1984), 424–432.

Ward, Bruce K. "The Recovery of Helen: Albert Camus's Attempt to Restore the Greek Idea of Nature", *Dionysius* 14 (1990): 169–194.

———. "Christianity and the Modern Eclipse of Nature: Two Perspectives", *Journal of the American Academy of Religion* Vol. 63, No. 4, Winter, 1995: 823–843.

Warren, Thomas. "On the Mistranslation of *La Mesure* in Camus' Political Thought," *Journal of the History of Philosophy*, vol. 30, no. 1 (January 1992): 123–130.

Weyembergh, Maurice. "Camus et la Genie du consentement," in *Albert Camus et La Philosophie*, 117–132.

———. *Camus: our la mémoire des origins* (Paris: de Boeck & Larcier s.a. 1998).

———. "Réflections sur l'(in)actualité de Camus", in Christine Margerrison, Mark Orme, Lissa Lincoln eds., *Albert Camus in the 21st Century: A Reassessment of His Thinking at the Dawn of the New Millennium* (Amsterdam, New York: Editions Rodopi B.V., 2008), 22–41.

———. "L'unité, la totalité,"La tentation du 'tout est permis': Camus entre 'détour' et 'rétour' ", in D. Lyotard ed. *Albert Camus, Contemporain*, 61–76.

———. "L'unité, la totalité, et l'énigme ontologique", David H. Walker réunis et présentés par *Albert Camus: Les Extremes et L'Equilibre* (Amsterdam: Editions Rodopi B.V., 1993), 33–50.

Wheeler, Burton W. "Beyond Despair: Camus' *The Fall* and Van Eyck's 'Adoration of the Lamb' ", *Contemporary Literature* vol. 23, no. 3 (Summer 1982), 343–364.

Williams, Bernard. *Ethics and the Limits of Philosophy* (London: Routledge Classics [reedition], 2011).

Woelfel, James W. *Camus: A Theological Perspective* (New York: Abington, 1975).

Wolin, Richard. *The Wind from the East: French Intellectuals, the Cultural Revolution, and the Legacy of the 1960s* (USA: Princeton University Press, 2012).

Woolfolk, Alan. "The Artist as Cultural Guide: Camus' Post-Christian Asceticism", *Sociological Analysis* 47: 2 (Summer 1986): 93–110.

Worms, Frederic. *La philosophie en France au XXe siècle. Moments* (Paris: Broché, 2009).

Zaretsky, Robert. *Albert Camus: Elements of a Life* (USA: Cornell University Press, 2010).

———. *A Life Worth Living* (Harvard University Press. Kindle Edition, 2013).

Žižek, Slavoj. *Sublime Object of Ideology* (London: Verso, 1989).

———. *Ticklish Subject* (London: Verso, 1999).

———. *Plague of Fantasies* (London: Verso, 1997).

———. *On Violence* (London: Picador, 2008).

———. *Did Anybody Say Totalitarianism?* (London: Verso, 2011).

———. *Welcome to the Desert of the Real: Five Essays* (London and New York: Verso, 2002).

Žižek, Slavoj with Judith Butler and Ernesto Laclau, *Contingency, Hegemony, Universality* (London: Verso, 2000).

Index

1 General Index

Abbas, Ferhat   321
absolute affirmation   131–134
absolute negation   131
absurd, the   1–4, 16, 24–27, 35, 41–45, 47–48, 150, 152, 159–175, 180–182, 184, 186–197, 211–214, 218, 242, 254, 260, 331, 357–358, 366, 370, 384
Adorno and Horkheimer, *Dialectic of Enlightenment*   82, 85, 90–91, 97, 204
adversary, not enemy   230, 306, 353, 354
Agamben, Giorgio   11, 15n55, 93, 101, 236, 288, 291n1245, 293, 347
   See also homo sacer
Algeria   5, 7, 10, 29, 55, 57, 149, 172n708, 204, 219, 232, 235, 246, 253, 263–277, 318–330, 336, 348–357, 375–387
"all is well"   108, 306n1315
"all or nothing" absolute claims   6, 25, 50n187, 127, 131–132, 137n550, 176, 184, 189, 192, 195, 214, 222, 226, 300, 312, 327, 343, 344, 362
apocalyptism   38, 143, 335
Arab, the (in *The Outsider*)   176, 324–325
Arendt, Hannah   84, 87, 91, 98–99, 128n517, 197
Aristotle   19, 28, 33, 34, 36, 42n158, 43, 46, 184, 191, 192, 247, 267, 286, 298–299, 301, 306, 313, 363, 367, 391n1761
ascesis (and need for)   219n933, 358, 359, 367, 370, 371
Audi, Paul   35, 331, 337–340, 373
Augustinian theodicy   107, 114–118
Auschwitz   65, 107, 130, 226n961
   See also Shoah, the
authority versus power   18, 386
Ayer, A.J., review and critique of Camus   20

Bacon, Francis   19, 36n135, 38, 42n158, 43n159, 91, 106, 308, 361, 372n1659
Badiou, Alain   11, 15n55, 56, 101, 145, 236, 257, 288–292, 347, 356
balance   25, 133, 234, 260, 298, 361–363, 376
   See mesure, moderation, *sophosyne*
Barthes, Roland   62–63, 105, 207–208, 257n1103

Bataille, George   2, 6, 152, 167, 234
Bayle, Pierre   26, 38, 91, 108–111, 116, 117, 181, 244, 246
biopolitics   97
Blanchot, Maurice   2, 6, 238n1033
Blumenberg, Hans   55, 116–117, 122–124, 135–136, 164, 253
Bousquet, François   30–31, 224n960, 268n1147, 269
Breton, André   1–2, 18
Buber, Martin   201n861

Cádiz (in *Stage of Siege*)   65–68, 72, 92
Caligula (in *Caligula*)   171–174, 177, 179–182, 187, 238, 308, 362, 374n1675
camps, internment and concentration   17, 64, 78, 85, 95, 126–127, 134, 154n611, 199, 216, 223–224, 248, 300, 364
Carroll, David   10, 54, 219, 265n1135, 269n1154, 274, 323n1390, 327, 329–330, 351, 379, 382
Catholicism   61, 90, 101–102, 114, 117, 119, 179, 246, 309
cave, the (in Plato)   55–56, 331
Chamfort, Camus' preface to the maxims and anecdotes of   45, 206
Char, René   258n1113, 270, 285, 302, 363
"cheating"   16, 25
Chestov, Lev   47
Christ, Jesus   2n6, 114n456, 116, 149, 334, 343
Christianity   2n6, 31, 48n179, 101, 103, 109, 114–115, 118, 121n491, 123, 253, 268, 278, 287, 305n1313, 333–335, 343, 357
Cicero, Marcus Tullius   21n84, 33–34, 35n129, 39, 40, 58, 75, 248n1071
civilian truce, Camus' proposal for a   321–322, 352
Clamence, Jean-Baptiste (in *The Fall*)   1, 74, 114n456, 218, 325–326, 330, 332–348, 355, 362, 371, 372, 391
communicative ethics   88n337, 227–229, 258
Cormery, Jean   319, 377, 379n1693, 380, 383–385, 389
courage as a secondary virtue   364–365
culture war   14, 14n52
cynicism as the temptation of intelligence

51

Damiens (in *Discipline and Punish*) 69–70
de la Vigerie, Emmanuel d'Astier 54, 62, 105–106, 207, 237
death 65–68, 115, 124, 159–160, 171, 180, 188, 192, 216, 240n1033, 281, 315n1350, 329, 359, 362, 367–368, 370n1651, 371–372, 374, 386
death penalty 4, 23, 26, 74, 102n401, 243, 295, 336
deconstruction 4, 12, 55, 152, 156–157, 159, 162n653, 167–168, 183, 192, 267, 289–290, 293n1253
  See also logocentrism
Derrida, Jacques 4, 11–12, 16, 56, 64, 152, 154–159, 161–163, 167–168, 170, 184–185, 192–193, 195–196, 199, 222, 267, 288–293, 321n1376
Descartes, René 19, 24, 48, 106, 124, 155n617, 182–183, 212, 269, 289n1237
description, contrasted with explanation 46, 48, 163, 195
desire for unity/meaning 42, 47–49, 110, 126–127, 137, 166, 169, 171, 177, 182–183, 189, 193, 213, 224–225, 244, 289, 300–301, 311–312, 315, 346, 361
  See also subject, the
Dews, Peter 78–80
Diderot 38, 39
Diogenes Laertius 368n1633
Diplômes thesis, Camus' 30, 49, 104, 119, 190, 268, 272, 278, 286, 301, 334, 356
disciplines, Foucauldian 69–80, 242
Doctor Rieux (in *The Plague*) 46, 62–64, 75, 91–92, 93, 97, 118–121, 124–126, 209n886, 218, 284, 302n1289, 314, 365, 391
du Gard, Martin 174
Dunwoodie, Peter 54, 274, 379

Eagleton, Terry 14, 15, 101, 292n1248
emotions 36, 37, 43n158
  See passions
enlightenment, the 38–40, 81–82, 91, 108–109, 196, 217, 219, 242
Epictetus 224n960, 359, 372
epistemic pluralism 46, 162
  See knowledge, pluralistic conception of
eschatology 2n6, 9, 23, 115, 123, 136, 138, 142, 144, 273, 278, 285, 287–289, 389–390

evangelical (early) Christianity 114–117, 123, 278, 280, 286
Evian accords, end of French Algeria 58, 263, 319, 328, 348
evil 4, 10, 20, 26, 63, 96, 104–112, 114–119, 123–124, 128–133, 142, 172, 178, 183n773, 197, 211, 225, 250n1082, 262–263, 279–280, 283, 300, 304–306, 317, 343–344, 346, 363, 365
existentialism 6, 11, 29–30, 42, 144n582, 151–152, 189, 255n1091, 270n1161, 288–289, 307, 343
extremes 127, 228, 234, 243, 300–301
  See also moderation

fall, the (Christian-Augustinian view of) 117, 188, 334
fascism 38, 57, 78, 86, 98, 105, 124, 128–129, 133–134, 137, 154, 201–202, 248, 262, 273, 277, 285, 294, 316, 324
flesh, the 160, 205, 221, 266
FLN (*Front de Libération Nationale*) 8, 238n1032, 319, 321–322, 350–351, 354–355, 378
Foley, John 9n35, 237–238, 328n1421
formal (bourgeois) virtue 218–219
Foucault, Michel 8n32, 11–12, 14n50, 15, 32, 55–56, 68–80, 82, 85, 88–89, 94, 154, 167, 194, 216, 233, 253, 257, 267, 291, 370n1646
freedom 8, 15n55, 19
  See liberty
freedom and justice as a long distance race 368
French revolution 69, 103, 110, 322

Gay, Peter 38–39
general will 10, 132, 219
Germain, Louis (Camus' school teacher) 30, 385, 390
Gide, André 271, 358
Gilson, Étienne 33
Glucksmann, André 17, 77–79, 81–82
gnostic theodicy 115–116, 172, 262, 278, 356
"go back down" (into politics) 51, 248n1071, 331
grace, theological 102, 110, 115, 118, 121, 124–125, 280, 333, 342, 356

INDEX 439

Greeks, the   29, 79, 165n665, 192, 210, 218n929, 242, 244, 256, 260–262, 267–268, 270–271, 279, 281n1201, 283, 286–287, 295–296, 298–306, 311, 347, 356, 360, 384, 391n1761
Grenier, Jean   30, 135, 271, 302, 344, 386–387, 390
guilt   19, 26, 35, 44–46, 57, 92–94, 117, 193, 265, 282, 306, 326, 329, 333, 336, 339–355, 361, 378

Habermas, Jürgen   14, 56, 184, 197, 222–223, 227–229, 253, 258, 290, 353
Haddour, Azzedine   6, 8, 54, 172n708, 206n875, 257n1103, 259, 264, 266, 269, 277, 320, 326, 330, 380n1700, 381
Hadot, Pierre   22n85, 32–35, 188, 256, 267, 359n1591, 372n1659, 391
hand to hand combat   145
happiness   25, 50–54, 96, 124, 126, 149, 179, 204n866, 224, 253–254, 279, 285, 320, 346, 362, 367–369, 372–374, 390–391
health versus salvation (in *The Plague*)   125
Hegel, Georg W.F.   13, 19–20, 30, 48, 78–79, 109, 112, 129–130, 132, 133–134, 136–137, 140, 164, 204, 212, 240, 254–255, 257–258, 267–268, 285, 299, 303, 308, 386
Heidegger, Martin   3n12, 8n32, 15n55, 21, 30, 42, 93, 98, 124, 139, 153–156, 159, 184, 194, 258, 267, 289, 327, 347, 364, 371
Hellenism, neoHellenism   31, 249, 253, 260, 264, 271–272, 278–280, 299, 307, 331, 357
    See neoclassicism
historicism, philosophical   13, 14n51, 97, 220, 255–256, 259, 265, 308, 352
Hitler, Adolf   17, 63, 74, 77, 80, 82–84, 86–87, 89, 91–92, 98–100, 153–154, 277, 333
Holocaust, the   208n895
    See Shoah, the
homo sacer   93
    See also Agamben, Giorgio
honesty   24, 113n450, 239, 254, 357
humanism   11–12, 80, 88, 130, 141, 144, 151, 155–156, 246, 323
humility   26, 58, 295, 317, 334, 340, 360
Hunter, Ian   290–291, 292n1248
Husserl, Edmund   30, 43n161, 46n170, 50n187, 157–158, 161–164, 169–171, 175, 186, 192, 195, 196, 290

"I am returned to my beginnings" (*Je suis revenue à mon commencement*)   181, 183, 222, 375
ideology, critique of   140n566, 257, 287
imagination   36, 195, 203–207, 218, 276–277, 353, 361, 387n1739, 391n1760
    See also sympathetic imagination
indifference   69, 127, 175, 196, 270, 314, 354, 371, 374n1675
inhumanity in nature   63, 125, 180, 191, 316, 366
intellectual trial (*process intellectuelle*)   340
"I rebel, therefore we are"   210, 310
irrationalism   164, 170, 186, 192, 214, 222, 295, 312–313

Jacobins   105, 112, 129, 132, 134, 219, 221
Jameson, Frederic   208
Jaspers, Karl   21, 169, 175, 287, 294
Jeanson, Francis   1, 6, 19, 28, 54, 57, 105–106, 128n518, 135, 138, 207–208, 219–220, 226, 237, 259, 262–263, 265, 336–339, 343, 363, 380n1700
"judge-penitent"   57, 327, 336, 343, 345, 347, 350, 365
justice, feverish need or passion for   52, 142, 201, 208, 236, 363

Kabylie, Camus' articles on   205, 271
Karamazov, Ivan (in *Brothers Karamazov*)   111, 118, 125, 126, 132, 137n549, 196–197, 222
Kierkegaard, Søren   21, 47, 50n187, 161, 169–170, 175, 180, 182, 186, 192, 196
knowledge
    of one's ignorance   109, 166, 170, 186, 244, 365
    pluralistic conception of   46, 162
Koestler, Arthur   135, 237
Kojève, Alexandre   129n522, 133, 144, 344, 365, 386

language   36, 46, 50, 57, 70, 88n337, 92, 142, 145, 157–159, 173, 185n782, 226, 228–229, 257, 274, 289, 307, 339–340

"leap"   16, 131, 175, 222, 344
Lenin, Leninism   8, 18, 23, 38, 86, 90, 113, 128–129, 135–136, 139, 142–143, 236–237
level, notion of   170
   See also limits
Levinas, Emmanuel   12, 56, 152, 167, 196–197, 199–201, 204–205, 208, 211n897, 253, 258, 288, 293
Leynaud, René   205–206, 221
liberalism   15n55, 17, 81, 245n1058, 311
liberty   17, 26, 41, 51–52, 80, 85, 141, 150, 187–188, 197, 232–233, 236, 285, 349, 368, 372
   See freedom
life of the mind   5, 52, 346
limits   4, 16, 18, 23, 26, 47, 54, 89, 107n417, 114, 166–170, 181–185, 192, 195, 211, 234, 239, 261–262, 280, 289, 295, 297, 299, 301, 305–317, 337, 344, 352, 354, 358, 376
   See level, notion of
Lisbon earthquake   107–110, 117, 119
logocentrism   153, 156, 159, 289n1237
   See also deconstruction
love   2n6, 25, 41–42, 45–47, 50–53, 57, 96, 121–122, 131, 151n596, 164, 166, 188, 198, 216, 218, 253–254, 258, 270–271, 280, 296, 311, 316, 318, 326, 329, 334–336, 360, 362–365, 368, 375–377, 383–385, 388–389, 391
lucidity   45, 160, 171, 358, 364, 370, 373
lumières   38–40, 108, 245
Lyotard, Dolorès   10
Lyotard, Jean-François   11–12, 16, 112n444, 154, 267, 288, 290n1244
Lyssenko   140

Maison de la Culture   272–273, 276–277
Maoism   68, 101, 343
Marcus Aurelius   35, 189, 278, 359, 369
Marx, Karl   20, 48, 79, 102, 113, 132, 133, 134, 138–145, 167, 204, 240, 285, 288, 290–292
Marxism   1, 3n14, 13, 38, 77–78, 80, 90, 101, 106, 113, 124, 129, 133–143, 144n582, 154, 184, 233, 235–236, 287–288, 307
Mauriac, François   102, 209n891
Mediterranean, as sensibility, mode of life, thinking   30, 262–263, 271–284
megalopsychia (great-souledness)   367, 372, 374
memento mori   160n639, 370–371

Merleau-Ponty, Maurice   10, 27, 29n102, 106, 130, 143–144
messianic turn (in post-structuralism)   57, 93n358, 292, 307
messianism   16n55, 56, 58, 101, 113, 138–139, 145, 236–237, 240, 253, 284, 288–293, 299, 305–306, 320, 327, 335
   See also political theology, prophetism
mesure   3, 25, 31, 47, 52, 56–58, 145, 192, 234, 249, 260, 294, 297–307, 312, 339, 352, 360–362, 366, 376
   See balance, moderation, *sophrosyne*
   See also extremes
Meursault (in *The Outsider*)   47, 151, 171–180, 187, 235, 266, 283, 308, 314, 324, 328, 374n1675, 391
micro-practices/micro-power (in Foucault)   70, 76, 233
Milbank, John   100–101, 119, 123
moderation   25, 45, 55, 127, 145, 191–192, 226n958, 250n1082, 297–298, 344, 361, 363
   See balance, *mesure*, *sophrosyne*
   See also extremes
modernity, legitimacy and critique of   55, 81, 97–98, 100, 136, 143, 155–156, 210, 232–233, 284, 335, 338
modestie   39, 240, 245
Montaigne, Michel de   19, 26, 28n102, 38, 44, 91, 181, 188, 195, 244–246, 359–361, 370n1651
Montesquieu   38–39, 91, 247, 250
moral psychology   217, 346, 362–363
moral sentiments   38, 208, 217, 239, 361
   See also sympathetic imagination
moralism   1, 28, 45, 181, 196, 206, 274
murder, impermissibility of   23, 25–26, 126, 130–134, 143, 179, 192–193, 198, 200–202, 211–214, 218–219, 238, 240n1033, 243, 248, 259, 261, 293, 343, 351
Mussolini, Benito   76, 86, 275–277

natural beauty   2n6, 36, 160, 253–254, 297, 326
natural evil   105, 117, 119, 260, 283
nature, as opposed to history   25, 63, 88, 96, 140, 255–263, 300, 307–308, 311
Nazism   85–86, 92, 94, 103, 152–156, 183n774, 202

INDEX 441

Neiman, Susan   106–109, 182n773
neoclassicism   7, 25–26, 31, 59, 131, 254, 265, 267, 269, 272, 283, 297, 301, 331, 357
    See Hellenism, neoHellenism
Neumann, Franz   92n355, 232
Nietzsche, Friedrich   1, 13–14, 16, 20, 23, 30, 46, 100, 132, 133, 136, 151–152, 154, 167–168, 204, 228, 267, 271, 281, 285, 299, 303n1296, 356n1571
nihilism   23, 25, 34n124, 42, 51, 85, 91, 94, 100, 103–104, 123, 127, 129–131, 134, 172, 181, 183n773, 196, 199, 202, 203n861, 221–223, 234, 253, 262, 269, 308, 351
Nobel prize for literature, Camus'   4, 20, 247, 268, 322–323
nostalgia   44, 57, 145, 166, 171, 285, 289, 374n1673
nouveaux philosophes   8, 12, 17, 21, 40, 77–82, 90, 97, 113n450, 253
Nussbaum, Martha   36, 42n158, 45, 190n816, 346, 364n1617

"objective guilt"   333, 350, 361, 378
O'Brien, Conor Cruise   4n14, 263
Orme, Mark   10, 35n126, 54, 62n212, 129n521, 182n773, 210n893, 233
"Orwellian" claims   90, 350
Orwell, George   87, 88n338, 90, 229
Othon (in *The Plague*)   119, 122, 204, 357

panopticon   68, 72–73, 75, 79n298
paralogism   344–345
Paris, as glittering cave   56, 298, 308, 341
Parmenides   185, 268
Pascal, Blaise   6, 37, 297, 300
passions   32, 36, 107n417, 131, 183n773, 219n934, 245n1057, 291n1245, 329, 358–359, 361–363, 365–366, 376, 381
    See emotions
Paul, Saint   101, 142n576, 178n741, 292
pessimistic libertarianism   15
philosophical suicide   153, 171, 186, 213, 346, 357
    See "leap," "cheating"
philosophy
    as a way of life   32, 33n121, 36, 57, 246, 355, 370n1650
    as stand-in and mediator   346, 353

Plato   19, 21, 33, 34, 55, 57, 79, 102, 156, 163, 228, 248n1071, 258, 267, 289n1237, 301n1258, 347, 348, 359, 391, 392n1762
Plotinus, Neo-Platonism   21n84, 30, 49–50, 163, 166, 183, 268, 297, 356, 359
plurality, difference (as something to be defended)   16, 47, 231–232, 291n1245, 347
Plutarch of Chaeronia   33, 247, 359, 367n1631
political theology   100n386, 101, 132, 236, 246
polytheism   305
post-colonial critiques of Camus   8, 58, 128n518, 172n708, 263, 266, 272, 277, 318–330, 348
post-colonialism   242, 257
post-modernism   11, 14, 17
    See post-structuralism
post-prophetic philosopher   57, 346–355
post-structuralism   4, 7, 11, 16n59, 16, 56, 152, 159, 184, 185, 193, 231, 242, 267, 289–293, 307, 333
    See post-modernism
power, Caesarian as opposed to Promethean forms   16, 96, 125–126
practical wisdom   191, 363
problem of evil   104, 105–113, 115–118, 123, 129
Prometheus, meaning of   125–126, 267, 304–305
prophetism   58, 135, 138, 342, 355
Pucheu, Pierre   203

radical orthodoxy   100
    See also Milbank, John
rationalism (belief in the ability of reason to totally explain the world)   5, 13, 40, 95, 98, 161–163, 186, 192, 214, 260, 289
rebellion
    historical   112, 129, 196, 211, 219, 222, 239, 286
    metaphysical   105, 110–113, 117, 123, 130, 136, 137n549, 178, 196, 225, 242, 305
relativity   140, 312n1340
renaissance, Camus' hope for a second   34n124, 42
reoccupation versus secularisation (in Blumenberg)   136, 285, 288
rhetoric   7, 19, 34, 36, 46, 55–56, 155, 185, 216n918, 292n1248, 314, 382

Rochefoucauld, François de La 206
Romans, the 23, 31–33, 56, 58, 115, 172, 190, 234n996, 245, 266–267, 274, 276–278, 279n1197, 281n1202, 282–283, 359
romantics, romanticism 18, 66, 94, 111, 129, 132, 151, 177–178, 181, 297, 302, 304, 305n1313
Rousseau, Jean-Jacques 17, 109, 112, 129, 130n523, 132, 204, 219, 241, 285, 289n1237, 347
Russian nihilists 9

Sade, Marquis de 38n141, 109, 111, 129, 132, 171, 174n717, 177–180, 224, 246, 346
Said, Edward 6, 8, 54, 259, 323
Sartre, Jean-Paul 1–3, 6, 8, 10, 20–21, 27, 35, 36, 39n143, 54, 57, 98, 105–106, 128–129, 143–144, 150–152, 155, 166, 171–172, 173n716, 181–182, 200, 207–208, 221n941, 226, 247, 259, 262–263, 265, 281, 322, 332, 335–341, 363, 375, 380n1700
Schmitt, Carl 15n55, 98, 101, 137, 139, 153, 242, 365
science 13, 15n55, 38, 71, 79, 124, 136, 139–140, 156, 162, 164, 195, 230, 258n1109, 261, 308–309, 312–313, 347, 353n1549
secularisation thesis 98, 101, 105, 135–136, 253
"self-assertion" 123, 125, 135–136
    See "sufficient rationality"
Shakespeare, William 53, 150, 173
Sherman, David 10
Shoah, the 154, 199, 225, 333
    See Holocaust, the
show trials 89, 126
Socrates 32–33, 36n134, 51n193, 55, 175, 193, 225, 244, 245, 267, 279, 281, 295, 301n1285, 352, 363, 392n1762
solidarity between human beings 5, 25, 26, 103, 219–222, 225, 227–228, 233, 242–243, 300, 311, 345, 374, 389
Sophie's Choice 196
sophrosyne 31, 192, 298–299, 301
    See *mesure*, moderation, balance
    See also extremes
spiritual exercises 32, 35, 160n639 370, 375, 383
Srigley, Ronald 6, 10, 24, 29n104, 31, 37, 38n141, 42n156, 54, 97, 103, 114, 136–137,

164, 190n810, 210, 212, 224–225, 232, 310, 335–338, 340, 343, 372n1659, 389–390
Stalinism 5, 8, 10–11, 16, 18, 74, 76–93, 98–99, 104, 113, 127, 128n518, 129, 140, 142–145, 231, 235, 254, 273, 284, 295, 311, 316, 343
stoicism 30, 35n129, 36, 48n181, 117, 125, 131, 180, 188–190, 218, 248n1071, 267, 279, 284, 295–296, 346, 359, 361, 363, 365, 367, 371–374
Stockholm 268, 301n1285
Strauss, Leo 14, 151, 157, 183n774, 229, 230n985, 240
subject, the 3, 13, 71–72, 88, 93, 158–159, 167, 180, 183–184, 185n782, 193, 200
    See also desire for unity/meaning, the
suffering of innocents 106, 109, 111, 118, 125, 143, 196, 215, 246, 311, 316, 351
"sufficient rationality" (in Blumenberg) 124
    See "self-assertion"
sympathetic imagination 195–196, 203–207, 218, 353, 361
    See imagination

Taylor, Charles 100–101, 119, 123
technology 69, 83
terrorism 23, 58, 85, 87, 112, 216, 219, 223, 351, 380
theology 15n55, 17, 23, 26, 55, 98, 101, 104, 106, 110, 114, 116, 123n497, 124n501, 125, 136, 164, 170, 255, 281n1202 283, 287–288, 348
"Thou shalt not Kill" (6th Mosaic commandment) 127, 200
three pillars of the thesis that Camus is a *philosophe* 22–41
Tipasa 53, 253, 267, 270, 282, 296, 310, 362
"to live without appeal" 190
torture 9, 48n181, 69–70, 85, 89, 92, 96, 121, 196–197, 204, 219, 234, 309, 350
totalitarianism 17, 55, 76, 83–95, 98, 104–105, 128, 195, 255, 269
totality 26, 43, 47, 83–85, 89–90, 96, 125–127, 137, 156, 184, 201, 225–226, 254, 285, 291, 294
    See also unity
tragedy, Greek 61, 279n1197, 302n1289, 303–307, 391n1761

INDEX 443

unity   25, 42, 47–50, 110, 112, 126–127, 137, 166, 169, 171, 182–186, 189, 213, 217, 223–226, 254, 289, 300, 301, 311–312, 316, 346, 361
   See also totality
universe of the trial   345, 350

violence   4, 9–10, 27, 51, 66, 82, 128–131, 137, 142–145, 156, 180, 211, 222, 236–239, 262, 273n1171, 277, 291n1245, 300, 306, 319, 321–322, 328n1421, 341, 352, 354–355, 363, 370, 377–381, 387n1734, 388, 390
virtue ethics   43n160, 359
virtues, the   15, 50, 115, 117, 191, 233, 283, 355–365
Voegelin, Eric   84n323, 210, 286n1223
Voltaire   26, 38, 39, 91, 108–111, 120, 125–126, 136, 155n617, 245–246, 360

Weyembergh, Maurice   192, 21n84
wonder   36, 43, 103, 206, 254, 316, 355, 385, 391n1761, 392
world not meaningless   128, 134, 189, 255, 312

"yes" underlying rebellion   216–217, 260

Zaretsky, Eli   10, 28n102, 54, 126n508, 209n891, 299n1276
Žižek, Slavoj   84, 145, 208, 236, 257, 288, 291n1245, 292, 347, 356

2   Camus, Albert

academic philosopher, not an   20–22, 40, 54, 194, 268–269, 357
agnosticism, not atheism   6, 24, 31, 111–112, 269n1158
Alger Republicain   10, 45, 173, 204, 321
Algeria
   Camus' praises for virtues of native Algerians   327n1414
   failures in   246, 320, 356, 375
   family in   318–319, 323, 327, 351, 375, 382, 388–390
   change in Camus' political position on   349
   upbringing in   378

beautiful soul   220, 340

capital punishment, change of mind on   240n1033
   See "Mauriac was right"
Cartesian/para-Cartesian argumentation   24, 27, 56, 124, 182–183, 210–214, 218, 222, 228, 239, 269, 310
Combat   45, 62, 80n305, 102n401, 114n456, 144, 150, 152, 183, 197, 201–202, 205, 235–236, 321, 325, 337, 349n1533, 361
communion, longing for   47, 49, 50, 149, 217, 362
contemplative, contemplation   5, 40, 57, 58, 254, 256, 261, 296–297, 300, 308, 310, 362
contradictions in   1, 5, 149, 153, 165, 210, 240n1033, 309, 330
counts himself in (what he describes)   369
critique
   of academic philosophy   20, 39, 357
   of "all or nothing" positions   6, 25, 176, 184, 189, 214, 343
   of Christianity   40, 114, 118, 135, 335
   of heroism   364
   of Marx   38, 135–143, 285
   of "political theology"   117n477, 236
   of Sartre's *Nausea*   4, 151, 173

death of   5, 181, 246, 319, 320, 375
dialogue, as a philosopher of   88n337, 227–231, 236, 240, 258, 273n1171, 300
divided reception of   5

eudemonism   47, 53
excluding nothing   6, 25, 260, 294, 300, 365
exile, sense of   329
existentialist, not an   3, 29, 152

fierce love of justice   202, 208, 253, 362
fidelity   48, 175, 226, 235, 360, 364, 370

irony   45, 265, 324, 334, 340

journalism   22, 36, 41–42, 86n329, 196, 201, 204, 206, 209, 217, 227, 232, 271, 275, 328n1421
justifications for violence   81, 130n523, 222, 351

loneliness of, sense of solitude after 1952 333, 369
lyrical essays   19, 22, 41–42, 54, 268, 296, 360

master argument in   24–27
"Mauriac was right"   102n401
memory, call to memory   226, 367, 370–371, 375
middle path   164, 174, 195
Meursault and Caligula not as Camusian "heroes"   171–180
mysticism   50, 152, 187–188, 193, 297

naturalism   58, 249, 256, 257n1102, 260, 264, 308, 308n1325, 310

personal thinker   34
poverty, as ethical school   279n1198, 339, 373–375
praise for Marx as critic   112–113

questions (of philosophical import) posed by   22–24

read Epictetus in hospital   226n960, 359
reader of the Stoics   267, 279n1198, 296, 359, 372, 374n1675
republicanism   5, 17
response to the   1952
    Les Temps Moderns affair   336–339
rhetoric, use of   7, 19, 36, 56, 215, 259, 314, 382

Sartre's and Jeanson's criticisms of   57, 226, 259, 263, 336–339
scepticism in   12, 16, 25, 39, 94n365, 103, 182, 186–187, 213, 242, 244–245, 257, 260–261, 288, 295–297, 360–361
sense of the sacred in   6, 50
spanning of different genres   42, 47, 318
stages of literary and philosophical production   1, 41, 214
syndicalism, trade unionism   237
systematicity of his works   310

theatre, love of   51, 302
tuberculosis   160, 212n900, 281, 370
two-sided   50, 97, 364

3   Camus' Works

Algerian Chronicles   225, 266, 277, 320–321, 350, 353, 357, 365, 375

"Between Yes and No"   373

Carnets   20, 22, 33, 35, 37, 41–42, 51, 54, 62, 102, 118n479, 145, 160, 165n665, 172, 174n722, 189n806, 194, 204n866, 214, 239, 254–255, 257, 267, 288, 296, 302, 315, 329, 331, 336–337, 338, 341, 343, 359, 368–369, 370n1647, 372, 374, 376, 383–384
Christian Metaphysics and Neoplatonism 104, 114–116, 122, 268, 272, 278, 279n1197, 281n1202, 286, 295, 297
Chute, La   1, 7, 21, 44, 55, 57, 74, 94, 201, 210, 265, 287, 325, 326, 330–333, 336, 338, 341–343, 348, 350, 362, 375
    See *Fall, La*
"Crise de L'Homme, La"   5n18, 82n312, 98, 227, 248
"Create Dangerously"   20, 22

"Desert, The" (from *Nuptials*)   188, 296, 309, 315

"Enigma, The"   55, 174, 181, 283n1211, 308, 318, 360
Étranger, L'   2, 4n14, 7, 21, 44, 150, 172–173, 175, 214, 282, 314, 325, 328, 337
    See *Stranger, The*
Exile and the Kingdom   21, 54–55, 57, 223, 314n1348, 320, 332

Fall, The   1, 21, 44, 46, 54, 57, 74, 218, 325, 326, 330–335, 337, 340–341, 344–345, 355, 389
    See *Chute, La*
First Camus: Youthful Writings, The   43n162
First Man, The   21, 41, 54–55, 57, 236, 331, 375, 377, 379, 381, 382–383, 386, 388–390

"Helen's Exile" (from *Summer*)   34n125, 38, 256, 261, 268, 295, 298–299, 301, 309, 345, 360, 376

INDEX 445

Homme Révolté, L'   3, 9, 17, 19–20, 21, 24–25, 28, 38n2, 40, 45, 47, 49, 55, 82–85, 98, 102, 105, 109, 111, 123, 125–127, 129, 132–138, 143–145, 164, 178, 184, 188, 190n809, 197, 199, 201–202, 207, 210–212, 214–215, 217, 220, 222, 226, 228, 234–235, 246, 256, 259–260, 263n1130, 264, 267–268, 273, 279n1197, 285, 287, 301, 304, 310–311, 331, 333, 336–337, 339, 343, 350–351, 358, 370, 384, 389
   See *Rebel, The*
"Host, The" (from *Exile and the Kingdom*)   283n1212

"Intelligence and the Scaffold"   302, 358

Lecture in Athens on the Future of Tragedy   61n208, 302n1289, 303
Letter to the Editor of Les Temps Modernes, *A*   263n1130, 332, 338
Letters to a German Friend   24n88, 37n137, 128, 134n535, 202, 277, 364
"Love of Life" (from *The Wrong Side and the Right Side*)   5n22

"Minotaur, or Stopping in Oran, The" (from *Summer*)   268–269, 314
Myth de Sisyphe, Le   210
   See *Myth of Sisyphus, The*
Myth of Sisyphus, The   26, 28, 41, 43, 47, 50n187, 54, 74, 94n365, 150, 160, 162, 164–165, 171, 174, 182, 184–185, 190, 192–193, 211, 219n933, 267, 284, 294–295, 304, 345
   See *Myth de Sisyphe, Le*

"Neither Victims nor Executioners"   80, 145, 227, 239, 288
"New Mediterranean Culture, The"   272–274, 282
"Nuptials at Tipasa" (from *Nuptials*)   270, 282

Peste, La   7, 21, 44, 61, 63, 65–66, 75n276, 84, 87, 91, 93, 105, 118–119, 124, 137, 180, 201, 204, 207, 214, 218, 263, 283, 302n1289, 328, 337, 357, 362, 365, 380
   See *Plague, The*
Plague, The   21, 41, 54, 62, 66, 68, 74–75, 85, 96, 118, 121n491, 262, 277, 324, 377
   See *Peste, La*
"Prometheus in the Underworld" (from *Summer*)   38n140, 268, 305, 360, 364–365

Rebel, The   24n88, 26, 28, 35n126, 37, 38, 41, 45, 49, 51, 54, 56, 59, 74, 76, 80–82, 84n320, 93–94, 99, 105–106, 112, 124, 128, 130n523, 131, 135, 138, 145, 170, 177–178, 189, 193, 196–197, 200, 210–211, 213–215, 218–219, 221–225, 227, 242, 259–262, 265, 286, 294, 304, 310–311, 335, 338–346, 348, 351–352, 357, 375–376
   See *Homme Révolté, L'*
"Reflections on the Guillotine"   4, 26, 45, 241–242, 336
"Renegade, The"   46, 283, 332, 340, 344, 348
"Return to Tipasa" (from *Summer*)   53, 253, 310, 362

Stranger, The   21, 41, 54, 151, 171, 174–175, 177
   See *Étranger, L'*

"Témoin de la Liberté, Le"   88n337, 231n990
"Temps des Meurtrieurs, Le"   228

"Wager of our Generation"   51n191, 233
"Wind at Djemila" (from *Nuptials*)   160, 282–283, 367

www.ingramcontent.com/pod-product-compliance
Lightning Source LLC
Chambersburg PA
CBHW071137300426
44113CB00009B/1000